CW00828030

The Battle of the Peaks and Longstop Hill

Dedication

This book is very humbly but also proudly dedicated first to my parents

> Flying Officer Lionel Dennis Mitchell RAFVR and Corporal Adelina Fritze WAAF, later Mrs Lynn Mitchell

Also secondly with all my love to my wife Alison

And finally to all the officers and men of the First Army who fought in Tunisia, and especially to those who did not return home.

The Battle of the Peaks
and Longstop Hill

Tunisia, April–May 1943

Ian Mitchell

Helion & Company Limited

Helion & Company Limited
Unit 8 Amherst Business Centre
Budbrooke Road
Warwick
CV34 5WE
England
Tel. 01926 499 619

Email: info@helion.co.uk
Website: www.helion.co.uk
Twitter: @helionbooks
Visit our blog http://blog.helion.co.uk/

Published by Helion & Company 2019
Designed and typeset by Mary Woolley (www.battlefield-design.co.uk)
Cover designed by Paul Hewitt, Battlefield Design (www.battlefield-design.co.uk)
Printed by Gutenberg Press Limited, Tarxien, Malta

ISBN 978-1-911628-93-4

British Library Cataloguing-in-Publication Data.
A catalogue record for this book is available from the British Library.

For details of other military history titles published by Helion & Company Limited contact the
above address or visit our website: http://www.helion.co.uk.

We always welcome receiving book proposals from prospective authors.

Contents

List of Illustrations

In Photo Plate Section

List of Maps

In Map Plate Section

List of Abbreviations

Abbreviation	In full
AA	Assembly area
AA	Anti-Aircraft
AA & DQMG	Assistant Adjutant and Deputy Quartermaster General
ACC	Army Catering Corps
ADC	Aide de Camp
ADMS	Assistant Director Medical Services
ADS	Advanced Dressing Station
AFHQ	Allied Forces Headquarters
AGRA	Army Group Royal Artillery
BEF	British Expeditionary Force
BGS	Brigadier General Staff
BMRA	Brigade Major Royal Artillery
BSM	Battery Sergeant Major
CCB	Combat Command B
CCRA	Corps Commander Royal Artillery
CCS	Casualty Clearing Station
C-in-C	Commander-in-Chief
CO	Commanding Officer
CP	Command Post
CQMS	Company Quarter Master Sergeant
CRA	Commander Royal Artillery
CRASC	Commander Royal Army Service Corps
CRE	Commander Royal Engineers
CREME	Commander Royal Electrical and Mechanical Engineers
CSM	Company Sergeant Major
DAA & QMG	Deputy Assistant Adjutant and Quartermaster General
DCM	Distinguished Conduct Medal
DF	Defensive Fire (as in DF task)
DFC	Distinguished Flying Cross
DSO	Distinguished Service Order

FOO	Forward Observation Officer
FSU	Field Surgical Unit
FUP	Forming-up Point
GOC	General Officer Commanding
GSGS	Geographical Survey General Staff
GSO 1	General Staff Officer Grade 1
HQ	Headquarters
IO	Intelligence Officer (Battalion)
JNCO	Junior Non-Commissioned Officer
LAA	Light Anti-Aircraft
LAD	Light Aid Detachment
L/CPL	Lance Corporal
LMG	Light Machine Gun
LOB	Left out of Battle
LRC	Light Reconnaissance Car
LUP	Lying-up Position
MC	Military Cross
MDS	Main Dressing Station
MG	Machine Gun
MM	Military Medal
OCTU	Officer Cadet Training Unit
OC	Officer Commanding
OP	Observation Party (or Observation Post)
QAINS	Queen Alexandra's Imperial Nursing Service
PIAT	Projector Anti-Tank
POW	Prisoner of War
RA	Royal Artillery
RAC	Royal Armoured Corps
RAF	Royal Air Force
RAMC	Royal Army Medical Corps
RAOC	Royal Army Ordnance Corps
RAP	Regimental Aid Post
RASC	Royal Army Service Corps
RCAF	Royal Canadian Air Force
RE	Royal Engineers
REME	Royal Electrical and Mechanical Engineers
RHQ	Regimental Headquarters
RMO	Regimental Medical Officer
RN	Royal Navy
RSM	Regimental Sergeant Major
SNCO	Senior Non-Commissioned Officer
TA	Territorial Army

UGC   Universal Gun Carrier
VC   Victoria Cross

List of Abbreviated Titles of Units

Abbreviation	In full
1st East Surreys	1st Battalion East Surrey Regiment
1st North Irish	1st North Irish Horse
1st Royal Irish Fusiliers (Faughs)	1st Battalion Royal Irish Fusiliers
2nd Coldstreams	2nd Battalion the Coldstream Guards
2nd Hants	2nd Battalion the Royal Hampshire Regiment
2nd Lancs Fusiliers	2nd Battalion Lancashire Fusiliers
2nd London Irish	2nd Battalion of the London Irish Rifles
3rd Grenadiers	3rd Battalion of the Grenadier Guards
4th RTA	4th Regiment Tabor Algerian
5th Buffs	5th Battalion of the East Kent Regiment
5th Northants	5th Battalion of the Northamptonshire Regiment
6th Black Watch	6th Battalion of the Black Watch Regiment
6th Skins	6th Battalion of the Royal Inniskilling Fusiliers Regiment
6th West Kents	6th Battalion of the Queen's Own Royal West Kent Regiment
8th Argylls	8th Battalion of the Argyll and Sutherland Highlanders
16th DLI	16th Battalion of the Durham Light Infantry
17th Field	17th Field Regiment Royal Artillery
56th Heavy	56th Heavy Regiment Royal Artillery
56th Recce	56th Reconnaissance Regiment
71st Field	71st Field Regiment Royal Artillery
132nd Field	132nd Field Regiment Royal Artillery
138th Field	138th Field Regiment Royal Artillery
142nd RAC	142nd Regiment of the Royal Armoured Corps

Foreword

The Fourteenth Army in Burma under General Bill Slim was often called "The Forgotten Army", principally by themselves. In comparison, the British First Army in Tunisia in the winter of 1942/43 was the "Unknown Army", and its exploits were largely unheralded. This book helps in so many ways to correct this unfortunate injustice by highlighting the story of the very heavy fighting in the hills of Tunisia. The author's introduction paints very well the picture of why the intervention by the Allies in Algeria and Tunisia was so necessary. The United States had been in the war for almost a year, but within the agreed British-USA policy of giving priority to the defeat of Germany, US land forces had not yet seen action in Europe. The build-up of large US armies in Britain was far from complete: blooding at least some of them was important. At the same time, the USSR was understandably pressing for some relief for their armies by the opening of a Second Front. General Montgomery's Eighth Army, after the Battle of El Alamein, was at last making real progress across the Libyan Desert. Operation Torch, as the venture involving the landing of Allied troops in Morocco and Algeria was to be called, made total sense and increased the pressure on the German and Italian forces in North Africa. The Germans reacted extraordinary quickly to the British and US invasion, and after hurried negotiations the units of the Vichy French forces largely joined in on the Allies' side. The landings were followed by a rapid advance into Tunisia, but the Allied attack eventually became bogged down near Tunis, which was not taken until May 1943. Although the author narrates this background to Operation Torch and these early operations well, the primary aim of his book is to describe the operations of a single division in battle in the mountains near Tunis in April 1943. This was the 78th Division, known as the Battle-Axe Division because of the design of its divisional badge.

This rather different and fresh approach to military history creates an interesting and accurate portrait of a division and its men in battle against a stubborn enemy across windswept hills. The author lucidly describes the sometimes see-saw nature of the fighting, and yet also manages to provide a valuable and touching insight into the lives of the officers and men who fought and sadly often died during these battles.

My father, Lieutenant Colonel, later Brigadier, "Swifty" Howlett, was one of those men, and he played a major role in the battle for these hills, culminating in the capture of Longstop Hill. Firstly, he was the commanding officer (CO) of the 6th Battalion of the Queen's Own Royal West Kent Regiment; and secondly, he had commanded the 36th Infantry Brigade which successfully captured the hill. He won the first of his two Distinguished Service Orders (DSOs) at Longstop, but was killed nearly a year later in Italy. It was because of my close family connection with these battles that I was honoured and very pleased when the author invited me to write this Foreword.

General Sir Geoffrey Howlett KBE, MC

Preface

My original aim when I started this project was to write a book about the two battles to seize Longstop Hill, which started in December 1942 and ended in late April 1943. However, while I was researching the second battle it led me to study the 78th Infantry Division's operations in April 1943. Most soldiers called these operations the Battle of the Peaks, and they ended with the capture of Longstop Hill. It soon became apparent that it was not possible to tell the story of Longstop in isolation, without relating the story of the battles in the mountains, for these made the capture of Longstop possible. Secondly, the more I read and learned about those battles, the more I realised that there was a series of amazing stories which needed to be told. Most importantly, this is a story that has largely been overlooked, just as the operations of the First Army in northern Tunisia have generally been almost totally forgotten.

These were fierce and difficult battles conducted over extremely challenging terrain, against a desperate enemy. Yet unusually in writing on the military history of the Second World War, they have largely been forgotten. While over 250 books have now been written about Operation Market Garden, less than eight have appeared about the Tunisian campaign as a whole, and none of those specifically focus on Longstop and the Battle of the Peaks. This seemed to me a little surprising, as the operation was a significant victory for the Allies. In contrast to Arnhem, the Battle of the Peaks led rapidly to the surrender of a quarter of a million Axis troops and was the final nail in the coffin of Rommel's much-vaunted *Afrika Korps*. As we now pass the 75th anniversary of these key battles, it seems only fair to ensure that the gallantry and self-sacrifice of the forgotten men of the 78th Division and the supporting units of First Army be finally recognised and documented. This book will hopefully also encourage others to start the process of telling the wider and fascinating story of the operations of that army from November 1942 to May 1943, and particularly the final battles to capture Tunis. That story has been seriously neglected by modern military historians and is virtually unknown to the public at large. The time is long overdue for this unfortunate oversight to be reversed and for the public to learn more about those who served in that forgotten formation.

This book is deliberately restricted in time, by formation and by geographical area. The primary focus is on the operations conducted in April 1943 by the 78th Division and its supporting units in the hills north of the Medjerda River. It is a story of the 78th Division's first battle as a complete formation. It is one usually told at a level no higher than division, with a special focus on combat operations as seen from the perspective of companies, battalions and brigades. It is at this level that the nasty business of fighting largely takes place, though I have not ignored the importance of supporting units or the influence that planning at corps level can have on the divisional battle. I have tried to maintain a balance between providing a perspective of the wider operational picture, planning at divisional as well as brigade level, and telling the story of fighting as experienced by companies, especially that by individual soldiers. If I have failed to maintain that balance, the responsibility lies entirely with me. I have certainly made it a priority to try to highlight the experiences of ordinary soldiers in the Battle of the Peaks. I was in part inspired to do so as a result of a quotation made by an Italian historian, Fabio Toncelli, in a film about the Battle of Ortona. His words made a great impression upon me. He said: "But ordinary soldiers don't end up in history books, only the generals do."

The 78th Division and its attached 21st Tank Brigade were to fight and win many famous battles in the following three years. In doing so, they established a reputation for combat performance that became renowned across the Allied armies.

The foundations for that reputation were first laid, however, in April 1943 on a series of wind-blown djebels, or peaks, and at a place called Longstop Hill. This book is humbly dedicated to all the officers and soldiers of the 78th Division and its supporting units of V Corps, whose declining number of veterans can rightly say with quiet but great pride: "I fought with the First Army in Tunisia."

Ian Mitchell

Acknowledgements

I would like to start by thanking General Sir Geoffrey Howlett for kindly agreeing to write the foreword to this book. As the son of Brigadier "Swifty" Howlett, he has shown a great personal interest in the book and has followed its rather slow and jerky progress with much patience, but has also offered kind support. He had a very distinguished military career in his own right, so his comments on military matters were ones I valued greatly and rarely ignored. His eagle eye and excellent memory highlighted evidence that I had missed, and led me to significantly revise the penultimate chapter.

As a first-time author in a neglected field, I owe a debt of gratitude to several writers whose works provided encouragement and inspiration to complete this book. It was that able military historian, Gregory Blaxland, who first got me interested in Tunisia and Longstop Hill. I read his book *The Plain Cook and the Great Showman* in 1997, was struck by it and returned to it once again in April 2008. It was reading his book a second time, and a visit to the Medjez el Bab Commonwealth War Graves Commission cemetery and Longstop Hill during a holiday to Tunisia in September 2008, that led me to start this book. Sadly, I never got to meet Gregory as he died in the 1990s, but I owe a great debt to him. I would also like to thank David Rolf and Rick Atkinson, whose books have stimulated wider interest in the Tunisian campaign. Richard Doherty, a highly regarded Irish military historian, served as a mentor and provided inspiration and advice. I can truly say that through his own books, good humour and assistance, Richard more than anyone helped to really "Clear the Way" for the writing of this book.

Two other authors have influenced the way I approached this book and inspired me to finish the project. Mark Zuehlke, a gifted and distinguished Canadian military historian, had a significant influence on me when writing this story. If you have read any of his books, you will have been impressed by the way he combines a description of the actual operations with the ability to bring to life the people who took part in them. I have tried my best to follow his example and do the same, though I suspect rarely as well as he would have done. I would like to thank him for the example he sets to all those who write military history and for his interest in my work. The work of another eminent author, Peter Cozzens, who writes about the American Civil War, also impressed me and had its own effect on this book.

Mike Peters gave me valuable advice, even though he was in the process of writing his first book and serving in Afghanistan. Mike is now a well-established author, so it must have been good advice! I met Mike through the International Guild of Battlefield Guides (of which he is now Chairman) and would like to thank the many people in the Guild who have offered their advice and friendship over the years. I am especially grateful to Tony Smith, the Secretary of the Guild, a valued friend. His occasional and well-meant tendency to express publicly his scepticism that I would ever finish this book of course achieved its aim, spurring me on to do so.

I would like to recognise the invaluable assistance provided by that amazing community of curators, archivists and librarians from both the UK and the USA, who have responded to my constant requests for information and material. As my first career was working for the Royal Navy as a librarian, I believe I have a rather unusual insight into the skills and hard work required of librarians and archivists who respond to requests from budding authors. My debt to them is considerable. I would especially like to recognise the assistance provided by Tim Ward, now retired from the post of Chief Librarian, and his staff at the Prince Consort's Army Library at Aldershot. I have been very fortunate to have had constant access to this library, with its marvellous collection of military books, throughout the work on this story. Tim and his staff have responded to my innumerable requests over the years with both patience and enthusiasm. One very cold winters' day, they all went above and beyond their duties as library staff when they helped me to extract my hire car out of the snow in the car park. Lieutenant Colonel Peter Reese, an accomplished author of several military histories, was researching two books during my frequent visits to Aldershot and became a source of welcome encouragement and advice. Since Colonel Reese was a distinguished officer in the Royal Army Educational Corps, in which I also proudly served, his gentle prodding to complete the book carried much weight.

Rod Mackenzie, the Regimental Archivist of the Argyll and Sutherland Highlanders Museum in Stirling, was especially helpful at the start and end of the process of writing this book. He alerted me to Jock McKellar's account and other sources. Rob Layden, Chief Executive of the Argyll and Sutherland Highlanders Museum, also kindly gave permission for me to use the painting of the attack on Longstop Hill on this book's front cover, as did Stuart Brown, the artist who created it. I would be remiss if I did not thank the staff at the Surrey Historical Centre at Guildford for helping me gain access to some very useful documents on the East Surreys. The staff at the National Archives at Kew should have much more public recognition for their hard work in maintaining a priceless collection of war diaries. They responded cheerfully and professionally to my numerous requests during many visits to the Archives. I am grateful to Kimberley Kowal, the previous Curator of Maps at the British Library, and her staff for their patience and assistance in providing copies of the original military maps used at the time of the battle. I would also like to acknowledge the following for permission to quote from various sources: David Hamilton (his father's memoirs), Lieutenant Colonel Jeremy "Jez" Robinson (use of extracts from John Coldwell-Horsfall's book *The Wild Geese are Flighting*), Robbie Robinson (his unpublished memoirs) and Lillian Schayek (for her husband's recollections). Caroline Corvan, Curator of the Museum of the Royal Irish Fusiliers, also took a major weight off my mind when, on my behalf, she secured her trustees' permission to cite several key extracts from the Russell letters.

I wish to express my deep gratitude to Richard and Edmund O'Sullivan, who together set up a great website on the Irish Brigade several years ago. I would like to recognise their contribution to maintaining the history of that brigade and for all the help they have given me over the last five years. I would particularly like to thank them for agreeing to take time, while making a film about their father's war in Tunisia, to take photographs of selected locations and for allowing me to use them in this book. I also wish to mention and thank a talented Tunisian photographer, Ashref Khmeri, who took some of the photographs in the book, as well as Mike Macy, who introduced him to me.

I am grateful to Duncan Rogers, from Helion, for believing in this book when others did not, and my commissioning editor Tony for his eagle eye in identifying my various errors and also for improving an old soldiers grammar. I would like to recognise the contributions of Paul Hewitt of Battlefield Design, who produced its book cover, then also kindly agreed to help create the excellent maps used and went the extra mile to do so and Mary Woolley also from Battlefield Design who did the typesetting

On a more personal note, I have a number of people who are important to me whom I wish to recognise. Sadly, both my parents are long dead, but I would like to acknowledge the huge debt I owe them. They showed me by their example how to navigate your way through life with dignity, respect, integrity and hard work. They both inspired me to join the armed forces and set a standard about values that I try to live up to today. My father Dennis was a RAF Flying Officer who flew as a pilot in Training Command, and my mother Lynn an Air Mechanic in the WAAF, during the Second World War. Both later fought private battles with much the same courage I know they showed in that conflict. This book is dedicated to their memory, with all my love. I have been immensely privileged to have among my family and friends various people whom I would like to recognise and thank for their support and love. These include my brother Peter and his late wife Julie, and our two nieces Becky and Katy with their respective other halves. Another constant source of support and guidance in my life has been my father's cousin Shirley, who has acted as my unofficial aunt and so much more. I would also like to thank our old friends John and Carol Taylor, Paul and Sarah White, Peter and Liz Lockwood and Peter and Bridget Spring for their friendship, support, encouragement and constructive criticism over the years.

It would be remiss of me if I did not also recognise, thank and possibly embarrass two brave, modest, but irritatingly multi-talented men whom I have had the honor of calling my close friends for nearly 30 years: Paul "Batman" Murtha and Peter Philpott. Both of them have seen the ugly face of war, and showed courage in very different battles. I would like to thank them publicly for their distinguished service to their respective countries and express my gratitude for the privilege of their continued and much-valued friendship.

Both of these two old soldiers have been truly blessed by having wives who possess good humour, kindness, grace, patience and tolerance in abundance. I can only marvel at the bravery and love that enabled Sue to support Peter through his many dangerous operational tours. Andrea, Paul's wife, in her own calm, humorous and inimitable way, has also been a huge support to him over the years, and especially after his recent heart attack. Both women have a special place in my heart. I am sure Andrea would not be offended, though, if I especially single out Sue, for her love and support to my wife Alison during some quite difficult times over the last 20 years.

Finally, this book would never have been written without the love, patience and support of my wife Alison. She has now held down three of the toughest jobs in the world, having been first the wife of an officer in the Royal Navy, secondly of an officer in the British Army and finally of an author. She has endured far too many periods when I spent more time than I should in my study, and listened patiently to me talking way too much about this book. She is a jewel beyond price and I love her to bits.

1

Operation Torch and the Road to Longstop Hill

1.1 An Appointment in Algiers

According to contemporary accounts, Lieutenant T.J. Villis, the second-in-command of C Company, the 5th Battalion of the Northamptonshire Regiment (hereafter the 5th Northants), was determined to secure a place in history. His battalion was part of 11th Infantry Brigade of the 78th Infantry Division, a formation within the Eastern Task Force that was bound, on an early November morning, for landings near the North African port of Algiers. This task force was part of the new Allied force, under the command of a relatively unknown American general called Dwight D. Eisenhower, which was carrying out Operation Torch, the Allied invasion of French territories in North Africa. These territories, in Morocco, Algeria and Tunisia, were governed by the French government that had been established as a result of the defeat of France in 1940. The new government, based in and named after the town of Vichy, was allowed by the peace treaty between France and Germany in 1940 to rule the southern half of France while the Germans occupied northern France. The new government, under its titular head, Marshal Pétain, was right-wing, pro-Fascist and collaborated with the Germans. The peace accord with Hitler, however, had allowed the Vichy government to retain control of its territories in North Africa and maintain significant though ill equipped French forces under its command in North Africa. It was against these territories and forces that Prime Minister Winston Churchill and President Franklin Roosevelt had decided the Allies would carry out their first joint offensive of the war. The primary aim of Operation Torch was to relieve pressure on the beleaguered Russians. This would be achieved by attacking the Axis forces, which were retreating from Montgomery's Eighth Army through Libya, from their rear through French North-West Africa. The official position of the French forces in North Africa who might oppose Allied forces was clear. They were loyal to France, as represented by Pétain and his government, and would defend North Africa against any force that tried to invade. The reality was that secret discussions with elements of the French Army by local American consular officials provided hope that the planned Allied landings, especially in Algiers, might be supported, or at least not opposed.

As part of Operation Torch, at 0100 hours on the morning of 8 November 1942, landings were underway on a small and narrow beach codenamed Apples White. Lieutenant Villis was very keen to be the first person off his landing craft. He wanted to be the first soldier from his regiment, brigade, or ideally the whole task force, ashore. The lieutenant's eagerness to secure his role in history sadly proved to be his undoing. He jumped out of his landing craft before it had grounded on the beach, was struck by the craft, disappeared under it and was drowned.[1] In one of those ironic twists of fate, Villis still managed to secure a place in the history of Operation Torch, though not the one he would have desired. Lieutenant Villis became the first British soldier to die in the operation, and almost certainly the first Allied soldier to die in the invasion of North Africa. The 11th Infantry Brigade landings by the 5th Northants at Apples White Beach, and its sister battalion the 1st Battalion of the East Surrey Regiment (1st East Surreys) on Apples Green, were otherwise unopposed. There was, however, one additional casualty on the beach, for it was recorded that one dog was killed during the landings. Due to delays elsewhere, the 11th Brigade was also the first unit to land, minutes or hours ahead of any other Allied formation. The 2nd Battalion of the Lancashire Fusiliers (2nd Lancs Fusiliers), the third unit of the brigade, landed on Apples White less than two hours later and all three units moved quickly inland. The 11th Infantry Brigade, commanded by Brigadier Edward Cass (see Plate 2), known universally in the British Army by his nickname of "Copper" Cass, quickly secured all their D-Day objectives, all of the French Army units stationed nearby surrendering without firing a shot.

Within less than three days, and in cooperation with American forces of the 34th Infantry Division, the units of the Eastern Task Force took the city and key port of Algiers. There was resistance, but it was limited, and on 11 November, both the 11th and its sister unit, the 36th (Kent) Brigade of 78th Division, began operations intended to secure new objectives in eastern Algeria and Tunisia. Optimism among units was quite high that the division would race to and take these new objectives. These were the important Tunisian ports of Tunis and Bizerte, which were garrisoned by other Vichy French Forces. Seizing these two ports would enable the Allies to reinforce and supply their forces in North Africa while denying them to Italian and German troops.[2] Although held by French naval and army units, the Allies were optimistic that there would be no opposition to their advance. The result would be to place the Axis army (as it was known collectively) in Africa in a vice. The First and Eighth Armies would then squeeze the life out of all Axis forces in North Africa, leading to the destruction of Rommel's *Afrika Korps*. The plan was to take Tunis in less than a month and defeat Axis forces within another month, and while Lieutenant Villis did not live to see it, this is what happened, for Tunis was eventually captured.

There were, however, some key variations from the plan which directly affected the men in the 78th Infantry Division. The final capture of Tunis was to take seven months, not one, and in the process the 78th Division suffered more than 4,000 casualties and the First Army some 23,000. The culmination of that campaign occurred in April 1943 when the Battle Axe Division

---

1   The story of the death of Lieutenant Villis is based on W.F. Jervois, *History of Northamptonshire Regiment 1934-1948*, (Northampton: The Northamptonshire Regiment Museum, 1953), pp.109-10. There is some confusion as to whether Villis was in fact called Villiers, as Jervois cites this name on page 366 of his book.

2   The story of the landings at Apples Beach and in Algiers is based on TNA WO 175/196 11 Infantry Brigade WD November 1942; TNA WO 175/517 5th Northants WD November 1942; TNA WO 175/519 1st East Surreys WD November 1942; Geoffrey Blaxland, *The Plain Cook and the Great Showman* (Abingdon: Purnell Book Services Limited, 1977), pp.85-88; David S. Daniell, *History of the East Surrey Regiment, Volume IV 1920-1957* (London: Ernest Benn, 1957), pp.150-52; and W.J. Jervois, *History of Northants*, pp.110-13.

and supporting units carried out a forgotten but bloody series of battles for an area known as the Peaks and for a hill complex known as Longstop Hill. The success of that division in those operations, codenamed Sweep and Vulcan, was a key factor in ensuring the capture of Tunis and the surrender of over 250,000 Axis troops. If these operations had failed, the final push to seize Tunis would have taken longer and been more costly, and the invasion of both Sicily and Italy would have been delayed, with all the consequences that might have caused for the conduct of the war. The series of actions to complete victory in North Africa, despite having long been overlooked, were described at the time as 'As tough and prolonged a bit of work as has ever been undertaken by the British soldier.'[3] Most of the men who fought in those battles are dead and the battles largely forgotten. However, the 75th anniversary of those battles has just passed, so an account of their gallantry and sacrifice is now long overdue. This book tells their story.

1.2 Background to Operation Torch

The attack on Algiers which claimed Lieutenant Villis' life formed part of the wider Operation Torch. It is perhaps fortunate that Villis and other soldiers who died to carry it out never knew that the decision to execute it was born out of a compromise designed to resolve often bitter disagreements between three new allies. Although America's entry into the war against Germany was welcomed by Churchill, it soon became apparent that President Roosevelt and his military advisers did not necessarily share the British view about how to defeat their new enemy. Moreover, a third ally in the fight against Nazi Germany, Joseph Stalin's Soviet Union, had very clear views about what had to be done, and they could not be ignored. The first six months of America's participation in the war against Germany and Italy were often devoted to a difficult debate between the two Allies about what strategy they should adopt to defeat their new enemies. At the same time, Soviet Russia, facing the undistracted efforts of the German Army on the Eastern Front and struggling for survival, was clear about the need for the Allies to launch a major attack on France, the so-called Second Front. This debate was carried out on several levels, and although the details of those discussions are not relevant to this story, a brief summary is necessary to set the scene and understand why by April 1943 the British First Army was fighting in the mountains of Tunisia alongside its new former Vichy French and American allies.

In simple terms, the issue that divided the two allies was when, where and how to attack Germany. The American service chiefs, and especially the 62-year-old commander of the US Army, General George Marshall, believed that the fastest way of defeating Germany was also the shortest. In sharp contrast to the British senior commanders, General Marshall and his fellow Chief of Staff, 64-year-old Admiral Ernest King, the Chief of Naval Operations, believed that America and Great Britain should focus all their resources on building up troops in the United Kingdom, with the aim of attacking France in 1943. President Roosevelt was also keen to launch offensive operations in 1942 and through France, though for a different and more complex political reason: he wanted to ensure that Americans troops were committed to battle as soon as possible in Europe. It should be remembered that after Pearl Harbor, and despite

---

3   K.A.N. Anderson, *Official Dispatches on North West African Campaign* (London: *London Gazette*), p.5,459.

Hitler and Mussolini's surprising declaration of war against America on 11 December, there were many parts of the American population who wanted the US to focus the majority of its forces on defeating the Japanese. Roosevelt saw Hitler's Germany as the most dangerous threat and wanted to ensure support for his "Europe first" strategy. Churchill and his advisers were also strong supporters of a "Europe first" strategy, but had a rather different perspective on how best to defeat Germany and Italy. The Prime Minister and his senior military advisers believed that the best approach, due to various constraints, was to avoid attacking Germany directly. They wanted to weaken Germany by raids on the Atlantic coast, bombing attacks on Germany and reinforcing British forces in North Africa; only when forces had been built up in the UK, properly trained and equipped would the Allies launch an attack on France. The reality was that George Marshall's counterpart in the United Kingdom, the acerbic but brilliant 56-year-old Lieutenant General Alan Brooke, the Chief of the Imperial General Staff, was horrified by the inherent difficulties associated with launching an attack on the French coast, either in 1942 or 1943. He and his two other Service Chiefs, Air Marshal Charles Portal and Admiral Sir Dudley Pound, believed that at this stage of the war, the necessary resources - including troops, landing craft and shipping - were insufficient to conduct such an operation. They were also concerned about how to respond to the disasters that were overcoming British armies both in the Far East and later in North Africa, where during 1941 and early 1942 the Eighth Army was suffering from a series of defeats at the hands of a German general called Erwin Rommel. Moreover Churchill, a wily, devious and experienced political leader, was not averse to saying one thing at one time to please his new ally in the short-term, while actually working to persuade them to do something completely different. From the outset of US involvement in the war in December 1941, Churchill endeavoured to sell Roosevelt and his advisers a plan to attack Germany's weaker partners first, and specifically the Vichy French government. This plan, which gradually became known as Operation Gymnast, proposed that the Americans and the British devote their main effort in 1942 to an attack on Vichy France's North African possessions in West Africa (at Dakar), Morocco and Algeria. If successful, this would provide the Allies with excellent bases in the Mediterranean, protect British supply lines to Egypt and, most importantly, pose a threat to the German *Afrika Korps* in Tunisia and Libya.

The Americans, led by Marshall and his planners, headed by a bright but virtually unknown 50-year-old brigadier general called Dwight Eisenhower, saw Operation Gymnast as a dangerous distraction from their proposed build-up in Britain and attack on France in 1943. Their negotiating position was, however, complicated by a number of relevant factors. First, and unlike Churchill, President Roosevelt tended to keep his service chiefs at arm's length. He might not see them for weeks and would often change his position without informing them. Secondly, Admiral King had a rather unreasonable dislike of the British and also believed that the priority for America should be the Pacific theatre. Finally, Marshall and his advisers generally lacked recent experience of fighting the Germans, whereas their British counterparts had learned all too well what it was like to face the Third Reich's formidable war machine.

The unfortunate result of this essential difference in perspectives was a long, tedious and occasionally acrimonious debate conducted by the two allies, on paper and face-to-face, during the spring and early summer of 1942. It was also a debate complicated by the need for both the United States and United Kingdom to look to and support the third party in this relationship, Stalin and Soviet Russia, which had been desperately fighting for survival during 1941 and early 1942. Churchill and Roosevelt, whatever their other disagreements, fully recognised that it was essential to keep Russia in the war. By 1942, the majority of the German Army and the *Luftwaffe* were engaged on the Eastern Front; compared to this epic struggle, the British campaign in North Africa was almost a minor skirmish. If Russia was defeated or made a separate peace, all Germany's forces would be available to prosecute the war against Britain and the USA in the Mediterranean and prevent the possibility of an attack on France. Stalin and his advisers understandably felt that his allies were not doing enough of the fighting, and devoted much time and cunning to trying to force the Allies into opening a Second Front in 1942 by launching an attack which would divert German divisions from the Eastern Front. The Russian demand for action placed the Allied leaders, and especially the British Service Chiefs, in a very difficult position. Brooke and his colleagues recognised the grim reality that, despite Russian pressure, the British Army, either with or without the limited American forces in the UK, was not prepared for or capable of launching a major attack on France in the summer of 1942. Such a desperate venture would be bound to lead to major casualties for the largely British forces that would carry it out, while having a limited or no impact on events on the Eastern Front. Brooke's fears for an early attack on France were to be proved correct, for on 19 August 1942 a much smaller but still major raid on the port of Dieppe by a largely Canadian force was easily repulsed by the Germans, at a cost of 2,850 Allied servicemen killed or captured. As suspected by the American Service Chiefs, Churchill and his advisers also had grave reservations about launching Operation Round-Up, the proposed cross-Channel attack in 1943, although they kept these to themselves. Fortunately, almost a month earlier, President Roosevelt had, without consulting his military chiefs, decided to throw his support behind Gymnast, which on 25 July 1942 was officially named Operation Torch. Although the American Service Chiefs and key planners endeavoured to fight a rearguard action against the plan, their focus eventually became how to turn the plan into reality.

This planning took place against a background of several key events and fighting in Russia and North Africa. In Russia, the Germans launched their summer offensive in the south towards Stalingrad, which was initially very successful and placed even greater pressure on the Allies. In North Africa, events also favoured the Axis powers, as Rommel and his Italian allies defeated the Eighth Army at Gazala and successfully captured the vital port of Tobruk. Churchill learned this news while at a conference with Roosevelt in America, and declared it one of his worst moments in the war. The Eighth Army, now led directly by the Commander-in-Chief (C-in-C) Middle East General Claude Auchinleck, retreated and set up a new and hasty defence line anchored on a dusty, fly-infested railway stop known as El Alamein. Under Auchinleck's leadership, Rommel's attack on Egypt was halted at the First Battle of El Alamein, but this success did not save Auchinleck from Churchill's wrath over Tobruk. During a visit to Egypt by the Prime Minister in August 1942, Auchinleck was dismissed and replaced as C-in-C Middle East by General Harold Alexander and as commander of the Eighth Army by Lieutenant General William Gott. However, Gott was killed in an air crash while flying to take up his new command, and his role was taken, on Alexander and Brooke's joint advice, by a newcomer to the desert, a comparatively unknown lieutenant general with Ulster roots called Bernard Montgomery. These two appointments had more of an effect on the development of Torch than it might first appear, for Alexander had originally been assigned to lead the new First Army, the formation that would command British forces once Operation Torch had been launched. Alexander had succeeded Lieutenant General Schreiber, the original commander, who fell ill. Within days, Alexander had been sent to Egypt and was replaced in this role by

Montgomery, who in turn was dispatched to command the Eighth Army a few days later. This quick turnover in British commanders led Major General Mark Clark to say to his new boss, the future Allied Commander for Operation Torch, Lieutenant General Dwight D. Eisenhower: "I hope the turnover of American generals in Africa is less rapid."[4]

The fourth choice to command the future First Army was a 55-year-old Scotsman, Kenneth Arthur Noel Anderson (See Plate 1), who was the almost direct opposite in character of the man he replaced, Montgomery. Since Anderson would play a key role during the battle for Tunisia and would command the First Army during the Battle of the Peaks, it is worth spending a little time describing the career and personality of this forgotten Army commander. In stark contrast to Eisenhower, his initial superior until February 1943, Anderson had extensive experience of fighting the Germans. Born on Christmas Day 1891 in India, where his Scottish father worked as a railway engineer, Anderson was educated at Charterhouse public school. After training at the Royal Military Academy at Sandhurst, he was commissioned as an officer into the Seaforth Highlanders in September 1911. Anderson survived nearly three years of fighting Germans on the Western Front in France during the Great War. He was severely wounded on the fourth day of the Somme, during an action for which he earned a Military Cross (MC). After recovering from his wounds, Anderson rejoined his regiment, which by now was in Palestine, in time to celebrate victory over the Turks. During the inter-war years, Anderson was selected to attend Staff College at Quetta in India and completed a series of important appointments. He was appointed to command the 1st Battalion of the Seaforth Highlanders at the comparatively early age of 38. After commanding his battalion on active service in India and acting as the senior staff officer for an infantry division, Anderson was assigned in January 1938 as a brigadier to lead the 11th Infantry Brigade in the 4th Infantry Division. These appointments marked him out to be an officer destined for higher command. He trained and led his brigade from 1938-39, then served in 1940 as part of the British Expeditionary Force (BEF) in France, where he distinguished himself despite the chaos of that campaign. When Montgomery, at that time the commander of 3rd Division, was promoted to command II Corps at Dunkirk, Anderson, on General Brooke's recommendation, briefly took command of that division.

During the two years from Dunkirk to Torch, Anderson commanded successively another division, two different corps and was promoted to lieutenant general in 1941. His rapid rise to command of the First Army reflected his success in a series of demanding roles and the confidence that Brooke and other senior officers had in him as an officer.

In contrast to some other army commanders, Kenneth Anderson refused to write his memoirs, left no diary and has not attracted a biographer. Most accounts of Anderson have at best damned him with faint praise, or at worst suggested he was a poor commander. Much has later been made by historians of Anderson's dry, introverted, blunt and pessimistic personality, and it is certainly true that Anderson was not a dynamic or extrovert leader in the mould of Montgomery or Patton. He was self-effacing, taciturn and disliked the idea of promoting a public image for an army commander. However, in 1942 these characteristics did not in themselves prevent an officer from commanding an army successfully. This was to be proved by Generals Dempsey, McCreery and Slim, who all respectively commanded armies in Europe, Italy and Burma. All three of these officers shared Anderson's modesty and aversion to the limelight, but this did not

---

4   General Mark Clark, *Calculated Risk* (London: Hamilton Panther Books, 1956), p.42.

stop them from being highly effective army commanders. It is certainly possible that a balanced and objective biographer will in future conclude that Kenneth Anderson's shortcomings as an individual and a general did not make him best-suited to be selected as First Army commander. The rather glib and easy criticism he has incurred from his many detractors has, however, tended to overlook an inescapable truth: that an inexperienced, small and newly established First Army managed to rapidly recover from its early reverses to inflict a series of defeats on the much-vaunted veterans of the German *Afrika Korps*. It is also worth noting that although Anderson's British troops had a healthy respect for the ability of the Germans they faced, at no time did they suffer from any kind of inferiority complex that had been so prevalent in the Eighth Army from 1941-42. The official biographers of the Tunisian campaign, Brigadiers Playfair and Molony, though not uncritical of Anderson, perhaps gave a more balanced view when they stated: "The Army's achievements are the best witness to the qualities of its commander, General Anderson, a fine soldier."[5]

Kenneth Anderson's initial task, before the First Army was even formally established on 9 November 1942, was to work closely with General Eisenhower in planning Operation Torch. The core plan for Torch was based on a three-pronged assault on the coast of North-West Africa (see Map 1). In the west, on the Atlantic coast of Morocco, the Western Task Force of some 35,000 men, led by the comparatively unknown Lieutenant General George Patton, would land on beaches north and south of Casablanca. In Algeria, the Central Task Force, led by yet another unknown major general, Lloyd Fredenhall, was based around the 1st US Armoured and 1st US Infantry Division. This would land near to the port of Oran. Finally, the Eastern Task Force, commanded initially by Major General Charles Ryder and composed of the US 34th Infantry Division and two brigades from the British 78th Infantry Division, would land the furthest east at Algiers. The extensive use of US troops and the selection of American officers to command all three assault forces were deliberate. The Allies believed that Vichy forces would be less likely to resist an American-led operation, rather than one commanded by a British officer or apparently composed of British forces.

Most senior Vichy commanders were rabidly anti-British, due largely to memories arising from the Royal Navy's destruction of the French fleet in 1940 at Mers el Kebir near Oran in Algeria and the death of over 1,000 French sailors. Officially, Vichy France was at war with the Allies, and British and Vichy forces had fought each other several times since 1940. A key aspect of planning for Operation Torch was the use of every possible device or effort to avoid or limit the likely resistance of French forces. Some, though not all, of these efforts paid off, when all six major amphibious landings were launched with eventual success by three task forces on 8 November 1942. Ironically, and despite the emphasis on the use of US forces to limit conflict with the French, it was the US units landing in the west near Casablanca and in the centre near Oran that had the greater number of casualties, having encountered significant though short-lived resistance from French forces. In the east, French forces under General Mast rallied to the Allied cause and tried to seize key points and arrest leading Vichy officials, including Admiral Darlan. The confusion caused by this attempt was an important factor in enabling the Eastern Task Force to land almost unopposed east and west of Algiers. Although casualties

5   Ian Playfair, C.J.C. Molony *et al., The Mediterranean and Middle East, Volume 4: The Destruction of the Axis Forces in Africa* (London: HMSO, 1966), p.457.

were incurred during a failed attempt to seize the harbour in a direct naval assault, Algiers and its two airfields rapidly fell to the Allies, and with very few losses. This allowed Anderson to fly from Gibraltar to Algiers on 9 November and set up his headquarters in the city.[6]

1.3 Anderson's Army Moves East

The capture of Algiers was just the first step in an overall Allied strategy whose ambitious objectives were the seizure of eastern Algeria, northern Tunisia and the city of Tunis. This advance was designed to threaten the German *Afrika Korps* from the rear and, in cooperation with the Eighth Army, eject it from the shores of Africa. The challenging nature of Anderson's mission required him to move his forces some 560 miles east from Algiers to the city of Tunis using very limited roads and one railway through difficult terrain. Along the way, he might at best expect grudging cooperation from local French officials, and at worst active sabotage by those who opposed the Allied landings. He was dependent on reinforcements on shipping convoys that had to travel some 2,000 miles from the United Kingdom, running the gauntlet of German U-Boat attacks. There was also the small matter of the likely violent reaction of the Germans and their Italian allies. Although taken by surprise by the Torch landings, the Axis forces soon responded rapidly to the situation. In addition to these difficulties for Anderson, there was the minor problem that the First Army was an army in name only. Although nominally an army commander, Anderson had under his direct command the actual equivalent of an under-strength infantry division, composed primarily of two infantry brigades. The need to help secure Algiers, and American sensitivities, meant that the US 34th Infantry Division in that city was under Eisenhower's direct command and was not part of First Army. Furthermore, French units were ill-equipped and for political reasons could not be placed under Anderson's command. To add to his problems, shipping limitations meant that the two brigade groups had limited motor transport, though they could be moved using assigned shipping. There was also the issue of air cover. Although RAF fighters landed at airfields in Algiers on the first day, Anderson was hampered by the slow build-up of aircraft, the lack of all-weather airfields and the increasing distance they had to travel to provide air cover as British troops moved east. The situation was summed up with typical understatement by Anderson himself when he said in his official report: "The First Army did not spring from the sea fully formed like Aphrodite but grew in stature painfully slowly as convoys arrived at fortnightly intervals."[7]

In view of the very meagre means assigned to Anderson and the rather ambitious ends he was required to achieve, it is difficult not to come to the conclusion that from the outset the advance on Tunis would prove difficult. It is to Anderson's great credit that, despite the many difficulties facing the First Army, he and his small staff rapidly and aggressively moved very limited forces into eastern Algeria less than two days after he landed. In this task he was ably supported by 44-year-old Major General Vyvyan Evelegh (see Plate 1), who commanded Anderson's sole infantry division, the 78th, known as the "Battle-Axe" division from its divisional sign. Although Admiral Darlan, the senior Vichy commander in North-West Africa, did not declare

---

6   The story of the American landings is told in detail in chapters 10-13 of George Howe, *North West Africa: Seizing the Initiative in the West. US Army in World War II, The Mediterranean Theatre of Operations* (Washington DC, USA: Department of the Army, 1957).

7   Anderson, *Dispatches*, p.5,452.

that hostilities were over until 0700 hours on 11 November, two battalions of the 36th Infantry Brigade set out by sea on the night of 10 November and landed unopposed the following morning at the Algerian port of Bougie. An attempt to land near to and take the airfield at Djidjelli failed not as a result of enemy resistance, but due to very difficult sea conditions. In the meantime, the remaining battalion of the 36th Brigade used requisitioned local transport to move by road eastwards from Algiers. Less than five days after landing at Algiers, Anderson's forces had therefore already leapfrogged some 100 miles eastward.[8]

1.4 Von Nehring and the Germans React

On 9 November 1942, *General der Panzertruppe* Walther Nehring was in hospital near Berlin when he received a phone call summoning him to attend a meeting elsewhere in the city. Nehring was recovering from wounds incurred in August 1942 while serving with Rommel in North Africa. He had hoped to return to Egypt in October, but a wound in his arm was infected. The following day, Nehring was therefore available to attend a meeting on the new situation in North Africa with the Chief of Staff of the Italian-German *Panzer* Army, *Generalleutnant* Alfred Gause. This meeting initiated the chain of events that led Nehring to fly back to North Africa for a short visit on 14 November, and return on 16 November to assume command of a newly created German *XC* Corps that was beginning to be established in Tunis. General Nehring's first experience of Tunis was nearly his last, as the Junkers 52 transport aircraft in which he travelled had a bad landing at El Aouina airfield and he was lucky not to be killed. The reason that Nehring was able to fly into the airfield in the first place was because the Vichy French took no hostile action when the Germans landed on El Aouina in broad daylight with Junkers transports full of *Luftwaffe* troops.

The Allied landings in North Africa on 8 November came as an unexpected and very unwelcome surprise to Hitler and his headquarters in Berlin (OKW), though not to his Italian allies and Rommel, who had long been concerned about a landing in the rear of the Italian-German army in North Africa. However, their concerns had been completely dismissed by Hitler, who forbade them to carry out any preparatory planning to deal with such an event. Despite many indicators provided by the build-up of troops for Torch, the Axis forces were caught completely off-guard when they learned of the landings. Hitler and the OKW were focused on the situation on the Eastern Front at Stalingrad and Rommel's retreat from El Alamein. In Rome, *Luftwaffe* General Albert Kesselring, Hitler's military representative in Rome - known as "Smiling Albert" due to his constant optimism - was also surprised and concerned. Kesselring took charge of the German response to Torch and ensured Nehring received clear instructions on his task and responsibilities in Tunisia when he passed through Rome on 14 November. Nehring was ordered by Kesselring to push all his available forces to conduct an aggressive forward defence of Tunis by delaying Allied forces on the Algerian-Tunisian border. Upon his arrival in Tunis, he found himself in a not dissimilar position to his counterpart in Algiers, Kenneth Anderson: both had commanders who had set them

---

8   The story of the First Army's move east is derived from Anderson, *Dispatches*, pp.5,450-55; TNA WO 175/50 First Army HQs November 1942 WD; TNA WO 175/168 78th Division HQs G Branch November 1942 WD; TNA WO 175/196 11th Infantry Brigade November 1942 WD; and TNA WO 175/213 36th Infantry Brigade November 1942 WD.

very challenging ends but had assigned inadequate means to achieve them. Ironically, while General Anderson and his commanders worried at the problems facing them moving east to capture Tunis, and especially a future German response to their advance, Nehring looked at his threadbare resources and glanced anxiously west. Upon his return to Tunis on 16 November, his new *XC* Corps had available at most only some 3,500 German troops in Tunis and 4,000 Italians in Bizerte. Moreover, these units were lightly equipped parachute troops with no vehicles, and his only *Panzer* unit was a company of six-wheeled armoured cars. Although the total number of German and Italian troops in Tunisia was higher than Anderson headquarters estimated at that time, the reality was that Nehring's force initially lacked the communications and mobility to execute Kesselring's overly optimistic orders. The one key advantage the Germans did have was the ready availability of *Luftwaffe* aircraft, both locally in Tunis and from airfields in Sicily.

Units of the *Luftwaffe II. Fliegerkorps* were quickly put to use in attacking Allied shipping and troops, particularly those in Bougie harbour in eastern Algeria.[9] Due to the bad conditions at Djidjelli, it had not been possible to land the required British units to rapidly capture and prepare airfields there in time to support RAF fighters. German JU 88 bombers were able to sink two ships carrying key supplies for the British in Bougie harbour on 12 November. Among the losses that would be keenly felt during the cold and wet Tunisian winter were the greatcoats of the two leading brigades. British troops did not have sleeping bags in 1942, and relied heavily on these coats to keep them dry and warm at night when exposed to the elements.

Meanwhile, back in Germany, Hitler's commanders were desperately trying to find any formations and equipment that were not committed to the Eastern Front and could be moved quickly to Tunisia to help stop the Allied advance eastwards. Among the units that soon received orders to move to Tunisia was the 10th *Panzer* Division, which was resting and refitting near Amiens, France, when Torch began. It had been on occupation duty in southern France when it received its marching orders for Tunisia. The newly formed 334th Infantry Division, based near Nuremberg, was also alerted for its move to Tunisia by its parent *XIII* Corps on 9 November. The division staff had to rapidly reorganize the formation while still meeting an expected deployment date of 1 December. Further south, Kesselring's staff in Rome tried to secure from the Italians the necessary rail assets and shipping to move the 334th from Germany via Italy to Tunisia. The issue of limited transportation, especially shipping, was to hamper the Axis ability to react to the Allies throughout the campaign. In the meantime, however, General Nehring made the best of the very limited resources available to him. He issued orders for one of his best units, *OberstLeutnant* Walter Koch's 2nd *Fallschirmjäger* Regiment, to move out of Tunis down the Medjerda River valley to the market town of Medjez el Bab. He also instructed Major Witzig's Parachute Pioneer Battalion to move to Bizerte and advance on the Bizerte-Bone road to a road junction near the small town of Djebel Aboid. During this period, Nehring also visited Admiral Esteva; the political governor of Tunisia, and Admiral Derrien, the commander of the Bizerte garrison. Under orders still from the Vichy government, and despite the fact that the Germans were in the process of occupying the rest of France, both Esteva and Derrien reluctantly cooperated with the Axis forces. Nehring was also keen to meet the military commander of Tunisia, Major General Georges Barre, to ensure his forces were

9   The German response is based on Walter Nehring, *The First Phase of the Battle in Tunisia*, Foreign Military Studies (FMS) Reports D-086 and D-147 (US Army Historical Division Europe).

neutralised, but soon after the Germans landed in Tunis, Barre moved himself and many of his units some 50 miles west to the town of Beja. To the Germans' frustration, Barre managed to ensure he was always out of his command post when German emissaries visited. His subordinate officers also protested ignorance of orders issued from the Vichy government that required them to cooperate with the German commanders. By interposing his ill-equipped forces between the Germans and the allies, Barre effectively delayed the Germans and Italians from moving east to engage the advancing Allies. Both German political advisers and military staff were reluctant to provoke any incidents that might lead to hostilities while the Axis forces were weak. This reluctance to confront the French meant that even on 17 November, Barre's units still occupied the west bank of the Medjerda River running through Medjez el Bab. This prevented Koch's 2nd *Fallschirmjäger* Regiment from moving further west. The uneasy truce ended on 18 November when Kesselring in Rome issued orders to attack Barre's French units from the air.

1.5 Advance into Tunisia

Meanwhile, First Army headquarters had not been idle and had been aggressively pushing forces further east to Algeria and beyond. On 12 November, two companies of the British 3rd Parachute Battalion were air-dropped near the Algerian town of Bone and a Commando unit landed from the sea. The 78th Division used all available transport of the 11th Infantry Brigade in Algiers to move a small mobile unit called Hart Force, which was rushed east to Algeria. It also sent two battalions of the 36th Infantry Brigade by rail, road and sea to Bone and on to Bougie. The movement of British forces east was heavily constrained by very limited communications systems and the lack of sufficient transport vehicles. On 13 November, the British in Algeria received valuable reinforcements when a follow-up convoy docked in Algiers. It brought an armoured regiment, the 17/21st Lancers, the 1st Parachute Brigade and most importantly the balance of the vehicle transport for the 11th Brigade. It also carried Anderson's advanced First Army headquarters, which was established that day in the Hotel Albert in Algiers. The 17/21st Lancers soon became the core of a mobile formation called Blade Force, named after the 78th Division's Battle-Axe sign. The formation included various 11th Infantry Brigade units, including the 5th Northants, artillery, reconnaissance and anti-tank units. Rapidly assembled in two days, its advanced elements had moved some 379 miles east to arrive in Souk Ahras by 17 November. Within two further days it had moved onwards to the landing ground at Souk el Arba in Tunisia, located on the Medjerda River, some 130 miles south-west of Tunis. In the north, the 6th Battalion of the Queen's Own Royal West Kent Regiment (6th West Kents), part of the 36th Infantry Brigade, arrived in Bougie on 14 November. Transport was so scarce that the unit had to use 11 French charcoal-burning lorries to move to the coastal town of Tabarka, which was 5 miles inside Tunisia, on 16 November. The 6th West Kents were rapidly followed by the 8th Battalion of the Argyll and Sutherland Highlanders (8th Argylls), who arrived in Tabarka on 17 November.

By this date, General Anderson had issued additional orders to Major General Evelegh. The Battle-Axe Division was to concentrate all its units in the Tabarka-Souk el Arba area, advance on Tunis and destroy the Axis forces. The attack on Tunis was to be conducted using all available British forces on three routes. The first route was to be in the north, using an established road from Tabarka via Djebel Aboid to the town of Mateur and on to Tunis. The second route was from the market town of Beja via a back road to the railway station of Sidi Nisr, then over a low mountain pass called Chouigui down to Tunis. The third and final route started at Beja, running south-east to Medjez el Bab, up the north bank of the Medjerda River to Tebourba and on to Tunis. Anderson would later be criticized in retrospect by several authors and historians for not concentrating all his forces on a single thrust on Tunis. This criticism seems to have overlooked the fact that the hard realities of logistics interfered with such aspirations. The army commander and his staff were all too well aware that trying to sustain a single thrust down one road, especially one under regular German air attack, was likely to be impractical (see Map 2).[10] The poor nature of the road network, combined with the number of vehicles needed to maintain just one division, would have quickly resulted in the deterioration of the single highway. Any resulting traffic jams would be easily attacked from the air. Although it was by no means ideal, Anderson and Evelegh were forced to use a number of routes to maintain their advance. This inevitably reduced the strength of the blow that could be inflicted on the Germans at any one point. The difficulties encountered were not the result of failing to concentrate the forces down one single route, but because the forces made available to Anderson by General Eisenhower were entirely inadequate to achieve the ambitious objectives he set, especially in the face of German air superiority.

Anderson was severely hampered by his lack of control over American troops under Major General Charles Ryder. The sensitivity of senior US commanders to any suggestion of initially placing American troops under British command meant that in the first weeks after the landings in Algiers, Ryder reported directly to Eisenhower, who was located hundreds of miles away in Gibraltar. Anderson had no direct control over the 9,000 US troops of the 39th and 168th US Infantry Regiments who formed the garrison of Algiers. These forces, along with their ample artillery and transport assets, were not initially available to support the main Allied effort to seize Tunis. Furthermore, although Eisenhower was the Allied ground commander for Operation Torch, he did not actually move to North Africa until 13 November. His first visit outside his headquarters was to Casablanca on 19 November, arguably in the wrong direction, and his first visit to see Anderson was not until 28 November and that took place in Algeria some 170 miles from the front line. Eisenhower would eventually visit Tunisia for the first time on 24 December, by which time the race to Tunis was effectively over.[11]

It is arguable that much of the criticism often levelled at Anderson is perhaps better targeted on Eisenhower, who devoted far too much time and energy on political negotiations with the French and far too little ensuring that the maximum resources possible were concentrated in the right place. Certainly it is reasonable to state that Eisenhower's lack of command and combat experience was a little too readily apparent in the early days in Tunisia. He also benefitted from the fact that two of Anderson's strengths were his humility and loyalty. Though much more experienced than Eisenhower, Anderson did not complain when a comparative novice

10   See Richard Atkinson, *An Army at Dawn, The War in North Africa 1942-43* (London: Little Brown, 2003), pp.175-76, and David Rolf, *The Bloody Race to Tunis: Destruction of Axis forces in North Africa November 1942–May 1943*, (London: Greenhill Books, 2001), p.41, for criticisms of Anderson's plans.
11   The 39th and 168th RCTs formed the garrison of Algiers under Major General C. Ryder USA, who reported directly to Eisenhower and not Anderson. The 168th RCT eventually moved into Algeria to protect supply routes on 24 December 1942. Eisenhower visits are recorded in the diary of Captain Butcher USN, his naval aide. See H.C. Butcher, *My Three Years with Eisenhower* (New York: Simon and Schuster, 1946), pp.204-08.

was imposed over him, and moreover he loyally committed himself to support his new boss. It is worth considering what would have happened if Montgomery had been appointed as First Army commander. Later experience suggests that he would have been less loyal to and more impatient of Eisenhower's undoubted lack of grip of the situation. That national sensitivities could quickly be subordinated to the ruthless demands of the mission was demonstrated on 15 November. On this date, and to Eisenhower's credit, he finally decided to reinforce the First Army with Combat Command B (CCB) of the Old Ironsides of the 1st US Armoured Division and two US artillery battalions. The 1st Armoured Division had come ashore as part of Operation Torch and had overcome the short-lived resistance of French forces in Oran. CCB was a self-contained mobile task force. Since Anderson lacked mobile armoured units, it was a particularly useful and timely addition to the First Army.

This reinforcement came at most appropriate time, as the uneasy peace that had existed between the Axis forces and Major General Barre's troops came to an end. Both Nehring in Tunis and Kesselring in Rome had become increasingly impatient with and suspicious of General Barre's unwillingness to cooperate with the Axis commanders. They suspected him of using delaying tactics while awaiting the arrival of Allied forces so he could reveal his true sympathies with the Allies. German suspicions were accurate, for while Barre evaded contact with German representatives, he secretly met with one sent by the Allies. Major Henry Lovell, the second-in-command of the 6th West Kents, was sent to talk to Barre at his headquarters near Beja on 15 November. Soon afterwards, armoured cars of D Squadron of the 1st Derbyshire Yeomanry arrived in Beja and were reinforced by the arrival of the 1st Parachute Battalion. When aerial reconnaissance revealed the presence of 'American' armoured cars in Beja and Barre rejected a German ultimatum to surrender his forces on 19 November, German patience ran out. In his headquarters in Rome, Kesselring gave orders to attack Barre's French formations by air and on the ground at Medjez el Bab.[12]

1.6 First Skirmishes

The German attack on French forces on 19 November was not the first skirmish of the Tunisian campaign that had occurred at a road junction near a dusty small hamlet called Djebel Abiod east of Tabarka (see Map 2). After arriving at Tabarka on 16 November, the 6th West Kents, commanded by Lieutenant Colonel Bernard Howlett, had marched east to seize the important road junction at Djebel Abiod. At this hamlet the coastal roads going north-east to Mateur and Bizerte joined with the road south-east to Beja. The 6th West Kents was a territorial battalion and as one might expect for a unit recruited in Kent, it had many accomplished cricketers among its ranks. This included its Commanding Officer (CO), Bernard Howlett (see Plate 3), whose nickname in the army was "Swifty" due to his fast-bowling skills, which had been used to good effect while playing for Kent in the inter-war years. On arrival at Djebel Abiod on the morning of 17 November, Howlett deployed his companies and two scarce 2-pounder anti-tank guns under the command of Captain Bryan Valentine, whose pre-war role had been captain of the Kent county cricket team. While awaiting instructions, Howlett was alerted at about 1100

---

12   For details of General Barre's negotiations, see Blaxland, *The Plain Cook*, pp.102-03, and H.D. Chaplin, *Queen's Own West Kent Regiment 1920-1950* (Uckfield: Naval and Military Press, 2004), pp.227-28.

hours to the advance of a German column, including tanks, which were duly sighted by his hidden troops two-and-a-half hours later. Howlett is reputed to have observed: "Looks as if we'll be opening the batting for the Gentlemen versus the Players."[13]

The column wending its unsuspecting way down the road from Mateur was that commanded by Major Rudolf Witzig, who had been ordered by Nehring to delay the British forces. Witzig had won the Knight's Cross of the Iron Cross for his part in the daring attack on Fort Eben Emael in Belgium in May 1940. His force included two companies of his own Pioneer Engineer Battalion, a company of Mark IV tanks from the 190th *Panzer* Battalion and an artillery battery. Although his force also included six Italian armoured cars, Witzig failed to use them as scouts and was badly surprised when the 2-pounder anti-tank guns of the 6th West Kents, supported by the 25-pounder guns of the 138th Field Regiment, opened up at close range. Major Witzig's force recoiled up the road, but not before leaving behind at least five damaged tanks and some 50 dead. The German force quickly retaliated with shelling and managed to inflict casualties on the unfortunate gunners, whose positions had now been revealed. Witzig's initial repulse at Djebel Abiod, although a local success, could not be immediately exploited by the 54-year-old commander of 36th Infantry Brigade, Brigadier Arthur Kent-Lemon. Howlett's under-strength battalion was unable to move forward as it lacked additional supplies, transport and reinforcements. It was rather isolated and its exposed positions came under regular shelling from the Witzig battle group and *Luftwaffe* air attacks.[14] The vehicles lost during bombing attacks at Bougie, and tenuous lines of communications stretching back to Algiers, now began to make their impact, especially on Kent-Lemon's brigade. The lack of transport meant he was unable to rapidly build up the required supplies, and move them and troops forward to Djebel Abiod. These problems meant that the 36th Brigade attack could not be resumed until 26 November.

All British units in northern Tunisia were dependent on whatever supplies could be moved along the two main roads east and on a single railway line which could take no more than four to six trains each day. Another factor was that in the forward areas all vehicles suffered increasingly from the unwelcome attentions of the *Luftwaffe*. These matters all lead Kenneth Anderson to reluctantly order Evelegh on 21 November to temporarily suspend the advance eastwards until he could concentrate sufficient forces and supplies to resume the attack effectively. Meanwhile, in the south near Medjez el Bab, the uneasy truce between the French and Germans came to an end on 19 November. Major General Barre's forces at Medjez el Bab came under air attack, but twice successfully repulsed strong attacks by *Oberstleutnant* Koch's force of paratroopers. Although Barre's ill-equipped forces were reinforced, the French were eventually forced out of Medjez el Bab by Koch's *Kampfgruppe* (Battle Group) on 20 November. French and Allied forces were forced to withdraw west towards the town of Beja, which also suffered from constant air attacks. Barre's forces were not capable of retaking the town, so the task fell to Brigadier Edward "Copper" Cass and his troops from the 11th Brigade which had only just started arrive near Beja, having completed a 500-mile road march from Algiers. Brigadier Cass's Brigade used the time from 20-24 November to move up first to near Beja and to probe towards Medjez el Bab. In the meantime, the able 32-year-old Koch (who had also won a Knight's Cross for his part in the capture of Fort Eben Emael) ensured his battalion of paratroopers quickly dug in

---

13   See Blaxland, *The Plain Cook*, p.101.
14   For details of this action see Chaplin, *Queen's Own*, pp.228-30, and TNA WO 175/509 6th West Kents November 1942 WD.

their mortars and machine guns to defend the town. By taking and subsequently holding Medjez el Bab and the bridge over the Medjerda for nearly five days, Koch helped gain vital time for reinforcements to arrive. His commander, Nehring, and his Italian allies made maximum use of these days to bring in new units.

Both sides had made use of the short lull in the fighting to move up extra forces and supplies. Anderson was aware from intelligence of the German build-up and allowed less than four days to pass before ordering Vyvyan Evelegh to continue the advance on Tunis. As a result, on 24 November, Brigadier Cass and the units of 11th Infantry Brigade began operations to eject the Germans from Medjez el Bab. The 2nd Lancs Fusiliers, lead by Lieutenant Colonel L.A. "Monk" Manly, moved to attack Medjez from the north while the 5th Northants, under the command of Lieutenant Colonel Arthur Crook, were ordered to attack from the south-west. The attack of the 2nd Lancs Fusiliers began badly with delays in the dark and the death of Manly, who was killed just as the battalion crossed its start line for the attack. Despite four brave attempts to cross the river and over 160 casualties, the Fusiliers were unable to establish viable positions on the east side of the Medjerda River at Medjez. As the Fusiliers pulled back under the cover of artillery fire, they could also hear the sound of their objective, the ancient Roman bridge in the town, being blown up.[15] The attack by the 5th Northants also failed when Lieutenant Colonel Crook's battalion encountered German tanks and had to withdraw. A second attack by the brigade was not required as Koch's *Kampfgruppe* pulled out of Medjez early the following morning and withdrew up the valley.

On the northern route, the advance of the 36th Brigade resumed on 26 November but rapidly ran into trouble. In a reversal of roles, Major Witzig's paratrooper engineers executed a classic ambush on the 8th Argylls which destroyed two of the battalion's rifle companies near Jefna station. Thereafter the brigade's advance on the northern route was stalled in front of two hills, Djebels Azzag and Ajred, which were soon to be known as Green Hill and Bald Hill. In the centre, Blade Force, now reinforced by an American armoured regiment, advanced rapidly through the Chouigui pass and was briefly able to attack Djedeida airfield less than 20 miles from Tunis on the 25th. However, it lacked the strength to take on rapidly growing German forces and would eventually be forced to withdraw to Sidi Nisr. The pressure exerted by Blade Force had one positive outcome, for as previously mentioned, at 0400 hours on 26 November the bridge at Medjez el Bab was blown up and the Germans retreated towards Tunis. Brigadier Cass's brigade now advanced again, and vehicles of the 56th Reconnaissance Regiment (56th Recce) were at the ancient town of Tebourba by dusk. They were quickly followed by the infantry companies of the 1st East Surreys, apart from one company that secured two hills called Djebel el Ahmera and Djebel el Rhar. These dominated the Medjerda valley road to Tebourba some three miles east of Medjez. The CO of the East Surreys, 38-year-old Lieutenant Colonel William Basil Wilberforce, great grandson of the famous anti-slavery campaigner William Wilberforce, wanted to ensure that his rear was protected. Bill Wilberforce was born in Yorkshire and was also a keen cricketer. He named the location Longstop Hill, after the position on a cricket field designed to catch fast deliveries. In assigning one of his platoons to secure Longstop Hill,

15   For delays in operations and the attack on Medjez el Bab, see TNA WO 175/50 First Army November 1942 WD; TNA WO 175/168 78th Division Nov 1942 WD; TNA WO 175/196, 11th Infantry Brigade Nov 1942 WD; TNA WO 175/512, 2 Lancashire Fusiliers Nov 1942 WD; and John Hallam, *The History of the Lancashire Fusiliers, 1939-1945* (Stroud: Alan Sutton Publishing, 1993), pp.39-40.

Wilberforce displayed excellent judgement and a view that become quickly endorsed by his German military peers. Though the hills are less than 1,000ft in height, Longstop and the peaks to the north soon became the most fought-over terrain in Tunisia. Longstop itself would rapidly be recaptured by the Germans and would be held for over five long months.

In view of the central importance of the Longstop Hill area to this story, it is worthwhile devoting a few lines to a description of the area.[16] Perhaps the most important fact about the feature is that it is actually two distinct hills, Djebel Ahmera (loosely translated as the red hill) and its twin brother Djebel Rhar. These two hills, which are respectively some 290 and 243 metres in height, are divided by a small but significant depression or col. The importance of Djebel Rhar is that its retention by an opposing force ensures that ownership of Djebel Ahmera can be easily disputed. The existence of two separate hills is not immediately obvious to anyone viewing the location from the west. It was doubly unfortunate that Wilberforce, who was completely aware of this fact, sadly reinforced this misunderstanding among other units through his use of a phrase that suggested it was only one hill. Both hills are quite low features compared to some of the more lofty peaks which can be seen to their north, and which also have a key role to play in this story. Nonetheless, anyone attempting today to walk from the main road to the top of Ahmera today will quickly find out two facts: this is no easy Sunday stroll, and there is an unfettered view from the top of Ahmera along the Medjerda River valley. Furthermore, the ridges from these hills sprawl down and compress the road and the main railway line with its small rail stop against the Medjerda, which lies less than 200 metres away. The Longstop Hill complex forms a natural chokepoint to the primary west–east routes to Tunis from Algiers when held by the enemy. The rail stop located here, Halte d'El Heri, also lends its name to the small hamlet that had grown up around it by December 1942.[17] It was also not feasible to easily bypass Longstop Hill and the Medjerda valley to the north in 1942, for that is a relatively inaccessible area of some 20 square miles of rugged, bare mountains and hills. It contains two peaks over 2,000ft and 10 peaks over 1,500ft in height, and in 1943 it could only be traversed on foot or by mule. The very difficult nature of the terrain in this area, which came to be called the "Peaks" by veterans who suffered there, is not easy to convey, but one officer described it in this way: "The mountain area north of Medjez el Bab dominated the entire campaign, and it was so foul, broken, blasted and inhospitable the Devil himself was surely the principal agent in its creation."[18] The scarce resources available to Evelegh and Anderson, combined with the challenging terrain to the north, meant that any renewed attack on Tunis would be restricted to the Medjerda Valley.

16   The source of the name Longstop has been credited to an unnamed staff officer at 78th Division HQ, but Harry Smith, the second-in-command of the battalion, clearly states in his memoir that Bill Wilberforce gave the hill its name. See H.B. Smith, *Operations of the 1st East Surreys in 1939–45, Part 2: North Africa, Sicily and Italy* (London: Imperial War Museum Reference 02(41) 662), p.8.
17   The description of Djebel Ahmera, Rhar and Halte De Hieri is based on the author's visit to the Longstop Hill area in September 2008 and analysis of photographs showing the views to and from the hill.
18   See John Coldwell-Horsfall, *The Wild Geese are Flighting* (Kineton: Roundwood Press, 1976), p.26.

1.7 Battles of Djedeida and Tebourba

Anderson was not the only commander with limited resources, for the German withdrawal from Medjez el Bab reflected the meager forces available to General Nehring in Tunis, though this situation was about to change. As Bill Wilberforce and his battalion continued their attack up the Medjerda valley towards the village of Tebourba on the evening of 26 November and seized it the following morning, plans were already being made by Nehring to counterattack the 78th Division. After being alerted earlier in November, as Operation Torch began, the leading units of the 10th *Panzer* Division had completed their long journey and reached Tunisia. Their arrival, combined with that of other Axis units, was to signal a significant change in the fortunes of the Allied forces. Nehring's desperate situation at the end of November had led him to commit the leading units of the 10th *Panzer* Division before the whole formation had arrived. The result was that Wilberforce and his battalion found themselves facing a serious counterattack from a *Panzer* battalion on the morning of 27 November. During the rest of the day the battalion, ably supported by the 25-pounder guns of the 132nd Field Artillery Regiment, managed to fight off this initial attack, though not without the loss of six guns. The repulse of this attack was misconstrued by divisional staff as the commitment by the Germans of their last reserves, but additional units of the 10th Panzer Division were now landing at Tunis. This new threat was not apparent to General Anderson or Evelegh, and the latter therefore committed the rest of the 11th Infantry Brigade to an attack. This was led by the 5th Northants, supported by American Grant tanks, and its objective was the village of Djedeida a few miles east of Tebourba. When the armour-backed 5th Northants attacked the village they came under heavy German air, armoured and infantry attack. By the next day the division's relatively dispersed positions along the Medjerda valley made it vulnerable, with the result that when Nehring managed to launch a more powerful German counterattack, the 78th Division suffered a serious reverse.[19] The force of this attack over the next three days pushed the division and its attached forces back west along the river valley, but only after three of the battalions involved had fought some difficult delaying actions. These included the epic stand of the 2nd Battalion of the Hampshire Regiment (2nd Hants) east of Tebourba in which one of its officers, Major Le Patourel, won the Victoria Cross (VC). Both the 1st East Surreys and the 5th Northants suffered heavy casualties in these battles, with the 2nd Hants down to less than a third of its strength. As a result of these losses, the 11th Brigade had only limited value as a force and was withdrawn west. The consequence of this action was by 6 December the 78th Division's lead brigade had been forced back to the tactically important Tebourba Gap, where the Medjerda valley narrows between two large hills just west of the town. This location was now held by the 8th Argylls, reinforced with artillery and a US unit. Normally, and despite 11th Brigade's weakness, this strong tactical position should have been held. But at this juncture bad winter weather aided the Axis, heavy rain beginning on 7 December and continuing for two days. This,

19   The story of the Battles of Djedeida and Tebourba is described in detail in TNA WO 175/196 11 Brigade Dec 42 WD; TNA WO 175/499 2 Hants Dec 42 WD; TNA WO 175/519, 1st East Surreys Dec 42 WD; TNA WO 175/517; David S Daniell, *Regimental History of the Royal Hampshire Regiment Volume 3 1918-1954* (Aldershot: Gale and Polden, 1954), pp.90-99; Daniell, *History of East Surreys,* pp.152-57; and Jervois, *History of the Northants,* pp.120-24. See also M.C. Barton, 'The Hampshires at Tebourba, 1942', in *Army and Defence Quarterly April 1944,* pp.57-63.

combined with the constant German air attacks, led the newly arrived commander of V Corps, Lieutenant General Charles Allfrey (see Plate 1), to order a surprising withdrawal to Medjez el Bab. This order was carried out on the night of 10 December, and while the British troops were able to withdraw successfully, CCB of the 1st US Armoured Division was not so lucky, losing some 200 tanks and vehicles bogged down in a muddy river bed near Longstop Hill. The result was that by the 10th, the 78th Division was back to the start-line area from which it had begun its original attack to capture Tunis. Moreover, the position christened Longstop Hill had not fulfilled the tactical purpose envisioned by Bill Wilberforce and had now fallen back into the hands of the Germans.[20]

---

20 Brigadier General Lunsford Oliver, the CO of CCB, was required to write an official report on this unfortunate action to General Allfrey at V Corps. A copy of the report is in the V Corps War Diary for December 1942. See TNA WO 175/82 Dec 42 WD.

The Commanders

Plate 1 Kenneth Anderson (Left), Vyvyan Evelegh (Centre) and Charles Allfrey (right) in Tunisia 1943.
(Copyright IWM -TR 637)

Plate 2 Major General Evelegh, GOC 78th Division (Left) with Brigadier Edward Cass, 11th
Infantry Brigade Commander (second from right) talking to American officers in Sicily, August 1943.
(Copyright NAM - 1999-03-88-44)

Plate 3 Portrait of Brigadier Swifty Howlett
(36th Infantry Brigade Commander)
(Reproduced with the kind permission of
General Sir G Howlett KBE MC)

Plate 4 Photograph of Brigadier Nelson
Russell (38th Infantry Brigade Commander)
(Reproduced with the kind permission of the
Royal Irish Fusiliers Museum)

2

The First Battle of Longstop Hill and a Winter Stalemate

2.1 Plans for the First Battle for Longstop

Although General Eisenhower informed his superiors that the delay in taking Tunis was temporary, it was rapidly becoming apparent that the opportunity to quickly capture Tunis had probably been lost. The build-up of German ground forces in northern Tunisia in November and early December had created sufficient strength to deny the Allies an opportunity to rapidly take Tunis. Three other key factors assisted the Germans: the arrival of heavy rain on 7 December, which turned tracks into mud and made off-road movement difficult; the stretched Allied supply lines; and finally the constant German air attacks on Allied ground forces, made possible by the close proximity of *Luftwaffe* air bases to the front line. As a symbol of that stubborn German resistance, those forces soon received a new name, the 5th *Panzer* Army, and a new commander to replace Nehring, the 54-year-old Prussian General Hans Jurgen von Arnim. Field Marshal Kesselring, the commander of all German forces in the Mediterranean, had lost confidence in Nehring and replaced him with von Arnim, who moved from command of a corps in Russia to command an army in Tunisia. The importance of Longstop Hill as a defensive position was immediately obvious to the Germans. They rapidly established defensive positions in that area using troops from a battalion of the newly arrived 754th Grenadier Regiment from the 334th Infantry Division. This battalion formed part of a recently formed *Kampfgruppe* under the leadership of *Oberst* Rudolf Lang, commander of the 69th *Panzer* Grenadier Regiment. This included a battalion from the 69th and one from the 7th *Panzer* Regiment, both of which formed part of the 10th *Panzer* Division. The *Kampfgruppe* pushed forward to contact the 78th Division in its defensive positions just to the east and south-east of Medjez el Bab.[1] The increase in German forces was only partly matched on the ground by the First Army. The 1st Guards Brigade, the third brigade of the 78th Division, arrived to relieve the badly battered 11th Brigade at Medjez on the evening of 10 December. Though missing its third infantry battalion, the 2nd Hants, this brigade, along with its two other complete infantry battalions - the 2nd Battalion

---

1   Details of German forces on Longstop Hill are derived from Rudolf Lang, *The Battles of Kampfgruppe Lang in Tunisia (10 Panzer Division) December 1942 to 15 April 1943*, Part 1, Report D-173 (US Army Historical Division Europe), and Intelligence Summaries in TNA WO 175/168 78th Division December 1942 WD.

the Coldstream Guards and 3rd Battalion of the Grenadier Guards - and attached troops was at this time the strongest brigade at Lieutenant General Allfrey's disposal. The 36th Brigade, for example, was tied up near Djebel Aboid in front of Green Hill and was lacking its third battalion, the 8th Argylls, which had been attached to 11th Brigade to cover its withdrawal. The only other formation in the First Army was the 6th Armoured Division, which was just arriving to take up positions south of Medjez down to the town of Goubellat.[2]

The significant casualties incurred by the Battle-Axe Division and CCB of the 1st US Armoured Division as a result of the German counter-offensive, combined with constant German air attacks, had seriously dented the confidence of the Allied high command in northern Tunisia. Five days earlier, Allfrey, the newly arrived General Officer Commanding (GOC) of V Corps, recommended that his formation abandon Medjez el Bab and withdraw some 25 miles west to a line centred on the ancient town of Teboursouk (see Map 2). As Allfrey was new not only to corps command, but also to active operations against the German Army, this degree of pessimism was not entirely surprising. What was rather unusual was that Allfrey's recommendation was not only supported by Anderson, but may have been initiated by him. Allfrey's proposed withdrawal quickly met with opposition from Major General Barre, the local French commander, who knew the importance of holding the gateway to Tunis as he had previously fought to hold it. He was not alone, for his superiors General Juin and General Giraud were also vehemently opposed to the plan, but more importantly it was also resisted by General Eisenhower. The latter's natural inclination was to be optimistic about future chances to capture Tunis, and he was rightly reluctant to give up hard-won and vital tactical ground. Anderson and Allfrey were strongly advised by Eisenhower to hold on to the Medjez el Bab area, and plans for a withdrawal were shelved.

In the meantime, the task of defending Medjez against any future German attacks fell largely on 1st Guards Brigade, supported by the remaining armoured units of CCB of the 1st US Armoured Division. The 1st Guards Brigade was commanded by 48-year-old Brigadier Felix Copland-Griffiths, who had won a MC in the First World War and a DSO in 1940 for his role in the defence of Arras while in command of the 1st Battalion the Welsh Guards. Brigadier Copland-Griffith's two battalions arrived on the night of 10-11 December, which was the same night that CCB became mired in mud during its withdrawal. The 2nd Coldstream Guards had barely settled into defensive positions in a wood north-east of Medjez near the rail station, when they saw a long column of the remaining American vehicles moving down the road into the town. The Coldstream Guards quickly discovered that the armoured withdrawal had not been cleanly executed, as part of the column actually consisted of German tanks and captured American jeeps. The ensuing firefight was minor and the Germans were forced to retreat, though not before the battalion suffered its first seven wounded of the campaign.[3]

2   The 1st Guards Brigade was the third brigade of the 78th Division. It arrived with follow-up convoys and reached Beja on 6 December, but 2nd Hants had been sent ahead.
3   Unless otherwise noted, the description of events and plans prior to the Battle of Longstop Hill is based on the War diaries of the First Army TNA WO 175/50, V Corps TNA WO 175/82, 78th Infantry Division TNA WO 175/168 and 1st Guards Brigade TNA WO 175/186 for December 1942; also Blaxland, *Plain Cook*, pp.139-43; Michael Howard and John Sparrow, *The Coldstream Guards 1920-1946* (Oxford: Oxford University Press, 1951), pp.108-11; and N. Nicholson, *The Grenadier Guards in World War 2* (Aldershot: Gale and Polden, 1949), pp.267-70. Readers should also be aware of A. Robson's excellent book *Tunisia 1942-43 The Second Battalion Coldstream Guards* (A. Robson, 2015).

As the 2nd Battalion the Coldstream Guards (2nd Coldstreams) plays an important role in the story of Longstop Hill, it is worth devoting a little time to this unit. The Coldstream Guards, one of the oldest regiments in the British Army, takes its name from a small river on the border between England and Scotland, where it was founded in 1650 by General George Monck. It became part of The Lord General's Regiment of Foot Guards for the monarch on the restoration of King Charles II. Although the second Foot Guards unit to be formed, the Coldstream Guards did not consider themselves second to any other unit, as they had technically been formed first and adopted the motto *Nulli Secundus* (Second to None). Over the next 290 years the regiment set out to prove its motto was true through its deeds on the battlefields around the world. These included its epic defence of Hougoumont farmhouse at the Battle of Waterloo in 1815, at the Battles of Alma and Inkerman in the Crimean War and the Battles of Mons, Loos and Ypres during the First World War. The 2nd Coldstreams had been a part of the BEF sent to France in 1940 before being evacuated. The battalion was commanded by 42-year-old Lieutenant Colonel William Stewart-Brown, who joined it as a 2nd lieutenant in 1919. He had spent the next twenty years slowly being promoted before he had assumed command of the 2nd Coldstreams in September 1942.

While Stewart-Brown and his battalion settled into their position, the 3rd Battalion the Grenadier Guards (3rd Grenadiers) took over the defence of hills just south of Medjez el Bab. Their retention of these positions had been a close-run thing, for the battalion commander and his staff arrived to carry out a reconnaissance of their new positions just as a column of German tanks came up the road towards the hill. Fortunately, artillery and tanks were quickly summoned and the German advance was stopped. As the two battalions of the 1st Guards Brigade were establishing their defensive positions near Medjez, plans were being made at Army level to use them in a more offensive capacity. Eisenhower was keen to regain the initiative and continue the attack on Tunis, and pushed First Army commander Anderson to plan a new attack. Lieutenant General Anderson was much more circumspect about the ability of his limited forces to seize Tunis, and in messages to Eisenhower he rated his chances of success as only 50-50. This apparent pessimism did not please Ike, who privately criticised Anderson for undue pessimism, something often noted by other authors. It was of course very easy to be optimistic about the First Army's chances of capturing Tunis from the isolation and safety of Algiers, where Eisenhower's now burgeoning Allied Forces Headquarters (AFHQ) was being established. Anderson had a number of faults, but he differed from Eisenhower in one key area as he had extensive combat experience. Whatever criticisms have been made of Anderson, and he had a long line of detractors, they did not include any reference to his personal courage or his constant visits to the forward commanders. In stark contrast, it is almost incredible that Eisenhower's first visit to Tunisia and anywhere close to the front did not take place until almost seven weeks after the first Torch landings. Prior to that time he based his assessment of the situation almost entirely on messages and correspondence, supplemented by meetings with Anderson at the latter's rear HQ in eastern Algeria. Anderson may have been a pessimist, but Eisenhower was frankly completely out of touch with the realities facing his First Army commander. Despite his misgivings, Anderson tasked Allfrey, the V Corps commander, with planning a new attack designed to take Tunis, and the 1st Guards Brigade was assigned a key role in that plan.

V Corps' Lieutenant General Charles Allfrey was a tall, thin, bluff, jolly but shrewd 47-year-old former gunner who had been commissioned into the Royal Artillery in the month the First World War started. He had originally attended the Royal Naval College at Dartmouth, but actually became an Army officer. Allfrey had gained extensive experience of battle over four years in France, and was awarded a MC for bravery in 1918. Between the wars, Allfrey attended the Staff College at Camberley, after which he was seconded to the Colonial Office and then to the Iraqi Army, where he won a DSO. Allfrey spent three years instructing at Camberley, and at the start of the Second World War briefly served in the BEF. He took command of the 43rd Wessex Division in 1941 before taking over as V Corps commander in March 1942, arriving in Tunisia in December.[4]

Allfrey's plan to take Tunis was based on the premise that the main attack would be conducted by the newly arrived 6th Armoured Division along the road that runs through the small town of Massicault. In order to support this attack, the 78th Division - and more specifically the 1st Guards Brigade - was assigned the task of taking Longstop Hill. This attack was scheduled to start on the night of 22- 23 December. Brigadier Copland-Griffiths was handed a rather tough nut to crack, as he had only two infantry battalions rather than the usual three and the Longstop feature was expected to be held by strong Axis forces. The 1st Guards Brigade plan assigned the task of taking Longstop Hill to the 2nd Coldstreams, with that of securing Grich el Oued village to the south going to the 3rd Grenadiers. Due to the need to subsequently use the 1st Guards Brigade in follow-up operations and the shortage of British units, the 2nd Coldstreams would be relieved on Longstop Hill by the 1st Battalion of the 18th American Infantry Regiment, whose nickname was the Vanguards. In order to cover the northern flank of this attack, in the trackless and rugged hills north of Longstop, a French Algerian unit, the 4th Regiment Tabor Algerian (4th RTA), was to secure the dominating height of Djebel el Ang to the north-west of Longstop. As part of the wider plan, the 5th Northants, who had been in reserve, were assigned the very risky task of using mules to march the whole battalion 10 miles over the hills from the village of Heidous to get behind the German front line and threaten their positions near Tebourba. The assumption was that Longstop would quickly be taken, so when the attack continued , the threat to their rear posed by the 5th Northants would cause the Germans to withdraw.[5]

2.2 The Other Side of the Hill

That most professional of British soldiers, the Duke of Wellington, is generally credited with making the famous statement that the whole art of war consists of guessing at what is on the other side of the hill. Wellington's advice to officers was designed to stress the need to visualise the nature of terrain in front of them, and just as importantly the critical importance of good intelligence on enemy forces. Never was the importance of taking Wellington's sage advice more appropriate than in the case of the planning of the operation to take Longstop Hill. This quotation was particularly relevant to the first battle of Longstop for two reasons. The first and perhaps greatest irony was that Brigadier Copland-Griffiths and other planners had completely

---

4   The profile of Charles Allfrey is based on information in the Army List and the biographical entry in R. Mead, *Churchill's Lions; A Biographical Guide to British Generals of World War II* (Stroud: Spellmount Publishers, 2007), pp.46-48.

5   The V Corps and 78th Division plans for the attack towards Tebourba are to be found in the Operations Orders in the relevant war diaries – TNA WO 175/50 WD and TNA WO 175/168 WD respectively.

failed to grasp that on the other side of the hill was yet another hill. As previously noted, the Longstop feature is actually not one but two hills, for Djebel Ahmera and Djebel Rhar are separated by a deep gully. The latter is lower than Ahmera by 40 metres and is not visible when viewed from the west. Its existence, however, means that any attacking force that fails to take this feature exposes itself to both enemy fire and rapid counterattack. This gap in knowledge has often been justified by the fact that the British military maps available to the 1st Guards Brigade did not show this level of detail. Certainly this justification was used by Copland-Griffiths in a later letter on the subject and by authors of accounts which cover the battle. It is unfortunately incorrect to state that the maps used by the 1st Guards Brigade and the Coldstream Guards did not show Djebel Rhar as a distinct feature. The 1st Guards Brigade's own operations order (i.e. their plan) for the battle clearly cites three 1:50,000 scale GSGS sheet maps used to create, and needed by commanders to execute, the plan. The specific map covering Longstop clearly shows the existence of Djebel Rhar and the terrain.[6] In defence of Copland-Griffiths, it is worth noting that when he did his original reconnaissance, he could only view the hill from a distance and his patrols were unable to get close to it. It is also worth stating that the brigadier and his staff were implementing a divisional plan, and that unlike Copland-Griffiths, the staff at division level could consult those units who had occupied the hill and several of them had also visited the area over the last month. The division plan was approved by Major General Evelegh, who must have travelled past Longstop several times, but it makes no reference to Djebel Rhar.

The mistake in not analysing the terrain was compounded by a further error in underestimating German strength. The intelligence officers at division and brigade level provided estimates to their units that Longstop was held by a maximum of two companies. This fact is repeated in the various plans, but was probably just a guess and was in any case outdated. The reality was that the Germans were acutely aware of Longstop's tactical importance, and had thus decided to focus most of their limited forces in this area. On the evening of 22 December, Ahmera Longstop Hill area was defended by 2 companies of the 754th Grenadier Regiment who were supported by the veteran 1st Battalion of the 69th *Panzer* Grenadier Regiment. Moreover, the recently appointed local commander of the area, *Oberst* Rudolf Lang (the CO of the 69th), had a significant force to use in any counterattack, a routine tactic of the German Army. This force was based around the motorised 2nd Battalion of the 69th *Panzer* Grenadier Regiment, reinforced as a *Kampfgruppe* with artillery, armoured cars and tanks. This was located close by at the Tebourba gap, only a few kilometres east of Longstop Hill. In view of the obvious importance of Longstop to the Germans defence line west of Tebourba, it was unlikely that any attack on Longstop would be a surprise. The best that could be achieved was to conceal the timing of any attack. Sadly, even this was lost as German observers on the heights of Djebel Ahmera noted Allied aerial reconnaissance of Longstop and were alerted as to the likely timing of the forthcoming attack. It seems that the odds were actually already stacked against the success of this new operation.

A number of other contributing factors doomed the British plan to failure. Although the seizure of Longstop was a vital first-phase objective, Copland-Griffiths was allocated minimal artillery support. The plan assigned only one regiment of 25-pounders and one battery of

6   See 1st Guards Brigade Operation Order in the 1st Guards Brigade war diary for December 1942, TNA WO 175/186, and the original GSGS Series 4225, 1:50,000 map Sheet 19 Tebourba. Djebel Rhar is clearly shown as a separate feature.

medium guns to support the entire attack. A further problem was that 1st Guard Brigade was composed of only two battalions, yet Evelegh's plan required it to take not only Djebel Ahmera, but also the village of Grich el Oued. As a result, the 3rd Grenadier Guards were not available to support the attack. The one unit that could have provided assistance was the 5th Northants, but they had been despatched on an unusual mission that required them to move over the mountains and to establish a minefield near the Tebourba gap. The plan devised by Lieutenant Colonel Stewart-Brown of the 2nd Coldstreams also hamstrung the attack. Despite the relatively large size of Longstop Hill, Brown's plan dispersed his limited strength by assigning one of his rifle companies to attack the railway station at Halte d'El Heri, which was to the south of the hill next to the road. Despite the commonly accepted principle that an attacking force should outnumber the defence by a factor of two to one, the Coldstreams' plan committed only two companies initially to attack Longstop Hill, a position estimated to be defended by roughly the same number of German defenders. Two other factors definitely doomed the plan to almost certain failure: the complete lack of any air support for the operation and the decision to relieve the 2nd Coldstreams on Longstop at night with an American infantry battalion immediately after the capture of the hill. A relief in contact at night with a foreign unit, military parlance for taking over a location in the darkness and while the enemy is close by, is a very difficult task, yet this was part of the divisional plan.

2.3 The Christmas Battle

Although the focus of this story is on later operations, a limited description of the first battle and its effects is appropriate in order to illuminate subsequent chapters. Despite the many obstacles that faced the 2nd Coldstreams, the battalion approached its first battle in Tunisia on the afternoon of 22 December with a degree of optimism, though not without reservations. Stewart-Brown's plan was to launch a night attack preceded by a short artillery barrage, with No. 4 Company seizing a high col located on the western side of Djebel Ahmera. This col would provide a further launch point for No. 1 Company to climb up and attack the main ridgeline of the hill itself. In the meantime, his other company, No. 2, would attack Halte d'El Heri. No. 3 Company and the battalion headquarters would follow behind and take low ridges between the railway and the hill. The small hamlet of Chassert Teffaha, located about a mile west of the hill complex, provided the start line for the Coldstream Guards attack, led by No. 4 Company.[7] As darkness fell, it initially appeared that this plan would be successful as No. 4 Company seized the col between Ahmera and the large hill complex to the north without opposition. No. 1 Company, led by 28-year-old Major Arthur "Paddy" Chichester, next moved from the col to attack up the long ridge which leads to the top of Djebel Ahmera from the west. It was at this point that the Germans, who were fully alert to such an attack, fired flares to illuminate Paddy Chichester's company. They opened up with machine guns and mortars, and No. 1 Company suffered several casualties. These included Chichester, who was shot in the neck and mortally

---

7   The description of the first battle is based on documents in the war diaries of the 1st Guards Brigade and the 2nd Coldstream Guards, TNA WO 175/186 WD and TNA WO 175/487 WD for December 1942, and Robert Baumer, *American Iliad: The 18th Infantry Regiment in World War 2* (Bedford, USA: Aberjona Press, 2015), pp.44-71. The German side of the battle is derived largely from Lang, *The Battles of Kampfgruppe Lang.*

wounded, while his Company Sergeant Major was also killed, so two key leaders were lost rapidly. Nonetheless, No. 1 Company seized the ridge, gained the top of Ahmera and tried to dig in on stony ground under fire. (See Map 3A)

To the south, No. 2 Company seized Halte d'El Heri supported by artillery, but in a combination of events lost it to a rapid German counterattack and suffered losses. Due to various problems of communication and coordination, the 1st Battalion of the 18th US Infantry arrived later than expected to relieve the Coldstream Guards, who had moved Major Charles Harford's No. 4 Company up to reinforce No. 1 Company. The relief took place on a dark black cloudy night and took time, but eventually the battalion moved down the hill and marched back in heavy rain to Medjez el Bab. It seemed that a difficult task had been completed successfully, but the reality was different. While Oberst Lang and his men may have lost the peak of Ahmera, it still held on to Djebel Rhar just below it across a ravine, and also the lower south-east slopes. All this was unknown to the Vanguards of the 1/18th Infantry as they attempted to consolidate their hastily scratched positions on the ridge and eastern slopes of Ahmera.

Precisely what happened on the morning of 23 December is not easy to ascertain, as the various British, American and German accounts are often conflicting and confusing. Most sources agree that the Vanguards came under attack, lost possession of their positions on Djebel Ahmera and were pushed partway down the ridge and onto its lower southern slopes. Contrary to some accounts, they had not been completely pushed off the hill, but one of its rifle companies had been overrun by a German counterattack. As a result, by late evening of 23 December, Charles Harford and No. 4 Company of the 2nd Coldstreams, weary from 36 hours of marching and fighting, were ordered back to help support the Vanguards. Harford's company returned to the col, joined later that evening by the other two companies. Sometime on the following morning, Lieutenant Colonel Stewart-Brown was placed in command of a force called Wicket Keeper, which was composed of all the troops, both British and American, located on the western and southern slopes of Longstop Hill and was ordered to recapture that feature. Rain had fallen heavily and the tracks had become almost impassable other than to tracked vehicles and mules, so it was difficult to provide additional support and move supplies. Copland-Griffiths developed a new plan to recapture Djebel Ahmera, to be launched from the col captured earlier. Supported by artillery, Charles Harford's weary No. 4 Company attacked through US infantry positions up the western slope of the Ahmera ridgeline, supported by artillery. In hindsight it was obvious that an attack against an alert enemy by only one company, albeit backed up by another, was likely to fail. The responsibility for that failure and ensuing events has to be placed squarely on the British chain of command. The bitter truth was that if two companies of Coldstream Guards had failed to take Longstop Hill on 22 December, repeating the exercise on 24 December with the same but now very tired two rifle companies was unlikely to achieve a different outcome against a fully prepared German defence. There was, however, no lack of courage exhibited by Harford and the men of the Coldstream Guards. Leading the attack up the slopes on 24 December in the fading light, Harford had to use his revolver to shoot a German at close range. A trail of dead and wounded was left behind as No. 4 Company attacked to retake the top of Ahmera. It was at this point that daylight revealed the consequences of failing to appreciate the terrain, for across a deep gully appeared a second hill, Djebel Rhar. That and the other eastern slopes of Longstop Hill were by now held strongly, and mortar fire rained down on Harford's men.[8] A valiant but doomed attempt to cross the ravine was undertaken and repulsed with heavy casualties, and as a result No. 1 Company was forced to pull back from the top of Ahmera.

Daylight on Christmas Day revealed the Coldstreams just holding the ridge and western slopes, while on the northern slope of the main Ahmera ridge, an American company held the left flank but had suffered losses and was vulnerable to attack. There was little Yuletide spirit on the German side of the hill as *Oberst* Rudolf Lang, mindful of the importance of Longstop Hill to German defence plans, launched the inevitable counterattack. The Allied failure to anticipate such a strong counterattack - a standard feature of German tactics - by moving fresh additional forces to reinforce the original attack, doomed any chance of holding on to any part of Longstop. Ironically, while the Wicket Keeper force tried to hold on to their gains, a decision had already been made to end the attempt to take Tunis. That decision was made by Eisenhower on Christmas Eve at a meeting with Anderson at the First Army's headquarters 380 miles east of Algiers. This was of course not known by the Vanguards, the Coldstream Guards or - just as importantly - the 5th Northants, which had marched through the mountains to place a road block on the German supply lines. Meanwhile, *Oberst* Lang's Christmas present for the troops at Longstop was a three-pronged attack, with the main thrust being launched along the south-eastern slopes of Djebel Ahmera. A secondary diversionary attack was to be conducted in the high valley to the north of Rhar and Ahmera, and around to the col seized by the Coldstream Guards. This attack would be supported by fire from the top of Djebel Ahmera. The main attack, assisted by armoured cars which managed to move across the southern slopes of Ahmera, started early on Christmas morning. It soon became apparent that the Coldstream Guards and Vanguards would not be able to hold on to the hill in the face of this new attack, and orders were delivered to the remaining companies to withdraw. It is worth noting that only after orders were issued did the three remaining companies of the Vanguards withdraw, and only when under severe pressure on their northern flank. British post-battle reports singled out the contribution and courage of the weapons company of the Vanguards, though the same applied to both B and C companies of that unit. The Vanguards were not alone in their reluctance to withdraw under fire from Longstop or in the way they demonstrated courage under fire, in this, their first action against the Germans. The withdrawal from Longstop by the remaining companies of the 2nd Coldstreams was orderly, as one would expect from a battalion of the Guards Division, and distinguished by several acts of gallantry. Foremost among these were two contrasting but equally cool acts of courage by Lieutenant Henry Ronald Callander and Guardsman Richard Dean. Callander stayed with the remnants of his platoon fighting the Germans, enabling others to withdraw, and had no thought of retirement until ordered by his CO, Stewart-Brown. The latter reported that Callander displayed qualities of great courage and leadership, with his behavior an inspiration to those in his vicinity. Guardsman Dean, a company stretcher bearer, it was later reported: "Displayed great courage and devotion to duty while tending wounded men under fire and remaining consistently where the fighting was at

---

8   Details of the Coldstream Guards in the Longstop battle have been drawn from E.R. Hill, 'The Coldstreams at Longstop', *Army Quarterly and Defence Journal* Volume LXVIII, No. 2 (July 1944), pp.175-80, and Howard's *Second to None*. A. Robson's book on the Coldstreams provides perhaps the most detailed account of the battle.

the highest pitch he was totally indifferent to any personal danger."[9] Dean and Callander were recommended for immediate awards, respectively of the Military Medal (MM) and the MC, recommendations that were approved less than four weeks later. (See Map 3B)

The gallantry displayed by Dean and Callander could not, however, conceal the difficult truth that the attack on Longstop Hill had been poorly planned and led to significant casualties. Although involved in both attacks on Longstop, it was not the Coldstream Guards but the Vanguards' 1st Battalion that suffered the most casualties, losing nine officers and 347 men killed, captured or missing, almost half the battalion. The 2nd Coldstreams lost 178 men, with a high percentage of officers and Senior NCOs killed or wounded, including the CO William Stewart-Brown. *Oberst* Lang and his men probably lost some 300 casualties, but they regained control of the whole of the Longstop Hill area. German forces were to retain control of their positions on Longstop for four more months. From this hilltop fortress, the units who later relieved Lang and his men had an uninterrupted view across the Medjerda Valley and were able to dominate the area and prevent any attack towards Tunis.

The recapture of Longstop Hill by *Oberst* Lang on Christmas Day left the 5th Northants, having undertaken their part of the operation, isolated well behind the German lines. Problems with radio communications had made it impossible to order the battalion to withdraw. Lieutenant Colonel Arthur Crook, the CO of the battalion, fortunately recognised the dangerous situation that confronted him and made the sound decision to withdraw his battalion back to Allied lines.

On the Allied side, a degree of realism and some degree of pessimism seemed to spread across the 1st Guards Brigade, the Battle-Axe Division and at corps level. There was concern about whether the German attack on Longstop presaged a wider counterattack, though the Germans were just as exhausted as the British. More importantly, commanders at all levels no longer underestimated German forces and devoted more time to thinking through tactical problems. Proof of this change in outlook, some might call it increased professionalism, came quite quickly.[10] Less than a week after failing to take Longstop, Brigadier Copland-Griffiths was required to prepare a second plan to capture the hill, revealing that the giddy and amateur optimism that led to the bungled attack on Longstop had not been completely eliminated in First Army. What is more interesting is what then transpired. Copland-Griffiths spent time analysing his situation and produced an appreciation, i.e. an analysis of the tactical problem. Dated 31 December 1942, this highlights the fact that many of the issues identified here were considered more carefully and some lessons had been learned. Soon after it was issued, any ideas his more senior commanders and staff officers may have held of a further attempt to take Longstop were quickly overruled by wiser council and the plan shelved.[11] A number of key lessons had been learned. First, and most importantly, Evelegh's staff had learned a lot about the terrain on the Longstop Hill complex. This included the existence of Djebel Rhar, or at least its tactical importance, since it could be argued it had been ignored before. The division was also now fully aware of the size of the geography of the wider area and the dominating heights north of Longstop above the village of Heidous, which was inevitably nicknamed "hideous" by the

9   See the MM Citation for Guardsman Dean and MC Citation for Captain H. Callander of 2nd Coldstream Guards, both in TNA WO 173/1.
10   The operations of the 5th Northants are based on the WD of 5th Northants TNA WO 175/517 and Jervois, *The History of the Northants*, pp.125-31.
11   See Appreciation by Brigadier Griffiths in TNA WO 175/186 1st Guards Brigade January 1943 WD.

British troops, including Djebels Ang and Tanngoucha. Lessons were also learned, or arguably relearned, about communications, the importance of using artillery and airpower, deception, surprise and the need to allocate appropriate forces to seizing and holding large hill areas against subsequent counterattack. These lessons had to be been learned the hard way through the bitter taste of defeat at Longstop. It could be argued that in the race for Tunis, at Tebourba and at Longstop, the 78th Division received an education which would be subsequently applied to great effect in the later battle for those peaks in April 1943.

2.4 Winter Stalemate

After the failure to capture Longstop Hill, a period of just over three months expired before the start of the major operations which largely form the subject of this book. The events of that period, however, are of relevance to this story in illuminating the strategic and operational framework for later operations and the primary unit involved in those battles, the Battle-Axe Division. At a strategic level, the months of January to March 1943 witnessed a stalemate in which both the Allied and Axis forces carried out several operations which made only a limited difference to the overall situation. By January 1943, Rommel and his Italian allies had withdrawn from their original positions at El Alamein in October 1942 all the way back to Tunisia. They had linked up with Von Arnim's 5th *Panzer* Army, enabling the Axis forces to shorten their long lines of communication and develop a coherent defence in Tunisia. The winter period also saw the British Eighth Army involved in a series of battles designed to push Rommel further back into Tunisia, while the First Army faced the difficult problem of defending its recent gains against an aggressive and reinforced 5th *Panzer* Army. For good or ill, Kenneth Anderson found himself frequently moving his units around to shore up those areas of his long, mountainous and weakly held front line that were threatened. This led to the undesirable situation where units of the 78th Division moved in and out of its control and from one part of Tunisia to another.

In a masterly understatement, a Battle-Axe Division intelligence summary of the time used the phrase "the chain of command had become somewhat tangled". The 1st Guards Brigade, after a period defending the Medjez el Bab sector, subsequently moved out of the 78th Division's operational control in February and never returned. Meanwhile, many battalions within the two remaining brigades found themselves on a kind of Cook's tour of northern Tunisia, though without any time to take in the scenery or enjoy a rest. The unit which arguably most experienced the impact of emerging threats was the 8th Argylls, which had the dubious honour of coming under direct control of the First Army and was used to plug a range of gaps. During the next three months it came under the command of 1st Guards Brigade, 11th Infantry Brigade, the French and a newly arrived British formation, the 46th Infantry Division. In doing so it moved multiple times, travelling all over northern Tunisia. At the other end of the spectrum, the 5th Northants moved only twice and spent most of the winter months in or close by Medjez el Bab. Most other units in the 11th and 36th Brigades found themselves shifted in or out of the control of their brigade commanders to work with other brigades and divisions. That work involved fighting and losses, but was also undertaken against the backdrop of a muddy, cold and wet winter. Two points can be made: first, that few units, and especially the infantry battalions of the division, received any rest from the strain of being in the front line; and secondly, that they were often outside the control of both their parent brigade or division. This adversely affected the effectiveness of the division as a whole, and specifically at brigade level, as the most effective military teams are those that work and fight together regularly.

The challenges faced by the Battle-Axe Division were the result of a series of counterattacks conducted by von Arnim's Fifth Army, spearheaded by the 10th *Panzer* Division, which had to be repulsed by First Army. Three significant major counterattacks took place in January and February. The most damaging inflicted significant materiel and personnel losses on the 1st US Armoured Division, which was now operating in southern Tunisia, in a series of battles that forced it back to the Kasserine Pass. In order to shore up defences in the south, Kenneth Anderson, commander of First Army, decided to send British units, including ones from the Battle Axe Division, from the area around Medjez el Bab to the aid of both the French and Americans. Inevitably, this required Allfrey to weaken the defences around Medjez itself. As a result, von Arnim was able to gradually push back British and French units that defended the front line south and north of Medjez el Bab, creating a salient. The gradual development of the Medjez salient and the loss of ground north-east and north-west of that town would require the British V Corps, and specifically the 78th Division, to undertake operations that became known as the Battle of the Peaks. The process of eroding Allied gains achieved by December 1942 began when Operation *Eilboote*, a German counterattack in January 1943, forced Anderson to send 36th Brigade south to aid General Juin of the French Army. The attacks of the 10th *Panzer* Division forced the lightly armed French units off valuable mountain positions on the Eastern Dorsal mountain range 100 miles south of Medjez. Seizure of these positions provided the Germans with an excellent defensive line and reduced any serious threat to von Arnim's southern flank. The transfer of units like 36th Infantry Brigade weakened the forces available to conduct operations north-east of Beja and limited any offensive operations other than a limited, costly and unsuccessful attack on Green and Bald Hill by 5th Buffs in early January. Now that the threat of cutting off his links with Rommel in the south had been reduced, von Arnim was free to conduct additional counterattacks against British in the north. These followed in late January, with local attacks against positions held by the 6th Armoured Division around the town of Bou Arada, 25 miles south of Medjez. The next phase of exerting pressure on the Medjez area commenced in late February and early March, when the 5th *Panzer* Army launched a series of attacks north and south of Medjez. The pressure exerted by those attacks ensured that no forces were available to reinforce the lightly armed Algerian troops holding Djebel Ang north of Longstop Hill when they were attacked by the German 334th Infantry Division. The French were pushed off the dominating position of Djebel Ang and from the village of Heidous on 1 March. The next day, German pressure led to the Allies withdraingl from the key mountain villages of Toukabeur and Chaouach (see Plate II) which dominated Medjez. Soon afterwards, the Germans extended their gains to the west of the town by seizing hill positions which effectively overlooked and threatened the Oued Zarga-Medjez road. The First Army, and especially V Corps, would now be forced to recapture these important positions and restore its primary supply route. The scene was set for the launch of Operation Sweep and the Battle of the Peaks.

3

For Want Of A Road – Planning and Preparing for Operation Sweep

---

3.1 A More Favourable Strategic Situation

The German success in early March which captured key terrain from V Corps did not reflect the wider strategic situation in Tunisia. Von Arnim's advance was paid for with significant casualties in both personnel and tanks. Moreover, it was not mirrored by success in the south, where the combined German-Italian army had been forced back in a series of battles to a defensive line just north of Gabes. The new German front in the south at Wadi Akarit still lay some 200 miles south of Tunis, but north of this line the nearest possible defensive location was at Enfidaville, only 40 miles south of Tunis. Moreover, though von Arnim had been assigned command of an army group which combined the two original armies, his forces were particularly short of ammunition, food and fuel. This was due to the combined efforts of Allied air and Royal Navy submarine attacks on Axis shipping and air transport. His attacks in the north had weakened his existing forces, and they now had to defend a longer front line which stretched both their forces and the logistic system. In contrast, the situation for Anderson's First Army and the Allies had improved greatly in the three months that transpired between the loss of Longstop Hill and the onset of spring. The First Army was no longer an army in name only, for commencing in January 1943, new and fresh formations arrived in Tunisia. These included the 46th Infantry Division, which started to arrive on 6 January, followed by two other infantry divisions (the 1st and 4th) and two tank brigades (the 21st and 25th). To these forces were added further artillery, engineer and support units and replacements.

In early February, General Harold Alexander had also arrived in Algeria to assume ground command of all Allied forces in North-West Africa, including both the First and Eighth Armies. In order to control operations, Alexander established the Eighteenth Army Group, which took over control of all Allied forces. In August 1942, Harold Alexander was a 51-year-old Guards officer who had become the C-in-C Middle East Command and Montgomery's boss in North Africa. He had been commissioned into the Irish Guards in 1912 and compiled a distinguished record for bravery and leadership during the First World War, winning the DSO and an MC. He had led the rearguard at Dunkirk in 1940 and been on one of the last destroyers to leave, and then served in Burma until he took over his new command. It should be recalled that Alexander was originally scheduled to assume command of the First Army and Operation Torch, but had been sent to the Middle East instead. Alexander's arrival was a mixed blessing for Anderson, as it allowed him to focus on operations but also reduced his authority and brought his past and current leadership of First Army under the scrutiny of a very critical eye. One benefit that should have immediately come from Alexander's appointment was a closer coordination of ground operations against the Axis forces by both British armies. However, the need to set up his headquarters from scratch, the distance between Algeria and the Eighth Army headquarters in Libya, and especially Montgomery's tendency to do what he wanted irrespective of orders, meant such coordination took longer than it should have. By 1 April, Anderson had under his command not only V Corps but also the US II Corps, which included four infantry and armoured divisions, and the French XIX Corps, which was being equipped with more modern equipment. A further formation, IX Corps, had two divisions which formed a strategic army group reserve.

German air supremacy in the skies over northern Tunisia had been lost, and the best the *Luftwaffe* could do was launch limited local air attacks. Allied air forces now delivered constant air attacks, not only on Bizerte and Tunis but also on Axis airfields in Sicily. After a difficult period of hard fighting in March, which led to British forces being driven out of Sedjenane and Sidi Nsir in the north, a strong counterattack (which involved the 36th Infantry Brigade) enabled it to recover all the lost ground. The strategic situation thus now favoured the Allies, and this change in the balance of forces provided all formations, and especially the Battle-Axe Division, with the opportunity and resources needed to plan a new offensive. A critical objective for the new operation was to enable the Allies to regain access to their main supply route, the road from Beja through Oued Zarga to Medjez.[1]

3.2 The Birth of Operation Sweep

The attack by V Corps into the mountains north-west of Medjez el Bab formed part of a wider operation devised by Anderson and his staff to capture key positions from which to launch an attack on Tunis and in a subsequent phase to destroy the 5th *Panzer* Army. Although Anderson's plan formally responded to a directive from Alexander on 25 March to launch this offensive, the reality was that the attack into the area known as the Peaks had long been considered essential. Operation Sweep, as it was named, was originally conceived in early March by Anderson, his Brigadier General Staff (BGS) and his senior operations staff officer, another dour Scot, Lieutenant Colonel Colin McNabb. Although the Battle of the Peaks has often been closely linked with Operation Sweep, the latter was actually a wider plan that involved all four divisions of V Corps, the French and an American division. The attack by a reinforced 78th Division to recapture the high ground overlooking the Beja-Medjez road and regain Longstop Hill was also originally viewed by Anderson as only the preliminary move in an operation that would result in an assault to take high ground between Massicault, near Medjez, and El Bathan, just east of Tebourba. This would place First Army less than 15 miles from Tunis and in an ideal location to launch a final combined attack with Eighth Army to capture Tunis. Meanwhile, in the south, the British and French forces forming part of IX Corps would attack across the Goubellat Plain and swing north-east towards Ksar Tyar and Massicault to protect the southern flank of V Corps. Finally, a US division would replace the 46th Infantry Division and attack in the

1   This review of the strategic situation in Tunisia is based primarily on Blaxland, *Plain Cook*; Howe, *North West Africa*; Playfair, *Destruction of Axis Forces*; and the war diaries of the First Army, V Corps and 78th Infantry Division for March-April 1943, TNA WO 175/16, 175/83 and 175/168.

north to reoccupy positions around Sidi Nisr. V Corps' initial task in the Operation Sweep plan was, however, to: "Retake the high ground north of the Oued Zarga-Medjez road to include Toukabeur, Chaouach and the Djebel Ang."[2] After the corps had completed this task, it was to capture Longstop and seize the high ground north of Bou Arada, i.e. the hills just south of Medjez. At the level of strategic planning carried out by Anderson and his boss General Alexander, these operations were viewed only as preliminary moves for a large and wider end game in Tunisia. Anderson's focus quite rightly was on thinking ahead to the final attack on Tunis. The gritty operational reality at the level of the Battle-Axe Division and its fighting units turned out to be very different from the First Army's plans, and their part of Operation Sweep was to take over three weeks of hard fighting in the Battle of the Peaks before McNabb's planned objectives were achieved. During this time, McNabb was to gain a completely new and very personal introduction into the reality of executing high-level plans on the ground.

3.3 For Want of a Road

In April 1943, the most direct route to Medjez el Bab from the critical Allied supply bases in Algeria, over 500 miles away, started from Souk el Arba to Souk el Khemis. After leaving Souk el Khemis, the road passed just south of the town of Beja and through a small village called Oued Zarga. Between Oued Zarga and Medjez, this key road passes along a valley which is dominated to the north and south by a steadily rising range of hills. One consequence of the German attacks in March was that by April , the Germans held all the hills to the north of the road and those which overlooked Medjez el Bab. Although the Germans did not actually possess the road itself, their machine guns, mortars and occasionally artillery prevented transport vehicles from using the road. Moreover, as the Germans now had positions several miles to the north-west and south-east of the town, Medjez itself was the tip of a dangerous bulge or salient. The loss of the route proved a serious logistical inconvenience for the Allies, as this road had previously been heavily used as the easiest way for most of the supplies to be moved up from rear depots in Algeria to the units based around Medjez El Bab. As previous chapters have demonstrated, the logistical problems involved in supplying the First Army in Tunisia provided Anderson and his staff with a constant headache. The new situation now required all Allied vehicles supplying units in Medjez to travel over the mountains via Thibar, to Teboursouk and onwards via Testour to Medjez, a much slower and more difficult route. Supplying the units based around Oued Zarga and to the north became a major problem. The V Corps' engineers eventually overcame this problem by driving a road from a point near Testour in the Teboursouk valley over wild and broken country to link up with Oued Zarga from the rear. Although an immediate solution was in place, it was clearly recognised by all the senior commanders that the lack of this route would lead to major difficulties in the logistical build-up for the final attack on Tunis. There is an old saying that for want of a nail the battle was lost. In order to supply and sustain the final attack on Tunis, the First Army would need as many good roads as possible. New formations such as the 1st and 4th Infantry Divisions were already arriving in Algeria, and they could not be supported in the final attack without additional roads. In this case, the

2   One source (132nd Field Regiment War Diary) refers to this as Operation Alibi, but the majority of contemporary sources and the relevant operation orders use the code word Operation Sweep.

senior commanders fully recognised that for want of a road, the final attack on Tunis might not succeed. It was also critical to ensure that Medjez el Bab was secure from attack from the north, as it would be the base from which First Army would launch its next and final offensive to take Tunis. The words Medjez el Bab mean gateway, and for a good reason; ever since the days of Hannibal, it has been recognised that the location was the key to the gate to Tunis. The need to secure the heights north of Medjez el Bab and reopen this critical supply route was a key factor influencing operational planning at all levels of command, from Eighteenth Army Group down to the 78th Infantry Division, in the last two weeks of March 1943. As we have learned, initial planning for these new operations was initiated by the First Army on 23 March, with a target date to recapture all lost ground by the start of April and retake Longstop Hill a few days later. These timelines proved too optimistic, since hard fighting was still taking place in the north, but the process of planning the new attack had been well under way by 1 April.

3.4 Evelegh's Appreciation

The crucial importance of reopening the Beja-Medjez road had long been apparent to Major General Allfrey, the now well-established commander of V Corps. In March 1943, Allfrey's own corps headquarters was based in a farm near Souk el Khemis on the road that would normally lead directly via Oued Zarga to Medjez El Bab. As this road was now closed, every vehicle that needed to travel to Medjez, including Allfrey's personal staff car, had to follow a much longer route. This new road was a rough track which detoured over the hills just south of Oued Zarga. It next joined what was a minor road which ran from the town of Testour to Medjez from the south-west. In order for transport to be able to move once again along the road and support the future offensive, it was essential to take the hills to the north of the road. A further factor was that only by taking those hills would it be possible to attack and outflank the German positions on the mountains which dominated the Medjerda valley to the east. The peaks needed to be captured, and in late March Allfrey instructed one of his divisional commanders to prepare a plan to take them; the result was the birth of what became known as Operation Sweep. It was not surprising that Allfrey assigned this task in to Vyvyan Evelegh, the commander of the 78th Division. Evelegh and his staff fully recognised the vital importance of the area and were aware that any successful plan to seize it would require a deep understanding of the local terrain. During late March, Evelegh and his staff, including his GSO 1 (key plans officer) Lieutenant Colonel Reggie Hewetson, made a detailed analysis, or military appreciation, of the task. This planning process was taught to all British Army officers, especially at Staff College at Camberley, and was part of the training provided to prepare them for future positions as commanders and staff officers. Both Evelegh and Hewetson had attended Camberley, and the former had become an instructor there. The process is a simple analytical tool with a series of steps that enable officers to create an effective military plan. Evelegh's appreciation of the problems he faced for Operation Sweep fully demonstrates that he was an accomplished commander and planner who possessed a keen analytical mind. Even more importantly, he instinctively understood that to translate a plan into action required him to first convince his able subordinate commanders that the plan was viable, and then leave them with the freedom but also the means to make it work.

Evelegh began his analysis by looking carefully at the terrain over which his division would need to fight and examining the available intelligence on the German forces defending it.

The area immediately north of the Medjez to Oued Zarga road was dominated by a series of rugged hill ranges. The sector which the division was eventually required to seize was some 15 miles wide and six miles in depth, and includes 10 peaks over 2,000ft and many others over 1,500ft. His initial focus during planning was, however, on an area some eight miles wide and six miles deep north of the Oued Zarga-Medjez el Bab road, though later operations were to seize objectives north and east of Medjez el Bab. The area which Evelegh proposed to attack was inhospitable, unpopulated and had few roads or tracks in 1943. It has not greatly changed today some 75 years later. The terrain includes bare rolling hills, dry but occasionally muddy river beds and high craggy mountains covered in rocks sharp enough to rapidly destroy even tough infantry boots. The land was bare and had almost no vegetation for concealment, either from the enemy or the elements, which included rain, wind and, as the weather changed, the increasingly hot sun in early April. Moreover, the distances between locations are considerable and this, combined with the increasing heat, meant that troops carrying heavy loads, because of the lack of roads, could rapidly become exhausted. Some soldiers who fought there describe it as the worst place they fought during all their time in the Second World War. A key point to understand about the challenges posed by the terrain in northern Tunisia was that made by the commander of the First Army, General Anderson. He noted in his official report:

> This mountain land is a vast tract of country, every hill in which is large enough to swallow up a brigade of infantry, where consolidation on the rocky slopes is very difficult, in which Tanks can only operate in small numbers, where movement of guns and vehicles is very restricted, and where the division had to rely on pack mules for its supplies and to carry Wireless telegraphy sets, tools and mortars.
>
> The general impression is one of wide Spaciousness - a kind of Dartmoor or Central Sutherland, but with deeper valleys and steeper hills.[3]

The problems posed by the terrain both here and elsewhere in Tunisia led the taciturn Anderson on more than one occasion to say: "Never shall I forget those cursed Djebels of Tunisia."[4]

The western edge of the area which Evelegh was ordered to attack includes the large 1,200ft hill complex of Djebel Mahdi. This in turn dominates the Bed Valley to the east, which varies in width from a few hundred feet to approximately one mile. The valley is some six miles in length and captures three key tributaries of the Medjerda River, which all flow down to the small hamlet of Oued Zarga. It was important to both sides, providing a potential route for armour and infantry either north-east directly into the rear of German defences or south-west to attack the rear of any British advance into the mountains north of the road. On the eastern side of the valley, directly across from Djebel Mahdi, the ground is dominated by two peaks, Point 624 and Point 667, respectively named Djebels Mansourine and Bech Chekaoui. These two peaks provide observation and dominate the area to the south. South of these two peaks is a large hill mass called Mergueb Chaouach and a lozenge-like hill, Point 512. From Point 512, an observer can look down to the south-east on the ancient and remote Berber villages of Toukabeur and Chaouach, perched on hills close to Medjez and overlooking the eastern end of

3   Anderson, *Dispatches*, p.5,459.
4   Anderson, cited in A.B. Austin, *Birth of an Army* (London: Victor Gollanz Limited, 1943), p.23.

the road. The two villages had been captured by the Germans in late February and early March, their rocky outcrops enabling them to have excellent observation over all Allied activities in the Medjez el Bab area and the key supply route from Oued Zarga to Medjez. The area to the north-east of the two villages gradually rises across difficult terrain via several rocky hills to the key heights of Djebel el Ang (Point 667) and Djebel Tanngoucha. These two features were the high points in the Medjez area, dominating the Medjerda valley and Longstop Hill area, and could only be taken after securing a first line of German positions based on a series of hills south of these mountains and north of the Oued Zarga road. This line of five low-lying hills, some 600ft in height, began closest to Oued Zarga with Oubirah, moving on to Outiah and Nahel, via Point 343 to Dourat, located to the south-east, and Rouached (or Recce Ridge it as was known), directly to the east. Once these hills were taken, it was possible to move on to capture the next line of natural defences, including the key features of Point 512, Mergueb Chaouach and Djebel Bech Chekaoui. Evelegh recognised that advancing across this extensive area offered significant challenges for his division, even without opposition from Germans who were now well-established on these hills.[5]

3.5 The Germans' Perspective

While Evelegh did not underestimate the opposition he faced, he was aware from his intelligence sources that his opposite number, newly promoted Major General Frederich Weber, had more than his own fair share of problems. Weber, the 45-year-old commander of the 334th Infantry Division, looked the very image of a Prussian general with his squarish head, short-cut hair and an Adolf Hitler-type moustache, but was actually born in the old French department of Moselle, then part of Germany, in 1903. He had been commissioned into the artillery, fought in the First World War and was decorated. He managed to stay in the army and transferred to the infantry, but progress in the post-war German officer corps was very slow, so it was no surprise that Weber only became a lieutenant colonel in 1938. Thereafter his rise was fairly rapid, for he was promoted *Oberst* (full colonel) in 1940 and two years later was appointed commander of the newly formed 334th Division, which he led to Tunisia. Weber assumed temporary command of the German *XC* Corps in addition to his own division in February 1943. By the start of Operation Sweep he had returned to assume command of his division at his headquarters near the village of Chouigui, west of Tunis. Weber had commanded the 334th during the attacks in February and March which had enabled the Germans to seize control of the villages of Chaouach and Toukabeur and the heights above the road to Medjez. Although successful, this and other attacks had not only reduced the strength of his formation but also extended the area it had to defend.

By 5 April, Weber's weakened infantry regiments - the 754th, 755th and 756th - were very thinly spread across a front that began in the hills just west of the small village of Sidi Nisr, north-east of the town of Beja, and ended some 30 miles later just to the south of the Medjerda River. The divisional artillery regiment, the 334th, was also somewhat limited in firepower,

---

5   The description of the terrain over which the Battle of the Peaks was fought is based on Evelegh's appreciation. See TNA WO 175/168 the 78th Infantry Division March 1943 WD Appreciation of Situation by Commander 78 Division, dated 28 March 1943, and the author's analysis of the GSGS 1943 maps of the area.

with just one battalion of 12 short-range 75mm mountain guns and two further battalions with 16 105mm and eight 150mm field guns. The reduced firepower was slightly offset by the fact that each infantry regiment had a company which was equipped with infantry field guns and Pak anti-tank guns. Moreover, Weber, along with all German divisional commanders at the time in Tunisia, suffered from constant Allied interference with Axis supply routes, which meant that supplies of food, fuel and ammunition were becoming scarcer. Reduced supplies, increasing Allied air superiority and the growing British strength on the ground were all impacting adversely on the morale of German units. The reduction in morale in the 334th Division, which contained a significant proportion of Austrians, manifested itself in a steady trickle of desertions to British lines. The fruit of interrogations from these deserters, along with other prisoners captured during active patrolling in the days up to the start of Operation Sweep, enabled Evelegh's divisional intelligence staff to eventually compile a pretty accurate picture of enemy troop strength and locations. Evelegh's knowledge of German dispositions when he initially produced his appreciation and preliminary plan on 28 March was, as he stated, somewhat vague. His intelligence was that the Germans had a battalion on Djebel Mahdi and three companies spread over an area from Djebel Outiah to Recce Ridge. His information improved significantly over the next few days, enabling Evelegh to identify the location of specific units and helping him to produce a more accurate and detailed final plan. By the start of the attack, Evelegh therefore knew that the area of about eight miles over which he proposed to launch his division was actually held by three, not two, German battalions. On the western edge of the line, the 3rd Battalion of the 755th Grenadier Infantry Regiment, with three rifle and one heavy weapon companies, was positioned around Djebel Mahdi to dominate the valley to the east. Across the valley, the 3rd Battalion of the 756th Mountain Infantry Regiment, also with four companies, held the area around and to the north of Djebel Nahel. Finally, the 1st Battalion of the 756th held the ridge to the south around Djebel Outiah and on to Toukabeur and Chaouach. In addition to these three battalions holding positions on the rugged hills, further units of the 334th were held in reserve a few miles north up the Bed Valley from Oued Zarga.[6] The nature of the rugged terrain meant that German commanders believed that it was unsuitable country for operating tanks. A small number of tanks from the 10th *Panzer* Division were held in reserve at the top of the Bed Valley leading north from Oued Zarga. The Germans' view that it was difficult to operate their own tanks in the area led them to them to a similar conclusion about British armour in these hills, though this proved to be an unfortunate assumption.

In the light of the relative strength of the 78th Battle-Axe Division and the weakness of Weber's forces, it might seem that Evelegh's initial appreciation would conclude that the enemy was unlikely to provide much resistance to his future attack. However, Evelegh knew from bitter experience that even relatively understrength German units, when well-led and well-equipped, could be formidable opponents. The 334th Division's excellent positions on the hills were fortified with wire defences and often covered by a number of minefields. These positions

6   Details of German forces in the area are derived from analysis of the intelligence summaries which can be found in TNA WO 175/82 V Corps WD and TNA WO 175/168 78 Division WD both from March- April 1943. Information on German weapons from US War Department *Handbook on German Military Forces* 15 March 1943 TM E 30 451 Chapter VII obtained from US Army Combined Arms Centre Library. <www.usacac.army.mil.> (accessed June 2017).

enabled them to rapidly see and engage any attacking troops. The German units were equipped with numerous MG34 and MG42 machine guns and several 80mm mortars. The new-model MG42 machine gun was a formidable weapon which could accurately fire up to 1,500 rounds a minute out to an effective range of nearly 1,500 metres. Its predecessor, the MG34 model machine gun, was also robust, proven and capable of maintaining a good but slower rate of fire of 800 rounds a minute. Each of the 334th Infantry battalions was equipped with at least 30 MG34s or MG42s in three rifle and one heavy weapons companies. The heavier, tripod-mounted and telescope sight-equipped MG42 enabled them to fire out to 3,000 metres and sustain high rates of more inaccurate but lethal indirect fire. Each weapons company was usually equipped with some six or eight 80mm mortars. This was an excellent weapon in the mountains, as mortars were relatively mobile and their fire could be directed by forward observers, while the mortars themselves were hidden on the reverse of slope of German forward defences. Unlike their British equivalents, German rifle platoons were designed around their machine-gun crews, which supplied the main offensive and defensive power for their infantry units. Riflemen in platoons were equipped with the bolt-action KAR98 Mauser rifle and could lay down accurate, though slow, rifle fire, but their main role was to provide close defence to machine-gun crews and carry the large quantities of 7.92mm ammunition required by the MG42.

In contrast, British Army infantry battalions in Tunisia initially lacked an organic heavy machine gun with the range and rate of fire of the MG42. A decision had been made by the First Army to leave behind the battalion medium machine-gun platoon with their formidable Vickers guns. Infantry battalions were instead forced to rely for firepower on the Bren light machine guns (LMGs) carried in each platoon. The magazine-fed Bren had a much slower rate of fire and a reduced range when compared to the German weapons, though it was highly accurate and devastating at medium and short ranges in the right hands. British rifle companies were officially equipped with only nine Brens in each company, but after earlier experiences in combat in Tunisia, they soon found ways to acquire several more. The 78th was supposed to have a divisional support battalion equipped with both the heavy Vickers machine gun and mortars. Unfortunately, due to shipping constraints, the 78th Division's own support battalion, a battalion of the Kensington Regiment, had to be left behind in England along with their Vickers machine guns. Even when First Army eventually realised its mistake and managed to reissue the Vickers direct to infantry battalions, the rugged Tunisian mountains with their absence of roads made it difficult to move the guns and ammunition where they were needed.

All these factors meant that, although weak in artillery support, German infantry units were better-equipped with heavy weapons at the company and battalion level than their British counterparts. Moreover, the German units were located in excellent, well-protected defensive positions with good fields of fire for those weapons. This was certainly the case for Weber's units, which usually held all the important geographical features and had complete observation over all approaches, which was often barren rocky terrain devoid of vegetation for cover. Each key hill was also overlooked by German positions on several others. Seizing one or even two of the hills alone was not possible, as German observers and troops located on one of the several adjoining hills would be able to bring down artillery and mortar fire on Allied troops. Any attack on the German positions had to be made in strength and with sufficient reserve troops to hold all hills once captured. Kenneth Macksey, an accomplished soldier and military historian, would later write in his excellent history of the Tunisian campaign that: "The mountains and valleys of Tunisia can swallow an army when a myriad peaks, few absolute in domination of a wide area, but each a potential centre of prolonged resistance, can neither be occupied in detail, nor by passed or ignored without peril."[7]

3.6 Friendly Forces

After assessing the nature of the terrain, weather (it had rained hard for almost three months and the valley floors were muddy) and enemy forces, Evelegh came to some preliminary conclusions: the importance of developing improved communications (to resupply his units once the attack started), of active patrolling (to gain more detailed intelligence) and of achieving surprise. It is evident that he carefully considered the issue of his own forces. He was well aware that the infantry units in his division were tired. Eight of the nine battalions had been in constant contact with the Germans over a five-month period, with most units having spent less than a week of this time resting. The remaining battalion had lost two companies in a recent battle and would take a couple of weeks to be rebuilt before it could be used in operations. It is easy to forget that merely living in exposed positions, at the mercy of wind and rain, can gradually undermine a soldier's physical condition. When this was accompanied by constant exposure to danger, enemy fire, dirt, fear of death and little sleep, even highly disciplined soldiers eventually find it difficult to perform their duties effectively. Most units had suffered significant casualties and were well under their established strength, and while some reinforcements had arrived, time was needed to train them. Evelegh wrote: "Infantry units hardly fit, without several days rest for protracted operations in a difficult country although spirits and morale high – 11 Infantry Brigade in particular requires resting."[8]

Moreover, after bearing the brunt of the fighting across northern Tunisia, both junior officers and soldiers may have thought it was the turn of another, fresher unit to conduct the attack. As an experienced commander, Evelegh was far too canny to simply ignore the human element in operations. It was also true that Operation Sweep was the first time since December that the 78th had actually fought as a complete division, since prior to April its brigades were constantly moved around and placed under command of other formations. He was not alone in his concerns about his men's morale, for General Anderson, after being briefed by Evelegh on his plan, bluntly stated: "The plan's all right – but will the troops fight?" Several authors have simply viewed Anderson's comment to be yet another example of his considerable pessimism as an army commander, ignoring an essential principle of warfare which is that a commander must constantly concern himself with the morale and fighting spirit of his troops. Evelegh, who probably (from his notes) also entertained doubts about his tired troops, kept them to himself in front of the First Army commander and responded: "Well sir one can only plan in the expectation that they will."[9] Nonetheless, in his final plans he carefully took into account the fact that the division's combat units had been constantly fighting for five months.

---

7   K. Macksey, *Crucible of Power: The Fight for Tunisia 1942–43* (London: Hutchinson, 1969), p.92.
8   See the Evelegh Appreciation on p.2, TNA WO 175/168 78th Infantry Division March 1943 WD.
9   The quotes by Kenneth Anderson and Vyvyan Evelegh are in Blaxland, *Plain Cook*, p.227

3.7 Operation Order No. 7

After completing his initial appreciation and issuing it to his staff on 28 March, Evelegh spent the next seven days refining it, using new information provided by active patrolling and discussions with his staff before issuing Operation Order Number 7 on 5 April. The final plan reflected Evelegh's careful balancing of the main factors that he had considered in his appreciation: the difficult terrain, lack of communications, enemy strength or weakness and the state of his formations. The plan required the division to seize an area some 10 miles in length, from Djebel Mahdi in the west to Chaouach in the south-east. It was to wheel east some eight miles to seize key features north of Longstop Hill. The initial attacks had to penetrate distances varying from two to four miles from the start line on the Beja-Medjez El Bab road. Despite the comparatively thin Axis defences manned by only three German battalions, Evelegh did not make the mistake of underestimating the difficulty of the task he had been assigned. Based on the nature of the terrain and the German defences, Evelegh determined that in order to conduct an attack across a front of this nature, he would need not only his entire division, but also additional infantry battalions. He required these units to help take over and secure key hills, to release his own battalions to maintain the momentum of the advance. Evelegh ensured that his division was temporarily reinforced by four additional infantry battalions during the initial stages of the attack. These units were provided by his neighbouring formations, the 46th and 1st Infantry Divisions. He also requested and was provided with two tank battalions to support his attack, plus a significant amount of additional artillery. The plan was based on achieving a level of tactical surprise, which was to be attained first by moving his units to hidden assembly areas relatively close to the German front line and by attacking at night. The former was necessary in order to avoid a very long and tiring night march by infantry units before going into the attack, while the latter would limit the Germans' ability to detect and respond to the infantry's approach across open terrain. The GOC took the risk that the defenders would not detect the movement of his infantry battalions and artillery regiments to locations near German positions. Evelegh's plan was for his division to attack with all three brigades in line, though only two battalions would be attacking at any one time in each brigade, leaving the third in reserve. The initial phase of the attack would take place in the middle of the night at 0400 hours on 7 April, with 38th Irish Brigade to the west assigned the job of capturing Djebel Mahdi, the 11th Brigade in the centre capturing Djebel Outiah and Dourat, while the 36th Brigade on the east of the line took Djebel Nahel and the valley of the Oued Bouneb. All three brigade attacks would take place simultaneously in order to achieve maximum surprise. Synchronisation of all attacks was essential to ensure that the Germans in each brigade sector were far too busy dealing with the attack in their area to provide support for fellow units in other sectors.

After these objectives had been seized and secured, Phase B required the 11th Infantry Brigade to take Point 512 near Toukabeur and 36th Brigade to capture the large hill complex of Mergueb Chaouach. During Phases C and D of the advance, the division would secure Points 624 and 667, and finally the Chaouach /Toukabeur heights. Once this stage of the advance had been completed, it was anticipated that further operations would be carried out to exploit the situation (see Maps 5 & 6). The intention was for the division to continue on to capture the heights of Djebel el Ang and Tanngoucha prior to finally taking Longstop Hill. Further details of each of the brigade plans will be examined when we consider each brigade operation in turn.

Having completed his plan, Evelegh went to some lengths to ensure his subordinate commanders understood it. He had a scale model sand table of the terrain built, and used it on 3 April at a divisional conference to brief all his brigade commanders, their staffs and the battalion commanders. He used the same model when briefing his senior commanders. Throughout the planning process, Evelegh worked closely with his division staff and subordinate commanders to refine and improve his plan.[10]

3.8 Fire Plan

British Army doctrine, in 1942 as today, required a commander to carry out his appreciation and produce a formal plan. The next step in the procedure was for his subordinate commanders to carry out a similar process in the light of their commander's intention and create their own plans. Apart from Evelegh's subordinate infantry brigade commanders, the most important actor in this process was 50-year-old Brigadier John Wedderburn-Maxwell of the Royal Regiment of Artillery. As Evelegh's Commander Royal Artillery, or CRA, Wedderburn-Maxwell was in charge of all the Royal Artillery units in the division and was his personal adviser on all matters relating to fire support. The task of creating the fire plan for the 78th Division and Operation Sweep fell to Wedderburn-Maxwell and his staff officers. This plan, once produced, described how many artillery units, guns and shells would be needed to support the operation. It determined how units were allocated to meet the needs of the operation and defined to a certain level how, where and when the guns would be employed.

Brigadier Wedderburn-Maxwell was a tough Lowland Scot who had served as a gunner officer throughout his regular Army career, and had seen extensive action throughout the First World War. In December 1914 he witnessed the famous Christmas truce and football match that took place in no man's land, describing it in a much-published letter to his father. It was perhaps indicative of his confidence and strong personality that his first exchange with his new GOC might in other circumstances, and with another commander, have been his last. Wedderburn-Maxwell was aware that Evelegh, though younger than him, had something of a reputation for being ruthless and rather difficult with his subordinates and staff officers.[11] At his first meeting with Evelegh, he rapidly took the initiative, as he recalled later: "I said I would like a word on my position and told him that I had done the whole of the World War, while I knew that he had only short experience at its end; that he was five years younger than me and finally I was not to be bullied." Fortunately, his divisional commander liked strong subordinates, and after initially greeting this opening gambit with unconcealed surprise, soon established an excellent working relationship with his CRA. The two men were to have their disagreements, including, as Wedderburn-Maxwell stated: "Three major rows, which always ended on a good note." However, they formed a formidable team in Tunisia until Wedderburn-Maxwell left the division in June 1943 at the end of the campaign. The CRA of the Battle-Axe Division grew to have a great respect for his boss's abilities, and commented that his GOC's "speed in grasping

---

10   Details of Evelegh's plan are from Operation Order No. 7, dated 5 April 1943, in TNA WO 175/168 78th Infantry Division April 1943 WD.

11   The profile of John Wedderburn-Maxwell is based on information in the Army List 1940-46 and from an interview in the Oral History Collection of the Imperial War Museum, Catalogue Number 9146, 1985.

essentials was amazing, and his ability to read ground in the chess of moving warfare impressed me immensely".[12]

Wedderburn-Maxwell's fire plan for Operation Sweep reflected the wider divisional plan and focused specifically on allocating the considerable artillery resources made available to the CRA to support the attack. The successful completion of Operation Sweep was a top priority in the First Army, and for the 78th Division this situation was reflected in the artillery assets made available to Wedderburn-Maxwell and his boss. As a normal type of infantry division, the Battle-Axe Division had its three field regiments - the 17th, 132nd and 138th - each of which had three batteries of eight guns. A regiment had 24 25-pounder guns, so there were a total of 72 guns in a division. The 25-pounder, so named because of the average weight of the shell it fired, was a comparatively new gun that only started to enter service with the British Army in April 1940. The 25-pounder was usually manned by a crew of six and could fire high explosive, smoke or anti-tank rounds. A total of 1,351 of these guns were manufactured, and it became the standard field gun for the British and Commonwealth armies in the Second World War. The gun had an average range of 9,000-11,000 yards and a maximum range of 13,400 yards. It had a normal rate of fire of three rounds a minute, with a rapid rate of five rounds a minute. A picture of its crew serving the 25-pounder gun is perhaps the most common image many people recall of the Royal Artillery in the Second World War. British infantry divisions on operations overseas also had a medium artillery regiment as part of their formal organisation. A medium artillery regiment in early 1943 usually consisted of two batteries, each of eight 5.5in guns, for a total of 16 in each regiment. The 5.5in howitzer was very new to the British Army in 1943, having only been introduced into service in 1942. This howitzer could fire a shell weighing 100lb out to a maximum range of 16,000 yards. A division usually had 72 field and 16 medium guns assigned to it to provide fire support to three brigades, plus anti-tank and anti-aircraft (AA) guns. However, for Operation Sweep a further four field regiments, one medium regiment and several additional light and heavy anti-aircraft batteries were assigned to the division to support its attack. These units were divided into three artillery groups, assigned to support the three brigades and a reserve group, as illustrated in Table 1.

Table 1: Artillery Organisation for Operation Sweep

Left – 38th Brigade	Centre – 36th Brigade	Right 11th Brigade	Reserve Group
Brigadier T. Rigby	Lt Col G.A. Thomas	Lt Col T. Usher	Lt Col Denham
102nd Field Regiment Group	17th Field Regiment Group	138th Field Regiment	4th Medium Regiment (minus one battery)
71st Field Regiment Group	132nd Field Regiment	19th Field Regiment (-1 Battery)	18 Battery, 56th Heavy Regiment
5th Medium Regiment	9/13 Medium Battery 4th Medium Regiment		
456 Light Battery			
12 and 19 batteries 56th Heavy Regiment			

---

12   Wedderburn-Maxwell's comments on Evelegh are from Ken Ford, *Battleaxe Division* (Stroud: Sutton Publishing, 2003), pp.2-3.

In addition to its field regiments, the 78th Division also had an anti-tank regiment and light anti-aircraft regiment, respectively the 64th Anti-Tank and 49th Light Anti-Aircraft Regiment. The former included eight 17-pounder and 40 6-pounder anti-tank guns, while the latter usually had a total of 39 40mm Bofors AA guns. The division therefore began the operation with some 174 guns allocated to it: 130 25-pounders, 32 5.5in and 12 7.2in guns. It also had 40 6-pounder and eight 17-pounder anti-tank guns. Furthermore, the 49th Light AA Regiment, under the command of Lieutenant Colonel Hunt, was reinforced by batteries from other AA regiments. For Operation Sweep's early stages, Hunt commanded a considerable AA force with a total 67 light and 12 heavy AA guns. These were designed to protect movement of the 78th Division's forces near Oued Zarga from attacks by German aircraft in the opening stages of the operation. Although the Allied Air Forces had now achieved local air superiority, the *Luftwaffe* in Tunisia was still a threat, based as it was on airfields located less than 10 minutes' flying time away near Tunis. This artillery grouping proved to be a wise precaution in the first days of the operation. The artillery groups supporting 36th and 11th Brigades were directly commanded by the COs of the field artillery regiments that were usually assigned to support these brigades. The centre and right artillery groups were under the command of Lieutenant Colonels "Tommy" Thomas and Clive Usher of the 17th and 138th Field Regiments respectively. Unusually, the left artillery group in support of the 38th Irish Brigade was commanded by the CRA of 46th (Midlands) Infantry Division, Brigadier Terence Rigby, and was composed of units from that division and selected corps artillery units. Finally, a reserve artillery group called the Mike Group was commanded by Lieutenant Colonel Mike Denham, CO of the 4th Medium Regiment. Denham's regiment, though officially a V Corps Artillery asset, was usually assigned to support the Battle-Axe Division.

Wedderburn-Maxwell's fire plan for Operation Sweep was developed with the assistance of his Brigade Major Royal Artillery (BMRA) and senior RA staff officer, Major Geoff Ashmore. The plan allocated the various artillery assets to one of three main artillery groups, each of which supported a specific infantry brigade, or to the Mike Group in reserve. Wedderburn-Maxwell must have expected tougher resistance to the 38th Irish Brigade's attack, as he assigned the greatest number of guns (58) and heaviest firepower to the left artillery group. The artillery plan for the first phase of the operation reflected the GOC's desire to gain tactical surprise. It directed only short but heavy concentrations of artillery fire on all known enemy defensive positions for a period of 10 minutes before and after zero hour (the time of the infantry attacks). Thereafter, the artillery units would be "on call" to provide fire support as directed by the Forward Observation Officers (FOO) who accompanied infantry battalions. A key, albeit alarming feature of the plan for infantry troops was that the artillery concentrations were designed to be fired when companies had managed to get to within only 150 yards of key objectives. As a 25-pounder shell on landing was capable of wounding anyone in the open within a radius of 30-50 yards, and with the potential for errors during firing, the possibility of the artillery killing or wounding its own troops was not insignificant. The infantry commanders in the 78th had considerable experience of being supported by their gunners and accepted the danger. After five months of fighting, experienced company and battalion commanders knew that increasing the distance would simply give the Germans more time to recover before attacking troops closed with their positions, resulting in greater potential casualties in the attacking platoons. It was a calculated gamble. Brigadier Wedderburn-Maxwell delegated the task of devising plans for each brigade to the artillery group for that brigade, so the nature and results of those plans will be considered when describing the operations of each of the division's brigades in later chapters.[13]

3.9 Supporting Arms and Services

Although the division's nine infantry battalions and its artillery undoubtedly provided the cutting edge of the 78th Division, this sharp edge could not have been applied without the assistance provided by other supporting arms and services. Within the British Army, both the Royal Artillery and the Corps of Royal Engineers have the same Latin motto: *"Ubique"* (everywhere). An ongoing but friendly debate continues between the two as to which has best claim to the motto, but it is certainly true that during the preparations and conduct of Operation Sweep, sappers - the Army's slang for Royal Engineers - were everywhere. The dynamic CRE (Commander Royal Engineers) of the 78th Division was 43-year-old Lieutenant Colonel Edmund Blake RE, who acted as Evelegh's adviser on all combat engineering matters and oversaw the activities of all four organic RE companies in the division. In a similar vein to Wedderburn-Maxwell, Blake took his GOC's plan and used that to develop his own more detailed combat engineering plan. Blake's main combat engineer assets in the division - the 214th, 237th and 256th Field Companies RE - were supplemented for the initial stages of Operation Sweep by the loan of the 565th Armoured Field Company from the 6th Armoured Division and a platoon of a bridging company. Additional engineering equipment was allocated for the operation, including bulldozers and other types of bridging equipment. The sappers' key tasks, both before and during the initial stages of the battle, were concerned with removing obstacles to the division's mobility. The first main role allocated to Blake's troops was to improve existing roads and tracks up to the front line and strengthen bridges in the area. The second task assigned to the RE companies was to enable the fighting troops and tanks to cross any physical obstacles. The rugged nature of the terrain and the dry river beds in the area, particularly those of the Oued Zarga, Oued Bouneb and Bed, presented significant natural obstacles to vehicle and tank movement in the Bed Valley to the east of Mahdi. The field companies were therefore also tasked with building or improving bridges at Oued Zarga and in the Bed Valley to enable the division's tanks and vehicles to move forward. The third and most dangerous task was to remove any minefields that could impede the attack of the infantry and tank units. The Germans had become particularly adept at using anti-tank and anti-personnel mines on roads and tracks in North Africa to inflict casualties and delay on Allied forces. They also had a nasty habit of mining the soft verges of roads. One complication to the CRE's plans, and in part the reason for the presence of the 565th Company, was that he had been ordered to use one section each from the 214th and 237th Field Companies RE for a special task. This task force, called Joss Force, was required to support the 38th Infantry Brigade. These troops were only returned part way through the operation.[14]

---

13 Details of the artillery fire plans for the division are derived from RA Operation Order 13 dated 6 April 1943 in TNA WO 175/170 78th Infantry Division CRA WD April 1943 and Left Artillery Group Operation Order No. 1 in TNA WO 175/159 46th Infantry Division WD April 1943.

14 Details of RE operations during Operation Sweep were derived from Operation Order No. 7 dated 5 April 1943 in TNA WO 175/171 78th Infantry Division WD for the Commander RE, and the WDs for March and April 1943 in that file, plus the WDs for the 214th, 237th, 256th and 281st Divisional

In addition to the Royal Engineers, a number of other supporting services had to create their own plans and preparations for Operation Sweep. A range of supporting units wore the Battle-Axe divisional sign on their shoulder as they formed part of division. Of these, arguably two organisations were the most important in terms of their future contribution to the operation: the Royal Army Medical Corps (RAMC) and Royal Army Service Corps (RASC). This does not in any way undervalue the role of a range of other services, whose contribution will be related in the main part of this story. It is worth examining how these organisations were structured and commanded, and how they prepared and planned for the battle. The motto of the RAMC, "*In Ardis Fidelis*" (Steadfast in Adversity), is very appropriate as the officers and men of the corps often found themselves either on the front line or very close to it, exposed to considerable danger. It is an often overlooked fact that the largest number of VCs awarded to a single corps or regiment in the British Army (27, including two bars representing second awards) were earned not by fighting unit, but by officers and men of the RAMC. Medical units within the Battle-Axe Division were to play crucial roles in the forthcoming operations. Care of the sick and wounded in the Battle-Axe Division was entrusted to the officers and men of the RAMC, overseen by Vyvyan Evelegh's senior medical officer, 43-year-old Colonel Douglas Cheyne, a Scot who was Assistant Director of Medical Services (ADMS). A career RAMC officer, Cheyne was exceptionally well prepared for his role, having served throughout the First World War as a doctor, during which he had been awarded the MC for bravery at Asiago in Italy in 1918. After the First World War, Cheyne served in a range of challenging Army medical appointments in India, China and Africa. Cheyne's job was to plan and prepare the medical units in the 78th Division for the collection and care of the inevitable casualties that would arise from the battle. His plan was supposed to be informed by an estimate of the likely number of wounded provided by the operations staff of the division.

Medical services at the sharp end of battle were usually delivered by a RAMC captain acting as the Regimental Medical Officer (RMO) and one RAMC soldier held on the strength of the fighting units in infantry brigades. They were supported by 20 soldiers from each unit, assigned as stretcher bearers. This job, as shown by Guardsman Dean's MM award at Longstop Hill, could be hazardous and required dedication and a cool courage. The role of a RMO with an infantry battalion in action was also no sinecure, as witnessed by the award of several MCs to RMOs, both before and during Operation Sweep. These front-line medical posts were directly supported by three Field Ambulance units in the 78th Division: the 11th, 152nd and 217th Field Ambulances. The role of these units was to collect wounded and injured from the front line, move them out of danger and carry out very basic treatment before they were sent for surgery in a Field Surgical Unit (FSU) or a General Hospital. FSUs (mobile operating theatres) were a new development in the RAMC and were used for the first time in Tunisia. A Field Ambulance's role was to use its two companies to provide the modern equivalent of an ambulance service, paramedics and Accident and Emergency department, albeit during a major disaster. It was expected to be able to open and close one of its advanced dressing stations inside an hour and find, move and process over 150 casualties. A wounded man would be picked up from the Regimental Aid Post (RAP) by a motor ambulance, jeep or lorry fitted out for evacuation. They would be moved to the rear to an advanced or main dressing stations (ADS or MDS), where the soldier would be checked by medical staff and receive additional basic treatment before being sent on to the rear to be properly treated. The medical plan for Operation Sweep assigned three Field Ambulances - 11th, 152nd and 217th, commanded by RAMC Lieutenant Colonels Keeling, Lytle and Clark respectively - to direct support for 11th, 38th and 36th Brigades. These units were supplemented for the operation by 10th Field Ambulance of 1st Infantry Division and the provision of support by medical units of the 46th and 4th Infantry Divisions. Treatment of the more seriously wounded or injured, including operations, took place some 35 miles from the front line at other medical facilities, including at least two large tented hospitals set up near an old monastery at the village of Thibar in the hills north of the ancient Roman ruins at Dougga. Those casualties who required more advanced aid or would take time to recover were moved by road and rail through a medical evacuation chain that stretched 500 miles back to Algiers. The scale of the operation can be illustrated by the fact that the First Army alone had been assigned six hospitals with over 3,000 beds. The RAMC was thus ready to fulfil its role and look after the inevitable cost that battle would bring in terms of men whose bodies (and minds) had been mangled, burned or broken in the fighting.[15]

Another corps which was to play a crucial but often forgotten role in the forthcoming battles was the Royal Army Service Corps. The role of RASC units in the 78th Division was to supply and transport all the supplies required by its fighting units, including food, water, fuel, clothing and all other types of supplies and reinforcements. The storage and supply of ammunition was a task for the Royal Army Ordnance Corps (RAOC); the RASC was only required to move it. The RASC also had the task of evacuating the wounded, since its personnel acted as drivers in Field Ambulances, and of moving enemy prisoners from near the front line to safety. In addition to transport, the corps also managed supply depots and ran bakeries, but the key part of its role was moving supplies. In Tunisia alone, troops were supplied by over 50 RASC transport companies, each equipped with 60 lorries, in total some 3,000 vehicles. Fighting soldiers and their commanders were in no doubt about the critical importance of the corps' hard and difficult work. The motto of the RASC's successor in the modern British Army, the Royal Logistic Corps, is "We Sustain", a very accurate description of its tasks. The role of sustaining the fighting brigades was also not without its risks. RASC drivers in Tunisia often found themselves under attack, either from the air or by shelling. Within the 78th Division, the task of ensuring the movement of the massive amount of ammunition and supplies required for the attack by the fighting units fell to the Commander RASC (CRASC). In 1943 this was Lieutenant Colonel Bill Hart, and for the forthcoming operation he had four companies available for the task, each of which had 60 large Bedford 30 cwt trucks to carry various supplies. However, the scale of the logistics operation was much larger as many more non-divisional RASC motor transport

15   This account of the Battle-Axe Division's medical support is based on information from TNA WO 177/420 Assistant Director of Medical Services (ADMS) WD 78th Infantry Division for March and April 1943, and especially Operation Order No. 11 78th Division ADMS dated 3 April 1943. Other useful sources were the TNA WO 177/693,737 and 823 WDs of the 11th, 152nd and 217th Field Ambulances for April 1943, and F. Crew, *Army Medical Services: Campaigns Volume II* (Uckfield: Naval and Military Press, 2014). The profile of Colonel Cheyne is derived from details in the Army List and R. Butt, 'Biographical Dictionary of Medical Practitioners in Hong Kong', a blogpost, see http://hkmd1841-1941.blogspot.co.uk/2014/04/cheyne-douglas-gordon-1929.html.

companies were required to move all types of supplies from rear areas as far away as 500 miles in Algeria to divisional supply dumps. Bill Hart and his four company commanders not only had to resupply the division with its daily needs, for example daily rations, but also had to work out how to support the fighting brigades and artillery regiments, despite the difficult terrain with its poor track and road system. Artillery regiments created significant resupply challenges for the RASC companies because of their guns' massive appetite for shells. To illustrate this point more graphically, on one night alone during the Battle of the Peaks, that of 11 April, two RASC companies had to pick up 10,000 25-pounder shells and move them in darkness to battery positions in a few hours over difficult tracks and roads.

Although these truck companies tended to move much of the division's supplies, the very difficult mountainous terrain meant that the division and its fighting battalions also had need of the assistance of a very different type of RASC asset, a four-legged one: mules. The need for mules to move critical but heavy equipment and supplies (e.g. water, ammunition, radios, mortars and machine guns) had been recognised in the middle of 1942 (see Plates 7 & 21). The first mule company to be established in Tunisia was formed by another of those talented sportsmen who ended up serving in or supporting the Battle-Axe Division.[16] Major Joe Dudgeon was an accomplished horseman from Ireland who had been awarded the MC in 1918, and had gone on after the war to win the Dublin Grand Prix and captain the British Showjumping team. Although aged 47 at the start of the war and living in Eire, Dudgeon sought active service and by November 1942 was in Algeria. He almost single-handily set up the 10th Pack Transport Company RASC, purchasing the mules, enlisting, equipping and training all the company personnel. These included Arab mule handlers enlisted into Army service and British NCOs. This was a great achievement; it was accomplished in a remarkably short space of time, and as each troop was complete it was immediately put into action. By January 1943, Dudgeon was in command of and responsible for the training of another pack transport company, the 11th. This was organised into three troops with 10 French and British officers, 88 British, French and Arab NCOs, 226 Arab mule drivers and 320 very important mules. Dudgeon played a key role in highlighting the need for mules in the mountains of Tunisia, organising RASC mule companies and helping to supply the infantry battalions in the 78th Division with their own mule parties. Infantry battalions quickly realised the value of mules and found themselves learning, through on-the-job training, how to handle them properly in difficult terrain.[17] For example, the 5th Northants relied heavily on mules during its abortive attempt in mid- December to move through the hills north of Longstop and mine the Tebourba gap. Lack of experience in packing mules had damaged the battalion radio at a crucial point and meant it was effectively not in contact for three days. The mule teams were to play a key role in enabling the fighting brigades of the 78th Division to operate in the desolate and rugged Djebels.

16   The organisation of the RASC in the 78th Division is based on the WD of the Commander RASC for 78th Division for March and April 1943 and the four WDs of the RASC companies in that formation - TNA WO 175/173, 175/174, 175/925, 175/934 and 175/941. The source for the movement of 10,000 shells is from the CRASC War Diary with an Ammunition Order dated 11 April.

17   The story of mule transport companies is derived from TNA WO 175/823 and 822 WDs in 1943 of the 10th Pack Transport Company and the 4th Pack Transport Group. The profile of Lieutenant Colonel Joseph Hume Dudgeon reflects information from the Army List, the Peerage website www. thepeerage.com/p34726.html (accessed January 2018) and the citation for his OBE.

3.10 Preparing for the Attack

The final 10 days prior to the start of the Battle of the Peaks witnessed a significant level of effort by the Battle-Axe Division and the supporting units of V Corps. Allfrey's plan for the initial phase of an attack on Tunis required the success of operations near the mining town of Sedjenane. This would fulfill three essential requirements of the overall First Army plan to capture Tunis; firstly to retake lost positions and free up the 36th Infantry Brigade, so it could take part in the forthcoming 78th Division attack. The second requirement was to secure positions which could defend the northern front against German attacks using minimal forces, and release the 46th Division to be moved south to take part in the wider attack. The final requirement was to deceive the Germans and draw their reserves to the north, in order to weaken their lines around Medjez el Bab. The attack was launched on 28 March by the 46th Infantry Division, reinforced for this operation by the 1st Parachute and 36th Infantry Brigades. In four days of costly fighting, the 46th Infantry Division regained all the territory lost in early March and finally seized Djebel Aboid. The latter, which had resisted all attempts to capture it for nearly five months, fell to an attack by 1st Parachute Brigade. The operation was significant for three reasons: it drew enemy reserves north as intended and weakened the German forces near Medjez; it weakened Axis forces in the north, as over 800 prisoners were taken, although most were Italian and not German soldiers; and it involved all three battalions of the 36th Brigade on operations immediately prior to the launch of Operation Sweep. The 5th Buffs, for example, conducted attacks on 28 March in heavy rain on a hill east of Djebel Aboid, losin four killed, 11 wounded and one missing. The battalion spent three days in woods near Sedjenane before moving south to Teboursouk, where they managed only three days of rest after five months of constant operations. The 6th West Kents were also involved with the brigade in supporting the attack on Sedjenane. Meanwhile, the 8th Argylls lost key personnel in two incidents. The first was on 29 March, when an aircraft machine-gunned the battalion and its HQs in an exposed location. Four key officers were wounded, and in all nine men were killed and 25 wounded. This setback had poor timing, for the 8th Argylls was soon to find itself with a key role in the forthcoming battle on the Djebels. The fighting that ensued added another five dead and 27 wounded to an already high butchers bill. The following day, 31 March, was the battalion's last in the front line before being pulled out for a very short rest. It was therefore doubly unfortunate that two sentries stumbled into a minefield, and in an attempt to rescue them a number of medical staff and stretcher bearers were killed or injured. In an act of cold-blooded courage that undoubtedly upheld the RAMC motto *"In Ardis Fidelis"*, and despite the risks, the RMO, Captain Hugh Matheson Macfie, ventured in the darkness into the minefield that had already wounded or killed others, to treat the casualties. His actions that night earned him an MC for gallantry. The experience of both battalions of the 36th Brigade shows that even after nearly five months of constant operations, the brigade's key units had enjoyed very little rest before being committed to a very difficult series of mountain battles.[18]

18   The strafing and minefield incidents experienced by the 8th Argylls are from A.D. Malcolm, *History of the Argylls and Sutherland Highlanders 8th Battalion 1939-47* (London: Thomas Nelson and Sons Limited, 1949), pp.116-17, the 8th Argylls WD for March 1943 and the citation for Macfie's MC in TNA WO 373/1.

Meanwhile, all across the V Corps and 78th Division area, the supporting services worked feverishly to create forward dumps of ammunition, food, water and all other types of supplies. This was often done at night to avoid alerting the Germans of the future attack. A whole range of units, especially the artillery regiments chosen to provide crucial fire support, had to be moved to assembly positions close to the front line in the hills to the south of the Oued Zarga-Medjez road. The artillery regiments assigned to support the attack had a significant problem as the divisional artillery plan gave these units locations for their guns which lay in areas that were often overlooked in daylight by German positions. The placement of the guns so close to the Germans was necessary, not only to bring the initial objectives within range but to avoid the immediate need to move the guns when German positions further away had to be taken. RE companies also worked to strengthen and improve roads and bridges that would be needed to support the attack.

Both V Corps and the Battle-Axe Division entered the fight for the Peaks with five months of experience and a much more professional approach to operations. The hard lessons received in the race to Tunis and the attack on Longstop had been learned. The commanders, officers and men of the fighting brigades were now hardened veterans of numerous actions. They had tasted the bitterness of defeat, but also had their successes. A new sense of quiet competence and confidence pervaded the companies and battalions of the division that was about to be committed to its second major offensive. That confidence can be seen in the war diaries, plans, and letters and personal accounts of the officers and soldiers at that time. One of the lessons learned in December was the importance of having sufficient forces in mountainous terrain to both seize objectives and hold them. Evelegh's division was significantly reinforced for the tasks it had been allocated. The division was assigned the equivalent of an additional complete infantry brigade to support it and secure flanks in the first three to four days of the operation. The new battalions assigned for part or all of this initial period were the 16th Battalion of the Durham Light Infantry (16th DLI), the 6th Battalion The Black Watch (6th Black Watch) and the 2nd Battalion of the Hampshire Regiment (2nd Hants), plus two companies of the Sherwood Foresters Regiment. These units had to reposition themselves to be ready for their part in the attack, as did the five artillery and two armoured regiments tasked with the support of the division. Another sign of the increased power and professionalism of the Allied forces was that at 0415 hours in the morning of 6 April, the 50th and 51st Infantry Divisions of the Eighth Army launched their attack on German defensive position at Wadi Akarit. This and Operation Sweep would be launched within 24 hours and be mutually supporting. It would not be possible for von Arnim to move forces from the southern front to support the northern one or vice versa; each area of the front would have to react to the two attacks with the forces in place.

The last four days prior to the attacks on the night of 6/7 April were used to provide the fighting units of the 78th Division with a short period of rest and preparation. This was not easy, as all the infantry battalions needed to devote time to undertake standing patrols in the defensive area, receive reinforcements, conduct training, complete their initial reconnaissance of their objectives and finally move up to concealed new assembly positions. These were often almost in sight of the enemy, close to the start line for their attacks.

Clear The Way: 38th Irish Brigade's Battle for Djebel Mahdi

4.1 The Arrival of the Irish Brigade

In his appreciation for Operation Sweep, Vyvyan Evelegh highlighted the tactical importance of German positions on Djebel Mahdi. This large, pear-shaped mountain is nearly two miles long and a mile wide, and in 1943 was held by units of the 334th Infantry Division. It secured the right flank of their defence line above the Medjez to Oued Zarga road. From their positions high on Djebel Mahdi, the Germans had excellent views of the hills to the east, which were the objectives of 36th and 11th Brigades, and posed a threat to their operations (see Map 4). Evelegh and his staff fully recognised this fact, and in his appreciation he stressed the need for the German positions on Mahdi to be eliminated early in the division's attack. He allocated the task of taking the mountain to a relatively new arrival, the 38th Infantry Brigade, by now informally known as the Irish Brigade.[1] The Irish Brigade was not an established formation of the British Army, but was formed in January 1942 as a result of a memo from Winston Churchill to the Chief of the Imperial General Staff in October 1941: "Pray let me have your views, and if possible your plans, for the forming of an Irish Brigade."[2] Like many of the ideas listed in Churchill's memos, the formation of the brigade was one that attracted a degree of controversy. It was initially resisted by the government of Northern Ireland because the original Irish Brigade (often known as the Wild Geese) had been Irish mercenaries serving the French, who had fought against England in the days of Marlborough. Despite, or possibly because of,

---

1   Unless otherwise specifically stated, Chapter 4 is based on analysis of the following primary sources: TNA WO 175/170 78th Division CRA WD April 1943;, TNA WO 175/216 WD 38th Infantry Brigade WD April 1943; TNA WO 175/506 WD 1st Royal Irish Fusiliers January–April 1943; TNA WO 175/505 WD 6th Royal Inniskilling Fusiliers Jan–April 1943; TNA WO 175/294 WD 1 North Irish Horse March-April 1943; TNA WO 175/499 WD 2nd Hants Jan–April 1943; and WO 175/494 WD 6th Black Watch April 1943. The following published sources were invaluable: R. Doherty, *Clear the Way: A History of the 38th (Irish) Brigade 1941-1947* (Dublin: Irish Academic Press, 1993); R. Doherty, *The North Irish Horse: 100 years of service* (Staplehurst: Spellmount Publishers, 2002); and Coldwell-Horsfall, *The Wild Geese*.
2   Quoted in W. Churchill, *The Second World War* (London: Cassell, 1950) p.329, cited in R. Doherty, *Clear the Way*, p.6.

the opposition of the head of the Army and the government of Northern Ireland, the Prime Minister had his way and 38th Infantry Brigade was formed on 13 January 1942.

Although originally part of the 1st Infantry Division, the Irish Brigade became the supporting infantry brigade of the 6th Armoured Division in June 1942. Leading units from the brigade began to arrive in Algeria in late November 1942, and the remainder arrived in Tunisia in the first week of December. The whole brigade eventually took up positions in the front line near Goubellat in mid-December. At some point in March 1943, it was decided that the 38th Irish Brigade would move from the 6th Armoured to the 78th Division and be replaced by the 1st Guards Brigade. It is claimed that this happened because Brigadier Felix Copland-Griffiths, commander of the 1st Guards Brigade, was unhappy serving under Major General Evelegh. Copland-Griffiths was also reputed to have felt aggrieved by the fact that Evelegh had received command of the division, even though he was much younger than Copland-Griffiths, junior to him by date of commission and the former had been the senior brigade commander.[3] The 38th Brigade spent most of January to March 1943 near the town of Bou Arada, 30 miles south of Medjez el Bab, where it experienced some hard fighting against German mountain, paratrooper and *panzer* units. During those three months, the brigade gained invaluable experience in fighting some of the toughest and most capable of German troops. It also began to develop a well-earned reputation as a unit which could tackle and complete the most difficult of tasks, irrespective of the obstacles placed in front of it. Over the next three weeks, the brigade was to greatly enhance this reputation, and increase it even further in tough later battles in Sicily and Italy. In Tunisia, the brigade was commanded by the tall, quiet but imposing 45-year-old Brigadier Nelson Russell MC (see Plate 4), who had previously served as Commanding Officer of a Territorial Army (TA) battalion (the 6th) of the Royal Irish Fusiliers, one of the three infantry battalions which formed the core of the brigade. Russell assumed command of the brigade in England in June 1942 and led it until March 1944. Although 6ft 3in tall, Russell was a humble and self-effacing commander, who quickly earned and never lost the trust, respect and admiration of all the officers and men who served in his brigade during his long period of command. The other two battalions of the brigade were the 2nd Battalion, the London Irish Rifles and the 6th Battalion of the Royal Inniskilling Fusiliers.

Although the brigade was a new formation, two of the regiments under Brigadier Russell's command had a long and distinguished history. The 1st Battalion, the Princess Victoria's Royal Irish Fusiliers (Nelson Russell's old regiment) was the regular battalion of an established Irish regiment. It had been formed from the amalgamation of the 87th and 89th Regiments of Foot, both of which traced their ancestry back to 1793. The Royal Irish Fusiliers had long been known by their nickname in the British Army, the Faughs (which will be adopted hereafter to describe the battalion), from an eighteenth-century anglicised translation of the regiment's informal Gaelic battle cry, "*Faugh a Ballach*", which in English means "Clear the Way". Irish soldiers of the 87th Foot are reported to have screamed this phrase as they dashed to capture the first Imperial eagle of the French 8th Regiment at the Battle of Barossa in southern Spain in 1809, the first time one of these standards had been taken in battle. The event came to symbolise the wild fighting spirit and willingness to take on difficult tasks, of both the Faughs and arguably all

---

3   See Ford, *The Battle-Axe Division*, p.3. The author would note that Evelegh's later performance as GOC of the division fully demonstrated the confidence senior commanders had in both his ability and potential.

Irish regiments who served as part of the British Army. In 1939, the Royal Irish Fusiliers could look back at a distinguished history, including battles such as Talavera, Sebastopol, Ladysmith and the Somme. In France in 1940, the regiment and its first battalion had added to its laurels by holding up the advance of the 7th *Panzer* Division, commanded by a certain Erwin Rommel, for several days before it was evacuated at Dunkirk. It landed in Algiers with the other units in the brigade in December 1942 and experienced some tough fighting around the town of Bou Arada in early 1943. By March 1943, command of this now seasoned battalion had passed from its highly effective CO, Pat Scott, to his able second-in-command, Major Beauchamp Butler, who was already highly regarded within the Faughs for his judgement, leadership and calmness under fire. These qualities were even more in evidence when he became CO and stood him in good stead in the ensuing months.

The second Irish unit in the brigade with a distinguished past was the 6th Battalion of the Royal Inniskilling Fusiliers, known by their nickname the Skins. This had reputedly been acquired when a bathing party of one of its predecessors, the 27th Foot, was caught unawares by the French in Italy at the Battle of Maida in 1805 and its soldiers prepared to fight naked. The regiment started its existence as a band of men prepared to defend the town of Enniskillen in 1688. Since that date the regiment had added many famous battle honours to its colours, including Badajoz, Waterloo and Gallipoli. The 6th Battalion, a TA unit, was raised in Northern Ireland in October 1940 and had not seen action before coming to Tunisia and being deployed on the Goubellat plain south of Medjez el Bab. The battalion's baptism of fire came in January 1943 near the village of Bou Arada when it attempted to secure a feature called Two Tree Hill. The attack failed, though through no fault of their new CO, Lieutenant Colonel C.H.B. Allen. A Royal Ulster Rifles officer, Allen took over when the previous CO was wounded in an air attack and he proved his mettle in his new role, both in the attack on Two Tree Hill and later by holding his position against a major German counterattack.

The third unit in the brigade, which had a less established regimental history and moreover had a difficult start in Tunisia, was the 2nd Battalion, the London Irish Rifles (2nd London Irish). In contrast to the two other battalions in the brigade, this unit lacked a long regimental history and was not a part of the regular army. The regiment could claim to trace its ancestry back to the Corps of Irish Gentlemen at Arms, which was formed in 1859, while two battalions served in the Great War with distinction. In 1937, the 2nd Battalion the London Irish Rifles was created when the 18th Battalion of the London Regiment was broken up. This became part of the London Irish, the Royal Ulster Rifles as a TA battalion. The 2nd London Irish officially became part of the 38th Infantry Brigade in January 1942, and after landing in Algeria in December, initially entered the front lines south of Medjez el Bab near the town of Bou Arada. Its first major action took place on 20 January 1943 when an ill-advised attack on a hill named Point 286 led to heavy fighting. The unit's initiation into battle was a disastrous one, in which two companies were overrun by German infantry supported by tanks, and the 2nd London Irish suffered at least 26 killed, 78 wounded and 130 missing, most of the latter captured. As many of these casualties came from its rifle companies, which rarely numbered more than 400 men, it was not entirely surprising that by late February or early March, the possibility of disbanding the battalion was discussed. This move by First Army headquarters was strongly resisted by Nelson Russell as it would have threatened the future existence of the 38th Infantry Brigade, which would only have two battalions. Russell won his argument and the much-reduced battalion was retained, but there was a price to be paid and its CO was relieved of his command.

His replacement was 38-year-old Pat Scott, the previous CO of the 1st Battalion, the Royal Irish Fusiliers, who took over in March (See Plate 27). By April, Scott had already established a reputation as the highly capable commander of the 1st Royal Irish Fusiliers, and was well known for four key characteristics: an ability to inspire confidence in his Irish soldiers; an eye for detail; a feel for battle (what the Germans called *Fingerspitzengefühl*, a fingertip feeling for battle, which is a rare skill in a commander); and being well-known for his tendency to speak his mind, which was combined with his unwillingness to tolerate fools gladly, irrespective of their rank. Russell's decision to move Scott to command of the London Irish Rifles from the Faughs was a measure both of the seriousness of that battalion's condition and his confidence in Scott. Scott immediately started rebuilding the battalion with a large draft of replacements, and it was pulled out of the front line. The impact of this decision was that the other two battalions of the brigade remained in the front line almost until the time they were committed to Operation Sweep. The Faughs and the Skins had endured a difficult winter, much hard fighting and an extended period of over three months in front-line duty by the time the launched their attack on Mahdi. In place of the London Irish as its third battalion for the forthcoming operation, an English battalion, the 2nd Hampshires, became honorary Irishmen and temporarily joined the 38th Infantry Brigade. The brigade moved up to the area near the village of Oued Zarga, west of Medjez el Bab, in late March and prepared for the forthcoming offensive.[4]

4.2 An "Unconventional Tank Regiment"

Another Irish unit was to play a vital role in the operations of the 38th Brigade and the 78th Division. This was 1st North Irish Horse, part of the 25th Independent Tank Brigade. The North Irish Horse had much more in common with the Wild Geese of the Irish Brigade than simply their home island. The regiment, commanded by Lieutenant Colonel David Dawnay, was, like the Wild Geese of the 38th Irish Brigade, quickly to become famous for its willingness to tackle and overcome obstacles which might defeat lesser units. It was perhaps also no accident of history that it was equipped with a tank named after the Irish Brigade's founder, the Churchill. Winston would probably heartily approve of what could arguably be considered the unofficial motto of both the Irish Brigade and the North Irish Horse: "the difficult we do as a matter of routine, the impossible just takes a little longer!" The pairing of an unconventional Northern Irish Yeomanry unit with the newly upgraded Mark III Churchill tank in the middle of 1942 was to prove a fortuitous one for the infantry units of the Battle-Axe Division in Tunisia and a disaster for the Germans. However, the early days of the Churchill tank had not been promising, with many technical problems arising from the decision to go into large-scale production despite very limited time for trials. The Churchill's debut in combat during Operation Jubilee, the disastrous Dieppe raid, was inauspicious, as several became bogged down due to the peculiar nature of the chert beach at the port. The Germans captured, inspected and tested some Churchills, and their subsequent technical report rated the tank poorly, describing it as easy to combat.

---

4   The historical profiles of Irish battalions in Tunisia are based on regimental histories, while personal profiles of Russell, Scott and Butler are derived from biographies in R. Doherty, *Clear the Way*, and Coldwell-Horsfall, *Wild Geese*. A further source is Brigadier N. Russell's report entitled the *Irish Brigade in Tunisia* hereafter cited as The Irish Brigade. This document is from the Fusiliers Regimental Museum but is also available on line at <www.irishbrigade.com>.(accessed 15 October 2018)

Their tendency to underrate the Churchill tank was fortunate, as its deployment in Tunisia would cause the Germans to have some nasty surprises.[5] The Mark III Churchill still had many limitations by the time the North Irish Horse used it in Tunisia. The tank was very slow (its top speed was only 17mph), and it only had a 6-pounder gun, although it did have two Besa machine guns. The tank had one especially endearing characteristic for infantry soldiers and the Irish Brigade: its mobility. The Churchill could go places other tanks simply could not. Another very important feature of the Churchill was its excellent armoured protection. Its frontal armour was formidable, which was demonstrated at El Alamein when a small number were committed to battle and survived numerous hits by Axis anti-tank guns: one tank was finally disabled, but only after being hit over 50 times. These two features made the tank very effective in the infantry-support role, and the tank's effectiveness was further enhanced when these were coupled with a regiment that had an unconventional mindset and was willing to take risks some units would not.[6]

The North of Ireland Imperial Yeomanry was formed in 1902 just after the end of the Boer War, and renamed the North Irish Horse in 1908. It was a Territorial (part-time) unit, which was mobilised in 1914 and fought only as individual squadrons during the Great War. After the war the unit almost disappeared, and at one stage was the butt of jokes, being known as the one-man regiment as only one officer remained. However, the unit was rebuilt by 1939 and remobilised. The North Irish was initially trained as an armoured car unit, converting to the Churchill tank in 1942. The regiment's CO, Lieutenant Colonel David Dawnay, was a regular soldier with deep roots in the Northern Irish aristocracy. In contrast to some of his contemporaries in fashionable cavalry regiments, Dawnay was also a thoroughly professional officer with a very modern approach to training and operations. He began his career as an infantry soldier in the Rifle Brigade in 1924, but quickly transferred to a cavalry regiment, the 10th Hussars, that same year. Dawnay was, like many of his fellow commanding officers in Tunisia, a sportsman of ability. He was captain of the British polo team that won a silver medal at the Olympic Games in Nuremburg in 1936, and also played tennis at Army level. At the start of the war he was still a captain, but was promoted to temporary major and commanded a squadron of his regiment in France in 1940 before becoming second-in-command of the North Irish. After commanding a Reconnaissance Regiment he returned to command the North Irish Horse in 1940. His appointment to the North Irish Horse was an inspired one, as he quickly brought in regular instructors and through hard training forged his regiment into a highly professional armoured unit. During training near Westbury in Wiltshire, Dawnay, who had ensured he read debriefing reports of the Churchill tank's performance at Dieppe, insisted his tank crews operate their tanks on the steep slopes nearby to become familiar with its capabilities. Most crews could not understand why this was required, as they all expected to be sent to the desert, but this training was to have a huge pay-off the following year.[7]

5   For the problems encountered by Churchills at Dieppe, see H.G. Henry, 'The Calgary Tanks at Dieppe', *Canadian Military History* Vol. 4, Issue 1.6, pp.61-74, see www.scholars.wlu.ca/cmh/vol4/iss1/6 (accessed 30 January 2018).

6   An excellent source on the Churchill tank is Bryan Perrett, *The Churchill: Armour in Action* (Littlehampton: Book Services Limited, 1974).

7   Details of David Dawnay's career are derived from Doherty, *North Irish Horse*, and the Army list. The use of hills near Westbury is also from the same source.

The regiment landed in Tunisia as part of the 25th Tank Brigade, and in February and March 1943, under Dawnay's command, quickly proved its mettle in a series of engagements with more experienced German *panzers*. At Hunt's Gap near Beja, the North Irish Horse, led by Dawnay in his first battle, stopped and then out-fought and destroyed a German *panzer* attack. This dangerous German attack had already overrun part of an infantry battalion and 155 Battery of 166th Field Regiment during its legendary stand at Sidi Nisr. Dawnay's unit demonstrated its unconventional streak when it disregarded conventional doctrine by manning a key section of the front line in the face of German threat without infantry in support for over 60 hours. It also destroyed several German tanks and helped disable and capture the first German Tiger tank taken by the Allies, which can be seen today at the Royal Armoured Corps Museum at Bovington. During March the regiment gained further experience in tank-infantry cooperation with a range of units, and had already begun to build a reputation as a highly capable tank formation. Until early April it had been deployed east of Beja near Sedjenane, working under the command of the 46th Infantry Division. On 6 April, the majority of the regiment was ordered south and assigned to support the 78th Division. Its initial debut with the division would be during the battle for Djebel Nahel assisting the 36th Brigade, but it was also to provide crucial support for 38th Irish Brigade over the next three weeks.

4.3 Douglas-Pennant's Plan for the Battle

The plan for the attack on Djebel Mahdi was prepared by Brigadier Russell and his 35-year-old brigade major, Frank Douglas-Pennant, who later succeeded to the family title of Lord Penrhyn. In this role, Major Douglas-Pennant, a pre-war regular officer from the King's Royal Rifle Corps, acted as Brigadier Russell's key operations officer and ran the brigade staff. Douglas-Pennant was a cool and competent staff officer, quite unperturbed by enemy actions, according to the citation for the MBE that he would later be awarded. He had served with the 1st Battalion of the famous 60th Rifles in the UK and India, and attended Staff College in 1940 before being posted to 38th Brigade in 1943. Russell and Douglas-Pennant's plan for 38th Brigade's attack was developed through a careful study of the terrain, reports from patrols and observation posts, plus air photographs taken on 3 April. On this same day, Russell, his COs and their second-in-commands also attended the planning conference at the divisional headquarters where they were briefed on their roles in Operation Sweep using a sand table model of the area.[8] The brigade's task was to secure the division's left flank by ensuring it took Djebel Sidi Bel Mahdi, to give the hill its full title. Russell described Mahdi as:

> A particularly blood-some pear shaped feature – about 4 miles long and at the widest 2 miles. It rose in a fairly gradual slope to 1,400 feet. The sharp end of the rear was nearest to us and was encircled by a wide 20 foot deep wadi with steep side.
>
> The wadi was wired and mined. The only approach was through a narrow valley which was mined, booby trapped and within mortar range.

8   Profile and quote about Major Frank Douglas-Pennant derived from his Obituary in the *Daily Telegraph* on 9 December 2003.

Russell concluded his account in rather typical style by stating: "As an objective it lacked many qualities."[9]

The plan to take Mahdi identified the requirement to secure Mount Kachiba, a major hill to the west of Mahdi, which overlooked both the hill but also key approaches to it. The need to secure adjoining features and prevent the Germans from calling in artillery and mortar fire on newly taken positions was to be a constant refrain during Operation Sweep. Russell recognised that although intelligence indicated Mahdi and its sister peak Mount Kachiba were not strongly held, the large and rugged area would require all the Irish Brigade's resources to be used. The limited intelligence available to the brigade indicated that Mahdi and its approaches were probably held by two understrength German infantry companies of the 3rd Battalion of the 755th Grenadier Regiment from the 334th Infantry Division. These units, largely manned by Austrian troops, were well equipped with the highly effective MG34 Spandau machine guns and 8.1cm mortars. The companies occupied fortified positions and had laid a series of anti-personnel minefields across obvious approaches. The 3rd/755th Grenadiers occupied good positions, but like most German units during Operation Sweep, they were understrength and had a large area to defend. They also had no tanks and a very limited degree of artillery support. The latter consisted of a few short-barrelled infantry mountain guns that formed part of the regiment and a couple of batteries of 105mm guns of the 334th Artillery Regiment. While using a brigade of three battalions to attack two companies might seem like having a hammer to crack a nut, both Douglas-Pennant and Russell had considerable experience fighting in the Tunisian hills and recognised that taking large hills was one thing, yet holding them in the face of German counterattacks was another. They also understood that well-equipped German infantry units, holding high ground and defended by minefields, could take a considerable toll on attackers, especially if those attackers had lost the element of surprise. While the initial front line might be lightly held, German Army doctrine was to hold back units to enable them to rapidly counterattack and retake lost positions just when an enemy was trying to consolidate hard-won gains.

The plan to capture Mahdi used all the resources that Russell had in his unit and others Evelegh had made available to the 38th Brigade. These included two sections of sappers from the 214th and 237th Field Companies of the Royal Engineers, substantial artillery support and a most unusual, but vitally important unit composed of often very badly disciplined individuals: over 200 mules. Two pack transport companies were assigned to support the 78th Division in the south, with the 11th Pack Transport Company to support of the 38th Brigade for the attack on Mount Kachiba and Djebel Mahdi. Two troops of 72 mules were also assigned to the 2nd Hants and 6th Skins.[10]

The 38th Brigade's plan to seize Djebel Mahdi relied heavily on a stealthy approach, tactical surprise, heavy use of supporting artillery, the rapid seizure of key features and the use of follow-on units to reinforce and help consolidate objectives. Brigadier Russell had already recognised that he needed to protect his left flank by seizing Mount Kachiba, a large hill to

---

9   Russell's comments on Djebel Mahdi are in N. Russell, *Irish Brigade*, p.113.
10   The plan for the attack on Mahdi is described in Operational Order (OO) No. 15 dated 4 April 1943 in TNA WO 175/216 38 Infantry Brigade WD April 1943. For details of German forces on Mahdi, see the Intelligence summaries in the 38th Brigade WD April 1943 and Divisional Intelligence summaries in TNA WO 175/168 78th Division WD April 1943. The author used the GSGS maps from 1943.

the west of Mahdi. It was suspected that Kachiba was unoccupied, but leaving this to chance was not an option, as any troops on that hill would be able to observe and interfere with his planned attack. He assigned this task to the 2nd Hants, who would make a silent attack (i.e. without any supporting artillery) to capture and hold Kachiba. The actual seizure of Mahdi was to be completed in three phases, in a pattern that was to be repeated across the division during its initial attacks at the start of Operation Sweep. In Phase One, Lieutenant Colonel Allen's 6th Skins and Butler's Faughs would use the cover of night on 5/6 April to work their way forward some four miles. They would then lie up in assembly areas concealed in wadis, close to Mahdi, during the following day. Assuming they remained undetected - and this was, as Russell remarked with a typical degree of understatement, the tricky part - they would use the cover of the night to attack the German positions on the Mahdi. Allen's battalion was allocated a tough assignment, his 6th Skins having to use the cover of darkness to move out of their assembly area, up a long steep river bed or wadi, break through any German defences and finally gain a position on the southern end of the mountain at Point 355, all by 0400 hours on 7 April. Butler's battalion would act as the follow-on force to exploit Allen's expected success and move on to leapfrog through the 6th Skins to seize the actual top of the mountain, Point 437, and then its northern slopes. The 1st Royal Irish Fusiliers were also to prevent any attempt by the Germans to counterattack down the Bed Valley against other division units which would have seized objectives at its southern end. Once these objectives had been taken, the 16th DLI from the 46th Infantry Division would move forward to relieve the 6th Skins.[11]

4.4 Gunner Who?

In contrast to their German opponents, the two attacking battalions were to receive extensive artillery support. Brigadier Wedderburn-Maxwell, the CRA, had created a group of artillery units just to support Russell. The left artillery group was composed of three artillery regiments and was under the command of Wedderburn-Maxwell's counterpart as CRA in the 46th Division, Brigadier Rigby, for this specific phase of the 78th Division attack. Rigby's artillery group was composed of two smaller artillery groups organised around the 71st and 102nd Field Artillery Regiments and the 5th Medium Regiment. Rigby's group had a total of 34 25-pounder field guns, 16 5.5in guns and two batteries from the 54th and 56th Heavy Regiments, which had eight long-range 7.2in howitzers.[12] Unbeknownst to the Germans, the artillery units supporting the 78th Division's attack included within their ranks at least two secret weapons: Lance Bombardiers Harry Secombe and Spike Milligan. These two future Goons served in the 132nd Field Regiment and 56th Heavy Regiment respectively. Both had already seen considerable action, particularly Secombe, who had been at the Battle of Tebourba, while Milligan had worked as part of a FOO party. The two future comedians' units had an important role to play in support of Operation Sweep, though only Milligan's 56th Heavy Regiment actually directly supported the attack on Djebel Mahdi and Mount Kachiba. Secombe was part of the gun crew of a 132nd Field Regiment battery which fired in direct support of 36th Infantry Brigade when

---

11   Details of the attack plan by the 6th Skins are derived from TNA WO 175/505 6th Royal Inniskilling Fusiliers WD April 1943

12   The fire plan for Mahdi is described in Left Artillery Group Operational Order No. 1 dated 5 April 1943 in TNA WO 175/159 CRA 46 Infantry Division WD April 1943.

it attacked Djebel Nahel. Milligan was a signaller in Major Jack Chater's 19 Heavy Battery's command post (CP), which had moved close to the front line near the hamlet of Sidi Mahmoud. Major Chater's battery was in turn part of an artillery regimental grouping organised around the 71st Field Regiment. Due to his role and location next to a 71st Regiment observation post (OP), he was in a good position to hear the artillery battle, and by dawn it gave him a panoramic view to the nort- east of the area around Mount Kachiba and Djebel Mahdi. The left artillery group's operations began at precisely 0350 hours. The night was both windy and noisy, and Spike Milligan later recalled his experience of the gunner barrage in his autobiography:

> Midnight, the wind was almost a gale. In the back of the truck we sipped tea and played twilight pontoon, me with headphones listening on the infantry network. A silent attack was to go in and take objectives by 0400 [and] we were standing by if they called for fire. At 0350 on our right, an artillery barrage was to support the 78 Division attack – on the Munchar -Medjez el Bab front. As the hour came, I thought of all those young men going forward into the darkness towards death or mutilation. At 0350 the sky sang with flashing lights, a thunder of iron artillery rolled through the night.[13]

As the barrage went in, Milligan used his radio to tune in to the BBC briefly; the sound of the beautiful classical music and the thought of so many men dying caused him to burst into tears.

Another observer of the wider 78th Division artillery operations that night was A.B. Austin, a war correspondent of the *Daily Herald*. Austin had been in Tunisia since late November 1942 and had spent a lot of time at or near the front line. His account of the barrage that night is also worth quoting:

> Just after midnight on the morning of the 7th April, I went to a farm off the road on a high ridge above Oued Zarga … In the darkness of a grove of trees from which the ground dropped away there was nothing but a bitter night wind blowing across the knee high barley under cold stars … At four in the morning it began, first a few guns barking to the north-east and then a low growl running along the batteries that had been hidden in the hollows round a twelve-mile arc. And with each growl and bark a white flash of light. When the whole twelve miles of guns were firing together a white flicker like summer lightning ran up and down the valleys and ridges throwing the high ground into sudden relief, filling the hollows with light. It was as if the hill-waves were really pitching and rolling. I stood at the centre of the arc. The nearest gun was in shouting distance (if you could hear yourself shout), the furthest 6 miles away on either hand.
>
> The nearest gun would stab your ear and flood you with light so that you could have read a book at intervals of a few seconds. The others would dwindle away to left and right until the furthest had a muffled thud.[14]

---

13   See Spike Milligan's memoir *Rommel? Gunner Who? A Confrontation in the Desert* (London: Penguin, 1974), p.153.
14   See Austin, *Birth of An Army*, p.120.

4.5 The 2nd Hampshires Attack, "Benghazi"

The first phase of 38th Brigade's attack was planned to be completed by 0400 hours and required the 2nd Hants to capture Mount Kachiba and the 6th Skins to take the south end of Djebel Mahdi. The successful capture of Kachiba was to be reported to Russell using the code word "Benghazi". As a result, the CO of the 2nd Hants, Lieutenant Colonel Martin, and his battalion staff had to plan for the seizure of an objective (Kachiba) which was codenamed after a city which was actually located some 500 miles away to the east in Libya. Covered in trees, Mount Kachiba was not a large hill, but it was some 900ft high and, most importantly, looked down on Oued Kachiba, a dry river bed which the Faughs would use in the second phase of the 38th Brigade attack on Mahdi. To the north-east of Kachiba was Point 361, which also overlooked the same wadi. 2nd Hants were tasked to capture Kachiba and to consolidate defences there, before, and only if necessary, going on to attack Point 361. The battalion that carried out the attack on Kachiba was a very different unit from that which had landed in Tunisia in November 1942. Only six officers and 141 men survived the Battle of Tebourba in early December, and the original CO, Lieutenant Colonel James Lee, and most of the remaining original battalion were killed or captured. Although the strength of 2nd Hants was rapidly increased to 600 men by the arrival of large drafts of replacements over the next two months, it took time to develop a fighting unit. That task was gradually undertaken while it was moved as part of the 1st Guards Brigade in February 1943 all over northern Tunisia, until in early March it took up positions near Munchar east of Beja. Its sojourn there in defensive positions provided it with enough time on the front line to ensure it was capable as a unit of undertaking a more active role in early April. The plan to seize Kachiba required the unit to move from near Munchar to an assembly area in a dry wadi located on the slope of a hill some four miles from the objective on the night of 4 April. It was to remain in this area until the late evening of 6 April. Its rifle companies would then move off from the hill in the darkness and down into the valley of the Oued Zarga River to a start line based on the river bed. It would attack from here at about 0100 hours one mile up a steep hill slope to take Kachiba. The attack was to be a silent one with no preliminary barrage, though artillery was on call, and the mountain was to be captured by 0400 hours. Although it was unclear to intelligence if the Germans were on the peak, it was critical that it be secured and no chances were taken.

This was one of those unusual occasions in wartime where everything went to plan. Lieutenant Colonel Martin and three companies of his battalion, supported by 72 mules, left their start line right on time, and after climbing the hill took control of Kachiba by 0400 hours without any opposition or casualties. The battalion did not require artillery support, so those guns could be switched to assist the 36th Infantry Brigade, which was also attacking and faced opposition. The first part of 38th Brigade's operation had gone well.[15]

---

15   Details of the 2nd Hants' history and the attack on Kachiba are from Daniell, *Royal Hampshires*, pp.113-14, and TNA WO 175/499 2 Hants WD April 1943. The code-word "Benghazi" is from p.8 of Operational Order No. 15 in TNA WO 38 Infantry Brigade WD April 1943.

4.6 "It All Depends on Me" – The 6th Skins Attack Djebel Mahdi

At some time in his military career, the 37-year-old CO of the 6th Skins, Lieutenant Colonel Charles Allen, had acquired the rather unusual nickname of "Heaver", although it is not known how he assumed this name. The son of an Army vet, Heaver Allen was born in India and was commissioned into the Royal Ulster Rifles in 1926. He had spent his career with Irish units, having also served as the Adjutant and second-in-command of the London Irish Rifles, before assuming command of the 6th Skins in January 1943. By April 1943, Allen had commanded the battalion through three months of difficult fighting and was highly regarded by his officers, his tough Irish Fusiliers and his brigade commander. Nelson Russell described Allen thus:

> I could write a good deal about Heaver without hoping to do him justice. Put all the qualities of the fighting CO inside a thick set, hardy, clean shaven medium sized man, with a hooked nose and a good determined chin – the result would have been Heaver Allen. I believe his battalion would have followed him anywhere.[16]

Heaver Allen had no illusions that his part of the capture of Djebel Mahdi would be an easy task, for intelligence indicated that "Guide" Mountain, the rough translation of its Arabic name, would be defended and that obvious approaches would have barbed-wire obstacles and be mined. In order to ensure that the 6th Skins was ready to carry out its part in the battle, the unit had been pulled back into reserve from positions near Bou Arada in the middle of March to train and rest. It arrived on 30 March to occupy new positions about four miles south of Mahdi and north-west of the village of Oued Zarga. In contrast to other units in the division, it had six full days to conduct several patrols into the valley of the Oued Bouneb and up to the slopes of Djebel Mahdi to gain information and intelligence about the terrain and the German defenders. The information from these patrols was to prove invaluable in helping Allen and his staff identify the best routes to their objective, which was a height named Point 355 on the southern slope of the mountain. The intelligence provided by these patrols came with its own heavy price, as on the night of 4/5 April one of Allen's able young officers, Lieutenant Kenneth Beeching, and two of his men were killed, with three others wounded, by a booby-trapped German Teller mine. The Germans made liberal use of both anti-tank (Teller) and anti-personnel (S or *Schu*) mines in northern Tunisia to offset their limited numbers, extended front line and lack of tanks and artillery. They also created anti-handling devices for Teller mines to prevent their removal or found ways of exploding the mines using a booby trap. The S-35 mine was particularly devastating as they could be sown in large numbers (1.93 million were produced by 1945) and, when activated by more than by 15lb of pressure, shot a propelling charge in the air which exploded and sent 300 steel balls out at waist height. An S-mine's effective range was 20 metres, so it could inflict horrible injuries on a group of men.[17]

On the night of 5/6 April, Allen and his fighting companies, assisted by 65 mules, moved four miles across bare rocky slopes overlooked by the Germans. By 0530 hours on 6 April they arrived at two wadis south-west of the mountain, where they rested all day in positions

16   See Russell, *Irish Brigade*, p.113.
17   Details of the 6th Skins operations on Mahdi are from TNA WO 175/505 6th Royal Inniskilling Fusiliers March- April 1943 WD and Russell *Irish Brigade*, pp.44-49.

which concealed them from direct observation. Lieutenant Percy Hamilton, a young platoon commander in A Company, recalls that the march was not without incident:

> After we got on to the flat plain, I heard a noise around me, which sounded like thousands of little birds rustling through the long grass, and it seemed almost uncanny because it didn't seem to come from anywhere, but yet was all around. After five minutes or so, I found that one of the mules in front had caught a length of signal wire and was trailing it along beside the track making a swishing noise. The column halted, then moved forward a little and halted again. After some time, the MO and the padre came walking back and told us that one of the mules had refused to cross a wire and during the confusion, the rest of the column had disappeared into the night.[18]

Fortunately, Hamilton and his part of the column caught up with the rest of the battalion fairly quickly. The officers, men, mules and their handlers spent the rest of the day out in the open and visible from the air as they tried to rest and prepare for the attack. Sometime in the evening, Heaver Allen gave a speech which David Schayek, one of his subalterns, later described:

> Heaver Allen came in to give a pep talk to all of us. Instead of a helmet, he had a camouflage net on his head tied with a knot like a pirate. I heard one of the fusiliers mutter, "Oo does 'e think 'e is: Moby Dick?" Heaver Allen's speech had a theme, "it all depends on me". It was quite inspiring.[19]

Allen finished his eve-of-battle speech and ensured that his men received hot tea and a generous ration of rum. The original plan was for the battalion to move from its concealed assembly area to its start line at a dry river bed south of Point 355 at 0030 hours on 7 April. After a rest at the start line, it would start its attack up the hill slope with the aim of arriving at its objective by 0400 hours. It was supposed to be assisted by a section of Royal Engineers from Joss Force, who would detect and clear mines, while its own intelligence section put down white tape to show clear paths. In one of those unfortunate ironies of war, this group got lost and was blown up while attempting to cross a bridge that was mined. Another section was quickly brought up, but the delay meant that the battalion didn't start off from its assembly area until 0100 hours. As a result there was no time to rest at the start line as planned, and the battalion went straight into the attack. The southern slope of Guide Mountain was steep and divided in half by a significant gully leading up to Point 355. The two lead companies moved up on either side of this long gully, with C Company, commanded by Captain Ferris, taking the left-hand side, and A Company, led by Acting Major Sydney Bunch, the right. ,Bunch's stocky build, rugged face and bald head made him look much older than his 33 years, and due to the losses incurred previously he was the most senior of the company commanders in the battalion.[20] He had also

---

18   See Captain P. Hamilton, *Personal Memoirs of Captain Percy Hamilton MC* (unpublished), p.12.
19   Details of the preparations for the attack and the quote from Heaver Allen are from Hamilton, *Memoirs*, pp.1-2, and Captain D. Schayek, *Recollections* (unpublished memoirs, 1999), p.6.
20   Details of the attack and the incident with mines are from TNA WO 175/505 6th Skins WD April 1943 and TNA WO 175/216 38 Brigade WD April 1943. The latter includes a useful two-page account of the attack on Mahdi.

already demonstrated his coolness under fire, having been awarded a MC for leadership of his company in two separate actions in January 1943 near Bou Arada. The two lead companies were followed closely by Allen and his battalion headquarters. B Company was nearby and had the role of acting as a carrying party, bringing much-needed digging tools and ammunition. Bunch's lead platoons, commanded by Lieutenants Percy Hamilton and Basil Hewitt, found it difficult to keep control of their soldiers in the darkness and rough terrain, and were delayed getting to their interim objective, a large black bush close to Point 355, before the artillery began firing. Hamilton later recalled: "My platoon got stretched out. At this stage, I had trouble with a Lance Corporal who had too much rum. I should have knocked him cold, but I left him."[21]

C Company, on the left, western side of the steep southern slope, had fewer problems initially and reached a position below Point 355, just prior to the start of the artillery barrage.

Although the battalion's approach seemed to have been undetected, this was not a silent attack such as that carried out on Mount Kachiba. Out of a dark night, at 0350 hours, suddenly came a large number of artillery shells and life became very unpleasant for the Germans occupying the southern end of Djebel Mahdi. Brigadier Nelson Russell later noted that his lead battalion had the finest artillery support he could have wished for that night. A total of 58 guns fired in direct support of the 6th Skins: 34 25-pounders, 16 5.5in medium guns and eight 7.2 inch heavy guns, including four from Spike Milligan's battery. The area on and around Point 355 became a distinctly unhealthy place to be, as 1,680 shells of varying calibre exploded in 10 minutes. Exactly on time, this fire was lifted and moved to a range of other targets: track junctions, gullies and areas which were suspected of housing more troops, weapons or which could be used as approach routes for reinforcements. All four artillery regiments continued firing for the next 15 minutes, using over 1,900 shells to stop any attempt to interfere with the Inniskillings' task of capturing their objective.

The attacking companies had slightly differing experiences. C Company initially seemed to be meeting less resistance than A Company. Both companies initially benefitted from the fact that the Germans were occupying positions behind the objective, on a reverse slope, and the British troops were not at first exposed to fire until they moved on to the objective and skyline. Lieutenant Hamilton outlines what happened next to the two lead platoons, as A Company arrived on top of the slope to the east of Point 355:

> We climbed for a long time and my platoon dwindled, partly because of being stretched out but also because I was trying to catch up with the barrage and the chaps just couldn't make it. When I reached it, I found Basil Hewitt in the same state, so we had a dozen chaps and the two of us. This part of the hill was covered with heather, growing fairly thickly and about eighteen inches high. A couple of chaps got up as far as the skyline and Jerry, who was dug in on the reverse slope, opened up.
>
> He got both the two, one must have died outright, the other was hit in the guts, and we listened to him die. It didn't take long, his screams died down gradually to a moan, and then he passed out.[22]

---

21   The quote is from Hamilton, *Memoirs*, p.12.
22   The quote is from Hamilton, *Memoirs*, pp.12-13.

On the left side of the hill, C Company made it up to the top, but found itself under heavy fire from a German MG42 which held it up. By this time Allen, who always believed in staying close to his leading units, had arrived at C Company's location, he spotted a machine-gun post on the reverse slopes and directed the Bren gunner to the target. The gunner was unable to follow his directions, so Allen called for the Bren gun himself. Before it arrived, Allen looked up to keep the MG42 under observation and was shot through the head and killed. Heaver Allen's leadership at Mahdi certainly lived up to the motto he had set his battalion in his eve of battle speech: "it all depends on me". His conduct that morning was typical of the man, and one reason he was so highly regarded by his fusiliers, yet this would do little to ease the pain which would be so keenly felt in a small village near Doncaster in Yorkshire by his wife Katharine, a local surgeon, and their young daughter Elizabeth.[23] Since the second-in-command of the battalion, Major McCann, was located well to the rear, Sydney Bunch took over temporary command of the 6th Skins on the mountain. He coordinated the operations of the rest of the companies as their dispersed platoons came under mortar and machine-gun fire. Despite this unenviable position, the core fighting spirit of the Inniskillings was soon in evidence among its junior officers, and especially its junior NCOs, as can be noted from two extracts from citations that describe the actions of Lance Corporal Edward Teare and Lieutenant C. Clarke.

> On 7 April 1943, during the battalion attack on Djebel Mahdi, L/Cpl Teare was Bren gunner in a forward platoon, which was held up by a German machine gun. L/Cpl Teare went forward alone with his LMG and some grenades and silenced the machine gun, taking the survivors prisoner and occupying the position himself. Throughout the day, he displayed great personal initiative and his individual efforts were largely responsible for the gaining of the Company objectives.
>
> On 6 April 1943, Lieutenant C. Clarke entered an enemy minefield in daylight within easy range of the enemy and with the assistance of a Sgt helped to carry a wounded man a distance of three miles to comparative safety. The following day on Djebel Mahdi, under very heavy fire he walked around attending to wounded men regardless of the great personal risk to himself. Later on he went forward by himself with a Bren gun to tackle a MG post which was holding up the advance, and effectively silenced it.[24]

As we will see later, this would not be the only time that Edward Teare would demonstrate his raw courage and proficiency with a Bren gun in the mountains. Clarke's initial act of courage had undoubtedly taken place during the incident where Kenneth Beeching had been killed and he had gone on to further distinguish himself during this attack. Although there is some confusion about timings, by about 0515 hours, C Company had moved forward and was attacking Point 355. Meanwhile, A Company was still trying to move forward on the eastern slope of the mountain. Hamilton and Hewitt found themselves in a difficult position. Hamilton's account of their precarious situation is worth quoting in detail as it reveals a sense of the ridiculous of which Harry Secombe and Spike Milligan would have likely approved:

23   Details of Charles "Heaver" Allen's death and family are derived from N. Russell, *Irish Brigade*, p.44, and the 6th Skins WD for April 1943.
24   The citations for Teare and Clarke are from TNA WO 373/1 Gallantry citations for Tunisian campaign.

Dawn was breaking and it was getting light very fast as it does in that country. Basil and I, by mutual consent, started to crawl round to the right to try and work a flanking movement. Jerry must have spotted us because something went crack between us and Basil started to bleed from the forehead. He said he was ok and told me that I had been hit in the head too. Then blood started to run down the one lens of my glasses until I couldn't see. I took them off and put them in my pocket, but decided that I could see less without them, so I had to get them out and clean them. I don't know why, but at the time, it struck me as humorous that I should be lying on my belly cleaning my glasses, with Jerry only fifty yards away taking pot shots of us. I took a couple of pot shots in his general direction as I couldn't raise my head enough to see him without the certainty of getting shot. Basil was still near me and we crawled further over the hill. I was slightly in front and I felt something hit my back. I shouted to him not to come any further forward and I thought I had been hit. I crawled into a hole but found I was not hurt. When I undressed afterwards, I found a bullet had gone right through my haversack ripping everything but luckily missing the Hawkins mine I had on me; it had then come out and taken about an inch of the belt of my tunic away. The bullet must have passed through about half an inch from my spine.[25]

Soon after Hamilton was wounded, his men had managed to outflank the machine-gun position and were able to knock it out and take eight Germans prisoner. It was through a series of little actions such as this that by 1000 hours Brigadier Nelson Russell was able to receive a one word message, "Alamein", which told him Point 355 had been taken. The first stage of the attack on Mahdi had been completed.

Although the Inniskillings had taken their objective, the hold on their positions was initially quite tenuous, despite support from artillery, as hidden mortars and machine guns continued to inflict casualties. The Germans also carried out a counterattack at about midday, although most sources indicate this was not a serious attempt to dislodge the Skins. It did, however, lead to two further Goon-like moments worthy of a story from Milligan's *Rommel? Gunner Who?*, in which he described his experiences in Tunisia. The first was related in the war diary of 71st Field Regiment, which was supporting the attack and its aftermath. At about 0730 hours on 7 April, one of the officers in the 71st, Major Day, called for an Uncle target (all the guns of the division) to fire on what he believed was a vital target, a German field artillery battery. Soon after, to his eternal chagrin and much mirth within his regiment, he learned that he had actually brought down the ire of all the division's guns on a German field kitchen. In retrospect, it could be argued that since an army marches on its stomach, a German kitchen was actually a worthy target.[26] The second incident is told by Lieutenant David Schayek, a platoon commander in B Company at Mahdi:

On the crest of the mountain, I heard a shout that the enemy was counterattacking. My first thought was of the British square, as at Waterloo and I wondered if one could have close packed men facing every direction. I ordered fixed bayonets and ordered the fusiliers to form a ring of steel. The NCOs marshalled the fusiliers and we did create a big circle

25   See quote from Hamilton, *Memoirs*, p.13.
26   The field kitchen incident is from TNA WO 175/333 71st Field Regiment WD April 1943.

with quite a big distance between each man and all were facing outwards. I was carrying a rifle and bayonet as I did not want to be picked off by the enemy as an officer. Like the others, I drew a bayonet and found, to my horror, that the bayonet, which I had picked up the day before, was faulty and it would not fit onto the muzzle of the rifle. I did not want to show that I had a faulty bayonet, so I held it with my left hand near the muzzle of the rifle that I held in my right hand and made it look as though I had a fixed bayonet. The enemy counterattack either never came or petered out before it reached us.[27]

Enemy fire made it difficult for the 6th Skins to establish a secure location from which their sister battalion, the Faughs, could start the next stage of the attack on Mahdi. However, by 1030 hours the Faughs had managed to get up to the Skins' positions. Later that day, the Skins were relieved by a battalion of the Black Watch and returned to Plateau Farm, their headquarters just south of the Oued Zarga road, where they were greeted by new CO Lieutenant Colonel Neville Grazebrook. The unit was to spend the next 48 hours resting before returning to take part in operations north of Mahdi on 9 April.

The battalion history and its war diary do not mention the battalion's losses at Mahdi, and other sources seem to suggest that casualties were quite low. The reality was quite different, as was made clear by the author's own research, for the 6th Skins lost 18 dead and 99 wounded during the period 4-10 April. Since most of these casualties were concentrated in two companies and incurred mainly on 6/7 April, the unit's losses on Mahdi were quite significant. It is said that all losses are replaceable, but that of two men who died taking Mahdi were a particular blow to the battalion. The first was obviously Heaver Allen, and his death is relatively well recorded for history. Less well known was the death of Corporal Edward Brookes, a promising 29-year-old junior non-commissioned officer (JNCO) who had recently been awarded a MM for his gallantry in attacking single-handed two German machine-gun posts in January 1943. Brookes died on 6 April, almost certainly in the Teller mine incident in which Beeching was also killed.[28]

4.7 The Faughs Take "Tripoli"

The task of exploiting the success of the Skins on Djebel Mahdi by completing the second stage of Douglas-Pennant's plan fell to their sister regiment, the Faughs. In contrast to the Inniskillings, the Faughs were a regular battalion which had experienced hard fighting in France in 1940 and subsequently in the winter months of 1943 around Bou Arada. The regiment had suffered significant casualties on the Goubellat plain south of Medjez and especially at its positions on Grandstand Hill, where it had fought elite German parachute troops. It had emerged from these actions an experienced, veteran and confident unit. After being on the front

27   Captain D. Schayek, *Recollections*, p.7.
28   Lance Corporal Brookes' death is related in the records of the Commonwealth War Graves Commission (CWGC). The author's estimates of dead for this action were derived from a review of the records for CWGC cemeteries at Oued Zarga, Beja, Medjez el Bab and Thibar. The estimates of wounded reflect the records of admissions to Field Ambulances. This information is to be found in TNA WO 175/420 Assistant Director of Medical Services 78th Division WD April 1943. This methodology has been used throughout the book to provide a comparatively accurate estimate of unit casualties.

line for nearly three months, the battalion was relieved on 23 March and moved to the rear to rest, receive reinforcements and undergo training. By 5 April, the unit was in an assembly area south of Oued Zarga and found itself required to make a night approach march to get to its final positions. The battalion at this stage was commanded by 40-year-old Lieutenant Colonel Henry Beauchamp "Beau" Butler, who was attached to the battalion, having originally been commissioned into the Inniskilling Fusiliers. The practice of transferring officers between the various regiments of the Irish Brigade started well before the brigade arrived in Tunisia, and was to become standard routine during the rest of the war. For example, Pat Scott, the previous CO of the Faughs, had been sent to command the London Irish Rifles, and the new second-in-command in the 6th Skins, Major John McCann, had just been moved from the London Irish. The Irish Brigade at the field officer level (i.e. major and above) could almost be seen as an extended family. Although he only formally took command of the Faughs on 18 March, Butler had been acting as its commander for over a month, as his predecessor had spent a period as an acting brigade commander. His experience as an acting CO, combined with his extended time as second-in-command, meant that the transfer of command was almost seamless. Butler's character and personality were rather different to Pat Scott, who had a caustic wit and a well-earned reputation of not suffering fools gladly. One of his company commanders described Butler as follows:

> He, like many of my friends in different way, had a personality perfectly adapted to the mercurial temperament of our Irish soldiers, though his manner belied the rock beneath. He was sensitive and bashful, and he tended to blink and stutter when giving us unpalatable instructions. I recall no criticism from him ever, but when things went wrong he took all the blame on himself. He was a delight to serve under.[29]

Irrespective of his tendency to stutter under stress, Butler did have several characteristics also held by his brigade commander, Nelson Russell. He was totally imperturbable in battle, tactically astute and, irrespective of the circumstances, always able to inspire his officers and soldiers. Butler would command the Faughs with distinction for the next six months until his untimely death near the Trigno River in Italy in October 1943. Brigadier Russell, not an officer known for hyperbole, wrote later that Butler's loss in Italy "was a tragedy for the whole Brigade and the Faughs lost one of their best commanding officers they ever had in peace or war … gifted with a quiet sense of charm of manner, he was the most determined and skillful leader of troops in action."[30]

In view of Butlers' undoubted ability, it was unfortunate that the Faughs' move up to their assembly position for the attack on Mahdi on the night of 5/6th April did not go at all well. The battalion had spent a lot of time in static positions and was not practiced in battalion night moves. Furthermore, it had just been provided with a large number of mules, some 30 for each company, to aid it in moving its heavy weapons, food, radios and extra ammunition, and these arrived from a previous battalion location late in the day. Irrespective of their great value in the hills of Tunisia, few officers and men grew to like these animals. One company

29   Quote from Coldwell-Horsfall, *The Wild Geese*, p.22.
30   See N. Russell, *Irish Brigade*, p.113.The profile of Beauchamp Butler is derived from Russell, J. Coldwell-Horsfall, *The Wild Geese*, and analysis of the battalion's war diaries, TNA WO 175/506.

commander in the Faughs described them as "Fractious 4-legged Children of Satan … who had an infinite capacity for mischief."[31] The night march through hills proved difficult, with at least one company becoming lost. By dawn the whole battalion managed to get itself under cover in a series of wadis ending in a narrow long gorge. This was actually the dry river bed of the Oued Zarga just north of the town of that name. The Faughs laid up the rest of the day in this location with over 100 mules, out of the sight of the Germans, though visible from the air. Fortunately, no *Stukas* arrived that day and the unit was both intact and ready the following morning when it was ordered to move up to take on its role in the battle for Mahdi. The Faughs moved up under intermittent long-range shelling by German artillery, but the shells fell on either side of the wadi bed and the cliffs protected them from losses. The battalion's good fortune remained intact, despite the fact that as it was marching north to join the Skins, it came under air attack by some German ME-109s firing cannon. The attack upset the mules, but amazingly left the Faughs unscathed. After avoiding a number of minefields in and around the Oued Bouneb river bed, which circled the bottom end of Mahdi, the leading companies of the 1st Royal Irish Fusiliers - D Company, led by Major John Coldwell-Horsfall, and C Company under Major Desmond Gethin - climbed up the southern slope and met up with the Inniskillings.[32]

Butler's leading company commanders were comparatively young for their roles at 27 and 24 respectively, but both were capable officers. Coldwell-Horsfall was the more experienced of the two, having joined the Faughs in 1935 and commanded D Company in Belgium with considerable distinction, earning a MC for his defence of key bridges. He had continued in command of the company afterwards and earned a bar to his MC near Bou Arada in March 1943. Although Coldwell-Horsfall had no prior link to an Irish regiment, since he was born and brought up in the Midlands, he quickly adapted to effectively leading Irish fusiliers with their sometimes mercurial temperament. The outcome was that a mutual admiration society started between Coldwell-Horsfall, his soldiers and the regiment, which was to last throughout his long life. As a commander, he was tough, shrewd, a strict disciplinarian and an excellent tactician. In addition to being a very capable officer, he was also a keen observer, had a good memory and the ability to write fluently and wittily. These attributes he later put to excellent use in writing a three-volume memoir of his experiences at war. His middle volume, *The Wild Geese are Flighting*, covers his time in Tunisia and is one of the best accounts of a company in battle. Coldwell-Horsfall's book is a must read for anyone interested in the war in Tunisia, and was an invaluable source for this book.[33] In contrast to Coldwell-Horsfall, Gethin was only 24 when he became a company commander and was a very different character. He had joined the Faughs in 1940, largely through a family connection, as his father had served as an officer in the regiment. He had been a platoon commander under Coldwell-Horsfall in Belgium and France, and proved himself cool under fire: although isolated for two days, Gethin and his platoon of

---

31   Quote from Coldwell-Horsfall, *The Wild Geese*, p.98.

32   The details of the Faughs' attack on Mahdi are derived from TNA WO 175/506 1st Royal Irish Fusiliers WD April 1943, J. Coldwell-Horsfall's own description in *The Wild Geese*, pp.105-14, and two documents in TNA WO 175/216 38 Infantry Brigade WD April 1943, one entitled "Mahdi" and the other Appendix A Account of Operations 7-11 April 1943.

33   The profile of John Coldwell-Horsfall is based on R. Doherty, *Clear the Way*; his obituary in the *Daily Telegraph* on 22 January 2007; and analysis of the battalion war diaries and its regimental magazine *Faugh a Ballach*. The author also benefitted from talking to the author Richard Doherty, who met Coldwell-Horsfall several times.

fusiliers inflicted much execution on the attacking Germans, yet his only message back was to ask if they could have some more grub. Gethin extracted his platoon and withdrew with Coldwell-Horsfall back to Dunkirk and England. Gethin was known by the nickname "Dizzy", a moniker that had probably been bestowed on him by Coldwell-Horsfall, due to Gethin's tendency to be rather vague at times. Coldwell-Horsfall, who knew him very well and liked him a great deal, later told the story that when giving his orders, Gethin had adopted a slightly unusual tendency to mutter "Ours is not to reason why" before moving off to lead his platoon. Irrespective of, or even possibly due to, his slightly eccentric approach to leadership, Gethin was promoted to acting major and appointed to command C Company on 19 March 1943.

On arrival at the Skins' positions, Coldwell-Horsfall and Gethin found that the area originally chosen for them to start their attack was under sniper and machine-gun fire, and observation proved difficult. Nonetheless, both officers implemented a plan they had discussed the day before, once artillery support had been arranged. Their plan was for Gethin with C Company to attack on the left directly up the slope to capture the top of Mahdi, Point 437, while Coldwell-Horsfall would follow on the right of the hill (on the eastern slope) to protect his flank. Both companies would advance with one platoon forward and the other two platoons in support.[34] While accounts vary, it seems most likely that the companies took a while to sort themselves out and were not able to launch their attack until after 1300 hours. Immediately prior to their advance, the German defenders on the Faughs' objective were on the receiving end of a heavy artillery concentration. Coldwell-Horsfall later recalled in graphic detail what happened next:

> The crest line 400 yards in front of us disappeared under a tornado of fire and steel which smote upon it. Erupting into an ever increasing grey black cumulus shot through with orange flashes and the continuous flickering flame of lightning, the maelstrom gradually spread itself outwards and skywards until it blotted out all forward vision and hearing too for that matter. It was difficult to believe that any opposition could have been left when the firestorm ended.[35]

Instead of charging forward immediately afterwards, Coldwell-Horsfall used his two flank platoons to sweep each crest with fire before sending in his lead platoon. The process took slightly longer than simply charging across the open mountain ridgeline, but significantly reduced casualties. Although existing accounts are contradictory, by no later than 1500 or 1600 hours, both companies had reached the northern end of Mahdi just in time to see the defenders leave their positions and run for their lives down the mountain's northern slope. As they arrived on their objective, D Company had a fleeting opportunity to engage and kill their routed enemy, and for a few minutes Coldwell-Horsfall found himself caught up in the excitement of firing his rifle at running Germans. He eventually remembered that he was the company commander and had better things to do, stopped shooting and walked over to meet Gethin, and together they began to coordinate the defence of Point 437. Soon afterwards, "Beau" Butler was able to send Russell the one-word message he had been waiting for, "Tripoli", which confirmed that the Irish Brigade had captured the top of Djebel Mahdi.

---

34   Dizzy Gethin's profile and the quotation "Ours is not reason why" is from Coldwell-Horsfall, *Wild Geese*, pp.58-59, and *Say Not the Struggle* (Kineton: Roundwood Press, 1977).
35   Quote from Coldwell-Horsfall, *The Wild Geese*, p.108.

Although the highest point of Mahdi had been taken, the Faughs' situation was by no means that secure. A spur leading down from its northern end towards the wide Bed Valley was by now inhabited not only by the defenders who had fled the top, but also by additional German troops, and they opened fire on C and D companies. The situation was aggravated when German self-propelled guns started to shell their positions and other artillery priorities precluded any immediate response. It appears that at one point the Germans seemed to be assembling for a possible counterattack near some buildings, so to prevent this 17 Platoon of D Company under Lieutenant Jack Chapman was sent to attack them. Chapman and his platoon moved down the mountain slope towards the enemy location. His platoon sergeant, the highly capable Robert "Robbie" Robinson, described what happened next:

> Enemy movement was spotted about 100 yards away on our left and on higher ground. The Platoon commander immediately gave the order to wheel to the left and charge the enemy position. As we did, our opponents opened fire on us killing and wounding several in the platoon including the platoon commander who was badly wounded. We continued charging up the slope firing our weapons from the hip and screaming a variety of Irish obscenities, our opponents quickly put up the white flag and we were quite surprised to take the surrender of some 19 Germans in good health well dug in and in a good position. The ground we had to cover leading up to their position was flat and completely bare of cover and they could have picked us off one by one.[36]

The outcome could have been very different for Chapman's platoon, as despite being outnumbered, they had attacked a force of at least 33 dug-in Germans with three machine guns. Nonetheless, 17 Platoon defeated them, killed 12 Germans and captured the remainder. Irish luck and aggressiveness meant that 17 Platoon had only one fusilier killed and seven wounded, including Chapman. These losses and increasing machine-gun fire meant the platoon had to withdraw with its wounded, and Robinson led the platoon back. Jack Chapman's leadership of his platoon during this short violent skirmish was to be recognised by the award of an MC. The same skirmish almost certainly also led to the award of a MM to Sergeant J. Morrissey, who according to his citation took over from a severely wounded platoon commander and led his men forward with bomb and bayonet to force the enemy to surrender. After the action, Morrissey also spent two hours under shell-fire arranging the evacuation of the wounded of both sides.[37] Morrissey's citation indicates he was the platoon sergeant at the time, though we know from two sources that Robinson actually held that role. This is one of many little contradictions that emerged from various sources when investigating what happened at Mahdi. This minor action was, however, noteworthy for one of those incidents that no fiction writer could possibly dream up when creating a novel. Sergeant "Robbie" Robinson later recalled that "during the round up, disarming and searching the prisoners I was puzzled to see Fusilier H. Fisher behaving in a friendly way with one of my prisoners [in fact an amazed Robinson watched Fisher embrace one of the Germans] – under my startled gaze they were actually exchanging photographs."[38]

---

36   Captain R. Robinson, *Unpublished memoirs of the Tunisian campaign*, pp.15-16.
37   Details of this patrol action are from the MC citation for Lieutenant W. Chapman and the MM citation for Sergeant J. Morrissey See TNA WO 373/1.
38   See Robinson, *Unpublished Memoirs*, p.16.

It transpired that Fisher had been a very good amateur boxer and had reached the finals of the Golden Gloves championships in the USA. On a desolate hill in Tunisia, Fisher had met by chance one of his old boxing opponents who had fought for Germany in the same competition. The chances of that meeting must have been at least one in a million.

Although valuable, Chapman's platoon raid highlighted the fact that the Germans had significant forces nearby that could be used to counterattack the Faughs' new positions. Coldwell-Horsfall and Gethin were well aware that a successful attack against German troops was at its most vulnerable in the hours that followed the capture of an objective. Both company commanders therefore brought back their respective platoons and set about establishing a firm defence. The companies dug in and were reinforced by a section of Vickers machine guns, while the other two companies of the Faughs and battalion headquarters moved up to provide additional support. By early evening, the leading companies were being shelled by German mountain infantry guns and mortars, which made life quite unpleasant and added to casualties. One of those hit was the battalion's intelligence officer (IO), who despite lying on a stretcher with a painful and serious mouth wound, still proceeded to interrogate one of the many prisoners who had been captured. The exposed nature of two lead companies was quickly recognised by "Beau" Butler, and he gave permission for Coldwell-Horsfall and Gethin to pull back to the reverse, southern slopes of Point 437. Although counterattacks were usually almost an automatic German Army response, the night passed fairly peacefully, though no one had much sleep. At about midnight, however, the 6th Skins were relieved in their positions on the south end of Mahdi by the 16th DLI. This unit was part of the 4th Infantry Division, but had been placed under command of 38th Brigade for this operation, as was the 6th Black Watch. The assignment of these two battalions to serve under the command of Brigadier Nelson Russell was a clear recognition by his superiors that the lessons of Longstop Hill had been learned: there was no point in seizing critical terrain if you lacked the forces to subsequently defend it. The arrival of these additional battalions in supporting positions ensured that having seized Djebel Mahdi, the Irish Brigade had no intention of returning it to the enemy.

The capture of Mahdi was greeted with much relief at all levels of command, but especially by Vyvyan Evelegh. As the primary architect of the plan for Operation Sweep, he knew that taking Mahdi was vital to secure the left flank of his division. By holding Kachiba and Mahdi, the 38th Brigade could prevent any attempt to interfere with wider operations that required access to the southern end of the long broad valley that lay below Mahdi. This rugged valley was criss-crossed by multiple dry wadis and stretched north and east from the Oued Bouneb, and became known as the Bed Valley to troops fighting there. The battle for Mahdi was the first major action of 38th Irish Brigade under the command of the 78th Division, and was an impressive debut for Russell and his two battalions. It demonstrated convincingly the Irish Brigade was an extremely capable unit. Although the number of troops defending Mahdi had proved to be less than 250, it was a rugged and difficult feature to attack and, in the right hands, an easy one to defend. Between them, the Skins and the Faughs pried it loose from the grip of the 334th Infantry Division in less than 24 hours and effectively put out of action a grenadier battalion, inflicting more than 50 casualties and taking 50 prisoners by midnight on 7 April. The price of this achievement was not a small one, as between them the two battalions lost nearly 40 killed and at least 150 wounded in action during the initial assault.

4.8 Infantry sweeps, Stukas and Spitfires

Although reinforced and well supported by artillery, Nelson Russell and his Brigade Major, Frank Douglas-Pennant recognised that it was important to strengthen their grip on the area and exploit the tactical advantage it gave the division. To this end, Russell encouraged his forward battalion, the Faughs, to harass the Germans by conducting a series of infantry sweeps at company level. The first of these minor attacks took place at 1100 hours on the morning of 8 April when 22-year-old Captain David Nicholas "Nick" Jefferies led A Company down the north-east slope of Mahdi to investigate reports of Germans in a gully there. Jefferies had started out as a platoon commander in Tunisia in D Company before becoming Coldwell-Horsfall's second-in-command, and had been promoted to A Company's commander in late January 1943. His brother Gus was the adjutant of the Faughs at the time. Nick Jefferies followed D Company's tradition of having rather eccentric officers, as he appeared to relish the persona of a languid and laid-back officer. His relaxed style and impish sense of humour had often got him into trouble with superior officers, but he was devoted to his fusiliers and his regiment. Jefferies' ability and courage were in no doubt at any point during his time in Tunisia. Moreover, his fusiliers would follow him anywhere, despite him often referring to them in mocking terms. Two hours after moving down the north-eastern slope of Mahdi, Jefferies and his men encountered a force of German infantry which was equipped with three machine guns, and this time, well-supported by artillery, proceeded in good Irish style to clear them out of the way. A Company returned that evening having added two German officers and 30 soldiers to the increasing number of enemy who would end up inhabiting the divisional POW cage.

Almost at the same time that Nick Jefferies departed on his mission, the battalion forward positions sighted a build-up of tanks and infantry on the eastern edge of the Oued Bed Valley. For the next three to four hours, these German forces attempted to move down the valley and threaten the units of the 36th Brigade which were moving into the valley. The threat never really emerged, because the Faughs were now accompanied on the heights of Mahdi by forward artillery observers who were able to bring down the wrath of the left artillery group on the Germans. The 5.5in guns of the 5th Medium Regiment engaged both the tanks and infantry. The battalion was also supported by the gunners of 132nd Field Artillery Regiment (Harry Secombe's unit), which had a proprietary interest in keeping Coldwell-Horsfall's company on Mahdi, for Captain James Browne, one of their battery captains, was his cousin. Although the guns of the 5th Medium Regiment kept the German tanks at bay, it is likely that they managed to mistake Churchills of the North Irish Horse for German *panzers* on 8 April, accidentally shelling and damaging two of their tanks. Incidents of so-called friendly fire were sadly not uncommon in Tunisia, but fortunately no casualties arose from this one.[39]

Among the many benefits that the acquisition of Djebel Mahdi delivered to 78th Division was that it allowed several artillery units to move across the Oued Zarga-Beja road. This was no mean feat as it required large numbers of vehicles to move to new positions in the dark and across rugged terrain. Their new battery locations, combined with the artillery's excellent observation posts high on Mahdi, Kachiba and Djebel Nahel to the east, brought within range

---

39 Nick Jeffries' profile and the patrol action are based largely on Coldwell-Horsfall, *The Wild Geese*, pp.13-14, 114, his obituary in the Regimental magazine *Faugh a Ballach* and the battalion war diary. The friendly fire incident is detailed in TNA WO 175/338 132nd Field Regiment WD April 1943.

targets that previously they were unable to engage. Their new targets included tanks, troops, mortars and the few but dangerous artillery guns positioned locally and in the German rear areas. The number of mortars, infantry and self-propelled guns available to the German 334th Infantry Division for use in killing and wounding British troops started to rapidly decline, as each one was spotted, engaged and destroyed. The significant numbers of 80mm mortars available to the Germans, and the damage that their well-trained mortar crews could inflict on infantry, ensured that the destruction of these weapons became a key task for artillery units. The medium and heavy regiments were specifically tasked with making their destruction a priority, and for every mortar that fired, medium guns were told to reply with 10 rounds from their 5.5in guns.

The comparatively small number of artillery guns available to the 334th Infantry Division in this sector and the scale of British firepower created a significant problem for Major General Weber as he considered how to counter the 38th Brigade's success. His options were limited as he lacked enough troops and tanks to counterattack everywhere. He turned for assistance to a weapon that had previously been used most effectively; air attack by the *Luftwaffe* to balance out his weakness in artillery. Throughout the period from the morning of 7 April and for the next six days, the *Luftwaffe* used its bases near Tunis to launch a series of strafing and bombing attacks on 78th Division units both north and south of the Oued Zarga-Beja road. During this period, JU-87 *Stukas* dive-bombed infantry and tanks while ME-109 and FW-190 fighters strafed infantry, vehicles and rear areas. When the attacks began on 7 April, it seemed initially to the men of the 78th Division that the bad old days of December 1942 had returned, when the only aircraft in the sky were German and they had evil intent. But evidence that German air superiority was no longer guaranteed was soon forthcoming, and in a rather dramatic manner. At about 1630 hours that day, Major Eugene Strickland of A Squadron of the North Irish Horse, who was in his Churchill tank north of the Oued Bouneb River, watched as his squadron's tanks were exposed to air attack by a group of 15 *Stukas* escorted by three ME-109 fighters. After a few moments, bombs could be heard dropping, but the sound seemed not too close. Strickland recalled later: "I raised my [tank turret] flaps carefully and looked out [and] was amazed and delighted to see our Spitfires among the *Stukas* and causing havoc. Bombs were jettisoned in all directions, no direct hits were scored; the shrapnel from the bombs proved ineffectual against the tanks' armour plate. The tank crews waved their thanks to the Spitfire pilots."[40] The German *Stuka* pilots and their fighter escorts had become a little too complacent and had been intercepted over the Oued Zarga area by Spitfires of 243 Squadron led by 23-year-old Squadron Leader James "Jimmie" Walker. Although Jimmie Walker was extremely young to command a squadron, he was already an experienced fighter pilot who had flown in Russia before assuming command of 243 Squadron. Walker, who hailed from Edmonton in Canada and was the son of a minister, had already won a Distinguished Flying Cross (DFC) in 1942 and had previously shot down four aircraft. On this day his squadron, which included several other Canadians, tore into the Germans, shot down at least five *Stukas* and probably destroyed two others. Walker himself shot down one of the *Stukas* and later described how he led the squadron into a tearing dive. He first saw the enemy planes 1,000ft below him: "It was too easy… I picked one out and saw strikes all over the aircraft. The next thing the starboard undercarriage was shot away just

40   Doherty, *North Irish Horse*, p.98.

after the pilot jettisoned his bombs."[41] One of the *Stukas* plunged down in flames and blew up in full sight of John Coldwell-Horsfall and his men on Djebel Mahdi. The loss of five *Stukas* at 1640 hours was followed by a similar event at 1800 hours when 232 Squadron shot down four more *Stukas* near Medjez el Bab.

This and other actions, often in full view of ground troops, made clear that the Germans no longer enjoyed air superiority in the skies above the First Army. The considerable fighter and fighter-bomber support provided to the Battle-Axe Division for the next period of Operation Sweep led to more German losses, but did not stop the *Luftwaffe* from attacking ground troops. The first six days of the operation saw up to 15 air raids in the divisional area every day, and although some consisted of just two FW-190s, others were more significant in size and duration. The persistent air attacks proved to be more of a nuisance than a serious problem and resulted in no more than 15-20 reported casualties. The *Luftwaffe* aircrews, and especially the *Stuka* pilots, courageously continued their raids in the face of RAF fighters, and although their losses continued to climb, they made a major effort on 10 April. The RAF Spitfire pilots were responsible for shooting down a total of 30 aircraft in six days in the area around the division.

However, not all these losses were due to the RAF, as the Battle-Axe Division had its own antidote to bombing raids: the guns of 49th Light Anti-Aircraft (LAA) Regiment, the division's air defence battalion.[42] Under the command of Lieutenant Colonel Vivian Hunt, the 49th LAA Regiment had proved itself to be a highly capable unit early on during the 78th Division's time in northern Tunisia. They had not been able to prevent the heavy air attacks inflicted on the division during the initial advance towards Tebourba, but soon became efficient in imposing a price for such raids. Unusually for a Royal Artillery regiment, the 49th often found itself in direct battle with the enemy, although in this case it was in combat with German fighter and bombers, not usually with German tanks and infantry. As a result of these actions, by early April 1943, four members of the regiment had already been decorated for gallantry. They included Sergeant Farley, who won a MM while supporting Blade Force at Chouigui Pass, and Lieutenant Mathei, who was decorated for his leadership of his troop at Tebourba under constant bombing and strafing. The 49th's attrition of German aircraft had proved to be a thorn in the side of the *Luftwaffe* in Algeria and Tunisia, but had come at a price as the regiment had already lost 26 of its men by the end of March 1943. Vivian Hunt was one of several excellent TA officers whose skills and leadership were identified both before and early in the war, and cultivated through increasing responsibility and promotion. It had been Hunt who had highlighted to divisional staff the tactical importance of defending the natural route south-west from Mateur to Beja, by securing a narrow gap north of Beja between two hills, which was subsequently named Hunt's Gap after him. His advice ensured that V Corps had secured this vital position when Germans attacked it during Operation *Oschenkopf* in March. It was also Hunt's AA gunners who used their 40mm Bofors and 3in AA guns to protect the divisional rear areas with their fire, claiming 10 aircraft shot down between 7 and 12 April. The regiment's performance during the operation continued a high standard recognised across the Battle-Axe Division. It was a most unhappy

41   Quotation is from a *United Press* release 8 April 1943 cited in the website www.acesofww2.com (accessed 18 October 2017) under Canadian aces.
42   Air operations by 243 Squadron are described in C. Shores *Fighters over Tunisia* (London: Spearman, 1975), p.306.

accident when shrapnel falling to the ground from an exploded AA shell killed a sapper from 214th Field Company RE on 14 April.[43]

4.9 Only the enemy in Front

The attack of the 78th Division, and especially the 38th Infantry Brigade on Mahdi and onwards into the Bed Valley from 7-9 April, would be supported by a regiment from a corps which had not existed just over two years before: the 56th Reconnaissance Regiment of the Reconnaissance Corps. This corps was established on 14 January 1941 in order to respond to the lessons of the British Army's experience in France in 1940, which indicated that there were insufficient cavalry regiments available to conduct forward reconnaissance on the enemy's location and strength for the number of British infantry divisions. This conclusion led to the formation of a recce battalion or regiment for each infantry division. These would primarily be equipped with light armoured vehicles, including the tracked Universal Gun Carrier (UGC), better known as the Bren Gun Carrier, and the wheeled Humber Light Reconnaissance Car (LRC) (see Plate 6). Recce regiments were normally numbered the same as their parent divisions, and originally the 56th had been part of the 56th London Division. However, when the 78th Division was formed it was transferred to that formation, but retained its original number. It proved to be a most fortunate course of events for the division, and especially later for the 38th Irish Brigade.

In one of those happy coincidences, the CO of the 56th Recce was Lieutenant Colonel Kendall Chavasse (see Plate 6), who as a new second lieutenant had started his first day in his new regiment, the Faughs, in 1924 with another young officer, Pat Scott. Chavasse would later meet and get to know another captain in the regiment, Nelson Russell. Although now serving in the Recce Corps, it could reasonably be said that when his regiment arrived in North Africa, Chavasse was already part of the extended family that was the Faughs and the Irish Brigade. In common with many of the unit commanders in the 78th Division, Chavasse was an interesting character with an unusual background and career. He was born in Ireland near Waterford into a long-established Irish family. His father had served in the Army during the Boer War, but Chavasse was initially expected to follow his two older brothers into the Royal Navy. In 1919, at the age of 15, Kendall Chavasse became a naval cadet at the Royal Naval College at Osborne on the Isle of Wight, and subsequently moved to the Royal Naval College at Dartmouth. Unfortunately, or perhaps fortunately for the Army, while he was at Dartmouth Chavasse became ill, and by the time he had recovered he was too old to resume service as a naval cadet. Due to family connections he was able to join the Army at the Royal Military Academy at Sandhurst, and in 1924 was commissioned into the Faughs. A keen sportsman and hunter, he devoted much of his spare time in India to shooting, polo and pig-sticking. After serving with his battalion in Egypt, Sudan, Malta and Cyprus, and becoming its adjutant from 1937-39, he completed Staff College at Camberley in Surrey in 1939. Successful completion of the Army staff course in the thirties was an essential step for any officer who wished to rise to command of a battalion or regiment, and proved that Chavasse was marked for higher rank. After Staff

---

43   The profile of Vivian Hunt, Hunt's Gap and 49th LAA Regiment is derived from Blaxland, *The Plain Cook*, pp.174-75; TNA WO175/427 49 LAA Regiment WDs April 1943; Cyril Ray, *Algiers to Austria, A History of the 78th Division* (London: Eyre and Spottiswood, 1952), p.40; and CWGC records. 49th LAA Regiment gallantry awards are from TNA WO 373/1.

College he was appointed as a brigade major in the 151st Infantry Brigade and served with that formation in 1940 in France, where he experienced the British armoured counterattack on Rommel at Arras and was mentioned in dispatches. This experience may have influenced his decision to later join the new Recce Corps, and he was assigned first as second-in-command of a recce regiment and then, in May 1942, to command of the 56th Recce Regiment.

As a completely new organisation that lacked any traditions or history, the new Reconnaissance Corps had to establish its own culture. Historically, forward reconnaissance in front of the main army had been the task of cavalry regiments, and partly by design and partly by accident the Recce Corps adopted a cavalry culture. It called its sub-units squadrons and troops, while men became troopers and not privates. The nature of the task they performed required the corps' soldiers to exercise judgement and initiative, so recce units were granted permission to select recruits who had above average intelligence. When combined with intensive training, this made the 56th Recce Regiment a highly capable unit.

Soon after its arrival in Tunisia in November 1942, Chavasse and his regiment found themselves in the role for which they had been created, operating with the advance units of the First Army and the Battle-Axe Division. It is generally agreed that the first British troops into Tunisia were a troop of the 56th Recce. Both Chavasse and the regiment proved their abilities in a series of actions during the race to Tunis. It was one of the 56th Recce's troops that covered the withdrawal of the remnants of the 2nd Battalion of the Parachute Regiment into Allied lines after a disastrous parachute drop near Oudna in December 1942. If it had not been for the work of one of Chavasse's troops, a certain Lieutenant Colonel John Frost would never have commanded his battalion at Arnhem bridge in September 1944, as he would have been captured in Tunisia. Chavasse's leadership and personal courage during those first two months in Tunisia earned him the award of a DSO in January 1943.[44] In common with several units in the 78th Division, the regiment spent the winter months of 1943 constantly on the move around Tunisia. Its assignment to support the 38th Infantry Brigade was the first time it had worked with that brigade. Chavasse was already well known by its key officers and moreover had actually named his own light armoured car *Faugh A Ballach*, the anglicised version of the Faughs' regimental motto. Although Chavasse had a particular interest and fondness for the 38th Brigade, his regiment found itself supporting all three brigades of the 78th Division at one time or another during Operation Sweep. The primary tasks of the regiment at the outset of the operation were, however, for A and B Squadrons to support the 38th and indirectly the 36th Brigade by conducting patrolling in the Bed Valley to the east of Djebel Mahdi. C Squadron, Chavasse's most experienced squadron, was attached to 11th Infantry Brigade to protect its flank.

The lonely and dangerous job of conducting reconnaissance patrols in the Bed Valley was one that was quite familiar to many officers and men of the 56th Recce Regiment. Throughout the winter of 1943, when the 78th Division had control of the Beja-Medjez road, patrols from the 56th had regularly worked their way up both the Bed and Tine valleys in order to provide early warning of any German attempts to attack south via these routes. A Squadron had carried out

44   The profile of 56th Recce Regiment is derived from R. Doherty, *Only the Enemy in Front: History of the Reconnaissance Corps 1941-46* (Stroud: Spellmount, 1994), and TNA WO 175/178 56th Recce Regiment March- April 1943 WD. Details of Chavasse's career are from Doherty, *Clear the Way*, p.60, the Army List, Chavasse's Obituary in the *Daily Telegraph* on 12 May 2001 and details on the Army officers section of www.unithistories.com (accessed 14 January 2018).

a successful raid on the *Ferme de Bed* (Bed Farm) in March. When it was ordered on 8 April to move up the Bed Valley and screen the 38th Brigade operations on Mahdi, it was moving on to ground it knew well. The operation on that day was carried out by three troops of A Squadron, supported by a troop of 25-pounder field guns, and was led by the squadron commander, Major Daire Murray. It was designed to both probe enemy defences in the valley and act as an early warning screen for any counterattack. After starting their move at 0730 hours, Murray and his squadron had managed to cross the Oued Bouneb by 0845 hours and took 18 prisoners. Progress became more limited than expected, as the tracks were mined and soon after they were heavily shelled. The lead troop became pinned down and suffered casualties in men and vehicles. In a typical act of leadership, Daire Murray left his vehicle to move forward on foot to help extract the lead troop, but was killed by shelling. Squadron patrols tried to move forward during the rest of the day, but were held up by enemy fire and mines; nonetheless, they were able to provide warning of German tanks and bring them under fire. A Squadron's patrol up the Bed Valley proved costly, for as well as Murray loss, three troopers were killed and an officer and six other troopers wounded, while at least two recce vehicles were lost. It showed that the Germans were sensitive to any attempt to probe up the valley and care needed to be taken. The following day, Chavasse sent B Squadron to effectively repeat the same mission, unfortunately with the same result. The squadron vehicles came under heavy shelling, much of it directed from Djebel Djebel Rmel at the north end of the valley. A Humber armoured car was lost and two of its crew were killed, although eight prisoners were taken. Surprisingly, Chavasse, who was an effective leader, decided to repeat the exercise yet again on 10 April, this time with A Squadron, but any attempt to move up the valley attracted heavy machine-gun and mortar fire and was stalled, though fortunately no soldiers were lost.[45] The three expeditions up the Bed Valley from 8-10 April saw a number of acts of gallantry, including that on 8 April by Trooper Read of an assault troop in A Squadron in the southern Bed Valley. On that day, Read's recce section became pinned down by mortar and machine-gun fire, in a position separated from the rest of his squadron by open ground and in full view of the enemy. Despite the danger, Read volunteered to take a message to the rest of the squadron and moved across fire-swept ground to deliver it and return to his comrades. Although the message was delivered, additional support was not forthcoming, so he volunteered again to go with his Troop Leader to cross the dangerous ground and deliver a second message. His citation notes that during the action Trooper Read "Displayed the highest possible courage and bravery, with total disregard for his own safety."[46]

The one lesson learned from the 56th Recce Regiment's activities was that it was obvious that the German hold on the Bed Valley would only be broken by a strong attack supported by tanks. This caused the division to think carefully about its next move, and as a result 38th Brigade found that its plans were to change.

4.10 A Change of Plan

While considerable activity happened in the air, on the ground the pace of operations within the Irish Brigade continued. On 9 April 1943, B Company of the Faughs conducted yet another

---

45   Details of A Squadron's operations in the Bed Valley are largely from TNA WO 175/178 56th Recce Regiment WD April 1943 and R. Doherty, *Only the Enemy in Front*, pp.50-51.
46   Trooper Read was awarded the MM the citation is in TNA WO 373/1.

infantry sweep assisted by artillery. This one killed only two Germans but netted 47 prisoners, increasing the total number captured by the brigade to well over 200. This sweep and that on the previous day were completed at the cost of one fusilier dead and two wounded. The success of the operation on this day was in no small part due to the actions of Fusilier Reaney, whose citation notes:

> Fusilier Reaney's section came under very close range MG fire from a dug in position on the hill top. Although under fire and being subjected to bombing, Fusilier Reaney advanced up the hill firing his Bren from the hip until wounded in the leg. His action enabled other men of his platoon to outflank the enemy position and bring about his surrender of the enemy. Fusilier Reaney's action showed great dash and disregard of personal danger.[47]

Reaney was aided in his efforts by one of B Company's officers firing yet another Bren from the flank, which enabled the company to take the position. Reaney's bravery at Mahdi earned him the award of a MM.

By this time the Faughs had been actively engaged in marching or operations since 5 April, which would have taken its toll. It is important to realise the physical challenges infantry troops faced in northern Tunisia. The rocky and rugged terrain, with its steep climbs and broken wadis, made movement difficult. Soldiers had to dig slit trenches on hard ground, conduct patrols during the day and, when not on sentry duty, try to sleep in the most uncomfortable positions. In early April the temperature during the day was in the low 70s and there was very little shade. The physical exertion required just to survive and fight made men thirsty and tired, but water was rationed and sleep limited to a few hours if soldiers were lucky. The infantry also faced the problems of being dirty and the constant threat of injury from bullet or shell. Brigadier Nelson Russell was acutely aware of the challenges his men faced and the fact that his old battalion needed to be relieved so it could have a brief rest. He was nonetheless forced to retain the Faughs on Mahdi another day so that he could carry out a short operation designed to keep the Germans off-balance. In order to conduct what he saw as a mopping-up operation, Russell had to bring the 6th Skins out of reserve back up to Mahdi and also use the 2nd Hants, which had experienced a quiet, uneventful couple of days on Kachiba. The operation was designed to clear, but not hold, an area of high ground both west and north of Kachiba and west of the Oued Kachiba riverbed which separated the Hampshires' positions from Djebel Mahdi to the east.

The 6th Skins had spent less than 48 hours resting to the south when, under the command of new CO Neville Grazebrook, it moved up to Kachiba and on the night of 9 April sent A Company to seize a hill called Point 361 directly to the north of Kachiba. The operation started well, as the Skins took the hill and also eight prisoners who surrendered eagerly. While working its way up the Oued Kachiba riverbed, C Company managed to enter a known German anti-personnel minefield. They suffered four casualties, but supported from Point 361 they attacked a German position which yielded 40 prisoners and two mortars. After this success, B Company attempted to seize a further peak, but had not reached their objective when the message "Trumps", the order to withdraw, was received at 1810 hours. The Skins' operation delivered 48 more prisoners to the divisional cage, but the battalion had suffered at least two dead and 12 wounded in return,

---

47   The quotation from Fusilier Reaney's MM citation is also in TNA WO 373/1.

a stiff price for such a local attack. Although originally authorised to seize hills to the north and east, which were the objectives for this day's activity, the CO of the 2nd Hants, Lieutenant Colonel Martin, had initially concluded it was not necessary. Nelson Russell's decision to launch his mopping-up operation resulted in a change to Martin's plans. He committed the 2nd Hants to take a height, Point 331, 1km west of his location, and then to go north to take Point 372. Point 331 was captured with few casualties, but faced flanking machine-gun fire. The next stage of the mopping-up proved much more costly. Although successful in taking the next height, Point 372, the attackers came up against much more determined resistance and suffered additional losses. Heavy machine-gun fire further increased losses when a company moved to the north-east, attacked and finally captured Puits Zatriah, a hill some two miles directly north of Kachiba. The battalion took the hill, captured 35 prisoners and inflicted an estimated 10-15 enemy casualties, but this turned out to be a pyrrhic victory. As previously planned, the 2nd Hants withdrew from the area at about 1810 hours, returning ownership to the Germans. Moreover, the final price paid by the Hampshires for this minor operation ended up being 24 men dead and at least 40 wounded.

The battalion's history unusually fails to mention this costly action, and it is unclear what German unit the Hampshires encountered that day. Its war diary simply refers to a successful raid and provides no details of the losses incurred. This is surprising in view of the actual losses. The relative success, or lack of, of this action was in any case probably no solace to the parents of Lance Corporal Harold Salvage, who lived in Twyford, Berkshire, when they were told of his death, for he was one of the men killed that day. However, it may have been some small consolation for them in their grief, to learn much later that prior to his death their son had so distinguished himself in a previous action that he was recommended for a MM, which they received in 1946. In an age when few are aware of the battles in Tunisia, it is worth recording that 17 men from the 2nd Hants, whose gravestones state they were killed on 9 April 1943, today lie in an almost hidden cemetery in the centre of the town of Beja. Although serving in the Hampshires, these soldiers came from locations as far away from that county as Aberdeen, Durham and Leeds. Many were in their late 20s and three were married. Though killed in a forgotten action, in a forgotten campaign and now buried in a rarely visited cemetery, they need to be remembered. Loss is of course part of war, and loss creates grief, one of the hidden costs of war that families pay.[48]

The battalion's final role in the Battle of the Peaks was to take over and briefly hold positions on Djebel Oum Guerinat in the Bed Valley from 12-14 April. After the fall of Tunis, the battalion became part of the 128th Infantry Brigade of the 46th Division, suffered heavy casualties during the Salerno landings and fought its way through Italy. Irrespective of the relative merits of executing this operation, it had not been a good day for the Irish Brigade, after the loss of 60 men, or for its brigadier personally. It had started out poorly for Russell, when a mortar shell landed on his new CP, badly concussed him and killed his brigade signals officer, Captain Strange. A bad day grew worse, as four times during the day while he was visiting his units, he came under air attack from ME-109s and the observation post he had travelled to

48   See TNA WO 175/216, WO 175/506 and WO 175/499, the war diaries of the 38th Brigade, 1st Royal Irish Fusiliers and the 2nd Hants for April 1943. Information on Lance Corporal Savage and other soldiers buried in Beja is derived from analysis of CWGC records and also from Savage's MM citation in TNA WO 373/1.

was a prime target for a battery of mortars. During his return journey to his headquarters, his car fell into a shell hole and became stuck. The final bit of bad news came when he got back to his headquarters to learn that his intention to rest the brigade for a couple of days had been overruled by the divisional commander and his staff. Though still suffering from concussion from the blast, Russell was ordered at very short notice on the evening of 9 April to plan and carry out a brigade attack the next day. He later recalled:

> On the evening of April 9, I received orders to advance the next morning with my Brigade to some rugged heights, which was quite 5 miles away. I took a poor view of this idea. Not only might five miles hold a lot of Bosche [*sic*] – but the Brigade was tired. There had been little sleep for anyone during the last six days – and the latter four of those days had seen continuous and heavy fighting – most of it at close quarters. However my views – poor or otherwise cut no ice. I was ordered to get on with it.[49]

It is unclear why Russell and his brigade were tasked with a further attack on 10 April, especially since it had not appeared in the original plan and seemed quite ambitious. It was also unusual and poor leadership for the division to issue orders so late and allow very little time for reconnaissance and preparation. It had been similar inadequate staff work that had got the division into trouble in December 1942. Moreover, the events of the last two days had provided clear evidence that German resistance to further attacks in the area seemed to be stiffening. It is clear that the order was unexpected, as Russell had already issued a plan for the relief of the brigade that evening by units of the 12th Brigade of the 4th Division, including the 1st Battalion of the Royal West Kent Regiment and 6th Battalion of the Black Watch, and did not expect his battalions to conduct further operations. Furthermore, Russell was directed to seize two hills: Djebel Oum Guerinat, which was three miles north of Mahdi, and Djebel Rmel, located on the eastern side of the exposed river valley that had been used by the Germans for the last two days by tanks threatening counterattacks. This plan had all the hallmarks of a hastily created and amateur scheme for which the brigade would pay a price. What Russell didn't say, when he later recalled that his views were ignored, was that he had actually presented them in person. Despite his terrible day, he had taken the unusual step of going to see Vyvyan Evelegh at his divisional headquarters at 2300 hours that night to present his concerns. The extent of Russell's frustration with the orders from division can be gauged from the fact that the brigade war diary for that day unusually notes that the brigadier stated that the operation was "not practical politics unless the threat of enemy tanks in the area 4647 was neutralised. It was therefore necessary to use [the North Irish Horse's] Churchills to go in advance of the infantry on the night."[50] This veiled criticism, placed on formal record in a war diary, was unusual and showed how concerned Russell must have been. It also suggests that the original scheme created earlier that day may have proposed an attack without tank support. Evelegh apparently listened to but overruled Russell's objections, and the latter was forced by time constraints to call his battalion commanders to a conference at half past midnight. Russell spent the next couple of hours with his commanders and staff, creating a viable plan. One change that seems to have

---

49   See N. Russell, *Irish Brigade*, p.116.
50   TNA WO 175/216 38 Infantry Brigade WD April 1943.

been agreed, because of the threat from German tanks, was the commitment of the North Irish Horse's Churchill tanks to support the attack. In view of Russell's concerns about the original plan and its lack of tank support, it is possible to speculate that had this change not been agreed, Russell might have baulked at sending his beloved brigade three miles up a valley against alerted Germans and with a right flank exposed to tank attack. If he had done so, he would have been relieved, for Evelegh, who had many virtues, was known for at least two vices: his bad temper and his reputed dislike of any challenge to his authority, however well-intentioned. That would have been a great shame for both the division and the Irish Brigade, as they would have lost a fine battlefield commander. After a frantic night of effort, during which Russell managed only one hour of sleep, by 0400 hours plans were complete and the Irish Brigade was ready to launch its attack. It would be directly supported by a troop of C Squadron of the North Irish and significant artillery fire. A and B Squadrons of the North Irish Horse also prepared to move down into the Bed Valley to deal with any threats from German tanks or infantry which might come down the valley and try to interfere with the Irish Brigade's advance.

4.11 The Last Furlong up the Maze

By first light on 10 April, 1 Troop of C Squadron North Irish Horse was in position to directly support the attack of the Faughs. Meanwhile, across the Bed Valley to the east of Mahdi, the two squadrons of the North Irish Horse were positioned further down western slopes of Point 667, after moving their tanks down from near that height. They had reached this rather lofty location during operations in support of 36th Brigade over the last four days that had led to the capture of this tactically significant hill. The original objectives of A and B Squadrons were quite modest. They had been tasked with advancing to two locations from which they could watch over the valley. The first was for A Squadron to advance down a slope from Point 667 to a location that gave a good view of the Oued Tine river, which wandered down through the Bed Valley before branching out to the north-east and becoming a broad valley. B Squadron's task was to advance north-west to a hill down in the main valley. From this location the North Irish's tanks could watch any movement to the north and detect any threats. The Churchills of A and B Squadrons quickly moved over the rough ground and took their initial objectives without any opposition. It was at this point that Lieutenant Colonel Dawnay of the North Irish Horse identified the opportunity to assist 38th Brigade. As he noted afterwards:

> Realising that I could help the attack of 38th Brigade if I could reach Djebel Rmel, I wirelessed this proposal to my liaison officer with 38th Brigade and received an answer that this move would be very helpful. Consequently I ordered the advance to continue on a two Squadron front towards Djebel Rmel.[51]

This change in plan would prove very helpful for the Faughs, as they started to move from their positions on Mahdi towards the northern point of that hill at 0900 hours. They met no opposition but proceeded very cautiously, and by midday had only reached Sidi Ameur, a farm which lay about a mile south-east of Djebel Oum Guerinat. In the valley, the North Irish used

---

51   See *North Irish Battle Report: North Africa and Italy* (Belfast: W.G. Baird, 1946), p.18.

the protection offered by their tanks to move more rapidly up towards Djebel Rmel, one of the Irish Brigade's original objectives. Although A Squadron was held up by a minefield, B Squadron was able to move quickly up to some high ground to the west of Djebel Rmel. Dawnay followed B Squadron in his command tank and personally directed them on to Djebel Rmel, a long, thin, hilly ridge dominated by a western height which extended out from that ridge. It was occupied by B Squadron after they chased away German infantry with Besa machine-gun fire from their tanks. Soon afterwards, A Squadron got through the minefield and moved to a watching position south-east of Rmel farm. On the western side of the valley, the Faughs and their attached troop of Churchills met no opposition as they advanced on to Djebel Oum Guerinat by about 1515 hours. The brigade, ably assisted by the North Irish, had taken both its objectives with comparative ease. Nelson Russell, watching the attack from his observation post, saw Lieutenant Mann's troop of Churchills from C Squadron of the North Irish Horse moving up along the western valley to take Guerinat. Russell later described this scene in his inimitable style:

> This attack was made memorable by the North Irish Horse assisting the Irish Brigade. It was the first time we'd fought together and I hope it won't be the last. I cannot imagine a better tank battalion. Moreover it gave our chaps a homely feel to follow behind a female Churchill called "Lily from Pontaferry". Actually the line of our advance was unsuitable for tanks, and I employed the bulk of them on the right flank. But a few were allotted to our infantry route, and in spite of bad ground – sailed up the Djebel Oum Guerinat as if it were the last furlong at the Maze. There was hardly any fighting during the advance – the Boche wouldn't wait for the North Irish Horse. I wasn't particularly sorry about this. By the time, the "Faughs" and the "Skins" (who had followed up) had advanced five miles and dug in – they could well dispense with warlike trimmings.[52]

Russell's observation that there was hardly any fighting during the advance was technically correct, since he referred to his own brigade. The North Irish, in contrast, came under not only air attack that day, but also had encounters with both anti-tank guns and the silent enemy, minefields. A Squadron's advance led it to a heavily mined wadi, and during this period it came under heavy artillery and mortar fire. One of the Churchills had a track disabled trying to cross the wadi. Despite the heavy fire, its commander, Lieutenant George Gardiner, got out of his tank to try to mend the track but was wounded in the thigh. In spite of his wound, which later proved serious, Gardiner continued to work on his tank and afterwards, having refused evacuation, he led his troop for 14 more hours. Gardiner's gallantry was matched by that of his driver, Trooper George Martin, who left the tank on his own initiative without orders and under heavy fire cleared 12 Teller mines, which enabled the other tanks to proceed across the wadi. Martin was cited for the fact that he showed complete disregard for the heavy artillery and mortar fire landing nearby and the danger posed by the mines. It is highly probable that Lieutenant John Dudley Townsend-Rose of 256th Field Company RE was involved in the same incident. Indeed one account notes that a RE officer encouraged Martin and other men to help lift the mines, and that was almost certainly Townsend-Rose. Lieutenant Townsend-Rose was

---

52   See H. Russell, *Irish Brigade*, p.116.

in command of a section from 256th Field Company RE, which had been sent forward to aid the North Irish. While under fire, he calmly and coolly disarmed a total of 22 Teller mines. These anti-tank mines were notorious for being equipped with at least one and usually two anti-handling devices, so such work was very dangerous, even when not under fire. George Gardiner and John Townsend-Rose were both later awarded the MC for gallantry, while Trooper George Martin received a well-earned MM.

The two squadrons of the North Irish took up position at Djebel Rmel and were able not only to relieve the Faughs of one of their missions, but also ensure they were not threatened by any German tanks. Two tanks were spotted, but the North Irish could not engage them and eventually they withdrew. Nonetheless, Brigadier Russell had been correct to be concerned about the threat of tanks, as two days previously Major Strickland, in command of A Squadron, had spotted eight tanks which he believed were Mark VI Tigers in a hull-down position on the eastern side of the valley and others out in the open. These eventually withdrew to the north and didn't bother the brigade again. Apart from an isolated duel with a 50mm anti-tank gun, which ended when the gun was knocked out and the crew taken prisoner, no further actions took place that day. However, A and B Squadrons of the North Irish found themselves in the very uncomfortable position of occupying part of Djebel Rmel without any infantry support. The tanks used parachute flares and regular bursts of Besa machine-gun fire to discourage any attempt by the Germans to counterattack. It was not until midnight that the 6th Black Watch managed to arrive and take over defence of the position.[53]

Meanwhile, the Faughs, whom Russell had been forced to retain, moved slowly but steadily to the extreme northern end of Djebel Mahdi and over a wadi to eventually climb up and take Djebel Oum Guerinat by about 1515 hours. The leading companies saw Germans withdrawing to the north, but suffered no casualties in this part of their battle. The Skins moved up behind them to take up positions at Sidi Ameur farm about 1km north of Mahdi. Both the Faughs and Skins had no trouble retaining their positions on the night of 10/11 April before they were relieved and moved back to their original assembly positions for a rest late on 11 April. The Skins were relieved on Mahdi by the 16th Battalion of the Durham Light Infantry from the 46th "Midlands" Infantry Division. This battalion had experienced hard and bloody fighting around the town of Sedjenane before being loaned to the 78th Division to take over Mahdi. Its stay on the mountain was comparatively uneventful, though the battalion still lost four men killed and several wounded.[54] The battle to take and hold Djebel Mahdi had come to a close for the Irish Brigade.

It could be argued that Mahdi was actually comparatively lightly defended by the Germans and its capture was just a matter of time. However, such a view overlooks the fact that a rapid seizure of Mahdi was essential to protect the flank of the operations being conducted by the 11th and 36th Brigades. Moreover, the nature of the terrain and approach routes made Mahdi a quite difficult objective to take quickly, yet 38th Brigade captured the two main heights in less than 24 hours. In the process the brigade inflicted considerable damage on two German battalions and took at least 246 prisoners. The GOC of 78th Division considered the capture of

---

53   The details of this action are derived from the relevant gallantry citations in TNA WO 373/1, TNA WO 175/657 256th Field Company RE WD April 1943 and TNA WO 175/294 North Irish Horse WD April 1943, and Doherty, *North Irish Horse*, pp.99-102.

54   See TNA WO 175/498 16th Durham Light Infantry WD April 1943.

Mahdi to be an essential preliminary to the rest of his plan for Operation Sweep, and rightly so as it dominated the Bed Valley. By taking and securing the area on and around Mahdi, the Irish Brigade ensured the success of the division's other critical operations. Since this was the first occasion in Tunisia that the brigade had operated as a whole in a major attack, it was a creditable performance. Perhaps the best measure of the brigade's achievement is the special order of the day the division received from its army commander two days later, which congratulated the formation for its efforts.

On the battlefield there is always a price to be paid, and the fighting for Mahdi was no exception. The Irish Brigade's own summary of its casualties was almost certainly an underestimate, as it suggested that the brigade had incurred no more than 70 casualties from 7-10 April. A more realistic assessment can be derived from RAMC returns and the records of the Commonwealth War Graves Commission. These indicate that during the period from 4-11 April, the Faughs and Skins lost some 40 officers and men dead and 188 wounded. When the losses of the 2nd Hants (24 dead and 51 wounded) are added to this total, the bare accounting grows to a significant butcher's bill of 64 dead and 242 wounded. The latter figure excludes casualties incurred by supporting units, which probably added a further 15 casualties. In total the brigade incurred over 300 casualties. Almost all of these losses were incurred by the rifle companies in infantry battalions, resulting in the brigade's fighting power being significantly reduced. This fact has to be borne in mind when we later study the Irish Brigade's next set of battles. Bare statistics provide one insight, but they cannot capture the smells, sights and sounds of wounded men. Those who fought here recalled the wounded lying in pain under the hot sun on the rocky battlefield. Medical officers would always remember the sights seen in advanced and main dressing stations. Blast and shrapnel injuries from artillery and mine explosions disfigured some men horribly, while many others had to have limbs amputated.

4.12 Hell on Djebel Rmel

The job of taking and holding Mahdi had been completed and the 38th Brigade had been relieved, but there was one final chapter to the story of operations in this area. The 78th Division's focus was now moving east of the Bed Valley, but it retained responsibility for ensuring that the two newly seized outposts of Djebel Oum Guerinat and Rmel were defended. The first hill was held without any major incident by the 2nd Hants before it was taken over by the 4th Infantry Division. The experience of the 6th Black Watch on Djebel Rmel was, however, rather different. The job of relieving the North Irish Horse on Djebel Rmel and taking formal ownership of the position provided the 6th Battalion of the Black Watch with a rather unusual introduction to active operations. The battalion formed part of a Highland regiment that was formed in 1715 and is known in the British Army by its nickname, the "Forty Twa", referring to the fact that the Black Watch originated as the 42nd Regiment of Foot. The regiment's formal title probably arose from the fact that its original tartan was a dark colour and its job was to keep watch over the Highlands, which had just experienced the Jacobite rebellion. The regiment subsequently fought all over the world, earned multiple battle honours and a reputation as a tough Highland regiment. A TA battalion, the 6th had fought in Belgium in 1940, been evacuated from Dunkirk and had spent the next three years of the war training in Scotland. The battalion's transition to wartime operations in Tunisia was quite a rapid one. It had left Selkirk in the borders of Scotland on 14 March, and by 6 April was at Beja in Tunisia. By 10 April the battalion was on Mahdi and supposed to relieve the Faughs, but as we have seen the Faughs were committed to the attack on Djebel Oum Guerinat. It was only upon arriving on Mahdi that the battalion learned it was tasked to join the North Irish Horse on Djebel Rmel and hold the area. Furthermore, this move would be made in darkness across terrain with which the unit was not familiar, and the 6th Black Watch were not relieving another infantry battalion as would be the norm, but two squadrons of Churchill tanks.

The 6th Battalion of the "Forty Twa" moved cautiously across two miles of no man's land and arrived at the North Irish Horse's positions near Djebel Rmel at or about midnight. One problem that arose from trying to hold a hill ridge like Djebel Rmel with Churchill tanks was that the North Irish Horse didn't actually occupy the whole ridge, but were based on its lower slopes. The critical position on Djebel Rmel was Point 350, which dominated the ridgeline and the surrounding area. Unfortunately it seems that in the dark this was not apparent. All the evidence available indicates that three of the four companies dug in on the southern part of the Djebel Rmel ridgeline on three lower hills. The consequences of this error became apparent the following morning, when first light revealed that the Black Watch positions were overlooked by German observation positions on hills to the north and east. In addition, the battalion positions were in an exposed location, as the nearest friendly unit was nearly two miles away. The Germans started to direct mortar fire on to their locations, and continued to do so intermittently during the day. This fire inflicted a few casualties, but at this point posed no major threat, as the companies were under cover. However, the following day, someone, probably the CO Lieutenant Colonel Patrick Barclay, made the poor decision to change over the forward unit, A Company, in broad daylight with the southernmost one, D Company. German observers probably could not believe what they were seeing, but very rapidly brought down the fire of a hidden artillery battery on the exposed companies. Both companies were caught in the open and the resulting casualties were heavy, especially as A Company could not get into D Company's original trenches. The Germans took full advantage of the exposed location of the battalion and continued to shell incessantly for most of the day not only the positions of the three rifle companies, but also of the battalion headquarters. At 1730 hours, the CO of the 6th Black Watch was wounded and later evacuated, while command fell to his second-in-command, Major Madden. The troublesome German artillery battery was spotted that evening, but unfortunately it was outside the extreme range of British medium guns and it was not initially possible to suppress its fire. An attempt at 1900 hours that evening to raid German positions on Point 350 also proved unsuccessful, incurring additional casualties. The ordeal of the unit on the slopes of Djebel Rmel was much alleviated the following day, 13 April, when the enemy artillery battery which had caused so many casualties was targeted and destroyed by guns of a medium regiment which had been covertly moved forward. Thereafter, apart from patrolling and another abortive attack on Point 350, the battalion had a more peaceful time, until it was relieved by troops from the 1st US Armoured Division on 19 April. One clear lesson had been learned for the future, for changeover of the forward companies completed on both 15 and 17 April was carried out at night.

The "Forty Twa" had experienced a rude introduction into battle in Tunisia on and near Djebel Rmel, for during the nine days it was there it suffered 19 dead and numerous wounded in action. These included Colonel Barclay, who succumbed to his wounds in hospital on 21 May. Subsequently the battalion was to suffer more significant casualties in two major actions in Tunisia in late April and early May, before fighting through Italy. The Highlanders would nonetheless always remember their difficult stay on Djebel Rmel ridge.

This action brought to an end the 78th Division's role in operations in the Bed Valley on Mahdi, Kachiba and Djebel Rmel.[55] The area was transferred to the control of Americans, who later used it as a base from which to launch II US Corps' operation, under the command of Major General Omar Bradley, to seize Mateur and Bizerte. It was one of the ironies of history that Djebel Rmel was finally captured by an American battalion from the same regiment which had been involved in the First Battle for Longstop, the Vanguards, in this case the 2nd battalion of the US 18th Infantry. This battalion launched its own attack on the early morning of 23 April. In a further tragic irony, the 2nd Battalion went through a very similar experience on Djebel Rmel to that which the 1st Battalion had undergone on Longstop. The battalion attacked Djebel Rmel in darkness and captured it, then lost but regained it before finally being forced off the hill by a strong German counterattack. On this occasion, however, the Vanguards, under command of their own 1st US Infantry Division, were not to be denied their prize and in an attack, also ironically supported by tanks, the battalion took and held Djebel Rmel. The 2nd Battalion was commanded by the highly capable Lieutenant Colonel Ben Sternberg and, after four more months in Tunisia, was a much more experienced outfit than the unit involved at Longstop Hill. Nonetheless, its losses at Djebel Rmel were significant: 43 killed, 160 wounded and 20 missing.

Harold Alexander and several of his senior British staff officers had by April 1943 developed grave, though somewhat unfounded, doubts about the fighting capabilities of US units, conveniently forgetting the many reverses experienced by raw British troops in North Africa. These doubts sadly continued for some time after Tunisia, but if Alexander had bothered to check, which he didn't, the Vanguards' performance at Djebel Rmel provided clear evidence that when properly led and supported, American troops could beat the Germans. Incontrovertible evidence of the fighting spirt of the Vanguards would be provided on 6 June 1944 when the regiment landed on Omaha Beach. During the next eight hours, the regiment would show its true mettle while fighting off the beach in Easy Red sector. The battalion's reputation would be further enhanced at Aachen in September 1944 and finally in the Ardennes in December that year. Tunisia could be said to have provided a valuable proving ground where the regiment learned its trade.[56]

---

55   Details of the 6th Black Watch's ordeal on Djebel Rmel are from TNA WO 175/494 6 Black Watch WD April 1943 and B.J.G. Madden, *A History of the 6th Black Watch (Royal Highland Regiment) 1939-45* (Perth: Leslie, 1948), pp.17-24.
56   See Baumer, *An American Iliad,* pp.115-21, for details of the 18th Infantry's battle for Djebel Rmel.

5

Operation Sweep: 36th Brigade's Attacks in the Centre

5.1 Swifty and Windy's Plan

General Evelegh assigned the task of evicting the German grenadiers of the 334th Infantry Division from the key hills of Djebel Nahel and Mergueb Chaouach to the men of the relatively flat county of Kent, the 36th Infantry Brigade. The 36th "Kent" Brigade was commanded by 44-year-old Brigadier Bernard "Swifty" Howlett, who had originally commanded the 6th Battalion of the Queen's Own Royal West Kent Regiment (6th West Kents) during the initial unsuccessful advance on Tunis. A tough, quiet, modest and rather slight man who was an excellent battlefield commander, Swifty Howlett was promoted to command of 36th Brigade in late December 1942. Apart from a short period in command of another brigade and also of a provisional division, Howlett had been in command of the 36th Brigade since then. The 36th Brigade had been composed of three battalions from Kent when it had gone to France in 1940 as part of the 12th Division. After surviving a battering and evacuation from Dunkirk, it had been re-formed. The brigade had one of its Kent battalions replaced by the 8th Battalion of the Argyll and Sutherland Highlanders (8th Argylls) and been assigned to the new 78th Division. By March 1943 it was composed of Howlett's old battalion, the 6th West Kents, the 5th Battalion of the Buffs (The East Kent Regiment) and the 8th Argylls. The brigade also had a regiment of 25-pounder field guns from the Royal Artillery, the 17th Field Regiment and other supporting units, including Royal Engineers. The brigade was reinforced for Operation Sweep by the North Irish Horse, which would later operate in support of the 38th Brigade. This was the first time the brigade had been directly supported by Churchill tanks, and their deployment was to make a considerable difference.

Brigadier Howlett's plan was developed in conjunction with his newly appointed Brigade Major (plans and operations officer), Major John Windeatt from the Devonshire Regiment, who was inevitably nicknamed "Windy", and also the 78th Division staff. The plan on paper seemed quite simple and was divided into two phases (see Map 5). In Phase A of the initial divisional attack, on the night of 6/7 April, the brigade would take and hold a hill called Djebel Nahel located north of the Oued Zarga-Medjez road. Evelegh, in his appreciation, had determined the need for this feature to be seized: the eviction of its German defenders would remove their ability to have direct observation over the future main supply road. More importantly, it would prevent the same units bringing direct and indirect fire on the hills to the east and interfering with 11th Brigade operations. Howlett decided to assign the job of taking this hill to the 5th

Buffs, whom he also tasked with securing crossing points for tanks across the dry river named Oued Bouneb. Once this objective had been seized, Phase B would commence: the crossing of the Oued Bouneb and the seizure of a large hill to the north-east of Nahel, Mergueb Chaouach. The job of acquiring this hill was assigned by Howlett to his old battalion, the 6th West Kents, along with the 8th Argylls. Both of these units would be supported by Churchill tanks of the North Irish Horse once daylight came. The third phase of the plan, Phase C, required the brigade to help seize a height east of the Bed Valley called Point 667, which dominated the area north of the hilltop villages of Toukabeur and Chaouach. This task could only be completed after Nahel and Mergueb Chaouach had been taken[1].

5.2 Codename Canterbury – Seizing Nahel

The task of taking Nahel - codenamed Canterbury for the operation - was assigned to the CO of the 5th Buffs, 43-year-old Acting Lieutenant Colonel A.D. McKechnie. Alexander McKechnie had commanded the unit since 17 January 1943, and unusually had been assigned to it after serving previously in the 12th Honourable Artillery Company; a London-based TA artillery unit. Although a stockbroker by profession and not a regular officer or from the regiment, McKechnie soon established his credentials to command the unit by his cool and capable leadership under fire during a difficult battle on 31 January 1943 near Robaa, when the 5th Buffs had to stop an attack by German infantry supported for the very first time by two Tiger tanks. By April 1943, "Ginger" McKechnie, as he was nicknamed due to his reddish locks, was a fairly experienced CO who led his unit with an avuncular style of command. The battalion he commanded could trace its history as a regiment back to 1572 when it was part of Thomas Morgan's Company of Foot, The London Trained Bands. It was established as the 3rd Regiment of Foot in 1689 and could claim precedence as the third most senior infantry unit in the British Army. The regiment had earned its nickname in 1708 for the buff-coloured facings on its uniform, which distinguished it from another regiment. During the next 230 years it acquired over 80 battle honours and fought in many of the British Army's most famous battles, from Blenheim in Germany to Talavera in Spain and during the First World War at Ypres, the Somme and Passchendaele. As a Territorial battalion, the 5th Buffs was quickly mobilised in 1939, assigned to the BEF in Belgium and the 36th Kent Brigade. The battalion was almost wiped out as a result of fighting during the battle for Belgium and the retreat from Dunkirk, and it returned to its native Kent with less than 100 of the original 600 men in the unit. After being completely rebuilt in England, it landed with the 78th Division at Algiers in November 1942 and saw action at Djebel Aboid in the north, but avoided the heavy losses suffered by the brigade's other battalions in the fight for Tunis. During the following three months it held several sectors across Tunisia and took part in a number of sharp actions.

---

1   Unless otherwise stated, Chapter 5 is largely based on the following primary sources: TNA WO 175/213 WD 36th Infantry Brigade WD April 1943; TNA WO 175/506 WD 5th Buffs April 1943; TNA WO 175/495 WD 6th Queens Own Royal West Kents April 1943; TNA WO 175/491 8th Argylls April 1943 WD; TNA WO 175/282 142nd Regiment RAC April 1943 WD; and John Windeatt's memoirs *Very Ordinary Soldier* (Exeter: Oriel Press, 1989). Operational Order 25 in TNA WO 175/213 36 Infantry Brigade WD April 1943 outlines the brigade plan.

Just over two weeks after McKechnie took command of the battalion, he was involved in the Battle of Robaa. He survived this baptism of fire, and he and his battalion earned high praise from the First Army commander for the action. In common with its sister regiments in the Kent Brigade, the unit had received very little rest over the last five months before being committed to battle on 7 April 1943. It was, however, blessed with some veteran and capable company commanders, who in turn led excellent junior officers, NCOs and soldiers. The battalion's objective, Djebel Nahel, was a twin-topped hill whose lower slopes were covered by wheat and barley fields, located some five miles north-east of what was in 1943 the original hamlet of Oued Zarga. The hill is about a mile south, south-east of Djebel Mahdi, is over a mile in length and in some places half a mile deep. Its tactical value lay in its position overlooking the Beja-Medjez road and the fact that it dominated the Oued Bouneb river valley below it and overlooked the approaches to another key hill and objective for the wider plan, Mergueb Chaouach. Though on paper, and when viewing a map of the time, the plan to seize Nahel seemed simple and achievable, the reality of infantry operations on the ground - both in 1943 and today - is often very different. The plan required the 5th Buffs to navigate at night from its start line, commencing at 0130 hours across some four miles of trackless terrain, uphill and in silence, to arrive at a forming up point (FUP) just below the enemy positions. An FUP is a military term for a suitable location, usually out of sight of the enemy but within easy marching distance of the final objective. After arriving at the FUP, it had to wait for the barrage to start at 0345 hours, and when that finished attack Djebel Nahel and expel its German defenders, hold the position and move down to seize crossings over the riverbed or wadi of the Oued Bouneb below. The best information available to Ginger McKechnie was that Nahel and the slopes to the west of the hill were probably held by at least two, and possibly three companies of Austrian troops from the 3rd Battalion 755th Grenadier Regiment of the 334th Infantry Division. This information proved to be comparatively accurate, as we know from the excellent intelligence summaries, written both before and after the battle by the division staff and available in its war diaries. Later information indicated that Nahel and an adjoining smaller hill to the west were in fact defended by the 9th and 10th Companies of that battalion, supported by heavy machine guns from the 12th Company. The 11th Company was held in reserve, while two 75mm infantry guns were also dug-in behind the hill to support the defence. This unit, the 3rd/755th, had not received any reinforcements, despite having losses in previous battles, and had about 300 men in the forward fighting companies. All this information was usually derived from the interrogation of captured prisoners, who once captured proved very willing to share revealing and valuable tactical information about the location, morale and strength of their units and their view of their officers. It is worth noting that the 78th Division's intelligence staff also benefitted from a steady stream of Austrian and German troops who deserted and crossed over to British lines.

Lieutenant Colonel McKechnie's plan to complete this difficult task was based on assigning A Company to form a number of fighting patrols. Their job was to move ahead of the main body of the battalion to detect and avoid any enemy posts found along the way. The main attack on Nahel would be completed by the units that moved up behind the patrols, with B Company attacking on the left and C Company on the right, followed by D Company in support. There was much that could go wrong, for during its movement the unit could encounter minefields or new unidentified positions which would quickly bring down enemy fire. To help the Buffs overcome these obstacles and take Djebel Nahel, the battalion was allocated a significant degree of artillery support, a section of Royal Engineers and by daylight a squadron of Churchill tanks of the North Irish Horse.[2] Artillery support for the attack was provided by a regimental artillery group led by Lieutenant Colonel "Tommy" Thomas, the CO of the 17th Field Regiment, which included 48 25-pounder guns from both his own regiment and the 132nd Field Artillery Regiment and a battery of eight 5.5in medium guns. Thomas had also assigned a number of Auster artillery-spotting aircraft from 651 Army Observation Squadron and two troops of anti-tank guns of 256 Battery of the 64th Anti-Tank Regiment. By April 1943, the 17th Field Regiment had been in action for three months, and although it did not arrive in the front line until late December 1942, it had become an experienced and well-oiled machine for delivering death and destruction at a distance. Before it was transferred to the 78th Division it had gained valuable experience in fighting around Medjez el Bab and in the battles around Bou Arada. "Tommy" Thomas' second-in-command was Major Peter Pettit, who kept a diary of his time in Tunisia and later battles in North-West Europe. Pettit was another officer who demonstrated the value of the TA in wartime, having joined it before the war and worked his way up from the lowest rank of gunner to be commissioned as an officer. In one of those many coincidences, the unit Pettit joined was the Honourable Artillery Company and he knew Ginger McKechnie personally. Their relationship would prove to be useful in this and subsequent battles fought by the 78th Division.

Another crucial relationship for battle was that forged between the infantry commanders and their Forward Observation Officers (FOO) from their attached artillery regiment. Although different field regiments might support individual battalions, as a rule one regiment supported a particular brigade. Battalion and company commanders grew in time to know and trust the FOOs who worked with them on specific operations. The job of the officers and men assigned to this task meant they had to accompany their infantry colleagues in the front line. It was dangerous, tiring and stressful work, as at any time of day or night they could find themselves under fire and requested to bring down accurate and effective fire on multiple targets that might be close to their positions. This danger involved not only the FOO, but also the men assigned as plotters and radio operators. You may recall that the comedian Spike Milligan had worked in this role for the 56th Heavy Regiment.[3]

Despite the potential for problems in the attack on Nahel, events went largely to plan on the night of 6-7 April and the fighting patrols moved forward stealthily and without opposition. These were accompanied by the Brigade Intelligence Officer and his intelligence section. They had volunteered for the task of using white tape to show the 5th Buffs FUP for their attack. The two lead companies moved off at 0200 hours, and nearly two hours later were close to their objective. At 0345 hours, the sky above Oued Zarga was suddenly lit up with flashes as the

2   Details of the history of the 5th Buffs, the Robaa battle and the attack on Djebel Nahel are derived from C.R.B. Knight, *Historical Records of the Buffs Royal East Kent Regiment (3rd Foot) 1919-1948* (London: The Medici Society, 1951), especially Chapter 8; and TNA WO 175/495 5th Buffs WD January–April 1943. The war diary includes a useful account of 5th Buffs operations on Djebel Nahel and Mergueb Chaouach. The codename Canterbury is cited in Operational Order No. 25 in the April 1943 WD. Details of German forces on Djebel Nahel are from Intelligence summaries in TNA WO 175/168 78th Infantry Division Operations Branch April 1943 WD. The profile of Alexander McKechnie is compiled from information in Blaxland, *Plain Cook*, p.229, the Army List and C.R.B. Knight's book.
3   The story of Tommy Thomas and Peter Pettit is from John P. Jones, *Battles of a Gunner Officer: Tunisia, Sicily, Normandy, and the Long Road to Germany* (Barnsley: Pen and Sword, 2014), and TNA WO 175/326 17 Field Artillery Regiment April 1943 WD.

artillery barrage began, with the shells landing on Nahel. The leading companies moved up close behind the concentration of shells laid down by Thomas' artillery group, which made it easier for the two companies to reach their objective. As the lead companies arrived on top of the hill, however, they came under fire from a number of German MG42 posts set up to fire from the flanks onto the hill crest. One of the platoon commanders that night was Lieutenant Tony Money, who had been studying at Trinity College, Oxford, when the war interrupted his degree course. The citation for his MC states that when Money's platoon came under fire from one of the MG42 posts, he single-handedly charged the enemy position until he was seriously wounded, inspiring his men to attack and overcome the German defences. Money's MC citation told only the bare facts of the action, and the full story would laer be relayed in a letter written by Money to a friend after the war. According to Money, what actually happened that night was as follows:

> I led an attack on a hill on the outskirts of Tunis. I threw a grenade up a slope at a German. Unfortunately for me it rolled back down the hill, where it exploded close behind me; I was wounded by shrapnel in six or seven places. I did not realise I had been wounded as most of the wounds were out of sight on the back of my body, and I felt no pain then: my adrenaline was so high it blanketed it out.

According to other accounts, Money threw a second grenade which killed or wounded the Germans in the position, and he entered the post and took on one of the surviving Germans. Money described what happened next:

> I was grappling with a German on the ground when a member of the platoon took a shot at him from a few yards and hit him, and on its way hit me too. Just below the base of my spine. Again I felt someone up there was taking care of me.[4]

Despite these unusual events, which show that accidents that can happen in the chaos of a close infantry battle, there was no doubt of Lieutenant Money's personal courage that night. He received an immediate award of a MC but his serious wounds meant he spent several months in hospital, and throughout his long life his body bore the scars of that action at Nahel. After the war, Money resumed his studies and after earning his degree forged a successful career as a teacher, becoming a much-admired housemaster at Radley College in Oxfordshire. Money spent 20 years at Radley, where he positively influenced several generations of young pupils and was much-mourned by all those who knew him when he died at the age of 90.[5] Money's injuries may have removed him from this battle, but the fight to destroy the German MG 42 posts continued and casualties began to rise. At this point two JNCOs from the leading companies took on the task of dealing with the machine-gun positions. Lance Corporal Lumpkin and Corporal Chantry made a good double act, for while Lumpkin risked death by exposing himself to provide covering fire, Chantry charged the position. Chantry killed a German who tried to throw a grenade at him, as well as a second one who tried the same thing and also a

---

4   See *Old Radleian Magazine* 2008, Obituary for Tony Money pp.7-17.
5   See *Old Radleian Magazine*, pp.7-17, and the MC citation for Lieutenant A. Money in TNA WO 373/1.

third German. Chantry and Lumpkin next charged and captured the position together. Their initiative and gallantry that day was a great example of why the British Army has always placed such great importance on the training and development of its NCOs. It ensures that irrespective of what happens to junior officers in a rifle company, there will always be NCOs who take on the task of leadership, recognise what needs to be done and do it. Chantry and Lumpkin would each be awarded the MM for gallantry. The two young men were not alone in taking the fight to the enemy, for that night Private Frederick Coppard also did more than was expected of him, as his MM citation reveals:

> Although not a Bren gunner, he seized a light machine gun (LMG) rushed into the open and engaged one of the enemy posts, destroyed it and killed several of the enemy. By his gallant action he undoubtedly saved many lives. During the later phase of the battle he was continually at the forefront of any action.[6]

The task of destroying or capturing the troublesome machine-gun posts took until early morning, but was significantly aided by the arrival at dawn of Churchill tanks from David Dawnay's North Irish Horse. These had left their original positions near Oued Zarga at 0330 hours, and travelled in the dark to arrive on the lower slopes of Nahel at about 0430 hours. To the surprise and concern of the men of the 9th Company 3rd/755th Grenadiers who were defending Nahel, the Churchills drove up the incline of Nahel's southern slopes and on to the crest of the hill by 0500 hours. The Austrian troops had fought courageously to hold their positions, but even they were unwilling to take on tanks. By about 0600 hours, the 5th Buffs had taken their key objectives on Nahel and the defenders retreated from the crest down towards the Oued Bouneb valley and into the gullies of the northern slopes of Nahel. Among the troops leaving the hill were the crews of two 7.5cm infantry guns from the 14th Company which had been located just below the crest of the hill on its northern slope. The threat posed by the guns was real, but they were not used, as the highly effective artillery support landed over 300 shells nearby, dissuading the crews from leaving their trenches and manning the weapons. The arrival of Churchills soon afterwards made their next decision an easy one, and after firing three shots at the tanks they fled down the hill but were later captured. The Austrian defenders fought bravely and many continued to fire their weapons until they were killed, but once the position was taken many decided their war was over and quickly surrendered. The action that night effectively destroyed the 9th Company of the 3rd/755th Grenadiers, also inflicting losses on two other companies. As soon as Nahel was taken, D Company moved down to the Oued Bouneb to try and seize crossings, but was held up by considerable mortar and machine-gun fire from gullies on the hill. After some close fighting and taking of further prisoners, this time from the 12th and 13th Companies of the Grenadiers, opposition died down.

It was probably during this morning action that another young lance corporal showed how important it was to have good junior leaders. While his platoon commander was away attending a briefing, he had left 26-year-old Lance Corporal Walter Weaver temporarily in charge of the platoon. At this point the unit was attacked by German forces; Weaver took command and

---

6   The quotation from Coppard's citation is from TNA WO 373/1, which also has the MM citations for Lumpkin and Chantry.

led a counterattack which stopped the Germans and the platoon took 13 prisoners. Weaver's initiative, courage and leadership in a critical situation earned him a MM. By 1100 hours, Djebel Nahel was secured. Both A and B Companies moved platoons down the slope of the hill to take a small hill, Point 259, to the north-west and also reach the dry river bed of the Oued Bouneb. The arrival of daylight meant any movement towards the Oued Bouneb was overlooked by the Germans, and the companies came under artillery and mortar fire which caused a number of casualties. Several of those wounded might not have lived had it not been for the courage of Private Albert Stern of the battalion, whose citation for his Military Medal recorded: "In spite of heavy mortar and machine gun fire [Stern] continued to evacuate casualties, many of whom would have died otherwise."[7]

The price for taking Djebel Nahel was comparatively low compared to other battles the battalion fought. No precise figure exists for the operation that led to the success signal "Canterbury" being sent to 36th Brigade. The best estimate is that the 5th Buffs lost only one soldier killed, plus at least two officers and up to 40 men wounded in action on 6/7 April. In return, the battalion took approximately 70 prisoners and probably inflicted some 50-70 casualties on the 3rd Battalion of the 755th Grenadier Regiment. The survivors of the three companies of the 3rd Battalion withdrew up the Bed Valley and briefly occupied Djebel Rmel, where its remnants would encounter the Black Watch. Companies of this unit had also been involved in the fight for Mahdi, and with its losses there and at Nahel, it meant that it had been effectively destroyed as a battalion. The capture of Djebel Nahel was a short but bloody fight and an important first step in Operation Sweep. As an operation it was closely linked to and dependent on the attack on Mahdi, for both objectives had to be taken to ensure the security of the other. It pushed the 334th Infantry Division off their position overlooking the Beja-Medjez road. Moreover, it provided the 36th Brigade with access onto the eastern side of the Bouneb and lower Bed Valleys and a base from which to attack its next objectives, including a large hill complex called Mergueb Chaouach. By the late afternoon, Alexander McKechnie was cautiously pleased with the results of his first major attack in the role of CO of the 5th Buffs. However, there was not time for any rest and at 0600 hours on 8 April, the battalion found itself moving on to the recently secured western slopes of Mergueb Chaouach as its start line for another attack.

5.3 The capture of Mergueb Chaouach

The initial attacks of the Battle-Axe Division on 6/7 April breached the first line of German defences by securing the line Djebel Mahdi-Nahel-Outiah-Dourat. This enabled the 78th Division to carry out the next phase of the plan, which was to capture the main peaks, eliminate the Medjez salient and provide a firm base for attacking Tunis. On the left flank, the 38th Irish Brigade had now firmly established itself on Djebel Mahdi and up the Bed Valley. In the centre and on the right of the attack, the 36th and 11th Infantry Brigades now entered into a new and difficult phase of fighting which was soon to require all the strength and resources of the 78th Division. The seizure of Djebel Nahel by the 5th Buffs provided the division with the firm

---

7   The MM citations for Weaver and Stern are from TNA WO 373/1, while details of the action and German forces at Nahel are from the 78th Division intelligence summaries and Account of Operations of 5th Buffs 6-8 April 1943 in TNA WO 175/495 5th Buffs April 1943 WD.

base needed to commence the next stage of operations and take a new key feature, Mergueb Chaouach. Although this significant hill complex shares the same name as the village of Chaouach, it is located some four miles from the village and actually lies only two miles north-east of Djebel Nahel. The tactical importance of this hill area lay in its location. First of all, at over 1,500ft high, it overlooked the Oued Bouneb and Bed river valleys and the objectives being secured in the initial phase of the division's attack, such as Djebel Nahel. Secondly, intelligence had identified it as a likely location of the three German reserve infantry companies in the area. Finally, the capture of Mergueb Chaouach was an essential prerequisite to attacking the primary objectives for Operation Sweep: Points 667 and 624. Point 667 is a high point on a long ridge known as Djebel Bech Chekaoui, and Point 624 is the highest point of Djebel Mansourine. Both were identified as critical terrain objectives in General Evelegh's appreciation, and their capture was crucial in the plan for Operation Sweep. Evelegh himself noted:

> The most dominant feature is the high ground Point 624-Point 667. This ground dominates the mountains around Toukabeur and Chaouach and the valley of the Ferme du Bed and is the key position to any advance into the mountainous area.[8]

The seizure of Mergueb Chaouach was necessary, and was identified as Phase B of Operation Sweep in both the divisional and brigade plans. It could now take place as initial operations by all three brigades of the division had seized the line of high ground from Mahdi to Nahel and across to Djebels Dourat and Outiah. Given its size, height, tactical importance and the possible presence of three German companies, it is perhaps not surprising that Brigadier Howlett assigned a force of two of his three infantry battalions, plus two squadrons of Churchill tanks from the North Irish Horse, to take Mergueb Chaouach. The first of the two infantry units assigned to the task were the 6th West Kents, Howlett's own battalion which he had commanded with distinction until promoted to brigadier. The other battalion that surprisingly formed part of the 36th Infantry Brigade was the 8th Argylls. The Queen's Own Royal West Kent Regiment was the result of an amalgamation in 1881 of two existing regiments of Foot, the 50th and 97th, which can trace their history back to 1755 and 1824 respectively. In common with their sister regiments in the division, the West Kents could look back on a history that included participation in a number of famous battles and campaigns. It could also claim the unusual tradition and distinction of its officers and men having served in the role of marines on Royal Navy (RN) warships. The 6th West Kents were a TA battalion which had fought in France in 1940 and suffered considerable casualties in the BEF's retreat. After evacuation from Dunkirk it had been rebuilt and had undertaken extensive training, which included amphibious operations, before assignment to the 78th Division. Bernard Howlett had assumed command in summer 1942 and led the battalion during the tough and costly battles in the race for Tunis from November-December 1942. When he was promoted to brigadier in December, command of the unit was temporarily assumed by his second-in-command, Major Henry Lovell, and in February 1943 by Lieutenant Colonel Edward Heygate. Unsurprisingly for a battalion raised in Kent, a key characteristic of the battalion was the devotion of both officers and men to that most English of sports, county cricket. The 6th had taken this to a whole new level as it included

---

8   See Evelegh's appreciation.

Bryan Valentine, the county cricket captain for Kent, as one of its officers. Valentine, who served as platoon commander of the anti-tank platoon, added to the laurels he won as a cricketer when he was awarded the MC for his bravery in November 1942. The early months of 1943 saw the battalion (and the brigade) supporting French troops near Robaa some 50 miles south of Medjez el Bab. It returned to man positions near its old battle ground at Djebel Aboid in the middle of March and took part in a counterattack to retake positions near Sedjenane. Like other units in the division, the 6th West Kents was an experienced if rather tired battalion when it was assigned by Howlett to take Mergueb Chaouach, having been in the front line almost continually for some five months.[9]

The sister unit of the 6th West Kents was the 8th Argylls, which in common with most infantry battalions within the 78th Division had a long history, though the regiment was actually formed only in 1881 by combining the 91st and 93rd Highlanders. These two regiments, however, could both trace their lineage back to 1759 and had numerous battle honours. The 8th was also a TA battalion that had served in the BEF in the famous 51st Highland Division. Unlike many of the units in that ill-fated formation, the 8th was not trapped at St Valery and captured. It did, however, have a very difficult time, and less than 100 officers and men from the original battalion were evacuated from France. The battalion was rapidly rebuilt using reinforcements from the two regions from which it usually recruited: the rugged wooded coast, hills and islands of Argyll and the bare, heather-strewn moors and volcanic mountains of Sutherland. The men who formed the battalion were tough, quiet and undemonstrative, largely fishermen and farmers in peacetime. Yet they were all descended from close-knit Highland clans who knew each other and their families well. This meant that when roused through drink or anger, or both, they exhibited all the warrior characteristics that have long made Scottish Highlanders feared as soldiers around the world. The next two-and-a-half years were devoted to hard and extensive training across Britain under its new CO, Lieutenant Colonel J.G. "Jock" McKellar, who took command in July 1940. His personality, background and style of command were perfectly suited to command of what he called his jocks. Jock McKellar was a tough, calm, mature and cheerful but direct regular soldier, and was probably more than anyone responsible for making the battalion into the highly effective fighting unit it had become by April 1943. He personally shaped the unit during training and led it during five months of difficult fighting across northern Tunisia. During those months, a 40-year-old accredited war correspondent, Alexander Austin, who held the rank of wing commander, spent significant time with the battalion and gained its trust. The resulting portrait of the 8th Argylls in the front line provides an invaluable insight into life in the unit at that time and is captured in Austin's excellent memoir, *Birth of an Army*. Austin had reported on the Battle of Britain and landed with the Commandos at Dieppe before joining the First Army in Tunisia. Sadly, his life and a brilliant future career was to be cut short far too soon when he was killed with two other correspondents in September 1943 just north of Salerno in Italy.

For the first five months under McKellar's command, the battalion became something of a fire brigade unit, being moved constantly from one crisis to another, suffering significant

9   The profile of the 6th West Kents is based on P. Bryan, *Wool, War and Westminster* (Staplehurst: Spellmount, 1993); Chaplin, *The Queen's Own*; details in the Army list and www.unithistories.com (accessed 27 January 2018). Valentine and Howlett's cricketing records are available on the cricketing site www.espncricinfo.com (accessed 15 January 2018).

casualties and perhaps having only five days of rest in five months. During this time, and despite constant operations, McKellar managed to win and retain the affection and respect of every man in the battalion. His sterling qualities had not escaped his superior's attention, and he was not fated to lead the unit during Operation Sweep and at Longstop Hill. In early March he was selected to attend a senior staff course in England and was relieved as CO, initially by his second-in-command, Major Webb. Webb was wounded during fighting near Sedjenane in March and his place was taken by Lieutenant Colonel Colin McNabb in early April. In view of the key role played by the Argylls in taking Longstop Hill some three weeks later, it is perhaps only fair to recognise the vital contribution McKellar played in creating the unit that McNabb inherited. The battalion that subsequently captured Longstop, against almost impossible odds, was in all respects the product of McKellar's efforts, though as we shall see McNabb would lead it gallantly. The role played by McKellar in leading the unit prior to Longstop has almost universally been ignored in many accounts of the battle. However the officers and men who captured Longstop were trained and moulded in McKellar's image.[10]

The 39-year-old ex-Seaforth Highlander who now took command was, however, no lightweight, nor did he lack fighting spirit. Colin McNabb came to the unit after having served in the role of chief staff officer to General Kenneth Anderson at First Army HQ. According to those who met him, McNabb shared similar personality traits to his boss and was a dour, quiet but absolutely fearless Scot keen to get to grips with the Germans. He had requested command of an infantry battalion, and was so keen to do so that he willingly accepted a drop in two ranks from brigadier to lieutenant colonel. McNabb somehow managed to persuade his boss to let him take command of the Argylls, though it meant that Anderson lost a valued subordinate who had been with him for five months.

The task faced by 36th Brigade was no easy one, for Mergueb Chaouach is a large, rugged hill mass which was one of the features that dominated the Oued Bouneb and Maiou river valleys and the local area (see Map 5). This complex of hills, rising to over 400 metres, sprawls across an area some two miles wide and one mile deep to the north-east of Djebel Nahel. It also lies to the north of Point 512 and is the most obvious western approach to reach Points 667 and 624. The plan to take Mergueb Chaouach assigned Edward Heygate and his unit to initially move up the Oued Maiou riverbed, which lies on the north-east side of the Djebel Nahel hill complex and climb up a long western slope. Colin McNabb and his Argylls were assigned a separate approach route, moving up the Oued Bouneb riverbed to the south of Mergueb Chaouach and attacking up its slopes. The 6th West Kents had managed to have three days of rest before it moved to its assembly area north-east of Oued Zarga on the night of 6 April, arriving there at 0430 hours. It spent the morning laid up in this area and received intermittent artillery fire which caused a few casualties. At midday, the battalion moved off to carry out its approach north along a dry river valley before attacking its designated objective on Mergueb Chaouach. The 6th West Kents continued to come under shellfire during this period and was also delayed

10   Details of the 8th Argylls are derived from Malcolm, *History of the Argylls*, and Lieutenant Colonel J. McKellar, *Account of Operations of 8th Argylls in Tunisia* (unpublished memoirs held in the archives of the Argyll and Sutherland Highlanders, Stirling). Another valuable source on the 8th Argylls is Austin, *Birth of an Army*. Details of the battalion's operations and attack on Mergueb Chaouach are from TNA WO 175/491 April 1943 WD, which includes a document entitled "8th Argylls in 78th Division's attack on Mergueb Chaouach".

by booby traps, all of which led to further casualties. After a brief rest near Teboursouk, the 8th Argylls under McNabb had spent the night of 6-7 April travelling in lorries to an area near Oued Zarga, where they arrived at 0430 hours. The battalion took losses even before it started its main attack, for the rifle companies were observed by the Germans during their march to its lying up position (LUP). B and R companies were shelled and lost an officer killed and two soldiers wounded. The LUP was an area designated for the battalion to use prior to its main attack, and the 8th Argylls stayed here until 1300 hours on 7 April awaiting news that the 5th Buffs had taken Djebel Nahel. Once this had been confirmed, it moved forward to its starting position for the climb up the rugged Mergueb Chaouach. The move was led by R Company, which acquired this letter as its title since it was originally a reinforcement company after the battalion's heavy losses in December 1942. Unfortunately, R Company was mortared and ran into German S mines on the way to its start line near the Oued Bouneb. It suffered several casualties, so McNabb decided to send the rest of the battalion on a route slightly to the west to cross the Oued Bouneb river bed. Sadly, as B Company led the way they too ran into S mines and lost three men killed and seven wounded. The long approach march, combined with the hold-ups imposed by mines and mortars, caused a delay in start time for the attack of the two battalions, and a new zero hour was set for 1700 hours. The rugged terrain and other problems meant that the battalions were unable to meet even this new time.

The need to seize Mergueb Chaouach before dark was clearly understood by the officer in command of the two squadrons of the North Irish Horse assigned to assist this attack, Major Eugene Strickland. The crews of the Churchill tanks in A and B Squadrons of the North Irish had already had a pretty busy day by late afternoon. It had started at 0330 hours with a move to their start line for the attack on Nahel and their successful support of the 5th Buffs in that attack, so by late afternoon they had been active for 14 hours. Nonetheless, Strickland embraced the ethos imbued by David Dawnay into his unit, of finding ways to support the infantry even if it meant taking an unconventional approach to his mission. He therefore decided to commence his approach to the hill, even though his sole infantry support at this time comprised only a section of 10 men from the Argylls in Bren Gun Carriers. Strickland and his squadrons of Churchills crossed the river bed and moved up to a set of farm buildings known as Italian Farm. The tanks waited for the infantry for an hour, and when they had still not arrived Strickland didn't hesitate: at about 1730 hours he decided to move out on his own and attack up the hill without the two infantry battalions. Despite hardly being a text book manoeuvre, as tanks were not supposed to be unsupported, his idea worked. The sight of Strickland's Churchills climbing up slopes, which the Germans thought were impassable for tanks, unnerved the troops on Mergueb Chaouach. Strickland's tanks slowly climbed their way up the hill, wiping out any machine-gun posts they spotted along the way. As the Churchills ground their way up the hill and tackled the steeper slopes, the horrified Germans realised the tanks were not going to be prevented from reaching their positions. These defenders, who were primarily from a *Marsch* (reinforcement) battalion, quickly decided that discretion was the better part of valour and fled their positions. A troop of tanks was held up almost at the top of the hill by a deep ravine. This was found to house the German headquarters, whose staff officers fled so quickly that they left secret operational orders and radios strewn about in the area where they had set up residence.

The result of Strickland's efforts was that when the 6th West Kents and the 8th Argylls began their final attacks at about 1700 hours, they encountered very limited resistance from the Germans on the hill, apart from occasional sniper fire. Y Company of the Argylls moved up to reinforce the tanks, and the remainder of the Argylls and 6th West Kents made their way up to the top of the hill to help consolidate the position. While climbing towards their objective, the 6th West Kents noticed that they were about to be attacked from the air by *Stuka* dive bombers. Fortunately, a number of Spitfires arrived and forced the *Stukas* to jettison their bombs and flee. At least one of the *Stukas* was shot down in flames and another crashed, and the battalion later took prisoner a badly burned *Stuka* pilot.[11] Mergueb Chaouach was officially described as secured by about 1900 hours that evening. Contrary to expectations and the available intelligence from division, Mergueb Chaouach was not heavily defended by the Germans and casualties were comparatively low. However, to the 8th Argylls, who suffered a total of 12 dead and 28 wounded during the period of the operation, the term "light" may have had a hollow ring. While the West Kents did not come under much direct fire on their approach to Mergueb Chaouach, bombing by Stukas and artillery fire nonetheless took their toll. The battalion's casualties for that day are not formally recorded, but it is likely it lost at least 30 men to indirect fire. The battalion had a total of seven men killed from 7-9 April, with seven officers wounded and 42 other ranks admitted to medical units from 6-10 April. The capture of Mergueb Chaouach was, however, a significant tactical success for the 78th Division, as it removed a key defensivee position from German hands. The large hill overlooked Djebel Mahdi, the Bed Valley and the hills to the south, and had enabled German mortar and artillery observers to direct fire on troops in the valley. In the hands of the 78th Division, it now could provide an excellent position to direct similar fire on German positions to the north and east. It also provided an excellent base from which to launch attacks on other peaks that lay to the east.

5.4 Taking Hill 667 - Djebel Bech Chekaoui

The old saying "there is no rest for the wicked" could well have been applied to the situation confronting the 5th Buffs at dawn on 8 April, although in fairness the only wickedness exhibited by the battalion recently had been that shown to the king's enemies. It was, however, true that the unit had received precious little rest. Although the battalion had been constantly on the move and engaged in fighting for two days, it was up, ready and on the move by 0600 hours on 8 April. To add insult to injury, neither the unit's rations nor water had arrived by the time it started its move for the rendezvous point for its next attack. It was a fairly tired, rather hungry and thirsty set of infantry soldiers that prepared to attack their next objective, Djebel Bech Chekaoui. This long craggy ridge was one of the objectives for the next stage in the divisional plan. That plan had always envisaged that once Mergueb Chaouach had been captured it would be used as a good location from which to attack Point 667, which lay on the eastern end of Djebel Bech Chekaoui (see Map 7).

Djebel Bech Chekaoui stands high above the surrounding terrain, with a small summit area and steep slopes. The mountainous ridge rapidly gains height in just over a kilometre, from 585 metres in the west to 667 metres in the east. To the south-east is a small hill some 624 metres high called Djebel Mansourine. Bech Chekaoui is separated from the highest point on

---

11   Details of A and B Squadrons' operations at Mergueb Chaouach are from TNA WO 175/294, 1 North Irish Horse April 1943 WD, and *Battle Report North Irish*, pp.15-16; Doherty, *North Irish Horse*, pp.97-99; and Intelligence summaries in 78 Division WD April 1943. The JU-87 attack was the same one described in more detail in Chapter 4.

Mergueb Chaouach (Point 492) by a narrow and tactically difficult approach route, which rises first to Djebel Fernane at 541 metres and next to the start of Chekaoui itself. The capture of Bech Chekaoui and Point 667 would help remove any threats to the left flank of 11th Brigade as it turned eastwards from Djebel Outiah, Dourat and Point 343 to capture Point 512 and onwards to the hilltop villages of Toukabeur and Chaouach. The long thin ridge of Bech Chekaoui was also tactically important as it was higher than the two villages and could be used for observation and, if occupied by the Germans, would pose a threat to the troops who held Mergueb Chaouach. The height and all-round view provided by this mountain made it a location to be coveted by any artillery forward observer. The hill also overlooked the dry river valley the Oued Kranga further east, which ran from north to south straight down to the village of Chaouach. On the other side of the Kranga were the three key objectives for the second stage of the 78th Division's attack in Operation Sweep.

Evelegh had always identified Djebels Bou Diss, el Ang and Tanngoucha as the final and crucial objectives in the wider plan to outflank German defences in the Medjerda valley. Since the other two battalions of the 36th Brigade had just captured Mergueb Chaouach, the job of attacking Point 667 fell to the 5th Buffs, who had only just completed the capture of Djebel Nahel. The battalion began this operation at 0600 hours on 8 April by marching from Nahel across the Oued Bouneb to an initial assembly area on a track at the bottom of the western end of Mergueb Chaouach. The CO of the 5th Buffs, "Ginger" McKechnie, decided to approach Point 667 using a long and indirect route that required an extended march north to a junction of two wadis just to the east of Djebel Mahdi and well to the north of Mergueb Chaouach. The battalion would move north-east to its start line on a track running north-south, before moving east on to wider slopes that gradually rise to approach Djebel Bech Chekaoui from hills to its north-west. (See Map 7) It is not entirely clear why this long and complicated route was chosen, especially as it had risks, since parts of Djebel Mahdi remained in the hands of the Germans on the morning of 8 April and the battalion's initial approach would be in view of observers. It may be that this route was selected because it provided a less obvious and difficult one from which to attack Point 667, rather than through the lines of the battalions on Mergueb Chaouach. Another reason may have been that such a route enabled the 5th Buffs to be supported in the initial stages of its advance by Churchill tanks of A Squadron of the North Irish Horse, who were assigned to this task. If the Buffs had taken a route directly up the slopes of Mergueb Chaouach towards Point 667, it would have been difficult even for the adventurous North Irish Horse to have supported the unit.

Both the 5th Buffs and A Squadron's busy squadron commander, Major Strickland, once again started their day early. The main body of the battalion marched from the bivouac, where it had spent an uncomfortable night, to a location it would use as the FUP for its attack under the leadership of its adjutant Captain Collins. Collins was in charge as McKechnie and all of his company commanders had gone ahead of the battalion to conduct a reconnaissance from a good vantage point on the hillside. During its march along the valley, the battalion came under both mortar and machine-gun fire from nearby gullies, causing some casualties. The forward companies, led by their remaining officers, engaged the Germans until the CO and the company commanders returned soon after. According to the battalion history, McKechnie and his officers had hitched a lift on the turrets of Strickland's Churchill tanks which had started moving up the valley. The precise truth of this story is difficult to determine, since records conflict about the relative progress of the two units. It is, however, clear that Strickland and his tanks were delayed by the need to lift mines at the Oued Djeb, one of the river beds on the route north. It seems probable that one of his troops moved ahead and was available to support the forward companies when they were pinned down. The fire from multiple high-explosive rounds and Besa machine guns helped the Buffs to overcome any resistance. The German troops were forced to withdraw after losing dead, wounded and prisoners. The battalion resumed its march, and soon after the rest of Strickland's squadron arrived to accompany them. Fortunately, the Germans on the north end of Mahdi were too busy to bother the 5th Buffs when it carried on its march north. However, it seems that British forward observers mistook Strickland's tanks for German ones, and so for a period he and his tank crews had the uncomfortable experience of being shelled by their own artillery. It appears that FOOs from the left artillery group, which included 77th and 102nd Field Artillery Regiments and Spike Milligan's 56th Heavy Regiment, were probably the guilty parties. The 5th Buffs only narrowly avoided a similar fate: by this time they had arrived at a junction of two wadis, a waypoint on its route, and the nearby gullies provided useful cover when British artillery fire was switched briefly from the tanks to their location. It is unclear if their own gunners inflicted any casualties on the 5th Buffs during this unfortunate instance of friendly fire. Strickland's tanks survived the friendly barrage and positioned themselves to protect the 5th Buffs from a German tank attack down the Bed Valley.

These various delays meant that despite the early start, the planned start time of the attack, 1130 hours, had to be delayed one hour. By 1230 hours, the 5th Buffs were at the start line on the track, and after receiving rather more welcome support from the Royal Regiment of Artillery, in the form of an artillery concentration on the slopes ahead of them, began their attack.[12] The unit moved off, with C and B Companies leading the advance, and the headquarters with D and A Companies behind. The officer commanding C Company, Acting Captain Gordon Downes from Buckinghamshire, was a veteran in more ways than one. He had been commissioned a lieutenant from an Officer Cadet Training Unit (OCTU) at the grand old age of 36, was commissioned into the 5th Buffs in 1940 and sailed with them in November 1942 to North Africa. Downes quickly demonstrated his leadership ability, and in less than two years found himself in command of a company when he arrived in Tunisia. He had led the company through a series of difficult actions and was viewed as a veteran company commander by April 1943. He had not only survived, when some of his fellow officers had been killed, but at 38 was the "old man" among the younger new company commanders. At his age, and married, Downes probably need not have sought such an active fighting role, but had nonetheless done so.[13] It was probably no coincidence that McKechnie placed C Company and Downes in the van of his attack, as both had proven themselves time and again on the battlefield. It had been C Company, as well as B Company, that had led the successful attack on Nahel. Soon after starting their climb up the slopes of the hill, both C and B Company met opposition on the lower slopes of their objectives, which they rapidly overcame. Mopping-up parties provided by the rest of the battalion took several prisoners: these included *Hauptmann* Antritter, the CO of the 3rd Battalion of the 755th Grenadier Regiment. Antritter's unit had been constantly under

12   The story of the attack on Point 667 is from the 5th Buffs' April 1943 WD and C.R.B. Knight, *Historical Records*, pp.200-02. The friendly fire incident is from the *Battle Report North Irish*, pp.16-18, and TNA WO 175/338 132nd Field Regiment April 1943 WD.
13   Details of Captain Downes are from the Army List, *The Dragon – The Regimental Paper of the Buffs*, February 1941 issue, and Knight, *Historical Records*.

attack since 7 April, and had become so worn down that he had put his battalion staff into the firing line before he was captured. Prior to their capture, Antritter and his staff did not even have time to burn valuable confidential orders, so these were found and quickly forwarded to intelligence staff at division, where they proved useful. The 5th Buffs continued its attack and now moved up gradual slopes covered in bean and corn fields. By 1630 hours, Downes and his company, who had been leading the attack, had arrived on their objective, and by 1800 hours the rest of the battalion had joined them. A Company was sent on to secure Point 624, Djebel Mansourine, just to the south.

The success of the attack on these objectives owed much to the leadership of Downes as a company commander, combined with that of the senior NCOs in the 5th Buffs and the courage of individual soldiers in the rifle companies, including C Company. The importance of courageous leadership to success in battle, shown time and again by NCOs in infantry battalions in the Battle of the Peaks, cannot be understated. During the operations from 6-9 April, the distinguished conduct of two individuals in the battalion provided a perfect example of their courage and leadership.[14] The first of these was Sergeant Clarence Jeffery, who initially distinguished himself during the Buffs' approach march to Bech Chekaoui, when its forward companies were surprised and engaged on the morning of 8 April. Sergeant Jeffery was ordered by his platoon commander to flank the Germans and deal with them. Jeffery led the way and, followed by two others, crawled behind a sniper and forced him to surrender. He went straight to a German mortar position held by seven men and forced them to surrender too. Jeffery and his small group brought back eight prisoners, along with a mortar, machine gun and rifles. The following day, when the Acting CSM of his company was injured, Jeffery took over the role and was a great inspiration to his men in the company. He worked untiringly throughout the whole time his company, C Company, was on Point 667. Sergeant Jeffery's personal conduct and gallantry during the whole operation was of such a high standard that McKechnie had no hesitation in recommending him for an immediate award of the Distinguished Conduct Medal (DCM), which he quickly received. Many ordinary soldiers had demonstrated courage throughout the last three days. However, one private soldier's performance was considered unusual. According to the citation for his MM:

> Private Sydney Reed showed no signs of fear throughout the whole battle between the 7th and 9th April [sic]. When the battalion was temporarily held up on a track west of Mergueb Chaouach he went forward with an officer in full view of the enemy and shot at several enemy posts, and on one occasion when he was firing forward he walked straight at a machine gun post firing his rifle and put the post out of action.
>
> On another occasion he had to be called back. Throughout the operation he showed complete disregard for his own safety and set a magnificent example to his fellow men.[15]

Sydney Reed's almost suicidal bravery in the face of enemy fire demonstrated that ordinary soldiers could also inspire others in battle.

14   The story of *Hauptman* Antritter is from Intelligence Summary No. 126 8 April in TNA WO 175/82 April 1943 WD.
15   Both Jeffery's DCM citation and Reed's MM citation are from TNA WO 373/1.

Meanwhile, down in the Bed Valley, Strickland and his tanks continued to protect the flanks of the 5th Buffs' attack. Early in the afternoon, he and his tanks were joined on the south side of the Djebel Djeb by B Squadron of the regiment. Both squadrons were targeted by *Stuka* dive-bombers, being bombed and machine-gunned on three occasions in the afternoon. At last light, when the Buffs were firmly established on Point 667, the troops of A Squadron were withdrawn and spent the night in defensive positions on the western slope of Mergueb Chaouach. Strickland and A Squadron had been fortunate, despite being shelled by their own artillery, that of the Germans and also bombed by *Stukas*, since only two troopers had been wounded during the day.

The men of the 5th Buffs may have hoped that after nearly three days of tiring activity they might have a more restful time while securing Point 667, but this was not to be. The battalion had hardly managed to dig in on the mountain when at about midnight a 20-man German patrol approached the position and disturbed everyone's sleep. The patrol was driven off, but its purpose had been to learn about the strength and positions of the unit. The outcome was that the 5th Buffs' positions came under mortar and artillery fire, followed by a company-sized attack at dawn from a fresh German unit that had only just arrived in North Africa, the A-24 *Marsch* Battalion. *Marsch* Battalions were ad hoc units formed rapidly from available officers and men as reinforcements. Usually they were absorbed into existing units, but sometimes, when there was a crisis, they were committed to action as a complete unit. The German company used the cover of thick scrub to attack C Company's positions. The attack was vigorous and pressed home with courage, and was stopped only after close-in fighting. Tragically, it was during this fighting that Captain Gordon Downes was killed. The loss of Downes was a significant blow to his company and the 5th Buffs, but he had trained it well and his remaining platoon officer and one of his best SNCOs ensured the German company was forced to retreat. The individual in question was Sergeant Thomas Dobbins, and when two platoons lost their commanders he assumed command of both of them. He personally led the combined group in a successful bayonet charge against a large number of Germans, which saved the position. Dobbins was injured during his charge, but his initiative and personal gallantry that morning had been critical. The citation for the award of Dobbins' DCM noted that: "Throughout the whole battle he was a great source of inspiration to all the men under his command."[16] Although the DCM had been instituted in 1855 and had frequently been awarded to recognise gallantry of this nature, to many amongst the general public, the use of the words "Distinguished Conduct" to describe the medal had led to a misleading impression it was awarded for good service. The reality could not have been further from the truth, for until 1992 the DCM was the second-highest award for bravery that could be bestowed on NCOs in the British Army, one that was only awarded when a soldier's conduct did not merit a recommendation for a VC.

The soldiers of C Company received important assistance from 17th Field Regiment of the Royal Artillery during the German attack on the early morning of 9 April. This was provided first of all by defensive artillery fire and secondly by the personal intervention of two members of the FOO party that directed this fire. The FOO for the 5th Buffs that day was Temporary Major Donald Robertson, and his small party included Sergeant Norman Fowles. Robertson and his

16   Quotation from George Brown, *For Distinguished Conduct in the Field: The Register of the DCM* (Langley: Western Canadian Distributors, 1993), p.256.

group accompanied the 5th Buffs during their attack on Bech Chekaoui, and on their arrival established an observation post on the highest part of Point 667. At about midnight a strong German patrol approached Point 667 and drew close to the party's position. Sergeant Fowles showed complete disregard for his own safety by using his Tommy (Thompson submachine) gun and other infantry weapons to fire at the Germans who were closing on his party, forcing them to withdraw. The following morning, a stronger counterattack was launched on the 5th Buffs, and specifically C Company's positions. This was where the FOO party was located, resulted in casualties among its platoon officers and left some men without a leader. Donald Robertson noticed this and organized a group of 15 men, including his own party, which he personally led to help counterattack the German force. Robertson used a captured machine gun until that jammed, and then a rifle, with which he accounted for three Germans. He was assisted by Sergeant Fowles during the fighting, the latter personally killing several Germans. This action demonstrated an important truth that artillery observation parties often found themselves in the thick of the action and sometimes had to provide fire-support in a slightly more violent manner than simply directing their guns. During the next 24 hours ,Robertson, Fowles and the rest of the party continued to man their exposed position, despite heavy shelling. Fowles further distinguished himself that night when he twice ventured on his own out of the defensive position into no man's land to repair the OP party's telephone line link. The gallantry and dedication to duty exhibited by Major Robertson and Sergeant Fowles did not go unnoticed by the 5th Buffs, who in turn reported it to their regimental CO, Lieutenant Colonel Thomas. He had already been aware of the sterling qualities of these two men, which according to him they had demonstrated throughout the campaign and he needed little encouragement to recommend Robertson for a MC and Fowles a MM, which they were duly awarded. After the A-24 *Marsch* Battalion's attack on Point 667 was repulsed, the now-battered C Company came under intense shelling during the morning and early afternoon.[17] Since it had lost so many leaders, and with casualties mounting, it was decided to reinforce the company, and two companies (A and B) were moved forward to its aid. However, the Germans had shot their bolt and no further attack was forthcoming.

During 9 April, the North Irish Horse had also been busy. Two troops of Churchill tanks, commanded by Lieutenant Hern from A Squadron, had been sent forward and had taken up positions to cover the Bed Valley, probably on the slopes of the hill used by the Buffs to attack Point 667. They saw and fired on some German tanks that were probing south. Meanwhile, David Dawnay and Eugene Strickland had been active, and at midday had carried out a reconnaissance on foot of the same area. As a result, the tanks of B Squadron were dispatched to cross the Oued Djeb, move up the northern slopes of the same hill and take up hull-down positions. At 1700 hours that day, Dawnay had been visiting his troops when he saw what he reported as eight German Tiger tanks plus several Mark III and IV tanks. Dawnay called for artillery fire on the tanks, and one Mark IV tank was claimed as damaged. Although Dawnay was an excellent commander, it is questionable that he actually saw this many Tiger tanks. There was only one Tiger battalion in Tunisia and probably less than 20 operational Tiger tanks left in the country, and the vast majority of these were south of the Medjerda river. The North Irish

---

17   The story of Robertson and Fowles' actions on Point 667 is from their MC and MM citations in WO 373/1.

were continuing to add to their reputation as a unit keen to go to considerable risk to fulfill their mission of providing tank support to infantry units and uphold their unofficial motto.[18]

After four days of moving and fighting, the battalion was finally relieved in the early hours of 10 April by Lieutenant Colonel Heygate and the 6th West Kents. The battalion moved back to a bivouac on the western slopes of the Mergueb Chaouach to finally get some well-earned rest before their next operation. McKechnie's battalion was in sore need of time to recuperate and replace casualties. While Ginger McKechnie was dealing with this task, he was also kept busy writing citations for gallantry awards for his men. However, their CO's own performance on the battlefield had much impressed his brigadier, Bernard Howlett. The latter expected and set a high standard for command, so it was to McKechnie's great credit that Howlett strongly recommended him for the award of a DSO for his leadership on Nahel and Point 667. In his citation, Howlett noted that his leadership on 8 April when the battalion was under heavy fire was particularly important. When Lieutenant General Allfrey approved the recommendation for McKechnie's DSO, he unusually made a note that despite having taken over a battalion which had an unlucky run, his leadership had turned out a very good battalion. The price for taking both Nahel and Djebel Bech Chekaoui and Point 624 had been considerable. The 5th Buffs' history suggests that the unit lost 22 men killed and 102 wounded over the three days of the battle. It seems likely that this figure was actually much higher and that the battalion lost almost 25 percent of its strength in these attacks. A combination of records from other sources suggests that the 5th Buffs lost 26 killed and 209 wounded in this period. The battalion's officer casualties were considerable, with at least eight junior officers wounded sufficiently to spend significant time in hospital and eight others evacuated.[19] Arguably the most serious loss to the battalion was that of its well-respected and gallant C Company commander Gordon Downes. One would like to think that the leadership and gallantry shown by Downes on Nahel, on Point 667 and during several tough battles from November-April would have been recognised by a significant gallantry award. Unfortunately events don't always turn out that way, and the only recognition he received was a belated Mention in Dispatches in September 1943. It is not always the case that gallant men are remembered, and Downes was a brave man who left behind a wife, Pamela, and deserves more recognition. Downes is buried in a small CWGC cemetery in the centre of the town of Beja. He is not alone, and perhaps fittingly is surrounded by 10 men from the East Kents who were also killed during 8-9 April.[20]

The seizure of Point 667, the second-highest mountain in northern Tunisia and a key tactical feature, was an important blow to the defensive plans of Major General Weber, commander of the 334th Infantry Division. When it was accompanied by the subsequent capture of Point 512, Toukabeur and Chaouach to the south by 11th Brigade, which we will describe in the next chapter, it successfully completed the first phase of Vyvyan Evelegh's original plan for Operation Sweep. The period from 7–10 April saw Brigadier Bernard Howlett's 36th Brigade

---

18   The story of the North Irish Horse and the "Tiger" tanks is from *Battle Report North Irish Horse*, pp.16-18.

19   Allfrey's comment about Alexander McKechnie is from remarks on the citation for his DSO in TNA WO 373/1.

20   Information on Gordon Downes' family is from the CWGC gravestone. Downes lies in the same cemetery as Heaver Allen. Downes' Mention in Dispatches is from the *London Gazette* of 23 September 1943 and cited in the *Dragon; the Regimental Paper of the Buffs* from October 1943.

and its attached units conduct a successful series of operations in difficult terrain against a competent foe and seize all its assigned objectives. The brigade also captured in excess of 300 German prisoners and inflicted significant damage on at least one of the battalions of the 334th Infantry Division.[21]

---

21   The number of German POWs is based on V Corps and 78th Division Intelligence summaries and war diaries.

6

Operation Sweep and the 11th Brigade's Attack on the Right

6.1 "Copper" Cass and the 11th Infantry Brigade

The task of assaulting the German defences on the right flank of the attack during Operation Sweep fell to the 11th Infantry Brigade, a regular unit commanded by Brigadier Edward Cass known to his contemporaries as "Copper" because of his crop of red hair. Unlike its fellow brigades, the 11th lacked a specific regional identify. It was composed of two regular and one TA infantry battalions from all parts of England. These were respectively the 1st Battalion of the East Surrey Regiment (1st East Surreys) commanded by Lieutenant Colonel William Wilberforce and the 2nd Battalion of the Lancashire Fusiliers (2nd Lancs Fusiliers), which was commanded by Lieutenant Colonel Sydney Linden-Kelly. Last but not least was the 5th Battalion the Northamptonshire Regiment (5th Northants), whose CO was 44-year-old Lieutenant Colonel Arthur Crook. At the outbreak of the Second World War, the 11th Brigade had originally formed part of the 4th Division, and its brigadier from 1938-40 was the future First Army commander, Kenneth Anderson. The brigade and its battalions had experienced hard fighting in Belgium and France before their withdrawal from the beaches of Dunkirk. Anderson's performance in command of the 11th Brigade during the retreat had impressed his corps commander, Lieutenant General Alan Brooke, who took command of the British Army in 1941. It resulted in Anderson being assigned commander of the 4th Infantry Division during the last few days of the retreat and afterwards an appointment to lead a corps. Anderson knew the brigade and its accompanying units quite well. It could be said that his rise to command was in part due to the efforts of 11th Brigade. After Dunkirk, the 11th Brigade had formed part of the counter-invasion force, completed amphibious training and was assigned to the newly formed 78th Division in 1942. The commander, Brigadier "Copper" Cass, had served in India and in 1940 in Norway, before assuming command of the brigade in 1942. The brigade had landed in Algeria in November 1942 and taken a key role in the race to Tunis. In early December 1942, the 1st East Surreys and 2nd Hampshires (the latter detached from 1st Guards Brigade) had gallantly but unsuccessfully defended the key towns of Djedeida and Tebourba. There they had suffered significant losses as a result of the German superiority in both airpower and tanks. During the winter months, all three battalions had spent almost all their time in the front line and acting as reinforcements in threatened areas. Their front-line experience included time in the Medjez el Bab sector, where they had gained much useful knowledge of the local terrain.[1]

---

1   The story of the 11th Infantry Brigade and its CO is from Blaxland, *Plain Cook*, p.87, the Army List

The divisional plan assigned 11th Brigade the mission of seizing Point 512, a lozenge-like hill (see Plates I and II) to the west of the villages of Toukabeur and Chaouach (see Plate II). These two old Berber villages were perched on a mountain and overlooked the whole Medjez el Bab area. The villages and Point 512 had originally been taken and held by the 78th Division, but were lost in the German attacks in March. The villages and Point 512 provided the Germans with excellent locations from which to observe and shell any movement north of the Medjez-Oued Zarga road. Point 512 posed a significant threat to the operations of the division, especially the 11th Brigade's attacks, and had to be taken. In order to capture this feature, Cass and his brigade needed to clear the first set of hills located to the north and east of Oued Zarga and the road to Medjez.

Once Djebels Oubirah, Outiah and Dourat had been taken, the next phase of the attack could begin and the units of Cass's brigade would swing around to the east to attack and capture Point 512. This hill dominated the area around Toukabeur and Chaouach, and offered the ideal jumping-off point for attacks to recapture the two tactically important villages. It is probable that this tactical approach was adopted by the divisional commander and Cass, as it avoided the need for a frontal attack directly from the south and east against Point 512 and these two strongpoints. Both villages were perched on a high ridge that provided the Germans with direct observation of the Medjez el Bab area. They were likely to be much more strongly held than the ridges the unit was assigned to attack further west. It is almost certain that an attack directly from the south would have met with far stronger resistance and led to much greater casualties. The adoption of this more indirect approach may have been influenced by the costly failure of a raid on the feature known as Recce Ridge to the east of Toukabeur and Chaouach in late March 1943 by the Irish Guards. That operation had led to the death or capture of its entire No. 2 Company. Irrespective of the reason, Evelegh's plan proposed a flanking attack to seize the two villages and the 11th Brigade got the job of carrying it out. The brigade's detailed plan (Operation Order 21) assumed an attack in two phases. It is worth noting that the actual aim of that plan was the specific capture of Point 512. The seizure of the Berber villages was not an objective in the brigade plan, although the divisional operational order specifically required the capture of the Chaouach-Toukabeur area in Phase D of the attack. This fact may explain a degree of confusion that occurred about who was to attack and take the villages during later operations. Phase A of the brigade attack would take place on the night of 6/7 April. The 1st East Surreys would seize Djebel Outiah on the left while the 5th Northants attacked and captured Djebel Dourat, a rugged hill located about a half-mile south east of Outiah, and also a small hill known only as Point 343 on its right.[2]

In line with the wider divisional plan, the attack would receive considerable artillery and tank support. The CO of 138th Field Regiment, Lieutenant Colonel Clive Usher, had control of 40 25-pounder field guns from his own regiment and the 19th Field Artillery Regiment. Both infantry battalions would also benefit, once daylight arrived, from the direct support of Churchill tanks from A and C Squadrons of the 142nd Regiment of the RAC. A part of the

and TNA WO 175/196 11 Infantry Brigade November 1942 - April 1943 WD.

2   See Operation Order No. 21 dated 5 April 1943 in TNA WO 175/196 11 Infantry Brigade April 1943 WD for the brigade plan, and also the 78th Division Operation Order for Operation Sweep. The story of the tragic attack by the Irish Guards on Recce Ridge on 30 March 1943 is detailed in D.J. Fitzgerald's *The Irish Guards in the Second World War* (Aldershot: Gale and Polden, 1949), pp.139-42.

25th Tank Brigade, a separate armoured brigade designed for infantry support, the 142nd had been formed by converting the 7th Battalion of the Suffolk Regiment in 1941 to a tank regiment. The original CO of the 142nd, Lieutenant Colonel Maxwell, had demonstrated such ability that he was promoted to command the 25th Tank Brigade. Lieutenant Colonel Alec Birkbeck of the Royal Tank Regiment took his place in the summer of 1942. The brigade, which included the North Irish Horse and the 142nd Regiment, arrived in Tunisia in February 1943. After a difficult first engagement, the 142nd Regiment under Birkbeck learned quickly and in February 1943, at Bou Arada, its C Squadron destroyed several German tanks and helped stop a major counterattack. By the time it took part in Operation Sweep, the unit was well prepared for the challenges of supporting infantry units in rugged terrain.

One relevant feature of the 11th Brigade plan was that it did not require the capture of Djebel Oubirah, a hill immediately north of Oued Zarga. The East Surreys' attack was expected to bypass any defenders on Oubirah by seizing Djebel Outiah. This approach was almost certainly driven by the lack of sufficient troops. It required Brigadier Cass to take the calculated risk that Oubirah was not strongly held, or if there were any troops located there, they would withdraw when outflanked. To reduce this risk Cass assigned C Squadron of 56th Recce Regiment in his plan to move at daylight on 7 April and patrol up a dry valley to the south of Oubirah. C Squadron's Humber cars and Bren Gun Carriers would provide a screen which would detect any German attempt to outflank the brigade's attack. Once these features were seized, the brigade assigned the task of taking Point 512 in Phase B to the remaining infantry battalion in 11th Brigade, the 2nd Battalion of the Lancs Fusiliers. The possession of Point 512, with a height of 1,500ft, provided excellent observation of the area and directly overlooked the two villages. It would place the brigade in an excellent position to seize the two Berber villages, Toukabeur and Chaouach (or "Charwash", as it soon became called by the troops) during the exploitation phase (D) of the brigade plan. The original intent of the plan was that Point 512 would be attacked on 7 April, though this did not actually happen.[3]

6.2 Codenamed "Soldier" – The Capture of Djebel Outiah

The task of taking objective "Soldier", the brigade's original codeword for Djebel Outiah on the left of the brigade's sector, was assigned to the 1st Battalion of the East Surrey Regiment. The 1st East Surreys was a regular Army battalion with a history they could trace back to 1702 and the formation of a Regiment of Marines. The regiment had a slightly complex history, but included on its colours, among others the battle honours, Dettingen, Sebastopol and Ladysmith. The 1st Battalion deployed as part of the BEF to France in 1940 as part of the 11th Brigade, under the command of Kenneth Anderson. It had distinguished itself, but also incurred significant losses during the retreat to Dunkirk. It was re-formed and assigned to the 78th Division. The battalion's CO was 39-year-old Lieutenant Colonel William Basil Samuel Joseph Wilberforce, known as Bill. Bill Wilberforce inherited not only a rather long set of Christian names, but also a fairly distinguished family surname. He was the great-great grandson of

---

3   Details of the role of 142nd RAC Regiment are from W.R. Nicholson, *The History of the Suffolk Regiment* (Uckfield: Naval and Military Press, 2006), pp.254-55, 263-64, and TNA WO 175/282 142nd Regiment April 1943 WD. Information on the terrain and the plan is derived from analysis of the original GSGS maps and the 11th Brigade Op Order No. 21.

William Wilberforce, the famous campaigner against the slave trade. Wilberforce was not an East Surrey officer, and assumed command of the battalion only three weeks before it embarked for Tunisia. He was born in 1904, educated in Yorkshire and commissioned as an officer in the King's Own Yorkshire Light Infantry in 1924. After serving with his regiment in Germany, he met and married his wife Cecilia in 1926 before going on to India in 1933. In the next few years Bill and Cecilia Wilberforce had a son and daughter, and he attended the Army Staff College in 1935. He subsequently served in two staff appointments and commanded a Young Soldiers Battalion before being appointed to command of the 1st East Surreys in October 1942. Despite facing the significant problems of being a stranger, both to the regiment and combat, and taking command just before the unit embarked for Tunisia, the new CO quickly established his ability to command, since he was an able tactician and was always cool in a crisis. Tall and apparently imperturbable whatever the situation, Bill Wilberforce commanded the battalion during the landings at Algiers and through a series of engagements during the initial race to Tunis. It was at Tebourba, in early December, that both he and the East Surreys particularly demonstrated their mettle. After being attacked by German units and almost losing a company, they were ordered to counterattack strong German forces with two depleted companies to save three batteries of guns. Their successful attack enabled the guns to withdraw, but the East Surreys had to make a very hazardous retreat. The losses incurred since landing, and especially at Tebourba, meant that by the time the battle ended the battalion's strength had dropped from nearly 800 to 350. Wilberforce's performance as a leader in this battle and during the next three months meant that by the time of Operation Sweep, he was firmly established as an inspiring battalion commander who was trusted and widely admired by his officers and men. He was also highly regarded by Brigadier Copper Cass, although the two men were as different as chalk and cheese, for in contrast to Wilberforce, Cass was small and well-known for his fiery personality. Their strong relationship was aided, not only by Wilberforce's undoubted qualities, but also by the fact that both officers had belonged to the same regiment, the King's Own Yorkshire Light Infantry.[4] The battalion was also well respected, both in the brigade and across the division, for its courage and fighting ability. However, like all other units in the 78th Division, it had received little rest over the winter months and was tired.

The battalion's objective, Djebel Outiah, was the name assigned to a ridge of two relatively low but tactically significant hills, divided by a small stream, which were located about 1,500 yards north of the main Beja-Medjez road. Djebel Nahel, which we have previously seen was captured by the 5th Buffs, was located to the north-west of objective "Soldier", and Djebel Dourat, a rugged 900ft ridge, was to be found to the south-east. Wilberforce and his battalion faced similar difficulties to the other units involved in the division attack. They had to conduct a long approach march on the night of 5-6 April to an assembly area on the reverse slope of Djebel Touila, just under two miles south of the main road, in order to avoid being spotted when moving into position for their attack. The battalion had initially lacked a complete picture

4   The codeword "Soldier" is from 11th Brigade Op Order No. 21 in TNA WO 175/196 11 Infantry Brigade April 1943 WD. The historical profile of the Queen's Royal East Surreys is based on its history as described on the Regimental Association website www.queensroyalsurreys.org.uk (accessed 14 December 2018). The biographical sketch of Bill Wilberforce is also derived from the same source, combined with information from the Army List, the Wilberforce family website www.wilberforce.info (accessed 18 January 2018) and Blaxland, *Plain Cook*, pp.125-26.

of the likely strength of German troops and defences on "Soldier", as a patrol sent to the area on the night of 3 April was unable to gain any information. However, a combination of patrols conducted by other units and interrogation of deserters suggested that the area including Djebels Outiah and Dourat was thinly held by the 9th and 10th Companies of the 3rd Battalion of the 756th Mountain Infantry Regiment. The information provided by two deserters in late March was invaluable, as it revealed that the companies were understrength and largely made up of Austrian troops, whose morale was low. One of the deserters, who had been shot at when he ran away in daylight from his position, stated the view "that the troops were too thin on the ground to hold against a strong attack".[5] According to his report, the strongest position was on Djebel Dourat, with the forward trenches held by four weak platoons at night. Although it was unclear if Outiah was actually defended, Wilberforce had to act on the assumption that it would be. His plan required the three companies of the battalion to march at night some two-and-a-half miles from their assembly area over rugged terrain to their start line on the main road. It would use a clearly defined track leading north-east as the axis of the approach to and attack on Outiah. In order to prevent any nasty surprises on the way, a fighting patrol led by Captain P. Heal would move out in front of the two leading fighting companies, A and B. C Company would follow the other two companies and be ready to reinforce or exploit the initial attack. The leading companies would be accompanied by sappers from 237th Field Company RE to deal with any mines, booby traps or obstacles that were encountered. The threat of anti-personnel mines was real, for the Germans had held the area for a significant period.

Events on the night of 6/7 April initially followed the plan, as the second-in-command of the East Surreys, Major Smith, recalled later: "I can recall moving up to our start line on the road itself on this very dark still night shortly to be rent by the sounds of hundreds of shells passing overhead and the flicker of innumerable guns lighting up the whole scene." The initial advance of the East Surreys went well and according to the war diary, by 0450 hours, the first companies had seized their objectives on Outiah without any opposition. However, when C Company, commanded by Major Bill Caffyn, moved through the Surreys' positions on Outiah and advanced towards Point 322, which lay about a kilometre further north, the situation changed. Harry Smith, who had joined the regiment in 1929 and served in France and Tunisia, further recalled:

> To start with the attack went well, until we began to run into enemy wire, minefields and heavy mortar fire. The enemy was using Austrian mountain troops stiffened by Germans to hold Djebel Outiah ... they were well dug-in in a 1914-18 type of continuous trench system with deep dugouts ... I well remember that distinctive scented smell one had begun to associate with the enemy which was very much in evidence.[6]

The arrival of daylight at 0600 hours exposed all the companies and battalion HQ to the direct view of German troops, and both A and B Company came under machine-gun and heavy

---

5   The deserter's remark is from a report in Intelligence summary No. 3 in TNA WO 175/519 1st East Surreys March 1943 WD. Details of German dispositions are from this source and Intelligence summaries in 11 Infantry Brigade March-April 1943 WD.

6   Harry Smith's recollections are from H.B. Smith, *Operations of the 1st East Surreys, Part 2 - North Africa, Sicily and Italy* (London: Imperial War Museum Reference 02 (41) 662), p.15.

mortar fire. Since there had been no time to dig in, it was inevitable that by 0645 hours the two companies on Outiah began to suffer casualties. Moreover, radio contact with Caffyn's company was lost as it attempted to move up to capture Point 322. During this period the highly mobile armoured cars and Bren Gun Carriers of C Squadron 56th Recce had moved rapidly at daybreak across the road and up the valley to the west of Oubirah, and by 0700 hours had a troop on Point 235, to the north of Djebel Oubirah. These veteran troopers provided a constant stream of valuable radio reports. It was C Squadron that alerted Wilberforce to the fact that Caffyn's company had not reached its objective. It is unclear exactly what happened to C Company, as varying accounts give quite conflicting stories, but what is certain is that it was held up, probably by mortar and machine-gun fire, and had several casualties. Kendal Chavasse's recce troopers occupied Caffyn's objective first at about 0830 hours, a fact acknowledged by the East Surreys in their war diary. Caffyn and his company seem to have arrived over the next hour or so and began to dig in under fire either on Point 322 or just south of this feature. It was during the morning, and while his soldiers were distracted by rapidly digging trenches to get under cover, that Major Caffyn was taken prisoner and the company lost its commander. Caffyn would eventually return to the East Surreys, but only after an extended stay in a prisoner of war camp in Italy. Throughout the morning, C Company took control of the area around them, but came under increasingly heavy artillery and mortar fire. The effectiveness of this fire can be gauged by the fact that by lunchtime the company reported that it had 50 percent casualties.

Meanwhile, Wilberforce's other companies were also suffering from German shelling, mortar and sniper fire, but also held on to their positions. B Company's platoon officers were especially hard hit, as Lieutenants Watkyns and Heath were killed and Evans wounded. By the late evening, however, these two companies had managed to retain their grip on the new positions. The situation was much more serious for C Company at or near Point 322. An analysis of various, albeit contradictory, records indicate that from mid-morning onwards, C Company was not fully in control of the area in and around Point 322. It seems likely that certainly by mid-afternoon, all that was left was an understrength platoon, which was supported by a few recce vehicles from 56th Recce Regiment's C Squadron. The platoon was under heavy fire and was having great difficulty holding on to its location. It was fortunate that C Squadron of the 142nd RAC Regiment, under the able command of Major Trevor Roper, came to the rescue. The squadron had originally been tasked to support the 2nd Lancashire Fusiliers, but having started early was soon in advanced positions to the south-west of "Soldier". When it became obvious that the East Surreys might be in trouble, Roper moved his squadron up a wadi to the west of Outiah and swung right to arrive close to Point 322. Roper had 11 Churchills in his squadron when he reached and passed through the East Surreys' location and advanced against German machine-gun and mortar positions. Although Roper and his tanks briefly received some 50mm anti-tank fire, they rapidly dealt with two machine-gun posts, forced a mortar to withdraw and took a number of prisoners. The nature of the rugged terrain meant that the Germans did not really expect tanks to be able to operate in this area, so their appearance was an unpleasant surprise. Once again, the Churchill's heavy armour and mobility in difficult terrain had proven the wisdom of the decision to continue production and deploy this relatively unproven tank despite initial difficulties. Alexander Austin, a war correspondent who was present at this time, wrote:

> The tanks were doing something that had never been tried before. They were climbing the hills to get at the German machine gun nests and mortar posts. Anti-tank guns they did

not have to bother about, for the Germans had never suspected that tanks would wander so high up into these hills.

Austin personally observed the Churchills at work on 7 April and gave a vivid description of their activities:

> You could see the black beetle shapes of the Churchills against the green hillsides, moving stealthily upwards. Nothing seemed to stop them. When their guns and their machine guns came prodding over the skyline, and their tracks made that deliberate, crushing sound on the slopes on the edges of slit trenches and weapons pits, the German machine gunners fled out of their nests. The tanks rumbled on round the back of the hill, mechanical beaters driving the game.[7]

Major Roper and his tanks remained in this position well into the afternoon, when they were withdrawn to prepare for an attack on Point 512, which was later abandoned. Their initiative and intervention undoubtedly enabled the East Surreys to retain control over the area around Point 322, its furthest objective. The majority of the East Surreys' troubles on this day probably arose from accurate shelling and mortar fire directed on to them from positions to their east, and also from Mergueb Chaouach to the north. The 5th Northants on their eastern flank identified three heavy mortars located in a valley north-east of Djebel Dourat, and it is likely these mortars caused some of the casualties on 7 April.

It is often forgotten how devastating mortar and shellfire can be on troops caught without cover and in a rocky area. The experience of the East Surreys at Outiah shows how destructive such weapons could be. The battalion also faced the difficulty of evacuating a large number of wounded, a task that had to be undertaken primarily at night and across rugged terrain. Too many accounts of battle leave out the difficult and inconvenient details of how the battalion stretcher bearers had to carry the often mangled, but heavy bodies of their wounded colleagues down rocky and difficult tracks. The effects of jagged shrapnel from shells on young men also created horrible injuries, which marked them for life and provided lasting nightmares for others.

The following day, the battalion spent most of its time consolidating its hold on its new positions and supporting other attacks, including those of the 5th Northants on its right. While Bill Wilberforce and his battalion had captured and held objective "Soldier" and the ridge line to its north, the price of taking its objectives was rather higher than had been expected, as the original intelligence had stated that the line was thinly held. The best estimate of the East Surreys' casualties for the attack on Outiah and Point 322 from 7-8 April indicates the battalion lost eight dead and approximately 60 wounded. The latter figure represents only those who were evacuated: others may have received slight wounds which were treated on the front line. The East Surreys had, however, lost three platoon commanders, and as a result Wilberforce was forced to send John Woodhouse, his new 20-year-old anti-tank platoon commander, back to B Company as commander of his old platoon, 10 Platoon. Woodhouse had already proven his leadership skills leading dangerous patrols, and would continue to do so for the next few days in the battles that followed.[8]

7   Austin's description is from Austin, *Birth of an Army*, p.121.
8   The story of the East Surreys' attack on Outiah is based on the 1st East Surreys' war diary; Daniell,

Plate 5 View from south of Point 512 (Background left), Djebel Douriat (bottom left) and Recce Ridge (right) (A Khmeri , 2018 Author's collection)

Plate 6 Major Jack Forshaw MC (Far left) and Lieutenant Colonel Kendall Chavasse DSO (2nd from right) of 56 Recce Regiment with their Long Range Reconnaissance Cars (LRCs). (Copyright The Tank Museum)

Plate 7 Mules of 2nd Lancs Fusiliers taking jerricans of water to forward troops in the Chaouch area, April 1943. (Copyright NAM - 1999-03-88-18)

Plate 8 Sappers of 237th Field Company, Royal Engineers, clearing a minefield in the aftermath of the First Army's attack on Toukabeur and Chaouch, April 1943. (Copyright NAM - 1999-03-88-17)

Plate 9 Sergeant William Rowe MM of 256th Field Company RE. (Copyright IWM/ NA 433)

6.3 5th Northants take Djebel Dourat and Point 343

While Bill Wilberforce and the East Surreys captured and held Djebel Outiah, the second part of 11th Brigade's plan was being implemented by the 5th Northants. After its difficult battle near Djedeida in late November and its narrow escape in the hills north of Tebourba at Christmas, the battalion had a brief period out of the front line before spending 69 continuous days in defence positions north of Goubellat. It then had a brief rest before spending two weeks in positions on the hills directly across from Dourat and Recce Ridge. One of the few benefits of this further period in the line was that, unlike the East Surreys, the unit became quite familiar with the area it was to attack. The 5th Northants' role in the brigade's attack was to establish itself on a line running south-east to north-west between its objectives, Djebel Dourat and a feature named Point 343. Point 343 was the northernmost of the two locations and was just to the east of Djebel Outiah, the East Surreys' objective. Although it lacked a name, it could be argued that Point 343 was more important an objective than Djebel Dourat. This small oval hill was much higher than and dominated Djebel Outiah. It also overlooked both Djebel Nahel,

History of East Surreys, pp.166-67; H. Squire and P. Hill, *Algiers to Tunis: the 1st and 1st/6th Battalions of the East Surreys Regiment in North Africa 1942-43* (Queens Royal Surreys Association Museum, November 1993).

located to the north-west and the objective of the 5th Buffs, and all the ground below it to the south, including Dourat (See Map 6). At the other end of this imaginary line on the map was Djebel Dourat, a steep rocky hill forming part of a long ridge located just north of the Oued Zarga-Medjez road. The German positions on this long ridge completely overlooked both the road to the south and the western approaches to the villages of Toukabeur and Chaouach. Directly to the east of Dourat was a long extended ridge, composed of two hills called Djebel Rouached and Deraoain, which not only overlooked the main road but also created a threat to any attack on Dourat. Over the last few months, the long ridge had attracted the nickname "Recce Ridge".

The 5th Huntingdonshire Battalion of the long-established Northamptonshire Regiment was a TA unit which was activated in 1939. As part of the latter regiment, it could trace its lineage back to two regiments, founded in 1741 and 1755. After being formed in 1880, the Northamptonshire Regiment saw action in the Boer War and First World War. The territorials of the 5th Battalion became part of 11th Brigade in 1940, fighting in Belgium with the brigade before being evacuated in 1940. While training in England, the battalion became part of the 78th Division and landed with it at Algiers. By April 1943, the battalion had developed into a veteran unit, moreover one that was also blessed with an experienced and wily CO. Arthur Ainslie Crook had originally been commissioned into the Royal Artillery in 1918 and had seen action in France during the last months of the First World War. After the war, he served in Ireland and in an unusual change to the normal career of an artillery officer, spent time serving with the King's African Rifles in present-day Uganda. This experience led Crook to transfer to the infantry and the Northamptonshire Regiment. Although posted to Singapore at the time of the Japanese attack, he was one of the few in that unfortunate garrison who managed to escape. He took command of the 5th Northants in the autumn of 1942 at short notice, leading it with distinction and courage throughout the Tunisian campaign. By 1943, Crook was a seasoned officer of considerable tactical ability, and after his recent escape, some would say a very lucky one too.[9] The battalion he commanded had started its war in Algiers with over 750 men, but suffered significant casualties when ordered by Brigadier Cass to carry out attacks on Djedeida in late November 1942. The result had been the destruction of one of the battalion's companies and its reduction to only 350 men. It had taken time to rebuild the strength and morale of the battalion during its extended period in the line during the winter months.

Information gathered from aerial photographs, patrols, prisoners and other sources meant that when planning his attack, Crook had an accurate breakdown of the positions, strength and weapons of the German battalion on Djebel Dourat and Point 343. His operational order for the attack reflects this information and lists precise locations of German positions for the 3rd Battalion of the 756th Mountain Infantry Regiment. Unfortunately for Crook and the 5th Northants, intelligence had not detected the arrival to the area around Point 343 of a company of a different battalion, the 3rd Battalion of the 755th Grenadier Regiment. Crook's tactical plan required the battalion to move to and use concealed assembly areas behind Sidi Abd et Aziz a large hill south of the main road on the night of 5/6 April. It would lie low during the

9   The profile of Arthur Crook and the story of the attack on Djebel Dourat is largely based on TNA WO 175/517 5th Northants April 1943 WD, TNA WO 175/178 56th Recce Regiment April 1943 WD, and TNA WO 175/282 142nd Regiment RAC April 1943 WD, along with Jervois, *Northants*, pp.138-40.

next day and move at 2200 hours across rugged terrain to the start line, codenamed "Wind-Pump", an area on the Medjez el Bab-Beja road. The battalion plan assigned V Company to lead and secure the start line with series of outposts just north of the road. The battalion was scheduled to cross its start line at 0100 hours and arrive at its objectives three hours later. The plan of attack was for B Company on the left to seize Point 343 and C Company on the right to capture a feature just to the south of this location. It should be noted that Crook's plan differed slightly from that set down by 11th Brigade, which had directed him to capture Djebel Dourat. His plan was more ambitious, as it set Ae Derej, a small hamlet well to the north west of Dourat and only just south of Point 343, as an objective. This was despite the fact that his intelligence reports indicated this ridge was strongly held by the enemy. It is possible that Crook wanted to help secure the eastern flanks of Wilberforce's attack on Outiah. It is not clear whether or not this change in approach was endorsed by Brigadier Cass. It is apparent that Crook did not ignore the need to address the threat potentially posed by Dourat, as one of V Company's tasks for the attack was to capture the western end of this objective if events showed that this steep ridge was held by German forces. In the light of available intelligence this was a peculiar requirement, especially as it was tasked with securing a location well past Dourat and only just south of C Company's objective. The other company in the battalion, A Company, was scheduled to follow as a reserve. The 5th Northants could also rely on the support of the Churchill tanks of A Squadron of the 142nd Regiment RAC, under command of Major Gerald Heyland, and two sections of Royal Engineers. In line with the divisional and brigade plan, Dourat and Point 343 would be pounded for about 20 minutes from 0350 hours on 7 April by heavy concentrations of artillery fire.

Crook's plan required the 5th Northants to make an approach march at night over rugged terrain without any of the aids infantry units have today. It had to dig in and conceal itself at night, lie in concealed positions all day and then after dark, move nearly four miles and attack uphill in the middle of the night. Only a very fit, well-disciplined and confident unit could perform such a task. It was fortunate that under the command of Crook, the 5th Northants had gained a lot of experience of battle since landing near Algiers four months ago, including the actions at Djedeida and the Tebourba gap. More importantly, it had a lot of experience of moving across difficult country in the enemy's back yard. Indeed, in December 1942 it had completed a cross-country march over the mountains to the north of Djebel Ahmera in order to support the attack on that hill. The battalion lost radio contact at some point and did not know that a wider brigade attack on Longstop had failed. Eventually it had to conduct a fighting withdrawal all the way back to Allied lines east of Longstop. Crook's luck continued to hold good in Tunisia when on the night of the Northamptons' attack, the car in which he and his quartermaster were travelling hit a mine. The two officers were not hurt, but his driver was seriously wounded. It was perhaps fortunate that Crook's second-in-command, Major T. "Buck" Buchanan, was to lead the battalion during the first phase of the attack and Crook would be left out of battle (known as LOB). This practice was applied across the whole battalion to ensure that if disaster should befall a battalion attack, there would always be a cadre of officers, SNCOs and men who could be used to rebuild the battalion. Another aim of LOB was to be able to limit the casualties incurred by key commanders and give junior officers, such as second-in-commands of the companies or battalions, experience in leading attacks so they could take on this responsibility if promoted. The practice also ensured that the CO had an enforced rest from time to time and that his deputy got invaluable command experience.[10] Major Buchanan, who led the attack on this occasion, was a TA officer from the 1st East Surreys who had served briefly in 1940 in France. He had next commanded B Company of the East Surreys in Tunisia, including during the difficult battle of Tebourba, before being assigned by Brigadier Cass as second-in-command to the 5th Northants in February 1943. Crook's companies were all commanded by officers who had proved their leadership in action during the last five months in Tunisia, and in some cases before that in France. Typical of them was the officer commanding B Company, 30-year-old Major John Rayment from Essex, who had recently been informed that he had been decorated with a MC.

The battalion moved and laid low during 5 April without being detected. As soon as darkness fell, the battalion intelligence section, led by the IO, Captain Dudley Emmerton, taped the start line on the road while the majority of the battalion were moving up. It was a clear starlit night with no moon as the advance began in silence at 0100 hours. The ground to be covered to the German positions, about a mile-and-a-half away, was undulating but grew steeper, and was interspersed with cornfields and stone walls. At some point some elements of the original plan changed, since after crossing the start line both A and B Companies moved up to attack Point 343. V Company was directed to carry out the task of taking the western end of Dourat and moved off to the north-east after the rest of the battalion and headquarters passed through them. C Company moved almost directly north to take its objective, Ae Derej. It was a testimony to the battalion's training and skill, but also possibly to the lack of alertness by the Austrian mountain infantry defenders, that the companies managed to remain undetected during the majority of their climb to their objectives. It was also fortunate that their opponents had lacked either the time or resources to lay large-scale minefields. Exactly on time at 0350 hours, the silence of the night was broken by the opening of artillery fire. At 0410 hours, the barrage ended and signal flares shooting into the sky soon showed that both V and C Companies had been able to take their objectives without any significant opposition. Unfortunately, B Company was less fortunate and was held up by heavy mortar fire in the gully used as its line of approach to Point 343. Despite all the best efforts by Major John Rayment, the company commander, who was wounded in the face, it was unable to take Point 343. Moreover, as dawn broke the whole of the battalion and its advance headquarters started to come under heavy mortar fire. An attempt to move the battalion's medium machine guns in its Bren Gun Carriers along a valley on the north side of Dourat and to open fire on enemy positions proved costly. The open-topped carriers took the Vickers machine-gun crews to the location which had been selected and then withdrew. This area proved to be exposed to deadly machine-gun and mortar fire, and the Vickers crews quickly suffered heavy casualties. At this point a Bren Gun Carrier driven by Lance Corporal Stephen Brown moved forward to evacuate the wounded. Despite the hail of fire, and with complete disregard for his own safety, Brown left his carrier to find and carry two wounded soldiers back to his vehicle, before also returning to recover their heavy Vickers gun. Brown's unwavering devotion to duty that day was recognised by the immediate award of a MM.

Further north, B Company struggled to take their objective on Point 343 against heavy fire, and Major John Rayment was shot dead at 1030 hours while leading his company. Since

10   The practice of being LOB was quite usual at this time and is described in several war diaries and both published and unpublished memoirs.

the element of surprise had been lost and the company was exposed to heavy fire, it received orders at 1100 hours to withdraw. During the withdrawal, a young sergeant called Nixon Keir made several trips under fire to help evacuate the company's many casualties, his acts of cool gallantry only the first of several during the next two weeks. Keir was not the only NCO who distinguished himself that day looking after the wounded. Corporal Thomas Baker was in command of the stretcher bearers of C Company of the 5th Northants when it attacked Ae Derej. Although the company had successfully captured its objective, it had done so while under heavy mortar and machine-gun fire and had suffered considerable casualties. Corporal Baker and his party of stretcher bearers had to evacuate the wounded some two miles across rocky and difficult terrain, there and back to the Medjez road, all the while under fire from German positions on their flank. This work was difficult, exhausting and dangerous, as they had to carry heavy men down difficult tracks and had nothing to protect them from enemy fire. Baker and his men made this gruelling journey 10 times during 8 April, as a result of which 18 wounded men were evacuated and four lives were definitely saved. Although it could be argued this was a collective act of bravery, Baker was strongly recommended for the award of a DCM due to the personal example he set, but later received a MM.[11]

It was at this point, while 5th Northants struggled to take Point 343, Ae Derej and Dourat, that once again the Churchill tanks of the 142nd RAC Regiment intervened and proved their mettle. A Squadron, led by Major Heyland, had started their day well before dawn, moving by 0500 hours to the western end of Djebel Dourat. During this, move a 50mm anti-tank gun sited on Point 290, a feature to the north-east of Djebel Dourat, disabled or knocked out five of the squadron's tanks. Soon after its arrival, the squadron was split into two parts, with one section under its second-in-command assigned to help hold the right flank in the valley north of Dourat. The other group under the squadron commander was ordered to support the left flank. The Churchills on the right helped support the Bren Gun carriers that were under fire. When B Company withdrew, Heyland was asked to occupy its positions and he led all his 11 remaining tanks up towards Point 343. Despite heavy fire, including from anti-tank guns, A Squadron held on to the exposed but tactically important positions vacated by B Company and kept up a heavy fire on the Germans. It was fortunate that Churchills were well armoured, as they came under further mortar and anti-tank fire which, along with a mine strike, damaged but did not destroy four tanks. At about 1500 hours, A Company of the 5th Northants moved up to a position just below Point 343, allowing Heyland and his tanks to withdraw. The Germans, however, retained possession of the location. The squadron was originally expected to attack Point 512, but as we will see this planned assault was delayed for a day and his tanks ended the afternoon in hull-down positions dominating the east end of Dourat. While Churchill tanks were not expected to hold ground on their own, Heyland and his crews carried out this task effectively for four hours, by so doing playing a key role in ensuring the eventual success of 5th Northants.[12]

Another unit that played an important role in the attempt to secure Point 343, and also Djebel Outiah, was C Squadron of the 56th Recce Regiment under the command of Acting Major Jack Forshaw (see Plate 6). Both the 5th Northants and East Surreys were able to attack Point 343 and Djebel Outiah without much fear for their exposed left flanks due to C

---

11   The citations for the MMs for Brown, Baker and Keir are in TNA WO 373/1.
12   The details of this action are from A Squadron's own account in TNA WO 175/282 142nd Regiment April 1943 WD.

Squadron's operations. While his two sister squadrons had been assigned to try to probe the Bed Valley, Forshaw and C Squadron were handed a separate task: to move from the Oued Zarga-Medjez road on local tracks, get up to Djebel Oubirah and prevent any interference by German troops with the attacks launched by the 1st East Surreys. Fortunately for C Squadron, the tracks leading from the road were not mined and Oubirah was not defended. Forshaw's veteran recce vehicle commanders also used every opportunity to probe forward and provide reports back to him and the brigade commander. C Squadron had played an important role in supporting the 1st East Surreys to secure Point 322. Other recce troops in the squadron were tasked with covering 5th Northants' left flank as Major Rayment's company attempted to take Point 343. This proved to be a dangerous task, as one of its troops came under heavy fire from an anti-tank gun and three of the troop's Bren Gun Carriers were quickly knocked out. The action that followed led to C Squadron receiving a total of five gallantry awards, probably the largest number of decorations received on a single day by any Recce Corps unit and most likely by any similar-sized unit during the whole of the Battle of the Peaks. Perhaps the most unusual element of this action was that it is not mentioned by the 56th Recce Regiment's own war diary, nor has it appeared in any other account previously. The lead Bren Gun Carrier, driven by Trooper John Allsop, was hit three times by a 50mm anti-tank gun from the flank. All three crews were ordered to evacuate their carriers, but Allsop believed his vehicle might be salvaged. He requested and was granted permission to try. He returned to the vehicle and, despite being under heavy enemy fire, managed to start it and drive it to safety. Meanwhile, the carrier crews who left their vehicles had been forced to crawl across dead ground to relative safety under machine-gun and mortar fire. After reaching safety, it became apparent that one of the crew members had been wounded and left behind. Acting Corporal Charles Smith volunteered to go back to rescue his wounded comrade, who was lying in the open on an exposed forward slope. Corporal Smith crawled forward under enemy fire to reach the wounded man, but found that the soldier's wounds meant he could not move him. He then went to the abandoned carriers, found some blankets and returned to the man to make him as comfortable as possible. Smith returned to the carriers and removed anything of value from them before moving forward to find the position of two mortars that were firing on his troop. Smith used this information to inform a nearby tank commander, who moved his tank to a position from which he could silence the weapons. During this same period, Lance Sergeant Harold Dean was commanding a Humber LRC when the patrol on his right came under enemy fire and was held up. Dean led his patrol forward around the flank of the German position and captured a machine-gun post. An hour later, when an enemy submachine-gunner opened up on his patrol, Dean took one man with him and crawled up to where he though the gunner was hidden. He surprised the enemy post and took five Germans prisoner, learning from them the location of an anti-tank gun and a machine-gun position that had been firing on the Bren Gun Carriers in his troop. Dean reported this information to his troop leader, Lieutenant Eric Edwards, and volunteered to help him. Edwards' own vehicle was already committed, so he dismounted from his LRC and, accompanied only by Sergeant Dean, moved forward on foot and under fire to work around the flank of this post. Amazingly, Edwards and Dean managed to close on the German position and captured 18 prisoners, two anti-tank guns and three heavy machine guns. By silencing these enemy posts, Dean and Edwards enabled the infantry and tanks nearby to move forward and capture their objective and allow the rest of his troop's carriers to withdraw and reorganise. It was not surprising that their complete disregard for their own safety and coolness under heavy fire in the face of such odds led to Harold Dean being subsequently awarded a DCM and Edwards an MC. Furthermore, Allsop and Smith were both awarded MMs.

During 7 April, C Squadron managed to capture more than 60 German prisoners, a large number of weapons and considerable amount of supplies. This action and others over the period of 7-9 April were among several during which the squadron's commander, Jack Forshaw, demonstrated outstanding leadership. Although his unit was under attack from both the air and the ground, Forshaw constantly exposed himself in the open to organise his unit's operations, and was subsequently decorated with the DSO. It was almost entirely for this series of actions on 7 April that the 56th Regiment's most experienced squadron would receive five medals: a DSO, MC, DCM and two MMs. The reason why this most gallant series of acts was not celebrated in the regiment's war diary is, and will probably continue to be, a mystery.[13]

Despite the strenuous combined efforts of all the units involved, by the end of the day, the 5th Northants had only partly achieved the objectives assigned to it in the brigade plan. It had secured the Ae Derej position but had failed to completely secure Point 343, which created difficulties for the East Surreys on Outiah. Moreover, although it had taken the western end of Djebel Dourat, the Germans still held on to its eastern end and had strong positions on Recce Ridge to the east. All of the companies now devoted their efforts to consolidating their hold on the ground they had taken by digging in and preparing for a German counterattack. At intervals during the night they came under occasional heavy mortar fire, but no counterattack emerged. The German 334th Division was thinly spread in the area, and having come under attack across its sector, lacked sufficient reserves to mount such an attack. The 5th Northants spent the night bringing up ammunition, water, evacuating its wounded and preparing to renew operations the following day. First on Major Buchanan's task list on 8 April was securing Point 343, which fell to A Company 5th Northants, with the valuable support from A Company of the East Surreys led by Acting Captain Edward "Ned" Giles and assisted by a force of three tanks from the Regimental Headquarters Troop of the 142nd Regiment. The troop was commanded by the second-in-command of the regiment, Major Stuart Robertson. One of these tanks was usually commanded by the regimental intelligence officer, but he found himself demoted to the job of front gunner. Lieutenant Colonel Alec Birkbeck had been away at a conference, but on learning of the proposed attack, he exercised his prerogative to take part and took command of the tank. Despite being eager to participate, Birkbeck politely agreed that his deputy should continue to lead the troop. It is unclear what the original front gunner thought when ordered to give up his place in his tank, but perhaps he enjoyed the rest and questioned the sanity of his senior officers! The combination of two infantry companies, the tanks and the involvement of most of the regimental command group proved sufficient to take Point 343. Led by Major Robertson, the Churchill tanks destroyed one of the troublesome 50mm anti-tank guns and captured another. The tanks also helped both companies to capture some machine guns and take 52 prisoners from the 3rd Battalion of the 755th Regiment, the unit whose unexpected presence in the area had caused problems. Sadly, the operation was not without its price and the 28-year-old company commander of A Company 5th Northants, Captain Harold Morgan, was fatally wounded.

13   The story of C Squadron, 56th Recce Regiment, is derived from the five gallantry citations in TNA WO 373/1.

Captain Giles, the 23-year-old commander of A Company of the 1st East Surreys, took an active role in operations to capture Point 343. Giles had arrived in North Africa as a platoon commander, and though now commander of A Company, was still only an acting captain. His relative youth and comparative inexperience seemed to have had little impact on his ability to command his company in an exemplary manner. On 7 April, Giles went out and silenced a machine-gun post which was troubling his company. During the operations to capture Point 343, Giles ensured the battalion's 3in mortars were employed effectively to support the attack. He personally led A Company to aid the 5th Northants in seizing the location and helped capture 108 prisoners. Edward Giles and A Company were also to be active in the fighting to seize Toukabeur and Chaouach. During the action which led to the capture of Point 343, Sergeant Ernest Barber, an NCO in the 5th Northants, played a key role in assisting the attack. Barber was in command of a detachment of Vickers medium machine guns. At one point the Churchill tanks and rifle companies were held up by a position that included an anti-tank gun. Barber led his detachment forward under fire to a location from which his guns could engage this position. Throughout the time his Vickers guns were firing on the German position and gun, he and his crews were under continuous sniper and machine-gun fire. The devastating fire of the Vickers machine guns directed by Barber neutralised the anti-tank gun and enabled a successful attack on the left flank to be carried out, limiting the casualties incurred by the company he was supporting. The citation for Barber's MM highlighted that he stayed in a position of acute danger while leading his detachment, and also his coolness under fire. Barber was subsequently decorated with the MM.

The next job was to take control of the whole of Djebel Dourat, and this task was begun just after 1000 hours by V Company, assisted by tanks from A Squadron. The combined force had seized the eastern end of Dourat by late afternoon. The tanks later continued their advance to a position from which they could dominate Recce Ridge. This attack was not without incident, as three tanks were lost on a minefield during the day. During the assault V Company made a bayonet charge, but when it arrived on the eastern end of Dourat, it was pinned down by intense mortar fire. Shrapnel from exploding mortar shells caused several casualties across the company. Private John Welton was part of a platoon that was especially engaged in the fight. Welton spotted what he thought was a German mortar position which was causing damage, and climbed 150 yards up the steep slope of Djebel Dourat to inform his company commander. Throughout his climb, Welton was exposed to intense machine-gun and mortar fire which had killed three men in his platoon and wounded another. The V Company commander was then able to bring down artillery fire on and silence the position. Later inspection showed that Welton's information had been totally accurate, as the mortar and crew position was found exactly where he had said it would be. Welton's total disregard for his own safety in crossing such an exposed and fire-swept area to bring this news saved many lives. It is arguable that the act was worthy of a higher decoration, but it did result in him being decorated with a well-earned MM.

Two members of A Squadron 142nd Regiment RAC also particularly distinguished themselves during the difficult operations from 7-8 April. While acting as the turret gunner of a Churchill, Lance Corporal Sayer was wounded when fragments of a shell penetrated his tank and disabled the air conditioner. Sayer completely ignored his wounds and continued to engage the enemy. On the following day, when Sayer's Besa machine gun had a stoppage, he removed the gun and fired a Bren through an open aperture in the turret, despite the risk of incoming fire and while almost being suffocated by hot fumes, the air conditioner having not been fixed. He was also being constantly burned by hot cartridges spilling over him. According to the citation for his MM, Sayers' "determination to maintain fire support for the infantry with a total disregard for self, knowing full well that the ample enemy MGs would direct heavy fire on tank apertures and in particular his head was worthy of high praise". The same day saw Lieutenant George Smedley distinguish himself near Dourat when he and his crew were forced to evacuate their tank when it was hit by enemy fire and disabled. As the crew left the tank, they rapidly came under accurate small-arms fire, which Smedley spotted was coming from some trenches nearby. He attacked the trenches singlehanded and found four Germans, whom he captured and brought back. Throughout the entire action, the area was under fire from British artillery and Smedley was exposed to that fire. His brave actions ensured the safety of his crew led to him being awarded the MC.[14] The work of A Squadron and its commander's leadership was also recognised by the subsequent award of an MC to Major Heyland.

The 5th Northants ended the day concentrated to the east and north of Djebel Dourat. The following day, encountering no opposition, the battalion moved north-east to reach the line of the road running from the village of Toukabeur to Medjez. It had managed to capture two anti-tank guns and a heavy mortar. However, the ever-present threat posed by booby traps and mines surfaced that day, when the regiment's well-respected quartermaster, 42-year-old Lieutenant McLaughlin, was mortally wounded by a booby trap. Three days later, this tragedy was further compounded on the night of 11/12 April when a patrol entered a German-laid anti-personnel minefield. The patrol officer and five men were killed, and four wounded. During the following morning, in an attempt to recover the bodies, the Pioneer platoon set off more mines and its commander was wounded and Sergeant Young of the platoon was killed. In total, nine men lost their lives. Indeed, the seizure of Djebel Dourat and Point 343 by the 5th Northants and supporting units during 7-9 April came at some cost. In the hard fighting over three days, the battalion lost two officers and 23 other ranks killed, plus 80 wounded. In total, the battalion had 33 men killed and 93 wounded from 5-12 April. It could of course have been much worse had the Germans been more alert on Djebel Dourat, as the battalion could have been caught in the open climbing the slopes and suffered much heavier casualties, especially from artillery, mortars and machine guns. Nonetheless, this was quite a stiff price to take its first objective, and unfortunately the cost of completing its next tasks would rise even higher.

6.4 Satan and Sugarloaf are Secured (Point 512)

North of Djebel Dourat and one mile directly west of the clifftop Berber village of Toukabeur is a steep unnamed hill that rises to over 1,500ft (512 metres). The hill dominates the area around it, especially the western approaches to the village which was known in Roman times as Thuccabor. In April 1943, the hill was identifiable as Point 512 on military maps, but was often known as the Pimple or Sugarloaf, as this is how it appeared to those who viewed it from a distance. The formal codeword for the capture of this key location became Satan, so it could

14 See TNA WO 373/1 for Sayers' MM citation and also citations for all the other awards made to officers and men of the 5th Northants and 142nd RAC Regiment.

be said whoever captured it had an appointment with the devil.[15] There were three main reasons why 11th Brigade's planning had identified the necessity of capturing Point 512. The first was to deny it to the Germans, who could and did use it to bring down fire on British units. This had made life unpleasant for the 5th Northants during the operations to take Dourat, and was one reason why it had taken that unit considerable time to seize it. Secure possession of Point 512 would also enable British forward observers located there to repay the Germans for their previous attentions by bringing down artillery fire on Germans in Toukabeur. Perhaps most importantly, the capture of Point 512 would provide a firm base from which to outflank the Germans located there. The aim was to avoid a direct frontal assault by persuading the Austrian *Jaeger* troops located there that it was high time for them to leave their hilltop observation point. The removal of its undesirable and unwelcome occupants was a key part of the wider divisional plan to free the Oued Zarga to Medjez el Bab road from enemy fire.

The original plan scheduled the capture of Point 512 to take place sometime during daylight hours on 7 April. The units assigned to this task were Brigadier Cass's third infantry unit; the 2nd Battalion of the Lancashire Fusiliers and the Churchill tanks of C Squadron of the 142nd RAC Regiment. The opposition encountered by the 5th Northants on Dourat, and especially its B Company around Point 343, had necessitated the early and unscheduled commitment of the squadron to help clear and hold that feature. The removal of tank support for the 2nd Lancs Fusiliers and other events led to a delay in the timing of the attack on Point 512. During the afternoon, Lieutenant Colonel Linden-Kelly of the 2nd Lancs Fusiliers was called to attend two meetings with Brigadier Cass and his artillery and armour commanders. Cass's own observation of the objective with his commanders following the final meeting led to the decision that it was now too late to conduct the attack. It was decided to delay completing the capture of Satan until first light the following day. The delay gave Linden-Kelly, whose nickname was "Red", and his company commanders time to observe Point 512 more closely. More importantly, it ensured the unit would not only now attack with the support of tanks from the 142nd, but also that it would have a much greater level of fire support. Although the 2nd Lancs Fusiliers were a regular battalion, their commander, was not a regular officer for he had been a TA captain at the outbreak of war. Linden-Kelly's abilities led him to rise to become second-in-command of the 2nd Lancs Fusiliers when it landed on Apples Beach near Algiers five months previously. He assumed command of the battalion when the original CO, Monk Manly, was killed by a burst of machine-gun fire leading an attack to retake Medjez el Bab on 25 November 1942. The then Major Linden-Kelly's performance after assuming command during that first tough battle led to his confirmation in the role of CO and promotion to lieutenant colonel.[16] The battalion he commanded had a long and illustrious history. This included the famous incident in which it won "six VCs before breakfast" when landing as part of the first wave of troops at Gallipoli on 25 April 1915. The regiment and the 2nd Battalion had a reputation for their physical fitness

15   The codeword for the capture of Point 512 was originally designated as Silk, but the 11th Brigade used a different codeword for the actual operation on 8 April. The one used in 11th Brigade Op Order No. 22 dated 7 April for the capture of Point 512 was Satan. Point 512 was also known informally by two nicknames, Sugarloaf and the Pimple, as noted by A.B. Austin in *Birth of an Army*, p.124. It is worth noting that the other objective on 8 April, a point on the high ground west of Point 512 was codenamed Devil.
16   The profile of Linden-Kelly is from Hallam, *Lancs Fusiliers*, pp.39-41, and the Army List.

and of being tough fighters.[17] The 2nd Lancs Fusiliers had fought in Belgium and France as part of the 11th Brigade and been evacuated from Dunkirk. After the landings at Algiers and the tough fighting at Medjez el Bab, the battalion's losses of over 130 men, combined with its lack of immediate reinforcements, led to it being assigned largely defensive tasks. It had, however, earned a reputation for the excellence of its offensive patrolling.

The new plan for the seizure of Point 512 was based on a dawn attack on 8 April and was developed by Linden-Kelly with the aid of brigade staff and Clive Usher, the CO of 138th Field Artillery Regiment, who was in command of the 78th Division's right artillery group. This ad hoc unit included Usher's own regiment plus two batteries of 25-pounder guns from the 19th Field Artillery Regiment. To ensure that the battalion would have a trouble-free attack, Brigadier Wedderburn-Maxwell of the Royal Artillery assigned the additional support of the heavy guns of the Mike artillery group. The grouping of artillery consisted of eight 5.5in guns from the 4th Medium Regiment and four 7.2in guns from 18 Battery of the 56th Heavy Regiment under the command of Lieutenant Colonel Mike Denham of the 4th Medium Regiment. The resulting fierce bombardment that descended on Point 512, starting at 0500 hours on 8 April, was carried out by more than 100 guns. In addition to the guns, the Lancs Fusiliers were also assigned the support of the Churchill tanks of C Squadron of the 142nd Regiment Royal Armoured Corps. Though the squadron had a busy day on 7 April supporting the East Surreys, they had refuelled, rearmed and were on the move by 0315 hours the next morning. Unfortunately, visibility was poor and the drivers could not see well enough to move before 0515 hours. C Squadron arrived on the start line slightly late, to see the battalion already advancing in open formation in the valley below them.

Linden-Kelly's regiment stuck to the plan and moved out to attack the Sugarloaf precisely at 0600 hours in order to gain maximum benefit from the effects of the barrage that descended on the hill. His Fusiliers were probably less than happy soldiers that morning: they had been on the move for 36 hours without rest and had spent a cold and hungry night on the hills, their blankets and main rations having failed to arrive. The only food available to them was one tin of bully beef between two men. In these circumstances it was not surprising that they were impatient to be about the business of the day. The previous night had not, however, been without benefits for the unit, as while on patrol two fusiliers had spotted and fired on a group of Germans. The result, to their surprise, was that a German officer and 50 soldiers immediately surrendered. The attack was carried out at first light by cold, hungry and rather annoyed fusiliers, led by C and D Companies, with the former on the right and the latter on the left. Their direct approach to their objectives crossed rough and difficult country which proved unusable for tanks. C Squadron was forced to move forward by a different route on the other side of the valley leading to Point 512. After all the preparations, and despite its commanding position, the capture of Sugarloaf or Satan proved to be something of an anti-climax. By 0705 hours, the companies had reached and taken their intermediate objective, Point 406, without opposition, and by 0810 hours all four companies were on the feature. A total of 12 Germans, who had somehow managed to survive the intense barrage delivered that morning, were located by C Company and surrendered without a struggle. Though their numbers were small, their capture was highly significant

17   In an interesting coincidence, the author recently learned that one of his great uncles served as an officer and adjutant of a battalion of this regiment for a short period in 1918 before he was wounded.

as they were a party of forward observers from the German 334th Artillery Regiment and controlled batteries that had been shelling British units and impeding the advance. Deprived of both their forward observation team and the excellent view from Point 512, the German batteries' effectiveness was greatly reduced, though not completely eliminated. This enabled the division to bring supplies and fresh troops forward without major interference. Perhaps most importantly, the 78th Division's artillery units were now able to displace to new positions north and east of the Oued Zarga to Medjez road, allowing them to better support future advances. As the 2nd Lancs Fusiliers started to consolidate their defences on 512, the Churchill tanks of C Squadron 142nd RAC Regiment engaged to good effect enemy troops fleeing from Points 312 and 303 from the north-west and southern shoulders of the hill.

Not all the Germans were retreating, however, for when the tank commanded by Trooper Pullman and carrying the squadron's artillery observer, Captain John Dawson, moved over a crest to gain a better view, it was hit repeatedly by a 75mm anti-tank gun located on Point 312. The radio was put out of action and the tank was immobilised and under fire. The driver, Lance Corporal Brunt, got out of the tank and moved on foot under fire to inform his troop and squadron commanders of the situation. The latter ordered the crew to evacuate and his troop commander, Lieutenant Lister, was ordered to engage and destroy the anti-tank gun. Instead, and once the crew had been evacuated, Brunt volunteered to return to his tank and, operating the gun on his own, engaged and silenced the 75mm gun, while tanks in his troop fired on other gun positions. Despite his bravery under fire, there is no record that Brunt was ever decorated for gallantry, though this act was formally documented in C Squadron's war diary. There seems to be a degree of confusion as to who actually knocked out the anti-tank gun, for Lance Corporal Brunt was not the only person who didn't want to leave his tank. Unlike Brunt, the FOO from the 138th Field Regiment who had been with the same crew, Captain Dawson, later received the MC. This, according to his citation, was for staying with the tank after it had received two direct hits and directing artillery fire to silence the gun. Whatever the truth of the matter, Dawson certainly earned his MC for he was almost constantly in action leading FOO parties for over four weeks and later helped stop a German tank attack at Bou Aoukaz.

At midday, C Squadron was withdrawn and 2nd Lancs Fusiliers settled into its rather isolated positions under spasmodic shelling and mortar fire. The unit's left flank was rather exposed, as the 5th Buffs, its nearest neighbour, had moved on to attack and capture Hill 667 over two miles north of their position.[18] On that day, the bravery of soldiers like Brunt, the actions of C Squadron 142nd RAC and of the 2nd Lancs Fusiliers had an important impact in further loosening the Germans' grip on key positions in the hills north of the Oued Zarga-Medjez road. The taking of objective Satan, though it was something of an anti-climax, was significant as it undermined key defences to the west and provided 11th Brigade with the ideal position from which to overlook, attack and capture the village of Toukabeur to the east. While the Fusiliers and C Squadron of the 142nd were completing the capture of the Sugarloaf, Jack Forshaw's C Squadron was performing a dangerous but necessary task. C Squadron had been ordered to protect Lieutenant Colonel Linden-Kelly's start line by moving up to the north of that location, into the upper part of the Oued Bouneb river valley and by securing a hill north of Point

---

18   Brunt's actions are described on page 3 of C Squadron's Report in TNA WO 175/282 142nd Regiment RAC April 1943 WD. John Dawson's MC citation is in TNA WO 373/1.

512. Once it had finished that task, Forshaw was expected by 11th Brigade staff, somewhat optimistically, to push on to the village of Toukabeur and then south-east to the road that led from Medjez to that village. The only friendly troops to the north of C Squadron were the 8th Argylls and 6th West Kents on Mergueb Chaouach, some 1,000 yards to the north, and there was no information about enemy troops along its line of advance. It was just the kind of job that a recce squadron was meant to carry out: move patrols forward until the Germans or friendly forces were located. Yet it was a little optimistic to assume the squadron would be able to reach Toukabeur completely unsupported, and so it proved. The rugged dry wadis, minefields and enemy fire meant that the squadron made slow progress that day, but it did take and secure the hill north of Point 512 and protected the advance of the brigade. This was a fine achievement.

6.5 "Touk" is Took and "Charwash" captured

A cleverly crafted signal sent by the East Surrey Regiment to 11th Brigade headquarters, "Touk is Took", has led to the few historians who have studied the Battle of the Peaks to assign all the credit for the capture of Toukabeur to the East Surreys. The truth is slightly more complicated and confusing, as other units can reasonably claim to have contributed to the capture of this ancient mountain village. It is, however, fair to say that the East Surreys can legitimately claim to have occupied the whole village and claim the lion's share of the credit.[19] The seizure of Mergueb Chaouach late on 7 April, followed by the capture of both Point 667 and Point 512 by the Battle-Axe Division the next day, created the conditions that would enable it to go on to seize the villages of Toukabeur and Chaouach. These two villages were perched on clifftops within a mile of each other to the north-west of Medjez el Bab, and both had a grandstand view across the Medjez sector. Toukabeur on the left was an ancient village that contained an arch built by the Romans. Chaouach, about a mile east of Toukabeur, was famous for its old caves, or Hamouets, which had been created by excavating limestone hills in the area. To the north of the village lay a height, Point 542, which was named after the village, Djebel Chaouach. The tactical importance of both these locations had long been recognised by both V Corps and 78th Division headquarters. The villages had sweeping views of the country around and south of Medjez, which meant that whoever held them could dominate the local area. Any movement or activity could be observed and quickly made the target of artillery fire. When Medjez el Bab was captured in November, the two villages and the heights were quickly garrisoned by French units and rotating companies from various British battalions. The village of Toukabeur was also used as the jumping-off point for 5th Northants' abortive operation to try and cut German supply lines near Tebourba in late December. During the period from late December to mid-February, the villages were partly secured by the occupation of more forward positions on Djebel Ang, Heidous and Point 667 by the 3rd Regiment of Algerian Tiraulliers (3rd RTA). In order to provide additional security, British infantry units were sent to garrison Toukabeur, including companies from the East Surreys and the Lancashire Fusiliers, so both battalions had become familiar with the local geography.

---

19   The signal "Touk is Took" is cited in G. Blaxland, *Plain Cook*, p.229; see also Hill and Squire, *Algiers to Tunis*, p.1.

Despite the arrival of additional reinforcements in February, it was not possible for the First Army to strengthen the local garrison. A key reason was the need to send units south to respond to the pressures created by Rommel's attack towards Kasserine Pass which commenced on 14 February. In late February, von Arnim 5th *Panzer* Army launched a series of counterattacks against Allied units in the north. Initially the attack fell south of Medjez el Bab, but at the end of February, a German *Kampfgruppe* from the 334th Infantry Division, based around the 756th Mountain Infantry Regiment led by *Oberst* Eder, attacked through the weakly defended mountains north-east of Medjez. Although the area was defended by the French 3rd RTA, this unit was comparatively lightly armed and was forced by the superior strength of *Kampfgruppe* Eder to conduct a withdrawal from Point 667 in the north plus Djebel Ang and Heidous in the east. It was eventually pushed back by 1 March to positions near Chaouach, and soon afterwards ejected from both mountain villages. During their gallant defence of the area, the Algerian troops of the 3rd RTA suffered significant casualties and lost over 200 men captured.[20] The German attack continued west and led to the seizure of the line overlooking the Oued Zarga-Medjez road. The success of *Oberst* Eder's attack in the mountains created the conditions which directly led to the launch of the Battle of the Peaks. The lack of sufficient forces in the mountains near Medjez in late February proved to have unfortunate consequences, as the same hills which had been held by V Corps now had to be retaken one-by-one in bitter and costly fighting. Although the operation appeared to be a fine example of Teutonic military efficiency, it did contain elements of farce for one battalion. During the operation, two companies of the 3rd Battalion of the 755th Grenadier Regiment became so confused that they ended up firing on each other and some 22 casualties resulted. This resulted in the battalion commander being relieved of his command, an event that inadvertently caused the new CO, *Hauptmann* Antritter, to be captured by the 5th Buffs on 8 April.

Although the positions on Toukabeur and Chaouach may have appeared impregnable, by 9 April the Germans' hold on these clifftop villages was tenuous. Toukabeur was overlooked by Point 512, and by 8 April that was firmly in the hands of the Lancashire Fusiliers. British artillery observers on Point 512 now had an excellent vantage point from which to call down fire from multiple medium and field regiments to harass the Germans. To the north-west of Toukabeur, the 8th Argylls held Mergueb Chaouach, which overlooked its namesake village and also Djebel Chaouach. It was only a matter of time before the Austrian mountain troops would lose control of these clifftop fortresses.[21] The seizure of Point 512 by the 2nd Lancs Fusiliers, combined with the capture of a hill to the north by C Squadron 56th Recce Regiment, provided 11th Infantry Brigade with a secure base to the north from which to launch the final phase of its attack and seize Toukabeur and Chaouach. The right flank of any attack was largely protected by the leading companies of the 1st East Surreys, who had managed to make slow but useful progress and were well positioned to support the attack. Unfortunately, German positions on a hill called Point 290, which was to the east of Djebel Dourat, and also on Recce ridge, continued to create difficulties for movement in the area throughout the morning and

---

20   The story of the defence and loss of Chaouach and Toukabeur is from Howe, *North West Africa*, p.507, and an account of the operations of the 3rd RTA in Tunisia on the website www.les-tirailleurs.fr/unites/3-rta (accessed 17 January 2018).
21   The German friendly-fire incident is recorded in the 78th Division Intelligence Summary dated 9 April 1943.

early afternoon of 8 April. "Copper" Cass and his staff therefore ordered the 5th Northants, supported by tanks from the 142nd, to eliminate these positions, a task that was generally achieved by late afternoon. Once the threat from German troops in the area had been largely neutralised, it was possible to make the next move forward. There is some confusion about the sequence and nature of events that followed, but at 1645 hours Cass appears to have ordered the 2nd Lancs Fusiliers to carry out an attack on Toukabeur from the west. It was specifically instructed to secure tactically important high ground north of the village, including a feature called Point 447.

This attack was assisted by the tanks of the ubiquitous C Squadron of the 142nd Regiment RAC. The squadron surprisingly still had 13 operational Churchill tanks available to support the Lancs Fusiliers' attack. These had to be moved around the north end of Point 512 and took up hull-down positions on a high ridge looking towards Toukabeur. The leading 2nd Lancs Fusiliers company moved towards the village across two ridges and met some opposition during its attack. Due the nature of the terrain, the squadron's Churchill tanks found that they were able to engage the Germans most of the time, but there were occasions when they had to cease fire. This was necessary when the Fusiliers were moving over a ridge that would put them in the tanks' line of fire. At one point the leading B Company came under fire from high-explosive shells fired by an anti-tank gun and two machine guns, and as a result became pinned down. It would appear that at this time the tanks were not able to help the infantry, but fortunately the actions of three men in a platoon from the company played a key role in extracting it from this situation. Corporal Dennis Ryan from that platoon crawled forward, located the positions of the machine guns and directed his men's fire on to them. Meanwhile, he called forward two other men, Corporal Frank Nuttall and Lance Corporal Bernard Newsham, to accompany him on an assault on the anti-tank gun which was 150 yards away. The NCOs attacked the gun using their Thompson submachine guns and a Bren gun, killed one member of the gun crew and captured the rest. The three men used their position to turn the fire of their weapons on the machine guns, which enabled their section, encouraged by Corporal Ryan, to advance on to the posts under the cover of their fire. Both machine guns were silenced and enabled the attack which had been halted to resume.

As there is some confusion about who actually captured Toukabeur, it is worth noting that C Squadron recorded that the Lancs Fusiliers entered the village from the north-east at the same time as the East Surreys came in from the south-west.[22] As the primary effort against Toukabeur was supposedly to be made by Linden-Kelly's battalion, it is unclear why the 1st East Surreys later became involved in the seizure of the village. It is certain that B Company of the 2nd Lancs Fusiliers had secured the tactically important high ground to the north-west of the village which had to be taken if the village itself was to be occupied. Most accounts agree that a patrol from B Company was sent into the northern end of the village at about 1800 hours, but as darkness was soon to fall, it was decided that the patrol should withdraw from the village. The patrol's movement into the village may have been that reported by the tank crews as the arrival of the 2nd Lancs Fusiliers. The Lancashire Fusiliers could legitimately argue that it was the first British unit to take, or more accurately retake, Toukabeur. At some point, prior to or just after the Lancs Fusiliers had been in the village, a patrol from D Company of the 1st East Surreys

22   Newsham, Ryan and Nuttall all received the MM. See TNA WO 373/1.

entered the outskirts of the village. Due to previous heavy casualties, D Company was full of new, inexperienced soldiers, so Acting Major Pat Wadham, its company commander, personally led the patrol and his company in this action to inspire confidence and reassure his soldiers. The patrol was fired on and a short, sharp action ensued, but German opposition was quickly overcome. Various reports claim different timings for when the battalion actually occupied the village: one account states 1930 hours, another 2145 hours. At some point the 1st East Surreys had sufficient control of Toukabeur to enable its battalion CO and his headquarters to move into the village and send the signal "Touk is Took".[23]

While Bill Wilberforce and his battalion clearly broadcast their success with their triumphant radio signal and added the action to regimental folklore and its battle honours, the hard facts are that the capture of Toukabeur was a team effort. The East Surreys would not have been able to occupy the village had the Lancashire Fusiliers not taken the high ground to the north and held it. Moreover, the battalion's lead companies received critical support from tanks of C Squadron of the 142nd RAC Regiment. The latter's war diary makes clear that Churchill tanks were very active in the operation to seize the village. C Squadron of 56th Recce Regiment also played its part by protecting the flank and patrolling in advance of the two infantry battalions.

After a relatively quiet night in Toukabeur, Bill Wilberforce and two companies of the East Surreys had an early visitor at about 0800 in the morning. Brigadier Cass of 11th Brigade had come up to see the battalion and issue new orders. Wilberforce was ordered to attack and capture Chaouach, the sister village of Toukabeur, which lay about a mile to the east. Among ordinary soldiers the village quickly found its name amended from the difficult to pronounce Chaouach, to the rather easier to recall name of "Charwash". Cass ordered Lieutenant Colonel Linden-Kelly's battalion, positioned to the north of Toukabeur, to move east and secure the high ground north of Chaouach. Looking back on 8-9 April, it must have seemed unfair to Linden-Kelly and the Lancashire Fusiliers that while they kept being assigned the difficult task of working their way across rugged terrain to protect the 1st East Surreys, the latter obtained the publicity and fame that came with the capture of the villages. It is only just, some 75 years later, to recognise the critical importance the Fusiliers played in this operation, for without their unsung activities, Wilberforce's battalion would have found it much tougher to capture both villages.

While the Lancashire Fusiliers were embroiled in their skirmishes, the lead companies of the 1st East Surreys, supported as always by C Squadron of the 142nd Regiment RAC, advanced to take Point 542, otherwise known as Djebel Chaouach. B Company appears to have briefly encountered some half-hearted opposition from Austrian troops on the hill, but once their accompanying tanks appeared and fired several bursts from the Besa machine guns, the defenders very quickly gave themselves up and surrendered *en masse*. According to later reports, the Austrian soldiers captured at Chaouach had become demoralised by the fighting of the last three days. The key reason for their mass surrender was that their officers and veteran NCOs had slipped away and left them leaderless. Such behaviour by key leaders in the German Army in early 1943 was highly unusual, as in Tunisia the units of the 5th *Panzer* Army had fought effectively and remained both professional and disciplined. Although reports differ, it is probable that between 128 and 140 soldiers, most from the 10th Company of the 3rd Battalion

---

23   For timings on entry to Toukabeur, see Intelligence summary for 8 April in TNA WO 175/196 11 Infantry Brigade April 1943 WD, and also TNA WO 175/519 1st East Surreys April 1943 WD.

of the 756th Mountain Infantry Regiment, were captured when B Company of the 1st East Surreys occupied Point 542. Soon afterwards, the rest of the battalion moved into and occupied "Charwash". Later that day, the Lancashire Fusiliers relieved the East Surreys on the heights above Chaouach, including Point 542. It was a very hot day, and after nearly 72 hours of constant activity it was not surprising that the Fusiliers' war diary noted that the soldiers were tired and probably annoyed, as there seems to have been a shortage of food. The following day, the 1st East Surreys were ordered back from Chaouach to positions to the west, where they secured various locations, rested and reorganised. Linden-Kelly and his battalion took control of the village and its surrounding area, spending the next two days conducting patrols and resting.[24]

The capture of Toukabeur and Chaouach, and more importantly the heights to the north of both villages, returned two tactically important positions to the Allies and brought to a close the first stage of the 78th Division's operations in the Battle of the Peaks. Their original capture, along with the loss of Recce Ridge to the 334th Infantry Division in early March, had removed at a stroke one of the 78th Division's primary supply routes, the Oued Zarga-Medjez road. The elimination of German positions which dominated that road had been one of the primary aims of the plan for Operation Sweep, and with the taking of the two clifftop villages this had now been achieved. The cost of the operation to seize the villages may have seemed comparatively low, for the troops faced rugged terrain and a determined enemy. The 1st East Surreys' losses appear to have been four dead, though figures for wounded are not available. In what must have appeared to be a bitter irony, the Lancashire Fusiliers failed to get any credit for the capture of the villages but also suffered a higher casualty rate: the battalion lost 14 officers and men killed and approximately 54 wounded over the period.

6.6 Engineers at Work

It would not be fair to conclude this account of the first days of Operation Sweep without devoting time to a description of the invaluable contribution to these operations made by the officers and men of the Royal Engineers. The efforts of the sappers, as they are informally known in the British Army, has tended to be often ignored or overlooked in historical accounts. Yet the work of the Royal Engineers during the battle was not only vital but also difficult, dangerous and varied. A total of six companies were assigned to support the division. Two of these, the 237th and 256th Field Companies, were assigned to directly support 11th and 36th Brigades respectively. A hastily organized ad hoc unit of sappers named Joss Force assisted 38th Brigade. The 214th Field Company RE, 281st Field Park Company and a platoon from the 103rd Bridging Company RE were under the direct command of Lieutenant Colonel Edmund Blake, the CRE of the Battle-Axe Division. Two other companies assisted the engineering effort: the 137th Mechanical Equipment Company RE and 565th Armoured Field Companies.[25] The activities of 214th Field Company RE, commanded by Major R.B. Denton, offer an excellent

---

24 The war diaries of the East Surreys, Lancs Fusiliers and 142nd RAC give different and conflicting estimates of the actual number of prisoners captured and their location. See 1st East Surreys WD for April 1943 for the story of the leaderless company.

25 This account of the Sappers' activities is derived from TNA WO 175/171 78th Division CRE April 1943 WD, and those of the 214th, 237th and 256th Field Companies RE respectively TNA WO 175/645, 175/652 and 175/657.

example of how the expertise and courage of sappers often provided crucial support to the 78th Division. Denton's company was originally a TA unit from the Staffordshire area, and had served with the BEF in France before it was evacuated at Dunkirk. In 1942, after a brief period supporting 1st Guards Brigade, it was assigned to become the 78th Divisional Troop's RE Company. It arrived in Algiers in a follow-on convoy on 21 December 1942 and rapidly moved to Medjez el Bab, where it showed off its bridging skills when it built a 170ft double-tier Bailey bridge across the river in late December. At this time Denton was a captain, but in February 1943 the original Officer Commanding the company fell ill with malaria and Denton was promoted to major and assigned command. The role of divisional troops meant that the new OC worked directly for the CRE, 44-year-old Edmund Blake, and took on key tasks. Denton's assignment was not an easy one, for as the RE records show, Blake tended to be an energetic and hands-on commander who spent much time close to or on the front line supervising activities, especially those of Denton's unit.

When Operation Sweep started on the night of 6/7 April, a section (today it would be called a troop) of the company was already hard at work on two of the most critical engineering tasks required for the support of Operation Sweep: improving one vehicle crossing created on the riverbed north of Oued Zarga and starting to build an additional one for a bridge just next to it. The crossings had to be built if the division was going to successfully carry out the first stage of the attack. They were needed to enable brigade vehicles to get across the dry river beds and carry vital supplies and ammunition to forward units. These crossings would later be used to carry artillery guns, recce vehicles and tanks. The section had moved forward that night, and using picks and shovels only, was working on creating the crossing for vehicles over the Oued Zarga dry river bed just north of the village of that name. Work on this crossing was delayed until the early morning of 7 April, in order to avoid giving the Germans any notice that an attack was about to be launched in the area. The sappers of the company were joined at daylight by the bridging platoon, who brought pieces of trackway or matting that were used to improve access to and across a riverbed. Soon afterwards, a D-7 Caterpillar armoured bulldozer arrived to assist with the work. The two sections worked rapidly, and improved the first wadi crossing and laid matting by 0500 hours, and by 0930 hours had managed to build a box girder bridge next to it that would take vehicles up to 12 tons in weight. Two days later, to avoid holding up the advance, a third section of the company had to quickly build another bridge over the Oued Bouneb river bed as Churchill tanks were ruining an existing crossing area. This bridge allowed Churchills of the North Irish Horse to play a key role in putting 38th and 36th Brigade troops onto their objectives. There was, however, no rest for Denton's company, for after putting in the crossings, all three sections were assigned to clearing tracks and areas of Teller and S mines and farms of booby traps. During the afternoon a recce party came under fire and two sappers were wounded, one of whom died of his wounds.

The two other RE companies and the ad hoc Joss Force had been assigned largely to direct support of the three brigades and were very busy on all three days. One of the key tasks of these sappers during the next four days was clearing hills and tracks of mines, and improving tracks and building roads so they could be used by a range of vehicles. The task of improving existing tracks using bulldozers may on first glance appear to a mundane one, hardly worthy of mention. This was not the case near Djebel Mahdi on 7-8 April, as two sappers working as bulldozer operators showed that this routine role could involve many hazards. After the Skins and Faughs of 38th Brigade occupied Mahdi, any further advance required support from a range of tracked and wheeled vehicles. Only mule tracks existed, so a road had to be created across a deep wadi (Oued Bouneb) and up the Bed Valley. This required the use of a D-7 Caterpillar bulldozer manned by experienced bulldozer operators. Lance Corporal John Johnson and Sapper Hall, two members of 137th Mechanical Equipment (ME) Company RE, took on the job of cutting the road, though the tracks had not been cleared of mines. Working for several hours under intense mortar fire and enemy air attacks, the two men took turns to do the job. Their coolness and courage under fire was noted by Captain Adams, the officer in charge of Joss Force supporting the Irish Brigade, and led to both men being awarded a MM.[26]

While Johnson and Hall cut their road, and sappers built crossings and bridges, other engineer sections were busy with the dangerous but critical job of finding and clearing mines and booby traps. Within the constraints of time and resources available to them since they had occupied the area five weeks prior to April, the Germans had devoted considerable time to laying both anti-tank and anti-personnel mines on likely routes for British attacks. The job of finding them fell to sections of sappers from all three field companies, but particularly 237th and 256th Field Companies RE working in direct support of the attacking infantry battalions. Young NCOs led small parties of sappers equipped with mine detectors and sometimes bayonets to create gaps in minefields holding up tanks and infantry. This task was stressful enough in ordinary circumstances, but when conducted under mortar and other types of enemy fire it became extremely difficult. One of the terrible dilemmas of the sappers was how to balance safety against the need for speed. Sappers needed to work slowly in order to address obvious dangers posed by anti-handling devices on some mines, but they also had to remove large number of mines and all against time constraints. There was the added problem that the longer the infantry were held up, the more vulnerable they and the sappers became to enemy mortar and artillery fire.

As there was inherent danger in mine clearance and the active role played by 237th Field Company RE in this task during Operation Sweep, it was perhaps ironic that the officer commanding the company was Major T.E. Coffin RE. The 237th Field Company (often known as the Highland Company) hailed from Dundee and had originally been part of the 51st Highland Division, but had escaped capture in 1940 at St Valery as it was part of a brigade evacuated from Le Havre. The company was later transferred to the 78th Division and had been active ever since, gaining some fame for building a Bailey bridge under fire to span the demolished old Roman Arch Bridge at Medjez el Bab in November 1942. The unit's bridge-building skills were not, however, required for the first six days of Operation Sweep. All of its sections were assigned to carry out mine-clearance tasks in support of the 11th Infantry Brigade's attack on Djebels Outiah and Dourat, Point 343 and later Point 512 (see Plate 5 and Plate I). On 8 April, when 5th Northants and A Squadron of the 142nd Regiment RAC were trying to clear Djebel Dourat and advance on Recce Ridge, the tanks, and therefore the infantry, were held up by a minefield with both anti-tank and anti-personnel mines covered by enemy fire which had damaged three tanks. A sub-section of sappers led by Sergeant Charles Couchman moved forward to make gaps in the minefield. Although they were under heavy mortar fire, Couchman and his party never faltered, and despite the dangers cleared a 100-yard gap in the minefield which enabled the tanks and infantry to move forward, clear Dourat and later attack Recce Ridge. Unfortunately, the following day Couchman and two of his sappers were

26 Hall and Johnson's MM citations are described in TNA WO 373/1.

wounded while trying to remove an S mine. Sergeant Couchman recovered and his personal courage, and indirectly that of his men, were later recognised by the award of a MM. During the same period, Lance Corporal William Norrie from 237th Field Company RE also led a party that lifted 50 Teller and 24 *Schu* mines while under fire, for which Norrie was later also awarded a MM.

The Highland Company's third MM was awarded to Sergeant George Hickson, who was certainly the bravest man in the 237th Field Company RE, but was not actually Scottish, British or even a sergeant in the Royal Engineers. George Hickson was Canadian and a Sergeant in the Royal Canadian Engineers (RCE). He was on loan to the company under an innovative, though little-known scheme designed to provide officers and NCOs of the Canadian Army in England with battle experience in Tunisia. Hickson was somewhat different to many of the Canadians who served in Tunisia, as he already had a little battle experience before arriving in Tunisia. In Hickson's case this involved just two days on the beaches of Dieppe, but it was quite some experience. Soon after landing, he took command of a platoon after both his platoon officer and all the SNCOs were put out of action. During the day, Hickson, who was at that time a lance sergeant, personally led his sappers in knocking out German positions, including two large guns and two machine-gun posts. Hickson and his group were amongst the last to evacuate off the beach at Dieppe. In hindsight, Hickson's complete disregard for his own safety, leadership and courage on the beaches of Dieppe arguably should have merited the award of a VC, but instead he received a DCM. The fact that Hickson was subsequently assigned to join the group of Canadians sent to the First Army for additional experience shows how highly he was regarded, as only carefully selected and talented Canadian officers and SNCOs were sent to Tunisia. On 8 April, Hickson was supporting the 5th Northants near Recce Ridge, when the battalion and tanks of the 142nd were held up by a minefield. Hickson organised a detachment of sappers and led them to clear a 40-yard gap by lifting 100 mines in under an hour. Hickson and his party were under heavy fire at the time, but in a repeat of his actions at Dieppe he demonstrated complete disregard for his own safety and cool leadership by moving constantly in the open to encourage his men. George Hickson's second act of gallantry was noted and led, unusually, to Brigadier Cass to personally recommend him for a MM, which he subsequently received.[27]

Sergeant Hickson was not the only Royal Canadian Engineer active during Operation Sweep, for the 256th Field Company RE during this period was commanded by Major C.E. Brown of the RCE. Brown had already commanded an RCE company in England before arriving in Tunisia on the officer loan scheme and assuming command of 256th Company in February 1943. Brown's company was assigned to directly support the 36th Infantry Brigade during the first four days of Operation Sweep. One of his officers, Captain Peter Kidner RE, who had only recently joined the company after serving at V Corps headquarters, gave his impressions of the 256th and Brown in a diary he maintained: "On the whole, a first-class company, but discipline a bit weak, and an aversion to spit and polish! The O.C. is a Canadian, Brown – and very good, but also a bit 'anti-Blanco'. I think he is probably right."[28]

The sappers of 256th Company RE spent the first days of Operation Sweep in direct support of Howlett's 36th Brigade working on dangerous and tiring tasks. The most important was to clear

---

27   See G. Brown, *Register of DCM*, p.233, for his Dieppe award and WO 373/1 for his MM citation and those of Couchman and Norrie.
28   See *Kidner Diary*, 27 March 1943 entry.

mines and booby traps from the roads and tracks leading up to and onwards to Djebel Nahel and Dourat. The Germans regularly mined road verges, near likely roads and track junctions, with both anti-tank and anti-personnel mines. All of the company sections were employed to use mine detectors to find and, using hand tools and fingers, gingerly remove mines. This task was one that required sappers to have skill and nerve, and was tiring and stressful. Sergeant William Rowe RE (see Plate 9), who commanded a section, was typical of the brave sappers who carried out this task. By the morning of 7 April 1943, Rowe and his section had been working since 2000 hours the previous evening. During the morning, his section came under observed enemy mortar and shellfire and one of the company officers, Lieutenant Jackson, was killed and five sappers wounded. Although his section suffered casualties, he reorganised and continued the work, lifting many Teller and S mines and securing the safe passage of vehicles for the advance. Rowe's cool courage in difficult conditions set an outstanding example to his men under fire, and resulted later in the award of a MM.[29]

Over the first five days of Operation Sweep, the 256th Company's sappers were constantly on call and often over-committed, and it didn't help that they kept getting calls to tasks which proved either unnecessary or were previously allocated to other sappers. The majority of their work involved checking roads and other areas for mines so that other units could use them. Evidence of their hard work can be gained by the fact that during this period they lifted 600 Teller and 75 S mines. However, on 10 April, one section of the company received the task of installing a Class 40 Steel Girder Bridge (SGB) to enable tanks and heavy vehicles to move forward. This job was completed the following day and the company spent some time clearing the heavily mined area around Recce Ridge. All three of 78th Division's direct support companies, plus the two other companies attached for the operation, carried out critical tasks in dangerous conditions that were essential to the success of the division's early operations. They also demonstrated their skills and versatility of sappers as they rapidly moved with ease from building bridges to clearing mines, removing booby-traps and building roads. In this sense the sappers lived up to their motto, for they were truly "everywhere". The next two weeks of operations would continue to create challenges to test their commander, Edmund Blake, and his sappers, and they would continue to rise to that challenge.

7

No Place for Mules or Men

7.1 An Operational Pause

The capture of Toukabeur and Chaouach signalled the end of the first stage of Operation Sweep. Starting on 10 April, Major General Vyvyan Evelegh ordered what might best be described as an operational pause, a period during which no major attacks or advances were conducted. Evelegh understood all too well, as did his superiors Allfrey and Anderson, that after spending months on almost continuous operations followed by a period of four days of tough fighting in difficult terrain and varied weather conditions, the officers and men of the 78th Division were mentally and physically tired. Even the fittest and mentally toughest of soldiers eventually found that the combination of terrain, weather and intense physical activity over five months, combined with the added stress of combat, drained their ability and willingness to fight. Moreover, almost 72 hours of continuous operations meant that the men in almost every brigade and all the supporting units had hardly managed to get any sleep, and needed a brief interlude during which to rest. This did not mean that over the period of 10-12 April the division was inactive, or that it spent its time lazing about. For as we shall see, significant parts of the division were repositioned, while infantry units close to the enemy spent much of their time actively patrolling. Nonetheless, between 10 and 12 April, the three brigades of the division did not conduct any attacks. It is doubtful that Evelegh and his staff had much time to reflect on the last four days as they were heavily involved in planning for the next stage of operations. If they had taken time to do so, they might have been quietly satisfied, but not complacent, about the achievements of the last few days.

During the period since Operation Sweep commenced on the night of 6/7 April, the division had successfully completed each of the tasks outlined in Evelegh's original operational order issued on 5 April. All four phases of the order had been carried out and the division had captured all its assigned objectives. The division and its supporting units had captured over 1,000 prisoners, inflicted an estimated additional 300 dead and wounded on the German 334th Infantry Division and rendered two of its mountain infantry battalions almost completely combat ineffective. Furthermore, and of critical importance, it had reopened the Oued Zarga-Medjez el Bab road as a key supply route, which made it much easier to support the division in its operations in the mountains. Over the past four days, the *Luftwaffe* in Tunisia had been forced to commit significant resources to the battle and had suffered considerable aircraft losses that greatly reduced its effectiveness for future operations. There was another side to the ledger of battle, and a much more disagreeable one for the division's unit commanders to contemplate. The fighting in the hills had been tiring and probably more costly than had been originally envisaged. The best estimate is that between 0600 hours on 3 April and 0600 hours on10 April, the division and its attached units suffered some 159 men killed or died of wounds, plus 862 wounded in action. In total, the division and attached units had lost over 1,000 men dead or wounded, a stiff price to pay for completing the first stage of Operation Sweep and specifically reopening the Oued Zarga to Medjez el Bab road. These losses fell primarily on the division's three infantry brigades, which had already suffered considerable casualties over the last five months of the campaign. Among the nine battalions of the Battle-Axe Division, the unit which had probably been hardest hit from the last three days was the 5th Buffs, which had lost 26 men killed and 209 wounded; a casualty rate of approximately 30 percent. It was not surprising that the division needed time to rest, regroup and resupply its units while also receiving and rapidly integrating battle casualty replacements. The latter no doubt found the process of being moved to and incorporated into completely unfamiliar units unsettling, as they must have been acutely aware they were taking the place of men killed or wounded, and moreover they would quickly be committed to battle.[1]

7.2 The Wider Picture

Before reviewing the plans and preparations for the next stage of Operation Sweep and the subsequent fighting, it is worth briefly looking at the wider strategic picture and other developments in Tunisia. In retrospect, it is far too easy to conclude that by early April the fate of the German and Italian forces in Tunisia would be quickly sealed. For example, the combined Axis forces in the country at this time numbered some 190,000 troops, including veteran units of the *Afrika Korps*. Furthermore, now that the German-Italian forces had successfully withdrawn from Libya into Tunisia, they had linked up with the 5th *Panzer* Army in the north. The area that the Axis forces needed to defend had reduced significantly, and as a result their defensive line would be stronger and more difficult to break. The newly established *Armeegruppe Afrika* also received additional reinforcements, as the 999th Infantry and Hermann Goering Divisions had started to arrive. On the same day that Operation Sweep began, Adolf Hitler met Benito Mussolini at Klessheim Castle in Salzburg, Austria, to discuss the situation in North Africa. This led to a joint directive that the Axis bridgehead in Tunisia must be held at all costs. The two leaders considered it essential for the Axis position in Tunisia to be maintained to prevent any attack on Sicily and Italy until the autumn of 1943, at which point winter might delay any landings. If the Axis forces had managed to conserve, maintain and resupply their forces, it is possible that Allied victory in Tunisia might have been delayed for several months, with an adverse impact on the duration of the war.[2] There was, however, considerable evidence to

---

1   The figures reflect the casualties for the 78th Division and all attached units, including the losses of the 6th Black Watch and 16th Durham Light Infantry for the period up to 14 April when the former was relieved on Djebel Rmel. Although these losses were incurred outside of the period, they are included as their story is part of this book and the units were actively involved in Operation Sweep. The casualty estimates were derived using the sources previously cited: TNA WO 175/420 78th Division ADMS April 1943 WD and CWGC records.

2   Details of the strategic picture and planning are derived from H. Alexander, *Despatches, The African Campaign from El Alamein to Tunis* (London: *London Gazette*, February 1948); TNA WO 175/16

suggest that, irrespective of the apparent strength of the ground forces, the Axis hold on Tunisia had been gravely weakened and was unlikely to survive further attack.

The Achilles heel for the Axis forces in Tunisia was the vulnerability of their maritime supply routes from Sicily and Italy to Allied air and sea attacks. There was no point in reinforcing forces in the country if they could not be resupplied with equipment, spares, fuel and food. The threat against these supply routes had troubled Rommel when he commanded the *Afrika Korps*, and now that he had gone, left the new senior Axis commanders in Tunisia with their own kind of logistical nightmare. From the outset of the Tunisian campaign, Axis merchant ships using the main shipping routes from Sicily and Italy had come under attack by Royal Navy submarines, Royal Air Force (RAF) coastal command torpedo bombers and other Allied aircraft. This joint interdiction campaign sank precious and irreplaceable Italian merchant ships and sent critical heavy equipment, tanks, vehicles, fuel and men to the bottom of the sea. However, active countermeasures, including minefields and improved convoy escorts, had managed to limit but not slow these losses. The Germans also made extensive use of the *Luftwaffe* transport fleet, and particularly the JU-52 transport aircraft, to move men and supplies. This method could only solve part of the problem, and could not move tanks, vehicles or the scale of supplies required. For example, a successful voyage by just one 3,000 ton ship could deliver two days of supplies for the Axis forces. If the Axis had managed to use the winter period to build up considerable reserves of ammunition, fuel and equipment, they might have held out longer. Unfortunately, the Germans and Italians experienced a combination of bad luck and enemy action that precluded such an outcome. Their bad luck was that the weather in the southern Mediterranean between January and March was some of the worst in recent years, which significantly reduced their ability to move supplies.

The two key enemy actions were the increasing strength and effectiveness of Allied air power when directed against the Axis supply system and attacks by RN submarines. Allied aircraft began to target not only shipping but also both Tunisian and Italian ports. The most obvious evidence of the eventual fate of the Axis forces in Tunisia was that the last attempt by the Italian Navy to move large merchant ships in convoy to Tunisia ended in failure in early April and led to any future attempts being halted. The Axis supply situation had become critical, as insufficient reserves had been stockpiled and the movement of all supplies was totally reliant on small ships and air transport. As Allied air forces in Tunisia increased and more US fighter units arrived, these aerial supply routes became very vulnerable. This vulnerability was especially demonstrated when Operation Flax, an aerial offensive against Axis air supply routes, was unleashed at 0800 hours on 5 April. A fighter sweep by 26 American P38 Lightnings intercepted 50-70 JU-52s north-east of Cap Bon in Tunisia, with 15 of them being shot down. American fighters destroyed a total of 53 Junkers transport aircraft between 10 and 18 April. This level of losses could not be sustained by the *Luftwaffe*, and the fate of the *Armeegruppe Afrika* appeared to have been decided sooner, rather than later, though tough fighting remained ahead.[3]

As the long-term future of the Axis forces in Tunisia was being decided through increasing pressure on its supply routes, *Armeegruppe Afrika* also came under direct attack on land. On

18th Army Group April WD; WO 175/50 First Army April 1943 WD; Playfair, *Destruction of Axis*, Chapters 11-13; and Rolf, *Bloody Road to Tunis*, pp.146-49, 200-01.

3   See Alan Levine, *The War against Rommel's Supply lines 1942-43* (Westport, USA: Praeger, 1999), and Playfair, *Destruction of the Axis Forces*, pp.410-16, for details of the attack on Axis supply lines.

the night before Operation Sweep had been launched, Bernard Montgomery's Eighth Army commenced its attack on the German defensive line at Wadi Akarit. This offensive had been closely coordinated with the launch of First Army's own attack by Eighteenth Army Group headquarters to ensure that the Axis forces in Tunisia could not strip the southern front to reinforce the north or vice versa. The assault on Wadi Akarit began on the night of 5/6 April with a surprise attack on the mountains by 4th Indian Division. This was followed by operations to breach Wadi Akarit positions on the coast. The fighting lasted for 48 hours, during almost the same period as the first two days of Operation Sweep, and both operations were launched to benefit from each other. After difficult fighting and nearly 1,300 casualties, Montgomery's Eighth Army broke through the Axis defences and took over 7,000 prisoners. Originally Alexander had planned to take advantage of this attack by using his newly established Army Group strategic reserve, the British IX Corps, to attack well south of Medjez El Bab towards Pichon and Fondouk pass. The intention was to break through the Fondouk pass and drive down to cut off the retreat of the First Italian Army. Unfortunately, IX Corps, led by its commander Lieutenant General Crocker, underestimated the strength of resistance and a series of errors prevented the Allies from springing the trap before the Axis forces escaped north. One piece of good news was that at 1600 hours on 7 April, an American patrol from Patton's II US Corps met a unit of the 4th Indian Division and thereafter the two armies had soon made physical contact and were able to link up. Both the German and Italian forces were able to retreat to occupy the last feasible defensive line before Tunis, the formidable Enfidaville position, which comprised a narrow coastal strip with rugged and high mountains to the west. This defensive line included the highest mountain in Tunisia, Zaghouan, and a series of hills as rugged as any north of Medjez and was to prove very difficult to breach.

Although it seems that Alexander had probably concluded in March that the main attack on Tunis would be carried out by the First Army, he had still not formally informed his Eighth Army commander of this view by early April. Despite his new elevated status, Alexander sometimes disliked informing Montgomery of decisions the latter might question. It may be true that Alexander hadn't yet made the decision and wanted to confuse the Axis commanders on his intentions. If this was the case, the only result was that he managed to confuse both his army commanders, each of whom seemed to be planning separately to carry out the task. It was certainly true that, in the absence of clear orders, Montgomery continued to plan on the assumption that the final attack would be carried out by the Eighth and not the First Army. He ordered his subordinates to plan Operation Oration, an attack designed to break through part of the Enfidaville defences on or about 18 April. This task was to be carried out by two of his best formations; the 4th Indian and 2nd New Zealand Divisions. Their experienced commanders had considerable reservations about the likely success of this attack, but Montgomery ignored them. In contrast to Monty, the Axis commanders, and especially von Arnim, had significant confidence in their defensive lines, but they needed to as it was their last real line of defence. The consequence of these events was that the German forces in the north could focus all their efforts on dealing with the V Corps offensive (the second phase of Operation Sweep). Von Arnim also arranged to transfer key German units and equipment to the north to deal with the threat posed in that area.

Meanwhile, at Eighteenth Army Group headquarters, General Alexander and his staff were looking ahead and planning for the next stage of operations, specifically the final attack on Tunis. By 11 April, Alexander had finally decided that the First Army would carry out the main attack on Tunis and he informed Montgomery of this news. He also had a visit from his boss, General Eisenhower, and received some guidance he had not expected or desired. Eisenhower made clear that for political and military reasons he wanted the whole of the US II Corps to be used in a significant role in the forthcoming offensive. Alexander did not think highly of the American Army and had originally intended to employ only one US division; now he had to plan to insert the 90,000-man US II Corps into its own sector in the north of Tunisia. Finally, on 12 April, Alexander also directed Kenneth Anderson to plan and prepare for a full-scale attack designed to capture Tunis, commencing on or after 22 April. At this point Anderson and his staff were busy working with Allfrey's corps staff to launch the next phase of operations, and also directing the operations of IX Corps in its costly attack on the Fondouk pass. It was of course perfectly reasonable to task Anderson's staff with executing one operation and preparing and planning for another at the same time. The First Army staff were expected and resourced to execute and plan operations in varying degrees of maturity. Nonetheless, assigning a target date of 22 April for the final attack on Tunis indicates that someone in the new chain of command – Alexander, Anderson or Allfrey, or even all three – had become unrealistically optimistic about the German abilities to resist future attacks in the mountains. The first stage of operations in Operation Sweep had taken four days just to clear the Germans back from the main supply route from Beja to Medjez and had cost over 1,000 casualties.[4] A full-scale attack on Tunis was only possible if V Corps was able to remove the threat posed by the German forces located on the rugged mountains north of the Medjez to Tebourba road. This required the weary 78th Division to seize Djebels Ang and Tanngoucha, the mountain village of Heidous and of course also recapture Longstop Hill. The latter had been in German hands for almost four months and its defences had been significantly strengthened. According to Alexander's directive, V Corps and the 78th Division would have just four or five days after starting the next phase of operations, scheduled to start on 14 April, to finish Operation Sweep. Afterwards, it would have two to three days to rest and bring up supplies before taking part in Alexander's proposed attack on 22 April. This was a tall order even for any full-strength and fresh division, and the 78th Division met neither of those criteria.

The date in the directive demonstrates that Alexander and his staff, led by his normally capable Chief of Staff Richard McCreery, had unrealistic expectations. They appeared to have failed to understand how a combination of the terrain, German fighting skills and the gradually weakening fighting strength of the Battle-Axe Division was likely to require more time to finish off the Battle of the Peaks. Unfortunately, Anderson and his staff had either become victims to this new heady optimism, or were unwilling or unable to advise Eighteenth Army Group that their plans were unrealistic. Events would demonstrate clearly that this plan was far too optimistic. Another complication was that now that American concerns about their omission from the final attack had led to a change of heart by Alexander, the whole of US II Corps needed to be moved, along with its equipment, from Tebessa in the south over 200 miles north across

---

4   Alexander notified Montgomery formally in a signal on the evening of 11 April; see Playfair, *Destruction of the Axis Forces*, p.397. The official order was issued on 16 April; see Eighteenth Army Group Operational Instruction No. 12 16 April 1943 in TNA WO 175/16 18 Army Group April 1943 WD. It is worth noting that Anderson had already issued his own directive for the capture of Tunis two days previously; see Anderson's Personal Directive of First Army Commander dated 14 April in TNA WO 175/50 First Army April 1943 WD.

the main west-east supply routes of the First Army. The corps was now commanded by Major General Omar Bradley and had to be moved to gradually take over from British units holding positions north and east of Beja. One key benefit of this move was that it released the 4th and 46th Infantry Divisions for use in other operations. This process started on 14 April, when the US 9th Infantry Division started to take over the positions of the 46th Infantry Division west of Sidi Nisr. The forces in the upper Bed Valley, including 6th Black Watch on Djebel Rmel, were therefore relieved by units of the 1st US Armoured Division in mid-April. US forces were to carry out a supporting role by protecting the northern flank of V Corps by carrying out a supporting attack in the Tine valley and releasing others formations to concentrate for the attack further south. The II Corps attack did not occur until the morning of 23 April and was not part of the Battle of the Peaks, so it will not be considered here further, though like Sweep, it is a neglected operation worthy of attention.

Meanwhile, Anderson expected Allfrey and Evelegh to plan and execute the next stage of Operation Sweep. The main burden of this task appears to have fallen on Evelegh, although it is likely Allfrey provided oversight and guidance. The evidence shows that Evelegh did not, however, receive any formal orders for the next stage from his commander, for V Corps published no additional operational orders during this period. This was probably fine with the GOC 78th Division, as he had largely planned Operation Sweep's initial stage in his first operational order and was happy to plan and execute the next phase. Before we consider how Evelegh planned to carry out the next stage of the operation, it is worth briefly looking at the way in which the division was assisted in preparing for the next attack by its various logistic support units.

7.3 The Supporting Services

Far too many accounts of land battles ignore the unglamorous but critical role played by the various supporting services, as they are technically known. Yet without their efforts, the fighting battalions and their accompanying tanks and artillery could not do their job. It is perfectly fair that those who did the fighting should get much, if not all, of the credit and attention, but supporting services also deserve recognition, yet their work is so frequently ignored. In order to conduct its operations, the 78th Division had to be supplied with fuel, ammunition and food and receive replacements. The formation's three RASC direct support companies and a single divisional troops company, supplemented by other companies, conducted this task continuously and almost flawlessly during the battle. Each of the RASC companies had sixty 3-ton lorries for a combined total of 180 vehicles. Not every vehicle was, however, serviceable all the time, but the task had still to be performed. The primary task of the divisional RASC companies and their attached RAOC detachments, was to store and move food - usually comprised of Composite (Compo) rations - all types of ammunition, various supplies and fuel from divisional stores and ammunition dumps to forward brigade dumps, where individual units' own transport would collect them. Until the opening of the main Beja-Medjez road, this usually involved round trips of nearly 100 miles across poor roads over rugged terrain and at night. Later, the journey would be to bring ammunition from dumps at Dougga and Beja to the brigade ammunition point and other locations north of the Oued Zarga road. One of the critical tasks carried out by RASC drivers, in the lead-up to and during Operation Sweep, was bringing large quantities of ammunition for all the artillery regiments. For example, as part of the initial preparation for Operation Sweep's first stage, two RASC companies each had to load, move and dump

2,400 shells at 17th and 132nd Field Regiments' forward firing positions on just one day. Since these regiments were in concealed positions in the hills south of the Oued Zarga road, this task had to be largely completed at night so that dust clouds would not reveal the positions of the batteries. The process of moving ammunition and supplies of all types had to be continued once Operation Sweep began. For example, Major Broadbent's 328th RASC Company, which directly supported the 36th Infantry Brigade, was constantly at work moving bulk rations, fuel and large quantities of shells during the period from 6-10 April. Over this period, Broadbent's company made repeated journeys at night to move approximately 20,000 rounds of 25-pounder and 5,000 rounds of 5.5in gun ammunition from dumps at Dougga, Beja and Souk el Arba up to the brigade ammunition point. It also carried some 12,500 bulk rations up to brigade units, and next obtained a further 16,600 from division stores dumps, while also moving large amounts of fuel and oil.[5]

While the divisional RASC companies quietly but efficiently provided critical support to the three fighting brigades, a wide range of other supporting services also carried out important work. The rugged terrain and enemy action took its toll on the serviceability of divisional vehicles, but fortunately a brand new corps in the British Army was able to quickly repair all types of vehicles. The Corps of Royal Electrical and Mechanical Engineers (REME) had been formally established less than a month before the landings in North Africa on 1 October 1942. The majority of its 5,000 officers and 80,000 men had been transferred to this new corps from the RAOC. REME was deemed to be a tradesman corps, with private soldiers being called craftsmen. At this time, the Royal Engineers retained their responsibility for maintaining their own engineering equipment and the RASC still repaired their own vehicle fleet. The two main units of the REME, in or attached to the 78th Division, were three Infantry Brigade Workshops, a workshop for the 25th Tank Brigade and two individual Light Aid Detachments (LAD) which were attached to the tank battalions supporting the division. All these units worked hard under trying conditions to recover and repair all types of vehicles. The officer commanding these various units, with the title Commander REME (CREME), was Lieutenant Colonel T. Laird. REME workshop units were usually located well back from the front line so they would not be disturbed by enemy fire. Unfortunately, during the first two weeks of Operation Sweep, this did not mean they would not be exposed to the hostile attentions of the *Luftwaffe*. On the morning of 13 April, the newly established workshops of the LAD of the North Irish Horse at Oued Zarga was bombed and machine gunned. The LAD commander, Captain Leslie REME, was killed and two other members of the detachment wounded. The most exposed members of the REME were usually the recovery crews. Their job was to go forward to recover disabled or damaged vehicles and bring them back to the workshops, where they could be repaired and returned to the fight.[6]

Among additional services providing support to the division in a number of different ways at this time were members of the Corps of Military Police, or Redcaps as they were widely known due to the colour of their headdress, who manned lonely and sometimes dangerous crossroads to ensure vehicles did not stray into hazardous areas. They also helped guard German prisoners before they were sent back to the rear areas. Soldiers from the RAOC maintained supply dumps,

---

5   For the activities of the 328th RASC Company, see TNA WO 175/941 328 RASC Company April 1943 WD.

6   Details of the activities of the REME are from TNA WO 175/175 Commander REME April 1943 WD, and TNA WO 175/294 1 North Irish Horse April 1943 WD.

mended weapons and, upon the formation of the REME, took over responsibility for repairing RASC vehicles. The maintenance of signal communications within the Battle-Axe Division was the responsibility of the Royal Corps of Signals, which had to maintain radio networks and communication lines that enabled everyone above battalion level to communicate effectively. They also provided motorcycle dispatch riders who carried copies of vital orders and documents across the division. Other services such as the Intelligence Corps helped interrogate prisoners and disseminate vital information of enemy locations and strengths to the brigades.

Perhaps the two services who gained least recognition for their efforts, but nonetheless performed essential tasks, were the Army Catering Corps (ACC) and the Pioneer Corps. ACC cooks, supported by RASC bakers and butchers, were present in all units, including fighting battalions. They worked miracles in isolated and difficult locations to feed their officers and soldiers freshly cooked food instead of composite rations whenever possible. Napoleon is reputed to have said that an army marches on its stomach, and throughout history the quality and availability of fresh food - or its absence - has been a key factor in improving or lowering a soldier's morale. ACC chefs worked long hours during the operation to ensure that, whenever possible, hot and tasty food was available. The period from 10-13 April enabled several battalions to be briefly moved to locations where they could have access to their battalion chefs and be fed hot meals.

Last, but certainly not least, there were the officers and men of the newly established Pioneer Corps. Strictly speaking, the division did not include any pioneer companies within its organisation, but it would be remiss not to briefly note their contribution to the division. It is certainly true that their work was greatly valued in the 78th Division rear areas, as the division staff gave one of the key bridges west of Oued Zarga the name Pioneer Bridge. When formed in October 1940, the Pioneer Corps was the youngest corps in the British Army, but it could trace its origins much further back in time. The first record of pioneers goes back to 1346 at Calais, where the pay and muster rolls of the English garrison show pay records for pioneers. Many pioneers from the new corps served in France with the BEF and were lost when HMT *Lancastria* was sunk off the French port of St Nazaire in June 1940. The convoys which sailed to Tunisia from November 1942 onwards eventually included several pioneer groups and nearly 50 pioneer companies. These performed a wide range of manual labour tasks, whether it be unloading cargo from ships in Algerian ports, working on roads, bridges and airfields for the Royal Engineers or clearing debris from bombing raids. Pioneers also helped move supplies at depots near to the front, dug trenches and removed obstacles. In Tunisia, pioneers not only dug trenches but often occupied them, as on several occasions elements of pioneer companies took over infantry positions in the quieter areas of the front line. This was the case in April when elements of the 175th Pioneer Company took over front-line positions. On 11 April, pioneers of the 175th were protecting a road bridge near Medjez when a bombing raid killed two pioneers and wounded three others. Although not directly part of the Battle-Axe Division, pioneers provided important assistance to the formation, both in the forward areas and also as far back as Algiers. While they might appear to have a safer role than those in the front line, the men of the 175th Pioneer Company had the highest losses of any pioneer company in Tunisia, with 30 killed and 43 wounded in a company of only 289 officers and men. Although the work of the 175th Company stands out, many other pioneer companies made an invaluable indirect and direct contribution to the success of the operations in Tunisia. A total of 110 members of the Pioneer Corps were killed in Algeria and Tunisia before the Axis surrender. By end of the war, the Pioneer Corps numbered 12,000 officers and 166,000 men, and their efforts in support of victory were rewarded by the grant of the title Royal in 1946.[7]

7.4 Corps and Divisional Plan for Next Phase

While all the various supporting services were conducting a wide variety of essential tasks to support the next attack, the attention of Charles Allfrey and his staff was focused on tasks needed to execute Alexander's orders for a major offensive on 22 April. Two developments are particularly worth mentioning. Allfrey's main concern was to reorganise his corps prior to the proposed offensive and concentrate his three divisions - the 1st, 4th and 78th Infantry Divisions - around Medjez. He also had to give up the 46th Infantry Division, which had fought in the north, to IX Corps, which had become Alexander's strategic army group reserve and was based near Bou Arada. These moves were possible because, from 12 April, units of the US II Corps began arriving around Sedjenane and Beja, starting with 9th US Infantry Division. The 9th was followed by the Big Red One (1st US Infantry) on 16 April and two other divisions on the 22 April. The move of 90,000 US troops from the south to the north of Tunisia across the First Army lines of communications was a major achievement in operational logistics planning by officers from both American and British armies. These changes enabled Allfrey to gradually concentrate his corps around and to the south of Medjez el Bab. While Alexander and Anderson stressed the need to launch attacks on 22 April in their various plans and directives, Allfrey seems to have taken a rather different view. His instructions to his staff and commanders on 11 April called for planning and preparations to seize key objectives such as Longstop and the ground east of Medjez to be finished by 25 April, and attacks to take place subsequently.[8] In hindsight, this confusion indicates that there may have been a difference in thinking between that of Eighteenth Army Group and First Army, and that of Allfrey at V Corps. In retrospect, Allfrey's planning assumptions about how rapidly 78th Division would complete Operation Sweep seemed more realistic than his senior commanders. For example, the recapture of Longstop Hill actually took place from 23-26 April.

While Allfrey was working on future operations, Vyvyan Evelegh, GOC 78th Division, was focused on daily operations and rapid planning to launch that formation's next attack. In contrast to the initial stage of the operation, Evelegh and his staff did not have the luxury of spending time on a formal written appreciation, but this was not required, as by now he had a good grasp of the terrain in the future area of operations. His resulting plan, however, showed that Evelegh had grasped the essential details of the tactical challenge the division faced and clearly understood how to tackle it. Evelegh was ably assisted by his two key staff officers, Lieutenant Colonel Reggie Hewetson, his GSO 1 Operations, and his senior administrative officer, the Canadian Lieutenant Colonel W.A. Bean. The latter's title was a bit of a mouthful, the Assistant Adjutant and Quartermaster General (AA & QMG), but his job was important as he was responsible for all logistic planning. Bean also continued the new trend for Canadian

7   Details of the operations of the Pioneer Corps are from www.royalpioneercorps.co.uk (accessed 5 January 2018), M. Rhodes-Wood, *A War History of the Royal Pioneer Corps 1939-45* (Aldershot: Gale and Polden, 1960) and also from CWGC records.
8   See Operational Instruction No. 17 dated 11 April 1943 in TNA WO 175/82 V Corps April 1943 WD.

officers to fill selected roles in the Battle-Axe Division. He had led the first party of Canadians to Tunisia, spent time at First Army HQ and at V Corps, before temporarily taking on the vital post of AA & QMG in the 78th Division. Bean translated Evelegh's operational plans into sound administrative and logistic instructions in tandem with the commanders of all the supporting services in the division.[9]

The GOCs next operational order, no. 8, reconfirmed that the division's long-term objective remained the seizure of Djebel Tanngoucha, that high brooding mountain which overlooked the village of Heidous and Longstop Hill. This would allow V Corps to attack and seize Longstop and enable the rest of the corps and First Army carry out an advance toward Tunis south of the Medjerda valley. The operational order reflected the existing realities dictated by terrain, the enemy positions and the status of the division. Simply and crudely put, the Battle-Axe Division would be "Djebel hopping", for it would capture one line of djebels in order to secure positions from which to launch attacks on the next. It also had to ensure the flanks of any major attack were secured by taking additional flanking hills. As Anderson noted, the hill country could swallow up entire formations. The attacks would be carried out in four phases and two lines of advance: one from Point 667, east to Djebel Bou Diss and onwards to Djebel Ang and via a long ridge called Kef el Tiour to Tanngoucha itself; the second axis north-east from the village of Chaouach via Djebels Hamri, Kelbine, Bettiour and Mahdouma via Djebel Ang or Heidous to Tanngoucha. Evelegh chose Cass's 11th Brigade to conduct the majority of operations during the four phases of this part of Operation Sweep, although Howlett's brigade would play a brief role. He had little choice here, as 38th Irish Brigade had only completed operations in the Bed Valley on 10 April and needed time to rest and be resupplied. Moreover, of the remaining brigades, probably the best choice was the 11th Brigade, as it had suffered marginally fewer casualties than the 36th in the first five days. It is arguable that Evelegh was far too optimistic in his assumptions about the nature of German resistance, as his plan relied solely on Cass's brigade to conduct three out of the four phases of the plan and seize the most difficult objectives, Djebels Ang and Tanngoucha.

The reality is that Anderson's comment that the mountains swallowed entire formations proved uncannily accurate, and before the battle was over all three brigades would take part in the effort to capture Tanngoucha. Despite their extensive experience and skills, or the bitter lessons gained during winter fighting, the GOC, his staff and his commanders seriously underestimated the time and resources required for the forthcoming battle. Rocky crags defended by stubborn German units who launched frequent counterattacks would frustrate Evelegh's plans and upset an overly optimistic timetable set out at all levels, up to and including Alexander's Eighteenth Army Group HQ.[10]

9   The activities of Bean and other Canadians in Tunisia are recorded in R. Pellerin's article in the *Canadian Military Journal* Volume 17, No.1 (Winter 2016), 'Canadian Infantry in Tunisia', pp.47-56; and Report No. 95 'Attachment of Canadian Officers and soldiers to the First Army'. *Canadian Military History HQ* dated 12 May 1943.

10 Evelegh's plan is detailed in Operational Order No. 8 in TNA WO 175/168 78 Division April 1943 WD.

7.5 Preliminary Moves

The short interlude between the capture of Chaouach and the renewal of the 78th Division's attack allowed the infantry battalions in the 11th and 36th Infantry Brigades varying degrees of time for rest. Howlett's brigade was able to hand over control of the areas of Mergueb Chaouach, Point 667 and Nahel to battalions of the 4th Division, and two of the battalions were moved to near Toukabeur. Despite its reduced strength due to its losses over the last four days, the 5th Buffs were placed under command of 11th Brigade. The 6th West Kents handed over to a sister battalion, the 1st Queen's Own Royal West Kents, on Point 667, but next moved forward to tighten its control over Point 624, Djebel Mansourine. The latter mountain would provide an essential jumping-off point for the projected attack on Djebel Bou Diss to the east. Brigadier Cass kept his four battalions fairly busy conducting essential reconnaissance patrols from their existing positions north and east of Chaouach and securing key features needed for his brigade's attack on the night of 13/14 April towards Tanngoucha. Wilberforce's 1st East Surreys conducted patrols from their positions north of Chaouach to obtain information on German positions to the north-east. This showed that Djebel Bel Rherarif was not occupied, which was a pleasant surprise as Djebel Bel Rherarif was located south of Djebel Bou Diss and south-west of Djebel Mahdouma and Bettiour (see Plate III), both key objectives for the proposed attack. Wilberforce was quick to take advantage of the situation, and on 11 April moved A Company to secure this height. The following day, he started the process of "Djebel hopping" when he shifted the rest of the battalion to the same location. The bloodless occupation of Rherarif secured a useful position for the East Surreys' future attack and allowed Major Harry Smith, who was temporarily in command, to do the 6th West Kents a significant favour. The East Surreys could now protect the approach of the 6th West Kents from Point 624 via the deep river valley of the River Kranga when the latter attacked Djebel Bou Diss. The German 334th Infantry Division was now unable to use Rherarif to call in mortar and artillery fire to obstruct this move. The 5th Northants was also active with patrols during these three days, one of which on the 11/12 April had proved costly. The battalion's IO, Dudley Emmerton (see Plate 10), personally led one patrol which discovered that Djebel Kelbine north-east of Chaouach was also not occupied. Patrolling ensured that Kelbine was not used by the Germans and the hill acted as a valuable stepping stone for the unit's assault on Djebel Bettiour. When the 5th Northants moved up to Kelbine on 13 April, its presence on the peak provoked fire from German mortars, long-range machine guns and snipers during the day and led to the loss of one man killed and 19 others wounded. Though very unfortunate, this loss was more than counterbalanced by the tactical advantage the hill gave to the battalion in its attack that night. Brigadier Cass's units had been blessed with a decent streak of luck for three days, having secured these key locations without any loss, but now this good fortune started to come to an end. The other battalion in the brigade, the 2nd Lancs Fusiliers, spent 10 April retaining its hold on Chaouach and sending patrols to Bettiour. The last three days of operations, all completed in hot weather, had several negative effects on this unit. Both officers and fusiliers were hot, thirsty and fatigued, and the men were annoyed, since there was a shortage of food. The rigours of campaigning were also taking their toll. The CO of the 2nd Lancs Fusiliers, "Red" Kelly, who had already been hospitalized once in March, now fell ill with a septic leg and was sent off to hospital again, his deputy Major Garner-Smith assuming command. It is apparent from an unusually frank entry in the unit's war diary on 12 April that the men had been looking forward to a short well-earned rest, and

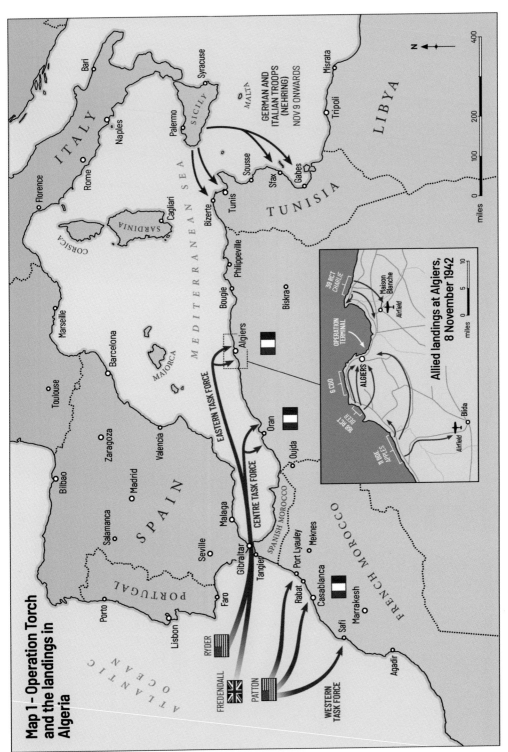

Map 1 – Operation Torch and the Landings in Algeria November 1942

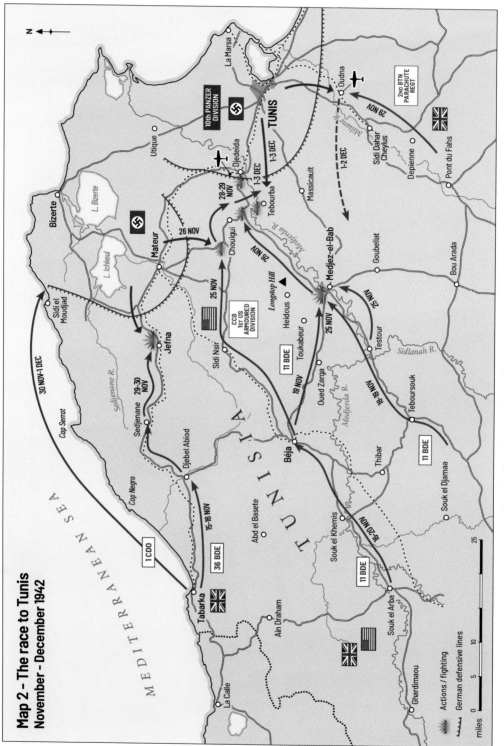

Map 2 – The race to Tunis
November – December 1942

Map 2 – The Race to Tunis, November–December 1942

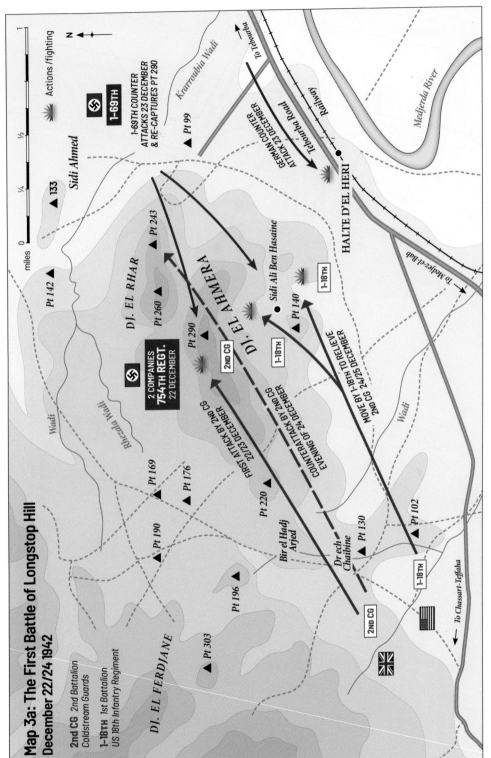

Map 3a – The First Battle for Longstop Hill, 22-24 December 1942

iii

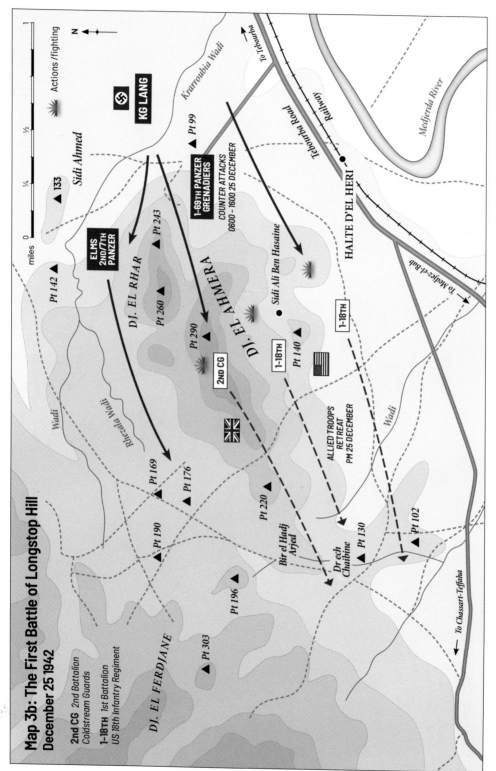

Map 3b: The First Battle of Longstop Hill December 25 1942

2nd CG *2nd Battalion Coldstream Guards*

1-18TH *1st Battalion US 18th Infantry Regiment*

Map 3b – The First Battle for Longstop Hill, 25 December 1942

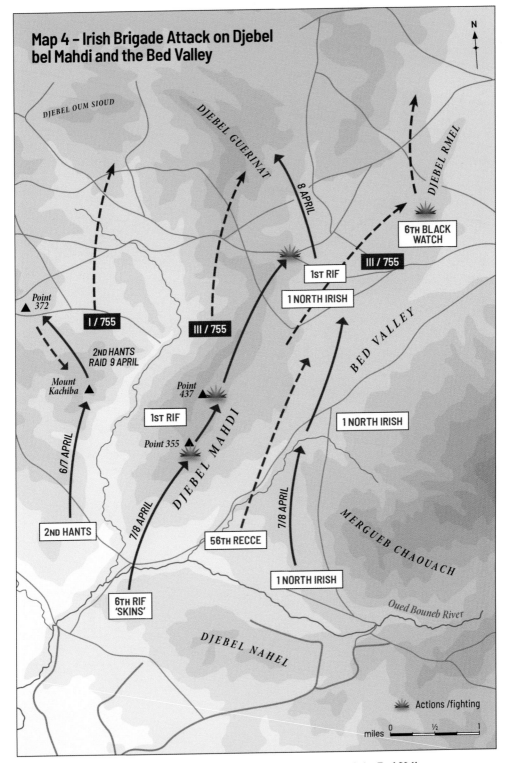

Map 4 – The Irish Brigade Attack on Djebel Mahdi and the Bed Valley

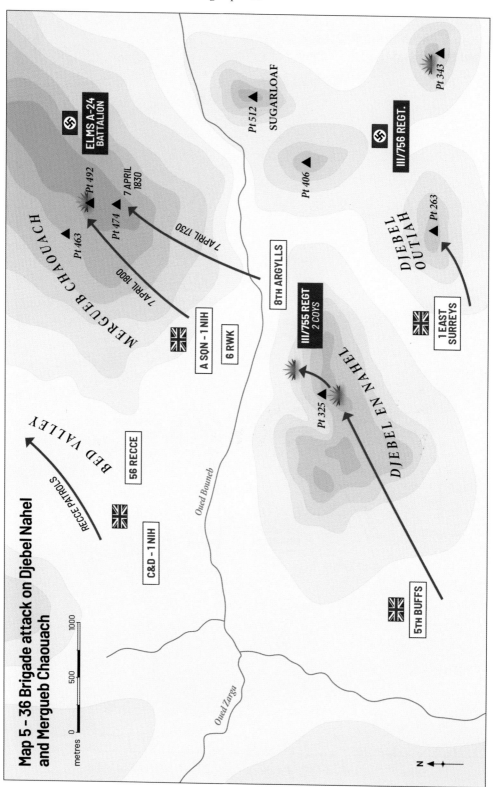

Map 5 – 36 Brigade attack on Djebel Nahel and Mergueb Chaouach

MERGUEB CHAOUACH

ELMS A-24 BATTALION

Pt 492

Pt 463

Pt 474

7 APRIL 1830

7 APRIL 1730

7 APRIL 1800

A SQN – 1 NIH

6 RWK

SUGARLOAF

Pt 512

Pt 406

Pt 343

III/756 REGT.

DJEBEL OUTIAH

Pt 263

1 EAST SURREYS

8TH ARGYLLS

III/755 REGT 2 COYS

DJEBEL EN NAHEL

Pt 325

BED VALLEY

RECCE PATROLS

56 RECCE

C&D – 1 NIH

Oued Bouneb

Oued Zarga

metres   0   500   1000

N

Map 5 – The 36th Brigade Attack on Djebel Nahel and Mergueb Chaouach

5TH BUFFS

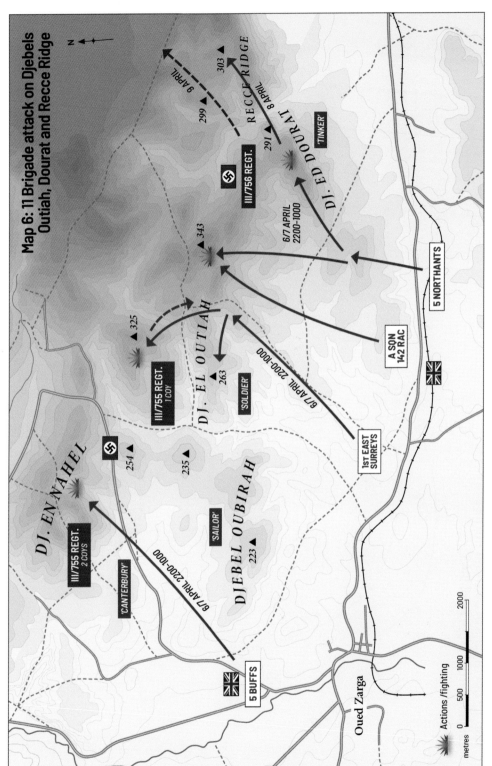

Map 6 – 11th Infantry Brigade's Attack on Djebel Outiah, Dourat and Recce Ridge

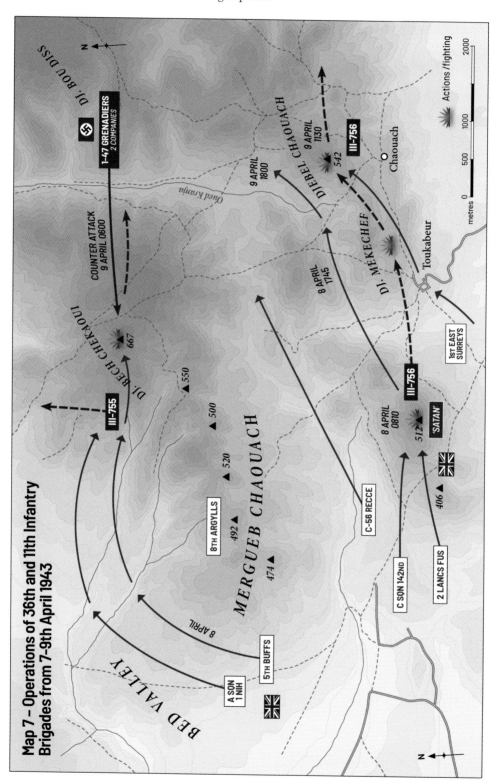

Map 7 – Operations of 36th and 11th Infantry Brigades from 7-9th April 1943

DJ. BOU DISS

1-47 GRENADIERS
2 COMPANIES

COUNTER ATTACK
9 APRIL 0600

Oued Kranfa

DJ. BECH CHEKAOUI

III-755

667

550

500

520

8TH ARGYLLS

492

MERGUEB CHAOUACH

474

8 APRIL

RED VALLEY

5TH BUFFS

A SQN
1 NIH

N

9 APRIL
1800

DJEBEL CHAOUACH

9 APRIL
1130

III-756

542

Chaouach

DJ. MEKECHEF

8 APRIL
1745

Toukabeur

1ST EAST
SURREYS

III-756

8 APRIL
0810

512

'SATAN'

406

C-56 RECCE

C SQN 142ND

2 LANCS FUS

N

metres
0   500   1000   2000

Actions / fighting

Map 7 – Operations of 36th and 11th Infantry Brigades from April 7-9 1943

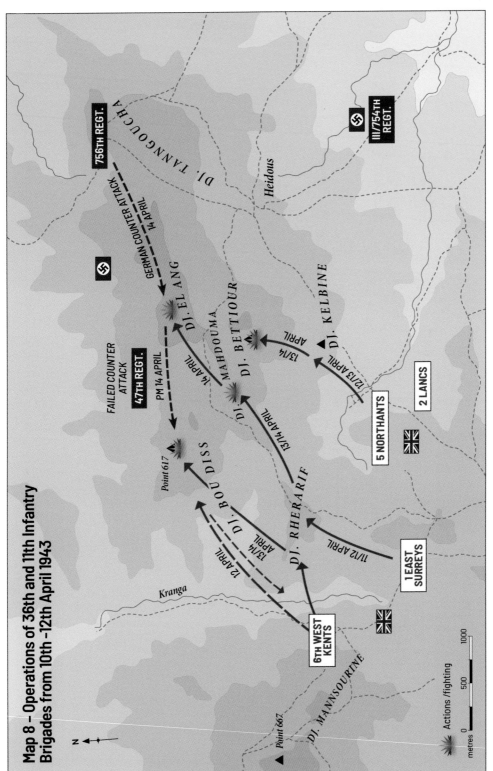

Map 8 – Operations of 36th and 11th Infantry Brigades from 10th –12th April 1943

Map 8 – Operations of the 36th and 11th Infantry Brigades from 10-12 April 1943

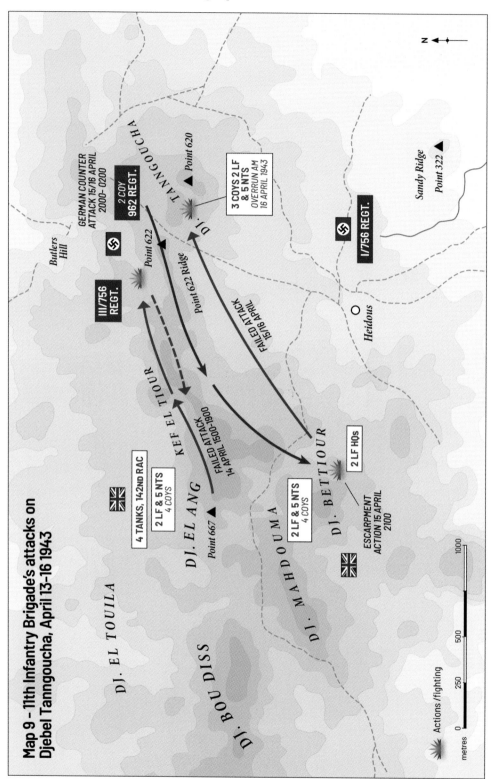

Map 9 – 11th Infantry Brigade's attacks on Djebel Tanngoucha, April 13–16 1943

DJ. EL TOUILA

DJ· BOU DISS

DJ· MAHDOUMA

DJ· EL ANG

KEF EL TIOUR

DJ· TANNGOUCHA

DJ· BETTIOUR

Butlers Hill

III/756 REGT.

GERMAN COUNTER ATTACK 15/16 APRIL 2000–0200

2 COY 962 REGT.

Point 622

Point 622 Ridge

Point 620

3 COYS 2 LF & 5 NTS OVERRUN AM 16 APRIL 1943

I/756 REGT.

Sandy Ridge
Point 322

Heidous

FAILED ATTACK 15/16 APRIL

FAILED ATTACK 14 APRIL 1500–1900

4 TANKS, 142ND RAC

2 LF & 5 NTS 4 COYS

Point 667

2 LF & 5 NTS 4 COYS

2 LF HQs

ESCARPMENT ACTION 15 APRIL 2100

Actions/fighting

metres

0   250   500   1000

N

Map 9 – 11th Infantry Brigade's Attacks on Djebel Tanngoucha, 13-16 April 1943

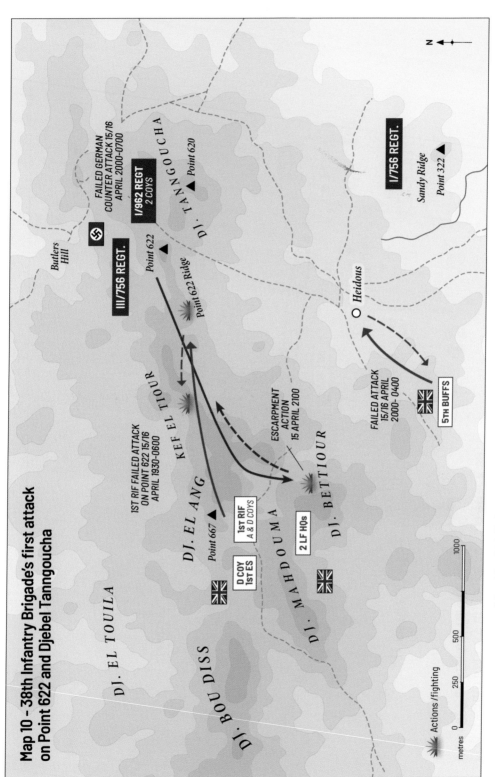

Map 10 – 38th Infantry Brigade's First Attack on Point 622 and Djebel Tanngoucha

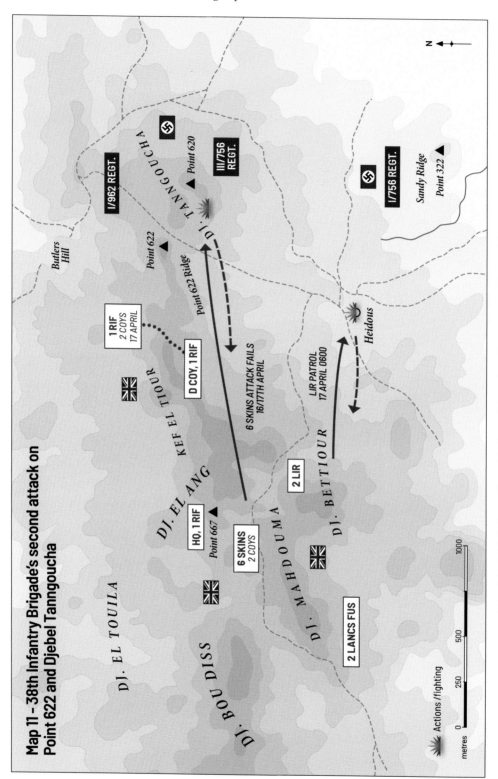

Map 11 – 38th Infantry Brigade's second attack on Point 622 and Djebel Tanngoucha

Map 11 – 38th Infantry Brigade's second attack on Point 622 and Djebel Tanngoucha

I/962 REGT.

III/756 REGT.

I/756 REGT.

Sandy Ridge
Point 322

Point 620

Point 622

DJ. TANNGOUCHA

Butlers Hill

Point 622 Ridge

1 RIF
2 COYS
17 APRIL

D COY, 1 RIF

KEF EL TIOUR

DJ. EL ANG

DJ. EL TOUILA

6 SKINS ATTACK FAILS
16/17TH APRIL

Heidous

LIR PATROL
17 APRIL 0600

2 LIR

DJ. BETTIOUR

HQ, 1 RIF
Point 667

6 SKINS
2 COYS

DJ. MAHDOUMA

DJ. BOU DISS

2 LANCS FUS

Actions / fighting

metres
0   250   500   1000

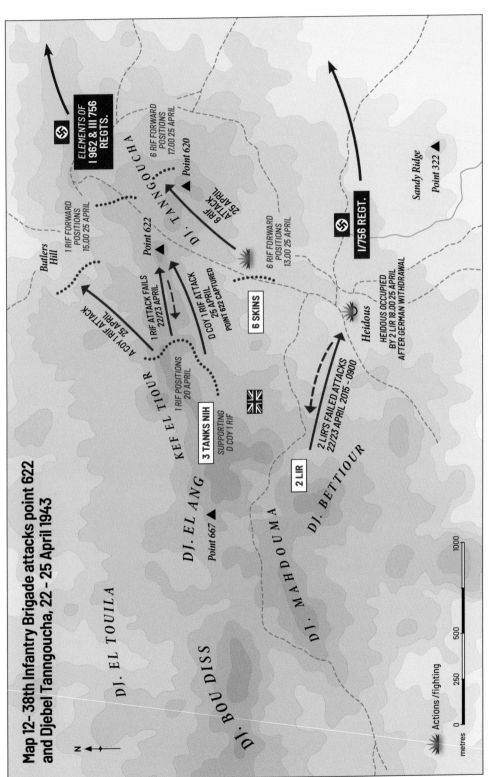

Map 12 – 38th Infantry Brigade Captures Point 622 and Djebel Tanngoucha, 22-25 April 1943

Map 12– 38th Infantry Brigade attacks point 622 and Djebel Tanngoucha, 22 – 25 April 1943

N

DJ. EL TOUILA

DJ. BOU DISS

DJ. EL ANG

Point 667 ▲

KEF EL TIOUR

1 RIF POSITIONS
20 APRIL

3 TANKS NIH
SUPPORTING
D COY 1 RIF

Butler's
Hill

A COY 1 RIF ATTACK
25 APRIL

1 RIF ATTACK FAILS
22/23 APRIL

D COY 1 RIF ATTACK
25 APRIL
POINT 622 CAPTURED

Point 622 ▲

DJ. TANNGOUCHA

Point 622 ▲

1 RIF FORWARD
POSITIONS
15.00 25 APRIL

6 RIF
ATTACK
25 APRIL

ELEMENTS OF
I 962 & III 756
REGTS.

6 RIF FORWARD
POSITIONS
17.00 25 APRIL

Point 620 ▲

6 RIF FORWARD
POSITIONS
13.00 25 APRIL

6 SKINS

Heidous

HEIDOUS OCCUPIED
BY 2 LIR 18.00 25 APRIL
AFTER GERMAN WITHDRAWAL

I/756 REGT.

Sandy Ridge
Point 322 ▲

DJ. MAHDOUMA

DJ. BETTIOUR

2 LIR

2 LIR'S FAILED ATTACKS
22/23 APRIL 2015 – 0900

Actions /fighting

metres   0   250   500   1000

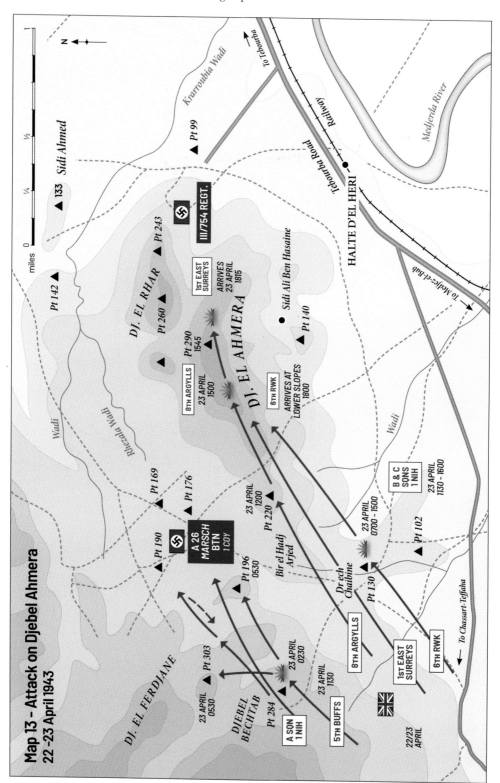

Map 13 – Attack on Djebel Ahmera
22 -23 April 1943

Map 13 – 36th Infantry Brigade's Attack on Djebel Ahmera 22-23 April 1943

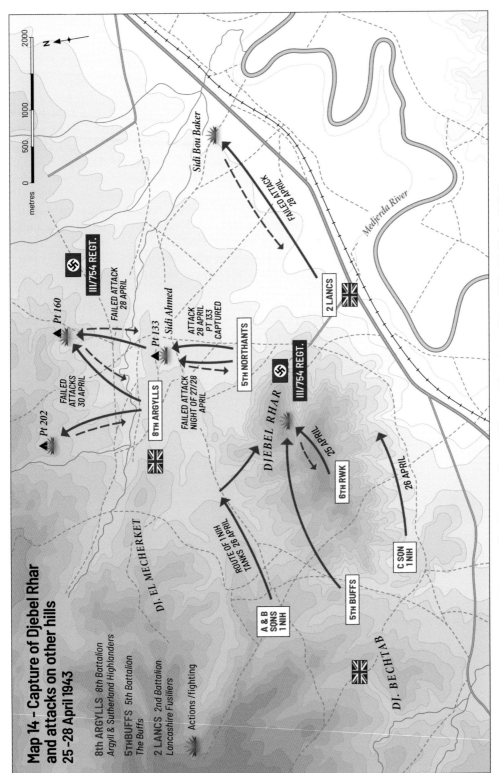

Map 14 - Capture of Djebel Rhar and attacks on other hills 25 -28 April 1943

8th ARGYLLS *8th Battalion Argyll & Sutherland Highlanders*

5TH BUFFS *5th Battalion The Buffs*

2 LANCS *2nd Battalion Lancashire Fusiliers*

🔥 *Actions / fighting*

2000

1000

500

metres

N

Pt 160

Pt 202

III/754 REGT.

FAILED ATTACK 28 APRIL

Pt 133

Sidi Ahmed

ATTACK 28 APRIL PT 133 CAPTURED

5TH NORTHANTS

FAILED ATTACKS 30 APRIL

8TH ARGYLLS

FAILED ATTACK NIGHT OF 27/28 APRIL

DJ. EL MECHERKET

ROUTE OF 1 NIH TANKS 26 APRIL

A & B SQNS 1 NIH

5TH BUFFS

C SQN 1 NIH

26 APRIL

DJEBEL RHAR

III/754 REGT.

6TH RWK

25 APRIL

DJ. BECHTAB

Sidi Bou Baker

FAILED ATTACK 28 APRIL

2 LANCS

Medjerda River

Map 14 – The Capture of Djebel Rhar and Attacks on Other Hills 25–30 April 1943

A Note about Maps in Battle of the Peaks and Longstop Hill

The reader should therefore note that even in 2019 no modern accurate topographical maps exist of the area in which the Battle of the Peaks was fought. Moreover the General Staff Geographical Division (GSGS) maps used by the British Army and referenced in war diaries were themselves based on inaccurate French maps.

As most records of the time refer to the existing GSGS maps the author chose to base the accompanying maps in this book and their references to specific heights on the information in the original maps rather than any more modern topographical information. The accompanying maps 1-14 thus reflect the information on the height of hills that was available in 1943 rather than that today as the descriptions of operations in the book are largely based on records of that time.

The difficult nature of the terrain combined with the absence of modern accurate maps has made it impossible to reproduce maps that exactly portray the terrain as it existed in 1943 and today. Despite these serious limitations Paul Hewitt from Battlefield Design has done an amazing job of creating maps that show the general movements on units around the terrain.

The reader should thus be aware that the maps in this book are not an exact match for the terrain but instead are meant to provide a general illustration of operations and actions. Any minor errors that may exist in these maps are solely the responsibility of the author.

were rather aggrieved when they learned this was not to be. Instead, the fusiliers had a mule transport company attached to them, received their orders for the attack and moved forward overnight on 12/13 April to a lying-up area in a dry river bed just south of Djebel Hamri, ready for its part in the next operation.

Other patrols confirmed that German troops were positioned on the four main peaks that were objectives for the brigade attack: Djebels Bou Diss, Mahdouma, Bettiour and Ang. The 5th Buffs sent A Company to secure Djebel Harig, a small height directly to the east of Chaouach, ensuring the southern flank of Cass's attack would be protected.[11] One reason it had proved possible to secure Rherarif, Kelbine and Harig at so little cost was that after losing over 1,000 men captured, Evelegh's counterpart, the 334th Division commander Friedrich Weber, lacked the strength to hold these locations. The division's withdrawal to the positions it held in February 1943 had shortened the length of its front line, but losses in local offensives in March, combined with those in Operation Sweep, had significantly weakened Weber's force. The 334th had to focus its limited strength to try to defend key heights such as Bou Diss, Bettiour, Ang and Tanngoucha. Weber had received as reinforcements two battalions of the 47th Grenadier Regiment on 9 April, though one of the regiment's companies was immediately lost in a fruitless counterattack on the 5th Buffs on Point 667. The 47th Grenadier Regiment had formed part of the German 22nd *Luftwaffe* Division, which had been part of the garrison on Crete until November 1942, when it was hurriedly moved to Tunisia. It spent most of its time in central Tunisia fighting as part of the Italian XXX Corps near Mont Pichon. It had been sent to Enfidaville on the coast for rest in early April, but had less than three days there before it was abruptly moved to the area near Djebel Bou Diss. In contrast to the other three battalions located nearby - the 1st Battalion of the 756th Mountain Infantry plus and 1st and 3rd Battalions of the 754th Grenadiers - the 47th Grenadier Regiments companies were at full strength.[12] Despite its comparative weakness, Weber's division could nonetheless maintain a formidable defence in the rugged mountains, as they were well equipped with machine guns and mortars. Evelegh must have realized that initially the relative balance of forces slightly favoured the Germans, for 11th Brigade was attacking with four battalions, but Weber's forces were defending with two or three understrength battalions and the two fresh units of the 47th Grenadiers. It has long been a military maxim that an attacking force should outnumber its opposing force by a factor of at least two and ideally three to one. This had not been the case for the initial or the next attack. In addition, on this occasion Cass's brigade would not be supported by any armoured units, for the 142nd RAC Regiment and C Squadron of the 56th Recce would not be available for the operation, though a troop of 142nd RAC tanks would be provided. The difficult terrain and the need for both units to repair and maintain their battered tanks and armoured vehicles precluded their use.

11   Details of the operations of the three battalions are from their respective war diaries for April 1943, regimental histories and also H. Smith, *Operations of East Surreys*.
12   The activities of the 47th Grenadier Regiment are from Intelligence summaries in TNA WO 175/82 V Corps March–April 1943 WD.

7.6 A Great Deal of Noise

In the absence of their usual tank support, Brigadier Cass looked to his other reliable supporting arms for generous assistance: his sappers and gunners. The often overlooked work of Edmund Blake's sappers in clearing mines and improving roads had borne useful fruit, as three regiments of Royal Artillery were able to move up to positions near Toukabeur and Chaouach. The 138th Field Regiment shifted its firing batteries quite early when it moved to Toukabeur at 1800 hours on 9 April. After a busy few days supporting the 5th Buffs, the 17th Field Regiment moved up to the same area on the night of 11/12 April, and the 132nd Field Regiment followed on the next night. There was very little cover for the batteries in the area, and the presence of three regiments plus two medium batteries and one heavy one led to a cramped situation. The second-in-command of 17th Field Regiment, Major Peter Pettit, kept a personal diary at this time, though this was against regulations. Pettit had recently had a brush with death when a lorry passing his vehicle was blown up on a mine, but he was only shaken. He recalled the problems of moving the regiment along difficult roads and tracks:

> I went ahead with dumping of ammo in new positions. Guides got lost … twenty four lorry loads of ammunition had to follow me up the mountain road, Dick Dobson, BSM (Battery Sergeant Major) Hamilton and I had to see to the unloading and assist the drivers … Btys [Batteries], very late in and RHQ [Regimental HQ] after them, appalling winding narrow road through mountains up and down and roundabout. No sleep. Only just got 10 and 13 Btys working parties away down the road which is in view by day from Longstop area. [13]

Artillery support for the operations on the night of 13/14 April would be provided by the three Field Regiments and the same artillery group which had supported the first attack. This was comprised of both batteries of 5.5in medium guns from Mike Denham's 4th Medium Regiment and the 7.2in guns from the 56th Heavy Regiment, including the battery in which Spike Milligan served, 19 Battery commanded by Major Jack Chater RA. Denham's artillery group was there to attack both enemy guns and lines of communication. Brigadier Cass was able to call on a total of 94 guns in direct support of the operation. Major Pettit's boss, "Tommy" Thomas, had the job of supporting Edward Heygate's battalion, while Clive Usher, the commander of the 138th Field Regiment, supported Arthur Crook's 5th Northants and the CO of the 132nd Field Regiment, Lieutenant Colonel Graham Tarr, assisted Bill Wilberforce's East Surreys. The fire plan for the attack was designed to keep the enemy defenders on Bou Diss, Mahdouma and Bettiour well down in their trenches during a period of about 30 minutes while the brigade's leading companies were exposed moving across open ground towards their objectives. The firing batteries would then increase their rate of fire for the last 15 minutes of the approach to make life especially unpleasant while the infantry companies closed on the three hills. While the field regiments fired on initial objectives, the medium and heavy guns would be targeting Djebel el Ang, the next major peak, to stop any reserves moving up to support the defenders. The technical details of the artillery plan need not be described, but it is worth noting the

---

13   See TNA WO 175/326, 337 and 338 – 17th, 132nd and 138th Field Regiments April 1943 WDs, TNA WO 175/363 4 Medium Regiment April 1943 WD, and Jones, *Battles of a Gunner Officer*, pp.44-46.

actual weight of fire directed during the attack on Djebel Bou Diss. The unfortunate defenders of this small hill would find themselves experiencing the terrible effects of more than 2,000 shells from 48 field guns landing in their vicinity for a 45-minute period of terror. Though the Germans would have been hugging the bottom of their trenches or dugouts, they could not have escaped the dust, smoke, noise and - worst of all - blast and concussion created by this number of shells. Any soldier of either side who was ever forced to endure constant shelling would never forget such a hellish experience. One of the staff officers responsible for planning this version of Dante's inferno must have been a sportsman, and possibly a keen tennis player, demonstrated by his choice of the codewords to be used for successful capture of the hills: 15 Love for Mahdouma, 30 Love for Bettiour and 40 Love for Bou Diss. In proper Wimbledon style, the future capture of Djebel Ang, Kef el Tiour and Tanngoucha would be notified by the words Game, Set and Match.[14]

7.7 Anyone for Tennis? – The Attack on Djebel Bou Diss

After spending a relatively quiet and restful couple of days on Point 667 once it had relieved 5th Buffs, the 6th West Kents was able, courtesy of the 1st East Surreys, to make an unhindered move on the night of 12 April some 300 metres down into the river bed below Point 667. This deep gully was probably the Oued Kranga, which ran directly north to south all the way from well north of Bech Chekaoui to just above Chaouach. The area provided access via a long climb to Djebel Bou Diss, the battalion's assigned objective, which some reports had suggested was not in fact occupied by the Germans. The 6th West Kents, under the command of Lieutenant Colonel Edward Heygate, had been allocated the task of taking Djebel Bou Diss in 11th Brigade's plan. Heygate had assumed command in February 1943 from Bernard Howlett's well respected deputy, Major Lovell.[15] It had been Lovell who had been sent to meet the French General Barre in those early days in Tunisia, and Howlett chose him as acting CO when he was promoted on 16 December 1942 to brigadier and took over command of 36th Brigade. Lovell commanded the battalion during the difficult battles in January and February, and arguably had earned the right to remain as CO, but it was not to be: instead Heygate assumed command. Heygate was no novice, having served with the 5th West Kents in Belgium and France in 1940, where he won a MC while commanding a company. He had previously commanded the 70th Young Soldiers Battalion of the regiment in England.

The new boss's first six weeks in charge were busy, but the battalion was in static positions and there were few actions of note, so he had time to get to know his men. The extended fighting over the last five months meant that the unit he encountered was very different to that which landed in November 1942. Only one of the four original company commanders who had landed at Algiers, Major Arthur "Bill" Miskin, still led a company, the other three having been killed or seriously wounded. A significant number of the original officers and SNCOs had been killed, wounded, captured or - in the case of Kent cricketer Captain Bryan Valentine - sent home to take up training posts. Although its losses had been considerable, the battalion had absorbed its

---

14   The codewords Game, Set and Match are from Operational Order No. 14 in TNA WO 175170 CRA 78 Division April 1943 WD.
15   Unless otherwise noted, the following account of the attack on Djebel Bou Diss is primarily derived from Chaplin, *Queen's Own*, pp.236-37, and TNA WO 175/409 6th QORWK April 1943 WD.

replacements and they had gained valuable battle experience. Despite the reports about Djebel Bou Diss being unoccupied, Heygate sensibly dispatched strong patrols to establish the nature of German defences on the hill. Most soldiers hated patrols and tried to avoid them, as they were usually conducted at night and were exhausting, stressful and occasionally lethal. The hazardous nature of patrolling was well illustrated by the 6th West Kents on 12 April. One of the strong patrols sent out on this day probed the positions on Diss but was attacked three times by Germans, and when it finally withdrew part of the platoon was cut off. This party was led by Sergeant Daniel Lenihan, who kept his men hidden and led them back by crawling through German lines. Meanwhile, another patrol led by Sergeant Ronald Benge was attacked while observing the enemy. Benge stood up in full view of the enemy, threw grenades and fired his Thompson submachine gun at the charging Germans. He then covered his section as they withdrew. This action showed that the infantry private's well-known military maxim, that nothing good comes from the results of a patrol, could be proven to be all too true. However, based on the information gathered by the patrols, Heygate learned that enemy positions close to Diss were well sited and strongly held.[16]

Nonetheless, he decided to take a calculated risk and dispatched two platoons from B Company, with its commander Major Bill Miskin, to attempt to seize part of Bou Diss. Miskin was to attempt to occupy it, but withdraw if this move elicited a strong response. It is unclear what Heygate felt he might gain from this decision, for he already knew that the Germans held Bou Diss, as previous patrols had been attacked, and Miskin would not have artillery support. Heygate may have felt that it would secure a better position for the attack on the hill. Whatever the rationale, Miskin and B Company ended up making the steep climb towards Bou Diss, and as they got close to the hill, they were promptly attacked by a larger German force. The melee that followed involved some close-quarter fighting, but the German attack was repulsed. Despite the fact his orders allowed him to withdraw if confronted by such a situation, Miskin proved reluctant to do so and reinforcements were sent to his aid. The Germans launched two more attacks, the latter, unusually for them, using a bayonet charge, which forced Miskin to withdraw 100 yards. After one final attempt to dislodge the determined Germans, Miskin finally admitted defeat and withdrew with his casualties south-west to Djebel Bel Rherarif, which was held by the East Surreys. Miskin's stubborn, cool and courageous leadership during this first abortive attempt to take Bou Diss was recognised later by the award of a MC.

The following day, Heygate decided to move the whole battalion to the same area (Point 564), as it placed it much closer to its proposed objective. The next day, the battalion tried to get as much rest as possible, while Heygate and his attached gunner officer developed a more formal plan to take Bou Diss. The new plan was executed on the night of 13/14 April, when the West Kents implemented 11th Brigade's wider attack by attacking Bou Diss as planned an hour or so earlier than the other units. The battalion was supposed to have captured the hill by one minute to midnight. The defenders of Bou Diss proved to be as determined as Miskin and B Company, for despite enduring a barrage of 2,000 shells they were still full of fight. The two leading companies in the attack, A and D, were only halfway to their objective when they came under heavy mortar and machine-gun fire. To avoid the attack stalling, D Company's commander, Captain Scott, moved to the front and, closely followed by a section commanded by Private

16   Both Lenihan and Benge were later awarded the MM; see TNA WO 373/1 for citations.

Rogan, led his men to the top of hill. Here the advance was delayed by fire from two Spandau machine guns. The Kentish men would not be denied their prize, and despite the risk Sergeant Bill Bryant led his platoon through them, charged and personally attacked the first Spandau post, though the platoon suffered severe casualties during this action. Bryant also inspired his platoon to hold on to his position while others took up the fight. At the same time, Private Bullock on the other flank rushed over the crest firing his Bren gun from the hip and forced the second Spandau crew to withdraw. The tough defenders of Bou Diss were only overcome after hand-to-hand fighting in which CSM Henry Dean played his part. Despite his English name and role as the CSM of a Kent battalion, Dean was actually from Renfrew in Scotland and had already distinguished himself in a series of actions during the last four days. His leadership and coolness under fire inspired his company during the successful fight to take Bou Diss. Major Miskin and B Company arrived in time to help claim the prize that had eluded them the previous day. As senior officer present, Miskin assumed command of the three companies along with Captain Kenneth Scott, as Captain Clarke, OC of A Company, had been wounded. By dawn they had secured the hill, positioned the platoons for its defence and evacuated wounded.

This time Miskin was determined that Bou Diss would be held against all comers. Inevitably the equally stubborn Germans had other ideas, and fairly rapidly the hill came under heavy infantry gun and mortar fire, which continued for some time. This fire was followed by a counterattack that afternoon by a company of the 47th Grenadier Regiment. When heavy mortar fire fell on Miskin's two Vickers machine-gun positions, their commander, Sergeant Kendall, ordered his crews to stay under cover, but remained with one gun in the open and despite the danger fired continuously at the advancing grenadiers, breaking up the assault in his sector. Artillery fire called down by a gunner officer, using a radio that had been carried up by mules, finally halted and drove back the counterattack. During this counterattack, Captain Scott, CSM Dean and Miskin continued to exhibit cool and determined leadership. Djebel Bou Diss was secure and this time there would be no doubt that it would stay in the hands of the 6th West Kents. In recognition of his gallantry in action for charging and destroying a Spandau post, Sergeant Bryant was subsequently awarded the DCM, while Bullock, Rogan and Kendall received the MM. CSM Dean would also receive the DCM for his several acts of cool, inspiring and courageous conduct under fire in and around Bou Diss, while Scott's determined leadership was rewarded when he received the MC. Miskin's conduct on this day would also provide further evidence to support a later award of an MC, which was earned partly for his earlier abortive attack on the mountain.[17]

The men of the West Kents were not the only soldiers who displayed courage and determination during the fighting for Bou Diss, for the officers and men of the 756th Mountain Infantry and the 47th Grenadier Regiments proved to be tough and gallant foes. Some of the defenders refused to give up and died at their posts, while many others only gave up when their situation was dire after fighting at close quarters. The West Kents eventually took some 70 prisoners during the capture and defence of Bou Diss. Many others were killed, including a considerable number of the company that attempted a counterattack on 14 April. The 6th West Kents respected the

17 The citations for these officers and men are available from TNA WO 373/1. Bryant and Dean's DCM citations are also in Brown, *For Distinguished Conduct*, pp.73, 143.

soldierly qualities of their opponents. For example, Bill Miskin, a most capable and determined officer, had the following to say about his foes:

> The Germans as soldiers were much better than we were. They were much more determined. When they got stopped they immediately tried to find a way round, to keep pushing on: and in defence they were stubborn much more than the British soldier of whom I was one. They were the first eleven. We were the second eleven. Not that we lacked training or lacked courage but it was a difference in attitude.[18]

Irrespective of which side was the better team - and after all the West Kents' supposedly lesser soldiers had prevailed at Bou Diss - there is a degree of truth in this statement. Among those German soldiers who put up such stubborn resistance were 60 men who had only landed in Tunis on 7 April, and had been sent up to join the 3rd/756th Mountain Infantry soon afterwards as replacements. They had not come from an elite unit, as they had been part of the reinforcement or A-50 *Marsch* Battalion. These recently arrived men had nonetheless been rapidly integrated into units and fought effectively against a veteran battalion. It may have been the fourth year of the war, but the organisational skills and fighting abilities of the German army in Tunisia still remained high. It was probably the key reason why the desire of senior Allied commanders for a rapid conclusion of the Battle of the Peaks in two or three days would be thwarted. Had the Germans in the Peaks been properly supported by sufficient artillery and well supplied with enough mines, barbed wire and ammunition, they might have held onto their positions for several months. Such a delay would have made a significant difference to the outcome of the war, as Italy may have stayed under Mussolini's leadership for longer and not been invaded until late 1943 or even 1944. The men of the 334th Infantry Division and attached units, though often manning isolated positions, fought skillfully and bravely, albeit for an evil cause, and 75 years later they certainly deserve our respect as soldiers. The fragmentary nature of German Army records and lack of personal accounts from the units that took part in the Battle of the Peaks makes it difficult to tell their side of this story in detail.[19] As always, the 6th West Kents had to pay a price for their eventual capture of Djebel Bou Diss. During the period from 11-16 April, it appears that the battalion lost 15 dead, plus five officers and 65 men wounded in action.

7.8 Fifteen Love - The Attack on Djebel Dar Mahdouma

When the East Surreys occupied Djebel Bel Rherarif, they undoubtedly did the 6th West Kents a favour, as it provided Edward Heygate's battalion a sound base from which to capture their objective. However, the West Kents could claim that they had returned that favour, as their seizure of Bou Diss now provided protection for the East Surreys' attack on Djebel Dhar Mahdouma. The eastern end of the latter was only separated from Bou Diss by a deep gully and could have posed a threat. The East Surreys' location on Bel Rherarif had provided the battalion with an excellent view of Djebel Mahdouma in the few days they occupied that feature. The

---

18   Julian Thompson, *Desert Victory: Forgotten Voices* (London: Ebury Press, 2011), p.280.
19   The author notes he made a deliberate decision to focus this book on the British side of the battle, as accessing German records in Germany and the USA would have incurred additional costs and time he could not afford.

top of Rherarif was only separated from the main height on Mahdouma by less than 1,000 yards and a small col which lay some 100-160 yards in a gully below Rherarif to the north-east. A deep valley lay between Rherarif and Bou Diss to the north. Brigadier Cass had assigned Wilberforce the job of taking Mahdouma, because one of the core rules of fighting in the Djebels was that to secure one peak, it was necessary to capture any adjoining ones that might be used to dispute your *de facto* possession. Wilberforce's veteran second-in-command, Major Harry Lockhart Smith, got the job because of that well-proven procedure called Left out of Battle (LOB). The value of Djebel Mahdouma for 11th Brigade was that it was located to the north-west of Djebel Bettiour (see Plate III), the initial objective for the 5th Northants, and could pose a threat to that attack. Secondly, possession of Mahdouma could provide ease of access for the attack on Djebel el Ang during the second phase of the wider 11th Brigade operation to take Djebel Tanngoucha. The other side of this coin was that if Mahdouma could provide access to Djebel el Ang, it could also be attacked from the same height (see Map 8). The key to success to fighting in these Djebels was to seize a chain of three or four adjoining peaks at virtually the same time. This in turn would enable the infantry battalions on each hill to provide mutual assistance to the other, by removing any troublesome occupants from that now slightly weary but still dangerous foe, the 334th Infantry Division.

The attack on Mahdouma was not in itself a complicated operation and was well within the undoubted abilities of Major Smith, known to his peers as Harry. Service in the Army and the East Surreys was a family tradition, for Harry's father had commanded the battalion for four years from 1907-11. An earlier, even more distinguished ancestor and soldier was Sir Harry Wakelyn–Smith, whose military career began in 1805 and covered 50 years. Wakelyn-Smith had served with the 95th Rifles and was an officer with Wellington in Spain at the siege of Badajoz, where he met and soon after married the 14-year-old Juana Maria de Los Doloros de Leon. Lady Juana accompanied Sir Harry to South Africa in the 1840s, where he was Governor General of the Cape Colony. It was after her that the town of Ladysmith was named. Harry Smith had some big shoes to fill when he was commissioned as a second lieutenant into the battalion in 1929 and spent nearly six years with them in India. He served at the regimental depot and was the adjutant for a TA battalion before he rejoined the 1st Battalion. He subsequently commanded the anti-tank company of the 11th Infantry Brigade in France and was well known to the brigade commander at the time, one Kenneth Anderson. Smith managed to be evacuated at Dunkirk and returned to the battalion as its second-in-command in September 1942. He and Wilberforce had made a strong leadership team during the dangerous and difficult months in Tunisia. Harry Smith later wrote a useful account of his time in Tunisia which has been a valuable source for this book.[20]

In addition to capturing Mahdouma, there seems to be some evidence that Brigadier Cass may have expected Harry Smith and the East Surreys to quickly secure Mahdouma and exploit onwards to capture Djebel el Ang. If so, Cass was more optimistic than his division commander Evelegh, whose plan clearly stated the need to seize Diss, Mahdouma and Bettiour first, before executing the next phase which was the capture of Djebel Ang. In contrast to the divisional plan, Cass's orders assumed a three-phase operation, the first phase of which would lead to capture

20   The profile of Harry Smith is from a biography on the regimental website www.queensroyalsurreys. org.uk (accessed 7 January 2018) and information from the entry on his ancestor in the *Encyclopaedia Britannica* (11th Edition) (Cambridge: Cambridge University Press) p.263.

of the line from Djebel Ang to Djebel Bettiour. The second phase covered the capture of Kef el Tiour ridge and the final phase the seizing of Djebel Tanngoucha. The four hills and ridges identified in Cass's plan encompass some of the most rugged and difficult terrain in northern Tunisia, and were described well by Brigadier Nelson Russell of 38th Brigade, someone who came to know them all too well:

> This hilly country north of Medjez merits description - but I doubt if I am able to describe it; I've never seen anything like it before …In a width of a couple of miles are the mountain villages of Toukabeur, Chaouach, Kelbine and Heidous … Between these villages are tracks, passable to goats, but which could be, and were, bulldozed into tracks for MT [motor transport]. To the east and the west of these villages is a jumble of bare rocky hills with no tracks at all; and north of Heidous, the last northern village, one runs into real tiger country and all civilization is left behind … This was our own particular bit of country, Bettiour, Tanngoucha (the most formidable of the lot), Pt 622, The Kefs, and a point to become famous as Butler's Hill. They all had one peculiar feature in common – their summits with stiff approaches were surmounted by long "dragon backs" about 20-40 yards wide – and with sheer sides, cliffs from 20 to 60 feet high.[21]

The physical defences of this area were formidable, and this in itself should have provided Cass pause for thought in his planning. Cass had commanded the 11th Infantry Brigade since the landings at Algiers and was an experienced brigade commander. He had many strengths, but one of his weaknesses was that he tended to be a very aggressive commander in Tunisia and sometimes took significant risks. There is an argument to be made that this tendency had been his undoing during the fighting at Djedieda and Tebourba. In retrospect, Cass's decision to compress his new attack into three phases in such difficult terrain may have reflected that tendency to take risks, and once again would get him and his brigade into trouble. Ironically, Cass and his brigade staff should have known a great deal about the topography of the area. Cass had commanded the brigade when it was operating in the Medjerda valley, from which Djebel el Ang and Kef el Tiour are clearly visible. His brigade had responsibility for defending the Medjez sector, including Toukabeur and Chaouach, on several occasions during the winter months, and patrols constantly roamed over the area. Moreover, Cass had sent Arthur Crook's battalion on its abortive raid to Tebourba back in December 1942, using a route that moved across this terrain. If Crook had been consulted, and we must assume he would have been, he would certainly have advised that the terrain around Djebel el Ang and the Kef was extremely difficult to cross but easy to defend. This relatively small area was to become a blood-stained battleground for the 11th and 38th Infantry Brigades over the next 10 days.

The attack on Mahdouma was scheduled to start at the same time as that on Djebel Bou Diss, which should have been captured by the 6th West Kents, but as previously described Heygate's battalion encountered more opposition than expected. The East Surreys' attack on Mahdouma was led by B and D Companies, with Captains Toby Taylor and Pat Wadham in command. Wadham was another relatively junior officer who had been a platoon leader when the battalion landed at Algiers but now commanded a company as an acting captain. He had previously

---

21   See N. Russell, *Irish Brigade*, pp.114-15.

distinguished himself during the Battle of Toukabeur. Captain Taylor was only 24, but had been an officer in the 1st East Surreys since 1938 and had served as a platoon commander with the battalion in France. He was a captain and the second-in-command of B Company when it landed at Algiers and had taken over as its commander. Taylor looked slightly older than his years as he was balding, and was the most experienced, at that time, of Wilberforce's company commanders. One of Taylor's claims to fame was that he had the audacity to take Bridget Anderson, the attractive daughter of the current GOC First Army, Lieutenant General Anderson, to various dances the previous summer.

It had been decided that the attack on Mahdouma would be conducted from a start line which ran along slopes in a gully below and to the east of Djebel Bel Rherarif, as these slopes provided access after a climb to Mahdouma. This gully provided an excellent reference point for the gunners, who had to adjust a creeping barrage designed to provide cover by moving 100 yards every minute up the mountain. This approach was a direct but also the obvious route to Mahdouma. Unfortunately, the Germans had also identified this fact and preregistered the area for mortars and artillery, which in technical artillery jargon is known as a DF (Defensive Fire) task. As B and D Companies were just leaving the start line at midnight, Harry Smith, along with battalion headquarters and C Company, had just arrived, along with a number of mules carrying heavy wireless sets, ammunition and equipment. It was at this point that all hell broke loose, German shells landing all over the start line and causing havoc and casualties among Smith's headquarters. The adjutant, signal and mortar officer were all wounded, while the mules, perhaps understandably, decided to move to a more desirable location and stampeded. Lieutenant John Woodhouse, who was a platoon commander in B Company during the attack, was caught in the shelling and provided a subsequent account of that experience:

We were shelled by the Germans on our start line before we got away. However with much shouting we got going behind our own artillery barrage which lifted forward in "steps" of 100 metres. It was essential to keep close to the barrage, so that there was as little a gap as possible in time between shells falling on German trenches and our arrival with bayonets fixed. In the lead of my platoon I kept close to the shell bursts until one shell passed over my head [and] it burst with a flash of red and a concussion wave which stunned me. My head rang like a bell as I lay flat smelling the fumes of the bursts. Luckily the shrapnel had all gone forward or sideways. Though temporarily deafened I had to press on as we were near the Germans on the summit who began firing in our direction. Thinking to distract them, I told my 2 inch mortar team to fire smoke to our flank. [It was] Not in the text book to fire smoke at night, but it succeeded in drawing the German fire. We staggered up the slopes and the Germans either ran or surrendered.[22]

While the lead companies were busy attacking Mahdouma, Harry Smith was trying to evacuate his wounded officers and men and recover the mules and crucial wireless sets. After a while the shelling stopped and most of the mules returned. The mules and their handlers came from 10th Pack Transport Company, which had British and French officers and largely Arab NCOs who

---

22   Bryn Evans, *With the East Surreys in Tunisia and Italy 1942-45* (Barnsley: Pen and Sword Military, 2012), p.41.

were from the French colonial army. The handlers were usually Algerian or Tunisian NCOs or soldiers. Mules were assigned to all the battalions who took part in this stage of the battle. The area in which the battle was fought was very rugged, not accessible by vehicles and exhausting to climb with heavy loads, so mules and their handlers played a critical role. They were used to carry heavy wireless sets, batteries, mortars, mortar bombs and other supplies. While Smith was trying to deal with the problems at battalion headquarters, Toby Taylor and Pat Wadham had completed their attack and in the early hours of the morning they secured Djebel Mahdouma, taking 25 prisoners. Their capture of Mahdouma was not without incident, as shown by the conduct of Lance Corporal Harold White, who was in command of one of the leading sections. During the attack White "kept his section right up to the barrage during the advance and when the barrage lifted he captured a machine gun post with his section leading the attack with great dash".[23] White was to demonstrate further coolness under fire at Djebel el Ang, and this performance combined, with that at Mahdouma, earned him the immediate award of a MM. Despite the chaos on the start line, the 1st East Surrey's had taken their first objective, which would enable Harry Smith and his depleted staff to organise a follow-on attack on Djebel Ang. In order to retain a degree of continuity, it is now necessary to leave Smith and East Surreys, but we will return later to briefly describe their involvement in the events that unfolded. It is now time to relate the operations of the two units involved in the concurrent capture of Djebel Bettiour; the 5th Northants and the 2nd Lancashire Fusiliers.

7.9 Thirty Love – The Capture of Djebel Bettiour

Lieutenant Colonel Arthur Crook and his battalion were tasked with taking the southernmost objective of those defined in Brigadier Cass's plan, Djebel Bettiour. At a height of 628 metres (2,060ft), Bettiour dominated the village of Heidous which lay to its south-east, but was in turn dominated by Djebel el Ang which at 668 metres (2,100ft) was located directly to its north. Mahdouma, the objective of the East Surreys, took up the area between Bettiour and El Ang, but was lower than either of the two hills. The importance of Bettiour lay in both its height and the fact it provided access via a saddle and a slope to Djebel el Ang. A long serrated saw-like ridge called Kef el Tiour ran from Djebel el Ang towards Djebel Tanngoucha. The southern slopes of Bettiour (see Plate III) are bare but cut by a series of gullies. The top of the hill appears uncluttered, but on the southern side, there is a surprise, a 25-40ft-high set of rocky limestone crags which are about 150 metres (160 yards) in length. The latter was to figure prominently in later fighting which swirled around the escarpment. The crest of the hill provides an extensive 360-degree view of surrounding countryside and on a clear day you can see for miles. The south-western slopes of Bettiour fall gradually towards Djebel Kelbine, some 900 yards away, which had been secured by Crook and the 5th Northants on the night of 12 April. Kelbine's rocky ridge provided an excellent base from which to launch the 5th Northants' attack on Bettiour on the night of 13/14 April.

This operation began after darkness fell, when at 2100 hours Captain Dudley Emmerton, the battalion's IO, and his intelligence section moved forward from Kelbine to choose a start line and lay white tape to mark it. Emmerton and his group selected a location just below a high 479

---

23   See TNA WO 373/1 for White's MM citation.

metre knoll north-east of Kelbine. During this period he and his section were under continuous mortar fire. The leading companies, V on the left and A on the right, moved off from Kelbine at about 2230 hours towards the start line for their attack. The two companies arrived without incident, and at 2330 hours they started their advance. Crook and the two company commanders, Captain J. McNeill and Acting Major Reginald Cook, must have seriously trusted Emmerton's navigational skills, as they agreed that he should personally lead the attacking companies on a compass bearing up the trackless slope to Bettiour. As the two lead companies moved steadily up the hill, they benefitted from the artillery shelling of Bettiour, which started at about 2350 hours, and by 0115 hours had secured the hill, though not without some close-in fighting. Emmerton's map-reading skills ensured the companies got to Bettiour, but the rocky crags at its top had to be scaled if the whole hill was to be taken. Cook and his company suddenly found themselves climbing hand-by-hand to scale these precipitous crags. They gained a foothold on top of the left of the crags and came under fire from a heavy machine gun. Cook led his soldiers in a charge, overran the gun and captured several prisoners. His action helped collapse the German resistance on Bettiour. While the lead companies were taking the hill, C Company followed them up on to the feature and went on to secure their left flank. At some time that morning the artillery observer attached to the 5th Northants ordered his wireless operator to send the signal with the codeword confirming the battalion's success in taking Bettiour, "Thirty Love".

The Germans responded to the loss of Bettiour by firing mortars on to the hill during the night. Soon after 0900 hours on 13 April, Lieutenant Colonel Crook and his battalion headquarters moved up and on to the hill. German shelling and mortars fell on Bettiour during the morning and took their toll. The casualties included one officer killed, one wounded and other soldiers wounded. This shelling also affected the officers and men of the 2nd Lancs Fusiliers. The battalion had spent the day of 13 April at Djebel Hamri trying to get as much rest as they could. Major Ken Garner-Smith, the second-in-command, led the battalion that night on a tiring march which placed it on the southern slopes of Djebel Bettiour as daylight broke on 14 April. The top of Bettiour was now a little crowded as two battalions occupied the area, yet the Fusiliers were lucky they lost only two men to this fire. Soon after arriving on the hill, Garner-Smith was also instructed to place a company of his battalion under the command of the East Surreys. According to Cass's plan, the 5th Northants were expected to have moved on to attack Kef el Tiour ridge to the east, but this had not been possible. The combination of the climb up to Bettiour, onto the crags and clearing the German positions had occupied the 5th Northants all night. In retrospect, this should have been anticipated, as night marches and fighting in mountains quickly tired men out, especially when the rifle companies had been so actively engaged in operations since 7 April. Cass, however, was impatient that the 5th Northants exploit their new position, and on the morning of 14 April radioed Crook and ordered him to confer with Garner-Smith and organise an attack to maintain the momentum and take Djebel Tanngoucha. While Crook and Garner-Smith worked on a plan to seize Tanngoucha, a determined effort was being made to pave the way for their attack by securing both Djebel Ang and the long narrow ridge called Kef el Tiour.[24]

---

24 The account of the attack on Djebel Bettiour is derived from Jervois *History of the Northants*, pp.140-142 and TNA WO 175/517 5th Northants April 1943 WD.

Plate 10 Captain D V Emmerton MC the Intelligence Officer who led the 5 Northants' attack on Djebel Bettiour. (Copyright IWM - NA 392)

Plate 11 Captain Eric Kerr RAMC, Regimental Medical Officer (RMO) of 5th Northants who was awarded a MC for his care of the wounded on Djebel Bettiour. (Copyright IWM - NA 393)

Plate 12 The headstone for Lance Corporal James Given's grave in Medjez el Bab CWGC cemetery. (Reproduced with the kind permission of R & E O'Sullivan, 2018)

Plate 13 A Mule train with French handlers passes 2 Churchill tanks on a mountain pass near Djebel Tanngoucha North Africa 1943. (Copyright NAM - 1999-03-88-21)

Plate 14 Sergeant Eddie Mayo MM of the 2nd London Irish Rifles. (Reproduced with the kind permission of Alan Mayo & R O'Sullivan)

7.10 "GAME" – The Initial Assault on Djebel Ang and Kef el Tiour

It is quite possible that Brigadier Cass may have originally planned that Djebel Ang be seized almost at the same time as the other peaks and be secured by dawn. At some time during the night it had become apparent that even if this was his intention, events had overtaken the plan. At dawn, the 5th Northants and 6th West Kents were fully occupied trying to secure Djebels Bettiour and Bou Diss, while the confusion of the night meant Harry Smith needed time to reorganise his battalion. It appears that during the early morning of 14 April, Cass, having been informed of the status of his battalions, made a decision about the next step. Smith received orders to attack Djebel el Ang just after daybreak, with the help of lavish artillery support, using A and C Companies. The East Surreys' war diary infers that Smith was concerned about the strength of such an attack, as it states that C Company was still weak. C Company had been fairly battered near Point 343 four days earlier, and also suffered during the previous night attack. John Woodhouse from C Company later noted that his platoon was reduced from 28 to 14 men by the morning of 14 April. It seems likely Smith expressed his concerns to Cass, for this was the reason why B Company of the 2nd Lancs Fusiliers was temporarily loaned to him so that it could form part of the attack on Djebel el Ang. The decision to split off a company from the Fusiliers and send it over to Smith on Mahdouma was a surprising one, highlighting the challenges facing the brigade even at this early stage. Battalion COs did not like their units being split up and committed in penny packets under the command of other officers, and had Lieutenant Colonel Linden-Kelly been present, he may have protested such an order. However, Garner-Smith was only the acting CO and a major, so he may have considered it difficult to challenge this order when issued by as experienced a commander as Cass.

The decision to commit two companies from separate battalions, who were originally on different hills, was not an ideal one. It was probably taken in a very short time and reflected what was available immediately to carry out an attack. It is possible that Cass should have ordered Garner-Smith to pass through the 5th Northants on Bettiour and attack Djebel el Ang with his whole battalion as soon as feasible after dawn. The Fusiliers were tired after their night march, but hadn't done any fighting and Bettiour provided a good jumping-off location to attack Ang. It is worth observing that the artillery plan devised the previous day provided a degree of flexibility on the exact timing for any attack on Ang, although the targets had already been worked out. Hindsight is of course a wonderful thing, and it is also true that at 0400 hours, after 24 hours of intense activity, it isn't easy to make good tactical decisions. Whatever the merit of this one, Djebel Ang would be attacked by two companies, A Company of the East Surreys, commanded by the capable Captain Edward Giles, and a company of the Fusiliers. Fortunately, artillery support for the next attack would prove to be considerable, with all four field regiments and the Mike group assigned to wreak havoc on Djebel el Ang, Kef el Tiour ridge and Tanngoucha. The gunners intended that the unfortunate defenders of Djebel el Ang should be on the wrong end of 1,200 25-pounder high-explosive shells in the relatively short period of 25 minutes from the order to fire. Any German infantryman on the narrow Kef el Tiour ridge would also be shelled by 880 rounds of HE and smoke for at least 45 minutes. Fire support for the attack was to be supplemented by that of the battalion mortar platoon. The mortar officer had been wounded early that morning, so this was now under the command of Lance Sergeant Straight. In order to better direct this fire, he decided to move forward on to the crest of a ridge to get a better view, despite information that the other side was occupied by Germans. When Straight crossed the top of the ridge, he was confronted by six Germans in a trench who levelled their weapons at him. Instead of surrendering, Straight drew his only weapon, a pistol, shot one of the Germans and the rest scattered when he fired at them. The incident further demonstrated Straight's coolness in a dangerous situation, for having scattered the Germans he obtained useful information for the subsequent attack before returning to friendly lines.

The gunners woke up any Germans who were still asleep in the trenches and dugouts when they started their artillery barrage 15 minutes after five in the morning. Captain Giles, in command of the attack, further distinguished himself that morning during this counterattack. His leadership and gallantry on both 8 April at Point 343 and during the early morning of 14 April at Djebel Ang, led to the later award of the MC. It appears that the Germans' initial resistance to this counterattack was limited, as by 0640 hours both companies reported that Djebel el Ang was taken. Twenty minutes later, Cass, back in his headquarters in Chaouach, was confident enough about the tactical situation to agree that the company of Fusiliers could return to Bettiour. This left Giles and his company in apparently sole control of Djebel el Ang. While Giles and his company were trying to get settled on the rocky mountain, using whatever trenches and dugouts existed, Harry Smith was briefly obliged to send D Company to the assistance of the 6th West Kents on Djebel Bou Diss, who had experienced trouble eliminating a pocket of enemy resistance. This task was duly completed, but hardly had it been done when Giles reported at 0740 hours that his company was under fire from some 150 Germans on a feature to the west of his position on Djebel Ang. These may have been Germans escaping from Mahdouma and Bou Diss, and soon after they were taken under fire by artillery observers.

Smith's problems were, however, only just beginning, as some two hours later he received the news that Giles's company was being counterattacked on Djebel Ang. Giles had taken some prisoners, but had eventually been forced to withdraw from that hill and ended up reforming behind Djebel Mahdouma to the west. It is worth wondering what the outcome might have been, had the company from the Fusiliers not been ordered back to Bettiour: Giles might not have needed to withdraw from Djebel Ang. This news could have put into jeopardy a plan that was being devised jointly by Crook and Garner-Smith to attack Djebel Tanngoucha, and it is not surprising that Smith was ordered by Cass to counterattack and recover the hill. Smith probably viewed this task with about as little enthusiasm as the weary Captain Pat Wadham from D Company, to whom he assigned it. Wadham and his company had spent the night taking Mahdouma and were exhausted, and were now asked to recapture Djebel el Ang on their own. It had previously taken two companies to take the hill, and having counterattacked, the Germans would no doubt wish to hold on to it. Wadham would therefore have only been human if he had expressed his doubts on the wisdom of this order. It seems that either Smith may also have had the confidence to express his doubts about the likelihood of success of this attack, or Cass had woken up to the reality of the situation. Whatever the cause, Cass agreed to stop the attack, but insisted that Mahdouma be held at all costs. He decided that the optimal way of dealing with the Germans on Ang was to shell them unmercifully. This proved one of the more sensible decisions he made at this time, as once they had experienced another artillery barrage, the Germans withdrew. This did not get Wadham completely off the hook, as he was told to reoccupy Djebel el Ang, but the good news was that he would be accompanied by two companies of the Lancashire Fusiliers.[25]

Hindsight is a wonderful thing, but is worth observing that Brigadier Edward Eden Earnshaw Cass, which was his full name, probably made a number of unfortunate tactical decisions during this period. It is possible to come to the view that he was suffering from the cumulative effect of five months of strenuous campaigning and a further week of intense fighting. Cass was probably tired and possibly a little out of touch with events. In his defence, it is worth noting two points: first, he was not alone, for even the normally unflappable Nelson Russell was not his usual self during this period. Moreover, Cass had not had an easy war. He had commanded the 1st King's Own Yorkshire Light Infantry during their short but difficult stay in Norway in 1940. His leadership in that campaign had earned him a bar to the DSO he had been awarded during the First World War. Afterwards, Cass had spent two years in India before assuming command of 11th Brigade in February 1942. He had led his brigade through difficult fighting since Algiers and had not really spared himself. His personal courage was never in doubt, but Cass was respected, rather than liked, by the officers and men of his brigade. Gregory Blaxland, an officer in the Buffs at this time, recalled that Cass was an expert shot and a martinet. He was, in the words of another of his officers, a fiery little man. The diminutive brigadier was known not only for his fighting spirit, but also for his temper, which someone or something would set off from time to time. There was another side of Edward Cass, for when he knew and trusted his subordinates he gave them a degree of latitude in critical decisions, and had done so with Bill Wilberforce when the latter asked for approval to withdraw in December 1942. He also had learned to trust Arthur Crook, although the two officers didn't always see eye-to-eye on all matters. Cass was always loyal to both his superiors, especially Evelegh, and his staff and subordinates. Whatever his faults during this period - and some of his tactical decisions are questionable - Cass was a highly experienced brigade commander, albeit a pretty tired one, who had to face difficult operational challenges.[26]

The situation on the morning of 14 April was that the brigade had a decent grip on Djebels Bou Diss, Mahdouma and Bettiour, although Bou Diss would soon be the subject of a counterattack. The brigade had apparently lost control of Djebel el Ang after initially capturing the hill, but the good news was that the Germans didn't seem to hold it either. After suffering the effects of a major artillery barrage that morning, they had vacated the hill. This withdrawal was exploited by the East Surreys when D Company, under Pat Wadham, advanced on to Djebel Ang at about 1300 hours, joined soon after by A Company. In tandem with this advance, two companies of Lancashire Fusiliers seem to have moved on to Kef el Tiour ridge, which they found clear of Germans. The precise sequence of events at this time is difficult to determine, as the war diaries of both units contradict each other, as do other sources. The degree of confusion that existed about who actually occupied Djebel Ang and what happened and when is considerable. The

---

25 Details of the attack on Djebel el Ang are derived from the following war diaries: TNA WO 175/196 11 Infantry Brigade April 1943; WO 175/519 1 East Surreys April 1943; and WO 175/512 2 Lancs Fusiliers April 1943; as well as H. Smith *Operations of East Surreys*, pp.166-67.

26 The profile of Edward Cass is based on Blaxland, *Plain Cook*, p.87; information from the Army List; the citations for his previous medals; and E. Ellenberger, *History of The King's Own Yorkshire Light Infantry 1939–1948* (Aldershot: Gale & Polden, 1961).

difficulty of providing a clear picture of events arises from the conflicting records of the East Surreys. The battalion's war diary infers that Wadham and D Company were sent to take Djebel Ang and occupied it with little or no resistance. On the other hand, the citation that led to the award of a MC to Wadham for his combined actions at Toukabeur and Ang states:

> Secondly in the attack on the Djebel Ang position on the 14 April [sic] he again led his company forward with great dash and established his company on the reverse slope of the hill while the enemy were on the other side. He carried out a personal recce of the enemy positions under heavy mortar and machine gun fire and subsequently occupied the whole feature.[27]

It is unclear which of the two sources is accurate, and the situation is further complicated by another piece of the tactical picture provided by the citation for a MM. This provides good evidence that the 1st East Surreys had never completely lost control of Djebel Ang at all. When Giles withdrew his company back, someone failed to ensure this order got to the section commanded by Lance Corporal Gerald Pearce. Pearce and his section found themselves under fire from two sides, for while they engaged the attacking Germans, they were also shelled by their own artillery. Pearce's section remained on the hill, though they were heavily shelled, until someone from the platoon finally reached him and he was told he could take his men back if he wanted to. Pearce decided not to pull back, remaining on the hill until his section was relieved later. Pearce's determined and courageous defence of his position led to him being recommended for the DCM, but he was actually awarded the MM.[28] This story illustrates the confused nature of operations on Djebel El Ang during this period and the inherent difficulty of reconciling the various different sources.

The possession of Djebel el Ang and the western end of Kef el Tiour offered a sound base for the attack on Tanngoucha, which was being organised by Arthur Crook with the aid of Ken Garner-Smith on orders from "Copper" Cass. Their plan was to attack Tanngoucha from Bettiour by initially taking the Point 622 ridgeline. The Kef el Tiour and Point 622 ridges now become central characters in the story of the next few bloody days in the history of the Battle-Axe Division. These two long narrow ridges would bear witness to the exertions, injuries and often violent deaths of soldiers from a total of five British battalions and three German regiments. The first and higher ridgeline, Kef el Tiour commenced at Djebel El Ang and extended east for over 600 yards before it linked eventually with Djebel Tanngoucha (see Plates IV, VI and VII). The ridge varied in height from 580-622 metres, and its top was a narrow 20-40ft flat rocky crest which restricted all movement (see Map 9). The top of the ridgeline was described by Major John Coldwell-Horsfall as a "fantastic serrated saw bladed crest".[29] In the middle of the ridgeline, the slopes fell away steeply, especially to the south and to a lesser degree in the north. It was possible for men to move around the ridge on both the north and south by using slopes further down, but these were quite steep, rugged and broken by gullies on the north end. To the south of Kef el Tour was a second steep and craggy dragon's tooth-type ridgeline. This was located below and slightly offset to the right of Kef el Tiour, and ended, according to the French

---

27   Quote from TNA WO 373/1 Captain Wadham's MC.
28   The MM citation for Lance Corporal Pearce is in TNA WO 373/1.
29   See J. Horsfall, *Wild Geese*, p.126.

maps of the time, at a height of 622 metres and thus became known as the Point 622 ridge. John Coldwell-Horsfall described the view towards Point 622 from his position on Kef el Tiour:

> The Point 622 ridge ran out from our right front in a kind of a curl. I described it as looking like a mammoth Hadrian's Wall. In fact it was more like a harbour mole jutting out over a steeply shelving beach. The thing was cliff sided, about ten feet high our end which we held, deepening to perhaps fifty feet at the other end of the feature. Nature had gone mad with its top, about twenty yards wide it was broken like a blown up rampart ... A little over 300 yards from us Point 622 itself projected above all this natural litter another slab of rock sticking up like a sawn off Martello tower with rubble all around it from apex to base.[30]

The Point 622 ridgeline started some 70 metres in height below and 200 metres in distance partly parallel to Kef el Tiour, and climbed gradually from 565 metres to the top. At the end of Kef el Tiour the ridgeline fell away to the right to meet up with the top of Point 622 ridgeline. The latter was linked in turn with Djebel Tanngoucha by a flat saddle or col. Djebel Tanngoucha was a big, long serrated slab of rock which lay at a slight angle but parallel to both the Kef el Tiour and Point 622 ridgelines (see Plates IV, VI and VII). The bottom of the Tanngoucha ridge was located below both Kef el Tiour and the Point 622 ridgeline at about 520 metres high, and extended north-east for about 800 metres, rising to a height of about 610 metres. A high saddle some 100 metres long provided easy access from Tanngoucha to the top of the Point 622 ridge. The land to the south of Djebel Tanngoucha sloped downwards towards the village of Heidous. This was located to the south of Djebel Tanngoucha and was dominated by its heights (see Plate VII). Of crucial importance to the 78th Division was the fact that Kef el Tiour ridge and Djebel Tanngoucha stood as twin sentinels watching over Longstop Hill and the Medjerda valley, which could be found nearly 1,000ft below to the south-east. German observers on Tanngoucha, Kef el Tiour and even in Heidous could see all movement towards Longstop and quickly call down artillery fire.

The twin sentinels had to be taken before a renewed attack on Longstop could be made. The terrain itself was formidable, but with their usual Teutonic efficiency the Germans had added a few interesting features, though not ones obvious to a casual visitor. Their engineers had tunnelled into the area around Point 622 and created underground dugouts within that feature which were virtually impervious to shellfire. The German defences on these heights were anchored on a line from Kef el Tiour ridge to Point 622 and then via the high col to Tanngoucha. The positions were mutually supporting and could bring sweeping fire across Kef el Tiour's narrow approaches. Any attack from Djebel Ang to Tanngoucha was also channelled neatly into the bottleneck that was "The Kefs", as the ridge was called by some observers. There was only one obvious feasible approach and it was difficult to achieve tactical surprise. The Germans had emplaced a couple of infantry guns in the area, but the terrain precluded the deployment of anti-tank guns: these were not expected to be needed, as it was not considered possible for tanks to reach the ridge. This was the terrain and the defences which faced any unit which wished to attempt to capture Djebel Tanngoucha, though none of this picture was known to the officers and men of the 5th Northants and 2nd Lancs Fusiliers as they prepared

---

30   J. Horsfall, *Wild Geese*, p.148.

for their attack. In the meantime, A and D Companies of the 1st East Surreys had settled in on Djebel El Ang and two parties of German prisoners had been sent back. The majority of these came from the 3rd Battalion of the 756th Mountain Infantry Regiment plus two replacement battalions, and interrogation of the prisoners revealed that the former battalion was now down to less than 250 men.

7.11 "SET" – The First Assault on Djebel Tanngoucha

If the German defenders had been able to get any rest that day, this was certainly disturbed in the afternoon when a strong artillery barrage fell on their positions. Under cover of the artillery, C and V Companies of the 5th Northants, plus C and D Companies of the 2nd Lancs Fusiliers, moved out to try to capture Point 622 and Djebel Tanngoucha. To compound their difficulties, the Germans would also have received a nasty shock at midday when their assumption that tanks could not operate on the hills around Bettiour and El Ang was rudely shattered by the sound of Churchills clanking into position to support the attack. Although the majority of 142nd RAC Regiment was not available, Cass had managed to have a troop of four Churchills commanded by Lieutenant Tony Jacques assigned to him for this operation. Both Jacques and his fellow troop commander Lieutenant Aylward, who was sent to support the 8th Argylls, had expressed their willingness to see if they could bring tanks up in support. Jacques had conducted a personal reconnaissance on the afternoon of 13 April and led his tanks on a difficult cross-country journey on the morning of 14 April. Jacques and his three Churchills arrived at Djebel Bettiour at 1230 hours, just in time to support the attack that afternoon.[31] According to one source, Jacques and the tanks used over 70 gallons of petrol to get up to Bettiour [32] and initially ran out of fuel, so mules had to be used to bring up more. Although the exact details are not clear, it appears that at least two Churchill tanks were able to move out from Bettiour up to Ang and towards Tanngoucha. The view of two tanks moving across such inaccessible country must have certainly shaken the morale of the German defenders, who thought this area was impassable to them. Howard Marshall, a BBC Radio reporter, witnessed the tanks in action and described them in a book he later published: "We watched our tanks playing a grim game of hide and seek with the German mortars, slipping round the rock face to have a smack at them and lumbering back into cover down a precipitous slope."[33]

Despite the initial shock of seeing tanks, the German reaction to the attack was swift and they shelled the 2nd Lancs Fusiliers' start line for the attack near Bettiour, and even the tough fusiliers of D Company started to look for cover. They had not, however, reckoned on the presence of their feared Regimental Sergeant Major (RSM) Robert Alexander at the start line. RSMs as a general rule don't usually lead troops into battle, but WO 1 Alexander had a different approach on this day. With complete disregard for his own safety, Alexander left shelter and walked out into the shell-swept area, stood in the open and encouraged the platoon to go forward into the attack. What encouragement he offered isn't recorded by history, but RSMs in 1943

---

31   In his account Nelson Russell suggested these tanks were from the North Irish Horse; however, it is clear from the war diary of 142nd RAC Regiment and the citation for the MC awarded to Jacques that they were from his troop of the 152nd RAC Regiment.
32   See Austin, *Birth of an Army*, p.126.
33   Howard Marshall, *Over to Tunis* (London: Eyre & Spottiswood, 1943) p.119.

generally preferred to be respected or even feared by their soldiers and the men of D Company probably didn't want to get on his bad side. By getting the platoon to move past the shelling, he undoubtedly saved more lives. Having encouraged his soldiers, the RSM returned to his normal job and, under fire, organised the collection and evacuation of wounded.[34] The two companies of the 5th Northants led by Major Reggie Cook were less fortunate, for as they started their attack heavy mortar fire inflicted many casualties, including Captain Wilkinson of C Company, who was killed. Nonetheless, the two companies continued their advance. The combination of two companies of the 5th Northants and two from the 2nd Lancashire Fusiliers, combined with the support of Jacques' Churchill tanks, did much to discourage the German defenders. They grudgingly withdrew towards Tanngoucha and the combined force now reached the top of the Point 622 ridge. Here the leading platoons were pinned down by a storm of machine-gun and mortar fire from both the OP on Point 622 and positions on Djebel Tanngoucha, and another company commander was taken out of the fight when Captain McNeill of the 5th Northants was wounded. The unsuccessful attack on Point 622 was, to use a misquote of Wellington's actual famous phrase, a damned close-run thing,[35] for at one point the 5th Northants were very close to taking Point 622. During the attack, Sergeant Pollett was in command of one of the platoons involved in the attack which came under heavy fire. Nonetheless, it appears that he and his men had managed to get to the bottom of Point 622 and the craggy Martello-like rocky tower structure that was probably the German OP. According to his MM citation:

> The only route to his objective open to Sgt Pollett was up a crack in the almost sheer rock-face 30 feet high. Under his directions two sections and Platoon HQ clambered up this crack and on reaching the top returned the enemy fire for 20 minutes until all but two Bren gun magazines had been exhausted and all 2" mortar bombs fired. The Platoon was then withdrawn 50 yards to a position on the ridge where more adequate cover could be obtained and the engagement continued.[36]

Throughout the incident, Pollett was observed constantly pointing out targets and encouraging his men to further efforts. His leadership and gallantry in action resulted in him being awarded a MM.

Although the leading platoons were eventually withdrawn from Point 622, the hard and rocky ground in their new location made it very difficult for the men to dig in and as dusk arrived it was decided to pull back up to Djebel Bettiour and consolidate a defence there. The withdrawal of the companies under fire at night was difficult, but was carried out effectively under the calm leadership of Major Reggie Cook. Cook's gallant conduct at Bettiour, during the attack to and withdrawal from the Point 622 ridge culminated five months of effective leadership, which was justifiably recognised by the immediate award of the MC. Another MC was awarded to Lieutenant Jacques of the redoubtable C Squadron 142nd RAC, in recognition of his sterling efforts in managing to get three Churchills up to Djebel Ang and leading two tanks in support of the attack.

---

34 RSM Alexander's role is described in Hallam, *History of Lancs Fusiliers*, p.46, and his DCM citation.
35 Wellington is actually reputed to have said "the nearest run thing".
36 See MM citation for Sergeant Pollett in TNA WO 373/1.

The first attempt to capture Point 622 ridge and Tanngoucha had failed. After discussion, Crook and Garner-Smith together decided that they would send in a new force. This would try to bypass the Kef el Tiour and Point 622 ridges and attempt to move around them to capture Tanngoucha, as this remained the 11th Brigade's final objective. The task of carrying this out was assigned to Acting Major J.F. Hudson of the 2nd Lancs Fusiliers, leading his own C Company together with A and B Companies of the 5th Northants. James Hudson was an experienced company commander who had won the battalion's first MC of the Second World War in France in 1940. He was supported by two young, but able, company commanders: Acting Captains Emery and Beagley. There was a great deal of pressure to capture Tanngoucha fast, and a hasty plan was devised which involved a significant risk. The new plan was innovative and might have worked if a 24-hour delay had been allowed and time provided to conduct a reconnaissance of unfamiliar ground. The rapidly devised plan required the three companies to bypass the main ridges by means of a night-time approach march across the lower slopes of Kef el Tiour and to attack Tanngoucha from below. The Germans expected attacks to come along the ridge and may have been less well prepared for a carefully executed surprise flanking attack. It was rather ironic that time, or more likely pressures from on high, prevented Hudson from sending out a patrol to carefully map a route, as one of his officers, Captain Latta, had established a reputation as a patrolling expert. No time was granted for such a delay, and instead Hudson and his troops began their approach at 2130 hours, making their way across the rugged steep lower southern slopes of Kef el Tiour. They planned to skirt the village of Heidous and climb to Tanngoucha (see also Plate VII) up the slope that led from north of the village to the summit of that hill. After marching for about half an hour across difficult ground, the companies found themselves enveloped in a dense mist and contact between the companies was completely lost. Hudson's C Company and A Company, led by Captain Emery, reported that they had managed to gain a foothold on the southern slopes of the mountain. Unfortunately, radio contact with the two companies was eventually lost at 0900 hours the next morning and no further word arrived until a few men from the force eventually returned on the afternoon of 15 April. There was little doubt that some form of disaster had befallen the attack.

It appears that A Company had reached the area of Tanngoucha at midnight after a difficult march across the rugged steep slopes, during which the fog rolled in and contact was lost with Hudson's company. At 0400 hours, Hudson and C Company arrived and the two company commanders took stock of their situation. They concluded that since their location would be under direct observation from positions held by the Germans on the heights, the best they could do was try to find some cover, dig in and wait. At dawn, Hudson's company positions was sighted and soon became the target for constant fire, and by 1000 hours C Company had been overrun.[37] Hudson, his deputy Captain R. Latta and two of his platoon officers were missing, although later it was confirmed they had been taken prisoner. The loss of Hudson, Latta and his company was a major blow to the battalion, as all three were highly regarded. The enemy next turned his attentions to A Company of the 5th Northants, led by Captain Emery, with mortar fire and sniping, while conditions became even worse when British gunners put heavy artillery fire down on the area. As this lifted, the Germans rushed their position and took as prisoners all

37   The story of the failed attack on Tanngoucha is based on the April 1943 war diaries of the 5th Northants and 2nd Lancs Fusiliers - TNA WO 175/512 and WO 175/517 - and the regimental histories.

those who had survived the experience of being shelled by their own side. This included Emery, his officers and most of his men. There was further bad news at first light, for B Company, led by Captain T.L. Beagley, had failed to reach its objective and learned that it was surrounded by German troops. It too found itself attracting artillery fire from its own gunners, which caused confusion and casualties. During the chaos caused by this fire, a number of the company managed to escape and even brought back 20 prisoners with them. Beagley himself was known to have been seriously wounded. He only managed to escape capture because he was found that morning and brought to safety by the battalion's medical sergeant, who demonstrated both dedication and cool courage.

Smith, Crook and Garner-Smith must have been alarmed when they eventually learned late on the morning of 15 April about the almost complete loss of the three companies in the nighttime attack. This, combined with other losses over the last few days, had much reduced the strength of their individual battalions. The impact of this action would have been slightly easier to take at their headquarters on Bettiour and Mahdouma if they had not both just started to recover from the receipt of some other bad news. This was the knowledge that a German counterattack had successfully recaptured Kef el Tiour and now threatened their positions on Djebel Ang and Bettiour.

7.12 Loss of the Kef and Djebel Ang

The unlikely source of 11th Brigade's troubles on the morning of 15 April was a German penal battalion, the 1st Battalion of the 962nd Schutzen Regiment of the newly formed 999th Infantry Division. The division had actually been formed in October 1942 as the 999th Brigade, which was composed of the 961st and 962nd Schutzen Regiments but was upgraded to a division in March 1943 with the addition of a third regiment, the 963rd. According to General von Vaerst, who commanded the 5th *Panzer* Army, apart from especially selected officers and men:

> The units of the 999 Inf. Div. consisted of men who had been punished for infractions of military discipline. For example, it contained officers and NCOs who had been reduced to the ranks, black butchers (*Schwarzschlächter*): military personnel caught killing live-stock for food illegally, etc. They had a chance to square their punishments by their behaviour in the presence of the enemy.[38]

Other sources suggest that 35 percent of the 999th Division's ranks were criminals or deserters and the rest had been political prisoners or other "undesirables". The division's officers and SNCOs were carefully selected for their ability to control and motivate this unusual group, and also for their political reliability, as most were members of the Nazi party. The division commander, Major General Kurt Thomas, was a committed Nazi who had served as an officer in the German Army battalion that had helped protect Hitler's headquarters. It is a symptom of the challenges the German high command faced in Tunisia that the 2nd Battalion of the 962nd Regiment only started to arrive by air in Tunisia on or about 11 April, but was committed to

38   See Vaerst, *Operations of the 5th Panzer Army*. FMS report D001 (US Army HQ ETOUSA) p.13.

battle by the night of 14/15 April.[39] Frederich Weber and his superior commanders were fully aware that the area around Djebel Ang and Tanngoucha was a crucial point in the mountain defences that protected Longstop Hill and the approaches to Tunis. They reacted accordingly by using this new fresh unit to recapture Kef el Tiour and Djebel el Ang. It would appear that initially the German commanders only committed two companies of the battalion in the counterattack that they unleashed during the early morning of 15 April.

The attack exploited the poor visibility at this time due to a combination of darkness and a mist that had come down that morning. It was preceded at 0430 hours by half an hour of ferocious artillery and mortar shelling on all the main British positions, including those on Kef el Tiour, Bettiour, Mahdouma and especially el Ang. Two companies of the regiment used the barrage to attack and force back the weakened A and B Companies of the 2nd Lancs Fusiliers, who had been holding the middle of Kef el Tiour ridge. Confronted by two full-strength and fresh Schutzen companies, the Fusiliers sustained considerable losses and withdrew to new positions near Djebel Ang. Soon afterwards, B Company, which had suffered especially bad casualties, was sent to Djebel Bettiour, but A Company held on to its positions on Djebel el Ang. A Company of the 2nd Lancashire Fusiliers may have felt it was defending Djebel el Ang on its own, but actually A and D Companies of the 1st East Surreys were also located nearby as they had been tasked with defending the hill. The mist, darkness and the unusual configuration of the ground around Djebel el Ang all contributed to the confusion about where both friends and foes were located and the surprising situation that soon ensued. The western end of Ang was divided into two spurs, the main height in the south and a subsidiary spur to the north. The slopes of the hill broadened out once the Kef el Tiour ridge came to an end and Djebel el Ang began, this terrain allowing Germans to slip around defences and attack other locations. Once the mist and darkness ended, visibility gradually improved and D Company of the 1st East Surreys, which was holding on to part of Djebel Ang, became aware of the German presence. It spotted some Germans attempting to infiltrate towards their positions and fairly quickly came under mortar and sniper fire. Soon afterwards, 50-60 Germans from one of the companies of the 2nd/962nd *Schutzen* Regiment had captured the northern spur of Djebel Ang. D Company was led by Captain Wadham, who organised his men to carry out a counterattack to remove them. Djebel Ang was not the only location under threat, for about this time Bettiour, which was occupied by two weak companies of the 2nd Lancs Fusiliers, also came under attack. This created confusion and problems for Garner-Smith, his battalion headquarters and B Company of his battalion, which had withdrawn to Bettiour to join the remnants of D Company. A Company remained on Ang, while as previously noted C Company had ceased to exist.

The melee in the dark created both opportunities and problems for the Germans: they exploited the confusion and chaos it created, but could also be vulnerable to the lack of awareness it created. The German attackers did not know, for example, that companies of the 1st Royal Irish Fusiliers had arrived at midnight and settled into the col between Djebels Bettiour and Ang. A further two companies were on their way and would arrive on Djebel Mahdouma by 1000 hours that morning. The Faughs' presence on Bettiour arose because Evelegh, possibly prompted by Brigadier Cass, had begun to understand that 11th Brigade in its weakening state

---

39   Information on the 999th Division is from the 78th Division Intelligence summaries and Samuel Mitcham, *German Army Order of Battle Volume 2* (Mechanicsburg, USA: Stackpole Books, 2009), pp.256-57.

was not capable of taking its objectives without additional reinforcements. Evelegh may also have already anticipated the need for another battalion, as he issued an order on 13 April which put the Faughs under Cass's command and placed it into a reserve position near Chaouach. This decision was taken well before 11th Brigade began to dash itself against the German defences on the heights of Ang and Tanngoucha. Evelegh had a good feel for terrain and the enemy, and he may have taken the precaution of providing a reserve nearby. After its last operation on 10 April, the Faughs had spent a fairly busy time by first marching 12 miles on the afternoon of 11 April from Djebel Oum Guerinat back to Plateau Farm, its start point six days before for the attack on Mahdi. It spent one day resting there, and early on 13 April carried out an exhausting 13-mile cross-country march to reach its reserve position in olive groves above Chaouach. After a short rest on 14 April, the battalion moved up in the dark and mist to establish itself near Bettiour and eventually around Mahdouma. The CO of the Faughs, Beauchamp Butler, had a new mission: to complete the capture of Point 622 and Djebel Tanngoucha.

It was Major John Coldwell-Horsfall of Mahdi fame, along with his D Company, that found himself in the uncomfortable position of discovering on the morning of 15 April that all was not well on Djebel Ang to his north or on Djebel Bettiour. In actuality there was little he and his men could initially do, and moreover he came to the incorrect conclusion that any friendly forces including the East Surreys had been completely ejected from Djebel Ang. The reality was different, for Wadham with D Company had attempted to eject the Germans on the northern slope of the hill, but this attack had failed. By 1000 hours Wadham and A Company of the Lancashire Fusiliers were still holding the southern slope of Djebel Ang, and did so from then onwards. They also stopped an attempt at 1000 hours to take their positions, aided by their own battalion's mortars and machine guns. By late afternoon a kind of stalemate had arisen, and there was ongoing dispute about who held Djebel Ang, with the Germans probably holding the northern part and the British the southern section. Meanwhile, Coldwell-Horsfall and his company spent the rest of their day in the col between Bettiour and Ang as targets for enemy mortar and machine-gun fire, though thankfully without incurring many casualties.

Across on Djebel Bou Diss, the 6th West Kents were not completely detached observers, for they too had been recipients of the nasty early morning barrage and continued to come under occasional fire throughout the day. The aggressive Germans also attempted a further counterattack to retake Bou Diss, but this was quickly repulsed by B and D Companies and several prisoners were taken. One of them, a German sergeant major, offered to go and bring in the remaining 40 men of his company, but he had been wounded, so his generous offer was rejected. In an interview 46 years later, Lieutenant John Williams, the battalion mortar officer, told a slightly different story about the sergeant major. He recalled that after all his officers had been wounded or killed, the latter had unsubtly marched his men up the hill to attack Diss and been heavily shelled before he was captured. The German NCO had served in the artillery during the First World War, and when questioned said that if his company had artillery support they would have retaken Bou Diss. He also asked if he could see the automatic field guns that had been shelling his unit, for he was sure they must be automatic as hand-served guns couldn't fire that fast. Williams, who despite serving in a Kent battalion actually came from Durham, felt he at least should relay the compliment to the gunners who supported the West Kents. The gunners, the 17th Field Regiment, were so pleased with his remark that they asked for the German sergeant major to be escorted to their battery positions. They showed him their "automatic" 25-pounder guns and looked after him before finally sending him on to the division

POW cage, which was now firmly established at Toukabeur and gratifyingly full.[40] The scale and ferocity of the artillery fire encountered by the German NCO was in no small part due to the efforts of the gunner officers and men, who as OP parties directed this fire while in exposed positions. One of those OP parties was led by Major Giles Brocklebank, an FOO from 138th Field Regiment who provided direct artillery support to the 5th Northants from 13-15 April. Throughout this period Brocklebank and his men manned an important OP which was under very accurate and constant enemy fire and faced with maintaining communications in very difficult circumstances. The citation for the MC which was later awarded to Brocklebank noted that: "It was solely due to his skill and perseverance that fire could be brought down on a heavy enemy counterattack, which was completely broken up before it could affect the situation."[41]

By the late afternoon of 15 April it was becoming obvious to all that 11th Infantry Brigade had shot its bolt and was unable to carry out any further attacks on Djebel Tanngoucha. After two days of hard fighting, all three of the brigade's battalions were reduced to the equivalent of two weak companies apiece. The only unit that wasn't seriously understrength was the 6th West Kents, and they had suffered casualties in their rifle companies. Fortunately, what had become very obvious to all three battalion commanders had now become obvious not only to Brigadier Cass but also to Vyvyan Evelegh. Cass and Evelegh had finally made their way up to Bettiour for the first time, and held a conference there at 1500 hours that afternoon. Evelegh had probably already made the difficult decision to replace Cass's battered 11th Brigade with the whole of 38th Irish Brigade, since he had summoned Nelson Russell, its commander, to his headquarters that morning. The latter almost certainly had been told what was to happen, since at 1535 hours, less than five minutes after this conference ended, Russell was able to issue the operational order for relief of 11th Brigade by the Irish Brigade. Evelegh would have been reluctant to commit the Irish Brigade to this renewed attack, as he was fully aware that the brigade had just completed five days of tough fighting and really needed a rest. Certainly Russell was not happy that his brigade was being asked to take over this difficult job. However, Evelegh was confronted with a nasty situation and had run out of options. He couldn't commit 36th Brigade, as the 5th Buffs had been battered and the 6th West Kents were holding Bou Diss. He also recognised he needed a full brigade for the job of clearing the Peaks, but Charles Allfrey didn't have one to spare, so his only option was to commit Nelson's brigade. Evelegh did manage to soften the blow, as he had arranged for the 2nd London Irish Rifles under Pat Scott to be moved from a rest area 20 miles south near Le Kef and brought rapidly up to join the brigade, so Russell now had three battalions at his disposal. Evelegh would have informed Cass that his brigade was to be gradually pulled out from its current positions and relieved by the Irish Brigade. This process couldn't happen overnight, as time was required to bring up its units, and Bou Diss, Mahdouma and Bettiour still needed to be held in the meantime. This news was unlikely to have been a surprise to him, but nonetheless it must have been a difficult pill for Cass to swallow. The truth was that both division and brigade commanders were tired and the former, if not also the latter, needed a rest.

Russell's plan demonstrated that either Evelegh was still in the dark about the real situation on the Peaks when he met Russell earlier, or Douglas Pennant wrote the plan the day before,

---

40   Imperial War Museum Oral Interview with John Williams 1989, reference 11839.
41   Quote from his MC citation in TNA WO 373/1.

when circumstances were different, before sending it out the following afternoon. This plan assumed that the Faughs and London Irish Rifles would carry out almost an administrative move in which they would "occupy" Kef el Tiour, Djebel Ang and Mahdouma. Unfortunately, the former was firmly back in German hands by the morning and possession of the latter was disputed, as Coldwell-Horsfall found out the night before. The Skins were ordered to move to a reserve position near Chaouach. The only part of the plan that was based on accurate information was that Mahdouma was still in friendly hands. Fortunately, the order to commit the Faughs from division reserve and move it up to Bettiour and the col with Djebel el Ang meant that one decision was quite easy for Russell. The Faughs' existing two companies nearby were already available to lead the brigade attack by ejecting the Germans from the northern slope of Ang and retaking Kef el Tiour ridge. The job of carrying out this attack was handed reluctantly by the CO of the Faughs, "Beau" Butler, at an "O" Group to A and D Companies, commanded by Nick Jefferies and John Coldwell-Horsfall. Coldwell-Horsfall recalled that:

> Beauchamp spoke to us in his usual apologetic manner, and explained that we had been brought in to restore a battle which seemed to have turned against us … He pointed out that nothing could be taken for granted and he could not truthfully say that we held any ground about us save where we now stood.[42]

Butler's guidance to his company commanders showed the degree of confusion that frankly existed in the area around Bettiour. His appraisal of the tactical situation was both honest and accurate. His point about possession of ground was soon shown to be particularly correct. In order to be freed to carry out this attack, A and D Companies of the 1st Royal Irish Fusiliers would be relieved by two companies of the 2nd London Irish Rifles and the rest would take over the Fusiliers' positions on Bettiour. Led by E Company, the 2nd London Irish left its assembly area around Chaouach at about 1730 hours and started a three-hour march which would take it to Bettiour.

7.13 The Defence of Bettiour

After a terrible night and a difficult morning, by early evening on 15 April, Major Ken Garner-Smith and his battalion headquarters must have been looking forward to a quick handover to the 2nd London Irish Rifles so they could move over to Mahdouma, join up with the East Surreys, rest and regroup. The battalion losses in missing, dead and wounded over the last four days meant that it had to be reorganised into just two composite companies, in addition to battalion headquarters and HQ Company. All told, the battalion probably had no more than 350 men left out of its original 650. Darkness had arrived and with it a thick mist. This cut visibility down to a few yards at battalion headquarters, which was located at the bottom of a 50ft-high rocky wall, at the top of which lay a flat bare escarpment. The lead elements of the 2nd London Irish were starting to arrive when the area around Bettiour came under heavy mortar fire at about 2000 hours. Soon after it became apparent that the Germans had managed to infiltrate through the British lines and launch a surprise raid or counterattack. A shower of long wooden-handled

---

42   See J. Horsfall, *Wild Geese*, p.122.

stick grenades were dropped from the top of the escarpment onto battalion headquarters and exploded. It seemed for a brief period that the headquarters might have to suffer the ignominy of having to rapidly vacate their quarters, and indeed some men started to fall back. At this point Lance Sergeant Stanley Myers, the pioneer platoon commander, intervened in a rather forcible manner. Myers rallied the men who had fallen back, seized a Bren gun and returned fire. He took a party of men and helped to restore the situation. At one point Myers resorted to an unusual and dangerous method of keeping the raiders at bay when he fused and threw live Hawkins anti-tank grenades at the Germans. The manual for Grenade Hand Anti-Tank No. 75 had probably never envisaged them being used this way, as they were intended to be laid so a tank would drive over an igniter, which would set off acid to explode a charge. Myers was an experienced pioneer so he knew that Hawkins grenades had another use; as demolition charges which could be set off using an alternative method. This was by fitting blasting caps or Cordtex, which was probably the way he utilised them. Nonetheless, even this method was pretty dangerous, but Myers' unorthodox use of Hawkins mines inflicted several casualties on the Germans and helped drive them back. In addition to this act, when the Bren gun was running low on ammunition, Myers exposed himself to go and get a resupply of magazines.

The situation appeared critical at one point, as there were relatively few men available to repel the unwelcome guests. While Myers and his party were harassing the raiders, Captain Pritchard, the adjutant of the 2nd Lancs Fusiliers, rallied every man he could, including signallers, clerks, batmen, RASC mule-handlers and members of the anti-aircraft platoon. This included the adjutant of the London Irish Rifles, Captain Wilson, who had arrived and helped with the defence. Pritchard then guided them into positions and their fire forced the Germans to withdraw. Despite being wounded in the face by a grenade fragment, the RSM WO 1 Robert Alexander insisted on carrying on with his job and would not allow his wounds to be dressed. Alexander eventually left to go to the rear some 24 hours later, and only after he was ordered to do so. Alexander's courage and devotion to duty on both days would result in the award of the DCM.[43]

Once this unpleasant incident was over, the Lancashire Fusiliers finally managed to hand over possession of Djebel Bettiour to the 2nd London Irish Rifles at midnight and, exhausted, battered but unbowed, they made their way down to Djebel Mahdouma. In a classic bit of English (or Irish) understatement, 38th Brigade's war diary noted about the handover by the Fusiliers to the London Irish that: "The position was fairly difficult to take over as 2 LF were repelling an enemy night attack. After this, however, the relief was accomplished."[44]

Stanley Myers' extraordinary disregard for his own safety in the fighting in the mist at Bettiour was later recognised by the award of a DCM, while Pritchard earned the MC for his leadership that night. The battalion stayed on Mahdouma for a short period before moving down to a rest area at Toukabeur on 17 April, and Lieutenant Colonel Linden-Kelly returned from hospital to resume command. Given the losses incurred by the battalion over the last six days, it would not have been surprising had Linden-Kelly been less than impressed with Garner-Smith's stewardship of his battalion during his absence. However, the day Linden-Kelly returned, the GOC V Corps, Allfrey, made a visit to the battalion and congratulated it on its part in the

---

43   See TNA WO 373/1 for DCM and MM citations for Alexander and Myers.
44   Quote from TNA WO 175/216 38 Infantry Brigade April 1943 WD (entry for 15 April 1943).

recent battle. This may have softened the blow of resuming command over a battalion that had lost over 250 officers and men during the period he was in hospital, including some of is best officers. Garner-Smith's period as acting battalion commander had been eventful. He left the battalion on 17 April upon his promotion to lieutenant colonel, and on the same day assumed command of a battalion of the Bedfordshire and Hertfordshire Regiment.

The adjutants of the London Irish and Lancashire Fusiliers were not the only ones to have an exciting night on 15 April. Although both A and D Companies of the Faughs were supposed to be in the midst of things, by participating in an attack that night, their battalion headquarters also found themselves under fire from German raiders. As the sky was filled with tracers and brightly coloured flares, Captain Richard "Dick" Jefferies, the brother of A Company commander Nick Jefferies, found himself obliged to grab a rifle and engage some Germans who were troubling his HQ. The Faughs launched their attack on Kef el Tiour while trying to defend their rear areas. Butler's earlier prediction about only controlling the ground around them had proved uncannily accurate. Fortunately, it didn't take long for Dick Jefferies and his men to get rid of the unpleasant Boche, as the Faughs tended to call them, and he was able to return to more normal adjutant duties, including monitoring the radio to follow the ensuing battle on Kef el Tiour. Captain Jefferies was especially interested in the progress of the attack as his brother Nick was leading A Company that night. The saga of the Faughs' battle on the Kefs and Point 622 on the night of 15/16 April and for the next 10 days is an extended one, and will be described later.

7.14 "In Arduis Fidelis"

The intensity of the fighting on the Four Peaks - Djebels Ang, Bettiour, Kef el Tiour and Tanngoucha - inevitably led to a significant number of wounded officers and men. These had to be found, treated, consoled and evacuated. This part of fighting is often ignored in accounts of battle, so it is fitting to end the story of 11th Brigade's sojourn in the mountains by briefly describing the role played not only by RAMC personnel but also the medical evacuation, treatment system and Army chaplains. The motto of the latter, "In this sign conquer", is perhaps less appropriate as a heading for such an account as that of the RAMC's Latin motto, which translates into English as "Steadfast in Adversity". This is a much more accurate phrase to describe the conduct of the doctors, medical orderlies, stretcher bearers and also the officers of the Royal Army Chaplains Department within the brigade's battalions during these difficult days from 13-17 April. The chaos, confusion, mist, constant shelling and mortar fire that became a constant feature of life in and around Mahdouma, Ang and Bettiour made it extraordinarily difficult to find and treat wounded men. The rocky crags could conceal those who needed aid, but also German soldiers, so anyone who ventured out in the day or in the mist during darkness faced an uncertain outcome. This danger does not seem to have discouraged Lance Corporal Leonard Bracegirdle of the 11th Field Ambulance, who was attached the Regimental Aid Post (RAP) of the 2nd Lancs Fusiliers for the period 14-16 April. The RAP and surrounding area was under continuous shell and mortar fire during this period, as well as intermittent small-arms fire. Bracegirdle nonetheless went out repeatedly to find and carry in wounded to the RAP. When a stretcher bearer was killed, Bracegirdle immediately volunteered to fetch his body in, and was only stopped from doing so by a direct order. After dusk he went out and searched for the man's body under heavy shell fire. Bracegirdle's conduct over those two days could be said to fully uphold the traditions of the RAMC, and were an inspiring personal example of the meaning of his corps' motto. The citation for the award of his MM was keen to note that throughout the action Bracegirdle showed exemplary qualities of leadership which inspired his medical section. While Bracegirdle was looking for wounded Fusiliers, Private Charles Morgan of the East Surreys was demonstrating a similar dedication to the needs of other men. Morgan was a stretcher bearer with C Company of the 1st East Surreys under the command of Pat Wadham on Djebel el Ang. Throughout the battalion's operations, Morgan tended and carried the wounded under heavy fire. He volunteered to replace another stretcher bearer who had been killed on Djebel Ang and continued doing useful work until he was wounded. In spite of his injuries, Morgan refused to go back to the rear until he was ordered by Wadham to do so.

When wounded men were found on Bettiour, their first stop, on a long but well-organised medical evacuation chain, was to be brought to the Fusiliers' RAP, which was run by the battalion's medical officer, Lieutenant Ringland Boyd. The RAP was located near the battalion headquarters on the reverse slope of the hill, but was fully exposed both to the elements and constant shelling. Though now out of the battle, the injured soldiers were not out of harm, and meanwhile lay in pain and great discomfort on the rocky ground. Boyd and his medical sergeant would try to give what immediate medical treatment they could to those at the RAP before they were evacuated. This would include stopping or reducing any bleeding, ensuring soldiers' wounds were quickly bandaged, trying to making patients comfortable with blankets and providing pain relief with morphine. The RAP was not a location where any real treatment could be provided: the priority was getting soldiers on to the next stage of the evacuation and treatment system. The evacuation of wounded proved difficult on Bettiour as there were no tracks or roads in the area, so a number of mules and handlers had been assigned to 11th Brigade for use in moving the wounded down from the RAP. These used mule litters to carry them to the road or track-head (i.e. where a track or road started) at Chaouach. A further problem during the four days of the battle was that the shelling and mortar fire became so bad that there were significant periods when the wounded had to stay at the RAP, it being too dangerous to move them. The medical staff led by Boyd worked tirelessly and without thought for their own safety under constant exposure to this fire, which sometimes landed on the crest of the escarpment just above them, for three harrowing days. Boyd's leadership, skills as a medical officer and devotion to duty on Bettiour undoubtedly helped save many lives. He and his aid team also fully lived up to their corps' motto.

While Boyd used his skill as a doctor to look after soldiers at the RAP at Bettiour, Chaplain 4th Class William Cooper, the Fusiliers' chaplain, demonstrated he too could be faithful in adversity. Throughout a four-day period on the rocky evil heights of Bettiour, as one officer later called them, the Fusiliers' padre ministered to his flock in his own inimitable style. During those days of constant shelling, Cooper stayed at the RAP and tended to both the spiritual and physical needs of his parishioners. He assisted Boyd in tending to the wounded, and when required helped evacuate them. Cooper was unsparing in his efforts to look after the wounded, continuing his ministry despite the inherent danger and difficulties. The combined efforts of Boyd and Cooper on the blood-sodden rocky crags of Bettiour would formally be recognised when both were later awarded the MC.

While Boyd and Cooper looked after the Fusiliers' wounded at their RAP, Captain Eric Kerr, the RMO of the 5th Northants (see Plate 11), cared for his wounded officers and men close by at his battalion's RAP, which was also on Djebel Bettiour, in his own way. As the morning of 15

April dawned, Kerr became aware that two companies of the battalion had been overrun near Tanngoucha and that several wounded lay out on its bare exposed slopes. He was determined that they should be treated and rescued, and made several journeys out into no man's land with parties of stretcher-bearers to bring back the men who had been wounded in the attack on Point 622 the previous afternoon or on Tanngoucha that night. Kerr and his gallant stretcher-bearers brought in 20 wounded men who might otherwise not have survived. This number included Captain Beagley, the B company commander, who was severely wounded. Beagley was carried back to the RAP by Kerr's Medical Sergeant. Kerr and his medical staff continued to treat wounded at the RAP despite the almost continuous shell and mortar fire falling on Bettiour. Sadly, we don't know the name of Kerr's gallant Medical Sergeant or those of his team of stretcher-bearers who helped to rescue the wounded, so their cool courage cannot be properly recognised. Kerr's personal courage and total disregard for his own safety were noticed and led to the immediate award of the MC.[45]

Padre Cooper's counterpart in the 5th Northants, Chaplain 4th Class the Reverend Ernest Elworthy, also took an active role in the effort to find, treat and recover the Northants' wounded. He did not spare himself either, and was wounded on the morning of 16 April while searching for casualties and had to be evacuated. In contrast to Cooper, Chaplain Elworthy's courage and dedication to his men was not formally recognised, but it was noted in the battalion war diary, which was in itself high praise. It also undoubtedly earned him something more priceless than any decoration: the respect and admiration of the soldiers of the battalion. Elworthy would continue his ministry with the 5th Northants in its battles in Sicily and throughout the long and hard Italian campaign. In July 1945, his courage and dedication to the battalion would finally be officially recognised when he was awarded a MC for his efforts during operations in April that year.

The wounded men who made it to the RAPs and were tended by the devoted medical staff had first to survive the dangers of constant shelling on Bettiour before being evacuated. At one point, the level of shelling prevented any evacuation of the wounded and they spent several hours at the RAP. Moreover, when they were evacuated their ordeal was sadly not yet over. An iconic image of the wounded of recent wars is that of them being moved by dedicated surgical teams in a Chinook helicopter. This demonstrates how much progress has been made in medical treatment on the battlefield in modern times. Unfortunately, helicopters didn't exist in 1943 in Tunisia, and the idea of a golden hour for life-saving surgery was only partly understood by medical staff. Transport options for the wounded in rugged mountains were much more limited. Instead of a rapid medevac by helicopter, during the Battle of the Peaks, when a wounded man was evacuated he was loaded on to a mule litter and faced a painful journey in that manner for one or two hours back down to Chaouach road-head. That was unless he was lucky enough to be wounded slightly later than 15 April, in which case he might have been evacuated on Bren

45   There is some evidence that this was actually Eric Kerr's second MC. The regimental history states he won his first in January 1943 for rescuing wounded. However, Kerr's award for Bettiour was cited in the *London Gazette* for May 1943 as his first MC rather than a bar to an existing one. The description of the activities and gallantry of attached RAMC doctors and staff and Chaplains are based on relevant citations in TNA WO 373/1 and the war diaries of the three infantry battalions.

Gun Carriers which were employed in that task.[46] At Chaouach, he would be unloaded by a section of the 11th Field Ambulance stationed there especially for that task, his injuries briefly checked and then be placed on a stretcher into a lorry designed to take wounded men. He would have made a further hour-long journey via Toukabeur down to the main Oued Zarga to Medjez road and moved to a farm on a track just off the main road. This was the location of a Main Dressing Station (MDS), which had doctors and medical orderlies who were able to review injuries, check blood loss, replace blood-sodden dressings, adjust splints and triage the casualties. The RAMC doctors would divide the wounded by priority, based on the chances of survival and seriousness of injuries. Seriously wounded men, who would survive if they could quickly get life-saving surgery, were sent direct to a Field Surgical Unit (FSU) at Beja about an hour and 20 miles away. The FSU was designed to perform life-saving surgery as close as possible to the front line. In one sense it showed that those who directed medical services fully recognised the importance of providing surgical treatment as early as possible. FSUs were simple but effective, and comprised a mobile operating theatre which was set up in a couple of large extended tents, carried by lorries, with a couple of surgeons and some theatre nurses. The remainder of the wounded, including those with potentially fatal wounds, were moved yet again, this time for a further hour to the mountain village of Thibar. At Thibar, the seminary or monastery of the White Fathers Order had been converted into a casualty clearing station, and in early April it was also the location of 70th Base General Hospital, which had an attached FSU. At this point the lightly wounded got to rest, while those who needed urgent attention were seen by skilled surgical and medical teams. In these more peaceful surrounds, X-rays could be taken, blood transfusions given and wounds cleaned much more thoroughly before surgical operations were conducted. Surgeons, doctors and male nurses would work in 12-hour shifts to provide a 24-hour service. Up until mid-April 1943, the supposed lack of female facilities meant female nurses were not allowed close to the front. This changed after the senior matron of the First Army visited the senior medical officer of V Corps and no doubt had a frank exchange of views. Members of the Queen Alexandra's Imperial Military Nursing Service (QAIMNS), who then, but not now, were exclusively female, were soon a common sight at Thibar and even Oued Zarga.

A wounded or sick soldier's journey, from the time of being hurt on Bettiour, was hopefully quite short to a RAP. Unfortunately, his subsequent journey to Thibar or Beja might last anything from five to 10 hours. Everyone in the medical evacuation chain, including Arab mule drivers, British RASC ambulance drivers, RAMC doctors, orderlies, QAIMNS nurses, pioneers, cooks and mechanics, all wanted to do their best for the wounded and worked to exhaustion and beyond to do so. The fate of wounded once they had reached Thibar Seminary depended on the seriousness of their wounds and the flow of casualties. Inevitably, some men didn't survive the traumatic experience of being wounded, lying out in the open at just below 2,000ft on bare slopes, followed by the tribulations of staying at the RAP, before being finally evacuated over several hours. Some seriously wounded men died before, during or after surgery in tents or in the monastery buildings. Today they lie among the 99 graves in five rows in the CWGC Cemetery which was established on the site of a temporary graveyard built in 1942. The

---

46   The profile of the medical evacuation chain is based on the 78th Divisional Medical Operation Order No. 12 dated 12 April 1943 in TNA WO 175/420 ADMS 78 Division April 1943 WD; and F. Crew, *Army Medical Services*, pp.345-46.

cemetery is less than 300 yards from the now-vacated Seminary building in the village of Thibar which was used as the hospital.[47]

The fate of those who survived their wounds depended on how long the doctors felt they would need to recover, combined with the pressures created by the ebb and flow of the battle. Thibar Hospital would by 16 April provide some 1,400 beds, where there was time for the less seriously wounded to recover. If, however, their wounds were serious and likely to require significant time to recover, they would be moved further back in the system. A wounded soldier would next be sent by vehicle to a railhead, usually at Souk El Khemis, and join a medical evacuation train with nurses on board, set up to take wounded back to hospitals at Bone in Algeria or all the way back to Algiers. Those who would take more than six months to recover for duty or would eventually be discharged as not physically able to serve, would be sent in a hospital or a merchant ship in a convoy back to the UK. When the fighting was intense and large numbers of wounded arrived at the various base hospitals, including Thibar, it was sometimes necessary to move existing occupants back to the rear area hospitals rapidly. This was done by rail, by special medical evacuation road convoys and increasingly by air using the now more common C-47 Dakota transport. Those who fully recovered from their wounds would spend time convalescing before reversing the same journey in slightly more uncomfortable transport back to their units.

7.15 The Price of Battle

The difficult fighting across Djebels Ang, Bou Diss, Mahdouma and Bettiour, and the failure to take Tanngoucha, exacted its own unique price in dead, wounded and missing. The brunt of these casualties was sustained by Brigadier Cass's 11th Infantry Brigade, which suffered considerably during the period from 10-17 April. Actual battle casualties for the Battle-Axe Division were significant, but surprisingly not as high as one might have expected for fighting of this intensity. They were, for example, lower than the initial four days of Operation Sweep. For a range of reasons, precise figures for casualties among 11th Brigade's infantry battalions are not simple to calculate, though it is clear that it was the fighting companies who suffered most. A reasonable estimate is that the three infantry battalions together lost some 52 men killed or died of wounds, 198 wounded and at least 248 missing in action, for a total of 498 casualties. The majority, though not all, of those missing were later found to have been captured and became prisoners of war. One of the interesting figures for 11th Infantry Brigade was the number of men from the infantry battalions that had been captured or were missing: this figure came directly as a result of the unsuccessful attack on Djebel Tanngoucha, where companies of the 2nd Lancs Fusiliers and the 5th Northants were effectively overrun and captured. It was perhaps inevitable that the fighting during this period took a significant toll of officers at company level, with six company commanders killed, wounded or captured. A further nine platoon commanders were also captured or killed in the battalions involved in this fighting. These losses had a serious impact on the effectiveness of the infantry companies, as they removed a valuable

47 Details of the cemetery at Thibar are from L. Harris's excellent book *Cemeteries and Memories: The Second World War in Tunisia* (Oxford: Milton Tompkinson, 2007), pp.105-09, and the CWGC website. The CWGC Cemetery remains intact, and in 2018 was still well cared for, but this sadly cannot be said for the graveyard of the monks, as their cemetery was recently heavily vandalised.

level of leadership. The unit that suffered the most in the brigade was, not surprisingly, the 2nd Lancs Fusiliers. The battalion originally declared in its war diary that it had lost eight killed, 75 wounded and 148 missing in action, but these figures were a significant underestimate as the actual losses inflicted came to 26 dead, 84 wounded and 148 missing. In comparison, Howlett's 36th Infantry Brigade was much less engaged in the fighting and consequentially suffered fewer casualties. Nonetheless, its three infantry battalions lost 35 men killed or died of wounds and 97 wounded in action during this period.

Casualties in all the units that directly and indirectly supported the attacks of the 78th Division, such as the Royal Artillery, Royal Engineers, Recce Corps, the tank regiments and logistic units, were quite low but added to the toll. In total from 11-19 April, the 78th Division incurred approximately 660 casualties in the battles to secure the four peaks. This excludes the casualties in the Irish Brigade incurred on its arrival and in the later fighting on Bettiour, Ang, Point 622 and Tanngoucha. But the figures do not reveal the impact of fighting in increasingly hot weather in rugged mountains on the health of the soldiers involved. All this exertion also came after spending nearly five months already involved in intensive operations in the hills and mountain of northern Tunisia, often constantly exposed to the elements. All these factors together had certainly reduced the overall fighting efficiency of the division's nine infantry battalions, and had its impact on its supporting units.[48]

Behind the cold statistics of warfare in the mountains are a range of personal stories of the dead and those missing or captured. It is not feasible here to relate all their stories, but a few examples may help to provide a fuller picture. The losses incurred by the 2nd Lancs Fusiliers included both the oldest and youngest men killed during this period. The dubious honour of falling into the latter category fell to 39-year-old Fusilier Campbell Hulme from Widnes in Lancashire. The youngest to fall was 18-year-old Fusilier Geoffrey Smith, who despite his presence in a Lancashire regiment was from Halifax in Yorkshire. The 1st East Surreys' losses included 2nd Lieutenants Kenneth Burch and Joseph Hicks, who at 24 and 31 respectively were both older than 23-year-old Captain Tony Wilkinson, who had commanded a company of the 5th Northants. The latter, though serving in a Northamptonshire Regiment, came from Felixstowe in Suffolk. Several of the soldiers who were killed were married, and thus wives became widows. This was especially unfortunate for one of the youngest soldiers to be killed in the 2nd Lancs Fusiliers, 20-year-old Private William Smith, as he had only been married for a short time to his wife Kathleen. The second-oldest man to be killed during this period, 38-year-old Sergeant Joseph Sullivan, was also married, though he had perhaps spent more time with his wife Jessie.[49]

The cost of this fighting was of course not just limited to the British troops in the 78th Division, for German units also had significant losses. It is much more difficult to assess the scale of those losses as the lack of good records make it hard to provide an accurate estimate. German casualties were likely to have been lower than those for the 78th Division as they were defending their positions. A very rough estimate is that the German units involved, and especially the

---

48 The estimates and breakdown of casualties for this phase of the battle were produced as a result of painstaking analysis of CWGC records, battalion war diaries for April 1943 and the 78th Division ADMS casualty records.

49 The stories of individual casualties for this period were obtained from analysis of CWGC records and the inscriptions on their headstones, which can be found on the CWGC website.

334th Infantry Division, lost 80-90 dead and 300 wounded. Records also indicate that the 78th Division took approximately 250 prisoners of war in the period from 11-17 April. The fighting certainly effectively put out of action the 3rd Battalion of the 756th Mountain Infantry Regiment and made ineffective as a unit the 1st Battalion of the 962nd *Schutzen* Regiment.[50]

50   The rough estimate of German casualties is based on figures in the intelligence summaries in the V Corps and 78th Division war diaries: see TNA WO 175/82 and 175/168 for April 1943 and analysis of battalion war diaries.

8

The Battle for Kef El Tiour and Tanngoucha

8.1 The Second Attack on Kef El Tiour and Point 622

At the critical division commanders' conference on Djebel Bettiour on 15 April, Brigadier Nelson Russell was instructed to take over the task of securing the 78th Division's final objective, Djebel Tanngoucha. His plan for that night required the Faughs to take Djebel Ang, Kef el Tiour and afterwards exploit towards the elusive Tanngoucha. A secondary attack was also to be launched against the hilltop village of Heidous, which lay just below that mountain, by the 5th Buffs. It is not clear from existing records where the supposedly bright idea for the secondary attack on Heidous - or as the troops soon came to call it with their gallows humour, "Hideous" - came from, but it was now part of the plan. Throughout the day, both companies of the Faughs assigned to the task, A and D, lay in their shallow trenches on the col below Bettiour and suffered from the nasty physical and psychological effects of regular mortar and artillery fire. At 1730 hours, "Beau" Butler came personally to give a final briefing to the two company commanders, Coldwell-Horsfall of D Company and Jefferies from A Company. Acting Captain Jefferies was the son of a Hertfordshire vicar and at 22 was one of the youngest company commanders in the British Army in April 1943. He had proven his worth as a soldier in battle several times since beginning the Tunisian campaign as a lieutenant commanding 17 Platoon. He had recently been awarded the MC for two patrols he led on Goubellat plain, during which he had shown the utmost coolness and courage in trying situations. He had led A Company since Major Murphy, the previous incumbent of this job, had been killed in January 1943 and his deputy blinded. Murphy, as befits a man who bears that distinguished Irish name, had been a very lively character who was highly regarded by his Fusiliers for his capacity for drink and bold leadership. He was not an easy act to follow, but despite his young age, Jefferies was a natural soldier and leader who rapidly won over the affections of the tough warriors of A Company. His soldiers quickly found out that Jefferies was tough or even tougher than they were. He led from the front, and on several occasions went on patrols on his own in no man's land, in one case joining a German mine-laying party briefly before detaching one of the men as a prisoner.[1] Jefferies appeared to have led an almost charmed existence under fire.

---

1   The profile of Nick Jefferies is largely based on J. Coldwell-Horsfall's books *Wild Geese*, pp.13-14, and *Say Not the Struggle*; Doherty, *Clear the Way*, pp.24, 32; and Jefferies' MC citation.

He was a close friend of Coldwell-Horsfall, the leader of D Company for the attack, and the two companies often worked together. Jefferies was usually a lively officer full of fun, but on the morning before the attack, when he and Coldwell-Horsfall used a position to examine the ground they would move over, the latter noticed his brother officer was unusually subdued, quiet and withdrawn. Coldwell-Horsfall asked him if anything was worrying him. Jefferies looked at him for a while and said nothing. As they began to leave, Jefferies turned to Coldwell-Horsfall, whom he admired greatly, and said "John I am glad we are doing this one together."[2]

One of the several tantalizing mysteries of the Battle of the Peaks for a serious historian is why Brigadier Russell and the Faughs appeared to believe Djebel Ang needed to be captured. An even greater mystery is how, when the battalion carried out its supposed attack, they managed to avoid bumping into the East Surreys' companies that partly occupied it. This was one of those situations where two separate parties have a completely different perspective and recollection of the same events. The war diary of the East Surreys makes clear that at 1900 hours on the evening of 15 April, D Company remained on the southern slopes of Djebel el Ang, but the top and northern slope were held by the Germans. It is also clear that when the 2nd London Irish arrived to take over the positions of the East Surreys and 5th Northants, B Company of the 1st East Surreys also moved up at about 1930 hours to aid D Company on Djebel Ang. It might be expected, therefore, that as two infantry companies were on the southern part of Djebel el Ang, when A and D Companies of the Faughs moved up to their start line to supposedly attack Djebel Ang, they might have noticed each other. The war diary of the Faughs is very clear that the battalion's task was first to retake Djebel el Ang and the Kef el Tiour ridge. It also notes that their start line was on the western edge of the former hill when their attack was launched at about 2045 hours that night. It is slightly perplexing that despite all the discussions between Cass, Evelegh and Russell and their staff, that no one appeared to have told the Irish that other British troops were occupying part of a hill they were about to attack![3] It seems probable and fortunate that that the gunners were, however, aware of these dispositions, as the East Surreys were not shelled as part of the artillery barrage. Unless all the records are wrong, somehow in the darkness, A and D Companies of the Faughs got to the start line, avoided the B and D Companies of the East Surreys and carried out a very noisy and violent attack on the eastern part of Djebel el Ang. It seems almost a miracle that the soldiers of both companies didn't end up shooting each other. However, like thieves in the night, the two companies of the Faughs managed to pass by the East Surreys and get to their start line. It is possible that the Faughs' approach from the col between Bettiour and Ang managed to hide the East Surreys' positions from them.

Immediately before Coldwell-Horsfall gradually led his company to the start line, he found himself having to quickly administer justice to one of the hard-bitten pre-war regular soldiers of his company, Lance Corporal Given. Given was an excellent soldier in battle, but a poor one

---

2   The quotation is from J. Coldwell-Horsfall, *Wild Geese*, p.123.
3   This mystery came to light when the author analysed the April 1943 war diaries of the 38th Infantry Brigade, 1st East Surreys and 1st Royal Irish Fusiliers for this book, and J. Coldwell-Horsfall's account in *Wild Geese*, pp.123-25. The rest of the story of the Faughs' attack on Kef el Tiour in the following pages was largely derived from the above sources and the following war diaries: TNA WO 175/170 CRA 78 Division April 1943; TNA WO 175/326 17 Field Regiment; TNA WO 175/337 132nd Field Regiment; and TNA WO 175/338 138 Field Regiment.

in barracks, as he and strong alcohol didn't mix well. His rank was a temporary one, as he had a fascinating set of conduct sheets which told the story of 23 charges of drunkenness. During the winter battles in Tunisia, the Faughs had made significant use of rum to ward off the cold and also when about to carry out an attack to fortify the men. That evening was no different, except that a new sergeant had left a jar with the remainder of 17 Platoon's rum ration within Given's easy reach, and the temptation had proved too much. Given was far too good a soldier to leave behind in any attack, but Coldwell-Horsfall made sure that he was reduced to fusilier and put under close arrest before the company moved out. Given's platoon sergeant, R.J. "Robbie" Robinson, was an extremely capable SNCO who knew all about his lance corporal's weakness for rum; it was unusual for Robinson to miss much, but he must have been distracted at some point and failed to notice the rum ration. Robinson was a highly regarded sergeant within the battalion with an unusual story behind his military career, though unlike his drunken fusilier, this was for all the right reasons. Robinson was only 18 years old when he became a platoon sergeant in the Faughs. In peacetime, the arduous path to rise from fusilier to this position might have taken 12 years or more, yet Robinson managed to achieve the same distinction in less than three years. He had enlisted under-age and had risen through pure ability to become a corporal by 1942. He was promoted to sergeant in March 1943 and became platoon sergeant by the time of the attack on Mahdi and the patrol in which Lieutenant Chapman was wounded. Sergeant Robinson was to be in the thickest of the fighting in Tunisia, Sicily and Italy, and later won the DCM. He survived the war and later wrote a short account for his children about his experiences in Tunisia. Those memoirs describe the night attack on Ang, the Kef el Tiour ridge and Point 622:

> Two companies A and D were ordered to retake a hill called Djebel Ang in a night attack … Ang was quite high, rocky and narrow with what I called a camels hump about three quarters of [the] way along from our attack start line, the ground sloped quite sharply down on either side particularly so on the left. Our two attacking companies formed a box formation because of the nature of the terrain. All automatic weapons were positioned along the front of the box and on the flanks so that maximum automatic fire could be directed at targets in every direction.[4]

The plan for the attack on the rest of Djebel Ang and the Kef el Tiour ridge was not that subtle: Coldwell-Horsfall's D Company was to attack on the left and Jefferies' A Company on the right. As Robinson accurately reports, Coldwell-Horsfall placed all his eight Bren light machine guns at the front to provide maximum firepower, and Jefferies did the same.

Fusilier Given continued to be under close arrest and couldn't carry a rifle, but was loaded down with Bren magazines. As the two companies formed up, and just before the barrage started, two German Spandau machine guns unexpectedly opened up on them in the darkness with tracer fire from the flanks. Butler, who was close by, wondered if his men would ever get off the start line, but soon afterwards Coldwell-Horsfall appeared, seemingly rather indignant that any German should have the temerity to interrupt his timetable, and reassured his CO that

---

4   The quotation is from Robinson, *Memoirs*, pp.16-17. The author is grateful to Robbie Robinson for granting permission to use extracts of these hitherto private and unpublished memoirs in this book.

both companies were ready to attack. The attack was preceded by a heavy artillery barrage on Heidous, Kef el Tiour, Tanngoucha and the surrounding area, which started at approximately 1930 hours, well before the companies reached their start line. The gunners did not stint on their provision of artillery support, for it was the one area where the Irish Brigade had the edge on the German defenders. The majority of the fire support initially was aimed at Heidous for the first 25 minutes of the barrage, and a total of 1,800 shells of various calibres fell on that unfortunate village. At 2030 hours, a further concentration of 2,200 shells fell in and around the Kef el Tiour ridgeline. The 132nd Field Regiment was also on call to fire on Kef el Tiour as and when ordered to do so.The barrage had been going for a while when the two companies began their advance and immediately they bumped into a German machine-gun position which opened fire. This proved a brave but rash act for it was immediately targeted by eight Bren light machine guns fired from the hip and 50 rifles, plus an Irish battle cry. The Germans didn't live long and the advance continued. A second Spandau opened up, and an account of the fight states: "The same thing happened 50 yards further on. The excitement was intense[,] men were cheering and shouting on all sides, those in the front firing from the hip with their tommy guns and Brens."[5]

The flight path of the shells from artillery positions near Chaouach to their targets, German artillery positions, caused the men of D Company some anxious moments as they began their advance. "Robbie" Robinson later noted;

> As we approached the Camels Hump, we became aware that our heavy artillery 5.5 inch guns were firing from their positions a couple of miles back from our right rear at enemy gun positions to our left front (i.e. a diagonal line of fire).
>
> It soon became apparent that these heavy shells were crossing the hump very close to its top and that sooner or later one or two of these shells would strike its top and probably cause casualties as we passed on either side.

In his memoirs, Robinson continued to describe the terrain and the movement of the lead wave of the two companies:

> I was in command of 17 Platoon on the left of the box formation and as we approached the hump which rose sharply, it became obvious that the two companies would have to continue to advance to the right of the hump and this would cause a degree of congestion due to the narrowness and steepness of the slope, the ground on the left dropped away very sharply. As I was about to direct my platoon over to the right, I noticed that there appeared to be a goat track running along the left of the hump and which appeared negotiable in a single file and I had a hunch that the track would converge with the right where the hump levelled off further along.[6]

---

5   See a two-page report entitled "The Kefs"in TNA WO 175/216 38 Infantry Brigade April 1943 WD, hereafter cited as "The Kefs". Details of the artillery support are from the Fire Plan for the attack in Operation Order No. 14 in TNA WO 175/170, the 78 Division CRA WD.

6   The quotation is from Robinson, *Memoirs*, pp.16-17.

It was at this juncture that Robinson's concerns about the artillery flight path were realised, as at least one of the 5.5in shells struck the top of the area called the camel hump and exploded. Robinson's men were showered with rock, but the shells' fragments missed them. A Company was not as lucky, and the shell killed Lieutenant Phil Slattery and a signaller instantly, seriously wounded Nick Jefferies and also injured several other soldiers. If Robinson hadn't noticed the goat track and followed it, his platoon would have been close to the explosion and he and his men would have been wounded or killed; such were the fortunes of war. Jefferies was required to relinquish control of A Company, and Captain R.L.G. "Tommy" Wood, the battalion mortar officer, temporarily took over its leadership. Despite this terrible friendly-fire incident, both companies managed to continue the attack, successfully seized the end of Kef el Tiour by 2300 hours and captured over 30 prisoners. Ironically, the German decision to launch their counterattack on Djebel Bettiour had made it considerably easier for the Faughs to take their first objective, as in order to do so the Germans had been required to weaken their defences on the ridge.

One of the other minor mysteries of this action is how the Germans avoided the Irish Fusilier companies, when the former moved along the Kef el Tiour ridge to attack Bettiour earlier that evening. Coldwell-Horsfall states in his book that the Germans launched their attack on Bettiour at the same time as his attack on Kef el Tiour, so both parties apparently passed each other in the night. Frankly this seems unlikely, as the Kef el Tiour ridge was narrow at the top (less than 60ft wide in most places) and at some points there was only one viable track. An alternative explanation is that though the mist and the darkness may have contributed to this situation, possibly it was simply a matter of timing. It seems likely that the men of the Schutzen battalion moved along the ridge and deployed off it at least 45 minutes before the Faughs started their attack. Most accounts agree the 2nd Lancashire Fusiliers' headquarters on Bettiour came under attack at 2030 hours, while the Faughs launched their attack from the eastern end of Djebel el Ang at 2045 hours after being delayed by Spandau MG42s. Since it would have taken at least 30 minutes in the darkness to move off the western end of Kef el Tiour and down to the escarpment on Bettiour, it seems much more probable that the Germans troops finished their move at 2000 hours, long before the Faughs started their attack. The outcome, whatever the cause, was that the Faughs now had possession of the extreme eastern end of the Kef el Tiour ridge, with a platoon from D Company on the reverse northern slope of Point 622. Although Point 622 and Tanngoucha were the officially recorded objectives of the attack, a decision was quickly made not to try to move further forwards as the mist was thickening. The leading companies had also reached a relatively flat area where digging in was possible, and Coldwell-Horsfall and his boss, "Beau" Butler, were especially conscious that one of the problems 11th Brigade had encountered here was holding onto its gains. Butler was perfectly able to assess the situation, as he had followed behind the lead companies in their attack and he quickly joined them as they were starting to consolidate their positions, despite the obvious dangers. It was typical of Butler's leadership style that he could often be found walking up to see how his fighting companies were doing in front-line positions. This discomforted officers like his adjutant Dick Jefferies and Coldwell-Horsfall, who felt it was improper and far too dangerous for him to be so far forward on a night attack. Despite their polite requests, Butler continued to want to be close to the action throughout his period in command of the Faughs. He did, however, appear to make one concession: he seems to have later reluctantly accepted the regular presence of whoever his exasperated adjutant assigned to be his bodyguard, and the latter had explicit instructions to follow him everywhere. Butler's tendency to wander about up to and on the front line at night, to see how his chaps were getting on and to encourage them with his presence, would sadly later prove his undoing.

While Butler tried to reorganise his companies, the badly wounded Captain Jefferies was carried to the rear by stretcher-bearers. At some point in the darkness and terrain, like so many others, the men carrying him became disorientated and nearly lost their way. Despite his wounds, Jefferies raised himself on the stretcher, looked at the stars, which had finally become visible, used his compass and brought them home to safety with the unerring navigation skills that had made him a superb patrol leader. He was evacuated off the mountain via the RAP to one of the casualty clearing stations, and on to Beja. Sadly his wounds were too great, and at midday the battalion adjutant, his brother Gus, shielding his own grief, recorded in the war diary the simple news that Captain D.L. Jefferies MC was reported having died of wounds in Beja.[7] His loss was mourned not only by his brother and his close friend Coldwell-Horsfall, but also by almost everyone who knew him. This was especially the case among the ordinary fusiliers of A Company, whose view of their new young boss had changed in less than three short months from grave concern that he had replaced Murphy, to the eventual awe in which he was to be held by them at the time of his death.

Lieutenant Slattery, who died instantly from the shell that injured Jefferies, had been part of the battalion since it landed in Tunisia but had only just rejoined the battalion three days previously. His death was also not easy to take, as he had only just recovered from being seriously wounded during the attack that killed Major Murphy on 18 January. Slattery's loss was also mourned within A Company, and it meant that other than Tommy Wood the company had no officers. One benefit of the CO being so far forward was that he could very quickly react to events, and as a result Coldwell-Horsfall was told apologetically that he would lose his deputy, the highly capable Captain Michael MacDonald, to A Company. MacDonald was a mature officer who had been commissioned from the Irish Guards and was a good choice to take over command of A Company from Wood.

Sometime after 2330 hours, C and D Companies of the battalion also moved up and along the ridgeline and were in position to ensure that any counterattack would be thwarted. The battalion's mules also arrived with mortars, ammunition, picks and shovels, and the companies began digging in. The mist that came down around the ridge reduced visibility to just a few yards, which made life difficult for the adjutant and the support troops that were trying to move up to assist the leading companies. In addition, wireless communication had broken down from the forward companies to the rear, and eventually Coldwell-Horsfall had to send men back to find the rear parties. The situation became even more confused during the night, as German troops withdrawing from their attack discovered parts of Coldwell-Horsfall's company who were holding the right-hand (southern) side of the Kef el Tiour ridge and the reverse northern slope of Point 622. One of the German officers leading a large group literally bumped into 20-year-old Lieutenant Peter Sillem, the commander of 18 Platoon, and in a moment worthy of a Hollywood action movie, Sillem shot him with his revolver and the German reportedly fell off

---

7   Today Nick Jefferies lies buried in the CWGC cemetery in Beja, Tunisia, while Phil Slattery is buried at Medjez el Bab CWGC cemetery.

the sheer crags some 100ft to his death. The rest of this group were killed, captured or rapidly managed to disappear into the night.

By the time it started to get light at 0530 hours, A, C and D Companies of the Faughs were quite well established on the eastern end of the Kef el Tiour. Moreover, Butler's signals team, various company personnel, mortars and some Vickers machine guns had arrived, though not his adjutant who had been seriously delayed. The problems experienced in getting forward various battalion headquarters groups had also made life difficult for Coldwell-Horsfall's cousin, Captain James Browne of the 132nd Field Artillery Regiment. Browne had been assigned to act as the observer for the Faughs while they were on the ridge. He had led a five-man party and two mules on to the ridge, but his progress up to the leading companies had been delayed by the darkness, mist and slow progress of battalion headquarters personnel. He finally arrived at a most inconvenient time, for visibility was rapidly improving and this meant there was little time to plan artillery defensive fire concentrations before the front-line positions were exposed to enemy observation and shelling. The failure by Butler and his team to accord Browne and his party the priority they undoubtedly required to move along the ridge was to prove unfortunate. As daylight broke, Coldwell-Horsfall started to push forward a couple of patrols to probe in the mist up the slope to the Point 622 ridgeline and decided to accompany one of them to get a better feel for the area. This must have been a slightly nerve-wracking business for all concerned, and it would have been surprising in such a situation if everyone in the patrol had not had their fingers close to the trigger of their weapons. The patrol with Coldwell-Horsfall was making its way along and up a rocky crag, when at the same time a nine-man German patrol led by an officer had arrived at the same point. Coldwell-Horsfall reacted rapidly and shot the German officer, while the other members of the patrol fired at the rest. This group of Germans must have been a recce party for a bigger group, as quickly afterwards the patrol sighted a different party which engaged them with machine pistols. These were all dispersed after an exchange of fire.

By this time, at about 0900 or 1000 hours in the morning, it should have been apparent that the Germans were determined to dispute the Faughs possession of the ridgeline and everyone should have been fully alert. The poor visibility caused by the mist, however, enabled the Germans to get very close to A Company on the north side of Kef el Tiour ridge, and it was here that their counterattack was especially damaging. The forward platoons had only seconds before Germans came out of the mist firing weapons and throwing grenades, and as a result inevitably suffered several casualties. One of the lead sections was overrun and the artillery OP party led by Browne found itself too far forward and under imminent threat. Browne's group managed to briefly bring down some artillery support before the leading German infantry threw grenades at their position, which killed two of his party. His OP sergeant gallantly moved forward from this post to engage the Germans with his Thompson submachine gun and killed an officer who fell close by. This gave Browne time to call down fire almost on top of his own position, and he told his sergeant to flee. Browne completed his fire mission and ran at full speed back to positions to the rear, vacating his previous lodgings, which were now a target for British guns, but not before he was hit and seriously wounded by machine-gun fire. Despite his wounds, Browne made it to friendly lines and soon afterwards got his revenge when the Germans who had shot him became ground zero for an Uncle target which he had requested. An Uncle target was the gunners' term for firing all available guns from within a division on a designated location. Browne would have sent a simple radio message with the words "Uncle Target" followed by the grid reference; in certain cases the number of rounds to be fired would be added, known as scale, so scale 10 would be to fire 10 rounds from all available guns in the division. In view of the critical importance of retaining hold of the eastern end of Kef el Tiour, Browne's request would have had the highest priority and at the very least the fire of 72 25-pounder field guns and probably that of 16 5.5in guns would have descended on the Germans. This fire resulted in the failure of the German counterattack, though not before A and C Companies had suffered many casualties. These included most of the men of the section of Vickers medium machine guns, who were posted in an exposed location on D Company's flank. They had opened up and promptly became the target of several MG42 machine guns.

By 1100 hours the situation was well in hand, and daylight provided the artillery observer who replaced Browne with the visibility required to prevent any repetition of the night's counterattack. By 1230 hours the adjutant had been able to join up with his CO and had brought with him a wireless set, which enabled the latter to update a concerned Brigadier Russell at his brigade headquarters. The absence of any communication, combined with constant calls for artillery fire on the gunners' net, can have done little to reassure Russell that all was well on the ridge. It would have come as some relief to make contact with Butler and learn that the situation was much better than it might appear.[8] This did not mean that life in the Faughs' positions at the eastern end of the ridge became any more pleasant, for regular though intermittent mortar fire, sniping and machine-gun bursts on the narrow ridge led to inevitable casualties. Among these were the battalion's RMO, Captain Harvey, who was wounded by a splinter from a mortar bomb when working on the wounded. The artillery fire ensured that on this occasion the Battle-Axe Division retained its grip on this vital location. The rest of day was spent by the three companies of the Faughs digging in further when possible, evacuating their wounded and bringing up supplies.

A final fitting postscript to the capture of Kef el Tiour by the Irish Fusiliers was written in his own inimitable style by 33-year-old Fusilier James Given from the town of Omagh in Northern Ireland. Given had taken his usual active part in the fighting, but was then wounded in the line two days later and sent back to be treated at the aid post. In view of his unerring ability to find alcohol, it did not take long for Given to find the store of medicinal rum that was kept there and he quickly consumed much of it. Whatever might be said about his ability to handle his alcohol, one thing could be said about Fusilier Given: he was a fighting soldier. Thus, after fortifying himself with medicinal rum, he headed back to join the battle on the front line. Given acquired a rifle and, roaring drunk but also fighting mad to the last, conducted his own personal battle with the enemy. A few days later his body was found on the slopes near Djebel Tanngoucha surrounded by several dead Germans. Given would probably not have survived the peacetime Army or civilian life, but his fighting spirit could only be admired by D Company and all those who knew him. His company commander, Coldwell-Horsfall, said of Fusilier Given: "He was a true faugh, with simple tastes, rum and the regiment." He may have gone into battle under close arrest and as a fusilier, but someone in the battalion, probably Coldwell-Horsfall, as a mark of respect for his courage, ensured that today, as he rests (sadly without access to his favourite

8   The story of James Browne's troubles is derived from the war diary of the 132nd Regiment and the account called *The Kefs*.

tipple) in Medjez el Bab CWGC cemetery, the rank on his headstone reads "Lance Corporal" (see Plate 12).[9]

8.2 5th Buffs' Attack on Heidous

It is often forgotten that the attack on Tanngoucha was planned to be a joint effort which would involve both the Faughs and the 5th Buffs. The latter had been tasked with capturing the Berber village of Heidous (see Plate VII). Once Heidous was taken, the 5th Buffs were to join with the Faughs in a joint attack on Djebel Tanngoucha. It is unclear who precisely decided that the 5th Buffs should capture Heidous, as the battalion was not at that point under Russell's command and the operation order he issued for the 38th Brigade made no mention of a role for the battalion. It seems probable that the capture of Heidous was definitely an objective at some point in division planning. The detailed division fire plan created for the attack on night of 15/16 April, for example, originally made Heidous a priority target for artillery fire. However, irrespective of what might have been planned at divisional level, it is clear that the 5th Buffs were not allowed much time to prepare for this attack. The regimental history frankly notes that "To the Buffs on the 15th April [*sic*], at very short notice and without time to arrange adequate artillery support, fell the task of trying to dislodge the enemy from their stronghold."[10]

In view of its important tactical position north-west of Longstop and immediately south of Tanngoucha, Heidous was always going to be defended by the Germans with determination as its loss would threaten both those critical defence positions. Any attack on Heidous would have to be carefully planned and well executed. Ginger McKechnie, the CO of the 5th Buffs, was unfortunately afforded precious little time to do either. To make life even more difficult, and for reasons that are not obvious, it seems the lavish artillery barrage which the gunners had originally planned to aid the Buffs could not be provided. The 5th Buffs started their attack by climbing up towards the village from north-east of the village of Chaouach at 1930 hours. There are few details of the operation, except that as they got closer to Heidous the lead unit, A Company, found out quickly that Germans had mortar and machine-gun positions in the village and on the slopes above it. The battalion had managed to get within 300 yards south-west of the village when Captain Freak and 16 of his men were wounded and one man was killed in A Company. It became obvious that any attempt to eject the Germans from the village would lead to unnecessary losses, and the 5th Buffs was already well understrength due to previous casualties. The CO therefore took the sound decision to call off the attack and the battalion withdrew to near Chaouach. Intelligence later discovered that the village was defended by two companies of the 1st Battalion of the 756th Mountain Infantry Regiment, who made skillful use of existing caves and cellars as shelters from artillery fire. Heidous was to continue to be a thorn in the side of the 78th Division, and especially the Irish Brigade, until eight days later.

---

9   The quotation is from Coldwell-Horsfall *Wild Geese*, p.144, while the rank on his headstone was confirmed by the CWGC website and a photograph of his grave kindly provided to the author by Richard O'Sullivan.

10   C.R.B. Knight, *Historical records*, p.202.

8.3 The 6th Skins Attack Tanngoucha: 16-17 April

On the morning of 16 April, Brigadier Russell met Lieutenant Colonel Neville Grazebrook, the CO of the 6th Skins, and assigned him the job of attacking and capturing Djebel Tanngoucha that night. Grazebrook must have been aware that his battalion would be making the Battle-Axe Division's third attempt to take the mountain. Moreover, the first attempt had met disaster and the second had achieved only partial success when Kef el Tiour was taken, but strong enemy defences on Point 622 had precluded any advance on Tanngoucha. The failure of the 5th Buffs' attack on Heidous had further confirmed the strength of the German defences on the mountain. In view of the information available about the difficulty of attacking Tanngoucha and the weakened state of his division, it is surprising that Vyvyan Evelegh agreed to carry out yet another attack on the mountain so quickly after the previous ones. Perhaps he felt one last hard push would be sufficient to release the German grip on Tanngoucha. Although there is no direct evidence of this, it is probable he was under pressure from senior commanders to complete the current operation to enable the division to be prepared for the attack on Tunis. At this stage, the 78th Division's sole priority was the capture of Tanngoucha and Heidous, so Evelegh almost daily visited Russell at his brigade headquarters to assess the situation and provide guidance. The decision to send in the Skins to complete yet another attack, on such a constricted approach, would have been made by Russell and approved by Evelegh. It seems likely that the latter would have asked the advice of Russell about the proposed attack, as Russell had long since proven to be a capable commander with a good feel for the battle. Normally it would have been sensible to trust his judgement but unfortunately on this occasion it may not have been wise to do so.

There is good evidence that Russell was not his usual capable self at this point in the battle and was not thinking as clearly as he would normally have done. Coldwell-Horsfall, an unabashed admirer of Russell's ability as a brigade commander, noted that he had been concussed in a bombing raid and was also shaken by the death of his signals officer. It was perfectly natural for Russell to have been adversely affected by these two incidents, but unfortunately this happened at the most inconvenient of times, for the brigade was in the middle of a very tough battle. It is difficult to escape the conclusion that after the problems of the last five days everyone was tired and not thinking as clearly as they might by deciding to conduct yet another frontal attack on Tanngoucha. It did not take a military genius to conclude that the Germans had a strong position and would be expecting a further attack using a similar or the same route. Wellington, that master of the battlefield, is reputed to have once said about Napoleon's predictable use of the columns at Waterloo that they came on in the same old way and he defeated them in the same old way. The Germans might be forgiven for thinking that Wellington's remarks about the French could be equally applied to the tactics applied by the British in their recent gallant but unsuccessful attempts to capture Tanngoucha. There is a good case that if a third assault was warranted, the brigade and the division should have taken the time to more thoroughly plan the next attack on this final objective. The German position on Tanngoucha and at Heidous was a tough nut to crack and would have presented the most able of commanders with a serious challenge. The height of the mountain and its position meant that any approach which attempted to flank the mountain using slopes and hills to the north and north-west would usually be detected and halted. The primary access route from the west to the highest point on Tanngoucha was along the Kef el Tiour ridge, then via the top of the Point 622 ridge and on to Tanngoucha (see Plate IV). However, the latter was a mini-fortress well protected by positions on its flanks.

These included Point 620, the highest feature on Tanngoucha itself, and the long ridge curving away to the north-east from Kef el Tiour which led to the grassy hill of Point 585, which was soon to be named Butler's Hill. The slopes running south from Kef el Tiour to the Point 622 ridgeline were difficult to cross and could in any case be observed from positions at Heidous.

The Germans lacked the generous artillery support which was available to the 78th Division, but had compensated for that by providing a large number of 80mm mortars and a few mobile but deadly infantry guns. The mortars were formed into mini-batteries and hidden in gullies to the east of Tanngoucha, where they were difficult to destroy but could be easily directed by German observers on that mountain. The rocky terrain magnified the effects from the explosions from mortar shells with the rock fragments that were also created.

Even if the Allied air forces had been able to provide air support, which they were not, the troops were far too close to each other to risk aerial bombing. The difficulties inherent in securing the division's primary objective surely required more careful consideration before launching the next attack. Unfortunately, Lieutenant Colonel Grazebrook was not to be afforded such a luxury and at 1245 hours on 16 April he was ordered to attack and capture Djebel Tanngoucha that night. Planning was rushed, for at 1415 hours the CO led his company commanders to view the ground as best they could from their positions near Chaouach, but at 1500 hours he had to attend a conference at brigade headquarters to discuss the fire support plan. At 1730 hours the main part of the battalion left its positions north of Chaouach to march to its assembly area via Djebel Kelbine and arrived there at 1930 hours after a tiring four-mile approach march. It is apparent from the Skins' own war diary and other sources that some officers in the battalion felt that preparations and planning for the attack were far too rushed. Russell and his brigade staff also seemed either out of touch with the tactical situation or very poor at communicating it to the Skins. Grazebrook's original plan was based on the assumption that the Faughs held Point 622 and the 6th Skins could use this as a springboard for their attack. He had been told at his meeting with Russell at 1245 hours that the East Surreys and 2nd London Irish held Bettiour and Djebel el Ang, and that Butler and the Faughs held Point 622.

"Beau" Butler knew that he didn't hold the Point 622 ridge, but Grazebrook didn't until he met Butler at the Faughs' main battalion HQ on the western end of Kef el Tiour at about 1900 hours that evening. It is puzzling how this obvious piece of crucial information was not provided to Grazebrook when it was well understood by Butler. The confusion about the occupants of Point 622 was not limited only to Grazebrook, for the East Surreys reported both at 1635 hours and again at 1852 hours that the Irish Fusiliers had two companies on Point 622. The reality was different, for although Coldwell-Horsfall and his company were located just above and on the edge of the Point 622 ridgeline, they had not captured either the ridgeline or Point 622 itself. Grazebrook was forced to revise his original plan at very short notice and communicate this to his companies. What is both mystifying and confusing is that according to the Skins' war diary, the new plan assumed the Irish Fusiliers would now capture Point 622 as the first phase of the Skins' attack. There is no evidence that Butler and his lead companies either prepared for or undertook such an attack. The Skins' approach to its start line was not without its dangers, as it appears they were fired on while moving up towards it, probably from Bettiour by soldiers of the 2nd London Irish. Lieutenant Percy Hamilton, whom we last met on Djebel Mahdi, was leading a platoon of A Company; he later recalled the incident:

We started soon after we had given our section commanders what information we could; [Captain] Bradley was in the lead and my platoon was first. He was a tall fellow and led off at a great rate, and my chaps could not keep up. In addition, one of the units we passed on our way out, machine gunned the end of the second platoon so the company got strung out considerably. After a mile, we had to stop to reorganise.[11]

Someone had obviously not got the message that the Skins were moving up, or possibly some of the newer arrivals to the London Irish had become a little jumpy. The relatively short period of time for preparation and the problems faced in conducting a proper reconnaissance of the ground, combined with the difficult terrain, created a number of problems for the unit. It is unclear which route the 6th Skins used to reach their proposed start line near Point 622. In any case, sometime before midnight and despite this series of problems, somehow they were in position on their start line and about to attack Tanngoucha. Just after midnight, the gunners opened up on the mountain with a large barrage and soon afterwards the two leading companies of the 6th Skins started their attack. The artillery plan for the attack involved a creeping barrage. This required the gun batteries to change the angle of the guns at prescribed intervals so the shells they fired moved forward 100 yards every minute or so. On this night sadly something went wrong and a shell from one of the guns failed to lift its fire and wounded 12 of D Company, including Captain McCaldin and Lieutenant Porter. The problems continued as the advance began, for during the attack, A Company under Captain Bradley, one of the leading companies, was somehow overtaken by B Company, which was supposed to follow it. The immediate result was described by Lieutenant Hamilton:

There was a level part on the left, which was actually a grassy strip, and as we approached this, we saw figures walking on the skyline. We lay down and fired at them and they fired back. This battle seemed to last for a few minutes, but perhaps it was not as long, and then someone from the other party shouted that they were Skins so we stopped firing.[12]

The people firing at Hamilton were soldiers from B Company, led by Major Bayley, which had got ahead of A Company. The surprising thing about these two exchanges of gunfire was that no one was hit, which suggests all concerned required more marksmanship training. This was the third friendly-fire incident of the night, and two of them demonstrated a lack of coordination between the various companies, which did not bode well for the rest of the advance. The luck of the Irish on this occasion seemed on this occasion to have temporarily deserted the 6th Skins. However, luck is a strange and fickle thing, which can change rapidly, and this proved to be the case on this night. Surprisingly, and despite the apparent odds against the battalion, B and D Companies of the Skins managed to move forward and get on to their objective without much opposition and with no further casualties. They also managed to capture five machine guns and take 16 prisoners. For a brief moment it seemed that the Skins might achieve what three other battalions had failed to do and capture Djebel Tanngoucha. Unfortunately, when artillery support stopped, this enabled the German defenders to come out of their dugouts

11   See Hamilton, *Memoirs*, p.16.
12   See Hamilton, *Memoirs*, p.16. The story of the 6th Skins' attack is largely derived from its war diary for April 1943 and a report entitled Tanngoucha in TNA WO 175/216 38 Brigade April 1943 WD.

and trenches located on the flanks of the two companies and open up with machine guns and mortars. This fire started to take its toll on the 6th Skins, who found themselves out in the open with no obvious shelter. At this point luck once again deserted the Skins, for the mule column carrying the picks and shovels needed for them to dig in never arrived. The mules and their Arab muleteers were spotted in the moonlight and shot at from the flanks. According to one source, the muleteers panicked and would not move forward, so the lead companies never got these vital items. Other sources make no suggestion of panic, merely stating that that the mules were targeted by heavy machine-gun fire and dispersed. Whatever the truth of the story, it is worth noting in their defence that most muleteers had effectively been conscripted into the Colonial French Army and might have been somewhat reluctant soldiers. The officers, NCOs and men of the RASC Pack Transport companies had already compiled an excellent record of service in Tunisia for their bravery under fire. One of the Arab muleteers, Sergeant Sifi, had been awarded a MM for his gallantry in a previous action. Furthermore, it appears that the German machine-gun and mortar fire was sufficiently bad not only to disperse the mules, but also to pin down the following Skins' companies and prevent them from moving through to continue the attack.

In the fine tradition of their regiment, the officers and fusiliers of the leading companies tried to silence the German weapons by sending forward patrols to identify and destroy the positions. One patrol tried to knock out a machine gun on a cliff face using the unusual method of firing a newly issued weapon, the Projector Infantry Anti-Tank, later popularly known as the PIAT, which was designed to take on tanks at short range with a rocket but on this occasion the fusiliers tried to adapt it for other purposes. Unfortunately this and other attempts failed, and the machine gun continued to cause problems. Battalion headquarters joined in the action and sent out a patrol to tackle a machine gun firing from the left flank, but this was found to be sited in a cave on the cliff face and couldn't be reached. Lieutenant Percy Hamilton was in the forefront of the attack, had placed his platoon under a cliff for protection and looked for a way forward. After he rescued a wounded man and tried to operate a wireless set he had discovered, Hamilton found himself in the uncomfortable position of being directly targeted by a machine gun. As he later recalled:

> I dropped the wireless mighty quick and ducked under the cliff, where I met Sgt (now Major) Richards. Richards and I chatted for a bit and discussed the possibilities of getting up the cliff. We decided it was impossible. Next thing we heard was someone loading a two inch mortar about fifty or a hundred yards away and Stephens' voice shouting to aim at the cliff; we shouted to hold on as we were at the bottom and Richards ran to the right and I to the left. Then we shouted for him to carry on. Jerry must have heard too as he wounded one of the mortar men and chucked a couple of grenades down where we had been.[13]

The Skins' attack had stalled, and by an additional stroke of bad luck the wireless sets of C and D Companies were put out of action. It rapidly became obvious that it was not possible to go forward, but also that the companies couldn't stay where they were or they would be destroyed

---

13   The quotation is from Hamilton, *Memoirs*, p.17, which is also the source of the tale of Hamilton's evacuation which is described below.

by enemy fire. Neville Grazebrook made the difficult but sensible decision to order a withdrawal to their start line and leave Tanngoucha back in the hands of its tough German defenders. Hamilton and his platoon were amongst the last of the Skins to pull back. He was delayed because he and a few of his men were assisting one of his lance corporals who had hurt his ankle. Dawn had by now broken, and Hamilton and his party were clearly visible to the German defenders, but perhaps because they were helping a wounded man, the Germans didn't fire. Soon afterwards the group found two mules wondering around, and having loaded the injured man on one of the mules managed to get back to friendly lines.

The 6th Skins' unsuccessful attempt to capture Djebel Tanngoucha on the night of 16/17 April was not as costly as might have been expected, based on the likely level of German resistance. The battalion reported casualties of only four dead and 36 wounded in action for the engagement, but it is likely that at least seven Skins lost their lives during the action. The failure of a third direct attempt to capture Djebel Tanngoucha in less than four days seems to have alerted V Corps' commander Lieutenant General Allfrey that a review was required of 78th Division's current approach to operations. Allfrey travelled up from his headquarters and met first with Evelegh, then went forward to visit Brigadier Russell at the Irish Brigade's headquarters near Chaouach at 1400 hours that afternoon. He took the opportunity to go up to a newly established brigade OP which provided a good vantage point of the rugged nature of the terrain of the peaks. There is no record of their meeting, but it is not difficult to conclude that the focus of their conversation was the desirability of continuing further attacks against Tanngoucha. Russell may have pointed out that the only fresh and strong battalion available to be thrown against this objective was the 2nd London Irish. The other two battalions in his brigade were understrength and tired; the Faughs were holding on to the Kef el Tiour ridge and the 6th Skins were about to relieve the tired battalions of 11th Brigade on Djebel Ang and Bettiour. After talking to Russell, Allfrey would probably have met again with Evelegh. While we do not know what was said, we do know from the 38th Brigade war diary that Russell and his divisional commander met at 1600 hours that day. The outcome of that meeting was very clear: "It was decided that there was no object in attacking Heidous and Tanngoucha at present and that it would be better to coordinate a new plan."[14]

Allfrey, Evelegh and Russell had finally come to accept the unpalatable truth that the current approach of launching one frontal attack after another on Djebel Tanngoucha could not be sustained any longer. It is reasonable to suggest that this conclusion should have been reached earlier, for example after the second attack had failed so badly, but hindsight is a wonderful thing. The order to suspend attacks on Tanngoucha reflected a hard-headed decision that the division lacked the strength to accomplish this mission and still be a viable formation capable of conducting future operations. Allfrey needed the division to be able to participate in a new operation, codenamed Vulcan, where its role would be to capture Longstop Hill. This task would have to be carried out by the 11th and 36th Infantry Brigades, which would need a brief period of rest and reorganisation. The Irish Brigade was already committed to retaining its hold on Djebel Ang and Kef el Tiour, and then it would be required to complete the task of capturing Tanngoucha. Allfrey's intervention created the conditions for the long-overdue withdrawal of "Copper" Cass's battered 11th Infantry Brigade from their positions on the peaks

14   TNA WO 175/216 38 Infantry Brigade April 1943 WD.

and the return to 36th Infantry Brigade of its two battalions. While the Irish Brigade had been conducting its attacks on Point 622 and Tanngoucha, these five battalions had played an important, exhausting though overlooked role of holding onto the division's initial objectives, Djebels Bettiour, Mahdouma and Ang.

The long overdue relief of the tired and understrength battalions of 11th Infantry Brigade necessitated a complicated juggling act, in which units were gradually replaced and pulled back from the more exposed front-line positions. The first of these moves took place in less than ideal circumstances on the night of 15/16 April, when after finally repulsing the attack of the 962nd *Schutzen* Regiment, the 2nd Lancashire Fusiliers were relieved by the 2nd London Irish Rifles at midnight and were pulled back from Bettiour to Djebel Mahdouma. Gravely weakened by its losses on Tanngoucha, the battalion's four rifle companies had to be reorganised into just two fighting companies when it arrived at Mahdouma. After just a day at Mahdouma, the battalion was pulled back to the austere but comparatively peaceful environment of Toukabeur. It is hardly surprising that, after its exertions over the previous 10 days, the Fusiliers' war diary noted that everyone was extremely tired. However, the battalion's performance over the last six months, and especially latterly, had not gone unnoticed. On 18 April, Linden-Kelly, its CO, was summoned to meet General Harold Alexander, the new Army Group commander. When he was introduced to Linden-Kelly, Alexander praised his battalion and gave it a great compliment as he said: "I hear your men are tough."[15] Linden-Kelly and his Fusiliers were later shifted to take over positions at Djebel Bou Diss, but played no further significant role in this story. This was not surprising as the unit had lost two of its companies on Tanngoucha and was greatly reduced in numbers. The 2nd Battalion Lancashire Fusiliers would eventually be rebuilt and play a key role in later operations of the 78th Division in Sicily and Italy.

Unsurprisingly, the next battalion within Cass's brigade to be moved was the 5th Northants, as it too had suffered at Tanngoucha. The battalion was actually the most understrength of all the units in the brigade, as it had been reduced to only 16 officers and 479 men from its usual establishment of nearly 750. It was moved south from near Bettiour on the evening of 16 April to near Djebel Bel Rherarif, and subsequently to Toukabeur. In a sign of how much had changed in less than seven days, this village could now be considered in the rear area, as it contained the brigade headquarters, a number of artillery regiments and several support units.

The 1st East Surreys was the last of the 11th Brigade units to leave the desolate and hazardous hills of Djebel Mahdouma, Ang and Bettiour. By this time, Wilberforce had resumed command of the battalion and Harry Smith had returned to his role as second-in-command. After its successful attack on Mahdouma and involvement in the battle for Kef el Tiour, the unit had taken over responsibility for Djebel Ang, where it had been the target for enemy artillery and mortars for two days. It was relieved on the night of 17/18 April by Grazebrook's 6th Skins and was able to move back to Djebel Bel Rherarif, its original start point for recent operations. Major Smith's courageous leadership of the East Surreys during the last difficult five days had continued a long-established military tradition established in the nineteenth century by his illustrious relative. It would be more formally recognised by the later award of a well-earned MC. Wilberforce and his unit spent the next two days in and around Djebel Bel Rherarif before being sent to relieve Eric Heygate's battalion, which was located near Djebel Bou Diss, on the

---

15   The quotation is from Hallam, *History of the Lancs Fusiliers*, p.48.

night of 20/21 April. Any hope that the battalion might be allowed time to rest was dashed the next day when it received orders to support 36th Brigade in its attack. It was a fairly tired infantry battalion that eventually moved by foot and vehicle to its new location near Chassert Teffaha.

Brigadier Cass had managed to pull back all of his battalions from the front line and provide some rest for the 2nd Lancashire Fusiliers and 5th Northants, though not for the East Surreys. Rest, in this case, proved to involve occupying slightly safer positions, albeit quite uncomfortable ones. Cass learned soon afterwards that he was to place the 1st East Surreys under the command of 36th Brigade for the forthcoming attack on Longstop Hill.

8.4 Resurrection and Preparation

Despite enduring an equally arduous fortnight of operations, the Faughs and the Skins were not immediately relieved in their mountaintop trenches and dugouts on Kef el Tiour and Djebel Ang. Both battalions had unfinished business to attend to, as the Point 622 ridge and Djebel Tanngoucha continued to be held by the Germans. The return to the fold of their newly resurrected third sister battalion, the 2nd London Irish Rifles, was however welcomed by all in the Irish Brigade, and especially by Russell. It now provided him with a more rounded brigade, for Pat Scott's unit was at full strength having completed a significant recovery since it was almost disbanded in mid-February. The battalion had suffered from significant losses, especially as a result of the decision to recapture Point 286 in January. This action had almost destroyed the battalion's rifle companies (E, F, G and H), as the London Irish lost 248 men, with 26 killed, 86 wounded and 136 missing, many of the latter later confirmed as wounded and captured. Losses were especially high among officers, with 20 killed, wounded or missing, and also among NCOs. Just over a month later, on 26 February, the battalion's positions came under a determined attack by tanks and German paratroopers and it suffered 21 killed, 48 wounded and 25 missing. Once again officer losses were high, with one killed and eight wounded. All told, the battalion had lost over 400 casualties in less than three months, due to which the idea of disbanding the battalion was actively considered, though it was eventually rejected.[16] Initially little could be done about rebuilding the battalion, as the tactical situation required it continue to hold its positions, but on 16 March it was moved to the Medjez sector and a number of changes were made. Although the battalion's losses were often due to other factors, the existing CO and his second in command were relieved and Pat Scott from the Faughs was assigned to take command. As a proven battalion commander from within the Irish Brigade, Scott provided the London Irish with a familiar face, which must have reassured the remaining officers and SNCOs. He joined only a couple of days after one of his more experienced officers, Major James Dunnill, from the Faughs. Dunnill had commanded a company in the Irish Fusiliers since they had arrived in Tunisia and would take over F Company, which had been hit badly in the February battles.

The next stage in the resurrection of the London Irish was carried out as new drafts of officers and men helped rebuild the battalion in February and March. Most of these were, surprisingly,

16   The story of the battalion's survival and resurrection is largely derived from Russell, *Irish Brigade*, pp.109-13; R. Doherty, *Clear the Way*, pp.36-42; and TNA WO 175/515 2nd London Irish Rifles January-April 1943 WD.

soldiers from the battalion's parent regiment, the Royal Ulster Rifles, and many were of Irish descent. These measures enabled the battalion to start to rebuild the rifle companies that had been hit so hard. A further step in the process of resurrecting the London Irish as a fighting unit was taken when the battalion was moved out of the front line on 30 March and managed to spend two weeks absorbing its new men and conducting extensive and realistic training exercises under Scott's critical eye. One problem the battalion faced was the loss of so many officers: four of its company commanders had, for example, been killed or wounded in two months. One way this problem was resolved in the short term was to temporarily assign Captain Strome Galloway, a Canadian infantry officer, as a company commander, and another Canadian officer as a company second-in-command. Both officers were part of the small but carefully selected group of Canadian infantry officers who had been sent to Tunisia in January 1943 to gain battle experience serving with the First Army. The assignment of Galloway to command a rifle company was heartily approved of by the London Irish, as was his magnificent bristling moustache. Galloway was to later recall that for a brief period three of the London Irish Rifles companies were in fact commanded by Canadian officers.[17]

Through this series of both orthodox and more unorthodox measures, the 2nd Battalion of the London Irish Rifles was resurrected almost from near death and prepared itself for future battle. The decision not to disband the battalion proved to be a wise one, not only because it would have left the Irish Brigade with only two battalions, but it would make the brigade vulnerable to being disbanded itself. Another reason was that under Scott's excellent leadership, the London Irish Rifles would prove itself to be an excellent fighting unit again and again in a series of tough battles in Sicily and Italy. The arrival of the London Irish Rifles enabled Russell to start to plan a further attempt on the elusive objective of Tanngoucha, which was scheduled to take place some four days later on the night of 22 April. During this period, the Faughs and the Skins spent an uncomfortable four days maintaining their positions on the eastern end of Kef el Tiour and Djebel Ang respectively, while the London Irish Rifles took up residence west of Djebel Bettiour. Although none of the three battalions was attacked directly, each of them had to occupy exposed positions, but probably the most isolated unit was the Faughs on Kef el Tiour. Its forward companies were situated very close to the enemy stronghold on Point 622, and at a height of 1,800ft were exposed to all the elements and any nasty objects the Germans might decide to throw at them at a moments' notice. It was also often very difficult to create viable trenches due to the rocky nature of the terrain, so many soldiers lived in small weapons pits scraped out of the ground. The Faughs stayed in cramped conditions, unable to move much in daylight, exposed to wind and a boiling hot sun, while trying to stay alert as any minute they could be targeted by artillery and mortar fire. It was impossible to wash, so clothes stayed grimy and sweat-stained, and water was scarce. Unless you have experienced such conditions, it is difficult to describe the misery they inflict upon the body. Everyone was exhausted, some more than others from the constant exertion and tensions that came with being exposed to battle conditions. This four-day period was frequently characterised by the battalion war diary as a quiet period in the various entries, but the chronicler of these events, almost certainly the

---

17   Captain Galloway later wrote a memoir, "With the Irish against Rommel", and on returning to the Canadian Army went on to command a company in his regiment with distinction for 25 months in Sicily and Italy. He survived the war, became a colonel, wrote nine books and died at the age of 88 in 2004.

battalion adjutant, had a funny, understated way with words. He stated that 19 April was quiet and that nothing of interest occurred on 20 April, the date of Hitler's birthday. However, he also went on to say that on 19 April there was severe mortaring of the company areas, and on 20 April they were under constant mortar attack. There was nothing routine about coming under attack by mortars, even if you were not injured or hurt. The concussion from the blast explosions affected people physically and mentally, while each mortar round kicked up dust and rocks which blew over the positions, leaving an acrid smell drifting across the ridge. The constant threat of mortar rounds stretched some men's nerves to breaking point and beyond. Major Coldwell-Horsfall recalled that 20 April was spent under the rays of a Tunisian sun, and at midday one of his fusiliers "suddenly jumped out of his trench and went berserk. He ran completely amok and started screaming and waving his rifle."[18] Coldwell-Horsfall's able Company Sergeant Major Fred Fincham initially wandered over to consult with his boss about what action to take, but decided to turn around. He walked over to the fusilier, looked at him, flattened him with a single punch, dragged him to a nearby trench and dropped him back into it. The CSM next walked over to Coldwell-Horsfall and mentioned that the day was getting a trifle warm.

The previous day saw another Faugh stalwart removed from the forward positions; Major Dizzy Gethin's luck could have been said to have ran out, but perhaps it was only badly dented. After sending out a successful patrol late on the evening of 18 April which seized a hated mortar and its crew, Gethin and C Company headquarters took a direct hit from either another mortar or a mountain gun. Amazingly, Gethin survived the blast but he was seriously wounded and was evacuated along with one of his subalterns on 19 April. Gethin spent considerable time in hospital and never returned to the Faughs. After a long recovery he went on to serve in and command a company in the 6th Airborne Division. "Dizzy" Gethin's luck continued to hold for he survived the war unscathed despite parachuting into Germany as part of Operation Varsity. Desmond Gethin died at the age of 65 in 1984.

Coldwell-Horsfall's depleted company, for it now had only one officer, Lieutenant Sillem, and 50 men, continued to hold on to its positions and prepared as best it could for its next attack. Death could still strike randomly in these forward positions, and on 21 April, the day before the attack, Coldwell-Horsfall and CSM Fincham were informed of the death of Fusilier Porter. Porter was an experienced and trusted 24-year-old soldier who both had known for four years, and was Coldwell-Horsfall's dispatch rider. Porter, who was killed by a shell from the dreaded mortars while coming up with the mules, left a young wife and daughter back in Liverpool and is buried in Medjez el Bab cemetery. Mortars continued to cause problems for the Faughs on Kef el Tiour, as on the afternoon of 21 April the battalion headquarters was hit hard and Butler's signals officer, Lieutenant Emmins, was killed; the shells also killed a fusilier and wounded an officer.

The experience of the Faughs was mirrored to some degree or another across the two other battalions during this period of relative calm before the coming storm. The Skins occupied Djebel Ang and its environs and lost seven men wounded by mortars on 20 April. Another grave problem, especially in the hot sun, was the scarcity of water. This was a particular challenge for

---

18 The quotation is from J. Coldwell-Horsfall, *Wild Geese*, p.145. Fred Fincham sadly died of wounds he received in the final attack on Point 622.

the Skins as it had insufficient containers to move the precious commodity forward. The whole battalion had to make do with only 32 gallons a day, which meant water was severely rationed and most soldiers received less than half a pint each day. Meanwhile, in their positions to the west of Djebel Bettiour, the London Irish Rifles found themselves troubled, like the Faughs, by almost constant mortar fire, and also the unwelcome attentions of German long-range gunners and air raids. The battalion's war diary differs from that of the Faughs, as it records in some detail what happened over the four days before the next attack. The diary provides an almost constant litany of reports of shelling on Bettiour and the surrounding area and shows that the battalion was continually harassed day and night. Though not exciting in their own right, these events have been described because they demonstrate the dangers and difficulties that an infantry battalion faced in Tunisia. Every-day, almost routine, death and injury in the front line created its own drama and adversely affected a unit's fighting capacity.

8.5 Sappers at Work: Roads, Beehives and Tellers

Throughout the period from 10 April to the launch of the next attack on 22 April, Lieutenant Colonel Edmund Blake, the CRE of 78th Division, and his three RE companies were as busy as bees working on a beehive. Their work did not involve closing with or shelling the enemy, as did that of the infantry, tanks and artillery, but it was just as vital. The three field companies also demonstrated their wide range of skills and sheer versatility as sub-units and showed why they were viewed as such valuable and scarce assets by commanders at all levels. One of the most important contributions made by the sappers was their work creating, and on a few occasions repairing, roads. This work stemmed from the difficult nature of the terrain in which the Battle-Axe Division was operating during the middle two weeks of April 1943. The only road venturing north of the Medjez to Oued Zarga road was the winding route or track going from Medjez to Toukabeur and thence to Chaouach. The whole area to the north of Toukabeur and Chaouach was inaccessible to vehicles, as it had no roads and what tracks existed were not designed for vehicles, one reason why mules were used so extensively at this time. However, this was the area across which the division was advancing and it had to be supported in the hills. All of Blake's companies, and also two additional RE companies (565th and 137th), were at one time or another involved in building a total of 11 sections of road or rough tracks. The companies worked, often at night, with a mixture of compressor drills, bulldozers and, when required, hand tools. One of the first and most resource-intensive road projects required at various times three sapper companies and involved building a new route with an easier gradient that would allow RASC four-wheeled lorries to travel from the Oued Zarga-Medjez road to Toukabeur.[19] This new route was critical if the 11th and 38th Brigades were to be resupplied and wounded to be evacuated rapidly. It also meant that the division's 25-pounder field guns could be moved up to Chaouach and Toukabeur to provide critical fire support in the mountains. The task took two days and nights and was viewed as so important that the CRE himself, Blake, helped survey the route and operated one of the bulldozers that cut the first route. A RASC truck was sent on it to test it out carrying supplies, and a RASC major declared it formally open at 1800 hours on 11 April.

19   Details of RE operations were derived from the same sources as those cited in Chapter 6.

The road construction and repair kings during this period were undoubtedly the 214th Field Company, as they completed or worked on seven separate road construction projects. This work often had to be carried out at night or under intermittent enemy mortar fire during the day. The results included the vital Toukabeur route and, most important of all, the road or track they created which ran from Chaouach to Djebel Kelbine and onwards to Djebel Bettiour. Initially this was used by four-wheeled vehicles and improved to allow Bren Gun Carriers and finally Churchill tanks. If the company had not completed this work, the North Irish Horse would not have been able to drive their troop of tanks up to assist the Faughs during the later successful attack on 25 April. The work included the vital task of building a crossing capable of taking Churchill tanks over a stream near Djebel Kelbine to allow access to the hills. Blake came up to watch the crossing being opened and used for the first time by the North Irish Horse. In view of the effort involved, he was therefore rather less than impressed when the tanks arrived but ignored the crossing and tried a line of their own. The result was one track came off a tank and another tank became bogged down. The last tank followed orders and crossed successfully. Although there is no formal record to confirm this, it was likely that the Churchill troop commander received both the rough end of the CRE's tongue and what was known in those days as a first-class bollocking!

The work of creating roads would have been so much more difficult had the sappers not been able to use D4 and D7 bulldozers up on the hills to remove obstacles, shift rocks or dirt and break up rocks into rubble for use in road construction. The division was allocated two of the larger D7 armoured bulldozers and four smaller D4 types for the operation, and they proved worth every penny the War Office paid for them. The 214th Field Company made extensive use of the D7 and D4 machines assigned to it. They were especially valuable when employed cutting a road east from Djebel Tanngoucha down a slope into the hamlet of Bergerie from 25 April onwards. Originally this task had been ordered and cancelled, but Major Denton, the company commander, decided that it would continue the work. This proved to be a fortunate decision, as the expected access road, which would have been used to support 38th Brigade, was not secured as planned and Denton's highway became crucial to get supplies to Russell's Irish Brigade.

The versatility of the direct support sapper companies in 78th Division was particularly demonstrated by their completion of a different, less routine but also important task: the construction of a small airfield or landing ground for RA Air Observation Post (AOP) aircraft. The task of completing a small landing ground for Auster AOP aircraft of 651 RAF AOP Squadron was assigned to the 214th Field Company RE. The job was not an especially onerous one, because the Auster Mark 1 required less than 100ft in which to take off and just over 150ft to land. The very short airfield proved to be remarkably useful as it enabled aerial observation for medium and heavy guns by the Royal Artillery well behind German lines. However, for one sapper officer it was to prove a mixed blessing. Lieutenant English, who worked directly for the CRE, was ordered by him to complete an aerial reconnaissance of the important bridge at Bordj Toum. This bridge near Tebourba spanned the Medjerda River and might need replacing if the Germans blew it up. English took off from the landing ground with his Auster pilot, but the aircraft was shot down and English was later posted missing believed captured.

The importance of these units' work in the direct support of the infantry cannot be overestimated, for without the efforts of the small sub-sections of sappers, the infantry battalions they aided would have been prevented from capturing their objectives except at much greater cost in dead and wounded. During all phases of the fighting, small sub-sections of no more than

10-15 men, led by a junior officer or SNCO, used mine detectors and other equipment to find, mark and clear gaps in minefields. The most numerous mines encountered were Teller mines, but S or *Schu* mines were the most dangerous as they were difficult to locate. Another task regularly completed by the busy sappers was helping the infantry to dig trenches by blasting holes in the rocky terrain. This was completed by using a four-pronged steel device full of explosives, which when triggered directed its blast downwards into the ground. The device was called a Beehive by the Royal Engineers because with its four prongs it resembled one, and over 300 of them were provided to the sapper parties.

The nature and dangers of this type of work are excellently illustrated through the stories of four young officers who led small parties doing this work in the hills: Lieutenants Murkitt, Pring, Maycock and Harris. All four of these officers, three of them from Major Coffin's 237th Field Company RE, were to be awarded the MC for gallantry, which emphasises the dangers of supporting the forward troops. The story of Lieutenant Frederick Murkitt provides a useful insight into the operations of sections. He led his party of sappers from the night of 6/7 April until he was wounded on 17 April. During the first five days, up until 11 April, Murkitt and his men detected and lifted more than 800 Teller and 75 *Schu* mines, creating two gaps in minefields that had been holding up troops from the 11th Infantry Brigade. Murkitt supervised the blasting of slit trenches for the East Surreys and London Irish Rifles by his sappers, using Beehives, on the following four nights until wounded by a rifle grenade and evacuated. Lieutenant David Pring led his section from 237th Field Company RE for 10 days from the evening of 6 April to the 15th, in support of the 2nd Lancs Fusiliers and 5th Northants in their advance from their start line near Oued Zarga all the way to Djebel Kelbine. Pring and his men blasted slit trenches using Beehives, while they were frequently under both machine-gun and mortar fire. At one point, in order to be able to clear tracks of mines, Pring rode on the leading tank of the 142nd RAC Regiment so he could carry out his task. In common with his other two fellow officers from the 237th, Murkitt and Alan Maycock, Pring had very little sleep during this period and distinguished himself by his personal courage and devotion to duty. Maycock and his party worked tirelessly from the night of 13/14 to the night of 16/17 April to support the troops attacking Tanngoucha and Heidous. Another lieutenant who led his sappers in support of troops on Tanngoucha was David Harris of the 214th Field Company RE. Harris and his section assisted the troops during the 6th Skins' attack on that feature. He distinguished himself while exposing himself constantly to enemy fire to supervise blasting of positions in the rocks to enable troops to gain shelter from enemy fire. The decision to approve recommendations for three MCs to the same unit meant that 237th was one of the most highly decorated RE companies in the First Army; its officers and men having received three MCs and four MMs.

The mine clearance efforts of all the direct support companies, and especially the removal of Teller anti-tank mines, made a vital contribution to the success of Operation Sweep. It included completing clearing all the mines from at least nine significant minefields. In total the three companies managed to detect and lift a total of 1,500 Teller and 250 *Schu* mines by 10 April, and many more in the following days. Without their efforts, it would not have been possible to so effectively deploy the Churchill tanks of the 142nd RAC Regiment and North Irish Horse in spearheading the advance. The level of effort required can be judged by the fact that the 78th Division's sappers lifted more than 1,000 Teller mines in just the first two days of Operation Sweep. This achievement drew praise from a number of officers, including commanders of the RAC, RA and RAMC units who benefitted from their work. However, this work was not

Plate I Point 512 from near the village of Toukabeur (A Khmeri, 2018 Author's collection)

Plate II The clifftop Berber village of Chaouach in 2018. (A Khmeri, 2018 Author's collection)

Plate III View of Djebel Bettiour (left) and Djebel Mahdouma (middle distance) with Djebel Ang at the top right above a building. Picture taken from Heidous Village in 2018 (note the escarpment on Djebel Bettiour) (Reproduced with the kind permission of R & E O' Sullivan, 2018)

Plate IV Djebel Ang and the Kef el Tiour ridge (top left), the Point 622 ridge (below it) and the saddle linking them with Djebel Tanngoucha (on the right). Note Djebel Bettiour is on the extreme centre left. (Reproduced with the kind permission of R & E O'Sullivan, 2018)

Plate V Longstop Hill viewed from Djebel Tanngoucha – Djebel Rhar is on the left Djebel Ahmera on the right and the saddle or col in the middle. (Reproduced with the kind permission of R and E O'Sullivan, 2018)

Plate VI The Kef el Tiour Ridge (note how narrow the ridge is) (Reproduced with the kind permission of R & E O' Sullivan, 2018)

Plate VII A view of the village of Heidous (centre), Djebel Tanngoucha (the hill to the right of Heidous), the Point 622 ridge (the ridge above Heidous) and Kef el Tiour (above Pt 622) from Medjerda Valley note that the Djebel Ahmera ridge is at the lower right. (Reproduced with the kind permission of R & E O'Sullivan, 2018)

Plate VIII View of the open fields on the approach route to Chaibane ridge and Djebel Ahmera used by the East Surrey's and 8th Argylls. (Author's collection, 2008)

without its dangers and these were clearly demonstrated at Sidi Medakrine farm just below Recce Ridge west of Medjez el Bab. A section of the 214th Field Company was clearing mines in the farm when an S mine was triggered and several sappers were wounded. In a desire to help their comrades, several men from sections of both the 214th and 237th Field Companies rushed to the aid of the wounded, a natural but sadly flawed professional response. As was too often the case, additional hidden S mines and/or booby traps caused further casualties. The casualties inflicted by these horrible devices included Major T. Coffin from 237th Field Company and one of his most experienced SNCOs, Sergeant David Laird, who had won a MM earlier in the campaign. Both were evacuated to a casualty clearing station and were visited there by the 78th Division's CFE, Lieutenant Colonel Blake. Coffin survived his wounds, though he had to relinquish command of his company, but sadly Laird did not and died of his wounds on 24 April, and is now buried in Oued Zarga cemetery. Three NCOs and three other sappers were killed or died of their wounds in this tragic incident, with nine men wounded.[20] While the bravery of the Royal Engineers in this incident cannot be doubted, the casualty toll brought home a critical lesson which sadly had to be relearned again and again in Tunisia and Italy. All too often when men were wounded in minefields, their comrades moved forward to give them urgent medical aid without taking the time and care to clear a safe path. As a result further men were wounded or killed, and since these had to be extracted as well, this actually delayed medical treatment for the initial casualties. Despite this, too many soldiers found themselves unable to resist the urge to immediately move to aid their friends when they heard their anguished cries for help. The terrible dilemma created by this nightmare scenario has sadly repeated itself in multiple wars up to and including the present day. The efforts of the 78th Division's Royal Engineers in Tunisia during April 1943 did not go unnoticed, and were later praised by the Chief Engineer of the British Army, who said their work was one of the finest engineer achievements of the whole campaign.

8.6 Plans and Reality Make Poor Companions

The next four days allowed Brigadier Nelson Russell, Major Frank Douglas-Pennant to devote time to planning their next move. Records show that Russell had a series of meetings with all three of his battalion commanders in this period to plan the next attack. The 38th Brigade was also visited by Kenneth Anderson, the First Army commander, who spent time at an observation post which provided a good view of the Kef el Tiour and Tanngoucha area. Anderson used the opportunity to address all the senior officers in the brigade about future plans. In the light of the problems that Russell and his brigade had faced over the last 10 days, it seems puzzling that key elements of their plan appear, even in retrospect 75 years later, hopelessly optimistic. It is also interesting to note that although Tanngoucha had been the 78th Division's key objective, previously the focus of the brigade plan was the capture of Heidous. The focus on Heidous is actually easily explained, once it is understood that the Irish Brigade's proposed operations on 22/23 April were only a subordinate part of the 78th Division's attempt to capture Longstop Hill. German positions in and around Heidous overlooked Longstop Hill and posed a serious

---

20   The relevant citations are available in TNA WO 373/1. The story of the tragic incident at Sidi Medakrine farm is based on the war diaries of the 214th and 237th Field Companies, respectively TNA WO 175/645 and 175/652.

threat to any attack. It was sensible to make Heidous a key objective, as this would help remove the threat it posed. The Longstop operation, which will be described in full in the closing chapters of this book, had one direct and negative influence on Russell's planning for his next attack. Previous attacks on Tanngoucha and Heidous had been preceded and supported by generous artillery fire from several regiments, most of whom had remained on call to repel any counterattacks. Unfortunately this was not feasible on the night of 22 April. Once the divisional artillery had provided fire support for Russell's attack, it was allocated to assist Brigadier Howlett's 36th Infantry Brigade, which would be attacking Longstop at 2200 hours that night. After that hour, Russell would have to rely upon the support of only one regiment, albeit the well-regarded 132nd Field Regiment, to deal with any problems.

Despite this serious drawback, it does appear that some hard lessons from previous attacks had been learned. Russell's plan involved his whole brigade, and each of the three proposed attacks would be mutually supporting. The London Irish would attack and capture Heidous and go on to seize two key ridges, one just below Tanngoucha and the other to the south-east, which the battalion called Sandy Ridge. The latter, though lower in height than Heidous, was believed to have five machine guns and a reinforced platoon of Germans. Both ridge positions could harass troops in Heidous, while Sandy Ridge also threatened troops advancing on Longstop. The job of capturing Tanngoucha went yet again to the Skins, who had prior experience of the approaches to the mountain and its defences. The final part of the plan was referred to as a subsidiary operation, in which the Faughs would attack and seize Point 622 and what were described as spurs 300 yards east of that feature. On reflection, much of Russell's plan seems sensible, as all the attacks were to be made on the same night and the strongest unit, the London Irish Rifles, had been allocated the primary objective of Heidous. There was, however, little finesse in the plan, but the nature of the terrain made that impossible. Yet the concurrent attack on Longstop by 36th Brigade would stop any reinforcements being diverted to higher up the mountains and prevent the Germans concentrating all their artillery against the Irish Brigade. The requirements of a later part of his overall plan were an entirely different matter, as they established very ambitious objectives for an understrength and tired infantry brigade to achieve. This part of the plan assumed that once it seized its assigned three objectives, the brigade would easily advance across eight miles of rugged and trackless hills to a new invisible line on the map. This line was drawn from the small hamlet of Montrosier, west of the Medjerda River, to a place called Sidi Hadday some three miles away to the northwest. Previous advances of this distance in the mountains had taken two weeks of tough fighting, so the author of the plan must have assumed that any German defenders would almost melt away once Tanngoucha and Heidous were taken. This was a flawed assumption, as any planner would have access to the information included in division intelligence summaries that identified at least three German battalions who might oppose such an advance. The third and final phase of the plan required the brigade to continue to move forward two more miles across the hills to seize another invisible phase line in the same mountain range, just marginally closer to the Tebourba Gap.

We may never know why a plan that included two hopelessly optimistic and unrealistic sets of objectives was created. While the plan bears the signature of the brigade major and must have been approved by Russell, it is difficult to envisage that two such capable officers would have been solely responsible for such a fatally flawed document. Perhaps the only saving grace of the plan is that it did not specify times and dates for such an advance. Russell and Major Douglas-Pennant both knew all too well that after 17 days of fighting and significant casualties, the rifle companies of the London Irish Rifles and Inniskilling Fusiliers had been drastically reduced in strength. As an example, John Coldwell-Horsfall's D Company, normally 160-strong, was reduced to only 50 men when it started its attack on Point 622. The Germans were almost certain to inflict even more casualties when the brigade once again attacked objectives which they had been unable to take at least three times previously. Any advance would still come under fire from German mortar and artillery positions, which could easily be relocated eastwards. The hills that lie to the east of Heidous and Tanngoucha rise to 400-450 metres (some 1,300-1,500ft), are cut with deep wadis and have steep slopes, so just moving across them is very difficult. Russell later described this terrain as amongst the worst he had encountered. It appears that another bout of heady optimism had resulted in someone at the 78th Division becoming over-optimistic about what could be achieved by a tired brigade. The brutal reality of fighting in the Battle of the Peaks soon imposed its own ruthless logic on events and rendered the plan almost immediately obsolete.

8.7 The London Irish Attack "Hades"

Although all three battalions conducted attacks of differing strengths on the night of 22 April, the London Irish Rifles were the first to attack and had a higher-priority objective. In the usual manner, the objectives for that night had been allocated codewords which would be transmitted when they were successfully captured. Whoever allocated the codewords this night may have had a classical education, as he used Greek gods for inspiration. In consequence, the capture of Heidous would be notified using the codeword "Hades", that of Tanngoucha would use the god "Olympus" and two other key features became "Apollo" and "Juno". It is noteworthy that the capture of Point 622, arguably a key objective based on its location, was not distinguished by any codename. In Greek mythology, Hades was the god who ruled the underworld, the kingdom of the dead which was guarded by Cerberus, a three-headed dog. In 1943, Heidous was not guarded by a three-headed dog, but it was defended by tough German infantrymen, including soldiers from the 1st Battalion of the 756th Mountain Infantry Regiment. Moreover, just as the dead had to pay a price to cross into the underworld of Hades, the Germans would make the London Irish pay a price in lives to enter Heidous.

Pat Scott's plan for the attack on Hades required an attack by two of his rifle companies making different approaches from the heights of Djebel Bettiour down to the village of Heidous. The approaches that were adopted had been determined as a result of two reconnaissance patrols conducted very early on the morning of 22 April. The attack on the village would be carried out under the cover of a 30-minute artillery concentration on the village and several nearby features commencing at 1945 hours. One of the companies moved from Bettiour using a route to the north of the village, while the second used one from the south into the village. In 1943, Heidous was divided into an upper and lower village, both of which were now in ruins due to the amount of artillery fire directed at the location. The two lead companies were F Company, led by Major James "Jimmy" Dunnill, and Captain Thornton's G Company. It is not surprising that Scott assigned Dunnill the task of actually taking the village: Scott knew Dunnill well as he had commanded a company under the former in the Faughs. Thornton was tasked with taking a small feature on the right of the village. Although Dunnill had commanded companies in two Irish regiments, his original regiment was the Green Howards and he hailed from Huddersfield in West Yorkshire. The evening of 22 April was quite dark, and the moon would not come out until 2200 hours, so Dunnill was forced to lead his whole company down the slopes of Bettiour towards his FUP on the outskirts of Heidous using a compass bearing. When Dunnill's two leading platoons started to advance on the edge of the village, they quickly came under heavy machine-gun and sniper fire. They moved on the village slowly but lost contact with Dunnill and his reserve platoon in the mist and darkness. Eventually news came that 10 and 11 Platoons were held up, so Dunnill sent his reserve platoon forward to see if it could flank the village from the south. Thornton's G Company was not able to support F Company as it was tied up on a rocky feature to the south of the village, and was also unable to contact F Company by wireless. One of Dunnill's platoon commanders, Lieutenant Rowlette, managed to get a forward section into the lower village and sent a message to this effect to his company commander. After delivering the message, Corporal Palmer began to lead Dunnill and his headquarters party back to link up, but this group got lost and at the edge of the village Palmer was killed by a machine gun. Dunnill, assisted by his runner Rifleman Whiteside, tried to find a way forward, but as they moved over a crest another machine gun opened up and Whiteside was hit. Dunnill used a Bren gun to fire upon and silence the German Spandau. The darkness and a mist hanging over the area created considerable confusion, so Thornton tried to go into Heidous to discover what was happening. He managed to meet Lieutenant Rowlette, but soon afterwards was hit by machine gun fire in the legs and taken prisoner. Dunnill, who by now had also been wounded, walked back to find and brief Scott, who sent E Company under Major Lofting to support F Company.

It was now 0300 hours and time was not on the side of the London Irish when E Company arrived outside the village. It soon became obvious that as the moon was now up, an attack on the village would be difficult and costly. Although Lofting was able to make contact with a section of G Company, there was no word about where the rest of G and F Companies might be. Lofting reviewed the situation and concluded that any further attack was likely to lead to unnecessary casualties. He withdrew E Company and moved back up to Bettiour. His decision was a sensible one in the circumstances and was the one made by the three platoons of G Company, who had reached their objective, but having had no contact also pulled back at dawn. Dunnill and his headquarters group withdrew, but what remained of the three platoons of F Company were surrounded and soon wounded or captured. Lieutenants Rowlette and Hughes narrowly escaped being taken prisoner by feigning death, and managed to crawl away at dawn and return to the battalion. According to the battalion war diary, only 30 men from F Company managed to get back to the battalion. The attack on Heidous had proved a failure, largely because German positions on ridges and within the village were well hidden, well protected and contained multiple machine guns. The majority of losses for the battalion were inflicted on Dunnill's F Company, but one of the few pieces of good news was that most of these, including the wounded, became prisoners. Despite the tough resistance it encountered, the battalion was lucky and lost only six killed on 22 and 23 April.

During the fighting in and around Heidous, 23-year-old Corporal Edward Mayo from Dagenham in east London demonstrated that the qualities that won him a prize as a star recruit in 1939 also made him a fine battlefield leader. Mayo had joined the London Irish in 1939 along with two other men, and each of them had been rapidly promoted. The others were Edmund Sullivan, who was now the CQMS of E Company, and Joe Ward, also now a NCO. Mayo had only just recently returned to the London Irish after recovering from his wounds sustained in battle around Bou Arada. He was married, had a young child back in England and was a quiet but effective JNCO, who was well liked and respected by his men. During the battle for Heidous:

Mayo personally destroyed a German machine gun post. Later, he rallied his platoon under heavy mortar fire and machine gun fire and, in spite of being wounded in both legs, succeeded in leading a fresh sortie on the enemy. Corporal Mayo had previously distinguished himself at Bou Arada on 20 January in leading his section with great gallantry in an attack on Hill 286, where he was wounded. He had only been back from hospital two weeks before the attack on Heidous. The way his men followed him on this last occasion was a tribute to his previous courage.[21]

Mayo's gallantry during the battle led to the award of the MM (see Plate 14). He was not the only member of the London Irish to be recognised for gallantry, for Dunnill's leadership, both previously in Tunisia and especially at Heidous, was recognised by the award of a DSO. Dunnill's runner, Rifleman Whiteside, also received a MM for his bravery that night.

The decision by Major Lofting to withdraw from "Hades" and the failure of the London Irish to capture the village could be viewed as a threat to the attack on Longstop, especially as this was not going to plan. It was probably not the news that the division commander, Evelegh, wanted to hear. After learning that Heidous had not been captured, Evelegh signalled Russell at midday on 23 April that the village must be taken. It seems likely that Russell expressed his concerns about another attack, as Evelegh decided to consult personally with him. He visited the 38th Brigade's command post, now situated near Djebel Kelbine south of Bettiour, in the afternoon. Although we don't know precisely what was said, the war diary for the brigade says the two men discussed the advisability of attacking Heidous. By the afternoon it was clear that both the Faughs and the Skins had also failed to take and secure their objectives, Point 622 and Tanngoucha, both of which posed a threat to any new attack on Heidous. Evelegh was persuaded to change his mind about a new attack on the village and instead ordered that strong patrols be sent to observe Heidous.

8.8 The Skins attack "Olympus"

The unknown officer who selected the codename "Olympus" for a successful capture of Tanngoucha was obviously very familiar both with the mountain and Greek mythology. The Greeks believed that the gods lived high above Mount Olympus in a palace in the clouds, and from there they kept an eye on life below. The gods could send storms if they were angry and decide who was victorious in wars. Some 1,800ft high and occasionally shrouded in clouds, Djebel el Tanngoucha must at times have appeared to be the home of the gods looking down with disdain on the puny efforts of the Battle-Axe Division's attempts to capture this height. When the 6th Skins launched their attack on the evening of 22 April, it was the fourth attempt by the 78th Infantry Division to seize this mountain top. The elusive objective had already repulsed two attacks by the 11th Infantry Brigade, seriously depleting that formation in that process. The 38th Irish Brigade had also launched one unsuccessful attempt and its strength was rapidly being eroded too. Although the 6th Skins had four days to prepare for a second attack, their CO, Grazebrook, still faced the same intractable problems his battalion had encountered

---

21   See TNA WO 373/1 for Corporal Mayo's MM citation. The story of the London Irish Rifles' attack on Heidous is from TNA WO 175/515 2 LIR April 1943 WD; Russell, *Irish Brigade*; and a letter written by Major J. Dunnill to Pat Scott held by the London Irish Rifles Museum.

during their first attack. The German position on Tanngoucha was mutually supporting, anchored on its right (north) by defences on Point 622 and on the left (south) by Heidous. Their defences ran across a saddle from the Point 622 ridge to Point 620, the highest point on Tanngoucha. Only two approaches were possible from the Faughs' positions, either via the Point 622 ridge and along the saddle to Tanngoucha or via the steep southern slopes below Kef el Tiour ridge and up to the mountain.

The plan for the night of 22/23 April required the Faughs to use one of their companies to attack and seize Point 622 and its ridgeline, so this approach was not available to Grazebrook. He was keen to learn as much as possible about the terrain, so he ordered his new IO, the bespectacled Lieutenant Percy Hamilton, to arrange for his officers to view the area from the Faughs' positions. This was a very sensible decision, but when Hamilton tried to visit the forward positions, he quickly discovered that the location was difficult and dangerous to access. The troops in the forward positions were not pleased to see him, as any movement attracted German mortar and machine-gun fire. Hamilton's request to bring forward the company commanders to view the terrain in daylight met with forceful opposition from the Faughs' CO, Lieutenant Colonel Butler. The latter refused to allow access to the forward positions during the day because of the likely enemy reaction. Hamilton did manage to gain Butlers' agreement to bring forward two company commanders with the mule trains that resupplied the Faughs at night. The officers soon discovered the perils of moving around the Kef el Tiour ridge and its slopes at night, as their movement was spotted and they attracted mortar fire. The recce provided the two company commanders, Captains Bayley and Duddington, with an uncomfortable experience but an improved understanding of the difficulties faced by their sister regiment, though only limited information about their objective. Grazebrook assigned D Company, led by Captain Blake Duddington, and B Company, led by Captain Bayley, to lead the 6th Skins' attack on the mountain. There was little room for subtlety, so the plan for the night required the two companies to move from Djebel Mahdouma to a start line on a track located on steep slopes just south of Point 622, then climb up to make a frontal assault on Tanngoucha. D Company was to attack on the right and take the highest point of Tanngoucha (Point 620) ,while B Company was to attack on the left to seize the saddle that lay between Point 620 and the Point 622 ridge. The attack was scheduled for 2100 hours and would follow that of the London Irish on Heidous which began at 2015 hours.

The Skins' advance was preceded by a period of 30 minutes during which five regiments of artillery fired on various targets, including Heidous and Tanngoucha. The timing of the brigade's attacks and this barrage was largely dictated by the timing of 36th Brigade's attack later that evening on Longstop. The 17th, 132nd and 138th Field, 4th Medium and 56th Heavy Artillery Regiments had just half an hour to fire in support of the Irish Brigade. The three Field regiments were also limited to the use of only one of their three batteries plus 457 Light Battery, a total of 30 25-pounder guns, and carried out this task along with 16 5.5in and 12 7.2in guns. The number of guns used may have been limited, but the fire plan allocated them a generous amount of ammunition and they laid down an intense fire. The two leading companies of the Skins reached and crossed their start line on schedule and seemed to have achieved a degree of surprise. Although German artillery fire fell between Tanngoucha and Bettiour about 30 minutes later, the troops didn't receive any small-arms fire and both companies managed to reach their objectives: D Company reached the base of Tanngoucha and B Company the saddle. At this point communications with Duddington and D Company were lost by battalion

HQ, which was following on behind the lead companies, along with A and C Companies. Although D Company reached its objective, it was unable to dislodge its determined defenders, who were concealed in caves, and it became pinned down under heavy fire. Bayley's B Company came under fire from both flanks but managed to get into the German trenches on the saddle and took a number of prisoners. Grazebrook ordered A Company, one of his reserve units, to go forward and support D Company. Battalion HQ arrived and established itself in a very exposed position relatively close to the forward companies. Soon afterwards, Lieutenant John McClinton, a platoon commander from D Company, arrived to ask for more ammunition and provide a report of events. McClinton was a very experienced platoon commander who had previously shown a high degree of leadership and courage. He reported that D Company's two platoons were pinned down by point-blank enemy fire below the rocky crags near Point 620 and were running low on ammunition. McClinton returned to his unit with ammunition, while additional rounds were also sent forward to B Company. Bayley's B Company was in trenches on the saddle when it received a fierce German counterattack supported by the crossfire of no less than 15 machine guns. A short and deadly hand-to-hand struggle ensued, but the tough German troops of the 756th Mountain Infantry Regiment overran B Company. When what remained of the company arrived back at battalion HQ, only Captain Bayley and 22 other ranks were left. At least two officers were killed and one captured, along with a number of other NCOs and fusiliers. Once again the gods on Olympus seem to have been frowning on the efforts of the Irish Brigade to secure the mountain-top fortress of Tanngoucha.

At this point it became obvious that the Faughs' subsidiary operation to capture Point 622 had been unsuccessful, and since machine guns at that location threatened the Skins flank, Grazebrook decided to send his one remaining reserve company to try and help the Faughs to seize that objective. C Company managed to find their way up the very steep slopes below that feature and meet up with a platoon of D Company. However, even this further addition of strength was insufficient to dislodge the German defenders. As dawn broke on "Olympus", the 6th Skins found itself in a tight spot. B Company had been overrun and C Company was up on Point 622 but pinned down, while A Company was on the forward southern slopes of the mountain dug in, but in full view of the Germans. Duddington and his severely weakened D Company were pinned down next to a rocky crag. The area between battalion headquarters and D Company was completely open and exposed to enemy fire, and it was not possible to communicate with Duddington. The survival of the company in its present location was doubtful, so Grazebrook asked his FOO to use smoke shells to provide cover for Duddington to withdraw. Acting on his own initiative, without any guidance from his CO, Duddington adopted a very different course of action. He led his remaining fusiliers under the cover of smoke, scrambled up and on to the crags and attacked the German defenders. The latter were completely surprised and Duddington's bold move paid off, for he and his men captured five machine guns and 35 prisoners and took over the position of Point 620. By this time Duddington had only 16 men left, of whom eight were wounded including him. Despite his best efforts, the weakened condition of D Company meant it lacked the strength to hold the position it had captured and this gallant effort came to naught, as Duddington was forced to withdraw down the mountain slopes.

Among those still standing were two platoon commanders, Lieutenants McClinton and Charles Clarke, and both had distinguished themselves throughout the last 12 hours of fighting by D Company. McClinton risked considerable danger to return for ammunition and led his platoon in seizing their objective. When D Company was eventually forced to pull back, it was his platoon that covered the withdrawal and managed to bring back many German prisoners. Clarke had already demonstrated considerable leadership and bravery on Djebel Mahdi when he rescued a wounded man from a minefield and on the following day ignored enemy fire while he walked around looking after his wounded men. Later he went forward by himself with a Bren gun to tackle a machine-gun post which was holding up the advance, and effectively silenced it. During the attack on Tanngoucha, he further distinguished himself by his fighting spirit. When D Company was pinned down by fire at point-blank range, Clarke succeeded in crawling forward with a Bren gun to a position from where he could fire into the caves and fissures occupied by the enemy. His position here, only a few yards from the enemy, enabled the remains of another platoon to advance up the rocks and wipe out the enemy. Clarke and McClinton were not the only men who distinguished themselves during this attack. As B Company attacked the saddle area, one of its platoon sergeants, Sergeant Ramsell, was the first man on the objective, despite fierce machine-gun fire from the flanks. When the company was counterattacked, Ramsell, who had taken over command of the platoon, was ordered to cover the withdrawal of the remainder of the company. He personally fired a Bren gun with great effect until all his magazines were empty. He continued to fire at the enemy with a captured German machine gun until ammunition for that was exhausted. During the final phases of the German counterattack, Ramsell was wounded in the head, face and arms, but in spite of these injuries he remained at his post and was the last to leave the position. Ramsell was subsequently awarded the MM, while McClinton and Clarke each received a MC.

The 6th Skins' failure to retain control of their objective of Tanngoucha seemed to be another repeat of past attempts to take the mountain. However, this time the situation was somewhat different, for although they had been forced to withdraw from the saddle and Point 620, the Skins had managed to dig in below their original objectives on the slopes of the mountain. On this occasion perhaps the gods were looking down on events and decided to intervene and allow the Inniskillings to hang on to some of their gains. However in typical god-like fashion, they also delighted in making things difficult for ordinary mortals. The battalion's new position was a perilous one for two reasons: it was in full view of the enemy and any movement drew fire, and the battalion strength had been seriously depleted by casualties. It had already suffered significant losses during the previous 16 days of operations, and now had lost a further four officers and 43 other ranks in the last 24 hours. The situation was so grave that Grazebrook placed his own battalion headquarters into an exposed position along with C Company on his left and A Company on the right. The remnants of B and D Company were combined into a single company, which was strengthened by using the anti-tank platoon as infantry. Percy Hamilton, the new Intelligence Officer, later recorded the problems facing battalion headquarters:

> The situation at HQ was somewhat critical. We were up in front like a rifle company and the only chaps for our defence were about six pioneers, a few Intelligence chaps and our batman. We had one Bren gun which would work, but with no other automatic weapons. Jerry was about four hundred yards away. We were situated on a reverse slope of a flattish sort of pimple, but there was enough cover to be able to move about in daylight and by going carefully round the dead ground, one could get to the two companies. We dug slit trenches on the reverse slope and a couple on the top of us at night. The CO said we would remain where we were, and we stayed there … At night, we manned the two slits on the

top of the mound. There were four officers, apart from the CO, and two of us split the night in the slits, while the other two shared the night on the wireless. There was a misty moon during the best part of the night, and the rations were brought up by mules to the hump behind us.[22]

The Skins clung on to their isolated positions and were subjected to intermittent mortar and sniper fire during the remainder of 23 April and throughout the next day. Surprisingly, and despite their exposed location, the unit suffered only eight more casualties over this 36-hour period while it waited for new orders.

8.9 The Second Attack on Point 622

One of the reasons why the attack on Tanngoucha had failed was that a concurrent effort by the Faughs on the night of 22/23 April had been unable to capture and secure the German stronghold on Point 622 and the ridge it occupied. Various sources refer to this attack as a subsidiary operation to the main attack, and unlike the other objectives it was not important enough to attract a codename for when it was captured. It is a sad and tragic irony that this position was actually the lynchpin of the whole German defensive line. In view of the amount of time they had now devoted to operations around Tanngoucha and Heidous, it was doubly unfortunate that Evelegh and especially Russell had become overly focused on the capture of these two objectives, at the expense of giving proper emphasis to the capture of Point 622. In stark contrast to this view, the Germans clearly understood that whoever held Point 622 and the ridge on which it stood, along with Djebel Tanngoucha, could dominate Heidous. The position provided a natural bottleneck as the ridge was narrow, rocky and had exposed slopes on both sides. All of these factors channelled any attacking troops into a narrow killing zone. Coldwell-Horsfall, albeit with the benefit of hindsight, noted that the area was "Literally the key point of this their Siegfried Line as they described it".[23] The position's strength was improved upon by German engineers, and it could be said to be defended by a "battalion of the damned". This was the 1st Battalion of the 962nd Schutzen Regiment, and the men of that penal battalion were all too aware that any withdrawal or attempted surrender could lead to summary execution by officers and NCOs behind them. On the other hand, if they stayed in their positions eventually they would be killed by the troops of the Irish Brigade. Any other troops might have surrendered once pressed and Point 622 would have fallen, though not without loss. Instead, this "battalion of the damned" stayed, fought tenaciously and in the case of the mini-fortress of Point 622 did so to the last man.

Looking back today, it is apparent that the capture of 622 should have been allocated greater priority in terms of men and other resources. The feature had played a key role in frustrating all previous efforts to seize Tanngoucha. The latter may have started out as the crucial end objective, but hard experience and observation should by now have demonstrated that the key terrain feature was no longer "Olympus" but an unnamed rocky ridge designated as a minor objective. Evelegh and Russell were both capable commanders, so it is unfortunate that they

---

22   See Hamilton, *Memoirs*, pp.19-20.
23   J. Coldwell-Horsfall, *Wild Geese*, p.148.

continued to focus most of their resources and attention on Tanngoucha and Heidous. In their defence, it may have seemed that seizing Tanngoucha might unlock the defensive line based on Point 622 from the rear. Since his two other battalions were assigned to take the other objectives, Russell had no choice but to give the task to Butler and the Faughs. The latter were also in position and available, while relieving them with another unit might be costly. The Faughs had not been inactive during the period from their capture of forward positions on Kef el Tiour. The Point 622 ridge had been raided at least twice during on the night of 16/17 April, once by a patrol led by one of Coldwell-Horsfall's capable platoon commanders, Peter Sillem. The latter had led a short patrol towards 622 on the evening of 16 April, and encountered and taken prisoner an unwary German machine-gun crew setting up in the mist. Another patrol that night towards 622, led by Sergeant White of 16 platoon, had even greater success and nearly got on to the feature, while capturing four prisoners and five machine guns.

For the rest of the period, the forward companies continued to hold their exposed positions, despite being regularly harassed by fire and the elements for nearly a week, until Nelson Russell was ready to launch his next attack. This was of course planned for 22/23 April, and on the afternoon of 22 April, Butler met with his company commanders and gave orders for the night operation to follow. The restrictive nature of the terrain would undoubtedly have offered Butler little room to be innovative. The plan required Coldwell-Horsfall with D Company to seize Point 622, while A Company under Captain Mike "Mac" MacDonald was assigned to assist them. The war diary makes clear that A Company moved into D Company's old positions on the east end of Kef el Tiour when Coldwell-Horsfall attacked Point 622. The essential problems facing Coldwell-Horsfall and D Company in their gallant attempt to take Point 622 remained the same as before; an entrenched and alert enemy and the difficulty of conducting flanking attacks due to the nature of the terrain.. The key point of the ensuing action is that the rocky, saw tooth-like nature of the ridge made it difficult to coordinate the efforts of the whole company. Sillem led his platoon on one side of the ridge, while Coldwell-Horsfall tried to control his other two platoons on a different part. All three platoons rapidly came under a storm of machine-gun fire. Sergeant Robbie Robinson, acting platoon sergeant of 17 Platoon in the action, later recalled the fighting in an account provided to the author:

> I remember as we advanced we thought every German machine gun in Tunisia was firing, most on fixed lines covering every possible line of approach to their positions. Our problem was finding the gaps not covered. When we reached the forward slopes of 622 it was a case of crawling from rock to rock, the objective stood out above us like a flat top loaf … another memory was how verbal the German defenders were during the early stages of the attack, they appeared to be shouting encouragement, giving orders or asking for information [but] on the other hand we were keeping very quiet … the noise of battle was quite horrendous, artillery shells and mortar bombs exploding in large numbers all over our area, added [to] by grenades and mg fire.

Robinson recorded that:

> I took over a Bren gun and got into a position behind a large rock and started to pick off the enemy machine guns one at a time. Up to this point they were not firing at us but appeared to be firing on fixed lines into an area behind us. I would watch for their muzzle flash, aim

at it and then fire a long burst, this appeared to be effective as at least 2 of their machine guns ceased firing. Another of the guns must have spotted my muzzle flash and returned fire. The German m/g could fire up to 1,200 rounds per minute, on this occasion a burst of 15-20 rounds was fired at the rock in front of me and I could feel the rock shudder with the impact of so many bullets.[24]

Robinson went on to recall quite clearly that at one point he heard Coldwell-Horsfall giving orders to fire from a position behind him and realised that his platoon would be the target for that fire. Robinson crawled back to Coldwell-Horsfall and informed him of his platoon's position, while narrowly avoiding being fired on by fellow fusiliers. Immediately prior to this incident, Robinson, along with Sergeant Morrissey, the acting platoon commander of 17 Platoon, some JNCOs and fusiliers had managed to get on to the forward slopes of Point 622. There they became involved in an exchange of fire with German defenders manning at least three machine guns, some as close as 20 yards away. While 17 Platoon was attempting to move forward, Lieutenant Sillem with 18 Platoon had advanced but had come under heavy fire and had limited success in moving forward. Coldwell-Horsfall had also been moving forward with his tactical headquarters when his group were fired on, first unsuccessfully by a mountain gun and afterwards more effectively by a Spandau. Coldwell-Horsfall was untouched, but the machine-gun burst wounded both his signallers and his batman, Fusilier Clanachan, who was from County Fermanagh. Clanachan had been Coldwell-Horsfall's batman and bodyguard since 1940, so it was a blow to him when he was wounded. Fortunately, Clanachan survived his wounds and later returned to duty with Coldwell-Horsfall in Italy.

Coldwell-Horsfall now met up with Sillem and soon afterwards sent off both 16 and 17 Platoons to try to find a route on up onto the ridge. Sergeant Fred White and 16 Platoon found a way to scramble up a steep rock face and get on top of the ridge, despite being showered constantly by hand grenades, which fortunately bounced off the rocks and didn't explode until they landed much further down the slope. White and his platoon ejected the defenders and after allowing a decent interval, Sergeant Morrissey decided it was safe to follow. Unfortunately, in the short time that elapsed, White and his men were subjected to a rapid counterattack. When Morrissey's unit attempted the climb, they were greeted not by the friendly banter of White, but by angry Germans. In the darkness and chaos, confusion reigned supreme with the Germans shooting indiscriminately. At one point one of Coldwell-Horsfall's men, Corporal Jennings, had managed to get to the top of the feature, but soon recognised he was being greeted by several Germans. When he tried to climb back down, he was mistaken as a German and shot five times by Fusilier Bill Mallon, though amazingly he survived. Mallon and Corporal Thomas Swain were well known to their company commander for their occasional lapses of discipline while in barracks, and in his book Coldwell-Horsfall referred to them good naturedly as his two" scallywags". While both may have had some vices as soldiers in barracks, he was clear that these were more than outweighed by their performance on the battlefield. During the attack on 22/23 April, both Swain and Mallon were in the forefront of the attack on Point 622, and Mallon's conduct especially was noted as he urged on his fellow fusiliers despite heavy fire. Swain was the first man to reach the objective, and along with Mallon they attacked and destroyed

---

24   Both quotations are from Robinson *Memoirs*, pp.18-19.

two German machine guns that threatened their platoon. Eventually, after a hard fight, D Company managed to secure part of the Point 622 ridge, but not Point 622 itself. Coldwell-Horsfall's situation was not good, but he believed one last effort might enable the company to capture Point 622. As he was leading an attempt to do so, he was knocked unconscious and temporarily blinded by a German stick grenade. After coming round, he handed over command to 20-year-old Lieutenant Sillem and was evacuated to the rear. His last advice to Sillem was to try to get on to Point 622, but if he couldn't, to find his men and get them back to cover before daylight arrived. When daylight dawned, the Germans were still holding out in the main part of the rocky stronghold, so Sillem ordered a withdrawal. Fusilier Mallon was among the last to leave, gallantly assisting the wounded back. Over the next couple of hours, Sillem risked his own life to round up the scattered soldiers of 16 and 17 Platoons before withdrawing from Point 622 and arriving back in their original positions.

Due to its losses, which included at least seven men killed and an estimated 20 wounded, D Company was replaced in the most forward positions by A Company. The attack had proved to be costly for D Company and it was now reduced to the strength of just 31 men, including cooks and mule teams; 18 Platoon, commanded by Sillem, was the strongest, but it had only 13 men including its commander. Coldwell-Horsfall was carried to the rear brooding that he had made a bit of a cock-up of the action. He would regain his sight and recover from his wounds, returning to his beloved Faughs in Italy. Interestingly, there is no mention of aid provided by the men of C Company of the 6th Skins by any of the Faughs involved in the fight on 622. This was probably just an unfortunate omission in later reports. The night operation to capture Point 622 only narrowly failed, and it is arguable that had Butler been provided with additional reserves, for example a couple of companies of the Skins or the London Irish, the Faughs might have broken the German hold on Point 622. Instead, the London Irish were committed on Evelegh's orders to attack Heidous, while the Skins made yet another unsuccessful attempt to take Tanngoucha.

As described previously, the latter attack was largely prevented due to flanking fire from Point 622. It is arguable that given the nature of the German position, an attack by a single understrength company with limited artillery support was likely to fail. However, the essential problem faced by the Faughs was that any attack on Point 622 placed its commander on the horns of a dilemma. While the difficult terrain made a two-company attack difficult and dangerous, a single-company attack would often suffer too many casualties to enable it to hold against any subsequent counterattack. The obvious solution seemed to be to commit one company and follow up with another to consolidate gains. Yet this plan also had deficiencies due to three factors: the weak nature of the forward companies, the threat posed by German artillery defensive fire and the problems of co-ordinating two infantry companies in the dark and on difficult terrain. It was now very obvious that the capture of Point 622 required a completely novel approach, one that the Germans would not expect.[25]

---

25   The story of the attack on Point 622 is based on Coldwell-Horsfall, *Wild Geese*, Chapter 13, and the war diary of the 1st Royal Irish Fusiliers for April 1943 WO TNA 175/ 506, which includes an account entitled "Point 622 and Butlers Hill".

8.10 One Last Desperate Attack

The failure of his second attack on the night of 22/23 April undoubtedly disappointed Brigadier Nelson Russell, but did not weaken his resolve to complete his mission. He was very aware of the significant casualties inflicted on the Skins and the Faughs, and the fact that these two battalions had been fighting for 17 days. He noted in a later account: "Something was due to crack soon … it wasn't going to be the Brigade. But we could expect little assistance … as the 11th Brigade was licking its wounds, and the 36th Brigade was in the middle of its bloody struggle for Longstop."[26] While the Skins clung tenaciously on to their positions on the slopes of Tanngoucha and the Faughs retained their grip on their forward positions near Point 622, Russell and his brigade staff wrestled with the apparently intractable problem of how to take these two objectives. At some point during this period it seems the gods on Olympus decided to smile down on the Irish Brigade and change sides. Someone on the brigade staff, probably Russell himself, had an unusual idea, one that would provide a nasty surprise for the Germans and break the deadlock. The proposed solution must have been under consideration for at least a couple of days, as it was incorporated in the new plan which Russell published on 23 April: the original idea involved the use of Churchill tanks to support an attack on Heidous. The idea for the use of Churchills in the hilly terrain was of course not new, the 142nd Regiment having already proved the feasibility of operating Churchills in the hills on 14 April. In that sense they had paved the way for the decision to use the North Irish Horse. The actions that followed subsequently led the North Irish Horse to receiving a great deal of praise and attention, all of which was very well earned, but it tended to gloss over the fact that the 142nd Regiment had already shown how it could be done. As a result of this decision, early on the morning of 23 April and in the aftermath of the previous night's failed attack, Captain R. Bowring, the commander of 1 Troop, A Squadron of the North Irish Horse, found himself at Russell's headquarters. According to Gerry Chester, who served in the North Irish Horse and briefly as part of Bowring's tank crew, Bowring was not a native Ulsterman but hailed from a distinguished family in Liverpool. His father ran a major shipping company and had been Lord Mayor of Liverpool. In addition to being a capable troop commander, Bowring was renowned in the regiment for being a very talented singer. The assignment of Bowring's troop to the 38th Brigade must have required a fair degree of persuasion by Russell, as the North Irish Horse were at this point almost totally committed to the battle for Longstop Hill. It is likely that Russell must have previously talked to David Dawnay, the CO of the North Irish Horse, and asked for his views on whether it was feasible to employ tanks in the hills. Dawnay must have known of the successful use of tanks by Lieutenant Jacques on 14 April, so he had not only replied in the affirmative, but also assigned tanks to help the Irish Brigade. Captain Bowring's troop had only two tanks left operational at this time, so he was allocated another tank from 5 Troop of the squadron. The 38th Brigade were left with just three tanks to support their attack. It is important to stress that originally Bowring and his tanks were to assist a future attack by the London Irish on Heidous, scheduled to have taken place on 24 April.

Bowring and his troop of three tanks spent the afternoon of 23 April negotiating some steep and winding tracks and managed to make their way up to Djebel Kelbine. Their move to

---

26   See Russell, *Irish Brigade*, p.115.

Kelbine was significantly aided by a track widened by a section of the Royal Engineers, who used a bulldozer to remove some obstacles. Bowring was taken up to Bettiour to see the enemy positions and determine the feasibility of using his tanks in the first case against Heidous. At Russell's request, Bowring next took his troop of tanks to investigate an approach to Heidous, and during this period one of the tanks suffered a direct hit from a German gun and the troop withdrew. At some point in the proceedings, what began as a proposal to use the Churchills to support an attack on Heidous developed into an idea that must previously have seemed so outlandish that it was not ever previously considered. When it was first discussed it may have seemed like a really stupid idea: why not try to get some tanks up on Kef el Tiour ridge to support any attack? When this idea was first posed, some staff officers may have questioned the sanity of the originator. It was, after all, already proving difficult to moving infantry along Kef el Tiour ridge. However, once they learned that it was "Beau" Butler who suggested the plan, they may have had second thoughts, for by now Butler knew the Kef el Tiour ridge rather well. In view of Russell's confidence in Butler, and perhaps recalling the adventurous spirit and adaptability of Dawnay's North Irish Horse and their Churchill tanks, Russell may have concluded that after all he had nothing to lose from making the attempt. Russell would have known that the 142nd managed to get their tanks at least on to Djebel Ang, so this would have given him more confidence on the feasibility of a more daring move. Bowring looked over the approaches, first to Djebel Ang and then along the Kef Ridge and concluded the route was difficult but not impossible. He noted, however, that his troop would require about 70 mules to carry a large amount of extra fuel, and also that while he might get his tanks up on to the mountain, he might not get them down again! Bowring's willingness to attempt what seemed an impossible task reflected the culture which Dawnay had instilled into his regiment. Coldwell-Horsfall, now safely ensconced in a hospital, later reflected:

> Our cavalry regiment, the North Irish Horse, were free of the inhibitions sometimes found in traditionally minded units. They did not consider that all hunting should be over flat country and they did not mind about their machines. Yes they might get a tank or two up the three thousand feet over Djebel Ang and if they couldn't get them down again they would no doubt be given others … I do not think that anyone can appreciate the achievement of the North Irish Horse tank crews unless they had carried out that climb, preferably in charge of a mule column.[27]

The decision to position three tanks within firing range of Point 622 and Tanngoucha provided the ace up their sleeve that Russell and his staff so clearly needed to break the stalemate on the ridge. Throughout this period, Russell was under considerable pressure from his GOC, for after an extended period when he had not visited Russell at all, suddenly Evelegh was visiting him every day. Despite the three aces in his hand and pressure to attack yet again, Russell questioned whether it was necessary to carry out another assault, as fresh US troops were now arriving and would soon outflank the Germans. Evelegh insisted a new attack was required, citing the problems Tanngoucha was creating for Howlett's brigade in its attack on Longstop Hill. He did agree a delay of one day and the attack was now scheduled for the morning of Easter Sunday, 25

---

27   Coldwell-Horsfall, *Wild Geese*, p.161.

April; as the tank commanders had to be able to see their targets, a night attack was out of the question. Russell's plan depended to a high degree on the shock and surprise that the presence of Bowring's tanks would create among the defenders, and their ability to suppress the German defences. Two companies of the Faughs, A and D, now each the strength of a platoon, would attack Point 622 and the feature called Butler's Hill to the north-east, but this time under cover of the Churchill tanks. While the Germans on Point 622 were otherwise engaged, the 6th Skins would move from their trenches and, with artillery support, attack Tanngoucha. No attack was to be mounted on Heidous at this stage.

The morning of 25 April came, but no attack was initially possible as mist on Kef el Tiour prevented Bowring and his tank commanders from seeing any targets. Russell agreed to a delay in the attack until the mist lifted, which did not happen until midday. Meanwhile, Russell received information that the defenders of Heidous might have withdrawn from that village, so patrols were despatched to confirm this. At midday, the mist having cleared, the Germans on Point 622 probably wondered if they were seeing things, for directly across from them on Kef el Tiour ridge were three large and extremely unwelcome guests: Bowring's Churchill tanks. Once their targets were visible, all three tanks started to blast them with high-explosive and Besa machine-gun fire. It appears that from their lofty perch, Bowring and his tanks were not only able to shoot at Point 622 and Butler's Hill, but also at targets on Tanngoucha. At 1235 hours, the combined force of about 60 men of A and D Companies of the Faughs started their advance from their start line. D Company was once again in the van, led by Lieutenant Sillem but assisted by Lieutenant Dennis Hayward. Young Hayward had only joined the battalion as a replacement two nights previously, and the fight for Point 622 would provide him with a rapid and rude introduction to combat. Fortunately, Hayward was a fairly robust subaltern and adapted quickly to his unusual debut in command of a platoon. He was allocated the task of leading a 10-man assault group, a kind of forlorn hope, whose job it was to attack and take the rocky tower that had withstood so many attacks. His assault group included two of Coldwell-Horsfall's rogues, Corporal Swain and Fusilier Mallon. The rest of the men from D Company, about 20 soldiers, were led by Sillem and Colour Sergeant David Bartram, who had replaced the wounded Sergeant White. Their job was to act as a fire-support or follow-up group, and they were equipped with all the Bren guns that were available. The attack by the Faughs and Skins would be directly supported by the North Irish Horse tank troop. The precise role Bowring's troop played in the attack creates a bit of a mystery. The first part of the puzzle is how the troop of tanks managed to get in a suitable position to support the Faughs and fire on Point 622 and Butler's Hill; the second part is what role they played. The approach to whatever position they reached was certainly a demanding one, as Sergeant Bullick, one of Dawnay's tank commanders, later described for an article in the *Belfast Telegraph*, the newspaper for which he had worked before joining the Army:

> Captain Bowring's troop advanced over country only fit for mountain goats. One tank got bogged down to the tops of its tracks. Under heavy fire the troop towed it out and went forward only to lose another in a deep wadi. Again the troops dismounted and towing started again. Luck was with the Ulster men once more and out she came. In this fashion the climb was made - on to a position where the Germans could feel, as well as see the menace of steel. It was not a speedy advance, nor a brilliant spectacle - just a lumbering and at times drunken amble, but nearer, always nearer to Tanngoucha and the sites of the

mortar men. And if anything these deliberate elephantine tactics increased the relentless threat of advancing steel. The Huns threw everything they had at the tanks but were getting a "bit windy" now - this was a slightly different matter to shelling unprotected infantry. At times they lost sight of the troop as it struggled through the usual interminable wadi, but sure enough it came into sight again and at last further ascent became impossible.[28]

Some accounts suggest that Bowring and his tanks actually travelled over the narrow, rocky and jagged ledge of Kef el Tiour ridge, until less than 150 yards away from Point 622. Another report claims that the tanks actually moved on to Butler's Hill to the north-east and supported the attack there, though this seems unlikely. A further account suggests that the tanks found it very difficult to fire, as snipers forced tank commanders to close their turret hatches so they couldn't see any targets. At least three accounts have nonetheless suggested that the tanks fired a large number of HE shells and machine-gun bullets at Point 622, and this was a key factor in enabling the Irish Brigade to capture their elusive objectives. Whatever actually happened, the German defenders must have suffered, both mentally and physically, from the presence of Bowring's tanks, but they still managed to put up a tenacious defence. As Hayward's assault group moved forward, they came under deadly machine-gun and sniper fire which killed five men and wounded another. It was a brutal introduction to combat for this young officer, who had lost 50 percent of his command. Despite these losses, Hayward didn't hesitate, especially since the survivors in the group included Swain, Mallon and a capable fusilier called Phillips. Hayward and his men were aided by the fact that the Skins on the slopes of Tanngoucha suppressed any machine-gun fire from Point 620. They also used their 2in mortars to fire smoke shells onto Point 622, and the depleted assault group advanced using the cover of the smoke to reach the enemy strongpoint on the ridgeline. Heywood, Swain and Mallon clambered up the rocky outcrop, firing their Thompson submachine guns and a Bren, and throwing hand grenades. Despite, or perhaps because of, his relative youth and inexperience, Hayward demonstrated a complete disregard for his safety. The citation for his MC later noted:

> By good leadership and splendid personal example Lieutenant Hayward got his group on using rocks as cover. About 20 yards from the objective, with only six men remaining, the party was finally pinned. Calling for a volunteer Haywood [sic], who realised, that if he failed the attack would be unsuccessful, crawled around the right flank under heavy fire from almost point blank range and assaulted the hill with grenades. This action caused the surrender of the position which allowed Lieutenant Haywood to get his group on the objective.

The citation did not mention that the volunteer was Corporal Swain, who was ably supported by Mallon. Swain's DCM citation stated:

> When the Group were held up within 100 yards of the objective, he voluntarily crept forward with his Platoon commander and in spite of accurate sniping, which killed four

---

men directly behind him, reached the rocks concealing an MG nest, climbed on top in the face of stick grenades and took prisoner the enemy gun crew.[29]

While Hayward and his men were trying to assault the German strongpoint, Sillem and his support platoon moved forward and tried to suppress the enemy fire. At some point during proceedings, Sillem advanced to reposition a light machine gun, but sadly as he did so a mortar shell exploded next to him and he was killed instantly, along with two stalwarts of his platoon. Twenty-year-old Sillem may not have known it when he was killed, but he had fulfilled the promise he made to Coldwell-Horsfall to have a go at capturing Point 622. When Swain and Mallon got on top of the outcrop with a Bren gun, it proved the final straw for the defenders; the white flags went up on the ridge, and also soon afterwards on Tanngoucha. When Coldwell-Horsfall's pair of "scallywags" took the surrender of the Germans, they were among the last men standing of the assault group. They had played a very deadly version of the old children's game, king of the castle. Mallon's aid to his fellow "scallywag" was critical in enabling him to get up onto the outcrop and use his Bren gun to induce the Germans to give up. The two men were not alone among those who contributed significantly to the capture of Point 622. Two members of Sillem's support group, Fusiliers Phillips and Heywood, risked their lives to provide critical fire support. Though originally a member of the support group, Phillips' citation noted that:

In spite of accurate sniper fire from the flanks, he crept forward through the wounded and killed, right up to a position between Corporal Swain and the Platoon Commander. He came alone and brought his own ammunition. His gun enabled the other two to get further forward again and into a better position for the assault. While changing his own position to one further forward he injured himself on a jagged rock and was unable to continue firing. When ordered back by Cpl Swain, he crawled back and tried to guide forward his No 2 and coolly collected magazines for him. His coolness and initiative under fire were an inspiration to his comrades at a critical moment.

At the same time, Fusilier Heywood distinguished himself:

The assault group was held up by a machine gun nest in the rock on the crest and was unable to get forward with covering fire. The CSM ordered Bren Groups forward and while others wavered and searched for positions, Heywood boldly rushed his [Bren] gun to a position to cover the isolated assaulting party ... Having fired some bursts, which temporarily silenced the gun and enabled the forward assaulting party to cover difficult ground, he manoeuvred his gun to a better position. As he took up this second position the MG again opened up and Fusilier Heywood was seriously wounded by the burst.[30]

The capture of Point 622 did not end the Faughs' woes, for the German infantrymen defending Butler's Hill to the north east did not immediately surrender, and A Company under Captain

29 The citations for Hayward's MC and Swain's DCM are from WO TNA WO 373/1.
30 The quotations are from the relevant citations in TNA WO 373/1. Mallon, Phillips and Heywood all received the Military Medal. The author was surprised to learn that all five of these men mentiond in this episode managed to survive the war, despite fighting in the brutal campaign in Sicily and Italy.

Mike MacDonald had a tough time. A platoon of Germans on Butler's Hill poured deadly fire on A Company and MacDonald as he led his men towards the feature. MacDonald and the company faced a series of challenges in attacking Butler's Hill. The German platoon there was supported by flanking fire from another platoon-sized position nearby on a feature known as Snipers' Ridge. A further challenge was that in their forward positions, A Company was perfectly visible to the enemy and as soon as they started their attack any movement out of their trenches would be noticed. According to one contemporary account, Bowring's Churchills also moved into position on the company's left flank to provide support. Captain MacDonald solved the issue of German observation of his position by the dangerous, though initially effective, means of getting his company out of their trenches while his supporting artillery was firing on Butler's Hill. Fortunately no shells fell short, and as the company advanced some 100 yards it appeared the attack would proceed without any losses. Sadly, when the company was about 300 yards from its objective, it came under heavy fire from mortars, machine guns and small arms before being pinned down. The company suffered a number of casualties, including MacDonald, who was seriously wounded by bullets in both legs, and the only remaining officer, Lieutenant Carr, took over command. Despite their losses, Carr and the rest of his Irish Fusiliers managed to cross the last 300 yards of open ground and take Butler's Hill, but half the company was lost in this effort. Although this attack has tended to be overlooked, A Company's capture of Butler's Hill ensured that the Faughs would hold on to Point 622, irrespective of what happened on Tanngoucha. The battalion account of the operation notes that this attack was actually much more difficult than that carried out by D Company, although Coldwell-Horsfall and his Irish Fusiliers would probably have contested that assertion. Later inspection of the German positions on Butler's Hill found that the defenders had exploited its natural rock fissures to create well-protected sangars which were difficult to see and provided complete protection from artillery fire. It was another formidable position, and it was to their great credit that A Company had taken it.

The success of the Faughs' attacks on Point 622 and Butler's Hill on 25 April was in no small part due to excellent support from artillery directed by FOOs of the Royal Artillery. One of these FOO parties was led by Lieutenant Lee from the 4th Medium Regiment, who was directing the 5.5in guns of that unit. Lee's wireless operator that day was Lance Bombardier Edward Morris. When Morris heard that Lee intended to go forward to an exposed position to better direct his guns, he volunteered to accompany him with his radio. In this position, both Lee and Morris were constantly exposed to mortar and machine-gun fire. Despite this danger, Morris never faltered in his duties and continued to relay clear and concise fire orders back to the guns on behalf of his officer.[31]

The seizure of Point 622 and Butler's Hill removed the threat of flanking fire against the 6th Skins in their planned attempt to capture Tanngoucha. The battalion had grimly held on to their exposed positions and ably supported the Faughs during their attack on 622, but once they saw the Faughs take the ridgeline, Neville Grazebrook and his men were determined to claim their own reward. On this occasion the Skins were not to be denied their prize, and it is likely the Germans may have realised this fact. When C Company climbed out of their trenches and assaulted the hill under cover of artillery fire and support from A Company, the

---

31   Morris was later awarded the MM for this and other acts of gallantry in Tunisia.

Germans quickly displayed white flags. Nonetheless, for the fusiliers of C Company who had been assigned the job of carrying out the attack, the time they spent waiting in their trenches that morning to attack the hill must have led to a difficult few hours. The stress and tension would have been considerable, as they faced the prospect of a frontal attack uphill, on a well-defended location, and the imminent death or wounding it might bring. The tension was not eased by the fact that at around midday, and during the artillery bombardment, several errant "friendly" artillery shells dropped close to the Skins' location. Fortunately, everyone was in their slit trenches and the incident caused no casualties. Despite the potential dangers when the order to attack came, the company nonetheless started their advance. According to Percy Hamilton, who was there:

> There was some fire from Jerry, but the attack had not been started long when a white flag appeared, followed by several more from different parts of the hill. There was a shout from our chaps that echoed right around the hill, and they went right up on the hill and completed the clearing up.[32]

It must have been a huge relief to many men when they saw a white flag raised on Tanngoucha. As soon as this was sighted, A Company also joined the attack and by 1430 hours "Olympus" had been secured, along with 20 prisoners. It was fitting that although the attack was made by C Company, Captain Desmond McCaldin, who had commanded D Company with distinction in the first attack, had recovered from his wound enough to return and witness this success. By 1500 hours all the objectives - Point 622, Butler's Hill and Tanngoucha - could be declared secure. Finally, Nelson Russell was able to send the signal which his GOC had waited so long to hear: "Olympus" and "Apollo" had been taken, though when he learned the cost, especially to the Faughs, he may have had felt it was a pyrrhic victory.

When they completed their attack on 25 April, Butler's battalion had been much reduced in strength compared to when Operation Sweep started. One battalion account states that it lost 18 officers and 218 other ranks in the period from 7 April to the end of the offensive in May. Coldwell-Horsfall and MacDonald's D and A Companies were especially hard hit. The Faughs, for example, lost 22 officers and men killed in the attacks between 21 and 26 April. In total, during the 26 days the battalion was engaged in operations in the Peaks, the Faughs lost 52 dead and more than 200 wounded. The 6th Skins had also suffered greatly during the last three weeks, and by the time it completed the capture of Tanngoucha was in a much weakened condition. It was inevitably the rifle companies which had been hardest hit, and by 25 April these had been reduced to platoon size. Only eight officers and 124 men remained in all four rifle companies out of the likely strength of over 550 men at the start of the operation. The 6th Skins had suffered 62 men killed and an estimated 200 wounded in less than 21 days. The Irish Brigade's third battalion, the London Irish Rifles, had sustained significantly fewer casualties than its sister units, as they did not become engaged in operations until the middle of the month. Nonetheless, during the 16 days it was engaged the unit lost some 15 dead and 60 wounded in action. These losses might have been higher had not the Germans voluntarily released their grip on "Hades" on 25 April. Scott's battalion finally occupied the village on 26 April after its patrols

32 Hamilton, *Memoirs*, p.20.

revealed that the Germans had pulled out. Russell was finally able to inform Evelegh that his last assigned objective, "Hades", had also been taken.

Sadly, despite their very high losses and weakened condition, the ordeal of the Irish Brigade in the Djebels was not yet over. Russell must have begun to dread his boss's visits, for Evelegh's arrival at his headquarters always seemed to bring pressure for further advances and never brought the longed-for news that the brigade was about to get a well-earned rest. Nor was it any different when Evelegh arrived at Russell's headquarters on the morning of 26 April, as the topic he wished to discuss was exploiting the brigade's recent success by an advance north-east into more mountains. Evelegh as an individual was not mean-spirited or completely uncaring, but he was an aggressive and ambitious commander, and one under pressure from all levels of the chain of command in North Africa to continue the advance. It is arguable that at this point it was both cruel and short-sighted to require the Irish Brigade to continue to advance to the original and unrealistic objectives they had been set, after all their efforts and losses. However, though the 38th Brigade was sorely in need of a break, it was not to be. Both the Faughs and the Skins, and soon afterwards the London Irish, received orders to attack north-east. The agony of the exhausted officers and men continued for six further days in terrain that was even worse than that which they had already encountered. Russell later wrote of this period:

> Over the Tanngoucha we found the nightmare country and the next five days will always remain as a nightmare to me. We reluctantly bade farewell to our three Churchills – even they couldn't take it. Great jagged hills with sheer sides – no saddle to get on and keep on – but dozens of hills intersected with valleys, with the dominating colour of blood red sand and grey rock … After three days fighting and clearing three miles of hills we came to a full stop.
>
> We could get no further. I doubt if we'd have got much further even if there had been no enemy at all. And the enemy was there and still fighting. We really had reached "impossible" country. It can't be described. I can only say that two of my signallers broke their legs trying to lay a line in the dark within 20 yards of my headquarters, and that Pat Scott - after one horrified look – said to me "My God. If we ever get out of this place alive, we can talk about it for the rest of our days."[33]

When the brigade embarked on his trek across this wilderness, one set of friendly faces had to be left behind, for although Captain Bowring vowed to follow the Irish Brigade wherever they went, the terrain proved too difficult even for them.[34] Bowring and his troop left having received a professional compliment of the highest order from an unusual but nonetheless welcome source. One of the German prisoners taken on Point 622 was being shepherded back to a prisoner of war cage when he passed the three Churchill tanks. He smiled at the commander, patted the tank and said in perfect English: "These are iron mules you've got."[35]

For the next six days, the brigade endeavoured to advance across a series of inaccessible Djebels, some with names such as Djebel Touila and others just numbered such as Point 484. The fighting was sometimes sporadic and other times fierce. The 6th Skins suffered the greatest

33   See Russell, *Irish Brigade*, p.115.
34   Captain Bowring served with the North Irish in Tunisia and Italy and survived the war.
35   See *Belfast Telegraph*, 16 June 1943.

losses during operations to seize Point 416 or Kef el Senrach, one of their platoons being overrun when it was counterattacked on the hill on 27 April. It was on this day that Lance Corporal Edward Teare of the 6th Skins, who had already distinguished himself by his bravery with a Bren gun on Djebel Mahdi, further demonstrated his courage. His DCM citation noted:

> On 27 Apr 43 during the battalion attack on Kef el Senrach, L/Cpl Teare was ordered to move to the left flank of the Company to a German MG post which was holding up the forward platoons. He succeeded in silencing this post with his Bren gun from an exposed position. Suddenly he was rushed at from a concealed position by 4 Germans led by an officer. With great coolness L/Cpl Teare opened fire, killing the officer and an NCO, after which the remainder gave them-selves up. The handling of his Bren Group continued to be of the greatest assistance to his company throughout the battle.

While his repeated acts of outstanding bravery later earned Teare the DCM, based on his citation, it is arguable he should have received the VC.[36]

This was one of the battalion's worst days in the campaign, as it lost 13 men killed and a significant number wounded. During this period the brigade lost at least 21 men killed and a great many wounded. It is noteworthy that in the advance, three of the FOO parties providing artillery support found themselves in such exposed positions that they were overrun by German troops. Only one of the officers, Lieutenant Goad from 4th Medium Regiment, managed to make his way back to friendly positions, the others in the parties being captured. Brigadier Russell suffered his own personal loss as his driver, Fusilier John Neil-Moores, who had been with him throughout the campaign, died later of wounds incurred in this period. Also among those killed in early May was Sergeant Frank McAleer of the 6th Skins, who had won the DCM with the regiment in January after conducting his own personal war against the Germans near Bou Arada. The agony of the brigade in the Battle of the Peaks finally ended on 3 May when it was relieved by two French battalions and the 1st/4th battalion of the Hampshires. The 38th Irish Brigade went into reserve, and subsequently gained the honour from Evelegh of being the first brigade of the division to enter Tunis on 8 May. While there may have been many in the brigade who would have preferred another unit to have this honour and to have a rest instead, the brigade encountered no opposition and enjoyed all the plaudits that arose with this move.

36   The extract is from Teare's DCM citation from G. Brown, *For Distinguished Conduct*, p.489; and TNA WO 373/1.

9

The Wider Picture & Planning for Operation Vulcan

9.1 The Global Picture

By the time the First Army launched its final operations in late April 1943, almost four years of war had elapsed, yet there was comparatively little good news for the long-suffering British people. The Battle of the Atlantic was reaching its peak at this time, and merchant ship losses in two critical convoys suggested the Allies might lose this most crucial of battles. Furthermore, the bombing campaign against Germany was inflicting heavy losses on the RAF. In the Pacific, after the costly battles for Guadalcanal and New Guinea, little progress seemed to be made, while in Burma, the Japanese were inflicting defeats on the British Fourteenth Army. Despite the surrender of the German Sixth Army at Stalingrad, the Russians also faced a resurgent *Wehrmacht*, which was preparing a major offensive that would eventually take place in the summer near a village called Kursk. With no sign of an imminent cross-Channel invasion of occupied France, it was only in the Mediterranean, and specifically in North Africa, that there seemed to be cautious grounds for optimism about the Allies' progress towards the defeat of the Axis forces. After the Battle of El Alamein in November 1942, the attention of both Churchill and the newspapers had inevitably been drawn to the operations of General Bernard Montgomery and the Eighth Army, which had secured Britain's first major victory of the Second World War during a dismal 12 months that had begun with Pearl Harbor and continued with the fall of Malaya, Singapore and finally of Tobruk. Monty's victory had been followed by the initial success of Operation Torch and the rapid advance of the First Army towards Tunis, which subsequently stalled. After tough fighting through the winter, both the First and Eighth Armies now seemed to be making progress and there was inevitably much political and military pressure to deliver a further victory to help sustain morale at home. At this stage of the war, a great deal of attention was thus focused on the operations in North Africa and its commanders. This came in the form of often unwelcome enquiries and pressure from both civilian and military leaders about the progress, or lack of it, in defeating the Axis forces in Tunisia. It also came in the form of numerous visitors, again both political and military, to Tunisia and a significant increase in the number of newspaper correspondents. All of these developments may have created unnecessary expectations and also some tensions among Allied commanders.

9.2 Eighteenth Army Group's Plan for Operation Vulcan

On 16 April, Eighteenth Army Group issued Operational Instruction No. 12 to both the First and Eighth Armies, outlining future offensive operations. This directive followed conversations which General Alexander had with Montgomery and the First Army's CO Anderson on 11 and 12 April respectively. In the document, Alexander made clear for the first time in writing that the First Army would be responsible for the main effort to capture Tunis, while the Eighth Army would play an important but supporting role. The task of the Eighth Army was to draw off forces from First Army by exerting pressure on the German defensive position near Enfidaville. As well as taking Tunis, Alexander assigned Anderson and the First Army the role of cooperating with the US II Corps in the capture of Bizerte and being prepared to work with the Eighth Army to prevent Axis forces withdrawing into a last-ditch stand on the Cap Bon peninsula. Alexander provided limited additional assistance to Anderson, ordering the British 1st Armoured Division to be temporarily transferred from the Eighth to the First Army. In a largely political move, designed to satisfy his boss Eisenhower, placate any external political pressures in the US and concerns expressed by Patton and Bradley, he placed the US II Corps under his own direct command. The more private reality was that as part of a separate operational instruction, he actually placed the Americans under Anderson's day-to-day tactical command. Alexander authorised Anderson to issue all orders and instructions necessary to coordinate the operations of the US II Corps with those of the First Army for the next phase of operations. Anderson was granted the authority to issue any necessary orders direct to US II Corps, without the need to gain approval from Eighteenth Army Group.[1] In a surprising move, and one that hardly signalled his confidence in Anderson, Alexander nonetheless granted Major General Bradley, the US II Corps commander, the right of access and appeal direct to him in the event he had concerns over any of Anderson's decisions.

The new operation was codenamed Vulcan and would incorporate the 78th Division's operations designed to recapture Longstop Hill. The Irish Brigade's moves from 16-26 April effectively drew Operation Sweep to its close. Officially, Operation Vulcan covered the actions of both First and Eighth Armies, but Monty and his staff hardly ever referred to it and continued to act independently. Monty had not completely accepted the idea that Eighth Army would take a secondary role in capturing Tunis, as highlighted by his ordering the launch of Operation Oration on 18/19 April, three days before Vulcan was to be undertaken. Oration was an attack on the Enfidaville defences, but was not coordinated with the wider offensive and had little impact on the German response to it. Although Oration was carried out by the Eighth Army's best divisions, it did not achieve its aim of breaking through the Axis defences or enabling Monty to secure for Eighth Army the credit of taking Tunis. Instead, the bloody and bitter fighting in the mountains cost Eighth Army over 1,500 casualties and demonstrated clearly the Axis troops' determination to defend their positions. It was also a second abject and rather humiliating lesson to Monty, the supposed master of the battlefield, on the challenges of fighting a determined enemy in mountain terrain. Monty had confidently told his sceptical commanders that the Eighth Army would breach the position, but he had failed to do so. One of Montgomery's unfortunate traits was his tendency to criticise other commanders in private

---

1   See Playfair *Destruction of Axis Forces,* p.430.

and in public. He had told Alexander that Anderson was unfit to command an army and that First Army was moving far too slowly in the Tunisian mountains.[2] Now the shoe was on the other foot, and Montgomery was learning why Anderson and First Army had encountered such difficulties in their advance on Tunis.

9.3 First Army and V Corps Plans

Montgomery consistently underestimated Anderson's ability as a commander. For example, Anderson had already anticipated and refined Alexander's order for the next operation. Two days prior to the issue of Alexander's operational instruction on 14 April, Anderson had issued a formal plan covering the First Army's part in Operation Vulcan. This differed only slightly in terms of Alexander's expressed intentions, but showed Anderson's clear understanding of the challenges he faced. Anderson's directive established the first task of his plan as not the seizure of a geographical location, but the annihilation of the Axis forces in Tunisia and thus the capture of Tunis and Bizerte. He clearly grasped that his subordinate commanders needed to focus on destroying the Axis armies, rather than being seduced into securing newsworthy, politically attractive but strategically irrelevant towns and cities. While the weakest strategic point for the Axis forces in Tunisia may have been their lines of communication, the First Army's critical objective was to destroy the Axis forces, and especially the famed *Afrika Korps*, in battle. Both Anderson and Montgomery clearly understood that defeating the Axis forces in battle in North Africa would further demonstrate that the German Army could be beaten. It would also improve the fighting spirit of Allied troops and provide a boost to civilian morale.

After careful review, Anderson and his staff decided that V Corps would launch the army's main effort along the Medjez-Massicault-Tunis axis. The task of breaking deep into the Axis main position on a narrow front was assigned to the 1st and 4th Infantry Divisions and the 25th Tank Brigade from V Corps. Charles Allfrey's corps had the role of advancing to critical high ground, on a phase line which ran from Peter's Corner, a road junction south of Medjez, to Longstop Hill. This ground included Longstop on the north side of the Medjerda River and a hill called Argoub es Seid on the south side. Once these objectives were secured, V Corps would advance to take the next line of hills, which included Gueriat el Atach and, most importantly, Djebel Bou Aoukaz. The reader will recall that American troops of the 1st US Armored Division under command of V Corps had already fought for and lost Bou Aoukaz during operations in December 1942. Although not mentioned in the directive, part of this operation, which was scheduled for 22/23 April, included the capture of Point 622, Tanngoucha and Heidous by the 78th Division. The division also had the role of taking Longstop Hill at the north-western end of Anderson's phase line. According to Alexander's original estimate earlier in the month, all these objectives were expected to have been secured by Evelegh's division well in time for the 78th Division to be made available for the main attack on 22 April. The Army Group staff's estimate of the time required to achieve this had proved woefully inaccurate, for the Irish Brigade would not secure the three peaks until 26 April and Longstop would finally be captured on the same day. As a result, the 78th Division would not be available to support

---

2   See Nigel Hamilton, *Monty: Master of the Battlefield* (London: Hamish Hamilton, 1983), pp.215, .232 for the unfit to command quotations.

Allfrey's attack. This error affected the plans of First Army and V Corps, for although Allfrey's corps made the main effort in Operation Vulcan for the First Army, he found himself attacking the teeth of the German defences with only two infantry divisions and one armoured brigade. Anderson's wider plan assumed that although V Corps would encounter bitter resistance, it would lead to the Germans committing their reserves, which could be destroyed on a ground of Anderson's own choosing. As part of the plan, once V Corps had launched its attack, the 1st and 6th Armoured Divisions in IX Corps south of Medjez would drive north-east to try to flank the German defensive positions near Massicault. Anderson hoped this attack would encounter and deplete German armoured reserves. As part of the plan for Operation Vulcan, the US II Corps would carry out an attack in the north in the Bed Valley towards its objective, Bizerte, and also seize the Chouigui pass. This attack would prevent the Axis forces redeploying troops from that sector, and might even force the enemy to commit some of his reserves. Finally, the French XIX Corps in the south would also attack to clear the road from Robaa to Pont du Fahs as part of these wider operations.

The First Army plan would later be criticised by Montgomery and other writers on a number of grounds. In Monty's case, he observed that Anderson's attack failed to concentrate all his strength on a narrow axis at this vital point. There is a degree of truth in this criticism, for the main blow comprised only one corps with just two divisions. It is true that Anderson could have reinforced V Corps for the main attack, perhaps by shifting the 46th Infantry Division to come under its command. This would of course have weakened IX Corps' attack in the south, as it would have lost its only infantry division and may have limited its ability to flank the main defences. One option Anderson was denied was to reinforce the corps using other Allied units. Anderson was aware of this potential solution, but was clear that he was constrained from adopting it as this would have disobeyed specific directive from Alexander, which required him to divide his army into three neat but inflexible national sectors. Anderson knew he had been the subject of much, sometimes unjustified, criticism by Alexander and other Allied officers earlier in the campaign for having a messy battlefield, where Allied units were intermingled irrespective of the nationality of their commander. Anderson later wrote (in April 1946) succinctly, and in the author's view pointedly, contrasting the restrictions on his planning with the freedom enjoyed by Montgomery, who was a frequent critic of his plans, and also Alexander, who had been far too quick to pass judgement and place restrictions upon him:

> Although I had a big total superiority in numbers and material, a limiting factor was the division of my army (including II Corps) into three national sectors; this naturally restricted the full freedom of movement of reserves which otherwise I would have enjoyed with a homogeneous army.[3]

One option that was discussed at this time was to delay any attack for a week to allow V Corps to be reinforced by 78th Division after it had completed its operations. Anderson was, however, under pressure from Alexander to attack on or about 22 April. He also believed strongly that an attack on that date would catch the Germans by surprise, and wanted to stick to his plan. There was one blindingly obvious option that was not considered at this time. This was the idea that

3   See Anderson, *Despatches*, p.5,459.

since the First Army was conducting the main attack, it should be significantly reinforced using several veteran divisions from Eighth Army. The main reason this solution was not adopted until later was that Alexander was always reluctant to impose his will on his friend Monty, despite him being an often prickly subordinate, and was perhaps uncomfortable with asking him to give up his formations. Anderson was thus forced to deal the cards he had been dealt rather than rightly demanding a new pack.

Whatever the potential flaws of Anderson's wider plan, Allfrey had the task of executing it in the best way that he could organise. The primary focus of his planning seems to have been the operations of the 1st and 4th Divisions. The 78th Division was, however, expected to attack on D-1 and be able to take Longstop Hill by 0200 hours on the day the rest of V Corps attacked. As the Germans had spent four months fortifying Longstop Hill, this estimate seems to be yet another example of a failure by Allfrey and his staff officers to confront hard tactical truths. Allfrey's plan for the rest of V Corps was designed to take place in five phases, and given the likely strength of German defences known at the time it appears to be also over-optimistic. The details of each phase need not concern us, as the operations of these two divisions are not part of this story, though it is one worth telling. Both divisions were expected to advance for between five to six miles, capture a whole series of hills along the right bank of the Medjerda, including Djebel Bou Aoukaz and Djebel Guessa, and finish their attack by capturing a crossing over the Medjerda at El Bathan. The Battle-Axe Division was expected to take Longstop Hill by 0200 hours on 22 April as the German positions there posed a threat to 1st Infantry Division's attack south of the Medjerda River. It was to continue to advance for some five miles across the mountains until it arrived at Djebel el Aroussa, six miles away near the Tebourba gap and across from El Bathan. Its task, and in part the reason why 38th Brigade received no relief after taking Tanngoucha, was to ensure it kept pace with the advance of the rest of the corps and protect its left flank. One key point to make is that the artillery support available to V Corps would be used first to support 36th Brigade's attack on Longstop and also the Irish Brigade's attack on Tanngoucha. The majority of artillery support against Longstop had to be completed in time for it to be available to support the other corps' attacks, which would begin at 0200 hours on 22 April. It is only fair to state that the limited amount of artillery available proved to be a major constraint on the plan devised by Allfrey and his staff. It is debatable that if the corps had been provided with more artillery, possibly by moving it over from II Corps, or more obviously from the Eighth Army, his plan may have been less inflexible.

9.4 Battle-Axe Division Plans and Preparations

The period (18-22 April) prior to the commencement of Operation Vulcan was a busy one for Evelegh and his staff. They had to simultaneously monitor the operations of the 38th Brigade in the mountains, develop a plan for Vulcan and also reorganise and prepare 11th and 36th Brigades for that operation. The division plan for the attack on Longstop assigned this task to Brigadier Howlett and 36th Infantry Brigade, as Howlett's was the stronger of the two battered brigades: Brigadier Cass's brigade had only recently been pulled out of the front line and two of his battalions, the 2nd Lancashire Fusiliers and 5th Northants, were seriously understrength. Howlett's brigade could hardly be said to be that much better off, but two of its battalions had suffered fewer personnel losses in its rifle companies during Operation Sweep. The strongest battalion in the division in mid-April was undoubtedly the 8th Argylls. It was inevitable that this battalion would play a key role in the forthcoming assault on Longstop.

One of the main tasks of Evelegh and his staff in the last few days leading up to the start of Vulcan was to reorganise and reposition the division's brigades, so they could implement the division plan. This process required a tired 11th Infantry Brigade to move back into the mountains to relieve those 36th Infantry Brigade units required for Vulcan. On the night of 20/21 April, the 5th Northants and 2nd Lancs Fusiliers marched up from Toukabeur and Chaouach to relieve the 8th Argylls and 1st East Surreys. The latter was tasked with taking over from Eric Heygate's 6th West Kents, so it would also be free for the attack. The move had to be completed by 0000 hours on 22 April and at this point Cass's brigade took over responsibility for the area.

The divisional plan for Operation Vulcan was issued as Operational Order No. 9 on 20 April, and was notable for being very detailed about what 36th Brigade had to do while providing little guidance on how it was to be done.[4] Objectives, tasks and phase lines for the attack were outlined with great abandon, and the plan addressed all aspects of coordinating 78th Division's attack with that of other corps units. In contrast to Operation Sweep, Evelegh did not carry out a detailed appreciation prior to creating his plan. This was surprising, since the first phase of the plan required the capture of arguably the strongest German position in Tunisia, if not the most difficult in the First Army's sector. It appears that Evelegh and/or his staff decided to largely entrust the task of planning the Longstop Hill attack to Brigadier "Swifty" Howlett and his brigade staff. It may be that Evelegh was busy focusing on 38th Irish Brigade's battle in the mountains and therefore provided limited input to the plan he issued. To his credit, he did make five positive contributions to the preparations for the Longstop Hill attack. The first was to reinforce Howlett's brigade for the attack by placing Bill Wilberforce's 1st East Surreys temporarily under the former's command. His second measure was to bring together all his senior commanders for a conference at divisional headquarters on the afternoon of 20 April and to brief them on the forthcoming operation, using a table-top model of the area. The third input was to ensure that Howlett would be supported by a substantial amount of fire support, which included, as will be seen, a large artillery group. He had also negotiated through the chain of command to secure a rare intervention in close tactical bombing by the Allied air forces. The result was that Longstop Hill was directly targeted by RAF Boston light bombers. The one area where Evelegh was able to have a direct influence on the outcome of the battle for Longstop Hill was ensuring that Howlett's attack would be supported by armour. When Allfrey issued his operational instruction for Vulcan on 11 April, it made no mention of providing the 78th Division with any armoured support. Evelegh noted this omission and responded on the same day by querying this fact. In his signal, Evelegh wrote politely but firmly: "May I pleased be informed if I shall have any tanks under command for this operation?" He then stated unequivocally: "I consider that tanks are essential for any attack on Longstop from the direction of Medjez."[5] Evelegh's timely intervention with his corps commander bore fruit, as the North Irish Horse was placed under his command for the attack. The assignment of Dawnay's regiment to support Howlett was to make a critical difference to the success of the

4   Operational Order No. 9 is to be found in TNA WO 175/168 78th Division April 1943 WD.
5   Signal reference O 486 Evelegh to Comd V Corps 11 April in TNA WO 175/168 78th Division WD April 1943.

second battle for Longstop Hill. It is an excellent example of the way the GOC of a division can, through personal intervention, directly influence the outcome of a battle. It is also one clear way Evelegh could be said to have provided direct assistance in answering the crucial question of how Longstop Hill was to be taken.

9.5 The Germans React – Operation Lilac Blossom

While Anderson, Allfrey and their staffs were busy planning how to land a knockout blow on the Axis forces, the German troops under von Arnim were not idly awaiting the Allies' attacks. The new commander of *Armeegruppe Afrika* and all Axis forces in Tunisia, General von Arnim was not convinced by intelligence reports that the attack would be made from Pont du Fahs in the French sector. A combination of radio intercepts and other sources had convinced him the main effort would be by the First Army and in exactly the place that Anderson chose. Von Arnim also had faith that any attack on the Enfidaville position would fail due to the inherent strength of that position, so he had no hesitation in moving German forces from this area north to confront Anderson's attack. More surprisingly, von Arnim agreed to use precious fuel and resources to launch a spoiling attack on V Corps as it was preparing for its advance. He seems to have believed that this surprise attack would inflict significant damage and delay any Allied attack on Tunis, thus gaining precious time. The attack would be codenamed Operation *Fleiderblute* (or Lilac Blossom in English). It would be launched by substantial forces from the Hermann Goering Division and the 10th Panzer Division against the British 1st and 4th Infantry Divisions just south of Medjez el Bab. The supposed originator of the plan for Lilac Blossom was *Luftwaffe* Major General Joseph Schmid, commander of the Hermann Goering Division. Schmid was a personal friend of Goering and had been his senior intelligence officer until late 1942, when he formed the division named after the *Reichsmarschall*. Prior to his arrival in Tunisia, Schmid had absolutely no experience of land operations and had a mixed record while leading the Hermann Goering Division from January-April 1943. In retrospect, it seems surprising that von Arnim was willing first to place such an inexperienced officer in command of such a critical operation, and secondly to launch it at all after his recent experience of such operations. During Operation *Oschenkopf* in February 1943, a similar attack by *Oberst* Lang, of Longstop Hill fame, had resulted in the loss of 71 tanks (including 19 Tigers) and had led Lang to be given the sobriquet "*Panzer* Killer Lang".

Operation Lilac Blossom was launched on the night of 20/21 April and had not dissimilar results to *Oschenkopf*, albeit in a shorter timeframe. After initial surprise, Schmid's troops met fierce resistance, especially once they were engaged by Royal Artillery field regiments, who were now in their nearby gun positions preparing to support Operation Vulcan. The spoiling attack cost the 5th *Panzer* Army 33 precious tanks, a significant number of dead and wounded, between 400 and 500 men captured and critical fuel supplies wasted. In return, the two formations largely involved in repulsing this attack, the 2nd and 10th Infantry Brigades of the 1st and 4th Infantry Divisions, lost approximately 350 men killed, wounded or missing and quickly recovered all positions initially lost. Most importantly, Lilac Blossom did not disrupt the corps' attack, leading to only a four-hour delay in launching Operation Vulcan and utterly failing to meet its original purpose. By launching Lilac Blossom, von Arnim provided Allfrey with an early and totally unexpected opportunity to destroy German armoured and infantry reserves. In view of the rapidly weakening strength of *Armeegruppe Afrika*, von Arnim could ill-afford such losses.

One of the key reasons why the overall fighting capability of *Armeegruppe Afrika* was declining, and that its likely demise was imminent, was its parlous logistics situation. This in turn was due to successful Allied attacks on its lines of communication. By 22 April, the Axis forces in Tunisia had very limited supplies of petrol and shortages in food. The latter was in part due to the need to feed large numbers of administrative and rear area personnel who had fallen back along with fighting troops when the Axis forces withdrew to Enfidaville. Normally these non-combatants would have been evacuated from Tunisia, but Hitler had forbidden any withdrawal of personnel, and furthermore, increasing Allied air attacks on the air supply routes meant it was dangerous to fly them out. It was becoming rapidly obvious that the almost complete loss of air superiority by the *Luftwaffe* would soon ensure the Axis forces in Tunisia would have to surrender. In a reversal of roles, it was now the turn of all Axis troops to be constantly harassed from the air. Moreover, Allied air forces were now able to attack Axis airfields in Italy which had been used to support *Armeegruppe Afrika*. An example of this deadly capability occurred on 20 April, when 63 B-24 Liberators of the US Army Air Forces attacked Bari airfield in southern Italy. The aircrews of the US 98th and 376th Bombardment Groups reported that they had destroyed 27 enemy aircraft in the raid. Unusually for air crews, who at this period of the war had a tendency to exaggerate actual results, they had seriously underestimated the destruction they had wreaked. German sources later revealed that the air strike destroyed 107 German and Italian aircraft on the ground, damaging a further 46. The aircraft destroyed at Bari included 40 brand new ME-109s awaiting assignment to *Luftwaffe* fighter squadrons. These could no longer be used to try to reverse Allied air superiority in Tunisia, and the *Luftwaffe* could not long survive losses on this scale.[6] It is, however, important to note that despite their worsening situation, both German and Italian troops were still willing to continue fighting. Indeed, as the end in North Africa drew closer, if anything their resistance to Allied attacks increased. Due to Hitler's orders, most front-line soldiers knew that their fate would either be death, injury or capture.

9.6 Operation Vulcan Commences

The willingness of Germans troops to continue fighting, irrespective of their eventual fate, was demonstrated all too clearly when Charles Allfrey launched the southern prong of his attack in Operation Vulcan on the early morning of 23 April. In spite of the losses incurred during Lilac Blossom, the Germans resisted fiercely the attacks carried out by the British 1st and 4th Infantry Divisions. Since these operations do not form part of this story, it is only necessary to provide a brief summary. The main attack was carried out on the left close to the south bank of the Medjerda River by the 1st Infantry Division and was initially repulsed with the loss of 500 casualties and 29 Churchill tanks. The majority of the tank losses were incurred by the 142nd RAC Regiment, which was now supporting the 1st Division after its efforts during Operation Sweep. During a counterattack that day, the regiment's commander, Lieutenant Colonel Birkbeck, and his crew

---

6   See Playfair, *Destruction of Axis Forces*, p.444. This source and also Rolf, *Bloody Road to Tunis*, pp.233-34, were used to derive details of Operation Lilac Blossom.

were sadly killed when a Tiger shell hit his tank. A second attack the next day was more successful and seized the Gueriat el Atach ridge. The 1st Infantry Division's next attack was designed to seize Djebel Bou Aoukaz, the hill disputed during operations in December 1942. Bou Aoukaz was relevant to operations on Longstop, as its height, 290 metres, gave it observation over some of the ground near Longstop. The attack, led by the 24th Guards Brigade, began on 26 April and was bitterly contested by the German defenders. Between 26 and 29 April, the Irish and Scots Guards battalions of the 24th Guards Brigade were gravely depleted in their attacks on this feature. The Bou changed hands several times until it was taken and held by the Irish Guards. Von Arnim clearly viewed the defensive line based on the Bou as critical to the effective defence of Tunis. He gathered together his few armoured reserves and created a *Kampfgruppe* which he launched in a counterattack on 29 April. This attack eventually failed, but when the Irish Guards were relieved they had less than 100 men left of their fighting companies.

As part of Operation Vulcan, the 4th Infantry Division conducted a series of attacks on 24 April to seize key terrain features and protect the right flank of the advance of the 1st Infantry Division. Over the next five days, the 12th Infantry Brigade advanced eastwards from near a feature called Banana Ridge towards Peter's Corner, a widely used name for the junction of the Medjez-Tunis road with another road leading south. The fighting was fierce and the 6th Black Watch, which had occupied Djebel Rmel, suffered considerable losses. Fighting over the next three days centred about the hamlet of Sidi Abdullah and what became known as Cactus farm. The German fought bitterly to defend and retake positions, including a counterattack on 29 April by the parachute regiment which had previously been commanded by the able *Oberst* Koch.

By 30 April, the V Corps offensive was slowing to a halt as German resistance became more desperate, casualties mounted and sheer exhaustion set in. In the south, to the east of the village of Goubellat, the British IX Corps launched their secondary supporting attack across the plain of Goubellat on 22 April. Corps operations started with an attack by the 46th Infantry Division to seize two important German defensive positons: one was called Argoub Sellah and the other originally named Two Tree Hill until shelling removed these two landmarks. The former was taken, though with much loss to the attacking battalion, but the latter remained in enemy hands until its occupants withdrew of their own accord. Two Tree Hill had been the source of much pain for the 38th Irish Brigade, and to the last it retained its evil reputation for inflicting damage on all who approached it. Both the 6th Armoured and later the 1st Armoured Divisions went into action in a move designed to outflank the German defences to the north, but quickly encountered the enemy's dreaded 88mm anti-tank guns and suffered significant tank losses. A costly attack on Djebel Bou Kournine followed, which brought much anguish to that veteran of Longstop Hill, the 2nd Coldstreams. By 30 April, it had become apparent that Operation Vulcan had run out of steam and that V Corps lacked the strength to break through the German defences. The attacks south of Medjez el Bab had weakened the German defences considerably and also secured the start line for an eventual attack on Tunis, but did not deliver the final blow.[7] One clear beneficiary of all these attacks was Evelegh's 78th Division, and especially Howlett's 36th Infantry Brigade. The attacks of both the 1st and 4th Infantry Division ensured that von Arnim had no reserves to throw in to counter the attack which Howlett now unleashed.

---

7   Details of Operation Vulcan were largely derived from Blaxland, *Plain Cook*, Chapters 13 and 14; and Hugh Williamson, *The Fourth Division 1939-1945* (London: Neame, 1951), Chapters 6 and 7.

10

Howlett's First Innings at Longstop Hill

10.1 The 36th Brigade Team and Operational Order No. 26

The Battle-Axe divisional plan allocated the task of taking the Longstop Hill area to the 36th Infantry Brigade and its commander, Brigadier Howlett, an accomplished amateur cricketer. When Howlett convened a final brigade conference of his COs at the headquarters of the 5th Buffs in the hamlet of Chassert Teffaha on the morning of 22 April, it could be reasonably said that he was planning how to win the last innings of a long series of matches in the battle to capture Longstop. By the middle of April, "Swifty" Howlett was an experienced brigade commander who had led 36th Brigade for just under three months in a series of hard-fought actions. He had also briefly commanded the 139th Infantry Brigade in March, before returning to the 36th. All of Howlett's units, and particularly his infantry regiments, had seen hard fighting, sustained considerable casualties and become experienced groups. During the last six months, his three infantry battalions had spent almost the entire time in the front line, often engaged in hard fighting, and had received little rest. His old regiment, the 6th West Kents, had spent less than 20 days in reserve and resting since they landed in Algiers in November 1942. Moreover, just existing in front-line trenches during a wet Tunisian winter and on exposed terrain was a challenge in itself, without an ever-present enemy who during January and February had complete control of the skies. It was surprising that despite these rigours, morale was good; units were physically fit and generally hardened to the adverse conditions. The brigade's infantry units were now even more tired due to taking part in Operation Sweep, for their actions had been conducted on difficult terrain and led to significant casualties.

The brigade plan was developed by Howlett and his Brigade Major (his key operations and planning officer), Major John Windeatt of the Devonshire Regiment. Windeatt, perhaps inevitably known to his colleagues as "Windy", had joined the brigade from England in January 1943. He had replaced the able Major Joe Kendrew on 11 February when the latter was promoted to take over a post in First Army headquarters. Kendrew, a noted Army rugby player, later earned great fame by winning four DSOs. Windeatt, though a graduate of the Staff College, had no previous combat experience on a brigade staff. Moreover, he had recently experienced a set of unnerving events. During operations near Sedjenane the previous month, he and his brigade signals staff had been caught in the open by German Me-109 fighters which had bombed and machine-gunned them. The brigade Signals Officer, Captain Hagger, and two signallers weres killed, and Windeatt narrowly escaped the same fate. It is to his credit that this harrowing experience did not affect his subsequent performance, as he learned his job quickly and had soon proven his mettle by helping Howlett to effectively plan operations in early April. There is no doubt that he and the whole team greatly benefited from Howlett's abilities, experience, calm leadership and guidance. Windeatt himself stated:

> As a completely inexperienced Brigade Major I was very lucky to find myself in Swifty's Brigade HQ where he treated all of us as part of his family. He was a kind and tolerant man … there was never any cursing or strip tearing and as a result we all did our stuff to the best of our abilities in the most pleasant and favourable atmosphere.[1]

Howlett was a natural commander and inspiring leader, who was not a fan of long, comprehensive and written operational orders, such as those covered at Staff College. It is perhaps ironic that Howlett, probably one of the more able brigade commanders in the First Army, never attended Staff College, as it is reputed that he failed one of the entrance exams.[2] "Swifty" tended to issue only verbal orders to his battalion commanders and expected Windeatt to follow these up with a short written brief covering the main essentials. The plan for the attack used a standard format of operational orders in the British Army. It outlined the situation, i.e. the background to the operation, described the terrain, provided details of the enemy, defined the friendly forces available and finally outlined the plan. Like most good plans, Howlett's was concise and simple. The actual operational order is less than six pages long, and in view of the outcome it would have been reasonable to believe that it was the result of long and detailed planning by the brigade team. In fact, Windeatt makes clear that he, the brigade staff and Howlett were less than delighted to be assigned the task and had very limited time for planning. Despite the time allocated to create Operation Order 26 (36th Brigade's plan), the resulting document indicates that someone, probably a combination of Howlett, Evelegh and the latter's talented GSO 1, Lieutenant Colonel Reggie Hewetson, had made a careful study of the terrain. They had next worked out how it could be used by both friendly and enemy forces to influence the outcome of the battle. Since a number of attempts had previously been made to seize Longstop, it is worth devoting time to examining the 36th Brigade's ultimately successful plan to seize Longstop by starting with a key perspective, that of the terrain and the enemy.

10.2 The Terrain and the Opposition

The divisional and brigade plan showed that its architects had clearly grasped that the Germans planned to hold Longstop Hill by exploiting its natural terrain features to conduct a defence in depth. They also understood five core facts that they and the Germans had learned over four months. The first was that taking and holding Longstop Hill could only be achieved if friendly forces secured the mountains above it (see Plate V). This would deny enemy observers the ability to make the hill untenable by shelling. The Battle-Axe Division's plan addressed this factor by its earlier operations and by requiring 38th Brigade (supported by some 11th Brigade units) to take Heidous and Tanngoucha. The second key point was that any direct attack on Longstop

---

1   Windeatt, *Very Ordinary Soldier*, p.87.
2   According to his son, General Sir Geoffrey Howlett, this paper was Imperial Geography!

would be exposed to fire from the ridges and hills that lie immediately north and west of the Longstop hill complex. These are the significant hills Djebel Bechtab, which is almost directly west of Longstop, and Djebel el Ferdjane (Point 303), to its north-west. Another key feature is Point 196, a small hill which dominates the gap between Ferdjane and Longstop which gave access around the right flank of German positions on Longstop. A third point is that Longstop Hill was actually not only two hills, but a hill mass comprised of several small ridges immediately to the west and east of the main peaks, Djebel Ahmera and Rhar. Any successful attack had to take and hold each ridge in turn, and this would require more than one battalion of troops. The fourth factor is that to the south of the hill complex, the ability to outflank or bypass the hill is limited by the hamlet of Chaibane on its lower slopes and the station and village of Halte d'El Heri. This settlement and the ridge above it provide an excellent position to dominate the ground to the south-west and stop attacks to outflank the hill along the road past the river near the railroad station. The fifth and final point, now well-known to both sides and learned through past and bloody experience, was that to take Longstop, a successful attacker had to take Djebel Ahmera and cross the saddle to secure Djebel Rhar (see Plate 15).

The challenges posed by the terrain would inevitably be aggravated by the presence of the enemy. The main German unit on Longstop Hill was the 3rd Battalion of the 754th Grenadier Regiment, which had three rifle or grenadier companies and a heavy weapons company. Each company had its own integral light machine guns (usually 12 per rifle company), and its weapons company (12 Company) also possessed 12 heavy machine guns and some four to six mortars. In or near the hill, the unit had some 48 light or heavy machine guns and at least four mortars. The battalion had arrived in Tunisia at the end of December 1942, initially without two of its companies which had been lost when its ship was sunk near Naples. These companies were later replaced using reinforcements. In contrast to many other battalions in the 334th Infantry Division, who had been used in various operations, the 3rd Battalion had spent most of the last three months in one location on Longstop. It had been slightly reduced in strength, having been required to send a platoon from each of its three infantry companies (9, 10 and 11) to reinforce a unit in an attack on Hunt's Gap in early March. However, at the time of the attack it was at almost 85 percent strength and a formidable force. The battalion, largely composed of soldiers from Austria and Bavaria, was very familiar with the terrain. It had also been granted time to make extensive defensive preparations to meet any attack. In addition to the 3rd Battalion on the hill itself, at least one or two companies of the A-26 *Marsch* Battalion occupied positions on Djebel Ferdjane (Point 303) just to the north of Djebel Ahmera.

The actual strength of German forces in and around the hill is not precisely known. A good estimate is that just prior to the attack, the forces on Longstop and to its north and immediate south totalled some 800 men.[3] The unit was well protected in positions across the hill complex, for it had dug or blasted deep trenches into the rock and extended existing caves by using explosives. The Germans also built a number of protected shelters and trenches on the reverse slopes of Longstop to provide shelter from British artillery fire. According to one account, the German engineers had excavated a tunnel almost all the way through the ridge on Djebel Rhar and created a shelter for the mules which brought supplies. They also wired their positions

3   Information on German troops on Longstop was obtained from intelligence summary No. 33 in TNA WO 175/68 78 Division April 1943 WD, and No 20 in TNA WO 175/213 36 Brigade April 1943 WD.

and made extensive use of mines on all the approaches. Finally, the position was directly supported by a number of 7.5cm anti-tank guns, emplaced on or near the hill, and by at least a couple of infantry mountain guns. More importantly, German forward observers on Longstop, Tanngoucha and at Heidous could call on fire from mortars and field artillery. The former was emplaced either in positions both on Ahmera or Rhar and the latter in camouflaged positions to the rear. The Germans' artillery staff had had ample time to survey and register artillery fire concentrations to cover key approaches.

10.3 The Home Team and Windeatt's Plan

The plan for the attack at both divisional and brigade level recognised the nature of the German defences and that they were held in depth. It assigned the whole of the 36th Brigade to the task, and also the 1st East Surreys. The remaining units of 11th Brigade were held in reserve locations vacated by Howlett's battalions. Howlett and his staff therefore had all his battalions available, though they were all understrength and very tired from constant operations. Howlett had been allocated operational command of the 1st East Surreys and of course the Churchill tanks of the 1st North Irish Horse Regiment of the 25th Tank Brigade. David Dawnay assigned all the squadrons of his regiment to direct support of the attack. He also had his attached RE Company, the 256th Field Company RE, and medical aid provided by 217th Field Ambulance RAMC. Finally, because of the minefields, the brigade was assigned three specially adapted Valentine tanks known as Scorpions, designed to clear mines using a set of metal chains rotating on a steel barrel, the forerunner of the famous flail tanks used on the Normandy Beaches.

Windeatt's plan recognised all the key factors described earlier, and especially the fact that the German defences were in-depth. It clearly showed that Howlett and Windeatt had grasped the need to progressively seize and hold key features. Their plan was to capture Longstop Hill in two phases, starting with a night attack. The first phase of the attack would start at 2100 hours, well after darkness had fallen, and was designed to reduce the effectiveness of the formidable German defences on Longstop. Most armies today are well-equipped with highly effective night vision devices, so it is easy to forget that this was not the case in 1943 for both British and German units. Darkness could be a friend and foe. For example, attacks at night were more difficult and could easily lead to confusion, but they also made surprise easier and could reduce the effects of enemy fire. The initial moves of the brigade attack would commence with the 5th Buffs starting their approach and attack on Djebel Bechtab and Point 303 on the left flank and the 6th West Kents taking Djebel Chaibane on the lower slopes of Ahmera on the right. These events would take place stealthily, but the final stages of the advance would be assisted by heavy artillery support. The aim was to take or neutralise positions to the north and south of Djebel Ahmera which otherwise could cause casualties with flanking fire to the units actually attacking Ahmera.

Once these positions were in British hands, phase two of the plan would be executed. In this phase of 36th Brigade's operation, the task of seizing Djebel Ahmera was originally assigned to Heygate's 6th West Kents, while Colin McNabb's 8th Argylls was to come up behind the 6th West Kents and go on to capture Djebel Rhar. The plan was designed to ensure that past errors were avoided and that both the key features of Longstop - Ahmera and Rhar - were captured on the same night. The third phase of the operation would begin once Longstop was taken, and required the commitment of the 1st East Surreys, the 5th Buffs, a section of sappers, two squadrons of the North Irish Horse and three Scorpion tanks. The East Surreys' first task was to advance to the south of Longstop, clear and open the road near Halte de Heri. The 5th Buffs would go on to advance about 1,000 metres to the north of Ahmera and Rhar to take two hills. The North Irish Horse would have the task of providing a squadron of Churchills to support the West Kents in mopping up on Longstop, while two squadrons would be available to deal with any counterattack. If this did not emerge, they were to assist the East Surreys and the Buffs in their advances. Operational Order No. 26 assumed that the attacks would be preceded by significant artillery support in the form of concentrated shelling of specific areas by an artillery group, and additional fire could be called upon if required. The gunners' plan for the attack on Longstop was comprehensive and will be considered later.

In summary, Windeatt's plan demonstrated that many lessons had been learned since the first attack on Longstop over four months earlier. A reinforced brigade would be used to provide sufficient infantry to seize and hold the whole Longstop hill area against any subsequent counterattack. The operation would have the support of a Churchill tank regiment, which could also stop any armoured counterattack. Moreover, in contrast to the original attack by the Coldstream Guards, the attackers would be supported by not just one but several regiments of artillery. Given the time allowed, it was a fairly sound plan, but as is so often the case, what the famous Clausewitz called the friction of war would prevent its smooth execution.[4]

10.4 36th Brigade Activities and Preparations

While Howlett and Windeatt were completing their plan for the attack on Longstop Hill, the units that would carry it out had varying levels of time to prepare for their role. After it had captured Mergueb Chaouach, the 8th Argylls had held its positions for two days before being allowed one day of rest and afterwards being shifted to occupy a new location near Djebel Mansourine (Point 624, east of Point 667). Based on the time the unit had spent on the front line, this new location could almost be counted as peaceful. It was, however, close enough to German positions to require vigilance and to receive the occasional shelling. The battalion had no contact with the Germans during the first five days of its sojourn in this area, but this changed on 16 April. Someone decided that the Argylls needed to be more active, and Y Company, under the command of Major Jack Anderson, was sent out to find out what the enemy was doing. He led a patrol which confirmed that the area to the north of the Argylls' positions was held by a German unit. The following day, Y Company, again led by Anderson, supported by a platoon of X Company, was sent out on the same route towards two features north-west of Djebel Bou Diss. The ensuing action between Y Company and a well-established German unit need not be described here, but was memorable for Anderson's unit not least due to the casualty list. Y Company was hard hit, and in a short bitter skirmish lost three dead, 10 wounded and nine missing in action: later investigation showed that all nine men reported as missing had been killed. This unfortunate loss was aggravated due to the fact that among those killed were four veteran NCOs, including two - Sergeant McInnis and Corporal Williamson - who had recently won MMs. The incident was noteworthy for two reasons: first, the extreme

---

4   Operational Order No. 26 dated 21 April 1943 is the 36th Brigade plan for the Longstop attack, which is in TNA WO 175/213 36 Brigade April 1943 WD.

courage displayed by Jack Anderson, Corporal Williamson and also another Highlander, Private William Irvine. The two men attacked three German positions until Williamson was killed, while Irvine displayed great courage acting as a Bren gunner in the same action. The second reason was Anderson's personal bitterness on being ordered to carry out a fruitless and unnecessary attack which led to the deaths of valuable men. He concluded a six-page report on the incident with the following:

> This attack seems to me a typical example of how the best men in a company can be dissipated in some small operation which has no definite end in view, and serves no useful purpose. I lost an officer and 5 NCOS who have been quite irreplaceable, as well as some of the bravest men in the company; we gained nothing but a certain amount of unwanted kudos and a rebellious attitude to all futile operations such as this was.[5]

After the tragic action of 17 April, the battalion spent a further three days in its positions before being relieved by another unit. It was perhaps a sign of the problems of the overstretched Battle-Axe Division that the only battalion that could be provided to relieve the Argylls in their positions was the severely weakened 2nd Lancs Fusiliers. The Argylls marched to Toukabeur, where they had one day's rest and time for baths before moving to their assembly area for the attack on Longstop.

Meanwhile, Heygate's West Kents had maintained a rather lonely but comparatively undisturbed grip on Djebel Bou Diss and its surrounding area until they had been relieved by the Argylls. They took over the Argylls' positions on Point 624 before being moved to Toukabeur on 20 April, and thence to their forming up location for the Longstop operation. The West Kents benefitted from the longest period away from the front line of all three battalions in the 36th Brigade, yet that lasted only three days. The second battalion in the brigade, the 5th Buffs, had spent the six days that followed their abortive attack on Heidous in a series of company positions dispersed north of the village of Chaouach. The battalion was located in a position designed to protect many of the artillery batteries and other supply units clustered around Chaouach. It too had a relatively uneventful period, apart from being shelled on two occasions, but it did not get a proper rest. All this juggling of understrength infantry units enabled Evelegh to create the conditions necessary to prepare for the very difficult proposition of undertaking the projected attack on Longstop Hill. Howlett's brigade was now reassembled, as both the 5th Buffs and 6th West Kents had been returned to his control. It was also reinforced with an additional battalion of infantry, with the 1st East Surreys under his command.

10.5 Making a Lot of Noise

A critical component of the plan was the provision of bountiful artillery support throughout all stages of the operation. A few days prior to Operation Vulcan, John Darcy-Dawson, a correspondent for the *Daily Herald*, interviewed Brigadier Pratt, the Chief Corps Royal Artillery Officer (CCRA) for V Corps. Dawson asked him if he had enough guns for the upcoming

---

5   See Report of Action of 17 April 1943 by John Anderson in TNA WO 175/491 8th Argylls April 1943 WD.

operation. Pratt smiled as he replied: "No Gunner ever has enough guns but we have enough guns to make a lot of noise."[6] Pratt's response to Dawson was almost certainly carefully phrased, as he was all too aware that the forthcoming operation would place major demands on available artillery support. The gunners first had to support 38th Brigade's attack on Tanngoucha, then 36th Brigade's attack on Longstop and finally the attacks by the 1st and 4th Infantry Divisions south of Medjez el Bab. These conflicting demands on artillery required the gunners to carefully plan and allocate the available fire support. This required Brigadier Wedderburn-Maxwell and his staff to plan how to place the artillery units assigned to the 78th Division in locations from which they could quickly bring down large amounts of shells on a range of different targets. As a result, at least three field regiments and a medium regiment were ordered to move at night to new locations east of Toukabeur. All this activity took take place on the night of 21/22 April, 24 hours before the attack was scheduled, and led to some pretty tired gunners. To support concurrent attacks on Longstop and Tanngoucha, Wedderburn-Maxwell had managed to put together another artillery group similar to that which started Operation Sweep. He appointed to command this group one of his more experienced commanders, Lieutenant Colonel G.A. "Tommy" Thomas of 17th Field Regiment. Thomas, his deputy Major Peter Pettit and the regiment had arrived in Tunisia in late December 1942 as part of 1st Guards Brigade. It had not been involved in the original attack on Longstop on Christmas Eve, but the regiment had quickly established an excellent reputation for its professionalism in a series of later battles. Wedderburn-Maxwell's decision to appoint Thomas to command this vital task reflected not only his confidence in his abilities but also that of more senior commanders, who had already determined that Thomas should be moved to a more important role. As a result, the command of the artillery group for Longstop would end up being Thomas' last job as CO of 17th Field Regiment. Immediately after the operation was concluded, Thomas discovered he was to move at very short notice to take up the important appointment of GSO 1 of the 4th Infantry Division just south of Medjez. If this was to be Thomas last task as a CO, then to use a terrible pun, he certainly went out with a bang! The artillery group assembled for the Longstop Hill attack included five 25-pounder artillery regiments: the 17th, 23rd, 132nd, 138th and 166th Field Regiments, plus 457 Light Battery. In addition to the 25-pounders, Thomas also had at his disposal the 5.5in guns of the 4th Medium Regiment and batteries of the 56th Heavy Regiment.

By coincidence, Thomas' last artillery mission would be aided by those two future Goons; Bombardier Harry Secombe from 132nd Field Regiment and Lance Bombardier Spike Milligan, who was serving in 56th Heavy Regiment. These two characters had met each other in what can only be termed Goon-like circumstances. During an operation in March 1943, Secombe was sleeping in a lorry near Le Kef when there was a tremendous crash outside. This was caused by an accident in which a 7.2in artillery gun had effectively blown itself off a cliff and landed near his lorry. Secombe's first introduction to his fellow Goon came when Milligan threw back the canvas cover of the lorry and shouted: "Anybody, seen a gun?" In classic Goon-like humour, Secombe responded immediately with "what colour!".[7] Newly promoted Bombardier Milligan was lucky not to end up in a POW camp at this time, for on the night of 21/22 April his regiment managed to lose yet another gun, this time to enemy action. One of the batteries of

---

6   Quotation is from John Dawson, *Tunisian Battle*, p.209.
7   Harry Seccombe, *Arias and Raspberries Volume 1: an Autobiography* (London: Robson Books, 1989), p.97.

Milligan's regiment was overrun when the Germans launched Operation Lilac Blossom. It lost a 7.2in gun, while two officers and 46 men were taken prisoner. Fortunately for Milligan, he did not serve in either of the two batteries that lost men captured.

The amount of artillery assigned to Thomas' group may seem a great deal, but it was probably much less than he would have wanted, for he had to support attacks against two very well-defended objectives. Another problem was that the 23rd and 166th Field Artillery and 56th Heavy Regiments were only available to provide support for four hours between 2200 hours on 22 April and 0200 hours on 23 April. His group also included one regiment, the 138th, which was fully committed to the support of 38th Irish Brigade's attacks on Point 622, Tanngoucha and Butler's Hill. Unfortunately, due to the wider attack planned under Operation Vulcan, it was not possible to use the artillery regiments of any other divisions. Although limited in the number of units, Thomas' fire plan was designed to ensure that he gained the maximum effect on the Germans. His plan achieved this by ensuring that the guns he controlled were liberally supplied with ammunition, which required the RASC to move large amounts of shells and dump them near to each gun battery. This demanding task provided a total of 400 rounds per gun for each 25-pounder, 300 for the medium 5.5in guns and 75 for the large 7.2in guns. It was a tiring couple of days for the gunners, as having moved during darkness on 21/22 April, they spent 22 April unloading and safely stacking the heavy shells and their charges.[8]

One additional fire-support asset was available: the use of tactical bombing. It was a method that until recently had not been employed in direct support of local ground operations against a specific target, as many senior RAF commanders believed this was not an appropriate use of their light bombers. However, on 28 March, South African-manned Boston bombers were used to attack specific enemy positions in a direct support mission for the Eighth Army with excellent effects. The air plan in support of Vulcan thus included a specific mission to bomb Longstop Hill. It was not the first time Longstop had been bombed, for on 14 and 17 April bombers had already attacked the hill. As part of Vulcan, Longstop had now become a priority target. The task was assigned to 18 and 114 Squadrons of 242 Group, and at 0945 hours on 21 April, 24 Boston bombers dropped their loads on Longstop Hill. It is not clear what, if any, effects this may have had on the garrison, as they were well dug in, but it may have improved the morale of British troops.

The strenuous efforts of Lieutenant Colonel Thomas and the hard-working officers and gunners of his units were, however, amply rewarded. Starting at 2000 hours on 22 April, the guns of five field, one medium and one heavy regiments of the Royal Artillery created what Brigadier Pratt had promised to Darcy-Dawson, "a great deal of noise". Just to add to the drama of the event, the night sky was lit up at about 1900 hours, just before the artillery started an hour later, by an electric storm, with lightning flashing across the mountains. There was no thunder, but commencing on the dot at 2000 hours, a total of 158 guns quickly provided this missing element. This initial fire support was delivered to assist the 38th Irish Brigade attack on Tanngoucha and Heidous. There was a short pause, and at 2200 hours the guns opened up in support of 36th Brigade's attack. The fire plan required over 900 shells to descend on enemy positions on Longstop and the surrounding German positions. The shells were to be delivered

8   See V Corps RA Operation Order 1 dated 19 April 1943 in WO TNA 175.86 V Corps CRA WD April 1943.

in 20 minutes of pre-planned concentrations fired on enemy positions by the four field and one medium regiments of the Royal Artillery. It was followed by a quick barrage on the Longstop Hill complex by the 17th and 132nd Field Regiments. The original plan assumed a pause of one hour and 15 minutes to enable the Argylls to close up and carry out the final assault, but as will be shown, this was not required. At the appointed hour, observers in the hills above Longstop at Chaouach watched as the Longstop Hill complex and other hills erupted in a cloud of flame and smoke caused by the barrage. By this time the troops of the leading units had started their approach march. The German reaction to this artillery barrage was to fire multi-coloured Verey lights into the sky and commence a degree of counter-shelling. When this happened, the troops of the leading units of 36th Brigade had already left their start lines and were well on the way to their objectives. The German troops on Longstop had over four months to dig in and had numerous caves and other shelters to protect them from artillery fire. Nonetheless, the barrage must have had some impact on their morale. A clerk from the battalion headquarters of the 3rd Battalion of the 754th Grenadier Regiment was present, and when he was later interrogated by an intelligence officer he described the barrage in the following terms: "About 2100, an artillery barrage opened up … none of us have ever seen the like before, even in Russia and so it went on all night long."[9] The most important contribution of the barrage was that it kept most of the troops on Djebel Ahmera and surrounding ridges in their dugouts and other shelters, and prevented them from initially responding to the advance.

10.6 5th Buffs' Attack on Djebels Bechtab and El Ferdjane

The 5th Buffs were allocated the task of attacking three key features that lay to the north of Djebel Ahmera. These were Djebel Bechtab (Point 284), an unnamed hill called Point 196 to the east of Bechtab and Djebel el Ferdjane (Point 303). The latter hill overlooked the highest point of Longstop and could pose a threat to any attack on Ahmera. The battalion, which was still commanded by "Ginger" McKechnie, was both understrength and very tired. As described, it had completed a series of demanding operations over the last two weeks, especially the struggle to take and hold Hill 667. Brigadier Howlett was very much aware that it should have a rest, and was not happy that 11th Brigade had insisted they carry out what had proved to be the unsuccessful attack on Heidous. According to his Brigade Major, John Windeatt, Howlett, "was very angry about the whole business, as the Buffs were exhausted before the battle started and we had been trying to give them a rest". He was not alone in his view, as Windeatt also related on 21 April: "On the way back from the forward defence lines two Buffs privates asked Swifty if they could have word with him and proceeded to tell him that the troops are dead beat and couldn't do another attack." It speaks volumes about Howlett's standing as a commander with his troops, that two private soldiers felt able to approach him directly and raise such concerns. What the two privates could not know was that both Howlett and Windeatt shared their fears, as the latter stated in his memoirs: "We know how damned tired they are but they've got to go in again."[10] All that Howlett could do was listen, which he did, but still require them to carry

---

9   The description is from Intelligence summary No. 148 in TNA WO 175/82 V Corps G Branch April 1943 WD.

10   See Windeatt, *Very Ordinary Soldier*, pp.41-43, for the quotations.

out the attack. He must have known that all the battalions in both his and the other brigades were all exhausted and long overdue a rest.

McKechnie's plan for the operation was to be carried out at night and in three phases. Djebel Bechtab was first to be taken by two rifle companies. The capture of Bechtab would be followed by an attack by the two remaining companies on both Point 196 and Point 303. It was important that each of the three main features were secured one after the other. The 5th Buffs had moved from its positions near Chaouach to new ones just north and east of Chassert Teffaha on 21 April, and had laid up in a gully just to the north of the hamlet on 22 April. Just after dark at 2015 hours, Colonel McKechnie took the sensible precaution of sending A Company to take and hold a small ridge north-east of the village which directly overlooked the battalion's start line. This also placed A Company just across from Djebel Bechtab, which meant that it simply joined in with the rest of the battalion as it went into the attack. The Buffs' advance from their start line commenced at 2115 hours, led by D Company on the left and B Company on the right, advancing to attack Djebel Bechtab. The battalion moved forward quietly until 2200 hours, when a heavy 20-minute artillery concentration was placed on the hill and surrounding area. This was followed by a further 40-minute barrage on Point 284. Both companies then came under heavy machine-gun and mortar fire, but by 0230 hours, and despite German opposition, Djebel Bechtab was in their hands and a number of prisoners taken. Colonel McKechnie left A Company to mop up the hill and then sent B and C Companies on to seize Points 196 and 303. They succeeded in doing this without difficulty by 0530 hours. The battalion now dug in, consolidated its positions and held them for the rest of the day. The seizure of these two key objectives was a fine piece of work by the 5th Buffs, as it required a night attack over relatively open terrain which had been held for some time. The men of the Buffs had no way of knowing whether or not the approaches were heavily mined or if the objectives were strongly held. The seizure of these positions to the north ensured that the Germans could not reinforce Longstop from its positions in Heidous. It also provided the battalion and its artillery observers with excellent views of the northern slopes of Longstop and to the east. There was of course a price to be paid for securing the new positions, and while it may have seemed rather a small one, this was probably no comfort for the parents and other relatives of the three private soldiers and one lance corporal who were killed on 23 April. Sadly, the lance corporal who lost his life was Walter Weaver, who had only recently won, but not yet received, his MM, awarded for his actions on Djebel Nahel less than two weeks previously.

10.7 The 6th West Kents' Opening Overs

The 5th Buffs was not the only unit that was tired and understrength prior to the attack on the night of 22/23 April. The 6th West Kents' losses on Djebel Bou Diss had been considerable. In the absence of reinforcements, the battalion strengthened its rifle companies for the attack with clerks, cooks and storemen from its headquarters. Even after this change, the rifle companies were less than 60 strong, when normally they would have over 120 men. The battalion moved from its original position in a gully south-east of the village of Chaouach on 21 April and spent the next day resting out of sight of the Germans. On the evening of 22 April it moved up a single lined track through minefields to its start line on a track junction just east of Chassert Teffaha. The battalion's task was to attack from Chassert Teffaha to the north-east via Point 139, seize Djebel bech Chaibane and then the hamlet of Hadj Ajred (see Plate VIII). These two objectives were located south and south-west of Djebel Ahmera and could be considered outer defences for that feature. The plan assumed that Heygate's battalion could capture these objectives under cover of the artillery by about 2300 hours. The 6th West Kents were to consolidate their positions and the 8th Argylls would have enough time to come up. The original brigade plan required another artillery barrage to be fired on Longstop Hill, starting at 0015 hours. The 6th West Kents would attack Djebel Ahmera and the 8th Argylls Djebel Rhar, commencing at 0030 hours. There is an old military idiom which states thaty the devil is always in the details, and this certainly proved true for the brigade plan, for the flaw in the detail of Windeatt and Howlett's plan was arguably its schedule for operations. This in turn was determined by the requirement that Longstop be taken by 0200 hours that morning which had been imposed upon them by Allfrey and by Evelegh in their respective operational orders. The need to comply with his superiors' orders meant that Howlett's planning flexibility was severely curtailed. It is possible Howlett understood the likely difficulty of capturing Longstop by 0200 hours, as his own orders avoided specifying a time for the capture of Ahmera and Rhar. In retrospect, it is evident that the timetable imposed for the attack on Longstop, and especially its first phase, the assault on Chaibane, was far too tight. The 6th West Kents had less than a couple of hours to move in the darkness from their start line, cross two miles of open fields and two dry river gullies, then attack and capture what was likely to be a well-defended location. The battalion had to mop up and within an hour and 15 minutes be prepared to go on to attack Djebel Ahmera, and also pass McNabb's battalion through them. All this was to be carried out with an understrength unit and at night. It was perhaps too much to ask of Heygate and his men ,and this in fact proved to be the case.

At first all seemed to go well, for the start line for the attack, a track just 300 yards east of Chassert Teffaha, was secured by a fighting patrol from the 6th West Kents without any problems. Heygate launched his attack exactly on time, starting at 2115 hours with C Company on the left, its objective the hamlet of Bir Hadj Ajred, and D Company attacking Djebel Chaibane on the right. The battalion headquarters and B Company followed the attacking companies. The leading companies achieved a degree of surprise and were not immediately detected, but soon afterwards it all started to go wrong. As they approached their objectives, both companies encountered problems from booby traps, barbed wire, machine guns and mortars. On the left, C Company, which was advancing towards Hadj Ajred, at first lost its way and attacked the wrong position, before realising its mistake and attacking the correct one. It was unable to reach its objective because of heavy German machine-gun fire and was forced to withdraw to a gully close by. D Company was able to cross both river gullies and despite the heavy machine-gun fire reached Djebel Chaibane and the small cluster of houses on its north-west slope. Despite numerous booby traps in the houses, D Company fought its way into the small hamlet but was unable to make further progress. During the attack on Chaibane, Ronald Lingham, though only a private, was commanding the lead section of his company when it encountered the main strongpoint on the hill, which had five machine guns. Despite the murderous fire, Lingham led his section against the strongpoint and did not stop attacking it until all of his men were killed or wounded in front of a barbed wire emplacement. Lingham personally dragged clear some of his soldiers from the obstacle and sent them back for medical aid. He continued to provide a great example to others during the rest of the attack. For his gallantry that night, Lingham was awarded the MM and later promoted to corporal.[11]

German resistance, particularly on Chaibane, proved to be too strong for Heygate's companies to overcome; D Company's position became untenable, so they were forced to withdraw, as were C Company. As the struggle continued and the hours passed from dark to dawn, it became evident that the second phase of the attack on Ahmera and Rhar could not be carried out in darkness. The 6th West Kents had not secured Chaibane, therefore it had not been possible to call forward McNabb's battalion. Heygate and his unit were, however, positioned at the foot of Djebel Chaibane and, according to the battalion war diary, just after dawn a second attempt was made to go forward, with limited success. There is something of a mystery around what the 6th West Kents did on the morning of 23 April. They appear to have had some support from the North Irish Horse's tanks, which enabled them to hold positions in a gully near to Chaibane or the hill itself. What does seem clear from available sources is that the battalion could not fulfil the second part of its mission, the capture of Djebel Ahmera, and spent the rest of the morning and early afternoon reorganising in positions near Chaibane. By now all surprise had been lost, and the German defenders on Longstop were fully alert and reacting in a most unfriendly fashion. Howlett's original plan, which had been to capture the whole of Longstop Hill by daylight, had unravelled and he had, to use a cricketing term, lost his first innings.[12]

11   The MM citation for Ronald Lingham is in TNA WO 373/1.
12   The story of the night attack of the 6th West Kents is derived from the battalion war diary for April 1943 and Chaplin, *West Kents*, pp.238-39.

11

Howlett's Second Innings at Longstop Hill

11.1 No Plan Survives

An old military saying states that no plan survives contact with the enemy, and certainly on the morning of 24 April Brigadier Howlett's original plan was no exception to this rule. While the attack of the 5th Buffs was successful, the advance of the 6th West Kents had foundered in the face of tenacious opposition and firepower from the 3rd Battalion of the 754th Grenadier Regiment in its fortifications on Djebel Ahmera and the surrounding area. Being such a keen cricketer, Howlett was well aware that a setback on the wicket during the opening innings could be reversed by good batting in the second. Just after daylight, at about 0600 hours, Howlett moved his brigade command post up to Chassert Teffaha from its previous location to get a better understanding of what was happening. He brought with him not only his brigade staff but also "Tommy" Thomas, his artillery commander. Howlett and his Brigade Major, Windeatt, quickly reappraised the situation before they devised and issued a new plan. Howlett turned to his remaining battalion, the 8th Argylls, to continue the attack. He was an excellent judge of the relative strengths and weaknesses of the battalions in his brigade. His style of command meant that he tended to spend much of his time well forward with his units as he always liked to be close to the front, and as a result frequently incurred his GOC's displeasure for being out of radio contact. Moreover, having served alongside the Argylls in tough fighting further to the north near Djebel Aboid and commanded the battalion as brigadier of the 139th Infantry Brigade near Sedjenane, he was familiar with their fighting spirit. He knew that they were capable of conducting what would be a very difficult attack against a well-defended position. In April 1943, Djebel Ahmera was covered in scrub that looked like the gorse of the Scottish Highlands. Photographs of the hill show that in 1943 it looked very like one of the rugged hills of Caithness and Sutherland. The 8th Argylls was composed of Highlanders who by tradition were disposed to terrifying their enemies in a fierce charge. It could be said they were well suited to both the task and terrain. In reality, Howlett was aware that although the Argylls may have been well matched to the role, the unpleasant fact was he had very little choice but to use them as he had no other units available. He knew that the 6th West Kents had been reduced in strength to the equivalent of just two rifle companies, and were also tired and understrength as a result of their recent operations. Although Howlett had run out of options and had to use the Argylls to break the deadlock, it was a case of having the right unit in the right place at the right time. He intended that the 8th Argylls be closely supported in the follow-up role by his only uncommitted battalion, the 1st East Surreys.

The brigade plan did not, however, rely alone on the raw courage and fighting spirit of the Highlanders and the East Surreys alone. Howlett was well aware that a lack of cover on the wheat fields close to Ahmera, combined with preregistered German artillery and mortars, created an ideal killing ground. Some 60 years later, little has changed in the area; the lack of cover and subsequent exposure to direct and indirect fire is apparent to any visitor with imagination. He therefore looked to one predictable asset and another surprise one to provide the battalion with the necessary edge to limit potential casualties and propel the Highlanders on to and up the hill. The first was the use of concentrated artillery, while the second was the deployment of tanks in direct support. At 0800 hours on 24 April, Howlett went forward in a Churchill to see the situation personally and met with his artillery and tank commanders; "Tommy" Thomas and Lieutenant Colonel Dawnay of the North Irish Horse. Thomas and his staff started to arrange a new artillery plan for an attack planned for 0930 hours, which was subsequently delayed to 1130 hours. At the same time, Dawnay talked to his staff about providing support to both the embattled West Kents and the Argylls. Dawnay and his regiment had only just arrived near Chassert Teffaha at first light, having moved from their previous location near Oued Zarga at 1930 hours the previous evening. Their journey had been both a frustrating and cold one, as it had encountered several traffic jams and created one of its own. The leading tank had been disabled by an anti-tank mine and briefly blocked the road until it could be moved. The regiment was also delayed by other vehicle traffic which it encountered on the single track to Chassert Teffaha. It was very fortunate that the hold-up which ensued was not detected by the Germans and was cleared before daylight. After his discussion with Howlett, Dawnay assigned B and C Squadrons of the North Irish Horse to provide direct support on the right, southern end of Ahmera to help the West Kents secure Djebel Chaibane. These two squadrons moved off quickly at about 0800 hours, and according to two accounts were instrumental in silencing some machine guns that were holding up Heygate's companies (see Plate 17).

11.2 Enter McNabb

Tank and artillery support would help, but fundamentally the only way Djebel Ahmera could be taken was by men on the ground, and that meant infantry. The task of leading the unit across the bare corn fields and taking the hill fell to the new CO of the 8th Argylls, Lieutenant Colonel Colin McNabb. The 39-year-old officer had assumed command of the battalion three weeks previously, having willingly taken a demotion of two ranks from his last role as Brigadier General Staff to First Army commander Kenneth Anderson, just to get command of a battalion. The Argylls' new boss had already shown his mettle five weeks before as General Anderson's liaison officer to the Allied forces at Thala. These units had subsequently slowed and stopped the hitherto successful *Afrika Korps* attack surging north from Kasserine pass. However, in one of his first acts as the new CO, McNabb did little to impress his new command. He called a conference of his officers and read from a First Army pamphlet entitled 'The Principles of Training in Battle' which was designed to help keep officers and men on their toes. McNabb insisted that the battalion, by now a veteran unit (which had received little or no rest recently), begin battle training. According to Major John "Hamish" Taylor, the second-in-command, McNabb's proposals were poorly received by his veteran company commanders, who felt that what their troops really needed was a short rest rather than retraining. In a most unusual move, a delegation of officers went to see Taylor and he was told in no uncertain terms to get the CO to stop this drilling and give the battalion a brief rest.

The leader of the delegation was the tall, dark but quiet commander of Y Company, Acting Major John "Jack" McKellar Anderson. At 26 years old, Anderson was relatively young to be a company commander, but like many other similar officers in the First Army he had gained experience the hard way. Anderson had arrived in France near Le Havre on 10 June 1940 as a second lieutenant leading a party of reinforcements, had spent exactly two days on the Continent and only narrowly escaped becoming a prisoner. He was born in January 1918 and spent his first years in Scotland until his parents moved to London. Two of his uncles on his mother's side of the family served and were killed in Highland regiments during the First World War. He was educated at Stowe public school in Buckinghamshire in the early 1930s. In one of those rare and unusual coincidences, he had shared his room with another schoolboy with whom he became close friends. They had a common interest in flying, and Anderson actually went on to learn to fly at the Royal Aero Club and gain his pilot's licence as early as 1935. The name of his close friend was Leonard Cheshire and he too would become a pilot, go on to join the RAF and become one of the most highly decorated bomber pilots of the Second World War. The two men would have one more thing in common, for both would win the Victoria Cross. After finishing his education at Stowe, Anderson moved on to Trinity College, Cambridge, and had completed a degree in History and Modern Languages by 1939. When war was declared he joined the Army as a soldier, but was rapidly sent to an OCTU and was commissioned in March 1940. He asked to join a Highland regiment because of his uncles, and was sent to the 8th Argylls. Anderson's qualities were quickly recognised during the two years of hard training that followed his short stay in France, and he was soon promoted. He also found time to get married and have a daughter before leaving for Tunisia in November 1942. He survived the difficult battles of the first two months, and by March 1943 was commanding Y Company as acting major. Anderson was highly respected by his men and was especially well known for his coolness under fire. He had only recently won an immediate DSO for his bravery during a difficult action at Hunt's Gap in March. There were some members of the battalion who felt that he had actually deserved to be awarded a VC instead. It had also been Anderson who had recently commanded Y Company so courageously during its unfortunate action on 17 April. While strict as a company commander, he also cared about his men. Hardly a rebel, nonetheless he was almost certainly the leader of the officer delegation to Major Taylor. Fortunately, Hamish Taylor intervened with his new CO, who sensibly relented and agreed the unit should have some rest, though it also did some training.

McNabb decision's may have been influenced by the fact that in his previous role at First Army headquarters, he had often been the staff officer responsible for issuing orders that moved the unit from one crisis to another. He would have been more aware than most of the relentless pace of operations it had endured. It was to McNabb's great credit as a person and as a new CO that he had listened to Taylor and his officers. Some new and inexperienced commanders would have viewed this move as a threat to their authority and reacted very negatively. McNabb, though somewhat dour as a person, was humble enough to admit when he was wrong. On the morning of the attack on Longstop, as he and his command team were about to assault

Longstop, he said to Taylor: "Do you remember the First Army Training in Battle [pamphlet]? – Taylor said he did. McNabb then said 'it is all balls and I wrote it'."[1]

11.3 The Argylls and East Surreys Move Up

The 8th Argylls' original role in Howlett's plan was to lie up during phase one and next pass through the 6th West Kents, once Chaibane had been taken, to commence a night attack on Djebel Ahmera. Howlett now asked McNabb and his Highlanders to carry out the same attack except in daylight and without a secure start line. The battalion moved up during the night of 21 April into gullies about a mile west of Chassert Teffaha, along with the other battalions of the brigade. The decision to move the Argylls and the other battalions into gullies, which were located in no man's land, was taken by Howlett himself. It was a calculated risk, since the move could have been discovered had the Germans sent out patrols, but fortunately they did not. The unit laid up in these gullies during the night of 21/ 22 April. At about 1900 hours, a mule convoy with the Argylls' heavy weapons and reserve ammunition moved off from Chaouach and joined the rifle companies by about 2030 hours. Forty-five minutes later, the lead companies marched off in the darkness and carried out their approach march, passing in single file through Chassert Teffaha early in the morning. The only noise that could be heard was the harness and creaking of the heavy loads of the mule parties. By 0200 hours, the battalion was lying up in the long corn on the flat fields a mile to the west of Longstop, waiting for the initial attack to be concluded. Unfortunately, it soon became obvious that the first phase of the attack had not been successful and that the Argylls would not be attacking that night. As daylight came, the unit moved into the gully to the north, out of sight of Germans observation, or so they thought. The location was overlooked by Djebel Bechtab (Point 284), which had been one of the objectives of the 5th Buffs. As a precautionary move, Y Company was ordered to send a platoon up to secure the hill. When the platoon arrived, it found the hill still had some German occupants, but it quickly attacked and soon afterwards 25 Germans surrendered. It is not clear how these individuals escaped the attention of the 5th Buffs, but it was night and things were confused so such events could easily occur. The platoon soon handed over the position to a party from the 5th Buffs and returned to the gully. The next few hours, from about 0400 to 1000 hours, were spent sheltering in the gully and being occasionally shelled, though with mercifully few casualties.

While the Argylls were trying to shelter near Djebel Chaibane, Bill Wilberforce and the 1st East Surreys were waiting in their own assembly area just west of Chassert Teffaha and were about to learn that their role in the Longstop attack had changed. Originally, the battalion was expected to carry out the third phase of the attack by advancing and capturing Halte De Hieri before moving up the Tebourba road, but this plan had been overtaken by events. The East Surreys had spent the daytime of 22 April having a brief but uncomfortable rest in heavy rain near Toukabeur. They left that night and enjoyed the relative luxury of a two-hour trip by lorry before arriving close to Howlett's headquarters at Ferme Rahal, two miles from Chassert Teffaha. The battalion received a poor welcome, for the companies had hardly left their vehicles before four men were wounded by stepping on S mines. The East Surreys marched up the crowded track to Chassert Teffaha to be further welcomed by mortar fire and artillery airbursts

---

1   Hamish Taylor, *Unpublished Memoirs*, p.26.

from a heavy German gun as they reached their assembly area in a cactus orchard at 0300 hours on 23 April. The troops spent the next few hours as close to the ground as possible, avoiding both German fire and cactus thorns, and managed by some miracle to suffer no further casualties. At 0750 hours, Wilberforce and his staff became aware that the plan was changing when they heard that the West Kents had not been able to clear the original start line for the Argylls' attack near Chaibane. Soon afterwards, Wilberforce and Harry Smith went to hear Howlett outlining his plan and orders for the next attack on Longstop at his command post in the farmhouse at Chassert Teffaha against the noisy background of heavy enemy shelling. It had only just concluded when Wilberforce suddenly collapsed, though he had not been wounded: he had fallen victim to an attack of muscular cramp which completely incapacitated him, and he had just enough time to hand over his marked map to Smith and tell him to assume command of the battalion, but didn't provide any details of their forthcoming task. Howlett had probably ordered Wilberforce to follow the Argylls and support them once they had carried out their attack on Djebel Ahmera, and also to go on to capture Djebel Rhar.

Smith later wrote that in the absence of information, he carried out a personal reconnaissance using a Bren Gun Carrier under heavy and accurate shellfire, to find his leading companies near to Djebel Bechtab. He observed a white tomb on a small feature which he suspected to be an enemy artillery observation post, so he ordered one of his companies to capture this first. The attack took place at 1130 hours, but very quickly bogged down due to intense enemy shelling and was stopped. It appears that about 30 minutes later, the whole battalion began their advance, moving up behind the Argylls, this time under the leadership of Wilberforce, who amazingly had managed to recover. Before describing what happened to the East Surreys, it is appropriate to relate the experience of McNabb and the 8th Argylls as they led the assault on Djebel Ahmera.

11.4 The Highlanders Advance

Sometime in the morning, McNabb had a meeting with Howlett, who briefly explained the situation and, no doubt reluctantly, ordered McNabb and the Argylls to attack Djebel Ahmera at about 1130 hours. McNabb's battalion was to be followed in its advance by the 1st East Surreys, who by now were located nearby. One of the factors driving the decision to attack so quickly was that the Germans were shelling the Argylls' forming-up area and tracks. Another problem was that having already fired one artillery concentration on Longstop early that morning, "Tommy" Thomas had been asked to fire a second one, but was forced to delay it for two hours. Thomas knew that given the amount of preparation required to fire the barrage, he could not easily delay it again. The revised plan for the Argylls' frontal attack was hazardous, for it would have to be carried out in daylight, in full view of German observers not only on Djebel Ahmera, but also on Tanngoucha and Heidous. The latter two hills had of course not been captured as originally intended. It required the battalion to move from its start line in a gully, drop over a small rise and advance across 500 metres or so of open fields past Djebel Chaibane on its right to reach the lower slope of Djebel Ahmera. McNabb had about an hour to prepare his unit for the attack, devise a swift plan, brief his company commanders and put in an attack. There was insufficient time to discuss the plan in detail with his officers, and instead he simply had to issue a rapid set of oral orders.

The battalion left the shelter of its positions in the gully and moved out in full view of the Germans towards their objective. At 1130 hours, the twice-delayed artillery barrage descended on Longstop Hill, which was immediately covered in shell bursts and smoke. The 8th Argylls moved to their start line for the attack on Djebel Ahmera, which was a small track running across the south-eastern slopes of Djebel Bechtab. The importance of the battalion's attack was underscored by the presence in an observation post on Chaouach of both Evelegh and Allfrey. John Darcy-Dawson, the war correspondent, was also present nearby and chatted to Evelegh and Allfrey while watching the artillery barrage. Dawson later wrote:

> We stood talking in the strong sunshine while below us the barrage was mounting in intensity and the flame from gun muzzles appeared to be continuous. Even at that distance the sound of the guns came up to us, making conversation difficult. I wanted to see how Longstop looked under this stream of shells and said goodbye to the two commanders. Over the shoulder of a hill a few hundred yards away I watched the last fight on Longstop. I could scarcely see the tops of the hills for smoke. The whole ridge seemed on fire but those machine guns kept up their insane chatter.[2]

Major Anderson, Y Company's commander, described the events that now unfolded:

> At about 1130 we moved in to the attack. The battalion advanced in the form of a box with Y and R, the left and right forward companies, battalion Headquarters in the centre and B and X behind. The companies were well split up. The attack was put in behind a heavy artillery barrage and was supported by fire from Churchill tanks in the rear. To reach the bottom of the hill the battalion had to pass through a large strip of corn which was completely dominated by the enemy. It was when we were about half way across the corn that enemy mortar and artillery shells started to fall among the companies, but this did not hinder our advance. Farther on machine gun fire opened up on us from Longstop itself and also from a hill on the left flank.
>
> My company being on the left suffered heavily from this enemy position which continued firing on us throughout this attack. Up to the base of the hill the battalion held its formation well despite heavy casualties.[3]

While Anderson was moving his company across poppy-covered open corn fields to the base of the hill, the reserve companies and Colonel McNabb and his O (Orders) Group (his immediate headquarters personnel) were moving across the fields following his forward companies (see Plate VIII). McNabb's headquarters group that day was rather larger than usual and would also have been easily identifiable by the number of wireless aerials. Officers watching the unit's move forward from the rear would have viewed the scene with a degree of mounting concern, for the Argylls' formation, and specifically the O Group, disappeared under the smoke and explosions

---

2   The quotation is from Dawson, *Tunisian Battle*, pp.214-15.
3   See Appendix D to TNA WO 175/491 8th Argylls April 1943 WD, Anderson's report on Longstop Hill p.1. The details of the Argylls' attack on Longstop are largely derived from Anderson's report; gallantry citations; Malcolm, *History of 8th Argylls*, pp.123-26; and Bryan Perrett, *At all Costs! Stories of Impossible Victories* (London: Orion, 1998), pp.154-70.

caused by the German mortar and artillery shellfire. This shelling was probably initiated by German observers located on Djebels Ahmera, Rhar and particularly Tanngoucha, for the latter had not yet been taken by the 38 Irish Brigade. From Tanngoucha, Heidous and Ahmera, German forward observers had a complete view of all approaches to Longstop. This fire could not be neutralised, either by artillery support or by the assistance that could be provided by A Squadron of the North Irish Horse. The other two squadrons, B and C, had also moved forward to try to support the West Kents. They assisted the Argylls' attack by firing on Djebel Ahmera from near Chaibane, but this move was of limited assistance as the majority of the fire on the Argylls was from artillery and mortars that were not visible.

11.5 Loss of the O Group

Any seasoned observer who watched as the Argylls' O Group disappeared beneath a barrage of German artillery and mortar fire, just before it reached the base of Djebel Ahmera, would have been left with few illusions about what fate had in store for McNabb and his staff. They may also, and understandably, have concluded that the Argylls' attack was now doomed to fail. While they would have been correct in their first conclusion, they would have been quite wrong on the second count. The precise cause of the demise of McNabb and his command team will never be known (see Plate 18). It is likely they were caught by either artillery or mortar shells close to or at the base of the hill. The most likely cause of their end was mortar fire, since according to accounts at the time, their bodies, when found, were badly mangled and such damage was usually inflicted by mortar rounds. What is certain is that the able 39-year-old CO was killed, as were his well-liked and popular Signals Officer, Captain Bobby Erskine, his adjutant, Lieutenant Bob McLeish, and all the other members of his immediate HQ staff. They included the Orderly Room Sergeant, Sergeant Sandy Mackinnon DCM (who had just been selected for an officer's commission), the Intelligence Sergeant, Sergeant McMillan, Pipe Major Sergeant Wilson and one of the rear link signallers. Five others in the group were also wounded. More importantly by this time, all of the Argylls' company commanders except Anderson had been wounded and were now for all intents and purposes out of the fight. Furthermore Captain David Browne RA, the attached artillery observer from 17th Field Regiment, had also been killed by the German shells. Fortunately, Captain Paul Lunn-Rockliffe, one of the other 17th Field Regiment observers, managed to survive unwounded, though members of his and Browne's parties were also hit. Losses among the leading companies of the Argylls had been considerable, and casualties were also mounting among the 1st East Surreys, which were following them in support.

The loss of the command group at this stage at the base of the hill, the removal of all key company commanders, the death of a key FOO and the consequent loss of coordination, could for a less seasoned unit have led to complete disaster. This would especially have been the case if the unit had been over-dependent on direction from its CO. Fortunately, this was not the case in the Argylls. Despite the losses incurred crossing the corn field, the leading unit, Y Company, had reached the bottom of the hill and continued the attack. It is impossible to know what motivated those men to continue to fight. One author speculates that one factor that may explain why the Argylls had quickly become what can best be described as "fighting mad", was an incident that occurred as Y Company cleared the lower part of Ahmera. After taking that part of the hill and capturing some Germans, the Highlanders were briefly resting and having a smoke. Next to them and sitting down was a small group of German prisoners, when suddenly, and for reasons that no one will ever know, one of them grabbed a machine pistol and killed a couple of Argylls. He and his fellow prisoners were quickly killed, but not before the damage had been done. According to Bryan Perret's excellent account of the attack, when the next phase of the assault resumed, the Argylls, "had been roused to a state of berserk fury, which bode ill for the remaining defenders of Ahmera". Perhaps they were angered by the death of so many colleagues, by their hatred for the enemy, thirst or even an element of rage, but the fighting spirit of the battalion unit came to the fore. After the battle, Anderson commented to Hamish Taylor: "We just had a hate for the Germans, the hill and everything."[4]

Irrespective of the causes, it appears that Brigadier Howlett had gauged the mettle of the Highlanders well, for their advance did not stop and they did not retreat, despite the difficult circumstances.

11.6 Anderson's One-Man Army

That morning, no one demonstrated that Highlander fighting spirit more than the only field officer still left in the fight, Major Anderson. He had led his company across the corn field despite the fierce shelling, which he later noted was less effective than fire from a troublesome machine gun on his left flank from a hill, one supposedly held by friendly troops. Anderson and his company arrived as a formed body at the base of Djebel Ahmera, but once they moved up it, the rocky terrain was so bad that units broke up and the fight became one carried out by individuals and sections. Anderson's final view of his CO and the battalion headquarters was just as the latter had reached the base of the hill. He did not personally see the loss of the command group, and nor did his men know about the death of the CO and his HQ staff, as they fought their own individual battles. These included the actions of Lieutenant Ernest Linklater, one of Anderson's own platoon commanders. As Anderson later wrote: "As far as I could see Lieutenant Linklater, my right hand forward platoon leader was the first man on the hill itself. He destroyed the first German machine gun post which continued firing at us right to the end." Soon after the Argylls arrived at the bottom of the hill, enemy machine-gun fire increased in severity, Anderson was slightly wounded in the leg and soon afterwards was told that the CO had been hit. Although we do not know what he thought at this time, it is likely he recognised that a crisis point had been reached and that action was required to maintain the momentum of the section attacks. What we do know is what he and his men did, and this is best described using Anderson's own words in a short report he wrote on 30 April, only six days after the battle ended. His account is a masterly piece of Scottish understatement:

> I therefore made my way to the front of the battalion to lead the men on, and we continued the advance. The men were in great heart, facing the enemy fire without flinching and I could see that Longstop was going to be taken by the 8th Argylls. Generally speaking the Boche stayed put and fired until we were right upon their positions. They then packed it in and tried to surrender but the Jocks were angry and in most cases they died pretty rapidly … Personally I ran into three positions on the way up the first rise; in each case I gave

4   Perrett, *At all Costs*, p.166 .

the occupants a full TSMG [Thompson submachine gun] magazine and when more men arrived they too joined the party. But this was only a small cross section of the main battle.[5]

As sources written at the time make clear, there are two lower summits (or rises, as Anderson describes them) on the ridge leading up the final summit of Djebel Ahmera. The best estimate is that by 1400 hours, Anderson and his men had managed to seize the first of these rises. This task was completed despite heavy fire and the hot sun, which added many heat exhaustion cases to the battle casualties, further reducing their ranks. Anderson makes clear in his report that the attack up the ridgeline to the top of Djebel Ahmera tended to become a fight by small groups of men rather than a coherent attack.

While Anderson was taking his part in the action, the acting commander of R Company, Captain David McNab, was leading another small group of men. McNab's normal role was to be second-in-command of R Company, but he had replaced the wounded company commander and had assumed command. When McNab arrived at the base of Ahmera, he encountered a machine-gun post which with an infantry section he attacked and overran, killing the gunners. He rallied the remainder of R Company and continued his advance. While moving up to the top of the hill, he knocked out two other enemy posts and led his group towards the top of Ahmera.

In a battle of this nature, it was inevitable that the momentum of the Argylls' leading platoons and sections was due to the courageous leadership of its NCOs, especially since the companies had lost several officers wounded. Four men stood out in this regard: Sergeants Fraser and McMillan and Lance Sergeants Bell and Hay. Their role in the battle for Longstop has been almost completely overlooked in accounts of the fighting. Sergeant John Fraser, for example, took command of his platoon when his officer was wounded, and despite being wounded himself, led his platoon with great skill and determination until it reached the summit. Lance Sergeant Bell also distinguished himself, for he not only took command of his platoon when his platoon commander was hit, but took over the company, rallied it and led it up the hill against heavy machine-gun fire. When he reached the top of Ahmera, he reorganised the survivors from his company. Sergeant Duncan McMillan's story at Longstop was similar to that of Lance Sergeant James Hay, for both took over platoons when their officers were hit and led them to attack German positions.[6] While there is no doubting the role played by Jack Anderson and officers such as David McNab, it is important to recognise that in the confused and chaotic fighting it was the gritty determination and leadership of these senior non-commissioned officers that made a huge difference. Their efforts ensured the Argylls continued to advance.

After taking the first summit, Anderson stopped his group of men and reorganised before continuing the attack up the ridge. As he describes it:

> Up to the top of the first hill we had kept well up behind the barrage with some of our shells falling behind us, but on this high ground I stopped and found that only Captain Macnabb [sic] and a handful of men were up with me and I was forced to let the barrage go on without us. Gradually more officers and men arrived all exhausted by the heat, the stiff climb and by the previous fortnight's fighting. In the end we collected about 4 officers and 30 men and

5   Both quotations are from Anderson's *Longstop Hill Report*, pp.1-3.
6   Details of the actions of McNab and the NCOs are from their MC and MM citations in TNA WO 373/1.

casualties had been so heavy that it seemed unlikely that many more would materialize. I therefore sent an officer to the East Surreys who were following us up to hurry up and hold the ground already taken, to enable us to go forward again.[7]

Behind the Argylls, the leading companies of the Easy Surreys moved up across the fire-swept corn fields, under the command of Wilberforce, arriving in time to enable Anderson and the Argylls to continue their assault. Wilberforce's two leading units, A and B Companies, had moved forward at about midday to follow in the footsteps of the Argylls. These were followed by the two remaining companies and Wilberforce with his headquarters. The move forward had been undertaken under fire, for his leading companies had been temporarily pinned down by the flanking machine-gun fire located near Point 196 to the north. This enemy position, possibly the one that had plagued Anderson's company so badly, was destroyed by a Churchill tank of A Squadron, North Irish Horse, while it was working its way north-east towards Point 196. Wilberforce could now move forward what remained of his battered lead companies. Despite the losses they had suffered on the way, they arrived at the base of the hill and also started climbing. As they did, they helped in mopping up any remaining enemy and securing positions. This allowed the Argylls to focus their efforts on their attack, a fact overlooked in some accounts of the battle. While the East Surreys arrived and had helped further secure the first summit (Point 220) between about 1445 and 1530 hours, Anderson and the Argylls had continued their climb, seized the second summit and were beginning their assault on the final summit of Djebel Ahmera (Point 280). Anderson concluded his account of events with the seizing of that final height:

> Finally we advanced on the last height. Shortly after starting, I came upon a mortar position and we all loosed off at the group of Germans in the dugouts. They promptly put up their hands and about twenty others flooded out of various holes and corners. I sent them back with a very belligerent private soldier. In the position we found four mortars complete with ammunition and also a great many stores. Later we captured a 75mm anti-tank gun after a brush with the crew. Otherwise our final advance was uneventful and we set about reorganising at the top.[8]

Although sources are contradictory on this subject, the final seizure of the summit of Ahmera was probably completed by about 1545 hours. Anderson's personal account of the battle is so matter-of-fact that on first reading it might sound like his company and the battalion had just completed a short live-fire exercise, rather than having taken Longstop against fierce enemy resistance. There was so much more to it than that. Despite the laconic and understated way in which Anderson describes it, the Argylls' assault and seizure of Djebel Ahmera was carried out against almost impossible odds. The hill was highly fortified, the defenders well dug in and liberally supplied with mortars, machine guns and access to artillery. Those who walk in Anderson's footsteps up Ahmera find it deceptively steep and rugged, and temperatures, even in spring, can often reach 80 degrees at midday. Most importantly, when it commenced the attack

---

7   The quotation is from Anderson's *Longstop Hill Report*, pp.2-3.
8   The quotation is from Anderson's *Longstop Hill Report*, p.3.

the unit had only 300 men and was very much understrength and tired. The battalion had been in action constantly since January and had been in two major battles over the previous three weeks. Furthermore, the approach was exposed and initial losses were high. A lesser unit might well have faltered without the kind of leadership exerted by Anderson. Taking all these factors into account, there is no doubt that the capture of Djebel Ahmera must rank as one of the finest feats of arms of the Tunisian campaign, indeed of the whole Second World War.

In achieving this success, four factors, two of them crucial, almost certainly made a critical difference. The first was the excellent artillery support provided by the 17th and 132nd Field Artillery Regiments. The 25-pounders fired a moving barrage which shelled German defences by targeting specific lines for eight minutes and next moving a further 200 yards to continue the exercise. A second factor was the role of the North Irish Horse, all of whose squadrons supported the attack with fire and a tank from A Squadron knocked out a troublesome machine-gun position located near Point 196 that had held up the East Surreys. Undoubtedly, the third crucial factor was the fighting spirit of the Highlanders, who continued the fight despite almost impossible odds. This was in part recognised by the award of MCs to Captain McNab and Lieutenant Linklater and the four MMs awarded to Sergeants Bell, Fraser, Hay and Macmillan. The final, and perhaps most crucial, factor on that day was that the men of the battalion were inspired by John Anderson's personal example of conspicuous gallantry as he led them from the front and attacked three enemy machine-gun posts in succession. The soldiers and officers in the Argylls and their senior commanders had no doubts about the critical role Anderson played in securing the hill. The citation for the Victoria Cross that Anderson was awarded on 29 June 1943, and which he so richly deserved, makes this quite clear:

> During the assault he personally led attacks on at least three enemy machine-gun positions and in every case was the first man in the enemy pits; he also led a successful assault on an enemy position of 4 mortars defended by at least 30 of the enemy. Major Anderson's force on the hill captured about 200 prisoners and killed many more during the attack. It is largely due to this officer's bravery and daring that Longstop Hill was captured, and it was the inspiration of his example that encouraged leaderless men to continue the advance.[9]

It is also a measure of the esteem in which Anderson was held by Brigadier Howlett, who was himself an officer of great personal courage, that on being notified of Anderson's VC, he had a special Brigade Order of the Day published. This contained the full citation of Anderson's VC and included his personal congratulations.[10]

The Highlanders' foes were also in no doubt as to the importance of their determination and fighting spirit in taking Longstop, since they knew how defensible they had considered their position. Possibly the greatest tribute to the Argylls' achievement came from the enemy. A captured German officer on the hill, almost certainly from the 754th Grenadiers, was seen to be staring at the unit patch of one of a group of Argylls reinforcements. These men had been sent up to the hill by the second-in-command, Hamish Taylor. Among those arriving on the hill was one soldier still wearing the regiment's tartan patch on his shoulder, although this was

9   Extract from Anderson's VC citation.
10   TNA WO 175/21, 36th Brigade July 1943 WD.

contrary to security regulations. The Germans had long had a healthy respect for, or even fear of, the fighting qualities of Highland troops, ever since the First World War when they called them devils in skirts. The tartan patch provided the officer with clear evidence that his unit's long hold on Longstop and Ahmera had now been ended by a Scottish Highland regiment. After a moment he shrugged and turned away, and speaking fluent English he made the comment: "So that explains it!"[11]

The costs to the Argyll and Sutherland Highlanders of getting to the top of Ahmera throughout that hot Good Friday afternoon had been heavy. Various sources record that four officers and 25 NCOs and men had been killed, 66 were wounded and 16 men were missing for a total of 111 casualties. These figures may have slightly underestimated the actual deaths during the battle on 23 April, for CWGC records show 33 men of the Argylls were killed on that day. These figures also do not include five soldiers killed between 24 and 26 April on Longstop Hill. In addition, at least two RA officers and one gunner were killed in the battle.[12] However, in return the Argylls and East Surreys had captured close to 300 German prisoners on the 23rd and were estimated to have inflicted a significant number of casualties on the defenders from the 334th Infantry Division. The attack on Djebel Ahmera was undoubtedly a tremendous feat of arms, but as past events had proved, taking the hill was one thing but holding it afterwards and taking the rest of Longstop was quite another. The defenders from the 3rd/754th Grenadier Regiment and other attached troops may have been forced off Ahmera, but they remained securely in possession of Djebel Rhar. The latter offered them a valuable platform to launch counterattacks on the British defenders of its sister peak. As we have seen previously, such German tactics were often highly successful, especially when made against weakened and exhausted survivors of an initial attack. The battle for Longstop was a long way from being over; indeed, to continue the cricketing analogy, the third, though final, innings was about to start.

11.7 Holding Djebel Ahmera

To counter such German tactics, Howlett and his commanders had taken a number of precautionary measures, most, though not all of which, were about to pay off. The first was to ensure that the Argylls would be supported and quickly reinforced by the East Surreys. This solution had been less successful than planned, since the 1st East Surreys had suffered a greater number of casualties than expected and were understrength when they arrived. By about 1800 hours, the Argylls on the final summit were reinforced by the rest of the rifle companies of the 1st East Surreys. On arrival at the top of the hill, Wilberforce, as the senior officer present, assumed command of all the defenders. Wilberforce moved about the hill, almost oblivious to enemy fire, wearing a soft cap rather than a helmet and puffing on his trademark pipe. His calmness and total disregard for his own safety, plus his presence on the hill that evening and throughout the operation, was an inspiration to all who saw him. Few who saw this coolness under fire would have guessed that less than seven hours previously he had been doubled over in agony from muscular cramps. Wilberforce must have been a very tough man to recover so

11   Perrett, *At all Costs*, p.167.
12   Revised casualty figures for the Argylls are based on analysis of CWGC records and 78th Division's casualty returns for that battalion. The original figures are from Perrett, *At all Costs*, pp.167-68.

quickly and lead his battalion for the next 48 hours, and was assuredly the best man to lead the defence of Ahmera.

Another help was that the units were accompanied by artillery observation parties who could call in artillery fire to stop any German counterattacks.[13] Although Captain Browne had been killed during the attack, Captain Paul Lunn-Rockliffe survived the assault and succeeded in establishing an observation post on Point 290 (Ahmera) with the remnants of the two original OP parties. These would be reinforced as further RA personnel arrived from other units, and the commander of the battery attached to the 8th Argylls, Major Venables, also moved forward. Lunn-Rockliffe was a highly regarded and experienced FOO who had already won an MC for gallantry earlier in the campaign and was exactly the kind of officer needed in this dangerous situation. His ability to request artillery fire, whenever it was required, was in no small part due to the efforts of two signals personnel from his own regiment: Sergeant George Heath and Bombardier Reginald Lawson. Both men had already previously distinguished themselves prior to the Longstop battle for their work in maintaining communications for the FOO parties. In Lawson's case, he had manned his wireless set, despite being under constant fire, during a tough battle for Djebel Mansour in February 1943. At Longstop Hill, he continued to do so for two days under similar conditions. He was also a member of the party which carried the heavy but critical artillery wireless set to the top of Djebel Ahmera. Lawson's steady courage during this period was a vital influence on his OP party and ensured its efficiency. Sergeant Heath was the NCO in charge of signals for the regiment and responsible for ensuring communications lines were working. At Longstop Hill, Heath repaired the command post line under heavy fire during the battle and therefore ensured viable communications. Both men would be recognised by the award of a MM for their critical contribution in ensuring that artillery fire was available to support the attack and defence of Djebel Ahmera. Another of the FOOs and his OP parties that made a significant contribution to the operations throughout the Battle of the Peaks, including those to capture Longstop Hill, was Temporary Captain Douglas Cond from the 4th Medium Regiment. Cond and his OP party had certainly lived up to the motto of the Royal Artillery, "*Ubique*", for they had seemed to be everywhere over the last two weeks. Cond had already demonstrated his skill and courage while acting as a battery officer at Bou Arada in February. He was subsequently assigned to become an FOO and led his OP party in the attacks on Mergueb Chaouach, at Bettiour and also at Heidous. Cond and his men took an active part in directing the 5.5in guns of his regiment while manning an observation post near Longstop, despite being under constant enemy fire, until the hill was captured. He and his men would be involved in supporting the attack on the Bou Aoukaz on 30 April. The conduct of Douglas Cond over this period resulted in the award of a MC. Hopefully the men in his OP party, who did not receive any awards, justifiably felt that Cond's MC was indirect recognition of their courage and determination.

Two other FOOs from the 17th Field Regiment had also been attached to and accompanied the North Irish Horse. They rode forward to the lower slopes of the hill in the comparative safety of Churchill tanks and were able to call down fire on any positions which they identified.[14] Throughout the day, the Churchill tanks of the North Irish Horse had made their presence

---

13   The tale of Wilberforce on Djebel Ahmera is from Daniell, *History of East Surrey Regiment*, p.171.
14   The story of the courage of the observer parties at Longstop is based on analysis of the relevant gallantry citations in TNA WO 373/1.

known to the Germans. They supported the attack, but even they could not climb the rugged main ridge of Djebel Ahmera. Nonetheless, A Squadron under Major Strickland was able to get its tanks into the valley that ran between Ahmera and the 5th Buffs' positions on Djebel el Ferdjane, although two tanks were hit by mines and the rest came under heavy shellfire. One tank from 5 Troop of A Squadron crossed a wadi, contacted men of the 5th Buffs on Point 303 and engaged German positions identified by them. Finally, at about 1800 hours, Strickland ordered all the tanks to withdraw as they would be vulnerable at night. Throughout the first part of the day, Strickland's recce officer, Captain Bill Mackean, had led the way for the squadron in his tank until it was disabled. Two members of his tank crew, Troopers Arthur Church and Samuel Johnston, left the tank to determine the nature of the problem, despite the tank being engaged by machine-gun fire. Mackean and his gunner engaged the rather foolhardy German post with their guns to provide cover, and one of the Germans soon raised a white flag and walked over to surrender. In one of those unusual incidents of war, the German soldier asked in English if he could go to get the rest of his crew, which he did, bringing back another four soldiers. Church and Johnston subsequently worked to repair the track, despite being in a German minefield and that by now night had fallen. They completed repairs to the track at 2130 hours and moved the tank out of the minefield, along with their prisoners. Unfortunately, the tank made it only another 300 yards before it broke down completely. During the rest of the night and that following morning, both troopers worked hard, often under fire, to prepare the tank for recovery by the regiment's REME mechanics. It was as a result of their courageous efforts that it was finally recovered and repaired. Trooper Johnston had already been recommended for a MM for an action in March when he had rescued his squadron leader from the turret of a tank. It was perhaps no surprise that Johnston was subsequently awarded the MM for this action, as was his fellow crewman, Trooper Church. In addition to the two MMs earned by the crew, their tank commander Bill Mackean would also earn an MC for his performance on 22 April, making the crew one of the most decorated Churchill crews in North Africa.[15]

The other reason why Ahmera remained in British hands this time was the fact that all three battalions, especially the 8th Argylls, had followed standard procedure, which led several key officers and men from the Argylls (including Major Taylor, the second-in-command) to be LOB. During the late afternoon of 23 April, Taylor, located at the rear battalion HQ and deliberately left out of battle, was informed by Major Alec Malcolm, the Argylls' Support Company Commander, who had just returned from the hill, that Colin McNabb was missing presumed dead. Malcolm had closely followed behind the attack, and as Anderson relates: "Major Malcolm appeared on top of the hill, shortly after we got there, to arrange about bringing up machine guns, mortars and supplies and he was able to take a message back to the Brigadier."[16] Majors Taylor and Malcolm had gone forward, first by Bren Gun Carrier, then afterwards on foot to Longstop. Both of the officers had carried a jerry-can of water up the hill, for they knew all too well of the likely thirst of the remaining troops. They arrived on the summit and together with Anderson they started to help reorganise the Argylls. In his own account, Taylor noted:

---

15   Sadly both Mackean and Johnson would later be killed in Italy.
16   The quote from Anderson is in the *Longstop Hill Report*, p.4.

When I arrived I found five officers and 40 men – this was what had captured Longstop. By nightfall we had gathered up 100 men. Some slightly wounded, some exhausted by the heat and the battle. The Battalion HQ was wiped out … Our artillery battery Commander Major Vaughan Venables was with us and his excellent radio link was invaluable. When I arrived I made a defensive fire plan with Major Venables.[17]

It was one of the Highlanders whom Taylor had managed to gather up and send forward that wore the tartan patch that led to the comment by the German officer about the capture of Djebel Ahmera.

One reason why additional communications were feasible was the devotion to duty that day of Corporal Harris from the Royal Corps of Signals, one of the rear link signallers in McNabb's Orders group who survived the shelling. Harris was responsible for the wireless communications to the brigade and carried a large man-pack radio linked by a cord to heavy batteries carried by another signaller. When the latter was killed, the radio link was broken. After the summit was taken, Harris retraced his steps, recovered the batteries from his colleagues' body, climbed the summit again and re-established radio contact. His general conduct that day was in the finest traditions of the Royal Corps of Signals.[18]

The efforts of Taylor and Venables in coordinating the work of OP parties already on the hill to establish communications and set up defensive tasks for artillery were to pay dividends later that night and over the next two days. Both officers and Anderson must have been acutely aware that their control over Ahmera was tenuous, since initially less than 100 exhausted men held the top of the Djebel. The Germans were masters of the art of the counterattack and had they launched one early that evening, the hill could well have been lost again. Howlett's grip on Ahmera was, however, tightened further by late evening, when companies of the 6th West Kents arrived on Longstop, though even with their addition the hill's defenders actually numbered less than a single weak battalion. After the attack on the night of 22/23 April, the 6th West Kents had spent the remainder of the afternoon in their positions near the village of Chaibane with the battalion HQ in a gully nearby. At about 1700 hours on the evening of 23 April, the understrength unit moved up on to Djebel Ahmera. It joined the East Surreys on the lower summit and slopes and began to dig in. At this moment Lieutenant Colonel Heygate, the CO, was wounded in the neck by fragments of either a booby trap or a German *Schu* or anti-personnel mine, and after first resisting his advice, was eventually persuaded by Major Bill Miskin of Bou Diss fame to be evacuated. In the temporary absence of the deputy, Henry Lovell, and despite the heavy shelling, his new adjutant Captain Gordon Defrates took over temporary command of the battalion and consolidated it under fire. For his coolness under fire, Defrates was awarded a MC. Later that day, Major Lovell arrived and took command of the battalion.

Why the German defenders did not launch an immediate counterattack that evening is not known. No detailed first-hand accounts remain from any of the enemy commanders, and the 334th Infantry Division was destroyed in detail in the final days before Tunis was taken, so records are patchy. It is possible that German communications were interrupted and this made

17   Hamish Taylor, *Memoirs*, p.28.
18   The role of Corporal Harris is covered in Perrett, *At all Costs*, p.167.

it difficult to launch a counterattack. Indications of a build-up and a heavy German mortar barrage at 0200 hours were the closest the Germans came to any attempt to retake the hill. The most likely explanation for the failure to do so is that after their losses over the last three weeks, the Germans simply lacked enough men to do so. The main German response to the seizure of Point 290 was largely restricted to small arms, constant mortar fire and shelling whenever movement was detected.

The 8th Argylls' attack and capture of Djebel Ahmera, aided by the East Surreys and North Irish Horse, had secured the first major objective of Howlett's plan for Longstop Hill. Previous events had shown that securing Djebel Ahmera did not necessarily lead to capture of the whole of Longstop Hill, but on this occasion Howlett and his brigade were to show anyone who doubted their ability to hold the hill to be mistaken.

Plate 15 Longstop Hill viewed from the east (NB The infamous col between Ahmera and Rhar) (Author's collection, 2008)

Plate 16 A Churchill Tank with Infantry on the lower slopes of Longstop Hil. (Copyright, Tank Museum)

Plate 17 Two Tanks of B Squadron, the North Irish Horse during the attack on Djebel Rhar (Note Djebel Rhar is on the left and Ahmera on the right) (Copyright, Tank Museum)

Plate 18 Lieutenant Colonel Pat Scott (bareheaded in the centre) CO of 2 LIR on a London Irish Rifles Bren Gun Carrier during the Tunis Victory parade. (Copyright IWM/NA 2562)

Plate 19 Lieutenant Colonel Colin McNabb's grave in Medjez CWGC cemetery. McNabb was killed leading his battalion at Longstop Hill. (Author's collection, 2008)

12

Finishing The Job – The Taking of Djebel Rhar

12.1 The East Surreys and the West Kents Attack

During the morning of 24 April, the Germans acknowledged the unwelcome presence of Bill Wilberforce's composite battalion on Djebel Ahmera by directing heavy mortar and artillery fire on the hill and its adjoining slopes. In doing so they provided a salutary reminder that however impressive the Argylls' achievement had been in taking Ahmera, Longstop as an objective could not properly be secured until its sister peak, Djebel Rhar, had been seized. The East Surreys who were located on the lower slopes of Ahmera suffered some 20 casualties from this fire, including the battalion's own IO, during the latter half of the morning. In the finest traditions of the RAMC, the RMO, Captain Bill Robinson, ignored his own safety to treat the wounded while the hill was being shelled. Earlier that morning, Wilberforce and his composite unit received much welcome support when a composite squadron of Churchill tanks from the North Irish Horse was assembled under the command of Captain Griffith and deployed to the southern slopes of Ahmera. At some point during Easter Saturday morning, Brigadier Howlett contacted Wilberforce by radio and gave him orders to coordinate an operation at 1330 hours against both Djebel Rhar and Sidi Ali Ben Hassine. The latter was an eastwards-jutting spur from Djebel Ahmera dominating the station and road at Halte d'El Heri. The plan was for Wilberforce's battalion to attack the feature that soldiers had now called Mosque Ridge, while the 6th West Kents under Henry Lovell would attack and capture Djebel Rhar. Both attacks would be supported by artillery and fire from tanks of the North Irish Horse. By midday, Griffith's composite squadron had been reinforced by two troops of tanks led by Major Paul Welch, who now assumed command of the whole force. The East Surreys' part of the operation was to be carried out under the command of Major Harry Smith, who had relieved Wilberforce in order to give him a short rest after his strenuous activities over the last two days. The actual job of taking Mosque Ridge was allocated to a couple of rapidly organised platoons under the command of a Major White and a troop of Churchills from the North Irish Horse.

The East Surreys' attack commenced at 1300 hours, when an artillery concentration was fired at Djebel Rhar and Mosque Ridge. In response to this, the East Surreys were heavily shelled and Major White wounded in a near miss. This removed the commander of the attack force at the outset. The situation for the Surreys was mainly retrieved by the actions of the North Irish Horse, whose troop of tanks moved up on the right to Mosque Ridge. However, they did so without infantry support, as the East Surreys' platoons were pinned down by German artillery and mortar fire followed by small-arms and machine-gun fire. Soon afterwards the battalion was notified by 36th Brigade that an enemy counterattack was about to take place. At this point the East Surreys' mortar platoon was employed usefully, firing a concentration on the slopes to the left of the 8th Argylls to break up any possible attempt, though none emerged. The tanks of the North Irish Horse managed to move up along the lower slopes of Ahmera and up to Mosque Ridge during the afternoon. They roamed around the ridge area, and using fire from their main guns and Besa machine guns suppressed any German positions. Later in the afternoon, the East Surreys sent out a relatively small party of infantry and a section of sappers from 256th Field Company to assist the tanks and occupy Point 140 on Mosque Ridge. Once this was in place, it was reinforced by 1800 hours by another platoon under the command of Lieutenant McMillan.[1] During this period Griffith and two troops of Churchills managed to move forward to the next ridge, accompanied by an artillery observer. The new location gave them excellent observation of German positions, and these were rapidly shelled. At the end of the day, the tanks withdrew back to Mosque Ridge, but on the way back Griffith's tank was disabled by a mine. Griffith and his crew found themselves in the unenviable situation of being forced to abandon the tank and remove any key pieces of equipment, while under fire from a German machine gun nearby. The tank's co-driver managed to achieve this by dropping a rubber groundsheet through a small 6in drain hole and by getting out of a side hatch and spreading it under the tank. The various important items, including gun sights, radio parts and documents, were next dropped through the drain hole onto the ground sheet and caught by the co-driver. He bundled up the items and carried his precious package across to another tank that had placed itself next to that of Griffith. One by one, the rest of the crew left through the escape hatch and crawled over and into the other tank. Sadly, history does not record the name of the co-driver who risked his life to help evacuate the tank, but he certainly deserved some form of recognition. The tanks withdrew back to Mosque Ridge, where they stayed all night with this small force in order to deal with any enemy counterattack that emerged during the night. The infantry responded by providing a small patrol to guard Griffith's tank, which was later recovered.

While the East Surreys had been attempting to neutralise German defences on Mosque Ridge, the 6th West Kents, under the command of Major Henry Lovell, had started their Saturday morning with the same heavy shelling and mortar fire experienced by the Surreys. This fell right across the summit of Ahmera, Point 290. By now C and D Companies were co-located with the remnants of the 8th Argylls, which comprised just over 100 men, on and around the summit. Towards midday, Lovell received his orders to attack Djebel Rhar at the same time as the East Surreys were due to tackle Mosque Ridge. The plan, hurriedly devised in response to the order by Lovell as acting CO, was for B and C Companies of the 6th West Kents to form up on the lower slopes of Ahmera, well below and out of sight of the German defenders on Rhar, and next attack across the col dividing the two hills. Sadly, Lovell's plan showed that some painful lessons about Longstop and its defences taught over the preceding months had not been learned. In daylight, the whole of Djebel Ahmera was under direct observation from German positions on Tanngoucha and Heidous, which had yet to be taken. As a result, even though the companies assembled in their FUPs on the reverse lower slopes

---

1   The story of the East Surreys and North Irish on 24 April is largely derived from their war diaries TNA WO 175/519 and 294 for April 1943; and Doherty, *North Irish Horse*, pp.106-07.

of Ahmera, the Germans on the heights directed a storm of shell and mortar fire onto them from their positions above and behind Rhar. After some delay, Captain Edward Weatherley, the commander of C Company, managed to inspire his men to move forward despite the fire. Soon afterwards Weatherley was hit by shrapnel in his leg, but despite the wound he continued to urge his men forward. As the company advanced, it was met by heavy machine-gun fire from German positions on Rhar itself. The NCO of the leading section was killed early on in this action by enemy fire, but Private Michael Sullivan took over and led it forward. As the section was nearing Djebel Rhar, it was fired on by a machine gun; Sullivan personally charged and destroyed the enemy post. Despite the gallantry of Weatherley and Sullivan, the German mortar, artillery and machine-gun fire had resulted in an increasing number of casualties. It was to his credit therefore that Brigadier Howlett, who was typically observing the attack from far forward, personally stopped the attack.

Casualties were significant, and included Lieutenant King and five men killed, with Weatherley plus at least 25 men wounded. These losses could be added to the six men killed and 30 wounded sustained on the previous day. The number of those who died would have been higher had it not been for the work of Sergeant Bourne, who risked his life to rescue a wounded man on 25 April, and Private James Cooper, who did so a day later. Bourne, who was in charge of the battalion's stretcher bearers, left the safety of his slit trench and made his way across ground swept by shellfire to tend to a member of an anti-tank gun crew wounded by a shell, and carried him to safety. Cooper was a member of the battalion's mortar platoon and was advancing to help secure Longstop on 26 April, when he found that one of the men of his company had been shot in the back and was lying out on an exposed slope. The man had been helping wounded back to the aid post, but had been shot while returning to action. He had been treated by a stretcher bearer who had gone back for help, but on return had found that enemy fire was too great to rescue him. On his own initiative, Cooper crawled out to the wounded man under fire, gave him a cigarette and crawled back to get the stretcher bearers, who he found had moved elsewhere. Cooper returned to the man and dragged him 70 yards to safety so he could be evacuated. It was not surprising that Weatherley would later be awarded a MC, while Sullivan, Bourne and Cooper all received MMs.[2]

The losses incurred by the 6th West Kents, both prior to and during Longstop, were so significant that when the battalion was reorganised later that evening there were only 80 men left in the four rifle companies, which at full strength would have comprised 480 officers and other ranks. As a result, these survivors were formed into two companies of 40 men each. These operations also resulted in the death of an officer much admired by Bombardier Spike Milligan: Lieutenant Tony Goldsmith, a FOO from 56th Heavy Regiment. At 31, Goldsmith was older than the average gunner officer in his role, moreover he was both liked and respected by his men, especially Milligan. Milligan greatly admired Goldsmith because of his courage, plus his ability to talk informally with his men and the fact they both shared a rather zany sense of humour. Goldsmith had demonstrated his courage when he had stoically manned a dangerous OP on 16 April despite being heavily mortared during the fighting on Tanngoucha. The latter characteristic was shown when he radioed back to Milligan and said: "Hello Milligan I am

2   The action by the 6th West Kents on the 24th is largely derived from Chaplin, *West Kents*, pp.239-40, and the citations for gallantry for the battalion in TNA WO 373/1.

going to have a nap, would they turn the volume down on the guns."[3] In his short life, Goldsmith had already shown great promise, having completed a degree at Balliol College, Oxford, and then worked as a writer and translator of French plays and impressed the playwright Terence Rattigan. His death hit Spike Milligan very hard, as he later wrote:

> When I knew he had been killed, I was stricken. He was the first really intellectual man I'd ever come across ... he never felt the need to pull rank on me and we talked to each other with such ease. I was very raw and unread ... he opened such doors for me.[4]

There was also one final gallantry award: the award of a MC was made to an officer of the 6th West Kents, 26-year-old Acting Major Paul Bryan. Bryan had been a captain when he landed in North Africa with the unit back in November 1942. He had served with the battalion through many of its battles, and by April 1943 was an acting major commanding headquarters company. During the battle for Longstop, Bryan was in charge of ensuring the battalion received vital ammunition, water and food. According to the citation for his MC, for three days Bryan personally led the mule parties, despite the fact they were heavily shelled, and it was largely due to his determination that these critical supplies reached the forward companies on Djebel Ahmera. Bryan would later write about what happened in an autobiography:

> I spent each night of this battle supervising the evacuation of the wounded and persuading the mules to take food and ammunition up to the troops. Every time I assembled a train of mules, got them loaded and the muleteers in some sort of order, all in the semi darkness, a shell would land among us and the mules and muleteers would scatter in all direction. The whole thing was a nightmare. I was awarded the Military Cross. My friends derisively called it the 'Mule Cross'.[5]

The failure by the 6th West Kents to capture Djebel Rhar required Brigadier Howlett and his staff to think again, and they were to spend most of 25 April planning a renewed attempt to complete the conquest of Longstop Hill.

12.2 Taking of Djebel Rhar

By midday on 25 April it must have become obvious to Howlett, that a direct assault on Djebel Rhar could not be achieved by the units tenuously holding Djebel Ahmera. It is debatable that Howlett and his commanders should have realised this earlier, well before the 6th West Kents' abortive attack. In retrospect, given the weakness of the units on Ahmera and the strength of the German position, on Djebel Rhar and on Tanngoucha and Heidous, it seems obvious any unsupported frontal attack was bound to fail. However, while it is easy with the benefit of hindsight to make such assessments, the hard reality of war is that commanders have to make quick decisions which are based on imperfect information. Howlett and his staff may have

---

3   Milligan, *Rommel? Gunner Who?*, p.178.
4   The quote is from an article on Milligan on the website www.creativecase.org.uk (accessed 15 February 2018).
5   Bryan, *Wool, War and Westminster*, p.87.

felt that one last push with his units could secure the rest of Longstop Hill: unfortunately for the Queen's West Kents they were wrong. Howlett spent most of the remainder of the day on Longstop encouraging the troops by personal example and planning with his subordinate commanders, especially Lieutenant Colonels Dawnay and Thomas. These discussions and events in the heights above Longstop led to a new and ultimately successful plan to take Djebel Rhar. The new brigade plan would not have required a lengthy appreciation, as given the exhaustion and weakness of the units on Ahmera, Howlett had really only one option: to use the 5th Buffs to attack and seize Djebel Rhar. Fortunately for Lieutenant Colonel McKechnie and his tired regiment, at 1230 hours on 25 April, the Faughs of the Irish Brigade began their successful attack on Point 622 and Butler's Hill. This enabled the Inniskillings to take Tanngoucha from the Germans later in the afternoon, and by that evening the London Irish had also taken Heidous. The loss of these key features meant that the Germans on Djebel Rhar could no longer expect their observers on these positions to bring down directly observed artillery and mortar fire on their attackers. The elimination of these posts was a vital step in spelling the end of resistance on Rhar. The remaining garrison from the 754th Grenadier Regiment largely occupied protected reverse-slope positions on Rhar and had only limited observation to direct approaches to the hill.

The revised plan produced by Howlett and his commanders on 25 April had the brigade feinting on the right and south side of Ahmera, but delivering its main punch on the left, taking Rhar from the north and west (see Plate V). Although tired, the 5th Buffs were now the strongest of 36th Brigade's units and were well established in positions on Points 303 and 196 to the west of the German defences on the hill. The battalion was well placed, if supported by artillery and tanks of the North Irish Horse, to strike the German defences on Djebel Rhar. It would achieve this by attacking north-east from Point 196 on the northern flank of Djebel Ahmera and turning eastwards to attack Rhar from the west. The feint on the right was to be carried out by Churchill tanks of C Squadron of the North Irish Horse and by a large fighting patrol from the 8th Argylls probing the southern slopes of Ahmera from Mosque Ridge.

An early morning mist prevented any detailed reconnaissance by the Buffs of the area they were attacking, though it must have helped cover the assembly of the leading companies on Point 196 at about 0830 hours. The 5th Buffs began their attack here, with D Company under Major Van Ammel on the left and A Company led by Captain Colley on the right, followed by B Company in reserve. The diversionary attack on the south towards Mosque Ridge by the 8th Argylls comprised only two officers and 30 other ranks, all of whom had been originally left out of battle. They had a busy day, as starting at 0200 hours that morning they had been involved in carrying rations to the forward companies and next found themselves tasked with this dangerous little venture. The patrol was led by Captain Scott and assisted by Captain Corlett, and as soon as it started they came under heavy mortar fire which delayed the advance of the infantry. The tanks of C Squadron nonetheless began their advance, and its leading troop quickly reached Mosque Ridge and worked forward to the next ridge. One of the Churchills carried Major Cary, the FOO from 17th Field Regiment. Upon arrival near Mosque Ridge, Cary was able to benefit from the view from his location and the substantial protection of a Churchill tank to call down accurate fire on Djebel Rhar. Eventually the small group of Argylls managed to work their way to Mosque Ridge, where they were initially held up by fire from German positions on Rhar. After a while the Highlanders received the aid of another troop of tanks which moved up to help. As a result the infantry moved on top of the ridge, cleared out all the snipers that were pinning them down, took a dozen prisoners and surprisingly suffered no casualties. This action was the end of the diversionary attack and was partly successful, in that the availability of an FOO helped to prevent a withdrawal to the north-east of the German troops on Rhar.

The main attack on Rhar from the west was unusually to be led by tanks of A and B Squadrons of the North Irish Horse, while the infantry followed. In accordance with his normal style of leadership, Howlett chose to be as close to the front as possible. In this case that turned out to be literally on the front line, as he was a passenger in Dawnay's own tank, just behind the advance. Although this approach became quite common later in the war, it was an unusual and innovative way of exercising command at this point in the conflict. However, it ensured that Howlett could monitor the battle closely, while avoiding exposing himself to enemy fire. The tanks of the North Irish formed up in front of the start line of the two leading companies of the Buffs at about 0830 hours, A on the right and D on the left, with B in reserve. Enemy shelling commenced before the assault was launched and partly delayed the initial attack, which eventually began at 0900 and was led by B Squadron. One of the tanks of B Squadron also carried an artillery observer, Captain Dennis Higgins, who although only 24 was an experienced veteran. Higgins had already distinguished himself for his coolness and bravery during an attack by a battalion of German infantry on the 3rd Parachute Battalion on 26 February. The attack overran a platoon and left Higgins cut off and with a complete German company behind him. Ignoring his precarious situation, Higgins continued to coolly call down artillery fire on the German attackers until he was rescued by a successful counterattack.

The 5th Buffs companies moved off from Point 196 and along the valley without incident. However, immediately that the companies started to move up towards the north-western slopes of Rhar, a hail of accurate shellfire descended upon them. Despite the German fire, the 5th Buffs' leading companies continued their attack, moving across the northern slope of Djebel Ahmera. According to one account, the "infantry resembled a line of guns and beaters walking up grouse on a Scottish moor on the glorious Twelfth".[6] The battalion's history was to later describe how the leading companies "without as much as a check – pressed on as if on a peacetime manoeuvre, notwithstanding that whole platoons disappeared in the smoke of bursting shells".[7] While the 5th Buffs' leading companies moved through shelling towards Djebel Rhar, their supporting tanks had already outpaced them and would prove to be the decisive element of the attack. A Squadron of the North Irish Horse moved along the lower northern slopes of Djebel Ahmera, while B Squadron was tasked with the job of moving along the valley to the north. The squadron commanders were the redoubtable Major Eugene Strickland and Major Gordon Russell, who had earlier been so active in the Bed Valley. Russell led his squadron in his tank named "Ballyrashane", and was accompanied by another tank called "Bangor" (see Plate 17). All the tanks in the North Irish Horse were named alphabetically after villages and towns in Northern Ireland. His leading troop (4 Troop) moved on the right on the lower northern slopes of Djebel Ahmera and in due course up Djebel Rhar. The troop was commanded by Lieutenant Michael Broomfield Pope and included a tank commanded by Troop Sergeant Edward O'Hare. As the Churchills of 4 Troop moved along the rough ground, a German machine-gun crew

6   Doherty, *North Irish Horse*, p.109.
7   C.R.B. Knight, *Historical Records*, p.207.

opened up on the advancing companies and was quickly silenced. Another crew now bravely tried to engage Pope's tanks. Pope later recalled:

> Sergeant O'Hare spotted it first and silenced it quickly. I had only proceeded a short distance further, when an almighty bang proclaimed a broken track due to a mine. The driver, Trooper P Abbott, a peacetime stable lad, laconically announced over the intercom, "That's buggered it Sir, the Old Cow's spread a plate".[8]

Pope ordered another tank of 4 Troop to come alongside, and despite being under machine-gun fire while he did so, he changed places with the tank commander so he could continue to lead the troop. The troop continued its forward movement and soon detected two further machine-gun crews on the western slopes of Rhar, which were quickly engaged and then their crews surrendered. Just after this action, the advancing companies of the 5th Buffs were once more engaged and held up by a machine gun on a spur of Djebel Rhar. Pope's troop again identified, engaged and silenced this position. He was now ordered by Russell to stop on the spur and allow the infantry to catch up before moving around the western flank of Djebel Rhar and working their way up the hill.

At this point there appears to have been a discussion between Russell and Lieutenant Colonel McKechnie of the 5th Buffs. During this talk, it was agreed that the final assault would be carried out initially by tanks alone, but that the infantry would follow on closely and mop up prisoners. While 4 Troop now had just three tanks left, it had moved so that it was positioned on a spur of the south-western flank of Djebel Rhar. Although accounts differ slightly on this question, it appears likely that both Pope and O'Hare started to climb up slightly different routes up the steep western slope of Rhar. Pope and his tank crew moved up a steep small wadi or re-entrant which led to the col between Ahmera and Rhar. The slope was steep and terrain rocky, so both tanks found the going difficult, and as a result their engines were over stressed and noisy. As Pope's tank moved up the steep wadi, it reached a cluster of rocks and was immediately confronted by an anti-tank gun just a few yards away. He gave some rapid and heartfelt fire orders: "Anti-tank gun, twelve o'clock, give it hell." The gunner fired his 6-pounder once and followed it up with a burst from his Besa machine gun. This quickly led to two of the German crew waving their hands and emerging from a hole to surrender. Pope now contacted O'Hare and asked him how he was progressing as the two tanks had lost visual contact. O'Hare replied: "Going well and taking prisoners. We've had to stop, oil pressure very low, we'll have to give her a drink."[9] According to one account, his driver got out of the tank as it lay among the German defences, with a revolver in one hand and oil can in the other, and topped up the engine oil. O'Hare and his crew continued their ascent and in an amazing feat, managed to get his tank all the way up to the top of Djebel Rhar and in the process, assisted by the infantry of the 5th Buffs, took over 50 German prisoners. O'Hare then navigated his tank down the rear, northern, slope of Rhar and at one point found himself required to simultaneously engage two machine-gun posts, one to his front and another to his rear. Meanwhile, Pope had taken a slightly different route and had managed to get on to the western slope of Rhar. During this

8   Doherty, *North Irish Horse*, p.109.
9   Doherty, *North Irish Horse*, p.110. This source, *Battle Report* and the Regimental war diary TNA WO 175/294 North Irish Horse April 1943 are the main sources for the activities of the regiment.

move he had encountered and captured Germans in both a machine-gun and a mortar position. When Pope turned a corner, he found a sheer cliff ahead of him which had 20 or more holes dug into it, out of which suddenly poured a large number of Germans holding anything white they could and yelling that they wished to surrender. It appears that many of the holes and caves were originally ancient tombs which had been used by the Germans as part of their defences.

By 1115 hours, the 5th Buffs' leading companies, A and D, had caught up and moved in to take the surrender of a large number of German prisoners. They included the Acting CO of the 3rd/754th Grenadier Regiment, all four of his company commanders and six other officers. In total, both units took over 300 prisoners of war that morning. These men were the rest of the battalion defending Longstop, as very few other Germans managed to escape from the hill. After moving the prisoners to the rear, the 5th Buffs immediately started to dig in, adapting existing fortifications or building new ones. The task of creating new trenches was made significantly easier by sappers from 256th Field Company, which helped blast new trenches in the rocks using beehive charges. The 5th Buffs had not emerged from the shelling and enemy machine-gun fire unscathed, with nine soldiers killed and 83 wounded during the attack. Among the wounded were six officers, all lieutenants, who as usual were leading from the front and most exposed to fire. Throughout the action, Regimental Sergeant Major J. Bell and Lance Sergeant Albert Nash distinguished themselves by their courage. Nash, who was only 21 years old and quite young to be a sergeant, had been attached to the battalion headquarters throughout the operation, but sadly lost his life in the battle. Despite their bravery, which was an inspiration to everyone who witnessed it, neither Bell nor Nash would be formally recognised for their gallantry. One NCO whose conduct was both noted and formally recognised was Sergeant Edward Foster, the platoon sergeant of the right-hand platoon of A Company of the 5th Buffs. His citation noted that when his platoon and A Company were about 200 yards from their objective, they came under heavy artillery and machine-gun fire and were pinned down. It reveals that the platoon suffered nearly 40 percent casualties in minutes, including the platoon commander, Lieutenant T. Smith. Despite the heavy fire, and accompanied only by another SNCO, Foster worked his way towards the objective and joined up with his company commander, Captain Davies Colley, who had a group of 14 men with him. Colley led the group to try to clear the left-hand side of the objective, while Foster, almost completely on his own, went around to the right. Foster stalked and killed a machine gunner with a hand grenade who was holding up the advance. Finally, assisted only by another officer, Second Lieutenant Webster, he entered four enemy dugouts and captured 70 German prisoners. Foster was deservedly later to be awarded the MM.

He was not the only member of the Buffs to be decorated for the attack, for Major Van Ammel, the company commander of D Company of the 5th Buffs, would also win the MC. Van Ammel had only just returned to the battalion, having being wounded earlier during the attack on Mergueb Chaouach. His Christian name was Adolf, so he must have had to endure considerable banter on this account from the other officers. It was one of those ironies of history that on this day it was a man named Adolf who was partially responsible for the demise or capture of a large number of Germans on Djebel Rhar. As they advanced, D Company was hit by the same artillery and machine-gun fire that caused problems for A Company, and might have become pinned down. Instead, Van Ammel, with complete disregard for his own life, continued to move forward and through his own personal example inspired his men to follow him and take their objective. The bravery of men like Bell, Nash, Foster and Van Ammel was not to be in vain on this occasion, for everyone from Howlett at brigade headquarters down to the most junior private in the 5th Buffs was grimly determined to secure and then retain possession of Djebel Rhar and the rest of Longstop. The two rear companies of the 5th Buffs quickly arrived to reinforce the position, and soon afterwards anti-guns of 254 Anti-Tank Battery were moved up to Chassert Teffaha to help prevent any *panzer*-led counterattack.[10]

While Pope and O'Hare were ensuring the capture of Djebel Rhar, the other forward troop of B Squadron, 1 Troop, had been coming up the valley on the left of 4 Troop. A combination of the terrain and other problems had reduced 1 Troop to only one tank commanded by the troop leader. In view of this situation, Major Russell ordered his tank and the only remaining one in 2 Troop, which was commanded by Lieutenant Pyl, to join up with Brown and for all three tanks to link up with 4 Troop. It was while the three Churchills were stationary on a spur of Djebel Rhar that they came under the fire of a 150mm artillery gun. Pyl spotted the flashes of the gun and was able to tell Captain Dennis Higgins, who was travelling in his tank, and he quickly started to direct guns on the target. Unfortunately, while doing this, one of the 150mm shells scored a direct hit on the Churchill tank in which Higgins was travelling and he was killed. Pyl and his crew were shaken, but unscathed by the hit. The tank was disabled, so for the second time that day Pyl had to transfer to another tank, though he ended the day in that one. The remaining tanks of A Squadron also arrived, though not without their own losses. One of the Churchills, commanded by Sergeant Des Kennedy of 5 Troop, had managed to travel over some very difficult terrain until it came to one obstacle too many. The tank stood almost on its front, before slowly rolling on its side. The following unusual and unforgettable exchange of messages now took place, with Kennedy radioing: "We have turned over, there are some big shells coming over. If somebody does not come and pull us over it will be all over - Over!" Major Strickland, who heard the message, was not very sympathetic and replied: "Sit tight baker 3 you are in an awfully big tank – Out."[11] Kennedy and his crew survived their rather precarious situation, and after a while received the assistance they needed.

While the 5th Buffs were tightening their grip on Djebel Rhar, A Squadron of the 56th Recce Regiment, which was located near Chassert Teffaha, now moved up to join C Squadron of the North Irish Horse. C Squadron's commander was able to show Major Webb, the recce squadron's commander, where some Germans might be holding out at two roadblocks on or near the Medjez to Tebourba road. Webb's troopers moved off to find them, and after a short engagement, in which four Germans were killed for no loss, an additional 30 prisoners were added to those already taken on the south flank of Ahmera, bringing this number to 56. The assault on Djebel Rhar added a further 350 prisoners to the divisional cage, which brought the total captured at Longstop to some 550 by 26 April. When added to all those captured by the 78th Division since the start of Operation Sweep, this made for a grand tally of 2,200 Germans captured.

The successful operations of C Squadron of the North Irish Horse on the south flank of Djebel Ahmera were unfortunately marred, not by enemy action, but by a freak accident of the weather. One of the tanks of C Squadron was hit by a bolt of lightning in its turret, which killed Lance Corporal Jamieson and burned two other crewmen in the turret, though the other

10   Details of the 5th Buffs' attack on Djebel Rhar were derived from C.R.B. Knight, *Historical Records*, pp.207-08; the citations in TNA WO 373/1; and the 5th Buffs' war diary TNA WO 175/495 April 1943.
11   Doherty, *North Irish Horse*, p.111.

two crew escaped without injury. Ironically, these were the only personnel casualties suffered by all three squadrons of the North Irish Horse during the attack on Longstop. Though tragic, this was a very small price to pay for their vital contribution to the capture of Djebel Ahmera and Djebel Rhar. Dawnay's insistence that his tank crews learn how to drive their Churchills up slopes in Wiltshire had completely paid off at Djebel Rhar. Despite, or perhaps because of, its unpromising start on the beaches of Dieppe, the Churchill tank had demonstrated its worth here at Longstop Hill, and the Germans were the first to acknowledge this fact. When interrogated shortly after being taken prisoner on Djebel Rhar, the battalion commander of the 3rd/754th Grenadier Regiment commented:

> The Djebel Rhar is one of the strongest defensive positions that one could ever occupy. I would have been prepared to hold it against a full scale British infantry brigade attack. When it was apparent that tanks were being used over the high ground I knew it was all over.

Another German officer is reported to have stated: "When information was first received that tanks were being used on the high ground at Longstop it was not believed by the officers."[12] The Germans, however, were not alone in their recognition of the worth of the regiment. In his post-operation report, Brigadier Howlett paid tribute to the regiment and also the role of the 5th Buffs in the capture of Djebel Rhar: "It is impossible to speak too highly of the support given by the North Irish Horse or of the steady advance of the Buffs under heavy shell fire, two factors which made the capture of Djebel Rhar possible."[13] The role played by the North Irish Horse, and especially B Squadron, in the capture of Rhar would also be recognised by the award of an MC to Gordon Russell and Michael Pope, and a MM to Sergeant Edward O'Hare. It was also one of the factors which contributed to the award of a DSO to its commander, Lieutenant Colonel Dawnay.

12.3 The Impact of the Capture of Longstop Hill

Although the capture of Longstop Hill did not end the fighting on the north side of the Medjerda River, news of this success had a major impact on the morale of both the British and German troops. Over the last four months, Longstop Hill had become a symbol to British troops of the difficulties of reaching Tunis and the determined resistance of the German troops. At a tactical level, it was clear to both the Allied and Axis soldiers that as long as the Germans held Longstop, the capture of Tunis was impossible. John Darcy-Dawson, the war correspondent, summed up the situation admirably when he had written:

> Longstop Hill remained the key position in an advance towards Tunis. It was the bolt that barred the gate and the bolt had to be withdrawn before we could push out along the Tebourba road from Medjez.[14]

12   Doherty, *North Irish Horse*, pp.111-12.
13   See "Capture of Longstop Hill" report attached to TNA WO 175/495 5th Buffs April 1943 WD.
14   Quotation is from Dawson, *Tunisian Battle*, p.209.

The news of the fall of Longstop spread rapidly, and made clear first that the long-awaited final attack on Tunis could now begin, and second that the fall of Tunis was almost inevitable. It also demonstrated conclusively that even the best-defended German defensive position could be overcome and that the Germans could be beaten. As a formation, the officers and men of the Battle-Axe Division had rarely suffered from any doubt that they could beat the Germans, but some newer formations had their reservations. The German defeat at Longstop removed any concerns they might have had on this subject. The news lifted morale across the whole of the 78th Division and the First Army, and to a degree this was reflected in the special order of the day written by a delighted Vyvyan Evelegh on 27 April:

> The divisional commander congratulates all ranks of 36th Brigade and the North Irish Horse on their magnificent success in capturing Longstop the finest feat of arms yet achieved by the First Army. In the opinion of the divisional commander no other infantry could have done that. Well done 36th Brigade.[15]

Evelegh's signal was probably not as well received in the other two brigades, and especially in the 38th Irish Brigade by their officers and men. The latter may have justifiably felt that it ignored the fact that the capture of Kef el Tiour, Point 622 and Tanngoucha was not only also a fine feat of arms, but was probably the reason why Longstop Hill was eventually captured. They would have been right on both counts, but Evelegh seemed to have been focused on the capture of Longstop. His congratulations were followed on the same day by a signal to 36th Brigade from the GOC of First Army, Anderson, announcing the immediate award of a DSO to "Swifty" Howlett.

> During the past two months your brigade has fought and won a succession of fights as fierce as any in the history of the British Army. The successful completion of the Longstop operation was splendid. My congratulations to every officer and man, I have great pleasure in awarding your-self an immediate DSO.[16]

The good news of the capture of Longstop Hill was well received across the whole of the First Army, and especially within V Corps, and provided a psychological boost for that formation. This information also quickly became known within the 334th Division and the German army in Tunisia, and Longstop's loss was a shock. The Germans had viewed the position as almost impregnable and a bulwark which was used to keep the British at bay, away from Tunis. When the battle was viewed from a strictly professional perspective, it clearly demonstrated that the Battle-Axe Division and V Corps had learned a great deal since the first engagement at Longstop and become much more competent. The contrast between the two battles was considerable, for in December the division attacked the hill using only two battalions, whereas in April a reinforced brigade of four battalions was committed to the fight. The first attack relied upon only one field artillery regiment for support, while in April five regiments of artillery were in direct support. Another key difference between the two battles was that the second battle was

---

15   See TNA WO 175/168 78th Division April 1943 WD.
16   See Appendix O to TNA WO 175/213 36th Brigade April 1943 WD.

a good example of one in which the infantry, armour, engineers, anti-tank guns and artillery all worked closely together to support each other. Finally, the first battle almost completely ignored the tactical importance of the peaks overlooking Longstop, while the second dedicated a full brigade to securing those heights. Longstop Hill proved that the 78th Division and its units had stopped the amateurish behaviour that had distinguished its earlier actions, including that at Longstop in December, and were as good if not better than any formation in the Eighth Army.

13

An Expensive Operation

13.1 Introduction

Most accounts of the 78th Division's operations tend to assume that very little of note occurred after the final battle for Longstop Hill. Actually, and in common with their brothers in the 38th Irish Brigade, three battalions from the remaining two brigades were involved in fighting that was both costly and of questionable value. While many historians have omitted an account of that fighting, this author felt he could not, as the units concerned suffered 200 casualties in less than five days. It was certainly surprising to discover that after all their exertions, at least three battalions in the 11th and 36th Brigades found themselves engaged in bitter fighting rather than resting. This unfortunate period commenced when, quite logically, Brigadier Cass and his brigade were allocated the task of retaining control of Longstop Hill. As a result, the 2nd Lancs Fusiliers left their rest area near Medjez el Bab and found themselves relieving the 5th Buffs on Djebel Rhar at midnight on 26 April. While this happened, the 5th Northants under Arthur Crook took over Djebel Ahmera from the 1st East Surreys early on the morning of 27 April. The third battalion to be relieved, and arguably not before time, was the 8th Argylls, who had been retained on Ahmera for two days after their costly capture of that feature, and they left for a short rest on the evening of 26 April. In view of the relative weakness of the two battalions that garrisoned Longstop Hill and the possibility of counterattacks, it was rather surprising that 11th Brigade was now ordered to attack. For reasons that are difficult to determine, someone gave orders for Brigadier Cass's understrength brigade to advance north and east from Longstop. The author's view is that the most likely explanation is that Vyvyan Evelegh was the source of these orders, though there is no written evidence to support this opinion. It is possible that Evelegh came under pressure from Charles Allfrey to keep the Germans north of the river in his sector fully occupied to prevent any men being moved to oppose the advance on Bou Aoukaz. If this was the rationale for the subsequent advance, it was a poor one, for the US II Corps had finally launched their offensive in the north on 23 April and the Germans were fully occupied with keeping them at bay. Moreover, from 25 April, the 38th Irish Brigade was gradually outflanking these German positions by its advance through the mountains. Whatever the rationale for the advance, the task of carrying it out fell to the officers and men of the 2nd Lancs Fusiliers, the 5th Northants and the 8th Argylls.

13.2 Lancashire Fusiliers Advance on Djebel Bou Baker

The first unit to be committed to operations was the Lancashire Fusiliers, at this point temporarily under the command of Major John Mackenzie, the new second-in-command of the battalion, as Linden-Kelly was in hospital. Upon arrival the battalion had one of its companies sent to probe up the Tebourba road. The rest of the battalion spent an uncomfortable day being shelled, before it received orders on the morning of 28 April to carry out a hastily devised attack to the east (see Map 14). Cass's instructions required the battalion to capture a small hill about 1,500 yards east of Djebel Rhar called Sidi Bou Baker, which overlooked the Medjez to Tebourba road and was close to the Medjerda River. The area from Djebel Rhar's south-eastern slopes to Sidi Bou Baker was completely overlooked by German positions in the hills north-east of Longstop. The task was complicated by the absence of any tank support and, inexplicably, the decision that the hill needed be captured before night fell. Therefore the battalion's leading companies assembled on the start line in the daylight at about 1900 hours.

To the impartial observer it must have seemed that hardly any lessons had been learned over the last few weeks of the necessity of carefully preparing for such an attack and carrying it out at night. The consequences of this decision were sadly both inevitable and costly. The two leading companies, A and B, were spotted and heavily shelled on the start line. Among those hit and killed that evening were Captain Coles, who had won a MC in February and led his company so effectively throughout Operation Sweep. Despite the shelling, both companies advanced across the open ground and managed to reach their objectives, but proved unable to capture them due to their casualties. Mackenzie was therefore forced to withdraw the two companies under fire as darkness fell. This desperate little skirmish cost the battalion a veteran company commander and four men killed, while 23 others were found to be missing believed captured and 16 men wounded. The loss of 44 men for no apparent reason obviously angered the battalion; an unusually forthright and critical entry in the war diary noted that: "It was an expensive operation with little achieved."[1] War diaries in 1943 were supposed to be purely factual records and not used to express critical comments. The inclusion of this remark in the battalion's diary is quite notable, and indicates how strongly Mackenzie and his staff felt about the value of this action. Unfortunately it will never be known whether the remark was aimed at "Copper" Cass or at the divisional commander. Immediately after the conclusion of the attack the battalion was relieved in its positions by the 1st East Surreys, withdrew the following day and took no further active part in operations.

13.3 The 5th Northants Advance to Sidi Ahmed Ridge

While the Lancashire Fusiliers had suffered the consequences of attacking Djebel Bou Baker, Arthur Crook's 5th Northants had been directed to carry out yet another very similar attack and one also conducted in daylight. The apparent reason for the commitment of Crook's battalion was the Germans' possession of a ridge known as Sidi Ben Ahmed, which was situated about 1,000 yards directly north of Djebel Rhar across completely open ground. The rationale for clearing the hill was similar to that used in justifying attacking Bou Baker and locations like

---

1   See TNA WO 175/512 2nd Lancs Fusiliers April 1943 WD.

Djebel Rmel in the Bed Valley. The attack was based on the assumption that it was necessary to take the hill as the Germans could use it to bring down fire which could cause harassment for troops on Longstop Hill. A core problem with this flawed argument was that as soon as you took the offending feature, you usually found yet another even higher hill which would pose a similar threat. It was ironic that less than two weeks after company commander Major Jack Anderson had pointed out the fallacy of conducting such unnecessary operations in his report on 17 April, that this lesson had still not yet been learned. A further irony was that his battalion would be one of those called upon to take part in a subsequent operation to take features immediately north of Sidi Ahmed ridge, once the 5th Northants had captured it, and it would suffer as a result. Anderson clearly understood that unless a feature had significant tactical importance, the best way to stop harassing fire was not to waste lives taking it, but to neutralise German fire by responding in kind with heavy artillery shelling. This usually tended to have a salutary effect on the offending parties and dissuade them from firing on your positions. When and if it was necessary to seize a hill, such operations were best completed after careful reconnaissance and carried out at night, or in daylight aided by tanks. By late April, all of the battalions in the division had considerably experience in conducting night attacks and were proficient in this task. It was unfortunate that despite these hard-earned lessons, Cass was apparently ordered to initiate yet another operation of this type.

Irrespective of why, or who initiated the operation, the job of seizing the ridgeline of Sidi Ahmed was to be carried out by 5th Northants in daylight and with very little time for planning and preparation. The battalion took over its positions on Djebel Ahmera by 0130 hours on the morning of 27 April, and having had very little rest that night were next ordered to take Sidi Ahmed ridge that morning. It is possible that Crook had been told by brigade staff that Sidi Ahmed was not occupied or defended, for the battalion war diary notes that it was ordered to move to rather than attack Sidi Ahmed. The lack of planning and preparation, combined with the decision to move in daylight and without any artillery and tank support, might just be explained by the assumption that the objective would not be defended. If this was the case, whoever believed such a move would not be contested was sadly mistaken. The two leading companies of the battalion, B and C, were prevented from reaching the ridge when they were shelled by mortars and artillery as they moved north-east along the valley between Rhar and the hills to the north. Crook and Captain Dudley Emmerton had a similar experience when they attempted to move to the same location with a carrier platoon using a route around the southern end of Djebel Rhar. The platoon attracted heavy shelling and was halted just north of the Medjez el Bab to Tebourba road. One section of the platoon did make it up to near the Sidi Ahmed ridge, so Crook and Emmerton dismounted and moved on foot to this position. Soon afterwards the area was heavily shelled and Emmerton was wounded, and Crook ordered the troops to pull back. The first attempt to seize Sidi Ahmed had ended in failure.

A second attempt in the early afternoon, this time by A and C Companies, was slightly more successful as they managed to reach and initially stay on their objective. C Company soon found itself pinned down by mortar and machine-gun fire and at dusk it was ordered to withdraw, but A Company managed to remain in positions near to, but not on the ridge, that night. This situation demonstrated clearly one of the basic rules of fighting in the peaks, for the Germans, having pulled back from Sidi Ahmed ridge on to three features to the north, now made life unpleasant for anyone who stayed on the ridgeline. During the evening of 27 April, Crook temporarily handed over command of the battalion to his deputy Major Buck Buchanan. At this point in the proceedings, Cass was confronted with a simple dilemma: should he withdraw the 5th Northants all the way back to Longstop or take the hills which he believed were a threat to the required positions on Sidi Ahmed? Cass made the decision to continue the attack, so on the morning of 28 April Buchanan directed his remaining rifle companies - B, C and V - to join up with A Company and attack again to regain control of Sidi Ahmed ridge. The attack was conducted at 1000 hours in complete view of the Germans, so it was no surprise that once again, after the companies had moved up to prepare for their assault, they were shelled and took casualties. This was sadly the inevitable consequence of conducting these types of attacks in daytime. By about 1430 hours that afternoon, Buchanan was able to get his lead companies close enough to Sidi Ahmed to join these up with A Company and conduct a proper attack on Sidi Ahmed. This was carried out with A Company attacking on the left, C on the right with B and V Companies behind them. Over the next few hours, the leading companies struggled to move forward and take their objectives. The deadlock appears to have been broken by V Company, led by Captain Morris Bennet and assisted by B Company, which managed to secure Sidi Ahmed despite fire from mortars.

One of the key reasons both A and C Companies made any progress in achieving the objectives were the efforts of two Bren gunners, Privates Harold Gillott and James Williams. When C Company became pinned down by mortar and machine-gun fire from a position on its flank, Gillott volunteered to go forward and dislodge the Germans. He took his Bren gun, engaged the German machine gun at close range and stopped it firing. Gillott continued onwards, engaged the enemy mortar post and silenced it as well. After these two posts were silenced, the whole company was eventually able to move forward onto its objective. Meanwhile, Private Williams was acting as the leading scout for A Company on the left when he encountered an enemy patrol of 14 men with a machine gun. Despite being unsupported, Williams engaged the patrol with his Bren gun and killed or wounded all its members. In doing so he removed a serious threat to the company and was considered personally responsible for the speed of its advance to Sidi Ahmed ridge.

That A Company was able to engage in this operation at all was a tribute to its new company commander, Captain John Pearcy, who had only joined the battalion on 24 April. Due to the losses that had been incurred previously on the slopes of Tanngoucha, his first task was to reform the remnants of that shattered company. He also had to do this while the battalion was in contact with the enemy. It was largely due to his leadership, and the support of his NCOs, that within three days, and by using reinforcements, it was capable of making any attack. Throughout 27-28 April, Pearcy's personal gallantry and leadership were in evidence as he led his new company through heavy fire to help seize the Sidi Ahmed ridge. At one point during the action on 27 April, when A Company had managed to get to Sidi Ahmed, communications with headquarters had broken down. It was essential to get information back to his CO, so Pearcy personally moved back under fire to battalion headquarters, briefed them on the location of his company and returned to it. It had been A Company that had managed to tenuously hold on to Sidi Ahmed on the night of 27 April and was counterattacked at first light. Pearcy had ensured that this attack was repulsed, but a second one had forced him to withdraw to positions close to Sidi Ahmed. It had been these positions which the company had occupied despite heavy fire and from which they relaunched the successful attack on the hill on the afternoon of 28 April.

Although it was now 1700 hours, and the day was drawing to a close, Bennet and V Company, in combination with C Company, were ordered after dark to move forward and seize Point 160. This was a conical hill also known as Sidi Ali Ben Aoune, which inevitably overlooked Sidi Ahmed. Captain Morris Bennet had already had a fairly eventful day before leading the attack. Sometime prior to this attack, V Company had been in positions in or near Sidi Ahmed, but was seriously harassed by a combination of machine guns, mortars and sniper fire. Two German snipers were especially causing problems and had led to a number of casualties in the company. Despite the grave risk of being shot by a sniper, Bennet moved out of cover to determine their location and used a 2in mortar to drop bombs which eventually dislodged them. At about 1930 hours, as night fell, Bennet led his company forward up the hill, and despite heavy enemy fire drove the Germans off the hill and took 10 prisoners. During this action Bennet was wounded in the head and temporarily blinded, but he would not leave his company until he ensured it had consolidated its hold on the hill. Even when he left the hill, guided by his batman, he made sure that they escorted the new prisoners down the hill.

At about 2130, V Company was reinforced when C Company managed to reach their positions on Point 160. Despite this success, it soon became apparent that the Germans had infiltrated around their location and had almost surrounded the two companies, so they were forced to withdraw back to Sidi Ahmed ridge. The battalion was able to hold its new position there, but it was apparent that it lacked the strength to conduct further attacks. The last two days had taken their toll on the battalion. The already depleted strength of its rifle companies had been further reduced by this series of attacks, which had resulted in at least three men killed, over 70 wounded and four missing in action. After the losses that the battalion had already incurred over the last three weeks, it could ill afford to lose the 77 officers and men who became casualties in this ill-advised venture.

The efforts of officers and men such as Bennet, Pearcy, Gillot and Williams that had enabled the battalion to capture and hold Sidi Ahmed were duly later recognized by the award of two MCs and two MMs. Another officer who made a significant contribution to maintaining the battalion's hold on the Sidi Ahmed ridge was Captain John Palmer, a FOO with the 4th Medium Regiment. Palmer manned an observation post on Point 154 from 27-30 April, since the presence of German tanks nearby meant he could not be relieved earlier. Throughout this period, Palmer and his party were under frequent artillery and mortar fire. Despite his situation, Palmer was able to send back valuable information which enabled the regiment to engage and damage four German tanks. His action helped to avert a serious threat to an artillery area located near Longstop. Palmer was later awarded the MC for this and a previous action at Djebel Bettiour on 17-18 April when he discovered and knocked out two German anti-tank guns.

Fortunately for the men of the 5th Northants, it had been decided that 11th Infantry Brigade would be pulled back from the Longstop area as they had been allocated another task. At midnight, the brigade and the two battalions still present - the 1st East Surreys and 5th Northants - were relieved by the 6th West Kents and 8th Argylls. Howlett and the 36th Infantry Brigade now assumed responsibility for Longstop Hill and the Sidi Ahmed ridge.

13.4 One Last Desperate Venture –the Attack on Mosque Ridge

Howlett's first action as brigade commander in this sector proved to be both surprising and tragic. He gave orders that the three features above Sidi Ahmed ridge had to be captured, assigning the task to the 8th Argylls. It is really difficult to understand and justify the decision to conduct yet another attack to take the hills above Sidi Ahmed, and especially to use the 8th Argylls. The two features which the Argylls were now ordered to take were some 1,000 yards north of Sidi Ahmed. They were Point 160, known as Sidi Ali Ben Aoune, and the unnamed Point 202. The latter feature lay to the north-west of Point 160, but was in turn dominated by two peaks, Djebel Touila, at some 328 metres, and Djebel el Hallouf, 428 metres. The capture of Points 160 and 202 might reduce enemy fire on Sidi Ahmed ridge, but it would also create another problem, for it would expose troops on these features to enemy machine-gun fire and shelling from yet other hills. It is important to note that in Howlett's defence, he was almost certainly implementing orders that he had received from his divisional commander, orders he did not approve of or like. Windeatt, his Brigade Major, noted: "The Divisional Commander wanted Swifty to attack down the road to Sidi Bou Baker as well as at Sidi Ahmed but he quite rightly refused to do it, in fact he is very much against the whole party."

The apparent reason for taking Sidi Ahmed, according to Windeatt, was to secure a start line for the Irish Brigade to conduct what he called "a fantastic scheme on foot for the Irish Brigade to make a terrific sweep to cut the main road from the north near Tebourba".[2] This was the ambitious operation which division staff had ordered Brigadier Russell and his weakened brigade to carry out and which led to difficult operations after Tanngoucha was captured. The actual reasons for these orders are difficult to determine. What is clear is that Evelegh and his staff committed a severely weakened battalion to an operation which at best was very difficult to justify.[3] There was a further reason for not ordering the Argylls to attack, which was after the death of Colin McNabb, it now had a new CO. Lieutenant Colonel Jim Scott-Elliott had only just assumed command on the night of 24 April, and in the most difficult of circumstances. It should have been apparent to Evelegh that the battalion was not ready to undertake operations and needed time to rest and reorganise. Finally, assuming that a divisional commander is allowed occasionally to consider human considerations, it seems a remarkably cruel decision to commit the Argylls to yet another attack so soon after they had secured, at such cost, such a victory for their division. It is likely that Howlett opposed the operation both on tactical grounds and because of the condition of Argylls. None of these reasons, unfortunately, seem to hold sway with Evelegh. The result of this rather poor planning was that this great fighting battalion would undergo one last but unnecessary ordeal in the Battle of the Peaks which would demand its own final price.

The commitment of the 8th Argylls to one final bloody attack commenced on the afternoon of 29 April, when it sent a small advanced party to the 5th Northants' positions on the Sidi Ahmed ridge to view their new location. Later, close to midnight, the battalion relieved the 5th

---

2   Windeatt, *Very Ordinary Soldier*, p.52.
3   The author's personal view that the operation was difficult to justify is based on extensive study of the relevant war diaries and reports of the 38th Brigade, 78th Division, the original GSGS maps and also a US Army official publication, *To Bizerte with II Corps* (Washington DC: Center of Military History, US Army, 1990).

Northants, who were probably more than happy to leave this location. Sometime during the early morning of 30 April, Scott-Elliott visited brigade headquarters and received orders for the battalion to attack Points 160 and 202 above Sidi Ahmed ridge. The attack was to be carried out that afternoon. It was once again in full view of Germans on these positions, but at least on this occasion the 8th Argylls were to be supported by a squadron of tanks from the North Irish Horse. Among the officers who were briefed by their new CO on their new task was Captain Lionel Sanderson, who had just joined the battalion the previous day and had been assigned by his new boss to take command of a company. In contrast to many replacements, Sanderson, nicknamed "Fuzzy" due to his curly hairstyle, was a regular officer who been commissioned into the King's Own Scottish Borderers (KOSB) in 1937. This was the same regiment into which his new CO, Scott-Elliott, had originally been commissioned before transferring to the Argylls. Sanderson had served in England in 1938 with the KOSB before he was selected to become Aide de Camp (ADC) to Major General Bernard Montgomery in Palestine and saw action in France with his regiment in 1940. During the BEF's retreat through Belgium to Dunkirk, Sanderson had assumed command of his company and it was largely due to his leadership that it was evacuated back to England. By 1943 he was an experienced veteran used to the chaos of war, but even he was more than a little discomforted by what he found on his arrival. After his meeting with Scott-Elliott that morning, Sanderson had walked over to some trees to learn that his new company was comprised of only one officer and 30 men, all of which looked dirty and tired. While Sanderson was trying to reorganise his new command into two understrength platoons, he learned to his concern that the battalion was moving up to the front line. The following morning, Sanderson's unease increased significantly when he was summoned to a briefing by his CO and learned that the battalion was about to carry out an attack on Points 160 and 202. The only good piece of news was that since his company was understrength, he and his men were assigned a supporting role. Sanderson was later to write:

> On hearing that we were to attack my heart sank with dismay. How would I be able to carry out my part of the attack knowing hardly a soul by name and still less about their capabilities or weaknesses?

This was Sanderson's first action in command of an Argyll company, so he was much relieved when, in a gesture that was typical of both his character and leadership, Jack Anderson, who was in reserve, quietly joined him and his company. Sanderson later wrote that Anderson's presence "lifted my morale and provided reassurance to those who had served with the battalion for several months. He was a far sighted officer and magnificent leader and example to all ranks."[4] There was no need for Anderson to have joined the company, as he had been told that he was to be kept in reserve during this action due to his efforts on Longstop. Another reason why Anderson was not supposed to take part in this action was that the citation for his VC was already working its way up the chain of command, and the new battalion CO wanted to ensure Anderson was alive to receive it.

---

4   The quotations are from Lionel Sanderson, *Variety is the Spice of Life* (London: Minerva Press, 1995), p.163.

The task that faced the battalion in capturing these two hills was not too dissimilar to that it had encountered in attacking Djebel Ahmera six days previously. The unit had to cross nearly 1,000 yards of open ground, attack uphill and in full view of the Germans. The plan for this attack was simple: the battalion would carry out a frontal attack in daylight, albeit with the support of an artillery concentration and with tanks in support. As a plan it was easy to understand, but did not involve any tactical change from previous attacks that had failed and was therefore very predictable. One key difference to this operation from the two previously conducted by Cass was the assignment of tanks. It is possible that Brigadier Howlett thought they might make a difference to this operation - after all, they had done so at Djebel Rhar - and therefore the battalion had the support of the Churchill tanks of C Squadron of the North Irish Horse, commanded by Major Paul Welch. At 1000 hours, the two leading companies of the 8th Argylls got out of their slit trenches on Sidi Ahmed and marched out on to the open ground leading north, while Welch's tanks moved ahead of the infantry. On the left was B Company led by Captain Scott, and on the right X Company, the latter led by another new ex-KOSB officer, Major Murch. These two companies were to be supported by R Company. Sadly, but predictably, the companies soon came under heavy machine-gun fire as they approached the two hills, started to take casualties and were unable to reach their objectives. Consequently, the Churchill tanks had moved well ahead of the majority of the infantry companies while negotiating two difficult wadis on the way. A key source of difficulty for the infantry proved to be long-range fire from hills to the north and north-east of their objectives. A young officer within B Company, Lieutenant John Urquhart, who was commanding the lead platoon in this attack, recalled:

> We had been under mortar and artillery fire for 15 minutes before crossing the start line and as the enemy saw the tanks and infantry advancing this fire became much [heavier] and a number of M.Gs opened up … as I reached a gulley junction about four hundred yards from the objective the fire became very hot and caused a number of casualties in my platoon but we pushed on and didn't suffer so badly from the mortar and air burst as the rest of the company who followed on. On reaching a point about a hundred yards from the objective we came under very heavy fire and the platoon took cover but I did not see them stop and pushed on … I spotted an enemy MG nest at the top of the ridge about 30 yards away and fired at it stopping their fire. I was then on the objective. I looked around for the rest of the platoon but only Private Neil had followed me.[5]

Urquhart and Private Neil were the only members of B Company to reach their objective, for the rest of the platoon, the company and also X Company became temporarily pinned down. The Churchill tanks were not delayed, and at one point one of C Squadron's tanks was in a hull-down position less than 20 yards from Urquhart. The latter dashed from the German slit trench he was occupying with Private Neil, moved to the rear of the tank and tried to communicate with its crew, but failed. Soon afterwards, Urquhart saw and took a German soldier prisoner, but found that he was forced to take cover in the German's slit trench and came under fire from one of the Churchill tank's Besa machine guns. Although C Squadron tanks got onto at least

5   Account by Urquhart in TNA WO 175/491 8th Argylls April 1943 WD.

one of the objectives, it proved difficult for the Argylls' infantry companies to move forward and join them. Moreover, Welch's Churchill tank crews became rapidly distracted from their infantry-support task as they came under fire from three German Mark IV *panzers*. This was the first time the North Irish Horse had encountered German tanks in the area in and around Longstop Hill. The Churchill crews quickly removed high-explosive shells, reloaded with armour-piercing ordnance and engaged the *panzers*, hitting two of them but suffering losses in return. After a short sharp action, which started at about 1115 hours and lasted about half an hour, the Mark IVs decided to withdraw. During this action, one *panzer* had knocked out a tank commanded by Sergeant Elliott, killed his gunner and forced the rest of the crew to evacuate the tank. It also hit the tank commanded by one of the troop leaders, Lieutenant R. Mann, the brother-in-law of Paul Welch. Sadly, Mann and his gunner, Trooper Whatley, were both killed. The driver, Trooper Neilson, was also wounded, so co-driver Trooper Eastwood drove the tank out of the action, but as it went down a hill it overturned. Both Eastwood and the other member of the crew, wireless operator Trooper Young, were injured in the accident. Despite his injuries, Neilson managed to evacuate Eastwood and Young from the Churchill and make his way under heavy machine-gun fire to report the situation to another officer and seek help for his crew. This act of courage and loyalty to his crew would later earn Neilson a MM.

Although C Squadron's tanks had originally got onto one of the objectives, both B and X Companies were only able to move forward to its lower slopes. As a result, Urquhart and his companion Private Neil found that they were cut off. Later, as darkness started to fall, Urquhart tried to move back to friendly lines along with his German prisoner, but was surrounded and captured, as was Private Neil. Urquhart would have a range of unusual adventures, which included being fired on yet again by friendly forces, in this case RAF fighters, while he was on an Italian POW ship, before he was eventually liberated and able to return to the battalion 10 days later.[6] Sanderson's company had been ordered to support B Company by attacking on their left, but they were quickly held up by enemy fire and unable to contribute much to the battle. This was fortunate for Sanderson, Anderson and the seriously understrength company.

The gallant efforts of Urquhart, Neil, the other officers and men of the Argylls and the North Irish Horse finally bore some fruit. At about 1515 hours that afternoon, Major Murch and about 40 men of X Company reached the lowest slopes of Point 202. It proved impossible for B Company to get any closer to Point 160, and its commander Captain Scott was wounded. Later, as darkness fell, two platoons of Y Company were sent up to relieve Murch and his men. The platoons now moved on to Point 160 and tried to occupy it, but found it still held by the Germans. For the rest of the night, the men of Y Company disputed possession of Point 160 with the Austrian troops who held it, but at first light, and in accordance with orders, they withdrew to Sidi Ahmed ridge and so ended the Argylls' last operation in Tunisia.

In a clear demonstration of the apparent futility of this attack, no further attempt was made by Howlett and 36th Brigade to capture these features, as no other battalion was now capable of mounting one. In any case, the tough Austrian troops of the 754th Grenadier Regiment who had held these positions so bravely were forced to withdraw when 38th Irish Brigade eventually started to flank their positions. The 8th Argylls spent the next 24 hours occupying Sidi Ahmed

---

6   Sadly, having survived this experience, John Urquhart was killed in August at the Battle of Centuripe in Sicily.

ridge before they were relieved on the night of 1 May without any real harassment. They were only able to do so because they had been reinforced by a company of the 5th Buffs. This attack was Howlett's last significant operation in Tunisia, so it was a pity that it proved a costly failure. It was even more tragic that the last attack of the 8th Argylls was such an expensive one for the battalion, which took 12 prisoners but failed to take its objectives and lost at least 12 men killed and nearly 90 wounded. The losses were largely concentrated among B and X Companies, and included many older and experienced soldiers in their mid to late 20s. These were men the battalion could ill afford to lose, given the fighting that lay ahead of the regiment in Sicily and Italy. Captain Sanderson was fortunately spared any losses in his company, and moreover Major Anderson also came through unscathed. A very observant and capable officer, Sanderson would go on to distinguish himself in Sicily, where he would win a MC, and also serve in Italy. In early 1944, Sanderson would personally be selected by Montgomery to be one of his famous liaison officers and serve in this role with distinction. Sanderson's personal recollection and judgement on these events are worth quoting:

> Fortunately my company's task was more of a supporting one than a major assault against the Germans in which two other companies were involved against stiff opposition with resulting heavy casualties ... it achieved nothing of consequence and seemed so futile at that stage of the campaign'[7]

Sanderson was not the only member of the unit who felt the operation was unnecessary, for unusually the regimental history stated that there was afterwards:

> a widespread feeling in the battalion that this was in Major Andersons' words (from his report on the action on the 17 April) "an operation which has no definite end in view and serves no useful purpose". It certainly induced a rebellious attitude to all futile operations.[8]

It is known that the Argylls were not reticent in expressing their views up the chain of command, and it is likely that their concerns were sympathetically received for Howlett almost certainly held similar views. His Brigade Major, John Windeatt, would later write:

> The attack on Sidi Ahmed was not a success, in fact it was the most futile show we've been put into which has cost the Argylls about a hundred casualties ... The Argylls were very bitter over this show as they consider and quite rightly so, that they suffered casualties for nothing.[9]

The Argylls' last action in the Tunisian campaign had been a bloody one, and tragically it had also been almost certainly unnecessary.

---

7   Sanderson, *Variety is the Spice of Life*, p.163.
8   See Malcolm, *History of 8th Argylls*, p.129.
9   Windeatt, *Very Ordinary Soldier*, pp.52-53.

13.5 The Last Shot of the Last Battle

The reason why "Copper" Cass and his brigade had been withdrawn from Longstop Hill was that they were needed to take over positions held by the 12th Brigade of the 4th Infantry Division south of the Medjerda River. This move was part of a shift in forces that would free up the latter brigade to continue their attack towards Tunis. Bill Wilberforce and the East Surreys were relieved by the 6th West Kents on Djebel Rhar on the night of 29 April, and were next sent to take over positions in the hills south of Medjez el Bab near Gueriat el Atach. They were subsequently moved to hold the left flank of the 4th Division in the area around a key road junction on the Medjez-Tunis road, long known as Peter's Corner. It had been so named in the early fighting for Tunis after the CO of the 1st Derbyshire Yeomanry, Peter Payne-Dalway. The battalion's positions were under direct observation and movement during the day was almost impossible, without eliciting enemy shelling or mortars. On 5 May, Wilberforce was able to tell his officers the good news that the final battle for Tunis was about to get under way. The next day, which was the start of Operation Strike, the battalion's positions were mortared heavily by the Germans, causing 11 casualties. On the morning of the same day, Wilberforce received the news that he had been given the immediate award of the DSO for his leadership at Longstop and during the Battle of the Peaks. It is possible that the likely end of the campaign made Wilberforce slightly less wary, for that afternoon for he was sitting in or standing next to his personal car in the open, along with his adjutant, at Peter's Corner. This proved to be a tragic error of judgment, for in literally the last shot of the last battle of the East Surreys in Tunisia, Lieutenant Colonel William Basil Wilberforce was killed. Harry Smith recalled the incident in a personal memoir he later wrote:

> He had unluckily parked his staff car behind a cactus hedge at Battalion Headquarters at Peter's Corner, and was sitting in it talking to Pat Wadham the Intelligence Officer when a German 88-mm gun loosed off one final round of solid shot which did all the damage. Pat Wadham had his kneecap removed by the same round … Our Commanding Officer was buried in the little cemetery in the farm garden near Medjez known as Beharine.[10]

The tragic death of Bill Wilberforce so close to the end of a long campaign hit the officers and men of the battalion very hard. It was also a great blow to the many officers across the division who had known him so well, including Cass, Howlett and Evelegh. The latter quickly confirmed Major Harry Smith in command of the battalion. This was a sound decision, for any other replacement might have been resented and Smith had proved his worth many times. It was one of those terrible examples of the capricious and senseless nature of war that Wilberforce, who had managed to survive the entire Tunisian campaign, should die so late in that campaign. Wilberforce's death created a widow of his wife Cecilia and took away a father from his son, who by family tradition had the first name of William, and his daughter Susan. The distinguished name of William Wilberforce continues on today in the form of Bill's great, great grandson William Daniel Wilberforce. Harry Smith would lead the battalion for the final few days of the campaign, though there would be no further fighting and Wilberforce was the last member of

10   Smith, *Operations of East Surreys*, p.5.

the battalion to die in Tunisia. Smith would justify the confidence placed in him by Cass and add further laurels to his distinguished family name during the campaign in Sicily and Italy as he continued in command of the battalion before being posted to a staff role in the Middle East. After the war, Smith would have a distinguished career, and in one of those little historical ironies was posted in 1956 to NATO headquarters, where he served under General Spiedel, who had been Rommel's Chief of Staff. Colonel Smith retired in 1961 and died in 1997.

Wilberforce's death on 6 May can reasonably be said to have brought to an end the participation of the Battle-Axe Division in the Battle of the Peaks. While some historians may argue that this actually happened when Operation Sweep ended on 20 April, this author's view is that the Battle of the Peaks continued in the mountains until early May. It seems appropriate to conclude this chapter with a short assessment of the 78th Division's period of four weeks of fighting in the mountains. During that time the division managed to achieve almost all the many difficult objectives it was assigned by V Corps to capture, though not always in the time frame originally allocated. The exceptions to this rule were the village of Heidous, which was evacuated by the enemy, and the unrealistic objectives near Tebourba assigned to it in late April. During those four weeks, the units of the Battle-Axe Division attacked, captured and held a total of 20 peaks in some of the most difficult terrain in northern Tunisia. They did so despite fierce resistance by veteran Austrian and German troops, many of whom had fought in Poland, France and Russia. In this period, the division captured in excess of 2,300 prisoners and effectively destroyed at least five battalions of enemy troops. A precise estimate of the casualties inflicted by the Battle-Axe Division and its supporting units on the Axis forces is difficult to determine. A rough estimate is that these casualties probably exceeded 900 men. It would be most convenient for this story to state that the 334th Infantry Division was effectively destroyed during the Battle of the Peaks, but that would not be true. The 78th Division's tough and wily opponents in the 334th Infantry Division would survive and continue to fight in the mountains, but it was certainly a shadow of the formation it had previously been when the attack commenced on 7 April. The German division had been seriously weakened by the fighting during Operation Sweep, and only survived due to reinforcements from so-called *Marsch* battalions or through the attachment of other regiments. The 334th Division, at the end of the Battle of the Peaks, came under the command of Major General Fritz Krause, as Friedrich Weber had been promoted to command of a corps. After fighting against the US II Corps, Krause would be among the German general officers who would surrender with their formations near Bizerte on 9 May 1943 to Major General Ernest Harmon of the 1st Armoured Division. The performance of the Battle-Axe Division during these four weeks of operations, and its capture of such difficult objectives as Djebels Mahdi, Bettiour, Ang, Kef el Tiour and Tanngoucha, and Longstop Hill, was remarkable. These achievements came after it had already established a fine reputation in five months of difficult fighting in the hills of Tunisia.

At the time, those who commanded the formation fully recognised its value. Kenneth Anderson, who commanded the First Army and set high standards, would write that: "I consider the 78 Division deserves high praise for as tough and prolonged a bit of fighting as has ever been undertaken by the British soldier."[11] Possibly the best tribute to the division, and especially to the Irish Brigade, came when the battle was over, for it was then that Brigadier

11   Anderson, *Despatches*, p.5,459.

Nelson Russell escorted Charles Allfrey, the GOC of V Corps, up into the Peaks and showed him the terrain that had been captured. When Allfrey finally saw the nature of the terrain the division had fought over, he was astonished and asked: "'How an earth did they do it?" Russell's honest but proud answer, one that might reasonably be applied to the whole 78th Division, though it referred to his own brigade, was "I'm damned if I know", though later noting that such a victory could "only have been done by the very best troops with first class junior leaders".[12]

12   Russell, *Irish Brigade*, p.115.

14

After The Battle

14.1 Operation Strike and the End of the Afrika Korps

While the 78th Division was involved in local attacks and holding its positions, a wider plan had been developed to attack and take Tunis and defeat the Axis forces in Tunisia. This new plan was agreed on 30 April after General Harold Alexander had finally decided to reinforce the First Army with divisions from Montgomery's Eighth Army for the final attack. Monty had reluctantly abandoned his ambition for the Eighth Army to strike the last blow, and to his credit had taken the initiative and suggested he loan some of his units to Kenneth Anderson. The plan required the transfer of the 7th Armoured and 4th Indian Divisions to the First Army and their relocation to the area south-east of Medjez el Bab. Lieutenant General Brian Horrocks was shifted from his job as commander of XXX Corps to take command of IX Corps, replacing John Crocker, who had been injured in an accident. Operation Strike was launched on 6 May, with V Corps and a reinforced IX Corps advancing against where the German defences were at their strongest, in the Massicault plain. The 6th and 7th Armoured Divisions attacked with the support of a large artillery barrage, supported by the infantry divisions. The 78th Division and Bernard Howlett's old battalion played a small part in the attack, as the 6th West Kents, now commanded by a newly promoted Lieutenant Colonel Henry Lovell, carried out a very limited advance to seize the start line for the 4th Infantry Division. The West Kents attacked on the night of 5 May and quickly took their objectives prior to the start of the main attack at 0300 hours. They held them during the day, and despite being mortared and shelled by Tiger tanks, only suffered one killed and 11 wounded in action. These casualties proved to be the last casualties suffered by the battalion and 36th Brigade in the Tunisian campaign.

The fighting over the period from 6-8 May was fierce, but ended with the commitment of the 1st Armoured Division in place of the 7th Armoured Division on that last day. This formation helped ensure the destruction of the few German armoured units left to defend the approaches to Tunis. It was fitting that playing their own role in Operation Strike were two regiments who had supported the Battle-Axe Division so well in the Battle of the Peaks and Operation Vulcan. Both the North Irish Horse and the 142nd Regiment RAC helped support infantry troops who took part in the final attack. At 1200 hours on 8 May, the West Kents entered the outskirts of Tunis to encounter thousands of German and Italian prisoners, with many in their own vehicles. The 1st East Surreys followed into the city soon after in the early afternoon, to be greeted by cheering French and curious though sometimes less than ecstatic Arab inhabitants. The capture of Tunis did not immediately lead to an end to the fighting, for the Axis forces around the Enfidaville position were still in place and some fighting continued near Bizerte. Moreover, von Arnim and his subordinate commanders were intent on withdrawing his battered formations into the Cap Bon peninsula, with the apparent intention of making a final stand. Von Arnim's orders to establish a final stronghold on Cap Bon were futile, as his lines of communication back to Sicily had now been completely severed and no further ammunition, fuel and food would be forthcoming. His plan was thwarted when the 6th Armoured Division attacked the troops of the Hermann Goering Division defending the town of Hamman Lif on 9 May. Their success here ensured that the Allies could and did cut off any serious withdrawal on to the Cap Bon peninsula. On the same day, the US II Corps cornered the commander of the 5th *Panzer* Army, Gustav von Vaerst, near Bizerte and took his surrender. In the south, French forces attacking in the mountainous Zaghouan sector secured the surrender of 22,000 Germans. The end in North Africa and the final destruction of the *Afrika Korps* came on the morning of 12 May, when von Arnim's Chief of Staff arrived at the headquarters of the 4th Indian Division to make arrangements for his boss's personal surrender. General von Arnim first destroyed all communications equipment which linked him to other Axis headquarters outside of Tunisia, then surrendered to Major General Tuker of the 4th Indian Division at his headquarters later that morning. Afterwards, Tuker took von Arnim to the headquarters of the First Army and into the presence of General Anderson. Von Arnim had been at pains to make clear that his personal surrender did not mean the formal surrender of all Axis troops, as his argument was that they were spread out too much for him to deliver this outcome. Nonetheless, despite the threats of some of his subordinates to fight on, the reality was that almost all Axis troops very quickly surrendered to the Allied forces. General Messe, the commander of the First Italian Army, was ordered by Mussolini at 1955 hours on 12 May to surrender his army. This he did to Lieutenant General Freyberg of the New Zealand Corps at Enfidaville at 1200 hours the following day. Anderson wrote in his official dispatch on the Tunisian campaign that:

> On the 12 May [*sic*] Colonel General Von Arnim Commanding General of Army Group Afrika surrendered with his staff at the headquarters of the 4th Indian Division and was brought to me at Headquarters First Army. The disaster was complete – the total of prisoners reached a quarter of a million ... the booty was immense. Dunkirk was amply revenged.[1]

Anderson's boss, General Alexander, was quick to send news of this great victory to England and Prime Minister Winston Churchill. Alexander knew that Churchill would appreciate a nice turn of phrase, so he spent time composing the message for maximum dramatic effect. The signal, which certainly made Alexander more famous, read: "Sir, it is my duty to report that the Tunisian Campaign is over. All enemy resistance has ceased. We are masters of the North African shores."[2]

There is no clear and agreed total for the number of officers and men of the Axis forces who surrendered in Tunisia. Anderson cited a quarter of a million. The figure cited in Playfair's

1   Anderson, *Dispatches*, p.5,462.
2   Alexander, *Dispatches*, p.884.

official history of the campaign indicates the Allies took 238,243 prisoners. Of these, 101,784 were Germans, 89,442 Italians and 47,017 others.[3] It is unclear who the others were, but they were most likely to have been Arab troops and other auxiliaries. American sources suggested that the Allies had taken a total of 275,000 prisoners by the end of the campaign, while von Arnim himself estimated that 100,000 German and 200,000 Italian prisoners had been taken. Whatever the actual figure, a serious blow had been struck against the Axis forces in the Mediterranean, one that ranked equal to the surrender of the German Sixth Army at Stalingrad. The officers and men lost included both veteran fighting troops and key technical and logistics personnel, all of whom could have made the subsequent Allied advance into Sicily and Italy even more difficult than it became. The initial destination of these tens of thousands of prisoners was a set of POW camps near Tunis, or the camps in the US or French sectors. The eventual destination for the members of the now defeated, though much-vaunted, *Afrika Korps* was quite varied, and included camps in Texas, Utah, Mississippi, Cornwall and Scotland. The equipment captured included large quantities of small arms, heavy weapons, artillery and vehicles, though most tanks had been disabled or destroyed. Despite the often-expressed view that the Axis forces had run out of food and ammunition, significant quantities of both were seized, though little fuel was left.

Very little of this was of much concern to the officers and men of the East Surreys as they entered the outskirts of Tunis on 8 May. This was the city that had been their objective ever since they had landed on the beaches outside of Algiers back in November 1942, although comparatively few of the officers and men who had then been with the battalion remained with the unit on this day. The East Surreys had been warned that they might be involved in mopping-up operations, so were wary as they moved into the outer suburbs of Tunis. An account from the battalion's records noted that:

> As the Surreys marched into to Tunis with loaded rifles and fixed bayonets, it became apparent that there would be no fighting. Crowds of civilians wild with excitement lined the route cheering and weeping by turns. The mopping up operation became a triumphal march.[4]

John Woodhouse of the East Surreys was present and recalled in a letter to his mother:

> At 1300 we marched in and rode part of the way in on trucks and Bren gun carriers. We were cheered almost the whole way and given drinks and flowers. At one place my truck was mobbed by people and couldn't move.[5]

The 6th West Kents, who entered the city just an hour earlier on a different route, had a similar experience:

> We were one of the first infantry units to enter the city and had a wonderful welcome from the civilians who were delighted to think that bombing had ceased. The population went

---

3   See Playfair, *Destruction of Axis Forces*, p.460.
4   See *Surreys in Tunisia* in TNA WO 175/ 519 1st East Surreys May 1943 WD.
5   Evans, *With the East Surreys*, p.50.

completely crazy rushing about the streets in any vehicle they could find, waving large flags and giving flowers and bottles of wine to the troops.[6]

The 6th Skins also managed to sample the delights of marching into and liberating the city of Tunis. They too had been warned they might be involved in mopping up, but found an ecstatic crowd. Their war diary noted:

> A tremendous welcome awaits the Battalion. Most of the public buildings are flying Tricolours. Groups of people stand on the road cheering, clapping and giving the V sign. Reaching the Rue de France, there was a crowd right across the road. The vehicles have to force a passage through a sea of people, waving flags and throwing roses to us. Some civilians asked us if we were the Eighth Army. They seemed badly informed about the situation of the war.[7]

It was fitting that at least one battalion from each of the three infantry brigades of the division were among the first infantry troops into Tunis, for the 78th Division had played a key role in ensuring that this moment had happened. The question by the French civilians, whether the Skins were from the Eighth Army, was symptomatic of a wider tendency for that organization to garner rather more publicity and credit than perhaps was its due for this victory. The Eighth Army was undoubtedly due a full share of the laurels, for it had endured some hard fighting, but it was the First Army which had first entered Tunisia and had experienced extensive fighting for nearly seven months. Unfortunately, over the next 75 years the myth has grown that it was just the Eighth Army which liberated Tunisia. Montgomery, to his eternal discredit, did very little to counter this view, both in the short and long term. Part of the reason for this unfortunate and enduring myth was that in contrast to Montgomery, Kenneth Anderson shunned publicity and believed his army's achievements would stand on their own merits without courting the media. Another issue was that frankly too many journalists cynically believed articles and references to the Eighth Army made for better copy. Sadly, Anderson was gravely misplaced in his belief that his army would receive the credit it was properly due. However, despite this slightly discordant note, the officers and men of both the 78th Division and the wider First Army took great pride in their key role in the capture of the first capital city to be liberated by Allied forces.

14.2 Appointment in Tunis

Although Lieutenant Villiers of the 5th Northants was tragically unable to keep his personal appointment in Tunis, the officers and men of his battalion, and many of those from the First Army who had landed in November 1942, were able to do so. Anderson and his First Army had their day in the spotlight, for in glorious sunshine on 20 May, a victory parade was held in the city of Tunis and it was their day. Harold Alexander had exercised sound judgment and made this a largely First Army affair. Montgomery was not invited, and the majority of troops who took part were from the First Army. It was, however, fitting that some Eighth Army

6   See TNA WO 175/509 6th West Kents May 1943 WD.
7   See the entry for 8 May in TNA WO 175/505 6th Skins May 1943 WD.

units did take part, for they had fought their way into Tunisia and to Enfidaville and taken part in Operation Strike. Nonetheless, it was rightly felt that the Eighth Army had completed its victory parade on 4 February 1943 in front of Winston Churchill in the city of Tripoli, and should take a back seat here. The saluting dais on the Rue de Gambetta in Tunis was appropriately flanked on both sides by a Churchill tank, with a squadron of Churchills in a row stationed just across from the street. The presence of these tanks was well deserved, for it was infantry tank regiments, such as the North Irish Horse and the 142nd Regiment RAC, that had done much to enable the parade to take place. Guards of Honour for the parade were provided by the British, Americans and French. The dais was occupied by a range of senior officers and civilians from several nations who had made varying contributions to ensuring the victory the parade celebrated. Taking the salute on the dais was General Dwight Eisenhower, accompanied by General Harold Alexander, Lieutenant General Kenneth Anderson, Admiral Andrew Cunningham, General Henri Giraud and Air Chief Marshal Arthur Tedder.

Although the Battle-Axe Division had certainly earned the right to lead the parade, diplomacy dictated that French units were at the head of the parade, and they were followed by the Americans. After them came the V Corps contingent, led by Lieutenant General Allfrey himself. This included the 78th Division, which was well represented by varying sized groups from each of its battalions and regiments. It was of course not feasible for entire units to take part, as such a parade would have taken far too long. In addition to other British units from the First Army, the 11th Hussars from the Eighth Army also participated. The presence of the French and the contingent from the American 34th Infantry Division should have reminded everyone that Anderson's First Army had the distinction of being the first truly Allied army in action. It is true that the Eighth Army had included a small number of French troops and many non-British formations, but the majority of these were from the British Empire. Monty had at this point in the war never commanded American troops and did not have any major French formations under his command in North Africa. Most of the battalions and regiments of the 78th Division that took part recall that the day was an extremely hot one, and those officers and men involved, though proud to do so, were happy when it was all over. Among those in the parade was Brigadier Nelson Russell, leading a contingent from the 38th Irish Brigade. Russell would later recall watching one of his COs:

> Pat Scott was on top of his carrier. His two great feet sticking out like twin bumpers, his pipe in his mouth and a wide grin on his face. Three flowers of sorts had got caught in his shirt collar. The happy warrior was at ease, surrounded by a seething mass of pleasant lunatics.[8] (see Plate 18)

14.3 The Fate of the First Army and its Commander

The First Army's moment in the spotlight was all too brief, for although Anderson and his men did not know it, the decision had already been made to disband it. Alexander had decided that only one army was required after the Tunisian campaign and that this would be the famed Eighth under Montgomery's command. The parade through Tunis was the last major

---

8   Russell, *Irish Brigade*, p.20.

official event which the First Army would carry out. The manner in which this decision was communicated to Anderson casts both Eisenhower and Alexander in a rather poor light. Despite loyally serving Eisenhower and helping Alexander deliver a major victory, Anderson was kept in the dark. He made several requests to both his superiors for information on the future of the First Army and his own situation, but his requests were ignored as neither of the men had the moral courage to tell him the bad news personally. Eisenhower fairly quickly ended any relationship with Anderson, who had so loyally supported him, and rapidly distanced himself from a man whose star was not in the ascendant or of value to him. The First Army was formally disbanded in July 1943, but by this point it was just a shell of its former self after its formations had been transferred to the Eighth Army. The same month Anderson was sent home, where he assumed command of the Second Army, supposedly to prepare it for the invasion of the France. His tenure as commander was brief, and when Montgomery arrived in January 1944 he was quickly replaced by Miles Dempsey. Montgomery had a low opinion of Anderson's abilities; for example, in March 1943 he had written to Alexander about Anderson, saying: "[I]t is obvious that Anderson is completely unfit to command any army."[9] It was also Montgomery who, in front of many junior officers, in appalling breach of etiquette and in a typically tactless manner, had offered his assessment that as an army commander, Anderson was a "Good Plain Cook".[10] It was therefore not a surprise that Anderson was replaced.

Anderson took his fate with good grace and finished the war as GOC East Africa Command. After the war he became a well-respected and admired Governor of Gibraltar, and he died there in 1958.

Despite their efforts and achievements, both Anderson and the First Army were to be consigned to obscurity. Anderson never wrote his memoirs and to this day lacks a biographer, while the First Army has yet to have its own historian. Monty's patronising description of Anderson joins a long list of many other famous British and American officers who have become his detractors. At some point a balanced and informed biography of Anderson will be written. It will no doubt highlight his several failings, but hopefully it will also show that he was a man of courage, integrity, considerable ability and loyalty. Such an account may well conclude that given the resources that he received, the enemy he faced and the challenges he overcame, Anderson was in fact a rather good chef. Hopefully his biographer may wish to consider in some depth how Monty might have been judged if he had been assigned command of the First Army, as originally intended, instead of Anderson. He would therefore have been required to fight the Germans in very different circumstances, with slender resources, a difficult logistic chain, German air superiority, an inexperienced Eisenhower and sometimes very difficult allies. Anderson's many critics, and those who have ignored the achievements of the First Army, might well again consult the view of the campaign's official historians. They stated that: "The Army's achievements are the best witnesses of the qualities of its commander, General Anderson, a fine soldier."[11] The First Army's achievements to which Playfair referred include the fact that its untested troops never had the inferiority complex which occasionally permeated the Eighth Army. They had also learned quickly how to fight and defeat veteran troops, advanced 600

9   As quoted in Hamilton, M*onty: Master of the Battlefield*, p.232.
10   See Blaxland, *Plain Cook*, p.266, for the quotation.
11   Playfair, *Destruction of the Axis Forces*, p. 457.

miles, liberated a capital city, captured over 100,000 German troops (more than at Stalingrad) and took 250,000 Axis troops prisoner. Not a bad record for any army or army commander.

14.4 The Path of the Battle-Axe

After a hard campaign that seriously depleted the ranks of the Battle-Axe Division, the formation spent the next two months recuperating, absorbing a large number of replacements and training. The division sorely needed a rest, for by May 1943 all of its men were exhausted both physically and mentally. The physical scars of the Tunisian campaign on men's bodies were easily seen on the sandy beaches of the coast, where they spent time relaxing. The mental ones were much more difficult to observe, but would have their impact later. In early July the 78th Division was transported to Sicily, where many of them would say they reluctantly joined the Eighth Army. It had not originally been intended that the division should take part in the invasion of Sicily, for it was recognised that it needed significant time to recover. However, when the Eighth Army was held up in the difficult terrain of the central mountains, the 78th Division was called to reinforce the attack being conducted by XIII Corps. Here the Germans had created formidable defences in the rugged terrain around the town of Centuripe. Evelegh and his division were committed to break the defences by capturing Centuripe, or as war correspondents soon renamed it, "Cherry Ripe". This location was so well defended that many thought it an impregnable position. It fell to Nelson Russell and the Irish Brigade to carry out the attack, which in due course captured the town, though the brigade had support from a range of other units. The brigade's seizure of Centuripe against difficult odds had caused the whole German line to Catania to crack and forced the Germans to withdraw to a new position: the Etna line. Centuripe, and the division's wider performance in Sicily, helped solidify its reputation as one of the best infantry divisions in the British Army at the time. It also impressed Bernard Montgomery, who having been shown Centuripe by Evelegh asked him to tell the 78th "that he considered the Division by capturing the position performed a wonderful feat of arms and he doubted that any other division in his army could have carried out this operation successfully". [12] Even greater praise came from Prime Minister Winston Churchill, who mentioned the news of its capture in the House of Commons and cited it as one of the greatest of achievements in storming a town.

After Sicily the division had a rest before it was committed to battle in Italy, this time back under the command of V Corps and Lieutenant General Charles Allfrey. The division earned high praise for its performance in the Battle of Termoli, the drive to the Moro River and at the Battle of the Sangro River in December 1943. It continued to maintain and enhance its reputation as one of the best divisions in the Eighth Army, and especially for its fighting abilities in the mountains. This was a skill it had learned in Tunisia during the Battle of the Peaks, and was again in evidence when it took part in the fighting at Cassino before being sent to Egypt for a well-earned rest in July 1944. Here the division blotted its copy book, its soldiers clashing with the many rear-area troops still in Cairo in what became known as the Cairo riots. Soon afterwards it was sent back to Italy, as the Eighth Army was bogged down in the mountains and took part in a series of bloody though successful battles at Trasimene and along the Gothic Line north of Rome. By autumn of 1944 the division was tired and felt that it had done more

---

12   Ford, *Battle Axe Division*, p.94.

than its fair share of fighting. As part of XIII Corps it had the dubious distinction of being part of the formation with the highest desertion rate in Italy, with 600 deserters coming from the division. This situation had arisen in part because eventually all soldiers had their limits, some of the original veterans had been fighting ever since November 1942 and many had been wounded at least once and felt that any luck they may have possessed had now run out. In addition to the levels of desertion, the rates of mental illness and sickness also rose alarmingly. After a winter period manning positions in the mountains, a new commander, Major General Robert Arbuthnott, and his staff helped revitalize what had become a tired formation. Arbuthnott had replaced Cass as commander of the 11th Infantry Brigade in Italy in 1943 and had gained the respect of many officers and men, so he was a good choice to assume command of the division at this time. During the final offensive in Italy, the Battle-Axe Division once again distinguished itself at the Battle of the Argenta Gap.

It ended the war near Trieste and finally took part in the occupation of Austria. Here its short but illustrious life ended, as it was disbanded in 1946, for it was not a regular Army formation. The 78th Division was created during wartime, had no history before it was formed and after the war it had no future. Historians have all too frequently overlooked the division's achievements and focused on the record of other formations. However, the division that began its wartime career landing on the beaches of Algiers, fought in the Battle of the Peaks and took Longstop had forged a reputation by May 1945 as one of the finest divisions in the British Army. The foundations for that reputation were laid down through the tough fighting that took place in Tunisia from November 1942 to April 1943, then was demonstrated for all to see in the Battle of the Peaks and the capture of Longstop Hill.

14.5 Action at Termoli and on the Sangro

The reader may well ask what happened to two of the principal characters in the Battle of the Peaks - John "Jack" Anderson and Bernard "Swifty" Howlett - and many of the others who took part? Major Anderson remained with the 8th Argylls, though he was moved to a safer job than commander of a rifle company. By late September 1943, when the Argylls landed in Italy, there were moves afoot to send him back home to take on a new job away from the front line. The British Army has an unwritten policy that those who survive the action in which they win a VC are usually pulled out of the fighting to ensure they become living examples of gallantry. Anderson initially resisted pressure to send him home and a compromise had been made which led to a role in command of Support Company, but by October it was apparent that he would be soon be ordered home. On 3 October, 1943 the Argylls were transported to the port of Termoli. They landed there the next day to reinforce the Commandos who had taken the port the previous day. The following day, on 5 October, the Argylls were ordered to attack and take positions near the village of San Giacomo. Lionel Sanderson and his company were leading the attack and they encountered significant opposition on a low ridge above a farm and near a brickworks. Although the Argylls' CO, Lieutenant Colonel Scott-Elliott, was not aware of it, the opposition came from part of a battlegroup of the 16th *Panzer* Division which had been sent to retake Termoli. When a further attack was launched on the village, the battalion and 36th Brigade became the subject of a wider and violent counterattack by the Germans. On the morning of 6 October, the battalion headquarters had withdrawn to the brickworks. This too soon came under heavy attack, and these Germans were repelled only by bringing the fire from a 25-pounder field regiment to within less than 100 yards of the building. After a while the situation became grave and the brickworks position became untenable, for shells from both sides were falling on the area, so Scott-Elliott ordered a further withdrawal. Unfortunately the brickworks were hit by artillery and Anderson was killed, in all likelihood and ironically by a shell from a British gun. The action at Termoli roughly handled the Argylls yet again and they lost over 170 casualties, including five officers killed. The most grievous loss and that most keenly felt was that of Major Anderson. The battalion history paid tribute to him: "His amazingly calm, unemotional courage and his unassuming modesty, which was combined with a resolute common sense, made him admired and loved by all who knew him."[13]

Battalion histories are not written by ordinary soldiers, so it is valuable to gain the perspective of one who knew Anderson well, a private in the 8th Argylls who was his personal batman. His views are especially relevant, for in a most eloquent, sincere and articulate letter written to Anderson's widow Moira, Private W. Irvine MM included the following comments:

> I was with your late husband from the time of my arrival out here in November. Was his Batman [and] went through all the battles with him … To me he was the finest lad I've ever met. Although I am only a private and he a major he treated me as a friend and not a batman. We had faith in each other while in action … Such a friendship grew up between us. He was a great fellow among the lads; we all thought the world of him. No one ever spoke against his fairness and consideration for others, [which] was well known in the ranks. Everyone was sorry to hear of his passing. No one will ever take his place in the eyes of the men he led into battle. To me he was the finest, I'll never do batman to another.

It had been Private Irving who had been with Jack Anderson in the engagement on 16 April near Djebel Bou Diss where he had won a well-deserved MM.[14] John Thompson McKellar Anderson was only 25 when he was killed, but in his short life he had achieved a great deal. His military career had been exemplary, and it is likely that had he survived, he may have eventually commanded a battalion, possibly the 8th Argylls. Anderson never formally received the VC, for that could only usually be presented by the king. It was his young widow Moira and his 2-year-old daughter who were to receive it on his behalf. In 2013, the Argyll and Sutherland Highlanders Regimental Association commissioned the respected military artist Stuart Brown to produce a painting of the battalion's attack on Longstop Hill. The resulting picture, which forms the front cover of this book, shows Jack Anderson leading that charge. A copy of the picture has hung in the authors' study just above his desk for the last three years and has inspired him to finish this book. Today, his VC is held by the regimental association and his medals, including a replica of the VC, are on show in the Regimental Museum at Stirling Castle. Jack Anderson lies in the CWGC cemetery near the Sangro River in eastern Italy. The inscription on his headstone reads: "As he trod that day to go, so walked he from his birth in simpleness and gentleness in honour and clean mirth."[15]

Sadly, Anderson is not the only veteran of the Battle of the Peaks who lies in the Sangro River cemetery, for the battle, though successful, was a costly one. Just a few rows in front of Anderson's

---

13   Quote from Malcolm, *History of 8th Argylls*, p.156.
14   J. Laffin, *British VCs of World War 2: A Study in Heroism* (Stroud: Sutton Publishing, 2000), p.234.
15   The quote is from one of Rudyard Kipling's poems.

headstone is located the grave of his brigade commander at Longstop Hill, Brigadier Bernard Howlett. After Longstop, "Swifty" Howlett continued to lead the 36th Infantry Brigade with distinction, earning a bar to the DSO awarded for that action in Sicily. Throughout his career, Howlett continued to subscribe to the view that in order to lead a brigade he had to be close to the action. On 29 November 1943, Howlett was typically near the front line, and was visiting the forward companies of his old regiment, the 6th West Kents, when he was killed. According to Lionel Sanderson, through whose company of Argylls he had travelled, Swifty had ignored his warnings about the exposed nature of the ground he crossed, and moreover returned the same route. Swifty had been accompanied on his visit by his close companion and friend, Clive Usher, the CO of the 138th Field Regiment. Usher survived, but was seriously wounded and had to briefly give up command of his regiment. Although not everyone was a fervent admirer of Howlett - Lionel Sanderson, for example, was a critic of his tactical abilities, though not of his leadership or courage - he was highly regarded by most subordinates. These included Lieutenant Colonel Paul Bryan, the new CO of the 6th West Kents, who had succeeded Eric Heygate. Bryan had been a captain under Howlett when the latter had first commanded the West Kents, and thought highly of his old CO. He recalled in his autobiography:

> This was a blow to the brigade for as I have repeatedly said he was a brilliant commander. It was a personal loss to me for he had taught me almost everything I knew about soldiering originally in the training period in England and then by example in battle.[16]

Howlett's ability as a commander had also been noted by his superiors and at the time of his death he had been assigned to command a division, and the appointment was not an ordinary one. Even though he was not an airborne officer, Howlett had been selected to command the 1st Airborne Division, as the previous GOC had been killed. His selection as the future GOC of the 1st Airborne owed a great deal not only to his performance as a commander, but also due to the fact that, on several occasions, he had under his command in Tunisia several parachute battalions. It is understood that Howlett was held in high regard by several seasoned commanders of the 1st Airborne, and his appointment would have been welcomed by that formation. Howlett's death meant that command of the division actually went to Roy Urquhart, who led it at Arnhem in September 1944. Though Swifty never commanded an airborne division, he would have been proud to know that his son Geoffrey would join that regiment, commanding a battalion and a brigade before rising to the rank of full general and Deputy Colonel in Chief of the Parachute Regiment.[17]

In addition to Howlett, at least two other senior officers of the Battle-Axe Division were to fall victim to enemy action at or near the Sangro. The beloved CO of the Royal Irish Fusiliers, Beauchamp Butler, finally pushed his luck too far, his tendency to wander up to his leading companies leading to him being killed near the Trigno River. Butler's desire to be close to the action was shared by the CRE of the 78th Division, Lieutenant Colonel Edmund Blake. It was

16   Bryan, *Wool, War and Westminster*, p.119.
17   The source for Brigadier Howlett's selection as GOC 1st Airborne Division is his son, General Sir Geoffrey Howlett, who later learned this from several senior veteran Parachute Regiment officers. Geoffrey Blaxland in his book also states Brigadier Howlett had been selected for divisional command; see Blaxland, *Plain Cook*, p.268.

sad, but not surprising, that Blake was also killed by mortar fire near the Sangro River, while supervising his sappers who were building a bridge. One final casualty of the Sangro campaign to mention was not an officer, but he had previously distinguished himself: Lance Corporal Ronald Lingham of the 6th West Kents. Lingham had earned the MM for his gallantry at Longstop Hill and been promoted to lance corporal. In Italy, at the Sangro River, he had taken part in a number of dangerous patrols into German lines, and was returning from an especially hazardous one when he drowned trying to return across the Sangro River back to Allied lines.

14.6 And What Happened to … ?

Many of the key participants in the Battle of the Peaks, both officers and men, went on to fight in Sicily and Italy and distinguished themselves in a number of ways, both in and outside of the Army. The later careers of the senior commanders involved in the Tunisian campaign - Dwight D. Eisenhower, Bernard Montgomery, Harold Alexander, George Patton and Omar Bradley - are well known to most readers, and will not be covered here. On the German side, General von Arnim spent four years interned as a POW in the USA and died back in Germany in 1962 at the age of 73. Friedrich Weber, the commander of the 334th Division, avoided being taken prisoner, as he was flown out of Tunisia. Weber commanded a further three infantry divisions over the next two years, survived the war and died in 1974 at the age of 82. Lieutenant General Charles Allfrey, the GOC of V Corps, led his formation through the fighting in Sicily and Italy for a total of 18 months. After leave in England in November 1944, Allfrey became GOC of British troops in Egypt; this was his last role, and he retired from the Army in 1948 and died at the age of 69 in 1964. Major General Vyvyan Evelegh, the ambitious and aggressive commander of the 78th, continued to command the Battle-Axe Division until December 1943, when he exchanged roles with Major General Charles Keightley, the GOC of the 6th Armoured Division. This was part of a process of broadening both senior officers' experience, but also a crude means of determining who would succeed to the command of V Corps. A combination of unfortunate tactical circumstances, and the problems that he encountered, meant that Evelegh's performance as GOC of the 6th Armoured was not a successful one. He therefore did not become a corps commander. Evelegh returned home to the UK, where he became Assistant Chief of the General Staff. He ended his career in 1950 still as a major general, and died in 1958. One officer within the 78th Division did rise to high rank, and that was Evelegh's GSO 1, Reggie Hewetson. Hewetson went on to become the BGS (Brigadier General Staff) of the Eighth Army and the British Army in Austria. After the war he rose to the rank of general, before retiring in 1961. He died in 1993 at the age of 83.

Both of the remaining brigade commanders of the 78th Division at the time of Longstop Hill, Nelson Russell and Edward Cass, surprisingly survived the war, despite the time they had spent close to the front line. Brigadier Russell commanded the Irish Brigade until February 1944, when, completely worn out from the pressures of command, he collapsed with exhaustion, was relieved and sent home to Ireland to rest. The shock to the brigade was mitigated by the news that his successor was none other than Pat Scott. Russell gradually recovered from the physical and mental exhaustion that had been caused by the pressures of serving as brigade commander for nearly a year. He missed out on further promotion and ended his career in command of an infantry brigade in 1950 in Northern Ireland. Although he never achieved higher rank, Russell must certainly be listed as one of the most able British infantry brigade commanders of the Second World War. He remained interested in all the officers and men who had served under his command throughout his life. They, in turn, held him in the highest esteem, and were much saddened by the news of his death at the age of 74 in 1971. The fiery Edward Cass continued to command 11th Infantry Brigade in Sicily, before being sent back to England to take over as commander of the 8th Infantry Brigade of the 3rd Infantry Division. "Copper" Cass was in command of the 8th Infantry Brigade when it landed at Sword Beach in Normandy on D-Day, and came ashore at about 0945 hours that morning. He ably commanded his brigade in Normandy, and for a brief 10 days, when the GOC was wounded, also the 3rd Infantry Division. He continued to command his brigade through France and into Holland until October 1944, when he was badly wounded by accidentally driving into a minefield while out partridge shooting near the Maas River. After recovery from his injuries, he commanded two further infantry brigades in 1945. He never achieved formal command of a division or rose higher in rank than brigadier. By the end of the war, Cass was one of the most experienced brigade commanders in the British Army, yet he is also one of the least-known today. He retired from the Army in 1948, and keeping up his interest in shooting (he had been a pre-war Army champion) became Secretary of the Army Rifle Association. Cass died in 1968 aged 70. A third brigadier served within the 78th Division in April 1943, and this was CRA, John Wedderburn-Maxwell. After acting as commander of Evelegh's gunners and surviving the latter's occasional outbursts of temper, Wedderburn-Maxwell was sent back to England and went on to have a successful military career, passing away in 1990.

Of the six battalion commanders within the 78th Division present when the formation landed in Algeria, only one of them, Arthur Crook, was alive and still in command of his original battalion at the end of the Tunisian campaign. Bernard Howlett became a brigade commander, Lieutenant Colonel Manly was killed at Medjez el Bab in December 1942, two other commanders returned home and Bill Wilberforce was killed. Despite the dangers of six months of often intense fighting, Crook's luck had continued to hold. Although his performance as battalion commander had been highly commendable, Crook was the only battalion commander in the division not to be awarded a DSO for his leadership, though many felt he certainly deserved one. It may be that his inability to suffer fools gladly meant that he missed out on such an award, or possibly it was his sometimes difficult relationship with Cass and Evelegh. Crook left his battalion a few days before the end of the campaign, but this was not the end of his career. After leave in England in August 1944, Crook was able to use his knowledge of Africa when he took command of the 6th West African Brigade. He led this unit with distinction in Burma and eventually won a DSO. Crook subsequently temporarily commanded the 81st West African Division in Burma, before returning to finish the campaign as brigade commander. After the war, Crook used his experience to good effect when he acted as an adviser to the Greek Army against communist guerillas from 1946-48, and was twice decorated by the Greek government. After Greece, Crook commanded forces in Cyprus and was a Defence Attaché in Thailand before he retired as a brigadier in 1953. Crook died in Windsor at the age of 82 in 1981. A very able tactician and strong leader, Arthur Crook's undoubted abilities were often underrated by his superiors.

The other battalion commanders in the 36th and 11th Brigade had mixed fortunes. Eric Heygate of the West Kents was quickly replaced by Paul Bryan soon after Tunisia, but the two amateurs, Lieutenant Colonels "Ginger" McKechnie and "Red" Linden-Kelly, stayed in command until the end of the campaign. McKechnie continued as CO until November 1943 and his abilities were further recognised. Although he was not a regular Army officer, he was promoted to brigadier, assumed command of two infantry brigades and was also decorated with the American Silver Star Medal. Alexander McKechnie continued to serve in the TA, and he finally retired from the Army in the 1960s, having been awarded an OBE. Linden-Kelly handed over command of his battalion in June 1943, but later commanded the 9th Battalion of the King's Own Yorkshire Light Infantry in Italy and won a bar to his DSO. He also survived the war and eventually retired from the TA in 1959. Only one of the COs of the Irish Brigade during the Battle of the Peaks ended the war with the Battle Axe Division, and that was Pat Scott. Neville Grazebrook commanded the Skins with distinction in Sicily and Italy, but was promoted to colonel in December 1943 and left the division. Scott commanded the London Irish Rifles in Sicily, before being promoted in July 1943 to command of the 12th Infantry Brigade in the 4th Infantry Division, and subsequently the 128th Infantry Brigade in the 46th Infantry Division. When Russell was sent home in March 1944, Scott was moved to command of 38th Irish Brigade. He led the brigade for the rest of the war, with his usual blend of tactical ability and inability to suffer fools at all. By the time Scott finished the war, he had spent nearly 29 months on operations, almost constantly in command of two battalions and three infantry brigades. In common with Cass and Russell, Scott's ability as a brigade commander has been almost completely overlooked by military historians. A future study of his career would be likely to reveal that he was a brilliant tactician and probably among the top five British brigade commanders of the Second World War. After the war, Scott rose to be a major general and held three further appointments before retiring in 1964.

The fate of the battalion commanders involved in the first attack on Longstop Hill was rather varied. The unfortunate American CO of the Vanguards during the Longstop Hill action, Lieutenant Colonel George Fricke, retained command of the battalion for only a few more weeks before being replaced. At the time William Stewart-Brown and Felix Copland-Griffiths from the 1st Guards Brigade were perhaps a little too quick to allocate blame to the Americans, and Fricke got most of it. A rather more objective review might indicate that Fricke was placed in a difficult situation by two officers, who in their respective accounts claimed to have more experience. Although Fricke lost command of his battalion, it did not end his career, since by April 1945 he rose to briefly serve as CO of a regiment. Fricke's later rise to regimental command contrasts significantly with the fate of Stewart-Brown, whose report on Longstop shifts perhaps too much blame onto the Vanguards. Although Stewart-Brown earned a DSO for Longstop, he only retained command of his battalion until February 1943. By 1944 he had dropped a rank and was a major and second-in-command of the 5th Battalion of the Coldstream Guards in Normandy, where he sadly died of wounds suffered in action in July 1944. The commander of the 1st Guards Brigade, Brigadier Copland-Griffiths, who had also criticized the American performance at Longstop, only stayed in command of the Guards until mid-April 1943. He was then replaced, and ironically sent to the capital of the nation whose army he had criticized, as Brigadier General Staff of the British Army Mission in Washington DC. Perhaps someone in Army appointments had a sense of humour, or more likely irony, when they decided on this posting. Copland-Griffiths retired from the Army in 1947 as a brigadier and died 20 years later. Two other COs from the division, who fought in the Battle of the Peaks, continued to lead their regiments after the Tunisian campaign with great distinction. David Dawnay, of the North Irish Horse, was promoted to command of the 21st Tank Brigade and led it in Italy, and next took command of the 26th Armoured Brigade of the 6th Armoured Division. After the war, Dawnay commanded two other armoured brigades, was promoted to the rank of major general and ended his career as Commandant of the Royal Military Academy at Sandhurst in 1953. After retiring, Dawnay continued to pursue his interests in equestrian matters and helped manage Ascot Racecourse before he died in 1971. Kendal Chavasse commanded the 56th Recce Regiment in Sicily and Italy. He won a bar to his DSO for his leadership at Termoli before he handed over command of his regiment in February 1945. Chavasse held a range of appointments prior to taking command of the Royal Irish Fusiliers in December 1945, and commanded the battalion in Egypt and Palestine. After he left the Army in 1948, Chavasse took up farming in Ireland and was active in several local organizations before his death in 1994.

The Tunisian campaign provided excellent combat experience for four young officers who had shown great promise as company commanders or in other roles. John Coldwell-Horsfall later became the CO of both the London Irish Rifles and the Faughs in Italy, at the early age of 28. Coldwell-Horsfall distinguished himself in both roles, and won a DSO to add to his two MCs. After the war, he left the Army to revitalize an ailing family business, but retained his interest in his old regiment and became Honorary Colonel of the 5th Battalion. He would later write three books about his experiences in the Second World War. John Coldwell-Horsfall, who was a natural battlefield leader, an astute businessman and an accomplished author, died in 2006. Gordon Defrates, the adjutant of the 6th West Kents who had won a MC at Longstop, also took command of his battalion in December 1944, when aged 29, and led it for the rest of the war. He earned a DSO and two MCs during the war, and went on to have a successful career in the food business. Unsurprisingly given his regiment, Defrates was passionately interested in cricket and played the game until 1968, when a successful operation for lung cancer forced him to give up his beloved sport. An unaffected, self-deprecating man, Defrates died in 2001. Paul Bryan, who had commanded HQ Company of the West Kents and also won an MC, later commanded the battalion, taking over in May 1943 at the age of 30, despite having only been commissioned into the Army in 1939. Bryan led the battalion in Sicily, where he won a DSO to add to his MC, and afterwards in Italy. In 1944 he was sent home to command an OCTU for the rest of the war. After the war, Bryan worked in the textile trade in Yorkshire, until he was invited to stand as Conservative candidate for his local constituency, entered politics and eventually won the election for the safe Tory constituency of Beverley in 1955. He held the seat until he retired in 1987, after serving as a Minister in Ted Heath's government and an adviser to Margaret Thatcher. Upon retirement from politics he wrote a very readable autobiography, *Wool, War and Westminster,* before he died at the age of 91 in 2004. James Dunnill, who had commanded companies in two battalions and had won an MC at Heidous, took command of the Faughs in 1944 at the age of 28, but was captured in September that year. He spent the rest of his war in a POW camp near Brunswick in Germany. During his stay in this camp, he is partly credited with the idea of setting up a network of what became known post-war as the Brunswick Boys Clubs.

It would be remiss not to refer to the later successful careers of those who served in the various supporting arms and services in Tunisia in April 1943. These included, Brigadier Jack Parham, the CCRA of V Corps, who became the Brigadier Royal Artillery of the Second Army for the whole of the North-West Europe campaign and retired as a major general. Lieutenant Colonel Mike Denham's performance during the Tunisian campaign so impressed his superiors that he was selected to take over as CRA of the Battle-Axe Division when Wedderburn-Maxwell left for other duties. Denham held this role right through Sicily and part of the Italian campaign until February 1944, when he was sent home. He survived the war, but died soon afterwards in 1947. Lieutenant Colonel Clive Usher recovered from his wounds and regained command of 138th Field Regiment until July 1944. He was promoted to brigadier and appointed CRA of 6th Armoured Division, a position he held to the end of the war. Usher earned two DSOs in 1943 and a CBE towards the end of the war. He stayed in the Army and finished his career as Defence Attaché in India before he retired in 1958. He died in 1982 aged 75. Lieutenant Colonel George "Tommy" Thomas, the previous CO of 17th Field Regiment before Usher, served as GSO 1 Operations for the 4th Infantry Division until April 1944. He returned to the 78th Division to assume command of the 138th Field Regiment. After the war, Thomas became the CRA of an airborne division and later rose to the rank of major general. The able Canadian commander of the 256th Field Company RE, Major Brown, returned to the UK after Tunisia. He used the experience gained there when he subsequently commanded 18th Field Company Royal Canadian Royal Engineers in Normandy and Holland. It is not clear what happened to Majors Coffin and Denton, the other two RE company commanders. Colonel Douglas Cheyne, the redoubtable ADMS of 78th Division, went on to serve as Director of Public Health services in Sicily. He later became the Deputy Director of Medical Services for XIII Corps in Italy and then Deputy Director of Medical Services, Land Forces Greece in 1945 as a brigadier. Cheyne retired from the Army in 1948 and died in 1966.

This review of the later careers of those involved in the Battle of the Peaks has been unfortunately limited to the more senior officers who took part. It would have been nice to have included some stories of junior officers, NCOs and also the soldiers who have been mentioned in this account. Unfortunately this has not been possible due to the absence of information on what happened to them after Tunisia. We can, however, mention one soldier's fate as an example. Sergeant Eddie Mayo of the London Irish Rifles, who won an MM at Heidous, missed the Sicily campaign due to his wounds but rejoined the battalion in Italy. He became a highly regarded platoon sergeant and was later slightly wounded a third time. The wound was minor and not recorded; had it been reported, under regulations Mayo would have been sent home. Sadly, he was killed at Monte Cassino. Mayo had wanted to ensure his soldiers were well entrenched after an attack, and was out in the open supervising them when killed by a shell. Mayo was universally liked and respected within his battalion, and this was reflected in letters his wife later received from both officers and soldiers. He is buried in the CWGC cemetery at Cassino. Hopefully the publication of this story may encourage relatives of other former First Army soldiers to provide this type of detail to military and regimental museums or other archives.

It is, however, possible to describe the later careers of two such soldiers, as they were went on to become the most famous veterans of the First Army. These were those irrepressible members of the Royal Regiment of Artillery, Spike Milligan and Harry Secombe. Milligan went on to serve in Italy, where he was hospitalized from wounds and nervous exhaustion, or as it is now termed, post-traumatic stress disorder. He carried out a number of rear-echelon jobs in Italy, eventually becoming a full-time entertainer in the Army and again meeting Secombe. After being demobilised, Milligan remained in Italy playing with a trio, but returned to Britain soon afterwards. While he was with the Central Pool of Artists (a group he described as composed "of bomb-happy squaddies") he began to write parodies of their mainstream plays. These displayed many of the key elements of what would later become *The Goon Show* with Secombe, Peter Sellers and Michael Bentine. Milligan became a celebrated comedian, actor, author, entertainer and campaigner. His achievements are perhaps more remarkable, as he suffered several mental breakdowns. He wrote a series of humorous accounts of his military service, including a book about his time in Tunisia. After a long and varied career, Milligan died aged 83 in February 2002. On his grave was his now legendary own epitaph, which translated from Gaelic reads "I told you I was ill". Bombardier Secombe met Milligan again in Italy and after serving to the end of the war with 132nd Field Regiment, also joined the pool of entertainers in Naples and formed a comedy duo with Milligan. He subsequently joined the Windmill Theatre in 1946 and worked with Milligan, Michael Bentine and Peter Sellers. Secombe went on to have a distinguished career as a singer, actor, comedian and member of *The Goon Show*. He was widely admired by the British public throughout his long career as a singer and entertainer, and was knighted in 1981 for his services to the theatre and television. He died from cancer in 2001 at the age of 79, less than a year before Milligan. His fellow gunner couldn't resist trying to have the last laugh at Secombe's funeral, saying: "I'm glad he died before me, because I didn't want him to sing at my funeral."[18] Given Milligan's zany sense of humour, it is likely he would have enjoyed learning that a recording of Secombe singing was subsequently played at his own funeral service.

---

18   See Milligan's obituary in Obituaries column of the *Daily Telegraph*, 17 October 2002.

Appendix A

British V Corps Order of Battle, 6 December 1942

Corps Troops:
  9 Battery, 13th Medium Regiment, RA
  14 Battery, 16th Medium Regiment, RA
  456 Light Battery, RA
  457 Light Battery, RA
  265/45th Light Anti-Aircraft Regiment, RA
  V Corps Signals
  564 Field Company, RE
  751 Field Company, RE
  103 Corps Bridging Company, RASC
78th Infantry Division: Major General V. Evelegh
Divisional Troops:
  56th Battalion, Reconnaissance Regiment
  132nd Field Regiment, RA
  138th Field Regiment, RA
  64th Anti-Tank Regiment, RA
  49th Light Anti-Aircraft Regiment, RA
  214th Field Company RE
  237th Field Company, RE
  256th Field Company, RE
  281st Field Park Company, RE
1st Guards Brigade: Brigadier R.A.V.Copland-Griffiths
  3rd Battalion, the Grenadier Guards
  2nd Battalion, the Coldstream Guards
  2nd Battalion, the Hampshire Regiment
11th Infantry Brigade: Brigadier E.E.E. Cass
  2nd Battalion, the Lancashire Fusiliers
  1st Battalion, the East Surrey Regiment
  5th Battalion, the Northamptonshire Regiment
36th Infantry Brigade: Brigadier A.L. Kent-Lemon
  5th Battalion, the Buffs
  6th Battalion, the Queen's Own Royal West Kent Regiment

8th Battalion, the Argyll and Sutherland Highlanders
1st Parachute Brigade: Brigadier E.W.C. Flavell
    1st Parachute Battalion
    2nd Parachute Battalion
    3rd Parachute Battalion
    6th Commando
6th Armoured Division: Major General C.F. Keightley
Divisional Troops:
    1st Derbyshire Yeomanry
    12th Regiment, RHA
    152nd Field Regiment, RA
    72nd Anti-Tank Regiment, RA
    51st Light Anti-Aircraft Regiment, RA
    5th Field Squadron, RE
26th Armoured Brigade: Brigadier C.A.L. Dunphie
    16/5th The Queen's Royal Lancers
    17/21st Lancers
    2nd Lothians and Border Horse
    10th Battalion, the Rifle Brigade
38th Infantry Brigade: Brigadier N. Russell
    6th Battalion, the Royal Inniskilling Fusiliers
    1st Battalion, the Royal Irish Fusiliers
    2nd Battalion, the London Irish Rifles
American Troops:
Combat Command "B": Brigadier-General Lunsford F. Oliver
    1st and 2nd Battalions, 13th Armored Regiment
    1/1st Armored Regiment
    1st and 2nd Battalions, 6th Armored Infantry Regiment
    27th Field Artillery Battalion
    701st Tank Destroyer Battalion (1 co.)
    16th Armored Engineers (1 co.)
Others:
    5th Field Artillery Battalion
    175th Field Artillery Battalion
    106th Coast Artillery (AA) Battalion
    701st Tank Destroyer Battalion (2 cos)
    3/39th Infantry Regiment
    67th Armoured Regiment (25 tanks)

Appendix B

Order of Battle for the 78th Infantry Division and supporting units. April-May 1943

78th Infantry Division: GOC, Major General V. Evelegh
Divisional Troops:
   56th Battalion, Reconnaissance Regiment
   78th Divisional Signals
   78th Division Provost Company
Royal Artillery
   17th Field Regiment, RA
   132nd Field Regiment, RA
   138th Field Regiment, RA
   64th Anti-Tank Regiment, RA
   49th Light Anti-Aircraft Regiment, RA
Royal Engineers
   214th Field Company, RE
   237th Field Company, RE
   256th Field Company, RE
   281st Field Park Company, RE
Royal Army Medical Corps
   11th Field Ambulance
   152nd Field Ambulance
   217th Field Ambulance
Royal Army Service Corps
   294 RASC Company
   328 RASC Company
11th Infantry Brigade: Brigadier E. Cass
   2nd Battalion, the Lancashire Fusiliers
   1st Battalion, the East Surrey Regiment
   5th Battalion, the Northamptonshire Regiment
36th Infantry Brigade: Brigadier A.L. Kent-Lemon
   5th Battalion, the Buffs
   6th Battalion, the Queen's Own Royal West Kent Regiment
   8th Battalion, the Argyll and Sutherland Highlanders

38th Infantry Brigade: Brigadier N. Russell
>   6th Battalion, the Royal Inniskilling Fusiliers
>   1st Battalion, the Royal Irish Fusiliers
>   2nd Battalion, the London Irish Rifles

Units attached to the 78th Infantry Division during Operations Sweep and Vulcan

Infantry Battalions
>   2nd Battalion, the Hampshire Regiment
>   16th Battalion, the Durham Light Infantry
>   6th Battalion, the Black Watch

Armoured Regiments
>   1st North Irish Horse
>   142nd Regiment RAC

Artillery Regiments
>   4th Medium Regiment, RA
>   56th Heavy Regiment, RA

Royal Engineers
>   565 Armoured Field Company RE

Royal Army Medical Corps
>   10th Field Ambulance

Appendix C

Order of Battle for the German 334th Infantry Division, 7-30 April 1943

Divisional Troops
   334th Infantry Division Headquarters
   334th Division Recce Unit
   334th *Schnelle Abteilung* (Anti-Tank companies)
   334th Artillery Regiment (two battalions)
   One Engineer Battalion, one Signal Battalion and Supply troops
Infantry Regiments
   754th Grenadier Regiment (three battalions, I, II and III)
   755th Grenadier Regiment (three battalions, I, II and III)
   756th Mountain Infantry Regiment (three battalions, I, II and III)
Attached units
   Various *Marsch* (Reinforcement /replacement) Battalions, including: A-24 *Marsch* Battalion
   47th Grenadier Regiment
   962nd Schutzen Regiment

A Note on Sources

War Diaries in the National Archives

The author has used the war diaries held in The National Archives (TNA), under the heading War Office (WO), which were produced either during or immediately after the Battle of the Peaks. These documents vary in quality but the files include many valuable additional reports and sketches. These documents provide a rich stream of original information, but as a trained historian I must issue the equivalent of a health warning: war diaries may be primary sources but they need to be treated with a degree of scepticism, for they were written in the field and after a battle and cannot be completely counted on for either accuracy or objectivity. A valuable source of information at Kew are the citations for gallantry medals awarded for actions in Tunisia. These citations are kept on microfilm and can be viewed there as part of two sets of records, WO 373/1 and WO 373/2. The citations often added key details of actions and/or helped confirm the accuracy of other records.

Foreign Military Studies

One useful source of information about German units is the US Army Foreign Military Studies (FMS) collection of reports. These were produced because US Army historians in Europe had the amazing foresight to require captured senior German officers to write over 3,000 accounts of their experiences and the operations of the units in which they served. This action has enabled the account by *Oberst* Rudolf Lang of German plans and operations at Longstop Hill to be available to historians. The author would like to publicly recognise the efforts of Richard Hedrick, the creator of the website www.sturm-panzer.com, for his painstaking work in obtaining and digitising many of the original FMS reports.

CWGC Records

The detailed records kept by the CWGC, easily accessible and searchable online through their website, provided critical information on unit casualties. The CWGC website enables anyone to download the records and filter them to determine specific information by unit or period. This data proved essential in understanding the actual scale of casualties (i.e. deaths) which were incurred by battalions and regiments during the Battle of the Peaks. This often contrasted significantly with that stated in other sources.

Maps

Unfortunately, no modern and reliable topographic maps exist for Tunisia. In the absence of modern topographical maps, the author was forced to rely on the original 1:50,000 and some 1:25,000 military maps used at the time. These are part of the General Staff Geographical Series (GSGS) produced for use by officers and men by the Royal Engineers mapping department. This has brought both benefits and penalties, for though it makes it easy to determine locations and grid references cited in war diaries, those maps were often based on French mapping, which was not that accurate. The ability to have at hand the original GSGS maps has been invaluable in understanding the terrain and also the information actually available at the time to those involved in the Battle of the Peaks.

Photographs

The ability to take photographs and film 75 years ago was entirely different to the situation today. As a result, a limited number of still photographs and films from that time now exist. The majority of these photographs were taken by official photographers and held by the Imperial War Museum and the National Army Museum. A number of the original still photographs used in this work are owned by private individuals, the Tank Museum collection and regimental museums.

Secondary Sources – Published

Books

There are numerous books on most other campaigns in the Second World War, but there are relatively few detailed accounts of the Tunisian campaign. The lack of interest in the Tunisia operations is sadly not new. Geoffrey Blaxland wrote the first non-official account of the First Army's actions because he felt it had been almost completely overlooked. Since his book in 1977, only two others have been devoted to the overall campaign: David Rolf's *Bloody Race to Tunis* in 2001 and Rick Atkinson's *The Army at Dawn* in 2002. Both books are highly recommended. There are, however, no detailed, recent accounts which cover the fighting in the north of Tunisia, and especially Operations Sweep and Vulcan, in any depth. This gap in the literature is surprising, but was welcomed by the author, for it provided that unexpected opportunity to write in detail about a campaign and a battle that has not been covered by any other author. Accomplished military writer Richard Doherty has, however, already done a sterling job of trying to fill in many of the gaps, and his books *Clear the Way: The 38th Irish Brigade*, *The North Irish Horse* and *Only the Enemy in Front* have provided valuable inspiration for this author. Recently, three further books have been written which ably tell specific stories of that campaign. These are Bryn Evans' *With the East Surreys in Tunisia and Italy*, Adam Robson's *Tunisia 1942-43 2nd Battalion Coldstream Guards* and John Phillip Jones' book on Major Peter Pettit; *Gunner Battles*. The regimental histories of the various units involved in the Battle of the Peaks vary in quality, depth and accuracy. Those authored by Chaplin, Daniell, Hallam, Jervois, Knight and Malcolm were of particular value. Three books published at the time by the war correspondents Alexander Austin, John Darcy Dawson and Howard Marshall are still available and offer objective, contemporary accounts. Accounts by war correspondents that provided useful perspectives were those by Divine, Jordan and Moorhead. Other books that have proved valuable in providing specific details include Bryan Perrett's *Impossible Odds*, Paul Bryan's *Wool, War and Westminster* and Lionel Sanderson's *Variety is the Spice of Life*.

Personal Memoirs

In contrast to many other battles of the Second World War, there are relatively few unpublished personal memoirs which are easily accessible. The Surrey Historical Centre provided access to the personal memoirs of Major H.B. Smith and Major Toby Taylor of the East Surreys. The archivist of the Argyll and Sutherland Highlanders, Rod Mackenzie, gave me access to their records, and especially to Lieutenant Colonel McKellar's personal account of the Argylls' operations from November 1942 to early April 1943 and Hamish Taylor's memoirs. General Howlett kindly alerted me to the personal memoir of John Windeatt, his father's brigade major, and allowed me to borrow his own treasured copy. The letters and personal memoir of Captain Peter Kidner of the Royal Engineers were also of value, and are published on the website www.simonkidner.co.uk.

Web-Based Material

The easy accessibility of information on the internet is both a blessing and a curse for most historians and authors. My personal view is that it is primarily a blessing, as it has made a significant amount of information available to the public and authors which would otherwise be difficult to find. However, a historian has to treat web-based information with scepticism and check on its veracity. There are three particular websites that provide information on the Tunisian campaign which the author can recommend. That created by Richard and Edmund O'Sullivan to honour their father, who served in the London Irish Rifles is especially to be commended. It is an excellent example of how the internet can be used to reach out, inform and educate the public about the operations of units in Tunisia. See www.irishbrigade.co.uk.

The website of the Queen's Own East Surreys Regimental Association is also a good example of a well-designed regimental association website where a range of useful information can be found. See www.queensroyalsurreys.org.uk.

Finally, the battlefield guide and amateur historian Paul Reed generously set up and maintains a valuable chat forum for those interested in the Second World War. This is a major repository of various useful documents. See www.ww2talk.com.

Bibliography

UNPUBLISHED MATERIAL FROM THE NATIONAL ARCHIVES

Eighteenth Army Group

WO 175/16 18th Army Group Headquarters G Ops section

First Army

WO 175 /50 to 63 - First Army War Diaries of various sections

Note: HQ First Army War Diaries and especially WO 175/50, 55 and 56 for the period include messages, situation reports and correspondence between Anderson and other commanders

Corps and Corps Level Organizations

WO 175/82-85 – War Diaries of V Corps G and A and Q sections

WO 175/86 - War Diary of the Commander Royal Artillery, V Corps

Divisions and Division Level Organizations

WO 175/168-169 - War Diaries of the 78th Infantry Division, G and Q Sections

WO 175/171, 173 & 175 - War Diaries of the Commander Royal Engineers, Commander RASC and Commander REME 78th Infantry Division

WO 175/170 - War Diary of the Commander Royal Artillery 78th Infantry Division

WO 175/136-137 - War Diaries of the 4th Infantry Division

WO 175/157-8 War Diaries of the 46th Infantry Division

WO 175/159 War Diary of the CRA 46th Infantry Division

Infantry Brigades & Regiments

WO 175/196, 213 & 216 - War Diaries of the 11th, 36th and 38th Infantry Brigades

WO 175/186 - War Diary of the 1st Guards Brigade

WO 175/490-520 Series – Infantry Battalions (individual numbers in brackets)

War Diaries of the 1st Irish Guards (488), 1st East Surreys (519), 1st Royal Irish Fusiliers (506), 2nd Battalion the Coldstream Guards (487), 2nd Battalion the Lancashire Fusiliers (512), 2nd London Irish Rifles (515), 2nd Battalion The Hampshire Regiment (499), 3rd Battalion The Grenadier Guards (485), 5th East Kents Regiment the Buffs (495), 5th Battalion Northamptonshire Regiment (517), 6th Battalion The Queen's Own Royal West Kents Regiment (509), 6th Battalion the Royal Inniskilling Fusiliers (505), 6th Battalion the Black Watch (494), 8th Battalion the Argyll and Sutherland Highlanders (491) and 16th Battalion Durham Light Infantry (498)

Tank Brigades & Regiments

WO 175/201 and 206 – War Diaries of the 21st and 25th Tank Brigades

WO 175/294 and 282 – War Diaries of the North Irish Horse and 142nd Regiment RAC

WO 175/178 – War Diary of the 56th Reconnaissance Regiment

WO 175/179 – War Diary of Blade Force

Artillery Units & Regiments

WO 175/296 – War Diary of First Army Group Royal Artillery

WO 175/326-350 - War Diaries of the 17th (326), 70th (332), 71st (333), 102nd (336), 132nd (337), 138th (338), 166th (341) and 172nd (342) Field Regiments of the Royal Regiment of Artillery

WO 175/361-362 - War Diaries of 456 and 457 Light Batteries of the Royal Regiment of Artillery

WO 175/ 363–364 - War Diaries of the 4th and 5th Medium Regiments of the Royal Regiment of Artillery

WO 175/311 - War Diary of the 64th Anti-Tank Regiment (Glasgow Yeomanry)

WO 175/351 - War Diary of the 56th Heavy Regiment of the Royal Regiment of Artillery

WO 175/427 - War Diary of the 49th Light Anti-Aircraft Regiment of the Royal Regiment of Artillery

Royal Engineer Units

WO 175/645, 652 & 657 - War Diaries of 214th , 237th and 256th Field Companies of the Corps of Royal Engineers

WO 175/675 - War Diary of 565th Armoured Field Company RE

Royal Army Medical Corps (RAMC) Units

WO 177/420 - War Diary of the Assistant Director of Medical Services (ADMS), 78th Infantry Division

WO 177/693 & 832 - War Diaries of the 11th and 217th Field Ambulances RAMC

Royal Army Service Corps RASC Transport & Mule Unit

WO 175/173 War Diary of the Commander RASC 78th Division

WO 175/174 War Diary of the RASC Divisional Troops Company

WO 175/925, 934 & 941 War Diaries of 237, 294 and 328 Companies of the RASC

WO 175/822 – War Diary of the 4th Pack Transport Group

WO 175/823 - War Diary of 10 Pack Transport Company

Gallantry Citations (Except for VCs)

See TNA WO 373/1 and 373/2 - Citations for Gallantry Awards for North Africa 1942-1943

PERSONAL MEMOIRS AND LETTERS

Dunnill, Major James, 'Letter to Lieutenant Colonel P. Scott entitled Report on action of F Company at Heidous on 23 April 1943' (unpublished, London Irish Rifles Museum)

Hamilton, Captain Percy, 'Personal Memoirs of Captain Percy Alexander Hamilton MC' (unpublished - courtesy of his son David Hamilton)

Kidner, Captain Peter RE, 'Personal Memoirs' (published on website www.simonkidner.co.uk, accessed 15 January 2018)

Manning, Hugh C., 'Operations of the 1st Battalion of the East Surrey Regiment in the 1939-45 War' (ESR /2 /15 /6) (Guildford: Surrey History Centre, undated)

McKellar, Lieutenant Colonel J., 'Account of Operations of the 8th Argylls in Tunisia' (this document is held in the Regimental Archives of the Argyll and Sutherland Highlanders)

Robinson, Captain Robert, 'Unpublished account of service in Tunisia' (extracts provided to author in 2008)

Russell, Brigadier Nelson, 'The Irish Brigade in Tunisia' (letters held in the Regimental Museum of the Royal Irish Fusiliers)

Schayek, Captain David, 'Recollections of service in Tunisia, an unpublished memoir' (Mrs L. Schayek)

Smith Major H.B., 'Operations of the 1st East Surreys in 1939-45, Part 2 - North Africa, Sicily and Italy' (London: Imperial War Museum, Reference 02(41) 662). This item is also available in the Surrey Historical Collection at Guildford (see reference ESR/2/15/6/5)

Squire, Lieutenant Colonel G.A. and Hill, Major P., 'Algiers to Tunis the 1st and 1st/6th Battalions of the East Surreys Regiment in North Africa 1942-43' (The Queen's Royal Surreys' Association Museum, November 1993)

Taylor, Major R.C., 'Seven Sunrays, One Morning in Tunisia: Return Visit to Tunisia' (London: Imperial War Museum Department of Documents, undated)

PUBLISHED SOURCES
Books

Atkinson, Richard *An Army at Dawn, The War in North Africa 1942-43* (London: Little Brown, 2003).

Austin, Alexander B *Birth of an Army*, (London: Victor Gollancz Limited, 1943).

Barthrop, Michael *the Northamptonshire Regiment 48th/58th Foot* (London: Cooper, 1974).

Baumer, Robert *An American Iliad the 18th Infantry Regiment in World War 2 (*Bedford, USA, The Aberjona Press: May 2015).

Blaxland, Geoffrey *The Plain Cook and the Great Showman*, (Abingdon: Purnell Book Services Limited, 1977).

Blaxland, Geoffrey *Destination Dunkirk: The story of Gorts Army* (London: Military Book Society, 1973).

Brooks, Stephen Editor, *Montgomery and the Eighth Army: A selection from the Dairies, Correspondence and other papers of Field Marshal the Viscount Montgomery of Alamein, August 1942 to December 1943* (Bodley Head for the Army Records Society; First Edition, 1991).

Brown, George A *For Distinguished Conduct in the Field: The Register of the DCM, 1939-1991* (Langley, Western Canadian Distributors, 1993).

Bryan, Paul *Wool, War and Westminster* (London: Tom Donovan, 1993)

Chaplin, HD *the Queens Own Royal West Kent Regiment 1920-1950*, (Uckfield: Naval and Military, 2004).

Churchill, Winston *the Second World War*, Volume 2, (London: Cassell Publishers, 1950).

Clark, Mark *Calculated Risk* (London: Hamilton Panther Books, 1956).

Cline, Ray *The Washington Command Post, the Operations Division*, (Washington DC: Center of Military History: US Army, 1951).

Crew, F A E Army, *Medical Services: Campaigns Volume II Hong Kong, Malaya, Iceland & the Faroes, Libya, 1942-1943, North-West Africa: Official History of the Second World War*, (Uckfield, Naval and Military Press, 2014).

Cunliffe, Marcus *The Royal Irish Fusiliers 1793-1950* (Oxford: Oxford University Press, 1952).

Dawson, John *Tunisian Battle.* (London: Macdonald & Company Limited, 1943).

Divine, A D *Road to Tunis*, (London: Collins, 1944).

D Este, Carlo *Eisenhower: A Soldiers Life* (New York: Henry Holt May 2003).

Doherty, Richard *Clear the Way, A history of the 38th Irish Brigade 1941-47*, (Dublin: Irish Academic Press 1993).

Doherty, Richard *the North Irish Horse. A hundred years of Service*, (Stroud: Spellmount Publishers, 2002).

Doherty, Richard *Only the Enemy in Front: History of the Reconnaissance Corps, 1941-46*, (Stroud: Spellmount Publishers, 1994).

Evans, Bryn *With the East Surreys in Tunisia and Italy 1942 - 1945: Fighting for Every River and Mountain*, (Barnsley: Pen & Sword Military, August, 2012).

Fitzgerald, D *History of the Irish Guards in the Second World War*, (Aldershot: Gale & Polden, 1949).

Ford, Ken *Battleaxe Division, From Africa to Italy with the 78th Division 1942-45*, (Stroud: Sutton Publishing, 2003).

Gelb, Norman *Desperate Venture: The Story of Operation Torch, The Allied Invasion of North Africa*, (London:Hodder and Stoughton, 1992).

Hallam, John *the History of the Lancashire Fusiliers 1939-1945*, (Stroud: Alan Sutton Publishing 1993).

Hamilton, Nigel *Monty. Master of the Battlefield 1942-44*, (London: Hamish Hamilton,1983).

Harris, Lillian *Cemeteries and Memories: The Second World War in Tunisia*, (Oxford: Milton Tompkinson, 2007).

Horsfall, John *The Wild Geese are Flighting*, (Kineton: Roundwood Press, 1976).

Horsfall, John *Say Not the Struggle*, (Kineton: Roundwood Press, 1977).

Howard, Michael *Official History of the Second World War, Grand Strategy Volume 4*, (London: HMSO 1972).

Howard, Michael *Mediterranean Strategy in the Second World War*, (London: Greenhill Books, March 1993).

Howard, Michael and Sparrow, J *The Coldstream Guards 1920-1946*, (Oxford: Oxford University Press, 1951).

Howe, George *the Battle History of the 1st Armoured Division*. (Washington D C :Combat Forces Press 1954, reprinted by Battery Press, 1979).

Howe, George *North West Africa Seizing the Initiative in the West US Army in World War 2 the Mediterranean Theatre of Operations*, (Washington DC USA: Department of the Army, 1957).

Jervois, W J *The History of the Northamptonshire Regiment 1934-1948*, (Northampton: The Northamptonshire Regiment Museum, 1953).

Jones, John P *Battles of a Gunner Officer Tunisia, Sicily, Normandy and the Long Road to Germany*. (Barnsley: Pen and Sword, 2014).

Jordan, Phillip *Jordan's Tunis Diary*, (London: Collins, 1943).

Knight, C R B *Historical Records of the Buffs Royal East Kent Regiment (3rd Foot) 1919-1948*, (London: The Medici Society, 1951).

Laffin, John *British VCs of the World War 2: A study in heroism* (Stroud: Sutton Publishing, 2000).

Levine, Alan J *the War against Rommel's Supply Lines, 1942-1943*, (Westport, Connecticut: Praeger, 1999).

Macksey, Kenneth *Crucible of Power: The Fight for Tunisia 1942-1943*, (London: Hutchinson, 1969).

Madden, B J G *A History of the 6th Battalion the Black Watch (Royal Highland Regiment)* 1939- 45, (Perth: Leslie, 1948).

Malcolm, A D *History of the Argylls and Sutherland Highlanders 8th Battalion 1939-47*, (London: Thomas Nelson and Sons Limited, 1949).

Malcolm, A D *Argyllshire Highlanders,1860-1960*, (Glasgow: The Halberd Press, 1960).

Marshall, Howard *Over to Tunis, The complete story of the North African Campaign* (London: Eyre and Spottiswood, 1943).

Matloff, Maurice and Snell, Edwin *Strategic Planning for Coalition Warfare 1941-42* (Washington DC: Center of Military History US Army, 1999)

Mead, Richard *Churchills Lions: A Biographical Guide to the Key British Generals of World War*, (Stroud: Spellmount, July 2007).

Milligan, Spike *Rommel? Gunner Who?* : A Confrontation in the Desert, (London: Penguin, 2012).

Mitcham, Samuel *German Order of Battle Volume Two: 291st-999th Divisions, Named Divisions and Special Divisions in World War 2*, (Mechanicsburg, USA: Stackpole Books, 2007).

Moorhead, Alan *African Trilogy: The North African Campaign, 1940-43* (W and N; New Edition, June 2000).

Nicholson, Nigel *The Grenadier Guards in World War 2 Volume 2*, (Aldershot: Gale and Polden, 1949).

Nicholson, W N *History of the Suffolk Regiment*, (Uckfield: Naval and Military Press, 2006)

North Irish Horse, *Battle Report of the North Irish North Africa and Italy*, (Belfast: W G Baird, 1946).

Paget, Julian *Second to None, The history of the Coldstream Guards 1650-2000*, (Barnsley: Pen and Sword, 2000).

Perrett, Bryan *At all costs, stories of impossible victories*, (London: Cassell Publishers, 1993).

Perrett, Bryan *The Churchill. Armour in action*, (Littlehampton Book Services Ltd 1st Edition, 1974).

Playfair, Ian and Molony, C *The Mediterranean and Middle East, Volume 4: The Destruction of the Axis Forces in Africa*, (London: HMSO, 1966).

Quilter, D C *No Dishonourable Name the record of the 2nd and 3rd Battalions of the Coldstream Guards 1939-46*,(London: W Clowes, 1947).

Ray, Cyril *Algiers to Austria: A History of the 78th Infantry Division in the Second World War*, (London: Eyre and Spottiswoode, 1952).

Rhodes-Wood, E *The War History of the Royal Pioneer Corps*, (Aldershot: Gale and Polden, 1960).

Riches, Paul A *The Spirit Lives on: Short History and Photographic Record of the 6th Battalion the Queen's Own Royal West Kent Regiment, 1939-46* (London: Tom Donovan, 1992).

Robson, Alan *Tunisia 1942-43: The Second Battalion Coldstream Guards*, (A Robson 2015).

Rolf, David *The Bloody Race to Tunis Destruction of Axis forces in North Africa November 1942 – May 1943*, (London: Greenhill Books, 2001).

Sanderson, Lionel *Variety is the Spice of Life*, (London: Minerva Press, 1995).

Scott-Daniell, David *History of the East Surreys Regiment: Volume IV 1920-1957* (London: Ernest Benn, 1957).

Scott-Daniell, David *Regimental History of the Royal Hampshire Regiment: Volume 3 1918-1954* (Aldershot: Gale and Polden, 1954).

Seccombe, Harry *Arias and Raspberries: An Autobiography Volume 1*, (London: Robson Books Limited, 1989).

Shores, Christopher *Fighters over Tunisia*, (London: Spearman, 1975).

Springer, Laurence E *History of the 16th Battalion the Durham Light Infantry 1940-46* (Laytonville, California: Styria, 1946)

Thompson, Julian *Forgotten Voices Desert Victory*, (London: Ebury Press, 2011).

Truscott, Lucian K *Command Missions: A Personal Story* (New York: E.P Dutton, 1954).

US Army Center of Military History *To Bizerte with II Corps (*US Army: Washington DC, 1990).

US War Department, *United States Handbook on German Military Forces, TM E30 451 (*Washington D.C: US War Department, 15 March 1945).

Williamson, H, *The Fourth Division 1939-1945,* (London: Neame, 1951).

Windeatt, John *Very Ordinary Soldier* (Exeter: Oriel Press, 1989)

Periodicals

Barton, M J, 'The Hampshire Regiment at Tebourba, 1942', *Army and Defence Quarterly and Defence Journal (April 1944)*: pp. 57-63.

Henry, H G 'The Calgary Tanks at Dieppe', *Canadian Military History*: Vol. 4: Issue 1.6, pp.61-74.

Hill, E R 'The Coldstreams at Longstop': *Army Quarterly and Defence Journal Volume XLVIII, No. 2 (July, 1944)*, pp. 175-80.

Obituary for Tony Money, *The Old Radleian Magazine, 2008,* pp. 7-19.

Pellerin R 'Canadian Infantry in Tunisia' *Canadian Military Journal Volume 17 No 1 Winter 2016,* pp. 47-56.

Reports

Foreign Military Studies (F.M.S) series produced by U.S Army European Theater of Operations Office of Chief of Military Historian

Buerker, Ulrich, *Commitment of 10th Panzer Division in Tunisia.* Report D215.

Lang, Rudolf, *Battles of Kampfgruppe* Lang in Tunisia. (10 Panzer Division) December 1942- to 15 April 1943 Part 1 Report D -173.

Lang, Rudolf, *Battles of Kampfgruppe* Lang in Tunisia. (10 Panzer Division) December 1942- to 15 April 1943 Part 2, Report D -166

Nehring, Walter, *First Phase of the Battle in Tunisia*, Report D-147.

Von Vaerst, G, *Operations of the 5th Panzer Army in Tunisia March 1943 – May 1943.* Report D001.

Weber, Friedrich, *Battles of the 334th Division and Group Weber December 1942 –January 1943.* Report D215

Other reports

Alexander, Harold Field Marshall, *Official Despatches: The African Campaign from El Alamein to Tunis* (London, London Gazette, February 1948).

Anderson, Kenneth Lieutenant General, *Official Despatch on Operations in North West Africa 8th November 1942 to 13th May 1943.*(London Gazette, November 1946).

Historical Officer, Canadian Military Headquarters. Report No 95 Attachment of Canadian Officers and Soldiers to the First Army. 12 May 1943.

Oral Interviews

Author's discussions with General Sir Geoffrey Howlett conducted in 2011, 2017 and 2018.

Imperial War Museum Oral History Collection:

Interview with Brigadier J Wedderburn-Maxwell RA Retired Catalogue Number 9146, 1985.

Interview with Captain J Williams Queens Own Royal Kents West Retired Catalogue Number 11939, 1989.

Index

FORMATIONS/UNITS

Armies

Allied

Axis

Corps

British/Dominion

United States

French

Axis

Commands/Task Forces

Allied
Blade Force 33, 37, 96, 335
Combat Command B (CCB) 35, 40, 44
Eastern Task Force 23–24, 29
Hart Force 33
Mike Group 66, 183

Axis
Kampfgruppe Eder 150
Kampfgruppe Koch 36–37, 43, 47, 150, 254, 340
Kampfgruppe Lang 43,47, 340

Divisions

British/Dominion
1st Airborne Division 320
1st Armoured Division 29, 35, 40, 44, 53, 107-108, 163, 166, 248-249, 309, 311
2nd New Zealand Division 161
4th Division 28, 69, 93, 102, 106, 128, 163, 168, 252–254, 261, 303, 308, 323, 325, 335
4th Indian Division 161, 311–312
6th Airborne Division 221
6th Armoured Division 44, 46, 53, 67, 74, 249, 254, 311–312, 321, 323, 325
7th Armoured Division 311
9th Division 163, 166
43rd (Wessex) Division 46
46th Division 52, 54–55, 63, 66, 69, 71, 78, 80, 101, 105, 163, 166, 249, 254, 323
50th Division 72
51st (Highland) Division 72, 117, 155
56th (London) Division 97
78th (Battleaxe) Division 23–24, 29, 33, 39–41, 43–44, 46, 51–53, 55–57, 60–61, 64–72, 74, 76, 78–81, 93–98, 105–106, 108–112, 115–117, 120–121, 128–131, 138, 147–149, 153–155, 157–159, 162–168, 187, 201–204, 211–214, 217–218, 222–225, 227, 229, 247–251, 254, 256, 260–261, 294, 296–298, 309–311, 314–315, 317–318, 320–322, 324–325, 327, 329–330, 335–336
81st (West African) Division 322

United States
1st Armored Division 29, 35, 40, 44, 53, 107, 163, 248, 309
1st Division 28–29, 108, 166
9th Division 163, 166
34th Division 24, 29–30, 315

German
10th *Panzer* Division 32, 39, 43, 53, 60, 252
334th Division 32, 43, 53, 59–61, 73, 79, 93, 95, 109, 111, 115, 126–127, 143, 150, 153, 158, 168–

169, 174–175, 203, 257, 278, 281, 296, 309, 321
999th Division 159, 191
Hermann Goering Division 159, 252, 312

Brigades

British/Dominion
2nd Brigade 252
8th Brigade 322
10th Brigade 252
11th Brigade 23–24, 28, 33, 36–37, 39, 41, 43–44, 52, 62–63, 65–66, 73, 98, 109, 115, 121, 126, 128–130, 137–139, 146–150, 152, 155, 167–169, 171–172, 175–176, 185, 190–194, 197–198, 201, 208, 217–218, 224, 229, 237, 251, 256, 258, 263, 298, 302, 318, 322
12th Brigade 102, 254, 308, 323
36th Brigade 31, 33, 36–37, 42, 44, 53, 55, 63, 65–66, 71, 73, 78, 80, 82, 94, 98, 103, 109–111, 115–116, 118, 121, 126, 154, 156, 164, 171, 194, 202, 218–219, 226, 230, 237, 250–251, 254–256, 258–263, 287, 290, 296, 302, 306, 311, 318, 320, 322
38th (Irish) Brigade 42, 63, 65–67, 73–79, 82, 89, 91, 93, 95, 97–99, 101, 103–106, 109, 115, 153–155, 167, 176, 194, 196, 202, 212, 217–220, 223, 225–226, 229–231, 233, 237, 240, 243–245, 247–248, 250–251, 254, 256, 261–262, 273, 290, 296, 298, 303, 306, 309, 315, 317, 321, 323
128th Brigade 101, 323
139th Brigade 255, 267
151st Brigade 98
1st Guards Brigade 43–48, 51–52, 74, 82, 128, 154, 261, 323, 327
24th Guards Brigade 254
1st Parachute Brigade 33, 71
21st Tank Brigade 323
25th Tank Brigade 76, 78, 129–130, 164, 248, 258
6th West African Brigade 322

Regiments

British
8th Argyll & Sutherland Highlanders 33, 37, 39, 44, 52, 71, 109–110, 116–117, 119–120, 149–150, 188, 251, 258–260, 263, 265, 267–280, 282, 286–287, 290, 298, 302–307, 318–320, 328–329, 335–336
6th Black Watch 32, 72, 88, 93, 102, 105–107, 115, 163, 254, 330, 335
5th Buffs 53, 71, 109–112, 114–115, 119–126, 131, 138, 148, 150, 159, 168–171, 194, 204, 212–213, 255, 258–260, 263–264, 267, 270, 280, 290–295, 298, 307
2nd Coldstream Guards 44–45, 47–51, 259, 323, 327, 333, 335